FAMILY LAW

D0635457

AUSTRALIA
Law Book Co.
Sydney

CANADA and USA
Carswell
Toronto

HONG KONG
Sweet & Maxwell Asia

NEW ZEALAND
Brookers
Wellington

SINGAPORE and MALAYSIA
Sweet & Maxwell Asia
Singapore and Kuala Lumpur

FAMILY LAW

Second Edition

Lilian Edwards, LL.B., LL.M., M.Sc.
Professor of Law at the University of Southampton,
formerly of the University of Edinburgh

and

Anne Griffiths, LL.B., Ph.D.
Professor of Law at the University of Edinburgh

THOMSON

™

W. GREEN

Published in 2006 by
W. Green & Son Ltd
21 Alva Street
Edinburgh EH2 4PS

www.wgreen.thomson.com

Typeset by Servis Filmsetting Ltd, Manchester
Printed and bound in Great Britain by
William Clowes Ltd, Beccles, Suffolk

No natural forests were destroyed to make this product;
only farmed timber was used and replanted

A CIP catalogue record for this book is available from
the British Library.

ISBN-10   0414 01395 6
ISBN-13   9780 414 01395 7

© W Green 2006

Crown Copyright legislation is reproduced under the terms of
Crown Copyright Policy Guidance issued by HMSO. All rights
reserved. No part of this publication may be reproduced or
transmitted in any form, or by any means stored in any retrieval
system of any nature without prior written permission, except for
permitted fair dealing under the Copyright, Designs and Patents
Act 1988, or in accordance with the terms of a licence issued by the
Copyright Licensing Agency in respect of photocopying and/or
reprographic reproduction. Application for permission for other use
of copyright material including permission to reproduce extracts in
other published work shall be made to the publishers. Full
acknowledgment of author, publisher and source must be given.

PREFACE

Ten years is a long time in family law. The first edition of this text appeared in 1997; the second appears almost a decade later, following the long-awaited appearance of the Family Law (Scotland) Act 2006. The new Act brings with it many crucial reforms which have been anticipated as far back as the Scottish Law Commission *Report on Family Law* in 1992. These include the granting of automatic parental rights and responsibilities to unmarried fathers; the reduction of the time periods for divorce to one and two years; the disappearance of desertion from the law of divorce; the award of a right (albeit limited) to financial provision after partners cease to cohabit, and on the intestate death of a cohabiting partner; the beginning of the end for marriage by cohabitation with habit and repute; and the final death rattle of the status of illegitimacy.

Impressive as this (partial) list is, the 2006 Act is only part of the avalanche of change which has descended on Scottish family law in the last decade. The last edition was written just after the implementation of the Children (Scotland) Act 1995, which effectively updated and codified much of Scottish child law. This edition has been equally transformed by the incorporation of the European Convention on Human Rights into UK domestic law in the Human Rights Act 1998. The policy of this volume has been to incorporate changes made as a result of the 1998 Act throughout, as appropriate, rather than to reserve a special section.

"Bringing rights back home" has most famously brought us so far a major challenge to the validity of the Scottish children's hearings system (*S v Miller*[1]) and a staunch assertion by the Inner House that human rights are compatible with the paramountcy of the welfare of the child in civil family actions (*White v White*[2]). As the dust settles on these cases, they leave us with a new system of legally-aided safeguarders for children coming before the hearing, and a potential new spirit of "rights discourse" for parents spreading through the courts. Other changes spurred on by Strasbourg and the Human Rights Act have been as various as the recognition, after years of struggle, of the rights of transsexuals in the Gender Recognition Act 2004; the restriction, though not the end, of the parental right of corporal punishment (see the Criminal Justice (Scotland) Act 2003); and the forthcoming reform of the law of freeing for adoption, which will for the first time enable "open adoption" contact orders with birth parents, even after a freeing order has been made. This book went to press as the Adoption and Children (Scotland) Bill 2006 was still in the throes of the Scottish Parliamentary progress; nonetheless, we have

---

[1] 2001 S.L.T. 531.
[2] 2001 S.L.T. 485.

attempted to anticipate the major changes it makes to the law of adoption, freeing for adoption and child care law in Chapters 6 and 8, wherever appropriate.

Perhaps the most significant change in the last 10 years, driven not just by Strasbourg or Westminster, but by Scotland's own demographic change, has been the full acceptance in Scots law of the unmarried heterosexual couple, and the same-sex couple, as a family unit, with or without children. Over a third of cohabiting couples in Scotland now have dependent children living with them, from that or previous relationships, according to the 2001 General Household Survey. And while the age of first marriage continues to rise, and the number of Scottish marriages declines, the number of stable cohabiting couples, both heterosexual and same-sex, continues to increase.[3] The new Adoption and Children (Scotland) Bill 2006 completes the process that was begun in the pioneering case of *T Petitioner*[4] by opening up adoption to gay couples. And the UK-wide Civil Partnership Act 2004 provides for same-sex marriage in all but name. The implications of the 2004 Act, along with the 2006 Act, for cohabiting and same-sex couples are explored in depth from Chapter 9 onwards.

Change, of course, does not always take as dramatic a form as landmark cases and ground-breaking new statutes. The 'meat and potatoes' of family law, financial provision on divorce, and disputes on residence and contact, continue to change in response to both legal challenge and social change. These topics are discussed in detail in Chapters 4 and 13. Family lawyers may be especially pleased to see the statutory demise of the much-mulled on *Wallis*[5] doctrine in the 2006 Act. In the world of child support, the much-needed changes made to the ailing Child Support Agency system by the Welfare Reform and Pensions Act 1999, and subsequent SIs, are analysed in Chapter 5. The demise of the Child Support Agency was announced subsequent to the going to press of this text: sometimes even 10 days are a long time in family law.

There are many people who have helped enormously in the writing of this second edition (the usual disclaimer of course applies). Ken Mason and Graeme Lawrie provided comments on Chapter 1 dealing with legal personality. John Fotheringham gave generously of his professional expertise by revising the section of Chapter 5 on child support law. Colin Moodie and Lexy Plumtree kindly revised Chapter 6 on adoption, both having played major roles on the Adoption Policy Review Group, whose work fed directly into the 2006 Bill. Louise Johnston and Alastair Henry gave helpful comments on Chapter 12 dealing with the Family Home. Dr David

---

[3] See Morrison, Headrick, Wasoff and Morton, *Family formation and dissolution: Trends and attitudes among the Scottish population* (2005, Scottish Executive)
[4] 1997 S.L.T. 724.
[5] 1993 S.L.T. 1358.

Nicholls reviewed draft chapters and provided many insightful comments. The authors would also like to thank all the students who helped as research assistants, with especial thanks to Paul Reid, now of Shepherd and Wedderburn, Solicitors, and Kirsteen Mackay, without whose capable and energetic work arranging and editing material for this edition, it might never have become a reality.

The law is stated as at February 2006; however, it has been possible to include later developments in places.

Finally, on a personal note, this second edition suitably marks one author's exit from the Scottish jurisdiction. Lilian Edwards began her academic career at Strathclyde University in 1986, teaching inter alia family law; 20 years later, and after 17 years at Edinburgh, she is moving on to a Chair at Southampton University, where more of her time will be dedicated to information technology law than family law. Lilian Edwards would therefore like to dedicate this edition to all her colleagues at Edinburgh and Strathclyde, who have offered so much wisdom, kindness and support over the last two decades.

Anne Griffiths would like to dedicate this edition to her husband, Ed Wilmsen, and all her colleagues who have provided so much support over the years, as well as to her students who have engaged in many stimulating and challenging discussions about the shape of family law in Scotland.

Lilian Edwards and Anne Griffiths
Edinburgh
July 2006

CONTENTS

Preface v
Table of Cases xi
Table of Statutes xxix
Table of Scottish Statutes xlvii
Tables of Statutory Instruments li
Tables of Scottish Statutory Instruments lv
Table of Conventions and European Directives and Regulations lvii

Chapter 1   Legal Personality and Family Relations 1
Chapter 2   The Child and Legal Capacity................................... 39
Chapter 3   Children and Parents 72
Chapter 4   Parental Responsibilities and Children's Rights I ... 112
Chapter 5   Parental Responsibilities and Children's Rights II... 169
Chapter 6   Children and Non-Parents 204
Chapter 7   The Child in Need of Care 240
Chapter 8   Needs not Deeds? The Children's Hearing
            System and Beyond 271
Chapter 9   Families, Marriage and Civil Partnership 312
Chapter 10 Domestic Relations, Persons and Property 349
Chapter 11 The Family Home 390
Chapter 12 Ownership of Family Property 424
Chapter 13 Financial Provision on Divorce and Dissolution
            of Civil Partnership.. 448
Chapter 14 Divorce: Grounds and Process 498
Chapter 15 Private Ordering: Minutes of Agreement and Joint
            Minutes of Agreement... 521

Index.. 547

TABLE OF CASES

A (ADOPTION: PLACEMENT), Re sub nom: Adoption Application (AA 113/67),
    Re [1988] 1 W.L.R. 229; [1988] 2 F.L.R. 133 6–35
A and B v C, 1987 S.C.L.R. 514 6–44
A and B v C (Adoption), 1977 S.C. 27 .... 6–58, 6–59
AB, Petitioner sub nom: AB v M, 1988 S.L.T. 652; 1987 S.C.L.R. 389 4–39
AB and CB, Petitioners (Adoption), 1990 S.C.L.R. 809 .... 6–40, 6–54
AB v CB sub nom: X v Y; AB v CD, 1959 S.C. 27; 1959 S.L.T. 111 14–15
AH and PH Petitioners, 1997 Fam. L.R. 84 4–83
AH and PH Petitioners sub nom: H and H Petitioners, unreported, Outer House,
    March 10, 1995 .... 5–17, 6–30
A v B (1925) 41 Sh. Ct. Rep. 23 12–38
——— v B, 1955 S.C. 378; 1955 S.L.T. 436 6–39
——— v B (Adoption), 1987 S.L.T. (Sh. Ct.) 121 .... 6–29, 6–66
——— v B & C *see* O'Connor v A and B
——— v Children's Hearing for the Tayside Region, 1987 S.L.T. (Sh. Ct.) 126 ... 6–41
——— v G, 1996 S.L.T. (Sh Ct) 123; 1997 S.C.L.R. 186 8–58
——— v Kennedy, 1992 S.C.L.R. 387 8–44
——— v Kennedy sub nom: JA v Kennedy, 1993 S.C. 131; 1993 S.L.T. 1188; 1993
    S.C.L.R. 107 .... 8–23, 8–24
——— v M, 1999 Fam. L.R. 42 .... 4–89, 6–07
——— v United Kingdom [1998] E.H.R.L.R 82; [1998] 2 F.L.R. 959; [1998]
    3 F.C.R. 597; (1999) 27 E.H.R.R. 611 .... 2–08, 4–22, 5–13
Aberdeenshire Council v R sub nom: Aberdeenshire Council, Petitioners, 2004
    Fam. L.R. 93; 2004 G.W.D. 23-494 4–79
Abrahams v Abrahams, 1989 S.L.T. (Sh. Ct.) 11; 1989 S.C.L.R. 102 10–59
Ackerman v Blackburn (No.1) sub nom: Ackerman v Logan's Executors (No.1),
    2002 S.L.T. 37; 2001 Fam. L.R. 90 9–56
Adams v Adams (No.1), 1997 S.L.T. 144 .... 13–44, 13–54, 13–63, 13–69
Adoption Application (Payment for Adoption), Re sub nom: Adoption
    Application (Surrogacy) (AA 212/86), Re [1987] Fam. 81; [1987] 3 W.L.R. 31;
    [1987] 2 All E.R. 826 3–83
Advocate, HM v Duffy, 1983 S.L.T. 7; 1982 S.C.C.R. 182 10–05
——— v Paxton, 1984 J.C. 105; 1985 S.L.T. 96 10–05
Ahmed v Ahmed, 2004 S.C.L.R. 247; 2004 Fam. L.R. 14 .... 10–48, 10–56
——— v Secretary of State for the Home Department [2002] UKIAT 439; [2002]
    Imm. A.R. 318; [2002] I.N.L.R. 345 9–05
Airedale NHS Trust v Bland [1993] A.C. 789; [1993] 2 W.L.R. 316 1–88
Airey v Ireland (A/32) (1979–80) 2 E.H.R.R. 305; Sries A No. 32 (1979) 8–33, 8–34
Aitken v Aitken, 1978 S.C. 297; 1978 S.L.T. 183 8–57
Akhtar v Secretary of State for the Home Department sub nom: Akhtar,
    Petitioner, 2001 S.L.T. 1239; 2000 G.W.D. 13-495 9–05
Akram v Akram, 1979 S.L.T. (Notes) 87 9–26
Alexander v Alexander, 1957 S.L.T. 298 10–38
Alexandra v Murphy, 2000 S.L.T. (Sh Ct) 44; 2000 S.C.L.R. 200 11–71
Allan v Greater Glasgow Health Board, 1998 S.L.T. 580; (1993) 17 B.M.L.R.
    135 1–32

Allardyce v Johnston, 1979 S.L.T. (Sh. Ct.) 54 3–39
Allen v Bloomsbury HA [1993] 1 All E.R. 651; [1992] P.I.Q.R. Q50 1–31
Anderson v Anderson, 1991 S.L.T. (Sh. Ct.) 11 .... 15–04, 15–13, 15–17
—— v Anderson, 1993 G.W.D. 35-2258 11–25
—— v Anderson, 1993 WL 966116 11–28
—— v Anderson's Trustees (1892) 19 R. 684 12–21
—— v Forth Valley Health Board, 1998 S.L.T. 588; 1998 S.C.L.R. 97 1–39
—— v Armitage (Husband & Wife: Evidence), 1993 S.C.L.R. 173 11–28
Assar v Assar, 1993 G.W.D. 2-102 11–15
—— v Assar, 1994 WL 1716350 11–28
Atkinson v Atkinson, 1988 S.C.L.R. 396 15–19
Attorney General's Reference (No. 3 of 1994) Re [1997] 3 W.L.R. 421; [1997] 3 All
    E.R. 936; [1996] Q.B 581; 2 W.L.R. 412; [1996] 2 All E.R. 10 .... 1–71, 1–72
Attorney-General (Cth) v Kevin and Jennifer [2003] Fam CA 94 (February 21,
    2003) (Australia) 9–38
Attorney General v X [1992] 2 C.M.L.R. 277; (1992) 15 BMLR 104 1–79

B (A Minor) (Adoption by Parent), Re sub nom: B (A Minor) (Adoption:
    Jurisdiction), Re [1975] Fam. 127; [1975] 2 W.L.R. 569 6–28
B (A Minor) (Wardship: Sterilisation), Re [1988] A.C. 199; [1987] 2 W.L.R.
    1213 .... 4–08, 4–09
B and G (Minors) (Custody), Re [1985] F.L.R. 134; [1985] Fam. Law 127 4–81
B v C, 1996 S.L.T. 1370; 1996 S.C.L.R. 874 .... 6–66, 6–67, 6–68
—— v Harris sub nom: C v Harris, 1989 S.C. 278; 1990 S.L.T. 208 .... 5.11
—— v Kennedy, 1987 S.C. 247; 1987 S.L.T. 765 8–44
—— v M (Child Support: Revocation of Order) [1994] 1 F.L.R. 342; [1994]
    1 F.C.R. 769 5–65
—— v United Kingdom [2000] 1 F.L.R. 1; [2000] 1 F.C.R. 289 9–07
Baehr v Miike, Civil Case No. 91 1394 (First Circuit Hawaii, December 3,
    1996) (United States) 9–38
Bangham v Bangham, 1992 G.W.D. 12-96; 1992 G.W.D. 23-1296 ... 3–19, 3–20, 4–77
Bannon v Bannon, 1993 S.L.T. 999 13–50
Barbour v Barbour, 1990 G.W.D. 3-135 11–28
Barclay v Barclay, 1991 S.C.L.R. 205 .... 13–77, 13–80
Barclays Bank Plc v O'Brien [1994] 1 A.C. 180; [1993] 3 W.L.R. 786;
    [1993] 4 All E.R. 417 .... 12–21, 12–28, 12–29, 12–31, 12–32
Baretdji v Baretdji, 1985 S.L.T. 126 4–81
Basinski v Basinski, 1993 G.W.D. 8-533 4–68
Bell v Bell, 1983 S.C. 182; 1983 S.L.T. 224 .... 11–26, 11–28
—— v Bell, 1988 S.C.L.R. 457 13–77
Bellinger v Bellinger [2001] EWCA Civ 1140; [2002] Fam. 150; [2002]
    2 W.L.R. 411; [2002] 1 All E.R. 311 9–40
Benham v United Kingdom (19380/92) (1996) 22 E.H.R.R. 293; Reports,
    1996–III 738 8–33
Berry v Berry (No.1), 1988 S.L.T. 650; 1988 S.C.L.R. 296 11–58
Bisset v Bisset (Husband & Wife: Aliment), 1993 S.C.L.R. 284 10–47
Black v Black, 1990 S.L.T. (Sh. Ct.) 42; 1990 S.C.L.R. 817 4–68
—— v McLeod, 1999 G.W.D. 1219 6–07
Blance v Blance, 1978 S.L.T. 74 .... 4–91, 4–95
Bolam v Friern Hospital Management Committee [1957] 1 W.L.R. 582;
    [1957] 2 All E.R. 118 1–29
Borland v Borland, 1990 G.W.D. 33-1883 4–84
Boyd v Boyd, 1978 S.L.T. (Notes) 55 14–25
Boyle v Boyle, 1977 S.L.T. (Notes) 69 14–20
Boyle's Trustee v Boyle, 1988 S.L.T. 581; 1987 S.C.L.R. 621 12–24
Brannigan v Brannigan, 1979 S.L.T. (Notes) 73 .... 4–91, 4–95
Breingan v Jamieson, 1993 S.L.T. 186 .... 3–21, 4–65, 4–67, 4–68, 4–77,
                                                                                                6–04

Brixey v Lynas (No.1) sub nom: B v L (No.1),1997 S.C. (H.L.) 1; 1996 S.L.T. 908; 1996 S.C.L.R. 856 HL; affirming 1994 S.C. 606; 1994 S.L.T. 847 .... 4–65, 4–68, 4–69, 4–79, 4–85, 4–86

Brodie v Secretary of State for Scotland, 2002 G.W.D. 20-698 12–17

Brooks v Brooks, 1993 S.L.T. 184 13–37

Brotherston v Brotherston (1938) 54 Sh. Ct. Rep. 218 10–47

Brown v Brown, 1985 S.L.T. 376 .... 11–27, 11–28

—— v Brown, 2003 Fam.L.B. 64-2 13–10

Buchan v Buchan, 1992 S.C.L.R. 766 13–39

—— v Buchan, 1993 G.W.D. 23-1515 13–64

—— v Buchan, 2001 Fam.L.R. 48; 2001 G.W.D. 6-226 13–58

Buckland v Buckland (otherwise Camilleri) [1968] P. 296; [1967] 2 W.L.R. 1506 9–31

Buczynska v Buczynski, 1989 S.L.T. 558; 1989 S.C.L.R. 224 .... 13–05, 13–10, 13–13, 13–14

Budge v Budge (No.1), 1990 S.L.T. 319; 1990 S.C.L.R. 144 13–42

—— v Budge, 1994 G.W.D. 38-2234 13–15

Burke v Burke, 1983 S.L.T. 331 9–24

Burnett's Trustee v Grainger [2004] UKHL 8; 2004 S.C. (H.L.) 19; 2004 S.L.T. 513 12–17

Burns v Burns [1984] Ch. 317; [1984] 2 W.L.R. 582 .... 12–10, 12–11

Burn's Trustees, 1961 S.C.17 10–89

Burton v Islington HA sub nom: B v Islington HA Joined Cases: De Martell v Merton and Sutton HA (No.1) [1993] Q.B. 204; [1992] 3 W.L.R. 637; [1992] 3 All E.R. 833 1–24

Bye v Bye, 1999 G.W.D. 33-1591 15–11

C (A MINOR) (Adoption Order: Conditions), Re sub nom: C (A Minor) (Adoption: Contract with Sibling), Re [1989] A.C. 1; [1988] 2 W.L.R. 474 ... 6–66

C (A Minor), Re [1985] F.L.R. 846 3–68

C and C v S sub nom: C, Petitioner; C v S, 1996 S.L.T. 1387; 1996 S.C.L.R ... 3–81, 3–84, 3–87, 6–36

C, Petitioner, 2002 Fam. L.R. 42 7–31

C, Petitioners (Parent and child: Adoption), 1993 S.L.T. (Sh Ct) 8; 1993 S.C.L.R. 14 6–72

C v C (A Minor) (Custody Appeal) sub nom: C (A Minor), Re [1991] 1 F.L.R. 223; [1991] F.C.R. 254 4–73

—— v K, 2004 G.W.D. 40-813 6–07

—— v Kennedy, 1991 S.C. 68; 1991 S.L.T. 755 8–28

—— v McM, 2005 Fam. L.R. 21 4–88

—— v Miller, sub nom: EC v Miller, 2003 S.L.T. 1379; 2004 S.C.L.R. 55; 2003 (October) SCOLAG 185 8–32

—— v S (Foetus: Unmarried Father) [1988] Q.B. 135; [1987] 2 W.L.R. 1108; [1987] 1 All E.R. 1230 1–83

Cahill v Cahill, 1998 S.L.T. (Sh Ct) 96; 1998 G.W.D. 11-556 13–59

Calleja v Calleja, 1996 S.C. 479; 1997 S.L.T. 579; 1996 S.C.L.R. 963 4–65

Cameron v Carr's Curator ad Litem sub nom: Cameron v Carr (No.1), 1998 S.L.T. (Sh Ct) 22; 1997 S.C.L.R. 1164 3–41

—— v MacIntyre's Executor sub nom: Cameron v Gibson, 2006 S.C. 283; 2006 S.L.T. 176; 2005 Fam. L.R. 108 6–33

—— v Stenhouse, 1998 G.W.D. 24-1230 5–07

Campbell and Cosans v United Kingdom (1982) 4 E.H.R.R. 293 .... 4–22, 5–12

—— v Campbell (1866) 4 M 867 9–56

—— v Campbell (1867) 5 M (HL) 115 9–57

—— v Grossart, 1988 G.W.D. 24-1004 3–30

Campins v Campins, 1979 S.L.T. (Notes) 41 4–65

Caparo Industries Plc v Dickman [1990] 2 A.C. 605; [1990] 2 W.L.R. 358 ...... 1–36, 1–38, 1–43, 1–47, 1–48

Carmichael v Carmichael's Executrix, 1920 S.C. (H.L.) 195; 1920 2 S.L.T. 285 ...   12–53
Carpenter v Carpenter, 1990 S.L.T. (Sh. Ct.) 68; 1990 S.C.L.R. 206   13–90
Carroll v Carroll, 2000 Fam. L.B. 58-6   13–12
Cattanach v Melchior [2003] HCA 38; [2003] Lloyd's Rep. Med. 447   1–38
Central RC v B, 1985 S.L.T. 413   6–60
Central RC v M (Parent & Child: Adoption), 1991 S.C.L.R. 300   6–40
Clark v Clark, 1987 G.W.D. 35-1240 ....   4–65, 6–03
Clarke v Hatten, 1987 S.C.L.R. 527   11–64
Clayton v Clayton, 1996 G.W.D. 18-1000   4–54
Clokie v Clokie, 1994 G.W.D. 35-2078   13–64
Clydesdale Bank Plc v Black, 2002 S.C. 555; 2002 S.L.T. 764   12–33
Coat's Trustees, Petitioners, 1914 S.C. 723; 1914 1 S.L.T. 504   5–94
Cohen v Shaw, 1992 S.L.T. 1022; 1992 S.C.L.R. 182   1–17
Colagiacomo v Colagiacomo, 1983 S.L.T. 559   11–27
Collins v Collins, 1993 G.W.D. 5-245   4–95
Cooke v Head (No.1) [1972] 1 W.L.R. 518; [1972] 2 All E.R. 38 ....   12–10, 12–11
Cooper v Cooper, 1989 S.C.L.R. 347   13–44
Cooper's Judicial Factor v Valentine, 1976 S.C. 63   10–89
Corbett v Corbett [1971] P. 83; [1970] 2 W.L.R. 1306 ....   9–37, 9–38
Cordiner v Cordiner, 2003 Fam. L.R. 39; 2003 G.W.D. 6-145   13–41
Cosh v Cosh, 1979 S.L.T. (Notes) 72   4–95
Cossey v United Kingdom sub nom: C v United Kingdom; Cossey v United
    Kingdom [1991] 2 F.L.R. 492; (1991) 13 E.H.R.R. 622   9–41
Costanda v M, 1997 S.L.T. 1396; 1997 G.W.D. 16-704 ....   8–21, 8–44
Cowen v Brown, 1991 G.W.D. 29-1718   4–86
Cower v Cower, 1969 S.L.T. (Notes) 78   4–95
Coyle v Coyle, 2004 Fam. L.R. 2; 2004 G.W.D. 2-30; 2004 Fam. L.B. 67-6,
    67-7   13–61
Crockett v Crockett, 1992 S.C.L.R. 591 ....   13–05, 13–24
Crosbie v Crosbie, 1995 Fam. L.B. 14-6   13–82
——— v Crosbie, 1996 S.L.T. (Sh Ct) 86; 1995 S.C.L.R. 399   13–37
Crozier v Crozier [1994] Fam. 114; [1994] 2 W.L.R. 444; [1994] 1 F.L.R. 126 ...   2–40
Crow v Crow (Divorce: Occupancy Rights), 1986 S.L.T. 270   11–57
Cunniff v Cunniff (Ex Div), 1999 S.C. 537; 1999 S.L.T. 992   13–22
Cunningham v Cunningham, 2001 Fam. L.R. 12; 2000 G.W.D. 36-1362   13–41
——— v M, 2005 S.L.T. (Sh Ct) 73; 2005 Fam. L.R. 14 ....   8–23, 8–24
Currie v Currie, 1950 S.C. 10; 1950 S.L.T. 15   3–57
Cuthbertson v Cuthbertson, 1993 G.W.D. 32-2020   4–95
Cuthill v Burns (1864) 24 D.849

D (An Infant) (Adoption: Parent's Consent), Re [1977] A.C. 602; [1977]
    2 W.L.R. 79; [1977] 1 All E.R. 145 ....   4–74, 6–58
D (A Minor), Re sub nom: D (A Minor) v Berkshire CC; D (A Minor), Re (Baby:
    Care Proceedings) [1987] A.C. 317; [1986] 3 W.L.R. 1080; [1987] 1 All E.R.
    20 ....   1–26, 8–22
D (A Minor) (Wardship: Sterilisation), Re [1976] Fam. 185; [1976] 2 W.L.R. 279;
    [1976] 1 All E.R. 326 ....   4–07, 4–08
D (Minors) (Adoption Reports: Confidentiality), Re [1996] A.C. 593; [1995]
    3 W.L.R. 483; [1995] 4 All E.R. 385   4–61
D v Berkshire County Council *see* D (A Minor), Re
D v D, 2005 G.W.D. 9-128   5–22
D & D v F (Parent & Child: Adoption), 1994 S.C.L.R. 417 ....   6–35, 6–54, 6–59
D v Grampian RC sub nom: D (Minors) (Adoption: Access), Re, 1995 S.C.
    (H.L.) 1; 1995 S.L.T. 519; 1995 S.C.L.R. 516 ....   4–40, 6–65, 7–64
——— v H, 2004 S.L.T. (Sh Ct) 73; 2004 Fam. L.R. 41   4–42
——— v Irvine, 2005 S.L.T. (Sh Ct) 131; 2005 Fam. L.R. 94   5–11
——— v Sinclair, 1973 S.L.T. (Sh. Ct.) 47   8–64
——— v Sinclair, 1995 G.W.D. 19-1053   8–22

D v Strathclyde, 1985 S.L.T. 114 .... 8–58, 8–60
Da Silva Mouta v Portugal [2001] 1 F.C.R. 653; (2001) 31 E.H.R.R. 47; 2001
    Fam. L.R. 2 .... 4–75, 9–05
Dance v Archibald, 1989 G.W.D. 13-535 4–65
Darrie v Duncan, 2001 S.L.T. 941; 2001 Fam. L.R. 81 15–32
Davidson v Davidson 1994 S.L.T. 506 13–41
De Winton v De Winton, 1996 Fam. L.B. 23-6 13–65
Dehvasati v Dehvasati, 2003 Fam. L.B. 63-3 13–57
Delaney v Delaney [1990] 2 F.L.R. 457; [1991] F.C.R. 161 5–53
Dever v Dever, 1988 S.C.L.R. 352 13–73
Dewar v Dewar, 1995 S.L.T. 467 9–56
Dible v Morton Fraser Partnership, 2001 Fam. L.R. 84; 2000 G.W.D.
    28-1097 15–32
Dickson v Dickson, 1990 S.C.L.R. 692 4–98
Docherty v McGlynn (No.1), 1983 S.C. 202; 1983 S.L.T. 645 ...... 3–39, 3–42, 3–45,
                                                      3–47, 3–49, 3–50, 3–53, 3–54
Dollar Land (Cumbernauld) Ltd v CIN Properties Ltd, 1996 S.C. 331; 1997
    S.L.T. 260 12–06
Donald v Donald (1862) 24 D. 499 10–47
Donnelly v Donnelly, 1959 S.C. 97; 1959 S.L.T. 327 10–42
Dosoo v Dosoo (No.1), 1999 S.L.T. (Sh Ct) 86; 1999 S.C.L.R. 905 .... 4–60, 4–61
Dougan v Dougan, 1998 S.L.T. (Sh Ct) 27; 1998 G.W.D. 4-182 13–60
Douglas v Duke of Hamilton (1769) 2 Pat.143 3–24
Dowswell v Dowswell, 1943 S.C. 23; 1943 S.L.T. 153 10–47
Drummond v Drummond, 1992 S.C.L.R. 473 15–13
Dundee City Council, Petitioners, 1999 Fam. L.R. 13; 1998 G.W.D. 9-465 5–21
Dundee City Council v K sub nom: Dundee City Council v GK, 2006 S.C. 326;
    2006 S.L.T. 63; 2006 Fam. L.R. 2; (2006) Fam. L.B. 79-5 4–41
—— v M sub nom: Dundee City Council v C, 2004 S.L.T. 640; 2004 Fam. L.R.
    79 6–31
Dyet v CICB, 1999 S.C.L.R. 1066 5–09
Dysart Peerage Case (1880–81) L.R. 6 App. Cas. 489 9–56

E (A Minor) (Wardship: Medical Treatment), Re [1993] 1 F.L.R. 386; [1994]
    5 Med. L.R. 73 4–10
E v E, 2004 Fam. L.R. 115; 2004 G.W.D. 26-548 4–42
—— v Kennedy, 1992 G.W.D. 25-1400 8–20
Early v Early, 1990 S.L.T. 221 IH (1 Div); affirming 1989 S.L.T. 114 ..... 4–69, 4–73,
                                                                4–79, 4–86
Ebrahem v Ebrahem, 1989 S.L.T. 808; 1989 S.C.L.R. 540 9–26
Edinburgh City Council v M, 1996 S.L.T. (Sh Ct) 112; 1996 S.C.L.R. 779 4–41
Edinburgh & District Tramways Co Ltd v Courtenay, 1909 S.C. 99; (1908)
    16 S.L.T. 548 .... 12–07, 12–08
Elder v Elder, 1985 S.L.T. 471 15–05
Elliot v Lord Joicey sub nom: Joicey, Re; Joicey v Elliot [1935] A.C. 209;
    1935 S.C. (H.L.) 57 1–16
Elsholtz v Elsholtz [2000] F.L.R. 497 2–11
Emeh v Kensington and Chelsea and Westminster AHA [1985] Q.B. 1012;
    [1985] 2 W.L.R. 233; [1984] 3 All E.R. 1044 1–31
Evans v Amicus Healthcare Ltd Joined Cases: Hadley v Midland Fertility
    Services Ltd [2004] EWCA Civ 727; [2005] Fam. 1; [2004] 3 W.L.R. 681; [2004]
    3 All E.R. 1025 3–94
—— v United Kingdom (6339/05) March 7, 2006; [2006] 1 F.C.R. 585; [2006]
    Fam. Law 35 3–94
Eves v Eves [1975] 1 W.L.R. 1338; [1975] 3 All E.R. 768 .... 12–10, 12–11

F (A Minor) (Blood Tests: Paternity Rights), Re [1993] Fam. 314; [1993] 3 W.L.R.
    369; [1993] 1 F.L.R. 598 3–55

F (A Parent) v Kennedy (Reporter to the Children's Panel) (No.1), 1992 S.C. 28;
  1993 S.L.T. 1277 .... 2–66, 2–67, 2–68
F (In Utero), Re [1988] Fam. 122; [1988] 2 W.L.R. 1288; [1988] 2 All E.R. 193 ....
  1–06, 1–07
F, Re sub nom: F v West Berkshire HA [1990] 2 A.C. 1; [1989] 2 W.L.R.
  1025 4–09
F v F Ancillary Relief: Substantial Assets) [1995] 2 F.L.R. 45; [1996] 2 F.C.R.
  397 .... 15–03, 15–26
—— v F sub nom: F v P, 1991 S.L.T. 357; 1991 S.C.L.R. 334 .... 4–39, 6–39
—— v Wirral MBC sub nom: Fitzpatrick v Wirral MBC [1991] Fam. 69; [1991]
  2 W.L.R. 1132; [1991] 2 All E.R. 648 4–12
Fairbairn v Fairbairn, 1998 G.W.D. 23-1149 4–87
Farrell v Farrell, 1990 S.C.L.R. 717 .... 13–54, 13–64
Fife Council, Applicant (2003) Fam. L.B. 63-5 7–28
Findlay v Findlay, 1991 S.L.T. 457 .... 14–01, 14–13
Finlayson, Applicant sub nom: Finlayson v I, 1989 S.C.L.R. 601 .... 4–10, 4–19,
  5–16, 8–22
Fitzpatrick v Sterling Housing Association Ltd [2001] 1 A.C. 27; [1999] 3 W.L.R.
  1113; [1999] 4 All E.R. 705; HL; reversing [1998] Ch. 304; [1998] 2 W.L.R. 225;
  [1997] 4 All E.R. 99 .... 4–75, 9–03, 10–29
Fleming v Fleming, 1993 G.W.D. 9-621 13–49
Fletcher v Young, 1936 S.L.T. 572 10–58
Flett v Flett, 1994 S.C.L.R. 189 .... 4–17, 5–22
Forrest Hamilton's Trustee v Forrest Hamilton, 1970 S.L.T. 338 12–49
Fourman v Fourman, 1998 Fam. L.R. 98; 1998 G.W.D. 32-1638 .... 2–45, 4–84
Fowler v Fowler, 1981 S.L.T. (Notes) 9 .... 4–20, 4–24, 4–87
Fraser v Fraser, 1994 Fam. L.B. 10-3 13–53
Frette v France [2003] 2 F.L.R. 9; [2003] 2 F.C.R. 39; (2004) 38 E.H.R.R. 21 ... 4–75
Friday v Friday [1970] 3 All E.R. 554 14–11
Frith v Frith, 1990 G.W.D. 5-266 10–38
Fullarton v Fullarton, 1976 S.L.T. 8; 1975 S.L.T. (Notes) 76 14–11
Fulton v Fulton, 1998 S.L.T. 1262; 2000 Fam. L.R. 8 13–20
Furber v Furber (No.1), 1999 S.L.T. (Sh Ct) 26; 1999 S.C.L.R. 145 11–71

G v G, 1999 Fam. L.R. 30; 1999 G.W.D. 10-447 4–96
—— v G, 2000 (59) Fam. L.B.5 4–48
—— v G, 2003 Fam. L.R. (Notes) 118 4–88
—— v H, 1999 G.W.D. 24-1125 8–29
—— v Templeton, 1998 S.C.L.R. 180 5–11
Gallacher v Gallacher, 1997 S.L.T. (Sh Ct) 42; 1997 S.C.L.R. 174 4–58
Galloway (Jean) v Galloway (John) sub nom: Tease v Galloway, 2003 Fam.
  L.R. 10; 2002 G.W.D. 40-1349; 2003 Fam. L.B. 61-5 .... 13–35, 13–77
Gardner v Gardner (1876) 3 R. 695 3–28
Geddes v Geddes, 1987 G.W.D. 11-349 4–69
—— v Geddes, 1993 S.L.T. 494; 1993 S.C.L.R. 299 .... 13–46, 13–88, 13–89
Ghaidan v Godin-Mendoza sub nom: Ghaidan v Mendoza; Godin-Mendoza v
  Ghaidan; Mendoza v Ghaidan [2002] EWCA Civ 1533; [2003] Ch. 380;
  [2003] 2 W.L.R. 478; [2002] 4 All E.R. 1162 .... 9–03, 10–16, 15–25
Gibson v Gibson, 1990 G.W.D. 4-213 13–26
Gibson v Hunter Home Designs Ltd, 11976 S.C. 23; 1976 S.L.T. 94 12–17
Gillick v West Norfolk and Wisbech AHA [1986] A.C. 112; [1985] 3 W.L.R. 830;
  [1985] 3 All E.R. 402 .... 2–10, 2–17, 2–29, 2–30, 2–31, 2–32, 3–33, 4–12,
  4–31, 4–34, 4–37
Gillon v Gillon (No.1), 1994 S.L.T. 978; 1993 S.C.L.R. 768 .... 15–15, 15–32
—— v Gillon (No.3), 1995 S.L.T. 678; 1995 S.C.L.R. 405 .... 15–16, 15–17
Gissing v Gissing [1971] A.C. 886; [1970] 3 W.L.R. 255 .... 12–10, 12–11
Glasgow City Council v H sub nom: Glasgow City Council v DH, 2004 S.C. 189;
  2003 S.L.T. 948 .... 7–53, 7–57

Glennan v McKinnon, 1998 SCCR 285 11–70
Goldie v Goldie, 1992 G.W.D. 21-1225 13–52
Gollins v Gollins [1964] A.C. 644; [1963] 3 W.L.R. 176 14–11
Goodwin and others v Department of Public Health 440 Mass. 309 798 N.E.
 2CD 941 (United States) 9–44
Goodwin v United Kingdom (1996) 22 E.H.R.R. 123; 1 B.H.R.C. 81 9–05
—— v United Kingdom (28957/95) [2002] I.R.L.R. 664; [2002] 2 F.L.R.
 487 .... 9–05, 9–41, 9–42
Grant v Edwards [1986] Ch. 638; [1986] 3 W.L.R. 114 12–10
—— v Grant, 2000 G.W.D. 5-177 4–62
—— v South West Trains Ltd (C249/96) [1998] All E.R. (EC) 193; [1998]
 E.C.R. I-621; [1998] I.C.R. 449 4–75
Gray v Gray, 1968 S.C. 185; 1968 S.L.T. 254 13–96
—— v Gray, 1991 G.W.D. 8-477 14–10
Greenwald, In Re Marriage of 454 N.W. 2d 34 (Wis.Ct.App. 1990) (United
 States) 15–26
Gribb v Gribb (No.2), 1996 S.L.T. 719; 1995 S.C.L.R. 1007 13–37
Grieve v Pringle (1797) Mor. 5951 10–06
Grimes v Grimes, 1995 S.C.L.R. 268 14–52
Guest v Annan, 1988 S.C.C.R. 275 5–11
Guillar v Scott, 1994 G.W.D. 33-1932 4–89
Guyan v Guyan (Note), 2001 Fam. L.R. 99 11–60

H (A CHILD) (Adoption: Consultation of Unmarried Fathers), Re sub nom:
 H (A Child) (Adoption: Disclosure), Re Joined Cases: G (A Child)
 (Adoption: Disclosure), Re [2001] 1 F.L.R. 646; [2001] 1 F.C.R. 726 9–07
H (A Minor) (Guardian ad Litem: Requirement), Re sub nom: H (A Minor) (Role
 of Official Solicitor), Re; H (A Minor) (Independent Representative),
 Re [1994] Fam. 11; [1993] 3 W.L.R. 1109; [1994] 4 All E.R. 762 2–44
HQ and LQ v CG, unreported, Inner House, October 16, 1992 6–29
H v H (Contact Order: Views of Child), 2000 Fam. L.R. 73; 2000 G.W.D.
 11-376 2–44
Haggerty v Woodrow (2005) G.W.D. 35-654 4–72
Hall v Hall (Husband & Wife: Occupancy Rights), 1987 S.L.T. (Sh. Ct.) 15;
 1987 S.C.L.R. 38 .... 11–57, 11–58
Hamilton v Fife Health Board, 1993 S.C. 369; 1993 S.L.T. 624; IH (Ex Div);
 reversing 1992 S.L.T. 1026; 1992 S.C.L.R. 288 .... 1–19, 1–20, 1–23, 1–24, 7–31
Hammond v Mitchell [1991] 1 W.L.R. 1127; [1992] 2 All E.R. 109 12–12
Hampsey v Hampsey, 1988 G.W.D. 24-1035 11–15
Hannah v Hannah (Parent and child: Custody), 1971 S.L.T. (Notes) 42 4–68
Hardman v Amin [2000] Lloyd's Rep. Med. 498; (2001) 59 B.M.L.R. 58 1–47,
 1–49, 1–51
Harper v Harper, 1990 G.W.D. 40-2322 10–39
Harris v F, 1991 S.L.T. 242; 1991 S.C.L.R. 124 8–44
Harriton v Stephens [2004] NSWCA 93 1–65
Harvey v Duff, 1995 G.W.D. 5-229 4–89
—— v Strathclyde RC, 1989 S.L.T. 612 5–21
Hastie v Hastie, 1985 S.L.T. 146 .... 4–68, 14–15
Hastings v Hastings, 1941 S.N. 69; 1941 S.L.T. 323 14–10
Haugan v Haugan (No.1) sub nom: Haughan v Haughan (No.1), 2002 S.C. 631;
 2002 S.L.T. 1349; IH (Ex Div); affirming 1996 S.L.T. 321 .... 13–78, 13–79, 13–80
Hay v Hay, 2000 Fam. L.B. 46-4 5–42
—— v Jamieson (1672) Mor. 1009 13–92
Hedley Byrne & Co Ltd v Heller & Partners Ltd [1964] A.C. 465; [1963] 3 W.L.R.
 101 .... 1 46
Heenan v Dillon, 1999 S.L.T. (Sh Ct) 32; 1999 S.C.L.R. 547 11–71
Henderson v Henderson, 1997 Fam. L.R. 120; 1997 G.W.D. 28-138 .... 2–44, 4–59
Henry v Henry, 1972 S.C. 134; 1972 S.L.T. (Notes) 26 .... 10–40, 10–81

Heritable Reversionary Co Ltd v Millar (1891) 19 R. (H.L.) 43 12–17
Hernandez-Cimorra v Hernandez-Cimorra, 1992 S.C.L.R. 611 13–91
Hewison v Hewison (1977) 7 Fam. Law 207 4–81
Higgins v Higgins, 2004 Fam. L.B. 67-7 10–52
Hill v Hill, 1991 S.L.T. 189; 1990 S.C.L.R. 238 4–73
Hoffmann v Austria [1994] 1 F.C.R. 193; (1994) 17 E.H.R.R. 293 4–82
Hogarth v Hogarth, 1991 G.W.D. 30-1771 4–79
Hood v Hood (1871) 9M 449 10–58
Horsburgh v Horsburgh (Husband and wife: Contract), 1949 S.C. 227; 1949
   S.L.T. 355 10–13
Horton v Horton, 1992 S.L.T. (Sh. Ct.) 37; 1992 S.C.L.R. 197 .... 15–05, 15–07
Houston, Applicant, 1996 S.C.L.R. 943; (1996) 32 B.M.L.R. 93 4–34
Huggins v Huggins, 1981 S.L.T. 179 2–46
Hume v Hume, 1926 S.C. 1008; 1926 S.L.T. 706 4–65
Hunter v Bradford Property Trust Ltd, 1977 S.L.T. (Notes) 33 9–31
——— v Hanley, 1955 S.C. 200; 1955 S.L.T. 213 1–29
——— v Hunter (1900) 2 F. 771 14–07
——— v Hunter, 1998 Fam. L.B. 33-5 4–96
Hussain v Hussain [1983] Fam. 26; [1982] 3 W.L.R. 679 9–24
Hyde v Hyde sub nom: Hyde v Hyde and Woodmansee (1865–69) L.R. 1 P. & D.
   130; [1861–73] All E.R. Rep. 175 9–10

I v ARGYLL AND CLYDE HEALTH BOARD, 2003 S.L.T. 231; 2002 G.W.D. 40-1319 ... 5–31
Imre v Mitchell, 1958 S.C. 439; 1959 S.L.T. 13 IH (1 Div); 1958 S.L.T. 57 3–38,
                                                                                                       3–49
Inglis v Inglis, 1987 S.C.L.R. 608 5–45
——— v Inglis, 1999 S.L.T. (Sh Ct) 59; 1998 G.W.D. 26-1335 15–16
Inland Revenue Commissioners v Duchess of Portland [1982] Ch. 314; [1982]
   2 W.L.R. 367; [1982] 1 All E.R. 784 10–03

J v C SUB NOM: C (An Infant), Re [1970] A.C. 668; [1969] 2 W.L.R. 540; [1969]
   1 All E.R. 788 4–63
Jacques v Jacques sub nom: Lightbody v Jacques, 1997 S.C. (H.L.) 20; 1997 S.L.T.
   459; HL; affirming 1995 S.C. 327; 1995 S.L.T. 963 ... 13–14, 13–20, 13–24, 13–40,
                                                                           13–42, 13–54, 13–96
Jamieson v McLeod (1880) 7 R. 1131 12–38
Jesner v Jesner (Divorce: Financial provision), 1992 S.L.T. 999 13–39
Joffre v Joffre, 1992 G.W.D. 27-1522 .... 4–20, 4–95
Johansen v Norway (1997) 23 E.H.R.R. 33 6–51
Johnson v Calvert (1993) 5 Cal 4th 84 .... 3–70, 3–88
——— v Francis, 1982 S.L.T. 285 4–79
——— v Johnson, 1972 S.L.T. (Notes) 15 4–79
Johnston v Johnston, 1996 S.L.T. 499 4–96
——— v Johnston, 2000 Fam. LB. 47-7 4–62
——— v Johnston, 2004 Fam. L.B. 70-6 13–60
Johnstone v Johnstone, 1990 S.L.T. (Sh. Ct.) 79; 1990 S.C.L.R. 358 ... 13–50, 13–77
Jongejan v Jongejan, 1993 S.L.T. 595 .... 15–13, 15–18
Jopp v Johnstone's Trustee (1904) 6 F. 1028 .... 12–15, 12–16

K AND F, APPLICANTS, 2002 S.L.T. (Sh Ct) 38; 2002 S.C.L.R. 769; 2002 Fam.
   L.R. 44 7–31
K Petitioners, 1994 Fam. L.B. 8-2 6–67
K v Finland Joined Cases: T v Finland [2000] 2 F.L.R. 79; [2000] 3 F.C.R. 248;
   (2001) 31 E.H.R.R. 18 6–51
——— v Finland (No.2) sub nom: T v Finland (No.2) [2001] 2 F.L.R. 707; [2001]
   2 F.C.R. 673; (2003) 36 E.H.R.R. 18 7–31
——— v K (Ancillary Relief: Prenuptial Agreement) [2003] 1 F.L.R. 120; [2002]
   Fam. Law 877 .... 15–03, 15–26

KD (A Minor) (Ward: Termination of Access), Re [1988] A.C. 806; [1988]
  2 W.L.R. 398; [1988] 1 All E.R. 57 4–92
Kamperman v MacIver, 1994 S.C. 230; 1994 S.L.T. 763 9–56
Katz v Katz [1972] 1 W.L.R. 955; [1972] 3 All E.R. 219 14–11
Keegan v Ireland [1994] 3 F.C.R. 165; (1994) 18 E.H.R.R. 342 6–44
Kelly v Gilmartin's Executrix, 2002 S.C. 602 5–07
—— v Kelly, 1997 S.C. 285; 1997 S.L.T. 896 .... 1–06, 1–79, 1–84
Kennedy v A (A Parent), 1993 S.L.T. 1134 .... 5–11, 8–20
—— v B (Supervision Requirement), 1991 S.C. 394; 1992 S.C.L.R. 55 8–44
—— v H, 1988 S.C. 114; 1988 S.L.T. 586 8–28
—— v M, 1992 G.W.D. 39-2283 8–20
—— v M, 1995 S.C. 121; 1995 S.L.T. 717; 1995 S.C.L.R. 88 8–57
—— v R's Curator ad litem, 1992 S.C. 300; 1993 S.L.T. 295 .... 8–23, 8–24
Kerr, Petitioner, 1968 S.L.T. (Sh. Ct.) 61 10–88
Kerrigan v Kerrigan, 1988 S.C.L.R. 603 13–41
Knight v Wedderburn (1778) Mor. 14545 1–03
Knox v Knox, 1993 S.C.L.R. 381 14–12
Koniarska v United Kingdom (Admissibility) (33670/96) sub nom: Koniarski v
  United Kingdom (Admissibility) (33670/96) (2000) 30 E.H.R.R. CD139;
  ECHR, 12 October 2000 8–54
Kyle v Stewart, 1989 G.W.D. 14-580 .... 4–68, 6–03

L, PETITIONERS (No.1) sub nom: L v Kennedy, 1993 S.L.T. 1310; 1993 S.C.L.R.
  693 8–47
L, Petitioners (No.2) (Children's Hearing), 1993 S.L.T. 1342 8–47
L v Central RC, 1990 S.L.T. 818 6–48
—— v H, 1996 S.C.L.R. 285 8–29
—— v L, 1996 S.L.T. 767; 1996 S.C.L.R. 11 2–66
—— v L's Curator ad Litem sub nom: Lawrence, Petitioner, 1997 S.L.T. 167;
  (1996) 32 B.M.L.R. 87 4–09
—— v Stott, 2002 G.W.D. 35-1163 5–14
Lang v Lang, 1921 S.C. 44; 1920 2 S.L.T. 353 9–28
Latter v Latter, 1990 S.L.T. 805 .... 13–18, 13–19, 13–39
Lavelle v Lavelle, 2001 G.W.D. 4-144 5–21
Law Hospital NHS Trust v Lord Advocate, 1996 S.C. 301; 1996 S.L.T. 848;
  [1996] 2 F.L.R. 407 4–36
Le Riche v Le Riche, 2001 Fam. L.B. 51-8 13–41
Lee v Lau [1967] P. 14; [1964] 3 W.L.R. 750 9–24
—— v Taunton and Somerset NHS Trust [2001] 1 F.L.R. 419; [2001] Fam. Law
  103 .... 1–49, 1–50, 1–51
Leeds Teaching Hospitals NHS Trust v Mr and Mrs A [2003] RWHC 259
  (QB) 3–77
Lewis v Lewis [1978] Fam. 60; [1978] 2 W.L.R. 644; [1978] 1 All E.R. 729 11–40
—— v Lewis, 1992 G.W.D. 27-1524 4–85
—— v Lewis, 1993 S.C.L.R. 32 .... 13–22, 13–24
Liddle v Morton 1996 G.W.D. 22-1292 11–39
Little v Little, 1990 S.L.T. 785; 1991 S.C.L.R. 47 ... 13–02, 13–42, 13–49, 13–95, 13–96
Lloyds Bank Plc v Rosset [1991] 1 A.C. 107; [1990] 2 W.L.R. 867 12–10
Logan v Logan, 2002 Fam. L.B. 55-4 13–32
Long v Long, 1950 S.L.T. (Notes) 32 9–27
Lothian RC v A, 1992 S.L.T. 858; 1992 S.C.L.R. 37 .... 6–48, 6–49, 6–52, 6–56,
                                                                                        6–57, 6–58
Louden v Louden, 1994 S.L.T. 381 (OH) 13–12, 13–64
Low v Gorman, 1970 S.L.T. 356 .... 9–56, 9–57

M (A MINOR) (Care Order: Threshold Conditions), Re sub nom: M (A Minor)
  (Care Order: Significant Harm), Re [1994] 2 A.C. 424; [1994] 3 W.L.R. 558;
  [1994] 3 All E.R. 298; [1994] 2 F.L.R. 577 7–30

M (I) v Kennedy, 1993 S.C. 115; 1993 S.C.L.R. 69 2–66
M v C (Children: Consent to Change of Name), 2002 S.L.T. (Sh Ct) 82; 2002
   G.W.D. 14-457 .... 5–15, 5–22
—— v Caldwell, 2001 S.L.T. (Sh Ct) 106; 2001 Fam. L.R. 76 8–34
—— v Children's Hearing for Strathclyde Region, 1988 S.C.L.R. 592 8–57
—— v D and Dumfries and Galloway Council, 2001 Fam. L.R. 58 7–21
—— v Dumfries and Galloway RC, 1991 S.C.L.R. 481 .... 4–41, 7–21
—— v M (Residence Order), 2000 Fam. L.R. 84; 2000 G.W.D. 21-826 4–84
—— v Netherlands App. No. 16944/90, 74 DR 120, February 8, 1993 4–77
M (A Parent) v Kennedy (Children's Hearing), 1993 S.L.T. 431; 1991 S.C.L.R.
   898 8–49
MB (Caesarean Section), Re sub nom: MB (Medical Treatment), Re [1997]
   2 F.L.R. 426; [1997] 2 F.C.R. 541; (1997) 38 B.M.L.R. 175 1–87
McAlinden v Bearsden and Milngavie DC, 1986 S.L.T. 191 11–74
McBain v McIntyre, 1997 S.C.L.R. 181 4–48
McAfee v McAfee, 1990 S.C.L.R. 805 .... 15–07, 15–14, 15–18
McCafferty v McCafferty, 1986 S.C. 178; 1986 S.L.T. 650 11–27
McCann v McGurran, 2002 S.L.T. 592; 2002 Fam. L.R. 74 11–72
McCaskill v McCaskill, 2004 Fam. L.B. 72-3 13–24
McClements v McClements, 1958 S.C. 286 4–80
Macleod v Macleod, 1990 G.W.D. 14-767 14–14
MacClue v MacClue, 1994 S.C.L.R. 933 13–88
McCluskey v HM Advocate, 1989 S.L.T. (Notes) 175 1–70
McColl v McColl, 1993 S.C. 276; 1993 S.L.T. 617 10–59
McConnell v McConnell, 1993 Fam. L.B. 6-7 13–25
McCormick v McCormick (Divorce: Financial Provision), 1994 S.C.L.R. 958;
   1994 G.W.D. 35-2078 .... 13–39, 13–64
McCreight v Edinburgh City Council, 2003 S.L.T. (Sh Ct) 45; 2003 Fam. L.R.
   2 6–68
McDonald v McDonald, 1953 S.L.T. (Sh. Ct.) 36; (1953) 69 Sh. Ct. Rep.
   125 12–44
MacDonald v MacDonald, 1985 S.L.T. 244 4–58
MacDonald v MacDonald, 1994 G.W.D. 76-104 .... 13–64, 13–67
Macdonald v MacDonald, 2000 Fam. L.B. 46-4 5–42
Macdonald's Tutor v Macleod, 1995 G.W.D. 28-1498 2–58
McFarlane v Tayside Health Board sub nom: Macfarlane v Tayside Health
   Board [2000] 2 A.C. 59; [1999] 3 W.L.R. 1301; [1999] 4 All E.R. 961; 2000 S.C.L.R.
   105 .... 1–31, 1–32, 1–36, 1–38, 1–39, 1–43, 1–47, 1–49, 1–52, 1–53, 1–54,
                           1–56, 1–57, 1–58, 1–60, 1–61
McGeachie v McGeachie, 1989 S.C.L.R. 99 10–37
McGowan v McGowan, 1986 S.L.T. 112 11–60
McGrath v McGrath, 1999 S.L.T. (Sh Ct) 90; 1999 S.C.L.R. 1121; 1999 Fam.
   L.R. 83 4–61
McGregor v D, 1977 S.C. 330; 1977 S.L.T. 182 8–44
—— v H, 1983 S.L.T. 626 8–23
—— v L, 1981 S.L.T. 194 8–22
McGuire v McGuire's Curator Bonis, 1991 S.L.T. (Sh. Ct.) 76; 1991 S.C.L.R.
   889 13–43
MacInnes v MacInnes (Interim Aliment), 1993 S.L.T. 1108 10–39
McKay v Essex AHA [1982] Q.B. 1166; [1982] 2 W.L.R. 890; [1982] 2 All E.R.
   771 .... 1–65, 1–66, 1–67, 1–68
McKay v McKay, 1957 S.L.T. (Notes) 17 4–80
Mackay v Murphy, 1995 S.L.T. (Sh Ct) 30 3–41
McKechnie v McKechnie, 1990 S.L.T. (Sh. Ct.) 75; 1990 S.C.L.R. 153 . 4–81, 15–29
McKeen v Chief Constable of Lothian and Borders, 1994 S.L.T. 93 4–12
McKenzie v McKenzie, 1935 S.L.T. 198 14–28
MacKenzie v MacKenzie, 1991 S.L.T. 461; 1991 S.L.C.R..252 ... 13–24, 13–77, 13–80
Mackenzie v Scott, 1980 S.L.T. (Notes) 9 9–56

Mackenzie's Tutrix v Mackenzie, 1928 S.L.T. 649 10–34
Mackin v Mackin, 1991 S.L.T. (Sh. Ct.) 22; 1990 S.C.L.R. 728 13–39
McKinnell v White, 1971 S.L.T. (Notes) 61 2–58
Maclachlan v Maclachlan, 1998 S.L.T. 693; 1997 G.W.D. 8-339 13–68
McLean v Dornan sub nom: McLean v Dorman, 2001 S.L.T. (Sh Ct) 97; 2001
    Fam. L.R. 58 4–41
McLean v McLean, 1947 S.C. 79; 1947 S.L.T. 36 4–85
MacLennan v MacLennan, 1958 S.C. 105; 1958 S.L.T. 12 14–07
Maclellan v Maclellan, 1988 S.C.L.R..399 .... 13–13, 13–14
McLelland v Greater Glasgow Health Board, 2001 S.L.T. 446; 2001 G.W.D.
    10-357 Court: IH (Ex Div); affirming in part 1999 S.C. 305; 1998 S.C.L.R.
    1081 .... 1–40, 1–41, 1–42, 1–43
MacLennan v MacLennan, 1958 S.C. 105; 1958 S.L.T. 12 3–60
Maclure v Maclure, 1911 S.C. 200; 1911 1 S.L.T. 84 11–05
McMichael v United Kingdom sub nom: McMichael v United Kingdom [1995]
    2 F.C.R. 718; (1995) 20 E.H.R.R. 205; [1995] Fam. Law 478 .... 3–14, 4–61, 8–39,
    9–06, 9–07
McMillan v Kyle and Carrick DC, 1996 S.L.T. 1149; 1995 S.C.L.R. 365 11–76
—— v McMillan (1871) 9 M. 1067 10–58
—— v McMillan, 2004 Fam. L.B. 70-5 11–60
McNaught v McNaught, 1955 S.L.T. (Sh. Ct.) 9; (1955) 71 Sh. Ct. Rep. 88 4–80
McNeill v McNeill (1997) Fam. L.B. 30-7 4–52
MacRitchie v MacRitchie, 1994 S.L.T. (Sh Ct) 72; 1994 S.C.L.R. 348 13–12
McVinnie v McVinnie (No.2), 1997 S.L.T. (Sh Ct) 12; 1996 G.W.D. 23-1383 . 13–95
McWilliams v Lord Advocate, 1992 S.L.T. 1045; 1992 S.C.L.R. 954 ...... 1–19, 1–21,
    1–23
Mahmood v Mahmood, 1993 S.L.T. 589; 1993 S.C.L.R. 64 ... 9–26, 9–32, 9–33, 9–34
Mahmud v Mahmud, 1977 S.L.T. (Notes) 17 9–26
—— v Mahmud, 1994 S.L.T. 599; 1993 S.C.L.R. 688 .... 9–32, 9–33, 9–34, 9–35
Marckx v Belgium (A/31) (1979–80) 2 E.H.R.R. 330 ... 3–14, 5–36, 9–05, 9–06, 9–07
Martin v N (A Child), 2004 S.C. 358; 2004 S.L.T. 249 .... 8–32, 8–55
Mather v Mather, 1987 S.L.T. 565 11–28
Matheson v Matheson, 1986 S.L.T. (Sh. Ct.) 2 11–28
Mayor v Mayor, 1995 S.L.T. 1097 14–46
Mazur v Mazur, 1990 G.W.D. 35-2011 11–13
Meikle v Meikle, 1987 G.W.D. 26-1005 14–12
Mendoza v Ghaidan *see* Ghaidan v Godin-Mendoza
Meredith v Meredith, 1994 G.W.D. 19-1150 4–73
Merrin (Reporter to the Children's Panel) v S, 1987 S.L.T. 193 .... 2–74, 8–19
Methven v Methven, 1999 S.L.T. (Sh Ct) 117; 1999 G.W.D. 28-1342 15–07
Midland Bank Plc v Cooke [1995] 4 All E.R. 562; [1997] 6 Bank. L.R. 147; [1995]
    2 F.L.R. 915 .... 12–11, 12–18
Midlothian Council v W, 2005 S.L.T. (Sh Ct) 146; 2005 Fam. L.R. 104 4–41
Millar v Millar, 1940 S.C. 56; 1940 S.L.T. 72 11–05
—— v Millar, 1990 S.C.L.R. 666 13–73
—— v Millar, 1991 S.C.L.R. 649 11–27
Miller v Miller sub nom: M v M (Short Marriage: Clean Break) Joined Cases:
    McFarlane v McFarlane [2006] UKHL 24; [2006] 2 W.L.R. 1283; [2006]
    3 All E.R. 1 .... 13–58, 13–75, 13–86, 13–97, 15 03
Milne v Milne, 1987 S.L.T. 45 15–05
—— v Milne, 1994 S.L.T. (Sh. Ct.) 57 .... 11–57, 11–58
Mitchell v H, sub nom: Mitchell v S, 2000 S.C. 334; 2000 S.L.T. 524 8–11
—— v Mitchell, 1994 S.C. 601; 1995 S.L.T. 426 .... 13–13, 13–16
Mitchell's Trustees v Cable (1893) 1 S.L.T. 156 5–38
Mooney, unreported, *Guardian*, October 15, 1994 6–35
Mooney v Mooney, 1987 G.W.D. 3-80 4–65
Morgan Guaranty Trust Co of New York v Lothian RC, 1995 S.C. 151; 1995
    S.L.T. 299 12–09

Morrison v Morrison, 1989 S.C.L.R. 574 13–67
—— v Morrison, 2000 Fam. L.B. (42) 15–07
Morrow v Morrow, 1989 G.W.D. 13-533 4–89
Muir v Muir, 1989 S.L.T. (Sh. Ct.) 20; 1989 S.C.L.R. 445 13–86
Muirhead v Ness, 1996 G.W.D. 30-1784 6–07
Mukhtar v Mukhtar, 2002 Fam. L.B. 60-7 13–41
Mullen v Mullen, 1991 S.L.T. 205 9–57
Munro v Munro, 1986 S.L.T. 72 10–38
Murdoch v Murdoch, 1973 S.L.T. (Notes) 13 11–35
Murley v Murley, 1995 S.C.L.R. 1138 13–88
Murphy v Murphy, 1992 S.C.L.R. 62 11–12
—— v Murphy, 1996 S.L.T. (Sh Ct) 91 13–44

N v L and Fife Council, 2004 G.W.D. 37-750 6–07
Neill v Neill, 1987 S.L.T. (Sh. Ct.) 143 10–42
Newton v Newton, 1923 S.C. 15; 1922 S.L.T. 567 .... 12–13, 12–38
—— v Newton, 1925 S.C. 715; 1925 S.L.T. 476 .... 12–07, 12–09
NHS Trust, An v MB [2006] EWHC 507; [2006] Fam. Law 445 4–10
Nolan v Nolan, 1979 S.C. 40; 1979 S.L.T. 293 14–26
Norfolk and Norwich Healthcare NHS Trust v W [1996] 2 F.L.R. 613; [1997]
    1 F.C.R. 269 1–87
Northampton HA v Official Solicitor [1994] 1 F.L.R. 162; [1994] 2 F.C.R. 206   2–35
Norris v Norris, 1992 S.L.T. (Sh. Ct.) 51; 1992 S.C.L.R. 395 14–25

O (Minors) (Care: Preliminary Hearing) 2003 UKHL 18 7–30
O v Rae, 1993 S.L.T. 570; 1992 S.C.L.R. 318 8–49
O'Connor v A and B sub nom: A&B, Petitioners; A v B & C [1971] 1 W.L.R.
    1227; [1971] 2 All E.R. 1230; 1971 S.C. (H.L.) 129 .... 6–49, 6–53
O'Hagan v Rea, 2001 S.L.T. (Sh Ct) 30; 2001 G.W.D. 2-94 5–21
O'Neill v O'Neill [1975] 1 W.L.R. 1118; [1975] 3 All E.R. 289 14–11
—— v O'Neill, 1987 S.L.T. (Sh. Ct.) 26 11–48
Orlandi v Castelli, 1961 S.C. 113; 1961 S.L.T. 118 9–26
Osborne v Matthan (No.1), 1997 S.C. 29; 1997 S.L.T. 811 4–83
—— v Matthan (No.3), 1998 S.C. 682; 1998 S.L.T. 1264 4–83
Oyeneyin v Oyeneyin, 1999 G.W.D. 38-1836 4–62

P and G (Transexuals) [1996] 2 FLR 90 9–40
P, C and S v United Kingdom (2003) 38 E.H.R.R. 28; 2002 Fam. L.B. 59-7 ...   7–31,
                                                                                                                    9–05
P (Minors) (Wardship: Surrogacy), Re [1987] 2 F.L.R. 421; [1988] F.C.R. 140 .   3–80
P v Kennedy, 1995 S.C. 47; 1995 S.L.T. 476 8–44
—— v Lothian RC, 1989 S.C. 200; 1989 S.L.T. 739 6–55
—— v P, 1999 S.C.L.R. 679 8–29
—— v P (Contact: Supervision), 2000 S.L.T. 781; 2000 S.C.L.R. 477 ..... 8–59, 8–60
Park v Park, 1988 S.C.L.R. 584 13–52
—— v Park, 2000 S.L.T. (Sh Ct) 65; 2000 G.W.D. 14-517 5–42
Parkinson v St James and Seacroft University Hospital NHS Trust [2001] EWCA
    Civ 530; [2002] Q.B. 266; [2001] 3 W.L.R. 376; [2001] 3 All E.R. 97 ...   1–52, 1–53,
                                                                                                         1–54, 1–55, 1–63
Paton v British Pregnancy Advisory Service Trustees [1979] Q.B. 276; [1978]
    3 W.L.R. 687 1–80
—— v United Kingdom (1981) 3 E.H.R.R. 408 .... 1–81, 1–82, 1–83
Patterson v Patterson, 1994 S.C.L.R. 166 15–39
Peacock v Peacock, 1994 S.L.T. 40; 1993 S.C. 88 .... 13–44, 13–67
Peebles v MacPhail, 1990 S.L.T. 245; 1989 S.C.C.R. 410 5–11
Perendes v Sim, 1998 S.L.T. 1382; 1998 G.W.D. 15-735 4–83
Perruche case (2003) 11 Med. L.R. 167 1–69
Petrie v Petrie, 1911 S.C. 360; 1911 1 S.L.T. 43 9–56

Petrie v Petrie, 1988 S.C.L.R. 390 .... 13–12, 13–43
—— v Petrie, 1988 S.C.L.R. 104 13–63
—— v Petrie, 1993 S.C.L.R. 392 .... 3–49, 3–52, 3–53, 3–54
Pettitt v Pettitt sub nom: P v P [1970] A.C. 777; [1969] 2 W.L.R. 966 ... 12–10, 12–11
Phillip v Phillip, 1988 S.C.L.R. 427 13–42
Porchetta v Porchetta, 1986 S.L.T. 105 4–91
Potter v Potter, 1993 S.L.T. (Sh. Ct.) 51; 1992 S.C.L.R. 788 4–52
Practice Note (Official Solicitor: Sterilisation) [1993] 3 All E.R. 222; [1993]
    2 F.L.R. 222 4–09
Preston v Preston, 1950 S.C. 253; 1950 S.L.T. 196 12–50
Preston-Jones v Preston-Jones [1951] A.C. 391; [1951] 1 All E.R. 124 3–57
Proctor v Proctor, 1994 G.W.D. 30-1814 13–69
Pryde v Pryde, 1991 S.L.T. (Sh. Ct.) 26 10–39
—— v Pryde, 1996 G.W.D. 39-2245 11–28
Puddinu v Puddinu, 1987 G.W.D. 4-105 4–91
Pyatt v Pyatt, 1966 S.L.T. (Notes) 73 12–50

Q (A Minor) (Parental Order), Re [1996] 1 F.L.R. 369; [1996] 2 F.C.R. 345 3–76
Quinn v Quinn, 2003 S.L.T. (Sh Ct) 5; 2002 G.W.D. 24-775 .... 13–24, 13–59

R (A Child) (IVF: Paternity of Child) [2005] UKHL 33; [2005] 2 A.C. 621 ... 3–76,
                                                                                            3–85
R (A Minor) [1991] 4 All E.R. 177 .... 2–25, 4–33, 4–34, 4–35
R (A Minor) (Residence: Religion), Re sub nom: R (A Minor) (Religious Sect),
    Re [1993] 2 F.L.R. 163; [1993] 2 F.C.R. 525; [1993] Fam. Law 460 4–81
R, Petitioner sub nom: AR v Reporter for Aberdeen Local Authority; R v
    Templeton; R v Walker, 1999 S.C. 380; 1999 S.L.T. 1233; 1999 Fam. L.R.
    20 2–66
R. (on the application of McCann) v Manchester Crown Court sub nom:
—— v Manchester Crown Court Ex p. M (A Child); R. (on the application of M
    (A Child)) v Manchester Crown Court Joined Cases: Clingham v Kensington
    and Chelsea RLBC [2002] UKHL 39; [2003] 1 A.C. 787; [2002] 3 W.L.R.
    1313 4–66
—— (on the application of Quintavalle) v Human Fertilisation and Embryology
    Authority sub nom: Quintavalle v Human Fertilisation and Embryology
    Authority [2003] EWCA Civ 667; [2004] Q.B. 168; [2003] 3 W.L.R. 878; [2003]
    3 All E.R. 257; CA (Civ Div); reversing [2002] EWHC 3000; [2003] 2 All E.R.
    105; [2003] 1 F.C.R. 664; (2003) 70 B.M.L.R. 236 3–92
—— (on the application of Rose) v Secretary of State for Health sub nom: Rose
    v Secretary of State for Health [2002] EWHC 1593; [2002] 2 F.L.R. 962; [2002]
    3 F.C.R. 731; (2003) 69 B.M.L.R. 83 3–98
—— (on the application of Williamson) v Secretary of State for Education and
    Employment sub nom: Williamson v Secretary of State for Education and
    Employment [2005] UKHL 15; [2005] 2 A.C. 246; [2005] 2 W.L.R. 590 5–18
—— v Bourne [1939] 1 K.B. 687 1–73
—— v Ethical Committee of St Mary's Hospital Ex p. Harriott sub nom: R. v St
    Mary's Hospital Ex p. Harriott [1988] 1 F.L.R. 512; [1988] Fam. Law 165 ... 3–96
—— v Human Fertilisation and Embryology Authority Ex p. Blood sub nom:
    R. v Human Fertilisation and Embryology Authority Ex p. DB [1999] Fam.
    151; [1997] 2 W.L.R. 807; [1997] 2 All E.R. 687 3–93
—— v Kennedy sub nom: R, Petitioner, 1993 S.C. 417; 1993 S.L.T. 910 8–47
—— v Legal Aid Board Ex p. W (Children) sub nom: W (Children) v Legal
    Services Commission [2000] 2 F.L.R. 154; [2000] 1 F.C.R. 165 2–44
—— v Lothian RC, 1987 S.C.L.R. 362 6–58
—— v Luton Magistrates Court Ex p. Sullivan [1992] 2 F.L.R. 196; [1992] F.C.R.
    475 5–79
—— v Morgenthaler [1988] 1 S.C.R. 30 (Canada) 1–74
—— v R, 2000 Fam. L.R. 43 13–41

R. v R (Rape: Marital Exemption) sub nom: R. v R (A Husband) [1992] 1 A.C.
599; [1991] 3 W.L.R. 767 10–05
—— v Smith (John Anthony James) [1973] 1 W.L.R. 1510; [1974] 1 All E.R.
376 1–78
R (Children) v Grant, 2000 S.L.T. 372; 2000 Fam. L.R. 2 2–42
Ramsay v Ramsay's Curator ad litem, 1986 S.L.T. 590 3–29
Ranaldi v Ranaldi, 1994 S.L.T. (Sh Ct) 25 .... 13–15, 13–64
Rand v East Dorset HA [2000] Lloyd's Rep. Med. 181; (2000) 56 B.M.L.R.
39 .... 1–44, 1–45, 1–46, 1–49, 1–50
Rashid v Rashid, 1999 Fam. L.R. 91;1998 G.W.D. 25-1241 6–07
Rees v Darlington Memorial Hospital NHS Trust [2003] UKHL 52; [2004] 1 A.C.
309; [2003] 3 W.L.R. 1091; [2003] 4 All E.R. 987; (2004) 75 B.M.L.R. 69 1–56,
1–57, 1–58, 1–59, 1–60,
1–61
—— v United Kingdom sub nom: Rees v United Kingdom [1987] 2 F.L.R. 111;
(1987) 9 E.H.R.R. 56 .... 9–39, 9–41
—— v Lowe, 1990 J.C. 96; 1990 S.L.T. 507 .... 2–61, 2–62, 2–69
Reynolds v Reynolds, 1991 S.C.L.R. 175 .... 13–24, 13–88
Richardson v LRC Products Ltd [2000] P.I.Q.R. P164; [2000] Lloyd's Rep. Med.
280; (2001) 59 B.M.L.R. 185 1–27
Riley v HM Advocate, 1999 J.C. 308; 1999 S.L.T. 1076; 1999 S.C.C.R. 644 ... 11–70
Rintoul's Trustees v Rintoul (Will: Construction), 1949 S.C. 297; 1949 S.L.T.
244 2–27
Ritchie v Ritchie, 1989 S.C. L.R (Notes) 768 5–46
Robertson v Hutchison, 1935 S.C. 708; 1935 S.L.T. 473 3–58
Roberton v Roberton, 1999 S.L.T. 38; 1998 G.W.D. 12-606 11–28
Roe v Wade, 93 S Ct 705 (1973) 1–74, 1–79
Ross v Ross (Divorce: Behaviour), 1997 S.L.T. (Sh Ct) 51; 1997 G.W.D.
14-618 4–52
Royal Bank of Scotland Plc v Etridge (No.2) Joined Cases: Barclays Bank Plc v
Coleman; Barclays Bank Plc v Harris; Midland Bank Plc v Wallace; National
Westminster Bank Plc v Gill; UCB Home Loans Corp Ltd v Moore; Bank of
Scotland v Bennett; Kenyon-Brown v Desmond Banks & Co (Undue Influence)
(No.2) [2001] UKHL 44; [2002] 2 A.C. 773; [2001] 3 W.L.R. 1021; [2001] 4 All
E.R. 449 .... 12–28, 12–31, 12–33, 15–16
Royal Bank of Scotland Plc v Wilson, 2004 S.C. 153; 2003 S.L.T. 910 12–33
Russell v Russell, 1991 S.C.L.R. 429 .... 4–20, 4–91, 4–95
—— v Russell, 1996 G.W.D. 15-895 13–52
—— v Russell, 1996 Fam. L.B. 21-5 13–69
—— v W, 1998 Fam. L.R. 25 7–50

S (A MINOR) (Independent Representation), Re [1993] Fam. 263; [1993] 2 W.L.R.
801; [1993] 2 F.L.R. 437 2–42
S (Adult: Refusal of Treatment), Re [1993] Fam. 123; [1992] 3 W.L.R. 806; [1992]
4 All E.R. 671 .... 1–87, 2–33
S (An Infant) v S sub nom: S v McC (formerly S) Joined Cases: W v W; W v
Official Solicitor (acting as Guardian ad Litem for a Male Infant named PHW)
[1972] A.C. 24; [1970] 3 W.L.R. 366 .... 3–42, 3–53, 3–55, 3–56
S and others v Murray and others, OH, August 20, 2004 at *www.scotcourts.gov.
uk/opinions/a/19100.hmtl* 5–07
S or B (AP) v M [2005] CSOH 70 5–08
S (G) v Kennedy, 1996 S.L.T. 1087 8–20
S v Glasgow City Council, 2004 S.L.T. (Sh Ct) 128; 2004 G.W.D. 30-616 5–20
—— v HM Advocate sub nom: Stallard v HM Advocate, 1989 S.L.T. 469; 1989
S.C.C.R. 248 10–05
—— v Lynch, 1997 S.L.T. 1377; 1997 S.C.L.R. 971 8–28
—— v Miller (No.1) sub nom: S v Principal Reporter (No.1), 2001 S.C. 977; 2001
S.L.T. 531 .... 2–07, 8–32, 8–33, 8–34, 8–35, 8–36, 8–37, 8–39, 8–54, 9–06

S v Miller (No.2) sub nom: S v Principal Reporter (No.2), 2001 S.L.T. 1304;
2001 G.W.D. 26-995 .... 8–34, 9–04
—— v N, 2002 S.L.T. 589; 2002 Fam. L.R. 40 8–28
—— v United Kingdom (1986) 47 D. & R. 271 9–05
SW v United Kingdom sub nom: SW v United Kingdom Joined Cases: CR v
United Kingdom [1996] 1 F.L.R. 434; (1996) 21 E.H.R.R. 363; [1996] Fam. Law
275 10–05
Saini v Secretary of State for the Home Department, 2001 S.C. 951; 2001 G.W.D.
13-507 9–05
St George's Healthcare NHS Trust v S Joined Cases: R. v Collins Ex p. S (No.1)
[1998] 3 W.L.R. 936; [1998] 3 All E.R. 673 1–88
Saleh v Saleh, 1987 S.L.T. 633 9–54
Salih v Enfield AHA [1991] 3 All E.R. 400; [1991] 2 Med. L.R. 235 1–45
Sanderson v McManus sub nom: S v M (A Minor: Access Order); Sanderson v
MacManus, 1997 S.C. (H.L.) 55; 1997 S.L.T. 629; 1997 S.C.L.R. 28 HL;
affirming 1996 S.L.T. 750; 1995 S.C.L.R. 902 .... 2–66, 4–53, 4–93, 4–94
Savage v Savage, 1993 G.W.D. 28-1779 13–25
Scoffier v Read (1783) Mor. 8936 2–24
Scott v Lothian RC, 1999 Rep. L.R. 15; 1998 G.W.D. 33-1719 7–67
—— v Occidental Petroleum (Caledonia) Ltd, 1990 S.C. 201; 1990 S.L.T.
882 .... 2–39, 4–13
Secretary of State for Health and Community Services v JWB and SMB, F.L.C. 92-3
(Australia) 4–99
Senna-Cheribbo v Wood, 1999 S.C. 328; 1999 G.W.D. 4-162; 1999 Fam. L.B.
4-162 6–07
Shand v Shand, 1994 S.L.T. 387 .... 13–05, 13–50
Sharp v Thomson sub nom: Sharp v Woolwich Building Society, 1997 S.C.
(H.L.) 66; 1997 S.L.T. 636; 1997 S.C.L.R. 328, HL; 1995 S.C. 455; 1995 S.L.T.
837 12–17
Shaw v Henderson, 1982 S.L.T. 211 9–56
Shearer v Shearer, 2004 G.W.D. 38-773 4–69
Sheffield (Kristina) v United Kingdom Joined Cases: Horsham v United
Kingdom [1998] 2 F.L.R. 928; [1998] 3 F.C.R. 141; (1999) 27 E.H.R.R. 163 9–41
Sheret v Sheret, 1990 S.C.L.R. 799 13–86
Sherwin v Trumayne, 1992 G.W.D. 29-1681 .... 5–68, 4–86
Shields v Shields sub nom: Cunningham v Shields, 2002 S.C. 246; 2002 S.L.T.
579 .... 4–84, 4–88
Shilliday v Smith, 1998 S.C. 725; 1998 S.L.T. 976 12–08
Shipton v Shipton, 1992 S.C.L.R. 23 .... 13–69, 13–86
Shishodia v Shishodia, 1995 G.W.D. 17-926 4–69
Short v Short, 1994 G.W.D. 21-1300 13–52
Simeone v Simeone, 581 A. 2d 162 (Pa. 1990) (United States) 15–26
Sinclair v Sinclair, 1988 S.L.T. 87; 1988 S.C.L.R. 44 4–65
Singh v Singh, 2005 S.L.T. 153 13–39
Skarpaas v Skarpaas, 1993 S.L.T. 343; 1992 S.C.L.R. 398; 1991 S.L.T. (Sh. Ct.)
15 .... 13–12, 13–43, 13–90
Skeikh v Skeikh, 2005 Fam. L.R. 7 9–56
Sloan (Reporter: Children's Hearings) v B (A Parent), 1991 S.C. 412; 1991 S.L.T.
530 .... 7–01, 8–25
Sloss v Taylor, 1989 S.C.L.R. 407 .... 3–19, 4–69
Smith v Bank of Scotland Joined Cases: Mumford v Bank of Scotland, 1997
S.C. (H.L.) 111; 1997 S.L.T. 1061 .... 12–28, 12–31, 12–33
—— v Greenhill, 1994 S.L.T. (Sh Ct) 22; 1993 S.C.L.R. 776 .... 3–49, 3–54, 3–56
—— v Smith, 1976 S.L.T. (Notes) 26 14–12
—— v Smith, 1983 S.L.T. 275 .... 11–26, 11–28
—— v Smith, 1989 S.L.T. 668; 1988 S.C. 253 13–12
—— v Smith, 1989 S.L.T. 668; 1988 S.C. 253; 1989 S.C.L.R. 308 13–26
—— v Smith, 1992 G.W.D. 23-1324 13–17

Smith v Woodhead, 1996 G.W.D. 10-533 .... 4–87, 6–04
Sochart v Sochart, 1988 S.L.T. 449 15–19
Soderback v Sweden [1999] 1 F.L.R. 250; (2000) 29 E.H.R.R. 95 .... 3–14, 6–51
Sohrab v Khan, 2002 S.C. 382; 2002 S.L.T. 1255 9–36
Soutar v Kilroe, 1994 S.C.L.R. 757 3–50
Starrs v Ruxton sub nom: Ruxton v Starrs, 2000 J.C. 208; 2000 S.L.T. 42 8–37
Stephen v Stephen, 1995 S.C.L.R. 175 .... 13–49, 13–50
Stevenson v Roy, 2002 S.L.T. 445; 2002 G.W.D. 10-316 11–64
Stewart v Monaghan, 1992 G.W.D. 23-1296 3–20
—— v Stewart, 1914 2 S.L.T. 310 14–06
—— v Stewart, 1959 S.L.T. (Notes) 70 10–03
—— v Stewart, 1987 S.L.T. (Sh. Ct.) 48 14–15
—— v Stewart, 2001 S.L.T. (Sh Ct) 114; 2001 Fam. L.R. 72 13–32
Stott v Stott, 1987 G.W.D. 17-645 13–71
Strathclyde RC v F, 1995 Fam. L.B. 17-6 6–61
Stubbings v Webb [1993] A.C. 498; [1993] 2 W.L.R. 120; [1993] 1 All E.R. 322;
    HL; reversing [1992] Q.B. 197; [1991] 3 W.L.R. 383; [1991] 3 All E.R. 949 ... 5–07
Sullivan v Sullivan, 2004 S.L.T. 118; 2003 Fam. L.R. 53 .... 13–72, 13–86
Surtees v Kingston upon Thames RBC Joined Cases: Surtees v Hughes [1991]
    2 F.L.R. 559; [1992] P.I.Q.R. P101 4–18
Sutherland v Sutherland, 2004 Fam. L.B. 70-04 10–50
Sweeney v Sweeney, 1993 S.L.T. (Sh. Ct.) 892 13–72
—— v Sweeney (No.1), 2004 S.C. 372; 2004 S.L.T. 125; 2004 S.C.L.R. 256; IH
    (Ex Div); reversing in part 2003 S.L.T. 892; 2003 S.C.L.R. 85 .... 13–39, 13–55
Symanski v Symanski, 2005 Fam. L.R. 2 13–59
Syme v Syme (1833) 11 S. 305 10–38
Symon v Symon, 1991 S.C.L.R. 414 .... 13–24, 13–69
Szechter v Szechter [1971] P. 286; [1971] 2 W.L.R. 170 9–33

T (A MINOR) (Adoption: Validity of Order), Re [1986] Fam. 160; [1986] 2 W.L.R.
    538; [1986] 1 All E.R. 817 6–31
T (A Minor) (Wardship: Representation), Re sub nom: CT (A Minor) (Wardship:
    Representation), Re [1994] Fam. 49; [1993] 3 W.L.R. 602 2–40
T (Adult: Refusal of Treatment), Re sub nom: T (Consent to Medical Treatment)
    (Adult Patient), Re [1993] Fam. 95; [1992] 3 W.L.R. 782; [1992] 4 All E.R.
    649 1–88
T (Minors) (Adopted Children: Contact), Re [1995] 2 F.L.R. 251; [1995] F.C.R.
    537 6–68
T, Petitioner sub nom: AMT, Petitioners, 1997 S.L.T. 724; 1996 S.C.L.R. 897;
    [1997] Fam. Law 8 .... 4–74, 6–32
T v A (Parental Rights), 2001 S.C.L.R. 647; 2001 G.W.D. 15-567 8–29
—— v T, 2000 S.C.L.R. 1057 .... 2–67, 2–68, 2–69, 2–71
—— v United Kingdom Joined Cases: V v United Kingdom [2000] 2 All E.R.
    1024 (Note); (2000) 30 E.H.R.R. 121 2–74
TP v United Kingdom (28945/95) [2001] 2 F.L.R. 549; [2001] 2 F.C.R. 289 7–67
Tahir v Tahir (No.2) 1995 S.L.T. 451 13–91
Tameside and Glossop Acute Services NHS Trust v CH (A Patient) [1996]
    1 F.L.R. 762; [1996] 1 F.C.R. 753; (1996) 31 B.M.L.R. 93 1–87
Tattersall v Tattersall, 1983 S.L.T. 506 11–35
Taylor v Taylor, 1988 S.C.L.R. 60 (Sh. Ct.) 14–20
Thake v Maurice [1986] Q.B. 644; [1986] 2 W.L.R. 337; [1986] 1 All E.R. 479 ... 1–31
Thomas v Fuller-Brown [1988] 1 F.L.R. 237; [1988] Fam. Law 53 ...... 12–10, 12–11
Thomson v Thomson, 2003 Fam. L.R. 22; 2002 G.W.D. 40-1352 13–88
Thurlow v Thurlow [1976] Fam. 32; [1975] 3 W.L.R. 161; [1975] 2 All E.R.
    979 14–11
Torrie v Turner, 1990 S.L.T. 718; 1991 S.C.L.R. 33 .... 3–39, 3–40, 3–42
Telfer v Kellock, 2004 S.L.T. 1290 10–16
Tyrrell v Tyrrell, 1990 S.L.T. 406; 1990 S.C.L.R. 244 13–12

U v W (ATTORNEY GENERAL INTERVENING) (No.2) [1998] Fam. 29; [1997]
3 W.L.R. 739; [1997] 2 F.L.R. 282 3–76
Udale v Bloomsbury Area Health Authority[1983] 1 W.L.R. 1098 [1983]
2 All E.R. 522 .... 1–30, 1–31

V v F, 1991 S.C.L.R. 225 4–34
Vance v Vance, 1997 S.L.T. (Sh Ct) 71 13–23
Vo v France [2004] 2 F.C.R. 577; (2005) 40 E.H.R.R. 12; 17 B.H.R.C. 1; (2004)
79 B.M.L.R. 71 .... 1–08, 1–09, 1–10, 1–15, 1–85

W, RE [1992] 4 All E.R. 62 .... 4–33, 4–35, 4–36
W (A Minor) (Adoption: Homosexual Adopter), Re [1998] Fam. 58; [1997]
3 W.L.R. 768; [1997] 3 All E.R. 620 4–74
W (An Infant), Re [1971] A.C. 682; [1971] 2 W.L.R. 1011 .... 6–55, 6–57
W (Minors) (Surrogacy), Re [1991] 1 F.L.R. 385; [1991] Fam. Law 180 3–86
W v B (Paternity: Parental Rights), 2000 G.W.D. 30-1166 6–04
W v H (Child Abduction: Surrogacy) (No.2) [2002] 2 F.L.R. 252; [2002] Fam. Law
501 3–68
W (A Parent) v Kennedy (Reporter to the Children's Hearing) 1988 S.C. 82; 1988
S.L.T. 583; 1988 S.C.L.R. 236 8–44
W v United Kingdom sub nom: W v United Kingdom (1988) 10 E.H.R.R. 29 ... 6–31
—— v W (Nullity: Gender) sub nom: W v W (Physical Inter-sex) [2001] Fam. 111;
[2001] 2 W.L.R. 674; [2001] 1 F.L.R. 324 9–40
Walker v C (No.1), 2003 S.L.T. (Sh Ct) 31; 2002 G.W.D. 5-142 8–11
—— v Walker sub nom: Walker v Walker's Trustees, 1911 S.C. 163; (1910)
2 S.L.T.306 14–28
—— v C (No.2) sub nom: Walker v SC, 2003 S.C. 570; 2003 S.L.T. 293 8–14
Wallis v Wallis, 1993 S.C. (H.L.) 49; 1993 S.L.T. 1348; HL; affirming 1992 S.C.
455; 1992 S.L.T. 676 .... 13–22, 13–24, 13–95, 15–28
Ward v Ward, 1983 S.L.T. 472 .... 11–27, 11–28
Watson v McLay, 2002 Fam. L.R. 20; 2002 G.W.D. 2-73 5–42
—— v Watson, 1994 S.C.L.R. 1097 .... 3–55, 5–42
Webster v Webster, 2003 Fam. L.B. 62-6, 62-7 .... 13–24, 13–32
Weir v Wier, 2005 Fam. L.B. 76-5 13–24
Welsh v Welsh, 1994 S.L.T. 828; 1994 S.C.L.R. 360 .... 13–63, 13–90
West Lothian Council v M sub nom: West Lothian Council v McG, 2002 S.C. 411;
2002 S.L.T. 1155 .... 4–41, 6–50, 6–68, 6–78
White v White, 1966 S.C. 187; 1966 S.L.T. 288 14–14
—— v White, 2001 S.C. 689; 2001 S.L.T. 485 .... 2–11, 4–22, 4–53, 4–94,
6–50
White (Pamela) v White (Martin) [2001] 1 A.C. 596; [2000] 3 W.L.R. 1571 12–03
Whitecross v Whitecross, 1977 S.L.T. 225 .... 4–65, 4–86
Whitehall v Whitehall, 1958 S.C. 252; 1958 S.L.T. 268 .... 3–38, 3–39, 3–40
Whittome v Whittome (No.1), 1994 S.L.T. 114; 1993 S.C.L.R. 137 13–19
Wilkie v Dunlop (1834) 12 S. 506 2–53
Williams v Williams [1964] A.C. 698; [1963] 3 W.L.R. 215 14–11
Wilson v Currie, 1991 G.W.D. 14-872 3–57
—— v Wilson, 1987 G.W.D. 4-106 5–45
—— v Wilson, 1999 S.L.T. 249, OH 13–59
Windeler v Whitehall (1990) 54 J.P. 29; [1990] 2 F.L.R. 505 12–11
Wiseman v Wiseman, 1989 S.C.L.R. 757 10–39
Woodhouse v Wright Johnston & Mackenzie, 2004 S.L.T. 911; 2005 S.C.L.R.
222 5–59
Worth v Worth, 1994 S.L.T. (Sh Ct) 54; 1994 S.C.L.R. 362 15–16
Wright v Wright, 1999 G.W.D. 3-119 6–07

X (MINORS) v BEDFORDSHIRE CC Joined Cases: M (A Minor) v Newham LBC;
E (A Minor) v Dorset CC (Appeal); Christmas v Hampshire CC (Duty of

Care); Keating v Bromley LBC (No.2) [1995] 2 A.C. 633; [1995] 3 W.L.R. 152 7–67

X, Petitioner (Public records: Alteration of entry), 1957 S.L.T. (Sh. Ct.) 61; (1957) 73 Sh. Ct. Rep. 203 9–40

X v Y, 2002 S.L.T. (Sh Ct) 161; (2002) Fam. L.R. 58 ...   4–39, 4–76, 4–77, 4–78, 8–28

X, Y and Z v United Kingdom (25680/94) (UK, European Commission of Human Rights, Information Note No. 129, 6) 9–05

YOUNG V RANKINE, 1934 S.C. 499 5–07

Z V UNITED KINGDOM (29392/95) [2001] 2 F.L.R. 612; [2001] 2 F.C.R. 246 7–67

TABLE OF STATUTES

1696 Blank Bonds and Trusts Act
(c.25) 12–12, 12–13
1849 Judicial Factors Act (12 &
13 Vict. c.51) 5–30
s.10 5–29
s.25(2) 5–29
1853 Evidence (Scotland) Act (16
& 17 Vict. c.112)
s.3 10–18
1861 Conjugal Rights (Scotland)
Amendment Act (24 & 25
Vict. c.96)
s.6 14–35
Offences Against the Person
Act (24 & 25 Vict. c.100)
s.58 1–73
s.59 1–73
1874 Evidence Further Amend-
ment (Scotland) Act (37 &
38 Vict. c.64)
s.1 10–18
1880 Married Women's Policies of
Assurance (Scotland) Act
(43 & 44 Vict. c.26) 12–25,
12–53
s.2 .... 10–29, 12–25,
12–53
1881 Married Women's Property
(Scotland) Act (44 & 45
Vict. c.21)
s.1 10–02
1886 Guardianship of Infants
Act (49 & 50 Vict. c.27) ... 4–04
1907 Deceased Wife's Sister Marriage Act (7 Edw.7 c.47) ... 9–17
1920 Married Women's Property
(Scotland) Act (10 & 11
Geo.5, c.64) 10–02
s.1 .... 10–13, 12–51
s.4 .... 10–14, 10–34
s.5 .... 12–22, 12–38
1921 Trusts (Scotland) Act (11 &
12 Geo.5 c.58) 5–29, 5–30
1925 Guardianship of Infants
Act (15 & 16 Geo.5
c.45) 4–04, 4–50

1929 Infant Life (Preservation)
Act (19 & 20 Geo. 5
c.34) 1–73
s.1(2) 1–73, 1–76, 1–83
Age of Marriage Act (19 &
20 Geo.5 c.36) 9–25
1930 Adoption (Scotland) Act
(20 & 21 Geo.5 c.37) 6–49
1931 Marriage (Prohibited
Degrees of Relationship)
Act (21 & 23 Geo. 5
c.31) 9–17
1937 Children and Young Persons
(Scotland) Act (1 Edw.8 &
1 Geo.6 c.37)
s.12 5–11
(7) 4–05, 5–14
1938 Divorce (Scotland) Act (1 &
2 Geo.6, c.50) ... 14–04, 14–10,
14–11, 14–14
1939 Marriage (Scotland) Act (2
& 3 Geo.6 c.34)
s.5 9–56
1949 Marriage Act (c.76) 9–10
Legal Aid and Solicitors
(Scotland) Act (12 & 13
Geo.6 c.63) 1–04
1962 Law Reform (Husband and
Wife) Act (10 & 11 Eliz. 2,
c.48)
s.2 10–14
1961 Trusts (Scotland) Act (9 &
10 Eliz. 2 c.57) 5–29
s.2 12–17
1964 Succession (Scotland) Act
(c.41) 5–95, 10–83,
10–84, 10–85,
10–97
s.2 10–86
(1)(a) 3–04, 5–95
(b) 3–04
(d) 3–04
s.5(1) 5–95
s.6 5–95
s.8 .... 5–95, 10–84
(1) 10–84

1964 Succession (Scotland)
Act—*contd*
s.8(6) 10–84
(b) 10–84
(c) 12–44
s.9 .... 5–95, 10–84
(3) 10–84
s.11 5–91
(2)(a) 5–91
(b) 5–91
s.23 5–91
(1) 6–26, 6–64
s.36 5–91
(1) 10–84
Divorce (Scotland) Act
(c.91)
s.5(2)(b) 14–11
1965 Registration of Births,
Deaths and Marriages
(Scotland) Act 1965
(c.49) 9–67
ss.13–20 1–06
s.18 3–34
s.20 6–27
s.48 14–56
1967 Abortion Act (c.87) 1–39,
1–45, 1–73, 1–75,
1–79, 1–80, 1–84,
1–86
s.1(1) 1–75, 1–77, 1–78
(a) 1–76, 1–77
(b) 1–77
(d) 1–77
(2) 1–76
(3) 1–77
(3A) 1–77
(4) 1–77
s.5(1) 1–76
1968 Social Work (Scotland) Act
(c.49) 7–05, 7–06, 7–19,
7–21, 7–28,
7–60, 7–61,
7–66, 8–02,
8–06, 8–07
s.12 7–10
(1) 7–10
(2) 7–10
(3) 7–10
(4) 7–10
s.13A 7–10
s.14 7–10
s.15 7–21
ss.16–18A 7–59
s.32(2)(c) 4–10
s.34A 7–07
s.37 7–27
s.42 2–66
s.78 .... 5–49, 7–63

1968 Law Reform (Miscellaneous
Provisions) (Scotland)
Act (c.70) 5–36, 5–38
s.5 5–38
s.11 14–31
1969 Tattooing of Minors Act
(c.24)
s.1 2–34
Age of Majority (Scotland)
Act (c.39) 2–17, 9–25
Family Law Reform Act
(c.46)
s.8 .... 2–29, 2–34
Children and Young Persons
Act (c.54) 1–26
1970 Conveyancing and Feudal
Reform (Scotland) Act
(c.35) 11–02
s.27 11–02
1971 Misuse of Drugs Act
(c.38) 8–15
Immigration Act (c.77) ... 10–08
1972 Road Traffic Act (c.20)
s.1 1–70
Matrimonial Proceedings
(Polygamous Marriages)
Act (c.38)
s.2 9–10
(2) 9–24
1973 Matrimonial Causes Act
(c.18)
s.12(e) 9–29
(f) 9–29
Domicile and Matrimonial
Proceedings Act
(c.45) 10–03, 14–47
s.1 10–03
s.7 .... 9–10, 14–36
s.8 9–10
(3) 14–36
s.22(3) 10–03
Sch.3 14–43
para.8 14–43
para.9 14–44
Prescription and Limitation
(Scotland) Act (c.52)
s.17(2) 5–07
(3) 5–07
s.19A 5–07, 5–08
1974 Land Tenure Reform (Scotland) Act (c.38) 11–03
1975 Children Act (c.72) ... 6–75, 8–06
ss.47–49 6–03
s.53 6–26
s.66 .... 7–07, 8–30
1976 Damages (Scotland) Act
(c.13) 1–17, 1–24
s.1 .... 1–17, 1–19, 10–15

1976 Damages (Scotland) Act—*contd*
   s.1(1) 1–19
     (4) 1–19
   s.10 10–15
     (2) 10–15
   Sch.1 10–15
     para.1(b) 1–17
   Congenital   Disabilities
    (Civil   Liability)   Act
    (c.28) 1–18, 1–68
   s.1(1) 1–18, 1–25
     (2) 1–25
     (2A) 1–68
     (2)(b) 1–68
     (3) 1–18
   Adoption Act (c.36) 3–83
   Divorce   (Scotland)   Act
    (c.39) ... 13–02, 14–02, 14–03,
                    14–27, 14–29
   s.1 .... 13–01, 14–04
     (1) 14–01
      (a)–(b) 13–03
     (2) 13–01, 14–01, 14–04
      (a) 10–04, 14–05
      (b) 3–60, 14–06, 14–08,
                 14–14, 14–15
      (d) 10–42, 14–16
      (e) 10–42, 14–22
     (3) 14–07
     (5) 14–24, 14–27, 14–30
     (6) 14–48
   s.2 14–32
     (4) 14–17, 14–19, 14–23
   s.3(1) 14–31
   s.3A 14–30
   s.4 14–31
     (1) 14–34
   s.5 13–02
   s.11 14–33
   s.13(2) 14–11, 14–17, 14–23
     (3A)(9) 14–30
   Domestic   Violence   and
    Matrimonial Proceedings
    Act (c.50) 11–10
   Licensing (Scotland) Act
    (c.66) 2–77
   Supplementary Benefits Act
    (c.71)
   s.17 5–52
1977 Marriage (Scotland) Act
    (c.15) 9–09, 9–10,
                    9–12, 9–50
   s.1 .... 9–09, 9–25, 9–55
   s.2 .... 9–09, 9–12, 9–13,
                 9–17, 9–21, 9–55
     (1A) 9–18
     (1B) 9–19
     (2)(a) 9–16

1977 Marriage (Scotland) Act—*contd*
   s.2(4) 9–16
   s.3(1) 9–50
     (4) 9–50
     (5) 9–50
   s.5(1) 9–54
     (2) 9–54
     (3) 9–54
     (4) 9–54, 9–55
      (a) 9–09
      (b) 9–09
      (c) 9–09
      (d) 9–09, 9–26
      (e) 9–09, 9–37
      (f) 9–09, 9–55
   s.6 9–50
     (1) 9–54
     (4) 9–50
   s.7 9–50
   s.8(1) 9–52
   ss.9–16 9–50
   s.9 9–52
     (3) 9–52
   s.12 9–52
   s.14(a) 9–52
     (b) 9–52
   s.15(2) 9–52
   ss.17–20 9–50
   s.17 9–51
   s.18(4)(a) 9–51
     (b) 9–51
   s.18A 9–51
   s.19(2) 9–51
   s.21 9–57
   s.23A 9–53
   s.24 9–53
   s.54 9–099
   s.20A 9–26, 9–27, 9–28
     (4) 9–36
   Sch.1 .... 9–09, 9–12, 9–13,
                 9–14, 9–17
     para.2A 9–19
     para.3 9–21
   Sch.5 para.8(1) 9–49
     para.8(2)–(5) 9–49
1978 Adoption (Scotland) Act
    (c.28) 3–87, 5–19, 6–16,
              6–17, 6–48, 6–82
   Pt I 6–21
   s.1(1)(b) 6–71
     (4) 6–21
   s.3 6–21
   s.4 6–21
   s.6 .... 6–30, 6–32, 6–49, 6–55
     (1)(a) 6–22
      (b) 6–23
      (ii) 5–17
     (2) 5–17, 6–23

1978 Adoption (Scotland) Act—*contd*
s.6A 6–23, 6–27
s.7 6–23
s.11 6–35
    (3) 6–26, 6–35
    (4) 6–26
s.12 6–91
    (1) 5–49, 6–33, 6–64
    (3) 6–64
       (b) 6–26, 6–64
    (5) 6–33
    (6) ... 5–17, 6–64, 6–66, 6–78
    (7) 6–33
    (8) 6–72
    (9) 6–41
s.13 .... 6–34, 6–38
s.14(1A) 6–24
    (1b) 6–24
s.15 6–24
    (1)(aa) 6–25
    (3) 6–25, 6–37
s.16 6–28
    (1) 6–42, 6–64
    (2) ... 3–87, 6–28, 6–48, 6–52
       (a) 5–52
       (b) 6–49, 6–52, 6–56,
                                   6–57
       (c) 6–62
       (d) 6–63
s.17 6–90
ss.18–21 6–75
s.18(1) 6–76
    (2)(b) 6–76
    (3) 6–75
    (5) 6–75
    (6) 6–77
    (7) 6–76
    (9) 6–41
s.19 6–77
s.20 6–77
    (1A) 6–77
    (3) 6–77
s.22 .... 6–38, 6–40, 6–89
s.22A 6–41
s.23 .... 6.40
s.24 6–36
    (3) 6–23, 6–26
s.25 6–40
s.25A 6–76
s.27 6–38
s.39 .... 6–25, 9–21
s.41 9–21
    (1) 6–64
    (2) 6–64
s.45 .... 3–98, 6–70
    (5) 6–39
    (6) 6–70
    (6A) 6–70

1978 Adoption (Scotland) Act—*contd*
s.50A 6–87
s.51 .... 3–83, 3–84, 6–36
s.51A 6–37
s.57 6–39
s.58 6–40
s.65(1) 6–21, 6–43, 6–44,
                            6–64, 7–61
1979 Land Registration (Scot-
     land) Act (c.33) 11–50
     Sale of Goods Act (c.54) ... 2–23
1980 Education (Scotland) Act
     (c.44) 6–08
s.8 5–17
s.9 5–17
s.28 5–21
    (1) 5–19
ss 28A–H 5–19
s.30(1) 5–19
s.35(1) 5–21
s.48A(1A) 5–12
     Solicitors (Scotland) Act
     (c.46) 1–04
     Law Reform (Miscellaneous
     Provisions) Scotland Act
     (c.55)
s.22(1)(d) 9–53
     Married Women's Policies of
     Assurance (Scotland)
     (Amendment) Act
     (c.56) 12–53
1981 Education (Scotland) Act
     (c.58) 5–19
     Matrimonial Homes
     (Family Protection) (Scot-
     land) Act (c.59) ... 4–98, 7–49,
          7–51, 7–54, 7–56, 7–58,
          7–69, 10–29, 11–04, 11–05,
          11–09, 11–12, 11–13, 11–14,
          11–15, 11–38, 11–41, 11–42,
          11–44, 11–50, 11–55,
          11–64, 11–65, 11–74,
          11–76, 12–01, 12–26,
          14–35
s.1 .... 11–12, 11–44, 12–35
    (1) 11–15, 11–44, 11–64
    (2) 11–12
    (3) 11–35
s.2(1) 11–20
    (a) 11–20
    (c) 11–20
    (e) 11–20
    (8) 10–29, 11–59
s.3 .... 11–23, 11–55
    (2) 11–20
    (3) 11–20, 11–57, 11–60
       (c) 11–15
    (4) 11–23

1981 Matrimonial Homes (Family
      Protection) (Scotland)
      Act—*contd*
      s.3(5) 11–23
         (7) 11–52
      s.4 .... 11–23, 11–27, 11–28,
               11–29, 11–36, 11–38,
               11–40, 11–44, 11–55
         (1) 11–55
         (2) 4–98, 11–24
         (3) 11–24, 11–25
            (b) 11–25
         (4) 11–30, 11–31, 11–40
         (5) 11–31, 11–40
            (a) 11–31
         (6) 11–28
         (7) 11–55
      s.5(1)(a) 11–41
         (b) 11–64
      s.6 ... 11–46, 11–54, 11–64, 12–26
         (1) 11–52
            (a) 11–46, 11–53
         (1A) 11–46
         (1)(b) 11–46
         (2) 11–46
         (3)(a) 11–48
            (i) 11–64
            (ii) 11–49, 11.64
            (b) 11–48
            (c) 11–54
            (d) 11–54
            (e) 11–50, 11–64
            (f) 11–64
         (4) 11–50
      s.7 11–48
         (1D) 11–48
         (3A) 11–48
      s.8(1) 12–26
         (2) 12–27
         (2A) 12–27
      s.9(1) 11–46, 11–56
         (a) 11–47
         (b) 11–47
      s.13 .... 11–60, 11–62, 11–63
         (1) 11–60
         (2)(a) 11–62
            (b) 11–62
         (3) 11–60
         (4) 11–61
         (5) 11–61
         (7) 11–61
         (9) 11–60
      s.14 11–37
         (1) 11–35, 11–55
         (2) 11–34, 11–40
            (a) 11–35
            (b)–(5) 11–35
            (b) ... 11–32, 11–35, 11–36

1981 Matrimonial Homes (Family
      Protection) (Scotland)
      Act—*contd*
      ss.15–17 .... 11–42, 11–68
      s.15(1)(a) 11–40
         (b) 11–40
         (1A) 11–67
         (3) 11–41, 11–65, 11–67
      s.18 11–09
         (1) 11–17, 11–18, 11–29,
                                11–65
         (2) 11–17
         (4) 11–63
      s.18A 11–33, 11–42, 11–43
         (3) 11–13, 11–19
         (4) 11–13
      s.18B 11–33, 11–43
      s.19 .... 11–47, 11–57, 11–58
         (a) 11–57
         (b) 11–57
      s.22 .... 11–12, 11–13, 11–14,
               11–15, 11–20, 12–35,
               12–42, 13–14
         (2) 11–13
      s.25(2) 12–47
      British   Nationality   Act
         (c. 61)
      s.6 10–06
      s.42 10–07
      s.42A 10–07
      s.42B 10–07
      Sch.1 para.1(1)(ca) 10–
            (2)(c) 10–07
         para.2(e) 10–07
         para.3(e) 10–07
         para.4 10–07
      Sch.5 10–07

1982 Administration of Justice
         Act (c.53) 10–15
      s.7 10–17
      s.8 10–17
      s.9 10–17
         (2) 10–15
      s.13(1)(a) 10–17
      s.14 10–15

1983 Divorce Jurisdiction, Court
         Fees and Legal Aid (Scot-
         land) Act (c.12)
      s.1 14–36
      Sch.1 para.18 14–36

1983 Education   (Fees   and
         Awards) Act (c.40)
      s.293 5–12
      s.294 5–12

1984 Law Reform (Husband and
         Wife)   (Scotland)   Act
         (c.15)
      s.2 10–04

1984 Law Reform (Husband and
Wife) (Scotland) Act—*contd*
s.4 10–03
s.6 10–14
(1) 12–21
(2) 12–21
s.7 .... 10–14, 12–21
Inheritance Tax Act (c.51)
s.18 10–21
s.22 10–21
Foster Children (Scotland)
Act (c.56) 6–89
Rent (Scotland) Act
(c.58) 11–01
Sch.1 para.2 10–29
1985 Companies Act (c.6) 1–04
Family Law (Scotland) Act
(c. 37) .... 5–41, 5–42 , 5–45,
5–58, 5–67, 10–52,
12–05, 12–19, 12–24, 12–45,
13–01, 13–02, 13–03, 13–96,
13–99, 14–34, 15–23, 15–26,
15–30
s.1 .... 5–42, 10–98
(1) 2–77, 10–14, 10–37
(a) 10–29
(bb) 10–14
(c) 5–42
(d) 3–21, 5–42, 5–49,
5–67, 6–09, 10–35, 10–41
(2) 10–37
(5) 2–77, 5–42
s.2 .... 10–43, 11–21
(2)(aa) 14–34
(e) 10–43
(3) 11–20
(4) 5–45
(a) 10–43
(b) 10–43
(c) 10–43
(5) 10–43
(6) 5–47, 10–44
(7) 10–44, 11–20
(8) 10–45
(9) 10–45
s.3(1) 11–22
(a) 5–46, 10–46, 10.61,
11–21, 11–22
(b) 5–46, 10–46
(c) 10–46, 10–58
(i) 10–58
(ii) 10–59
(d) 10–46
(2) 10–46
(3) 11–22
s.4 .... 5–46, 4–65
(1) 5–46, 10–36
(2) 5–45

1985 Family Law (Scotland)
Act—*contd*
s.4(3)(a) 5–46, 10–40, 10–55
(b) 5–46, 10–42
s.4(4) 10–55
s.5 .... 5–65, 10–47
(1) 10–47, 15–12
(1A) 5–65, 10–47, 15–12
s.5(4) 10–59
s.6 .... 5–65, 13–94
(1)(a) 10–43
(b) 10–43
(4) 10–47
s.7 .... 5–65, 10–57, 10–60
(1) 10–60
(1A) 5–65
(2) 10–56, 10–60, 15–12
(2A) 10–60, 15–12
(2ZA) 10–57
(2ZB) 10–57
(2ZC) 10–57
(3) 10–60
(5) 10–60
ss.8–10 12–04
ss.8–16 13–01
s.8(1)(a) 13–81
(aa) 13–23, 13–81
(b) 13–81
(ba) 13–83
(baa) 13–35, 13–51
(2) 13–05, 13–06, 13–92
(b) 13–22
(4) 13–35
(4A) 13–38
(5) 13–35
(6) 13–35
s.9 .... 10–22, 13–05, 13–06,
13–22, 13–41, 13–57,
13–76, 13–82, 13–86,
13–95, 13–97
(1)(a)–(c) 13–70
(a)–(d) 13–80
(a) ... 13–06, 13–07, 13–21,
13–39, 13–41, 13–57,
13–58, 13–63, 13–65,
13–67, 13–70, 13–95
(b)–(e) 13–06, 13–41,
13–60, 13–63, 13–64
(b) ... 12–04, 12–19, 13–57,
13–58, 13–65, 13–67,
12–79
(c) 4–69, 13–57, 13–66,
13–67, 13–68, 13–69,
13–76, 13–82
(d) ... 13–70, 13–71, 13–72,
13–74, 13–75, 13–77,
13–78, 13–79, 13–82,
13–86, 15–30

1985 Family Law (Scotland)
Act—*contd*
s.9(1)(e) ... 13–70, 13–76, 13–77,
13–78, 13–79, 13–80,
13–82
(2) 13–59
s.10 10–29
(1) 10–22, 13–05, 13–07,
13–22, 13–40, 13–41,
13–57, 13–58, 13–95
(2) 13–22, 13–39
(2A) 13–11, 13–23
(2B) 13–11, 13–23
(3A) 13–23
(3) 13–10
(a) 13–10
(b) 13–10
(4) 13–08, 13–13,
13–17,
13–41
(4A) 13–08, 13–13
(5) 13–26, 13–37,
14–27
(5A) 13–38
(6) 13–40, 13–42, 13–58
(a) 13–40, 13–42,
13–53, 13–54
(b) 13–20, 13–40,
13–41
(c) 13–51, 13–52
(d) 13–24, 13–42
(e) 13–54
(7) 13–10
(8) 13–32
(8A) 13–32
(8B) 13–38
(10) 13–26
s.11 13–42
(2) 13–60
(3) 13–66
(d) 13–66
(e) 13–66
(g) 13–66
(4) 13–72
(a) 13–71
(d) 13–71
(e) 13–71
(5)(a) 13–71, 13–80
(c) 13–80
(d) 13–71, 13–80
(e) 13–71
(6) 13–66, 13–71
(7) 10–42
(a)–(b) 13–55
(b) 13–71
s.12(1) 13–03
(2) 13–76, 13–82, 13–85
(3) 13–03, 13–76, 13–82

1985 Family Law (Scotland)
Act—*contd*
s.12(4) 13–82
s.12A 13–35, 13–50, 13–83,
13–84, 14–27, 15–31
(2) 13–38
(3) 13–38
s.13(2) 13–67, 13–82
(a)–(b) 13–03
(a) 13–74
(3) 13–76, 13–86
(4) 13–87, 15–11
(a) 13–87
(b) 13–87
(c) 13–87
(7)(a) 13–86
(b) 13–86
s.14(2) 13–81, 13–88, 13–90
(a) 13–24
(d) 11–41
(i) 11–41, 13–45
(ii) 13–45
(j) 13–89
(ja) 13–90
(k) 13–24, 13–88
s.16 .... 13–33, 13–99,
15–18, 15–20
(1) 13–99
(a) 15–11, 15–18
(b) 13–53, 15–13,
15–17, 15–18
(2) 15–18
(b) 15–18
(3) 15–11
(4) 15–13
s.17 13–32
(2) 10–43
s.18 .... 5–66, 12–38, 13–81,
13–91
s.18(1) 13–91
(i) 13–91
(2) 13–91
(3) 11–21, 13–91
(a) 13–92
(8) 5–65
s.19 .... 13–81, 13–93
(6)(d) 13–44
s.20 .... 10–46, 13–81, 13–93
s.24 .... 10–02, 10–22
(1) 15–03
s.25 .... 10–29, 11–20, 12–42,
12–47, 12–52, 13–98
(1) 12–42, 12–43, 12–44
(2) 12–40, 12–42
(3) 12–43
s.26 .... 10–29, 12–51, 12–52
s.27 .... 13–05, 13–35, 13–51
(1) 10–39, 10–43, 13–71

1985 Family Law (Scotland)
Act—*contd*
s.27(2) 13–10
s.28(1) 13–98
    (c) 13–98
    (2) 12–22
    (7)(a)–(b) 13–98
s.34 12–23
    (3) 12–23
    (4)(a) 12–23
    (b) 12–23
    (c) 12–23
s.74 12–23
Sch.2 12–22
Prohibition of Female Cir-
    cumcision Act (c.38) 5–16
Surrogacy   Arrangements
    Act (c.49) 3–68, 3–69
s.1A 3–68, 3–69
Child   Abduction   and
    Custody Act (c.60) 4–65
Bankruptcy (Scotland) Act
    (c.66) 12–23, 12–35
s.16 12–35
s.32 13–97
s.33 12–36
s.34 12–38
s.41 12–35
Law Reform (Miscellaneous
    Provisions)   (Scotland)
    Act (c.73)
s.8 15–10
s.9 15–10
s.13(5) 11–27
    (8) 12–27
1986 Law Reform (Parent and
    Child)   (Scotland)   Act
    (c.9) 3–23, 4–04, 6–10
s.1 .... 5–37, 5–40
    (1) 5–36, 9–03
    (4)(a) 5–39
    (b) 5–38
s.3 .... 3–19, 4–39, 4–40, 4–41
s.5 .... 3–26, 3–27, 3–37
    (1)(a) 3–27, 3–28, 3–29,
        3–30, 3–31, 3–33, 3–35,
            3–46, 3–54, 3–75
    (b) 3–33, 3–34
    (2) 3–27
    (3) 3–36
    (4) 3–26
s.6(2) 3–45
    (3) 3–41, 3–45
s.7 .... 3–24, 3–36, 3–37
    (2) 3–37
    (5) 3–37
s.9(1)(c) 5–40
Sch.1 para.17 9–16

1986 Marriage   (Prohibited
    Degrees of Relationship)
    Act (c.16) ... 9–09, 9–10, 9–18
Sch. 1 para.2 9–18
Sch. 2 para.2(b) 9–18
Incest and Related Offences
    (Scotland) Act (c.36) 9–20
Legal Aid (Scotland) Act
    (c.47)
s.17(2B) 13–35
s.29 2–43
s.29(4) 2–43
Social Security Act (c.50) 5–52
Family Law Act (c.55) 4–45,
                14–45
s.9(a) 4–44
    (b) 4–44
s.10(a) 4–44
    (b) 4–44
s.12 4–44
s.16 4–44
s.17A 4–45
s.44(2) 14–45
s.51(1) 14–45
    (2) 14–45
1987 Debtors   (Scotland)   Act
    (c.18) 10–62, 12–36
s.16 12–36
ss.51–56 10–62
Sch.5 para.5 12–36
Housing   (Scotland)   Act
    (c.26) 11–01, 11–60, 12–28
s.24(3) 11–75
s.26 11–74
    (1) 11–75
s.48 11–60
s.52(1) 10–29
    (2) 10–29
s.83 11–60
Sch.3. para.16 11–60
Sch.28. para.28 11–60
Family Law Reform Act
    (c.42)
Pt III 3–42
1988 Income and Corporation
    Taxes Act (c.1)
s.257(1) 10–20
    (6) 10–20
s.257A 10–20
s.279 10–20
s.282 10–21
Civil   Evidence   (Scotland)
    Act (c.32) 8–44
s.1(1) 14–48
s.2(1) 2–65
    (a) 2–68
    (b) 2–68
s.8(1) 14–48

1988 Civil Evidence (Scotland)
        Act—*contd*
        s.8(3) 14–48, 14–50
        (4) 14–50
        (5) 14–50
        s.9 8–44
        Finance Act (c.39)
        s.32 10–20
        s.36 10–39
        Housing (Scotland) Act
        (c.43) 11–01, 11–74, 11–75
        Road Traffic Act (c.52)
        s.101 2–77
1989 Children Act (c.41) 1–52,
        2–76, 4–11, 4–64,
        7–05, 7–26, 7–30, 7–68,
        9–07
        s.4 .... 3–16, 3–17, 9–07
        s.38(6) 7–35
        s.43 7–48
        s.44 7–47
1990 Human Fertilisation and
        Embryology   Act
        (c.37) 1–77, 3–61, 3–66,
        3–68, 3–69, 3–72,
        3–73, 3–77, 3–78,
        3–79, 3–86, 3–87,
        3–91, 3–92, 3–93,
        3–95, 3–97, 5–42
        s.13(5) 3–91
        s.27 .... 3–78, 3–86
        (1) 3–70
        s.28(2) 3–72, 3–74, 3–75,
        3–76, 3–77, 3–78, 3–85
        (3) 3–73, 3–74, 3–76,
        3–77, 3–85, 3–87
        (4) 3–74
        (5)(b) 3–75
        (6) ... 3–74, 3–77, 3–79, 4–77
        s.29(1) 3–70, 3–72
        (4) 3–70
        (5) 3–72
        s.30 ...... 3–84, 3–85, 3–86, 3–87,
        4–40, 6–36
        (7) 3–85
        s.31 3–97
        s.36 3–68
        s.37 .... 1–37, 1–75
        (4) 1–76
        s.44 1–68
        Sch.3 para.5 3–74
        Law Reform (Miscellaneous
        Provisions) (Scotland)
        Act (c.40) 11–75
        s.70 ...... 3–41, 3–43, 3–44, 3–49,
        3–51, 3–52, 3–55, 3–56
        (1)(a) 3–41, 3–43
        (b) 3–3–44, 3–45

1990 Law Reform (Miscellaneous
        Provisions) (Scotland)
        Act—*contd*
        s.70(2) 3–42
        s.74(1)—(2) 12–26
        Sch.8 para.31(2) 12–26
        para.34 13–81
        Sch.9 12–26
1991 Child Support Act (c.48) ... 3–14,
        3–41, 4–69, 4–98, 5–01,
        5–41, 5–42, 5–5, 5–51,
        5–57, 5–58, 5–59, 5–61,
        5–64, 5–67, 5–68, 5–77,
        5–80, 5–85, 5–86, 5–90,
        10–31, 10–32, 10–41,
        10–47, 10–60, 10–62,
        10–82, 13–04, 13–68,
        14–50, 15–12, 15–31
        s.1(1) 5–42
        (2) 5–58
        (3) 5–58
        s.2 .... 4–98, 5–50, 5–77
        s.4 .... 5–19, 5–61
        (10) 5–65, 15–12
        s.6 .... 5–61, 10–82
        (2) 5–61
        s.7 5–61
        (1) 15–12
        s.8 .... 5–59, 5–64
        (2) 5–64
        (5) 5–66
        (7) 5–67
        (8) 5–67
        (9) 5–67
        s.9 5–94
        s.14 5–77
        s.14A 5–77
        s.15 5–77
        ss.16–19 5–76
        s.18 5–76
        s.21 5–76
        s.24 5–76
        s.25 5–76
        (3A) 5–76
        s.29(3) 5–63
        s.31 5–78
        s.33 5–78
        s.38 5–79
        s.40A 5–79
        s.40B 5–79
        s.44 5–67
        s.46(3) 5–77
        (5) 5–77
        (7) 5–77
        s.54 .... 5–42, 5–49
        s.55 2–77
        (1)(b) 2–77
        Sch.1 5–68

1991 Child Support Act—*contd*
  Sch.1 Pt I 5–84
      para.2(1) 5–72
          (2) 5–73
      para.3 5–71
      para.4 5–71
          (1)(b) 5–84
      para.5 5–71
          (a) 5–84
      para.7 5–75
      para.8 5–75
      para.10(3) 5–67
      para.10C(2) 5–82
  Sch.3 5–76
  Sch.4B 5–80
      para.2 5–82
          (3)(e) 5–82
      para.3 5–83
      para.4 5–84
  Sch.5 10–62
  Age of Legal Capacity
    (Scotland) Act (c.50) ... 2–19,
          2–20, 2–22, 2–37, 2–38,
          2–42, 2–57, 4–30, 5–25,
          6–10, 9–25
  s.1 .... 4–17, 4–30, 5–94, 7–17
      (1) 5–07
      (a) 2–22, 2–23, 2–47,
          3–43
      (3)(c) 2–58, 2–74
      (d) 2–52–77
      (e) 2–45
      (f) 2–41
      (iii) 2–42
  s.2(1) 5–26
      (2) 2–27
      (3) 2–28
      (4) 2–29, 2–33, 2–35,
          2–36, 2–41, 3–43,
          4–34, 4–37, 5–06,
          7–35, 8–61
      (4A) 2–42, 2–44
      (4B) 2–42, 2–43, 5–07
  s.3 .... 2–40, 2–51, 2–52, 5–94
      (2) 2–50
      (3) 2–52
      (g) 2–52, 2–54
      (h) 2–54
  s.4 2–55
  s.4A 4–18
  s.5(2) 2–2, 2–47
      (3) 2–22
  s.7 10–04
  s.9 .... 2–38, 5–23
      (d) 3–43
  Agricultural Holdings
    (Scotland) Act (c.55)
  s.1 11–25

1992 Social Security Contribu-
    tions and Benefits Act
    (c.4) 10–63, 10–78
  s.37 9–48
  s.38 9–48
  s.39A 9–48
  s.40 9–48
  s.41 9–48
  s.44 9–48
  s.106 10–81
      (2) 10–81
  s.124 .... 10–66, 10–76
  s.130 .... 10–65, 10–74
  s.131(1)(a) 10–65, 10–74
      (3)–(5) 10–65, 10–74
  s.136(1) 10–78
  s.137(1) 10–79
  Social Security Administra-
    tion Act (c.5) ... 10–63, 10–81
  s.78 12–21
      (6) 10–32, 10–81
      (d) 10–81
  s.105 10–32
  s.106 10–81
  Taxation of Chargeable
    Gains Act (c.12)
  s.58 10–21
  s.222 10–21
  Local Government Finance
    Act (c.14)
  s.77 12–21
  Still-Birth (Definition) Act
    (c.29) 1–76
1993 Damages (Scotland) Act
    (c.5) 1–24, 10–15
1994 Local Government etc
    (Scotland) Act (c.39) 8–10
  s.22 8–12
  s.25 .... 8–12, 8–15
  s.40(1) 8–10
      (2) 8–10
  s.52(2) 8–11, 8–15
  s.56 8–11
      (4) 8–12
      (5) 8–12
      (6) 8–11
  s.63 8–13
  s.65(1) 8–11
1995 Civil Evidence (Family
    Mediation) (Scotland)
    Act (c.6) 15–39
  s.1(2) 14–55
  s.2 15–39
  Requirements of Writing
    (Scotland) Act (c.7) 12–13
  s.3(4)(c)(ii) 2–73
  s.14(2) 12–13
  Sch.5 12–13

1995 Jobseekers Act (c.18)
ss.1–3 10–65
s.2 10–66
s.3 10–66
s.3A 10–65
s.23 10–81
Sch.24 Pt 7 paras
118–125 10–81
Pensions Act (c.26)
s.167(1) 13–83
(2) 13–26, 13–37
(3) 13–26, 13–50
Child Support Act (c.34) ... 5–57,
5–80, 10–31, 13–04
Children (Scotland) Act
(c.36) 2–29, 2–41, 2–76,
3–05, 3–07, 4–14, 4–17,
4–18, 4–19, 4–21, 4–24,
4–26, 4–51, 4–52, 4–57,
4–64, 4–89, 5–04, 5–30,
5–36, 5–49, 6–22, 6–41,
7–21, 7–28, 7–66, 8–06,
8–11, 8–40, 11–15,
15–01, 15–31
Pt I 4–01, 4–67, 5–01, 6–29,
7–05, 7–07, 8–28
Pt II 1–26, 4–11, 5–49, 6–02,
7–04, 7–05, 7–09, 7–10,
7–61, 7–66, 7–68, 8–07,
8–67
Ch.3 7–26
s.1 .... 3–05, 4–15, 4–16, 4–18,
4–36, 4–54, 4–89, 5–02,
5–19, 6–03, 6–10,
7–63, 8–22
(1) 4–04, 5–02, 5–24,
5–33
(a) 5–22
(b) 4–05
(ii) 2–29, 3–05, 4–16,
6–12, 7–65
(c) 4–16, 7–33
(2) 4–16, 7–65
(a) 3–05
(3) 4–18, 5–07, 5–49, 6–43,
6–64, 7–63
s.2 .... 3–05, 4–16, 4–17, 4–36,
4–54, 4–89, 5–02, 5–19,
6–03, 6–10
(1) 2–22, 4–04, 4–16, 5–02
(a) 7–17, 7–18
(b) 4–82, 7–17
(c) 4–16, 7–23, 7–33
(d) 5–32
(2) 3–08, 4–48, 4–72, 4–81,
5–24, 6–11
(3) 4–84
(4) 6–43, 6–64, 7–63

1995 Children (Scotland) Act—*contd*
s.2(5) 2–22, 4–17
(7) 2–47, 3–05, 4–17, 4–29,
5–32, 6–12, 7–65
s.3 .... 2–22, 5–24
(1)(a) 3–06, 3–10, 8–28
(b) 3–06, 3–09, 3–17,
3–46, 3–73, 6–44, 8–28
(2)(a) 3–06
(b) 3–06
(5) 3–21, 4–13, 6–08
(6) 4–13, 6–08
s.4 .... 2–16, 3–16, 3–22, 3–73,
6–44, 6–76
(b)(i) ....
7–51, 7–52
s.5 .... 5–48, 6–08
(2) 6–08
s.6 .... 4–26, 4–56, 5–20
(1) 3–08, 4–25, 5–34, 6–11,
6–12
(2) 4–25, 5–34
ss.7–10 2–22
s.7 .... 2–22, 3–19, 6–10
(1) 6–10
(b) 6–10
(2) 56–10
(3) 6–10
(5) 5–24, 6–10, 6–12
(6) 6–12
s.8 6–10
(5)(a) 6–12
(b) 6–12
(c) 6–13
s.9 .... 4–45, 5–30, 5–31
(5) 5–30
(6)(a) 5–30
s.10 .... 5–30, 5–32, 6–13
(1) 5–32
(b) 5–27
(2) 5–32
s.11 ...... 2–22, 2–33, 2–40, 3–09,
3–18, 3–19, 3–20, 3–80,
4–13, 4–26, 4–36, 4–39,
4–40, 4–40, 4–41, 4–42,
4–44, 4–45, 4–47, 4–48,
4–49, 4–53, 4–54, 4–64,
4–71, 4–72, 4–82, 4–90,
4–92, 4–95, 4–99, 5–03,
5–15, 5–21, 5–24, 5–32,
6–03, 6–06, 6–26, 6–27,
6–44, 6–68, 6–76, 6–77,
6–78, 7–07, 7–21, 7–48,
7–64, 8–29, 8–48, 8–59,
8–60, 14–53, 14–54, 15–08
(1) ... 4–36, 4–44, 4–48, 6–35
(1A) 4–44
(2) 3–18, 6–03, 7–62

1995 Children (Scotland) Act—*contd*
    s.11(2)(a) 4–48
        (b) 4–42, 4–48
          (i) 4–43
        (c) 4–48, 7–18
        (d) 4–42, 4–48
        (e) 3–08, 4–48
        (f) 4–48, 6–11, 7–56
        (h) 4–48, 6–10, 6–13
      (3) 6–65
        (a)(i) 3–18, 4–39, 6–03
          (ii) 4–39
          (iii) ... 4–40, 6–78, 7–64
      (4) 4–40, 6–65
        (d) 7–64
      (5) ... 2–40, 4–39, 4–41, 4–42,
                      7–21, 7–64
      (7) ... 3–08, 4–04, 4–49, 4–87,
              4–88, 6–22, 14–53
        (a) 3–18, 4–20, 6–11,
               15–08, 15–29
      (7A) 4–71
      (7)(b) 3–18, 4–20, 4–24,
                4–87, 6–11
      (7B) 4–71
      (7C) 4–71
      (7D) 4–72
      (7E) 4–72
      (10) 3–18, 4–24, 4–55,
                   14–53
      (11) 4–54
      (12) 4–54, 6–05, 8–59
      (13) 4–48
    s.12 .... 15–08, 15–37
      (1) 4–47
      (2) 4–47
        (c) 14–53
      (3) 4–47
      (4) 4–47
      (8) 6–23
    s.13 .... 2–60, 4–45, 5–31
      (2) 2–60
      (3) 2–60
    s.14(1) 4–44
      (2) 4–44
      (5) 4–45, 5–25
    s.15(5)(a) 5–23
        (b) 2–43, 5–94
      (6) 2–42
    s.16 ..... 7–07, 7–62, 7–64, 11–15
      (1) ... 7–07, 7–32, 7–51, 8–40
      (2) 7–07, 7–52, 8–40
      (3) 7–07, 7–51, 8–40
      (4) 7–07
        (a) 7–07
        (b)(i)–(iii) 7–07
          (i) 7–07
          (iv) 7–07

1995 Children (Scotland) Act—*contd*
    s.16(4)(c) 7–07
      (5) 7–07, 8–41
    s.17 ...... 7–24, 7–25, 7–33, 8–57,
                 8–59, 8–69
      (1)(a)–(c) 7–25, 8–57
        (c) 7–23, 8–57
      (2) 7–25
      (3) 7–25, 8–57
      (4) 7–25
        (c) 5–17, 7–25
      (5) 7–25
      (6) 5–49, 7–24
    s.18 7–25
      (8) 6–23
    s.19 7–13
    s.21 7–13
    s.22 .... 2–48, 7–11
      (1)(b) 7–12
    s.23 7–13
    s.24 7–13
    s.25 ...... 5–49, 7–14, 7–17, 7–18,
             7–20, 7–26, 7–28
      (1) 7–14
      (2) 7–16
      (3) 7–16
      (5) 7–19
      (6) 7–17, 7–18
        (b) 7–20
    s.25(7) 7–20
        (a) 7–17
        (b) 7–18
    s.26 7–15
    s.27 7–13
    s.29 7–13
      (2) 7–13
    s.38 7–13
      (5) 7–13
    s.39 8–09
      (5) 8–09
    s.41 8–44
      (1) 8–30
      (2) 8–30
    s.42 8–44
    s.43 8–25
      (3)(a) 8–28
        (b) 8–28
      (4) 8–28
    s.45(1)(a)–(b) 8–25
      (2) 8–25, 8–43
      (3)–(6) 8–26
      (6) 8–26
      (7) 8–26
      (8) 8–28
    s.46(1) 8–38
      (2) 4–62, 8–38
    s.51 8–26
      (1) 8–63

1995 Children (Scotland) Act—*contd*
s.51(5) 8–63
    (c)(iii) 7–07, 8–63
  (8) 8–26
  (11) 8–64
    (a)(i) 8–64
    (ii) 8–46
    (b) 8–46, 8–64
  (14) 8–46
  (15) 7–42
s.52 7–37
  (1) 1–26
   (c) 4–10
  (2) 5–10, 7–22, 8–11,
                 8–15, 8–27
    (a)–(c) 8–15
    (c)(i) 5–10
    (e)–(g) ... 8–15, 8–23, 8–24
    (h) 8–15
    (i) 8–21
    (j)–(m) 8–15
s.54 ...... 2–48, 4–47, 6–03, 6–40,
                    14–53
s.55 .... 7–45, 7–48
  (1) 7–46
  (2) 7–47
  (3) 7–46, 7–48
  (4) 7–46
  (5) 7–46
s.56 8–11
  (4) 8–12
  (5) 8–12
  (6) 8–11
ss.57–60 7–28
s.57 1–26
  (1) 7–28, 7–29, 7–39
  (2) 7–28, 7–39
  (3) 7–32
  (4) 7–32
  (5) 7–28
  (6) 7–32
s.58 .... 7–34, 7–35, 7–39
  (1) 7–34
  (2) 7–34
  (4) 7–34
  (5) 7–34
  (6) 7–34
s.59(2) 7–37
  (3) 7–37
  (4) 7–37
s.60(1) 7–36
  (3) 7–37
  (6)(e) 7–38
  (7) 7–42
  (8) 7–39
   (b) 7–41
  (10) 7–39, 7–41
  (12) 7–39

1995 Children (Scotland) Act—*contd*
s.60(12)(d) 7–40
  (13) 7–39
s.61 7–44
  (4) 7–44
  (5) 7–44
  (6) 7–44
s.63 8–13
s.64 8–25
  (6) 8–43
s.65(1) 8–11, 8–27
  (2) 7–37, 7–41, 8–27
  (4) 8–42, 8–43
  (7) 8–42
  (9) 8–43
  (10) 8–43
s.66(1)–(3) 8–26
  (5) 8–26
  (6) 8–26
  (8) 8–26
s.67 8–26
  (2) 8–26
s.68 .... 8–42, 8–44, 8–49
  (2) 8–8–42
  (3)(b) 8–44
  (4) 8–44
  (5) 8–44
  (9) 8–45
  (10) 8–45, 8–47
s.68A 8–44
s.68B 8–44
s.69 8–42
  (1) 8–48
s.70 .... 8–48, 8–56, 8–63
  (3) 8–53, 8–72
  (3A)–(3E) 8–4
  (5) 8–61, 8–72
  (6) 8–53
  (7) 8–51
  (9) 8–53
  (10) 7–07, 8–26, 8–53
s.71 8–48
  (1A) 8–48
s.71A 8–48
s.73 6–41
  (1) 8–50
  (2) 8–50
  (3) 8–62
  (4) 7–62, 8–50
  (6) 8–51
  (8) 8–52
  (11) 8–53
s.75A 8–72
ss.76–80 .... 7–49, 7–58, 11–15
s.76 .... 7–58, 7–69, 11–15
  (2) 7–50, 7–53
  (5) 7–53
  (8) 7–50

1995	Children (Scotland) Act—*contd*	
	s.76(9)	7–51
	(10)	7–51
	(11)	7–51
	(12)	7–50, 7–53, 7–54
	s.77	7–54
	(1)	7–54
	(2)	7–54, 7–55
	(3)	7–54
	(d)	7–56
	(e)	7–56
	(f)	7–56
	s.78	7–54
	(1)	7–56
	(2)	7–54
	(3)	7–54
	(6)	7–54
	(7)	7–54
	(10)–(14)	7–54
	(b)	7–54
	(11)	7–54
	(13)	7–54
	s.79(1)	7–57
	(2)(a)	7–57
	(b)	7–57
	(4)	7–57
	s.85	8–47
	ss.86–89	7–59
	s.86	4–40, 5–49, 6–79, 7–60, 7–63
	(1)	7–63
	(2)	7–60
	(b)	7–60
	(3)	7–63, 7–64
	(4)	7–61
	(5)	7–64, 7–65
	s.88(1)	7–64
	s.90	7–35, 7–48, 8–61
	s.93	8–28
	(1)	7–37, 8–25
	(2)	2–48
	(a)	7–14
	(b)	2–48, 7–50, 8–08, 8–28, 8–71
	(4)(a)	7–11
	(5)	8–44
	s.95	5–17, 6–22, 6–30
	s.96	6–27
	s.97	6–25
	Sch.1 para.1	8–09
	para.2	8–37
	para.3	8–09
	para.8	8–09
	para.9	8–09
	para.11	8–09
	para.44	4–18
	Sch.2 para.16	6–26, 6–36
	para.7(d)	6–41

1995	Children (Scotland) Act—*contd*	
	Sch.2 para.11(d)	6–41
	para.29	6–44, 7–61
	Sch.4 para.2	5–30
	para.6	5–30
	para.15(11)	7–10
	para.26	6–03
	para.53	5–07
	(1)	2–41
	(3)	2–41
	Sch.5	6–26
	Criminal Law (Consolidation) (Scotland) Act (c.39)	9–20
	ss.1–3	8–15
	s.1	9–20
	s.5	9–25
	s.13	9–25
	Criminal Procedure (Consequential Provisions) (Scotland) Act (c.40)	
	Sch.4 para.97	8–15
	Private International Law (Miscellaneous Provisions) Act (c.42)	
	s.7	9–24
	Sch.	9–10, 9–24
	Criminal Procedure (Scotland) Act (c.46)	2–72, 11–73
	s.41	2–74, 8–14
	s.42	2–74, 8–14
	s.49(1)	8–08
	s.234A	11–73
	s.259	2–72
	s.264	10–18
	s.271A	2–72
	s.271B	2–72
	(3)	2–72
	s.271H	2–72
	Sch.1	8–20, 8–21, 822, 8–23, 8–24
	Sch.1.1	8–15
	Criminal Injuries Compensation Act (c.53)	5–09, 7–03
1996	Family Law Act (c.27)	15–01
	Pt II	14–30, 15–35
	Pt IV–10	11–10
	s.4	14–37
	s.29	15–35
	Trusts of Land and Appointment of Trustees Act (c.47)	12–11
1997	Protection from Harassment Act (c.40)	11–70, 11–73
	s.1(1)	11–70
	(2)	11.70
	s.8	11–71

1997 Protection from Harassment
Act—*contd*
s.8(3) 11–70
(4) 11–
(5)(a) 11–70
(b)(i) 11.70
(ii) 11.70, 11–71, 11–72
(6) 11–70
s.9 11–73
(1)(a)–(b) 11–73
1998 Crime and Disorder Act
(c.37) 8–65
Human Rights Act
(c.42) 2–01, 2–06, 2–15,
2–16, 3–14, 4–22,
6–44, 6–78, 7–70,
8–32, 9–03, 9–03,
9–04, 10–16, 15–25
s.1 9–04
s.2 9–04
s.3 .... 9–04, 10–16
s.4 9–04
s.6 9–04
s.7 9–04
s.10 9–04
1999 Adoption (Intercountry
Aspects) Act (c.18) 6–82,
6–83, 6–84
s.3 6–90
s.14 6–87
Access to Justice Act
(c.22) 15–35
Welfare Reform and Pen-
sions Act (c.30) 15–31
s.20 .... 13–35, 13–51
(3) 13–13–35
s.28(1)(f) 13–35, 13–51
(6) 13–35
s.29 13–35
s.84 13–35
s.55 9–48
Sch.12 para.6 13–35
Immigration and Asylum
Act (c.33) 10–08
s.10 (1)(b) 10–12
s.24 10–12
s.24A 10–12
s.41 10–11
2000 Child Support, Pensions
and Social Security Act
(c.19) 5–57, 5–60, 5–80,
10–31, 13–04
2001 Adoption (Intercountry
Aspects) Act (Northern
Ireland) 2001 (c.11) 6–83
2002 Tax Credits Act (c.21) 10–67
s.3(3) 10–65
(7) 10–65

2002 Tax Credits Act—*contd*
s.10 10–65
s.42 10–65
Employment Act (c.22) ... 10–26
Adoption and Children Act
(c.38) 3–17, 6–16, 6–82
s.52(1) 6–47
s.111 .... 3–16, 9–07
s.112 3–22
s.144(4) 6–24
(5) 6–24
Nationality, Immigration
and Asylum Act
(c.41) 10–07
ss.1–3 .... 10–07, 10–08
s.2(1)(a) 10–07
Sch.1 10–07
s.3 10–07
s.74 10–12
Sch.1 10–07
2003 Human Fertilisation and
Embryology (Deceased
Fathers) Act (c.24)
s.1 3–93
2004 Gender Recognition Act
(c.7) 9–01, 9–39, 9–43,
9–45, 9–63, 9–65,
13–03, 14–04
s.1 9–45
s.2 9–45
s.3 9–45
(6) 9–45
s.4(2) 9–45
(3) 9–45
s.5(1) 9–45
s.8(1) 9–45
s.9(1) 9–46, 9–47
(2) 9–46
s.10(4) 9–46
s.11 9–46
s 12 .... 3–24, 3–25, 9–47
s.15 9–47
s.18 9–47
s.20 9–47
Sch.2 Pt. 2 para.6 14–01, 14–04
Sch.3 9–46
Pt 2 9–46
Sch.4 Pt 2 9–46
Sch.5 9–48
paras 3–4 9–48
para.5 9–48
para.7 9–49
(2) 9–49
(3) 9–49
Asylum and Immigration
(Treatment of Claimants,
etc.) Act (c.19) 10–12
ss.19–25 10–12

2004 Civil Partnership Act (c.33) 4–69, 4–78, 6–24, 8–28, 9–01, 9–03, 9–08, 9–44, 9–60, 9–64, 9–67, 10–16, 10–79, 10–80, 11–04, 11–12, 11–12, 11–13, 11–14, 11–31, 11.42, 11–44, 11–48, 11–55, 13–03, 13–10, 14–32
Pt 3 Ch.3 ... 11–09, 11–12, 14–03
Ch.5 .... 13–01, 13–03
Pt 5 Ch.1 9–67
ss.11–30 13–01
s.11 10–14
s.85 9–67
s.86 9–61
(2) 9–61
(3) 9–61
(4) 9–63
(5)–(7) 9–63
(9) 9–63
s.87–100 9–64
s.87 9–64
s.88(2) 9–64
(3) 9–64
(5) 9–65
(6) 9–65
s.89 9–64
s.90 9–65
(2) 9–65
s.91 9–65
s.92 9–65
(4)(a) 9–66
(b) 9–66
(5) 9–66
(6) 9–65
s.93 9–67
(3) 9–67
s.94 9–67
s.95(1) 9–67
(2) 9–67
s.96 9–65
(2) 9–65
s.98 9–67
s.99 9–67
s.100(1) 9–68
(2)(a) 9–68
(b) 9–68
(c) 9–68
(d) 9–68
(e) 9–68
(f) 9–68
(3) 9–69
ss.101–112 11–12
ss.101–116 11–04
s.101 .... 11–09, 11–16, 11–44, 12–35

2004 Civil Partnership Act—*contd*
s.101(1) 11–44
(6) 11–64
(6A) 11–64
(7) 11–16
ss.102–112 11–09
s.102 11–20
(1)(a) 11–20
(c) 11–20
(e) 11–20
(3) 11–20
(7) 11–20
(8) 10–29, 11–59
s.103 11–23
(1) 11–22
(2) 11–20
(3) 11–20, 11–22, 11–60
(4) 11–23
(5) 11–23
(8) 11–52
s.104 .... 11–22, 11–38, 11–40, 11–44
(1) 11–55
(2) 11–24
(3) 11–25
(b) 11–25
(4) 11–30, 11–31, 11–40
(5) 11–40
(a) 11–31
(8) 11–55
s.105(2)(a) 11–41, 11–64
s.106 .... 11–46, 11–64, 12–26
(1) 11–50
(b) 11–46
(1A) 11–46, 11–53
(b)(i) 11–50
(ii) 11–50
(2) 11–46
(3) 11–49
(a) 11–48
(i)–(ii) 11–64
(c) 11–54
(d) 11–54
s.107 11–48
(1D) 11–48
(3A) 11–48
s.108 12–26
(1) 12–26
(2) 12–27
(3) 12–27
s.109 11–46
s.110 .... 11–57, 11–58
(b) 11–57
s.112(2) 11–62
(1) 11–60
(2)(a) 11–62
(b) 11–62
(3) 11–60

2004 Civil Partnership Act—*contd*
s.112(4) 11–61
    (5) 11–61
    (8) 11–61
    (10) 11–60
ss.113–116 11–09
s.113 .... 11–32, 11–37
    (2) 11–42
      (b) 11–32
ss 114–116 .... 11–42, 11–68
s.114 11–40
    (1)(b) 11–40
    (4) 11–41, 11–65, 11–67
ss.117–122 14–03
s.117 13–01
    (2)(a)–(b) 13–03, 14–03
s.117(3) 13–01, 14–20
    (a) 14–08
    (c) 14–16
    (d) 14–22
    (4) 14–20
    (6) 14–24, 14–27
    (8) 14–48
s.118 14–32
s.119(3) 14–19
s.120 .... 14–31, 14–34
s.121 14–31
    (2) 14–32
s.122 14–56
s.123(a) 9–70
    (b) 9–70
s.124 9–70
s.127 12–36
s.130 .... 10–18, 10–19
s.132 .... 10–29, 12–25, 12–38,
                 12–53
s.135 .... 11–13, 11–14, 11–20,
                 14–38
    (2) 11–13
s.233 14–46
s.249 .... 10–10, 10–81
s.254 .... 10–79, 10–80
s.261(1) 10–12
    (2) 10–17, 10–83, 12–04,
12–35, 12–38, 12–40, 13–97,
14–34, 14–48, 14–53, 14–55,
15–03, 15–11, 15–31

2004 Civil Partnership Act—*contd*
s.291(2) 15–08, 15–29
Sch.8 Pt 1 10–83
Sch.10 .... 9–61, 9–63
    para.2 .... 9–61, 9–63
    para.3 9–63
Sch.23 10–10
    Pt 1 10–10
    Pt 2 10–10
    Pt 3 10–10
Sch.24 10–80
    Pt 3 para.46 10–79
    Pt 4 para.61(4) 10–81
Sch.27 para.162 10–12
Sch.28 Pt 1 para.1(1) 10–84
    para.4 10–84
    para.6 10–85
    para.28 11–20
    Pt 2 13–01
    paras 11–13 ... 10–29,
                14–34
    para.11 10–35
    paras. 14–16 ... 12–04
    paras 16 10–29
    para.17 15–29
    para.19 15–31
    para.22 15–11
    para.24 12–38
    para.27 15–03
    para.28 12–40
    para.29 12–51
    Pt 3 12–36
    paras 31–41 12–23
    para.34 13–97
    para.37 12–35
    Pt 4 para.42 10–15
    para.47 10–15,
                10–17
    para.48–49 10–29
    para.55 14–48
    para.55 14–55
    para.60 14–53,
                15–08
    para.61 14–53
2004 Pensions Act (c.35) 13–38

TABLE OF SCOTTISH STATUTES

2000　Adults with Incapacity
　　　(Scotland) Act (asp
　　　4) 10–16, 11–50
　　　Standards in Scotland's
　　　School etc Act (asp 6)
　　　s.1 5–20
　　　s.2(1) 5–20
　　　　(2) 5–20
　　　s.16 5–12
　　　s.41 5–20
2001　Housing (Scotland) Act (asp
　　　10) 11–01, 12–28
　　　s.22 10–29
　　　s.108 9–03
　　　　(3) 10–29
　　　Sch.3 10–29
　　　Mortgage Rights (Scotland)
　　　Act (asp 11) 12–34
　　　s.1(2) 12–34
　　　　(b) 10–16
　　　　(3) 12–34
　　　s.2(2) 12–34
　　　Protection from Abuse
　　　(Scotland) Act (asp
　　　14) 11–42, 11–43, 11–65,
　　　　11–66, 11–69, 11–70, 11–75
　　　s.1(2) 11–43, 11–68
　　　　(b) 11–67
　　　　(3) 11–42, 11–64, 11–69
　　　s.1A(a) 11–42
　　　　(b) 11–42
　　　s.2(1) 11–42
　　　　(4) 11–69
　　　s.4 11–65
　　　　(1) 11–68
　　　　(a) 11–68
　　　　(b) 11–68
　　　　(2) 11–69
　　　s.6 11–67
　　　s.7 11–66
2002　Marriage (Scotland) Act
　　　2002 (asp 8) 9–50, 9–51
　　　Debt Arrangement and
　　　Attachment (Scotland)
　　　Act (asp 17)
　　　s.58(2) 12–36

2002　Debt Arrangement and Attach-
　　　ment (Scotland) Act —contd
　　　Sch.3 para.15 12–36
2003　Protection of Children
　　　(Scotland) Act (asp 5) ... 2–78
　　　Criminal Justice (Scotland)
　　　Act (asp 7)
　　　s.1 5–15
　　　s.49 11–73
　　　s.51 5–14
　　　Homelessness etc (Scotland)
　　　Act 2003 (asp 10) 11–75,
　　　　　　　　　　　　　　　12–28
　　　Commissioner for Children
　　　and Young People (Scot-
　　　land) Act (asp 17) 2–15
2004　Vulnerable Witnesses (Scot-
　　　land) Act (asp 3) 2–63,
　　　　2–69, 2–70, 2–72, 8–44
　　　s.1 2–72
　　　s.11 2–70
　　　　(1)(a) 2–70
　　　s.12(1) 2–70
　　　　(2) 2–70
　　　　(a) 2–70
　　　　(4) 2–70
　　　s.18 2–70
　　　s.24 .... 2–70, 2–72
　　　Antisocial Behaviour etc
　　　(Scotland) Act (asp 8) ... 8–01,
　　　　　　　　　　　　8–65, 8–70
　　　Pt 9 8–70
　　　s.2(4) 8–67
　　　s.4(1) 8–66
　　　　(2) 8–66
　　　　(4) 8–67
　　　s.5(2) 8–67
　　　s.7(3) 8–67
　　　s.9 8–66
　　　s.10 8–66
　　　s.12 8–67
　　　　(1) 8–27
　　　　(3) 8–27
　　　　(4) 8–27
　　　　(5) 8–52, 8–67
　　　s.13 8–70

2004	Antisocial Behaviour etc. (Scotland) Act —*contd*	
	s.102	8–70
	(3)	8–70
	(9)	8–70
	s.103	8–71
	s.107	8–71
	s.108(6)	8–71
	s.109(1)	8–71
	(2)	8–71
	s.114	8–70
	s.116	8–72
	s.117	8–70
	s.135	8–56
	s.136	8–48
	s.143(2)	8–66
2005	Protection of Children and Prevention of Sexual Offences (Scotland) Act (asp 9)	2–78
2006	Housing (Scotland) Act (asp 1)	11–01
	Family Law (Scotland) Act (asp 2)	3–11, 3–16, 3–17, 3–22, 4–41, 4–53, 4–69, 4–89, 5–37, 5–38, 5–39, 5–40, 6–07, 6–44, 7–17, 8–06, 8–29, 9–01, 9–02, 9–03, 9–08, 9–09, 9–58, 9–59, 10–16, 10–33, 10–35, 10–57, 11–32, 11–33, 11–65, 11–67, 13–10, 13–11, 13–97, 13–98, 13–99, 14–02, 14–30, 15–22, 15–25
	s.1	9–19, 14–16
	(1)	10–32
	(2)(a)	14–02
	(b)	14–02
	(c)	14–02
	(d)	14–02
	(e)	14–02
	(5)	10–35
	s.2	9–26, 9–27, 9–28
	s.3	9–56
	(1)	9–58
	(2)(a)	9–57, 9–58
	(b)	9–58
	(c)	9–58
	(3)	9–57
	(4)	9–57
	(a)	9–57
	(b)	9–57
	(d)	9–57
	s.5	11–64
	s.6(2)	11–46, 11–53
	(3)	11–50
	s.7	11–13, 11–48
	(1B)	11–48

2006	Family Law (Scotland) Act —*contd*	
	s.8	11–32
	s.10	11–32, 11–35, 13–23
	s.11	14–22, 14–30
	(a)	13–01
	s.12	14–30
	s.13	14–24, 14–27, 14–30
	s.14	14–07, 14–28, 14–30
	s.15	14–30
	s.16	13–05, 13–11, 13–21, 13–22, 13–23, 13–24, 15–28
	s.17	13–38
	(1)	9–55
	(2)	13–38
	s.18	13–90
	s.20	10–57
	s.21	3–49, 5–37
	(2)	3–37
	s.22	5–37
	(1)	10–03
	(2)	10–03
	s.22(6)	11–20
	s.23	3–18, 6–28, 6–44, 9–07
	(4)	3–17
	s.24	4–71, 4–72
	s.25	15–25
	(1)	10–90
	(3)	10–92
	s.26	10–29, 12–46, 12–47, 12–52, 15–20
	(4)	12–45
	s.27	10–29, 12–52, 15–20
	s.28	12–05, 12–19, 13–98, 15–20
	(2)(b)	12–19
	(3)(a)–(b)	12–19
	(8)	12–19
	(9)	12–19
	s.29	10–90
	(1)	10–92
	(2)(a)	10–92
	(3)	10–92
	(4)	10–94
	(5)(b)	10–92
	(c)	10–92
	(6)	10–92
	(7)(b)	10–94
	(9)	10–94
	(a)	12–19
	(b)	12–19
	(10)	10–93
	s.30	10–17
	s.31	11–09, 11–13, 11–17, 11–19, 11–29, 11–33, 11–43
	s.32	11–42, 11–43

2006 Family Law (Scotland)
Act —*contd*
s.33 .... 11–37, 11–48, 11–50,
11–53, 11–64, 12–26,
13–01, 14–03, 14–16, 14–22
s.34 11–21
s.37 14–47
s.40 10–57
s.41 5–40
s.42 9–59
s.45(1) 10–15, 15–18
(2) 11–42, 11–68, 14–03,
14–30
Sch.1 .... 13–01, 14–03
para.3 11–64

2006 Family Law (Scotland)
Act —*contd*
Sch.1 para.3(b) 11–16
para.5 .... 11–46, 11–50,
11–53, 12–26
para.6 11–48
para.8 11–37
para.9 .... 13–01, 14–16,
14–22
para.12 11–13
Sch.2 10–15
para.2 10–15
para.5 15–18
Sch.3 .... 11–42, 11–68, 14–03,
14–27, 14–30

TABLE OF STATUTORY INSTRUMENTS

1971 Registration of Births, Still-
     births, Deaths and Mar-
     riages (Prescription of
     Forms) (Scotland)
     Amendment Regulations
     (SI 1971/1158) 1–06
1976 Child Benefit (General) Reg-
     ulations (SI 1976/965)
     reg.5 10–77
1977 Marriage (Prescription of
     Religious Bodies) (Scot-
     land) Regulations SI
     1977/1670) 9–52
1982 Matrimonial Homes (Form
     of Consent) (Scotland)
     Regulations (SI 1982/
     971) 11–48
     Act of Sederunt (Rules of
     Court Amendment No.6)
     (Simplified Divorce Pro-
     cedure) (SI 1982/1679)
     r.49.23 .... 14–55, 15–39
     r.49.28(2) 14–48
     r.49–72 14–49
1987 Income Support (General)
     Regulations   (SI
     1987/1967) 10–76
     reg.2 10–77
     reg.4 10–77
     reg.4ZA 10–66
     reg.6 10–77
     reg.12 10–77
     Sch.1B 10–67
     Housing Benefit (General)
     Regulations (SI 1987/
     1971) 10–74
     reg.5 10–75
1992 Council   Tax   Benefit
     (General) Regulations (SI
     1992/1814) 10–74
     reg.7 10–74
1993 Act of Sederunt (Sheriff
     Court Ordinary Cause
     Rules) (SI 1993/1956)
     r.9.12 14–52
        (3)(a) 14–52

1993 Act of Sederunt—contd
     r.9.12(3)(b) 14–52
           (c) 14–52
           (4) 14–52
           (5) 14–52
           (7) 14–52
     r.33.7 4–58
           (7) 14–53
     r.33(16) 14–33
     r.33.19(2) 4–58
     r.33.20 4–58
     r.33.22 .... 4–56, 14–55, 15–39
     r.33.22A 14–54
           (1) 14–54
           (c) 14–54
           (5) 14–54
           (6) 14–54
     r.33.28(2) 14–48
     r.33.33(7) 4–58
     s.33.36 .... 14–52, 14–52
     r.33.37 14–52
     r.33.73 14–49
     r.33A.7(7) 14–53
     r.33A.22 .... 14–55, 15–39
     r.33A.23 14–54
           (1) 14–54
           (c) 14–54
           (5) 14–54
           (6) 14–54
           (1)(c) 14
     r.33A.28 14–48
     r.33A.36 14–52
     Sch.1 Ch.33A 14–21
           Ch.33A.18 14–21
1994 Immigration Rules (HC
     395) 10–08
     Rules of the Court of Ses-
     sions (SI 1994/1443) 6–82,
                                    6–90
     r.49.23 4–58
     Parental Orders (Human
     Fertilisation and Embry-
     ology) (Scotland) Regula-
     tions (SI 1994/2804) 3–85
1996 Jobseeker's Allowance Reg-
     ulations (SI 1996/207) ... 10–66

1996 Jobseeker's Allowance
Regulations—*contd*
reg.54 10–77
reg.169(2) 10–81
Act of Sederunt (Rules of
the Court of Session
Amendment No.3) (Mis-
cellaneous) (SI 1996/
1756)
para.2(17) 15–39
Divorce etc. (Pensions)
(Scotland) Regulations
(SI 1996/1901) 13–27
reg.3 .... 13–27, 13–28, 14–27
Child Support (Miscella-
neous Amendments) Reg-
ulations (SI 1996/1945) ... 577
Act of Sederunt (Family
Proceedings in the Sheriff
Court) (SI 1996/2167) ... 4–57,
15–38
Sch. para.12 15–39
Parental Responsibilities
and Parental Rights
Agreement (Scotland)
Regulations (SI
1996/2549) 3–16
Act of Sederunt (Rules of
the Court of Session
Amendment No.5)
(Family Actions and Mis-
cellaneous) (SI 1996/
2587)
para.2(16) 15–39
(20) 14–48
Secure Accommodation
(Scotland) Regulations
(SI 1996/3255)
r.11(1) 8–54
Adoption Allowance (Scot-
land) Regulations (SI
1996/3257) 6–37
Children's Hearings (Scotland) Rules (SI 1996/
3261) 8–42
r.11 .... 8–31, 8–35
r.13 8–29
Fostering of Children (Scot-
land) Regulations (SI
1996/3263) 5–49
Adoption Agencies (Scot-
land) Regulations (SI
1996/3266) ... 6–21, 6–30, 6–31
reg.10 6–30
reg.12(3) 6–44
reg.14 6–38
reg.15 6–38
reg.17 6–75

1996 Adoption Agencies (Scotland)
Regulations—*contd*
reg.18 6–75
reg.25 6–70
Sch.6 6–38
Sch.7 6–38
1997 Act of Sederunt (Child Care
and Maintenance Rules)
(SI 1997/291)
r.3.36 7–53
r.3.47(6) 8–44
Legal Aid (Scotland) (Chil-
dren) Regulations (SI
1997/1690) 2–43
2000 Pensions on Divorce etc.
(Pension Sharing) (Scot-
land) Regulations (SI
2000/1051)
reg.3 .... 13–35, 13–51
reg.5 .... 13–35, 13–51
Immigration (Transit Visa)
(Amendment) Order (SI
2000/1381) 10–11
Reporting of Suspicious
Marriages (Scotland)
Regulations (SI 2000/
3232) 10–12
2001 Child Support (Mainte-
nance Calculations and
Special Cases) Regula-
tions (SI 2001/155) 5–75
reg.3 5–71
reg.4 5–71
reg.5 5–71
Sch. paras 3–6 5–72
Child Support (Variations)
Regulations (SI 2001/
156)
reg.18 5–84
reg.19 5–84
2002 Working Tax Credit (Entitlement and Maximum
Rate) Regulations (SI
2002/2005) 10–67
Tax Credits (Definition and
Calculation of Income)
Regulations (SI 2002/
2006) 10–67
Child Tax Credit Regula-
tions (SI 2002 No.
2007) 10–67
Tax Credits (Income
Thresholds and Determi-
nation of Rates) Regula-
tions (SI 2002/2008) 10–67
Tax Credits (Claims and
Notifications) Regula-
tions (SI 2002/2014) 10–67

2002 Working Tax Credit
       (Payment by Employers)
       Regulations (SI 2002/
       2172) 10–67
      Tax Credits (Payments by
       the Board) Regulations
       (SI 2002/2173) 10–67
2003 Housing Benefit and
       Council Tax Benefit (State
       Pension Credit) Regula-
       tions (SI 2003/325) 10–74
      British Nationality (General
       Regulations) (SI 2003/
       548) 10–07
      British Nationality
       (General) (Amendment)
       Regulations (SI 2003/
       3158) 10–08

2004 Human Fertilisation and
       Embryology Act (Disclo-
       sure of Donor Informa-
       tion) Regulations (SI
       2004/1511) 3–98
      British Nationality (General)
       (Amendment) Regula-
       tions (SI 2004/31726) ... 10–08
      British Nationality
       (General) (Amendment
       No.2) Regulations (SI
       2004/2109) 10–07
2005 Tax and Civil Partnership
       Regulations (SI 2005/
       3229)
      reg.7(4) 10–21
      reg.62 10–21
      reg.107(2) 10–21

TABLE OF SCOTTISH STATUTORY INSTRUMENTS

2000 Divorce etc. (Pensions)
(Scotland) Regulations
(SSI 2000/112) 13–32
Debtors (Scotland) Act 1987
(Amendment) Regula-
tions (SSI 2000/189) 12–36

2001 European Communities
(Matrimonial Jurisdiction
and Judgments) (Scot-
land) Regulations (SSI
2001/36) 14–39
Adoption of Children from
Overseas (Scotland) Reg-
ulations (SSI 2001/236) ... 6–82
Panels of Persons to Safeguard the Interests of
Children (Scotland) Reg-
ulations 2001 (SSI
2001/476) 8–35
Curators ad Litem and
Reporting Officers
(Panels) (Scotland) Regu-
lations 2001 (SSI
2001/477) 8–35

2002 Children's Hearings (Legal
Representation) (Scot-
land) Rules (SSI 2002/
63) 8–35
r.3(1) 8–35
r.4 8–35
r.5 8–35
(3) 8–39
(b) 8–39
Marriage (Approval of
Places) (Scotland) Regu-
lations (SSI 2002/260) ... 9–51

2003 Act of Sederunt (Child Care
and Maintenance Rules)
Amendment (1993 Hague
Convention Adoption)
(SSI 2003/4) 6–82, 6–90
Intercountry Adoption
(Hague Convention)
(Scotland) Regulations
(SSI 2003/19) 6–82

2004 Act of Sederunt (Rules of
the Court of Session
Amendments) (Miscella-
neous) (SSI 2004/52) 6–82,
6–90
Act of Sederunt (Ordinary
Cause, Summary Appli-
cation and Small Claim
Rules) Amendment (Mis-
cellaneous) (SSI 2004/
197)
para.2(6) 14–52

2005 European Communities
(Matrimonial and Parent-
al Responsibility Jurisdic-
tion and Judgments)
(Scotland) Regulations
(SSI 2005/42) 4–45, 4–46,
14–39
reg.5 4–45
Intensive Support and Mon-
itoring (Scotland)
Regulations (SSI 2005/
129) 8–56
Prior Rights of Surviving
Spouse (Scotland) Order
(SSI 2005/252) 10–84
Civil Partnership (Jurisdic-
tion and Recognition of
Judgments) (Scotland)
Regulations (SSI 2005/
629) 14–38,
14–39
Act of Sederunt (Rules of
the Court of Session
Amendment No. 9) (Civil
Partnership Act 2004 etc)
(SSI 2005/632)
para.14 14–48
Act of Sederunt (Ordinary
Cause Rules) Amend-
ment (Civil Partnership
Act 2004) (SSI 2005/
638) 14–49
r.33A16 14–33

2006 Act of Sederunt (Rules of
the Court of Session
Amendment No. 3)
(Family Law (Scotland)
Act 2006) (SSI 2006/206)
para.15 14–49
Act of Sederunt (Ordinary
Cause Rules) Amendment
(Family Law (Scotland)
Act 2006 etc) (SSI 2006/
207) 9–55

2006 Family Law (Scotland) Act
2006 (Commencement,
Transitional Provisions
and Savings) Order (SSI
2006/212) 14–02

TABLE OF CONVENTIONS AND EUROPEAN DIRECTIVES AND REGULATIONS

Conventions

1950 European Convention on Human Rights 1–83, 2–01, 2–06, 2–07, 2–08, 2–10, 2–11, 2–12, 2–13, 2–74, 2–79, 4–22, 4–75, 4–76, 4–82, 4–90, 4–97, 4–99, 5–20, 5–36, 6–44, 6–51, 6–78, 7–05, 8–81, 9–03

    Art. 2 .... 1–11, 1–12, 1–13, 1–14, 1–15, 1–81, 1–83

    Art.3 .... 2–08, 2–09, 5–12, 5–13, 5–18

    Art.5 8–54

    Art.6 .... 2–09, 4–60, 4–62, 7–67, 8–36, 8–37, 8–39, 8–44, 9–05

    Art.6(1) 8–32, 8–33, 8–36

    (3) 8–32

    Art.7 8–72

    Art.8 .... 1–81, 1–82, 2–09, 2–11, 3–14, 3–94, 3–98, 4–10, 4–41, 4–60, 4–75, 4–77, 4–90, 4–97, 5–36, 6–31, 6–44, 6–78, 7–31, 7–64, 7–66, 8–36, 8–72, 9–03, 9–05, 9–06, 9–41, 9–42, 10–16

    (1) 3–14

    (2) 1–82, 1–83, 6–51, 9–06

    Art.9 .... 2–09, 4–82, 5–18

    Art.12 .... 9–05, 9–41, 9–42

    Art.14 .... 4–75, 5–36, 9–05, 9–06, 9–07, 10–16

    First Protocol, Art 2 .... 2–09, 5–12, 5–19

1980 Hague Convention on the International Abduction of Children 4–65, 4–98

    Art.2(11) 4–46

    Art.10 4–46

    Art.11 4–46

1981 European Convention on the Legal Status of Children Born out of Wedlock 5–36

1989 UN Convention on the Rights of the Child 2–06, 2–07, 2–10, 2–12, 2–13, 2–14, 2–15, 2–79, 4–17, 4–23, 4–87, 4–99, 6–22, 7–05, 9–03

    Art.1 2–79

    Art.3 2–10

    Art.5 2–10

    Art.12 .... 4–23, 4–24, 4–55, 4–60, 4–62, 4–87

    Art.19(1) 5–12

    Art.29 5–20

1993 Hague Convention on Protection of Children and Co-operation in Respect of Intercountry Adoption 6–83

2000 EU Charter of Rights

    Art.24(2) 2–11

2001 Convention of Jurisdiction and the Recognition and Enforcement of Judgments 14–39

    Art.1(2) 14–40

    Art.11(2) 14–41

    Art.16 14–39

Directives

2000 Dir. 2000/78 13–97

2004 Dir. 2004/38/EC 10–09

Regulations

2000 Reg. 1347/2000 ...... 4–45, 14–39

    Art.1(1) 4–46

    (2) 4–46

    (3) 4–46

2003 Reg. 2201/2003 .... 4–45, 4–98, 9–10, 13–39

    Art.1(1)(b) 14–40

2003 Reg. 2201/2003—*contd*
    Art.2(1) 14–39
    Art.8 4–46
    Art.9 4–46
    Art.11(2) 4–98
       (4) 4–98

2003 Reg. 2201/2003—*contd*
    Art.12 4–46
    Art.13 4–46
    Art.15 4–46
    Art.66 4–46

CHAPTER 1

LEGAL PERSONALITY AND FAMILY RELATIONS

This book is about the law of Scotland relating to families. The first **1–01** question that is logically raised by this statement is what we mean by a family. Unfortunately, there is no simple answer to this question. Although the stereotypical media image of the family may be of the "nuclear family", consisting of a married couple and two to three children, in reality family forms are widely disparate. A "family" may be comprised of adults in a married or cohabiting relationship, with or without children; couples who once shared such a relationship but are now divorced or separated but still have connections, possibly via their children; a single parent with a child or children; or multifarious other groupings made up of persons who have biological or social connections, including blood relations such as grandparents and also step relations.

Not only is there diversity in the form that families take but it is quite **1–02** possible for a person to be a member of more than one family at any given moment in time. So, for example, where a child has parents who split up, and each subsequently forms a new relationship, that child may be considered a member of both the new resulting families. It is important to accept that families are not static, but tend to progress through a life cycle; so, for example, the cohabiting couple without children may marry in time, have children who will become adults in due course and who, like their parents, may start their own family. The rights, duties, and obligations that exist between such persons, and their relationship with state agencies and institutions, such as courts and local authorities, are family law; the subject of this book.

The legal regulation of families thus revolves around relationships **1–03** between "natural persons" who have certain legal rights and are subject to certain legal duties. This raises the important question of when a "person" technically comes into existence in law, that is, when legal personality begins, for according to Scots law, all living human beings have legal personality.[1] The concept of legal personality is fundamental to the operation of the legal systems in the United Kingdom.

Only legal persons have standing in the courts and access to the **1–04** legal process, are able to hold and enforce legal rights and can be sued

---

[1] *Knight v Wedderburn* (1778) Mor. 14545.

and thus be held subject to legal duties. The category of legal persons is not confined to "natural" living persons but extends also to other entities endowed with legal personality: referred to as "artificial" or "juristic" persons. Juristic persons cover a whole range of bodies,[2] including those incorporated by or under statute,[3] or by Royal Charter,[4] or through custom and usage.[5] As the focus of this book is on the legal relationships between natural persons, as members of a family, we will restrict ourselves in this chapter to examining legal personality with respect to natural persons.

1–05   Just as families experience a life cycle, so do natural persons, who progress from birth to death, through childhood, adolescence, adulthood and old age. In the next seven chapters we will examine the legal problems associated with children. Subsequent chapters will deal with the regulation of adult domestic relationships. In this chapter we will be principally concerned with an area that has been the subject of intense debate over the years, namely the legal status of the unborn child or fetus, and, in particular, the issue of when legal personality commences. While this is too large an area to be covered in depth, we shall highlight important issues such as civil liability for ante-natal injury and negligence, criminal acts affecting the unborn child, and, in particular, abortion, and consider what the law in these areas says about the status of the unborn child in Scots law.

COMMENCEMENT OF LEGAL PERSONALITY

The General Rule

1–06   The general rule is that legal personality and the attendant rights commence at birth. A certificate of live birth is lodged with the appropriate registrar who issues a birth certificate.[6] Prior to birth, the fetus or unborn child has no legal rights and Scots law upholds the proposition put forward in *Re F*[7] that, "The fetus cannot . . . have any right of its own at least until it is born and has a separate existence from the mother".[8]

---

[2] See Gloag and Henderson, *The Law of Scotland* (10th edn, W.Green, Edinburgh, 1995) (hereafter "Gloag and Henderson"), Ch.52, pp.994–1000; *Stair Memorial Encyclopaedia of the Laws of Scotland* (hereafter "*Stair Encyclopaedia*"), Vol.11, paras 1041–1044.

[3] e.g. limited companies under the Companies Act 1985 or the Law Society of Scotland under the Solicitors (Scotland) Acts of 1949 and 1980.

[4] e.g. the Royal Bank of Scotland or the BBC.

[5] e.g. the Faculty of Advocates or the W.S. Society.

[6] Registration of Births, Deaths and Marriages (Scotland) Act 1965, ss.13–20 and SI 1971/1158.

[7] [1988] 2 All E.R. 193.

[8] *ibid.* May L.J. at p.195. See also the Scottish case of *Kelly v Kelly*, 1997 S.L.T. (2nd Div) 896.

It was held in *Re F* that the court had no power to ward an unborn **1–07** child. In reaching this decision the court observed that if there were such a power it would give rise to a conflict of interest between the mother and the child.

Attempts have been made to challenge this view, most notably in **1–08** the recent case of *Vo v France*[9] which went all the way to the European Court of Human Rights.

Vo v France[10]

In this case a Vietnamese women, Mrs Thi-Nho Vo, attended a hos- **1–09** pital in Lyon for a routine ante-natal appointment. There was another Vietnamese outpatient there whose name was also Vo and who was in attendance to have a contraceptive coil removed. Due to a lack of language skills, the medical staff had difficulty understanding the women with the result that there was a mix up and Mrs Thi-Nhos Vo's fetus's amniotic sac was penetrated eventually resulting in the death of the fetus.

Mrs Vo raised a case against the doctor under the French Criminal **1–10** Code for the offence of unintentional homicide. She opted to do this rather than pursue a civil remedy because she considered such a remedy was incapable of securing judicial acknowledgement of the homicide of her child. The issue for the court in this case was whether or not a fetus aged 20–21 weeks was a "human person" or "another" within the meaning of the French Criminal Code.

The court of first instance held that—at 21 weeks of gestation— **1–11** the fetus had not been viable, and therefore was not a human person. The Cour d'Appel, however, said that viability was an indefinite and uncertain concept and "reverted to the concept of the beginning of life".[11] The case was referred to the European Court of Human Rights where the central question before the Court was whether the absence of a criminal remedy within the French legal system to punish the unintentional destruction of a fetus constituted a failure on the part of the state to protect by law the right to life within the meaning of Art.2 of the European Convention on Human Rights and Fundamental Freedoms.[12]

Mrs Vo argued that: **1–12**

* it was now "scientifically proven" that all life begins at fertilisation;
* that the term "everyone" in Art.2 that provides that "Everyone's right to life shall be protected by law" was to be taken as referring to human beings rather than persons possessing legal personality;

---

[9] (2004) 79 BMLR 71.
[10] *ibid.*
[11] Mason, J.K., *Law and Medical Ethics* (7th edn, Oxford University Press, Oxford, 2006), p.5.10.
[12] For fuller discussion of the issues see J.K. Mason, "What's in a name?: The vagaries of Vo v France" (2005) 17 CFLQ 97.

- that subject to the exception provided in the law on abortion, French law guaranteed all human beings the right to life from conception;
- that the availability of abortion did not exonerate the State from its duty to protect the unborn child under the terms of Art.2.

1–13 In response, the French Government argued that Art.2 could not be intended to apply to the fetus (and that this must be so because the Article would otherwise be contrary to domestic legislation of those states that had enacted enabling legislation on abortion). In support of this claim it was argued that states other than France allowed terminations beyond 20-weeks gestation and that it would be paradoxical for states to have a margin of appreciation that excluded a protection of the fetus in the context of abortion without having a similar margin when a pregnancy was terminated as a result of unintentional negligence.

European Court's Ruling

1–14 The European Court asserted that it was still an unsettled question of what constitutes the "beginning" of "everyone's right to life" in the context of Art.2. So far, the issue had only been raised in the context of abortion, and the Court was reluctant to expound on this, noting that the question of when the right to life begins comes within the margin of appreciation that is attributed to individual states. In this situation, it was impossible to answer the question of whether or not the unborn child was a person for the purposes of Art.2 of the European Convention in the abstract. Moreover, there was no call to decide whether or not "the abrupt end of the applicant's pregnancy" fell within the scope of Art.2 in so far as there had been no failure on the part of France to comply with the requirements relating to the preservation of life in the public health sphere, that is, in relation to the law on abortion.

1–15 The Court then went on to debate the reverse side of Art.2—that is the duty of the state to take appropriate steps to enable other interested parties to establish liability and obtain compensation for a death, including one associated with either the public or private provision of medical services. The Court held that this obligation was satisfied "if the legal system affords victims a remedy in the civil courts, either alone or in conjunction with a remedy in the criminal courts, enabling any liability of the doctors concerned to be established and civil redress through damages". In this case Mrs Vo had opted not to pursue a civil remedy (which was now time barred). In any event, the Court held that even if Art.2 had applied to a fetus, there had been no legal procedural failure to provide the applicant with an effective remedy and thus no violation of Art.2.

The Nasciturus Exception

So far, attempts to attribute legal personality to a fetus before birth **1–16** have been unsuccessful. However, this general rule is subject to modification in certain circumstances, by virtue of the legal fiction referred to as the nasciturus rule,[13] which is applied where it would benefit the child to make such a modification.[14] The nasciturus rule provides that so long as that child is subsequently born alive, an unborn child can be regarded as being capable of having rights at a prenatal time, where that would be to his or her advantage. This fiction was first applied in the context of succession, to enable a child born posthumously to have a right of inheritance in a deceased parent's estate. The general rule for succession is that only those heirs who are alive and legal persons at the time of the deceased's death have a right to succeed to the deceased's estate.[15] Thus, if a father leaves a share of his estate to his children, a child still in utero at the time of his death strictly does not qualify to share in the estate. However, the nasciturus rule would enable such a child to share in the deceased father's estate by setting up the legal fiction that he or she should be deemed to have been born and to have become a legal person by the date of that father's death for the purposes of succession rights. Note that the rule only operates where its application will be to the child's direct advantage.[16]

The nasciturus rule has been extended beyond the context of suc- **1–17** cession. For example, in *Cohen v Shaw*[17] the court held that a child born after the death of his father —who had been negligently killed in a road accident by a third party—was entitled to sue for damages. Under the Damages (Scotland) Act 1976, the right to sue was only conferred on a relative,[18] defined to include a person who "was a child of the deceased".[19] The judge saw no reason to limit the application of the rule to succession cases.[20]

---

[13] Derived from the Latin maxim, *nasciturus pro jam nato habetur quando agitur de ejus commodo*. See Walker, *Principles of Scottish Private Law* (4th edn, Oxford University Press, Oxford, 1988), Vol.1, p.205.

[14] See *Stair Encyclopaedia*, who notes that "in all things ending in favour of the unborn, they are accounted as born", *The Institutions of the Law of Scotland*, III. v. 50 (Walker (ed.), 1981).

[15] Subject to the rules on deferred vesting in testamentary gifts, e.g. where a legacy is to vest subsequent to a liferent.

[16] *Elliot v Joicey*, 1935 S.C. (H.L.) 57.

[17] 1992 S.L.T. 1022.

[18] Damages (Scotland) Act 1976, s.1 and see also paras 10–15 to 10–17.

[19] *ibid.*, Sch.1, para.1(b).

[20] There is a body of opinion, however, which doubts that the rule, which originated in Roman law, was intended for use outside the realm of property and succession: see Norrie, "Liability for Injuries Caused Before Birth", 1992 S.L.T. 65 at 68; Rodger, "Case and Comment: Report of the Scottish Law Commission on Ante-Natal Injury", 1974 J.R. 83.

CIVIL ACTIONS RELATING TO ANTE-NATAL INJURY OR NEGLIGENCE

The Right to Sue in Respect of Ante-natal Injury: General Principles

1–18   Does the fact that legal personality does not commence until birth mean that a child (or his or her parents) cannot sue for injuries sustained *by the child* before birth as a result of another's negligence? This matter came to particular legal prominence in the 1970s after a large number of women, who had taken the drug Thalidomide during their pregnancies, gave birth to children with severe physical deformities. Injury to the fetuses those women were carrying had arguably occurred as a result of the negligent acts of the manufacturers of Thalidomide. The English Law Commission concluded that English law was so uncertain in this area that there should be legislation.[21] This took the form of the Congenital Disabilities (Civil Liability) Act 1976, which provides in ss.1(1) and (3) that anyone responsible for an "occurrence" affecting either parent of a child, or the child himself, which causes that child to be born disabled, will be answerable to the child if he or she was or would have been liable in tort to the parent.[22] This applies whether or not actual injury was caused to the parent. The Scottish Law Commission (hereafter "SLC") however, took the view that legislation was unnecessary in Scotland as there was no bar at common law to a person recovering damages for ante-natal injuries resulting from another's negligence.[23] The child once born alive is a legal person and has a right to sue in respect of personal injury, whether or not the act causing the injury occurred before or after *conception*. In the view of the SLC, parents also have a right to sue in respect of ante-natal injury to their unborn child. In Scotland, therefore, no legislation was passed and the matter has been left to be clarified by case law.

Case Law under the Damages (Scotland) Act 1976

1–19   In Scotland, two cases, *Hamilton v Fife Health Board*[24] and *McWilliams v Lord Advocate*,[25] have dealt with the issue of liability for ante-natal injury. In both these cases the parents of babies who died shortly after birth[26] sought damages in the form of a loss of society[27] award under the Damages (Scotland) Act 1976, s.1. The parents alleged negligence by medical personnel, prior to the birth of

---

[21] Report on Injuries to Unborn Children, Law Com. No.60, Cmnd.5709 (1974).

[22] For a fuller commentary, see Mason, *Medico-Legal Aspects of Reproduction and Parenthood* (2nd edn, Aldershot, Dartmouth, 1997), Ch.6.

[23] Liability for Ante-natal Injury, Scot. Law Com. No.30, Cmnd.5371 (1973).

[24] 1992 S.L.T. 1026 (O.H.), and 1993 S.L.T. 624 (Ex. Div.).

[25] 1992 S.L.T. 1045.

[26] In *Hamilton* the child died three days after birth and in *McWilliams*, after six weeks.

[27] s.1(4) enables a relative to claim damages by way of compensation for the loss of the benefits a relative might have expected to derive from a deceased's society as well as for grief and sorrow caused by the deceased's death.

their children, which resulted in their children's deaths after birth, caused by the injuries sustained ante-natally. The parents' claims were based on s.1(1) of the 1976 Act which provides that:

> "Where a *person* dies in consequence of *personal injuries sustained by him* as the result of an act or omission of another person . . . then . . . the person liable to pay those damages . . . shall also be liable to pay damages in accordance with this section to any relative of the deceased". [Emphasis added.]

The key issue at stake in these cases was whether or not it was necessary for there to be a legal person in existence at the time that the injuries were "sustained by him". The judges in the Outer House adopted different interpretations of the statute. In *Hamilton*, Lord Prosser reiterated the general legal rule that prior to being born, a child is not a "person" in legal terms. In his view, then, the "child had quite simply lacked the status of being a person when the injuries were sustained",[28] and so could not be said to have died "in consequence of personal injuries sustained by him".[29] The nasciturus rule had no application here, because it was not the child who was suing for damages and thereby benefiting directly from the action, but the parents. As we saw above, the nasciturus rule can only be invoked where it is directly to the benefit of the child. **1–20**

In *McWilliams*,[30] however, Lord Motion took another view, namely, that it was not necessary to rely on the nasciturus rule, a legal fiction: **1–21**

> "to give a child who is born alive a title to sue for injuries sustained in utero and . . . if a child dies after being born alive and the death is caused by injuries sustained in utero the parents of that child have a title to sue for damages for the death of that child".[31]

In his opinion, the fact that the injury caused by the negligent act was inflicted on a victim who was then in utero and therefore not yet a legal person, was not a bar to a subsequent right of reparation when that unborn child was later born alive. In other words, in His Lordship's view the act which causes injury and the sustaining of injury by a legal person need not occur simultaneously. **1–22**

When *Hamilton* was subsequently appealed to the Inner House[32] it was by and large the approach of Lord Morton in *McWilliams* which was upheld. The Inner House held that in order to sue for damages **1–23**

---

[28] 1992 S.L.T. 1026 at 1028
[29] *ibid.*
[30] 1992 S.L.T. 1045.
[31] *ibid.* at 1048.
[32] 1993 S.L.T. 624.

there must be both *injuria* (wrongful act) and *damnum* (loss). It noted that:

> "An unborn person, a fetus, is not a person in the eyes of the law – at least in relation to the law of civil remedies – and there can be no liability to pay damages to a fetus, even although the fetus has sustained injuries resulting from a negligent act or omission".

But that:

> "once the fetus ceases on birth to be a fetus and becomes a person there is a concurrence of injuria and damnum and the newly born child has a right to sue the person whose breach of duty has resulted in the child's loss. The coming into existence of that right to sue does not depend upon the application of any fiction".[33]

1–24   The end result then is that it is clearly possible in Scotland for parents to sue under the 1976 Act for injuries sustained by their child before birth as a result of the negligence of a third party, as long as the child is subsequently born alive.[34] It also seems now to be accepted even in England and Wales that the child him or herself, if born alive, can sue third parties at common law in respect of ante-natal injury.[35]

Child's Right to Sue Parents for Ante-natal Negligence

1–25   So far, we have considered cases involving children who have suffered ante-natal injury as a result of the negligent acts of third parties other than the mother. But can a child sue his or her mother where ante-natal injury has occurred as a result of their negligence (or, indeed, deliberate act)? The kind of situation where this might arise is where the mother has abused drugs or alcohol during pregnancy with resulting injury to the child in the womb. In theory there is no special reason why a child should not be able to sue a parent in respect of ante-natal injury; however the courts might well refuse such claims on the basis of public policy as undermining the stability of the family. It is also difficult in such cases to establish that the child's infirmities were wholly or even mainly caused by the ante-natal negligence of the mother, and not by other factors affecting the child before and during birth. In England, s.1(1) of the Congenital Disabilities (Civil Liability) Act 1976 makes it clear that a child cannot sue his or her mother for fetal neglect.[36] There is, however, no equivalent legislative guidance in Scotland.

---

[33] 1993 S.L.T. 624, *per* Lord McCluskey at p.629.

[34] The 1976 Act was amended by the Damages (Scotland) Act 1993 subsequent to the decision in *Hamilton*. The changes made do not, however, affect the ratio of that case.

[35] See English case of *Burton v Islington Health Authority* [1992] 3 All E.R. 833.

[36] Although see s.1(2) which provides that a pregnant woman driving a motor vehicle is under a duty to take care for her unborn child.

Although negligent acts by a mother affecting her unborn child may **1–26** not as yet clearly allow a claim for damages by the child once born, such acts are not wholly without legal consequence. Ante-natal parental negligence may be grounds for invoking the powers of the local authority and the courts to remove the child from the care of the parents to that of the state. Under the Children (Scotland) Act 1995, Pt II (see Chs 7 and 8), a fetus, not being a person in law, cannot be made the subject of legal action but the child subsequently born can be. The situation is similar in England. In *D (a minor) v Berkshire County Council*,[37] the mother of a child was a registered drug addict during her pregnancy, and continued to take drugs after the birth. Her child was born suffering from withdrawal symptoms so acute that it had to be kept in intensive care for several weeks after birth. The House of Lords[38] held that in deciding whether or not to make a care order under the Children and Young Persons Act 1969, which would enable the local authority to remove the child from the mother's care as soon as it was born, a court was required to consider whether there was any continuing impairment, neglect or ill-treatment of the child at the time immediately prior to the initiation of care proceedings. So, a court when considering the welfare of a child is entitled to look to the past, including to events before that child was born, in order to assess whether there might be problems that are likely to continue to affect the child's development in the future. In Scotland, although there is no equivalent case law, there seems no reason why a local authority might not obtain, inter alia, a child protection order[39] to remove a newly-born infant to a place of safety if there was evidence either that the child was already suffering "significant harm" or if not removed from the family home would be likely to do so, and that the making of such an order was necessary to prevent such harm occurring.[40]

Parents' Rights to Sue for Wrongful Pregnancy and Wrongful Birth

In some cases, pregnancy and birth may give rise to parents suing **1–27** health carers and, vicariously, health authorities on the grounds of "wrongful pregnancy" or "wrongful birth". A claim for damages on the ground of "wrongful pregnancy"[41] relates to an unplanned

---

[37] [1987] 1 All E.R. 20.

[38] *ibid.* at 33.

[39] From a court, by virtue of the powers in the Children (Scotland) Act 1995, s.57.

[40] See further Chs 7 and 8. Another option might be to refer the newborn child to the children's hearing on the ground that he or she was suffering from lack of parental care (Children (Scotland) Act 1995, s.52(1)(c)).

[41] J.K. Mason, R.A. McCall Smith, G.T. Laurie, *Law and Medical Ethics* (6th edn, LexisNexis, Edinburgh, 2002) the authors prefer to use the term 'uncovenanted pregnancy' which was first used by Kennedy J. in *Richardson v LRC Products Ltd* (2001) 59 BMLR 185 to cover this situation. Their reasoning is that they consider it undesirable to refer to a child who has come to be accepted as an "unwanted" child when what is really at stake is the fact that an unexpected happening, which was not-contemplated by the parties, namely a pregnancy, has occurred.

pregnancy which has occurred as the result of another's negligence. The term "wrongful conception" is sometimes used, however, as pregnancy without implantation causes no injury, the former phrase is to be preferred. A duty of care is owed by a doctor to a person who consults him or her about sterilisation or contraception. In particular, a duty is owed to both sexual partners if they come together to a doctor seeking an agreed limitation of fertility. A failure with respect to duty of care can be attributable either to:

- incompetent clinical expertise; or to
- inadequate explanation of the shortcomings of the procedure, in particular, as to the inherent possibility that conception might still occur after treatment due purely to the vagaries of nature.

1–28 A claim for damages on the ground of "wrongful birth" however, arises where the parents of a child who has been born disabled raise an action in negligence against a doctor or genetic counsellor who has failed either to:

- advise them of the risk of illness in their child(ren) prior to birth; or to
- carry out, and interpret correctly, appropriate diagnostic procedures which would have disclosed abnormality in the fetus.

In such a situation the health carer owes the parents a duty of care, which if breached, may result in the parents contending that they have been deprived of the opportunity to terminate the pregnancy as a result of which they are now faced with caring for a disabled child.

1–29 In assessing whether negligence has occurred in either of these cases, what constitutes a breach of a duty of care is largely governed by the principle laid down in *Bolam v Friern Hospital Management Committee*[42] that a doctor's action will not be held to be negligent if it conforms to a practice which would have been adopted by a responsible body of medical opinion. There are a number of cases establishing parameters of parents' right to sue in these circumstances that cover two heads of liability, being:

1) those that derive from pregnancy itself, including damages for pain and suffering of gestation and childbirth, and loss of earning, plus additional expenses resulting from pregnancy and convalescence; and
2) those relating to maintenance and upkeep of the child.

The question to be resolved is whether damages for upkeep of an uncovenanted[43] child should ever be awarded, and if so,

---

[42] [1957] 2 All E.R. 118. Note: popular usage is reference to 'Bolam', however in Scotland the principle was established in *Hunter v Hanley*, 1955 S.C. 200.

[43] *Op. cit* above, n.11.

whether the condition of the child or its mother should affect the quantum?

A conflict arises here because it has been widely argued that where a **1–30** healthy child is born this must always be regarded as a blessing and should never be regarded as a matter for compensation. This was the view taken by the judge in *Udale v Bloomsbury Area Health Authority*.[44] In this case the doctor negligently performed a sterilisation operation. As a result, an unwanted pregnancy occurred. The judge held that damages under the first head, that is for pain and suffering along with loss of earnings following a negligently performed operation were recoverable. However an award to cover the cost of bringing up the child was firmly rejected on the grounds that the joy of having a child and the benefits it brought in terms of love should be offset against any inconvenience and financial disadvantage resulting from its birth.

This view was criticised in the later case of *Emeh v Kensington Area* **1–31** *Health Authority*[45] which also involved negligent sterilisation of a woman who gave birth to a congenitally abnormal child. In this case the Court of Appeal awarded damages not only for pain and suffering and loss of earnings prior to birth but also for loss of future earnings, maintenance for the child up to trial and in the future, and for the plaintiff's future loss of amenity including the extra care that the child would require and the cost of rearing the child. Importantly it was held that damages would be awarded whether or not the child had been disabled. It rejected the objections against such recovery voiced in *Udale* and held that the fact that the women's pregnancy in this case was discovered in time for her to opt for an abortion did not limit her right to damages. A similar approach was adopted in *Thake v Maurice*[46] which attempted to lay to rest the distinction between entitlement to damages for pain and suffering and those representing the cost of the child's upbringing. The plea that the parent's damages should be cancelled out or reduced by their joy at the birth of a healthy baby was expressly dismissed. As a result, subsequent English cases came to cover damages under both heads of liability and, in some cases, even incorporating the costs of private education when that seemed appropriate[47] up until the House of Lords decision in *McFarlane v Tayside Health Board*,[48] that is.

The Scottish position

Prior to *McFarlane*, the case of *Allan v Greater Glasgow Health* **1–32** *Board*[49] accepted the proposition in Scots law that the unexpected birth of a healthy child due to another's negligence could give rise to

---

[44] [1983] 2 All E.R. 522.
[45] [1984] 3 All E.R. 1044.
[46] [1986] 1 All E.R. 479.
[47] *Allen v Bloomsbury Health Authority* [1993] 1 All E.R. 651.
[48] [2000] S.C.L.R. (HL) 105; 2 A.C. 59.
[49] (1998) S.L.T. 580.

damages. It held that there were no grounds in principle or policy to prevent an award of damages for the upbringing of a child born in such circumstances. However, the House of Lords decision in *McFarlane v Tayside Health Board*[50] has overturned established authority in this area and limited what is recoverable in *both* cases of wrongful pregnancy and wrongful birth.

McFarlane v Tayside Health Board[51]

1–33 The pursuers were a married couple with four children who decided that as they did not want any more children, the husband would undergo a vasectomy. The operation was performed by a surgeon employed by the defenders (the Health Board). When the husband later submitted sperm samples to the hospital for analysis he was informed by the surgeon that his sperm counts were negative and that contraceptive measures were no longer necessary. The pursuers acted on the advice received but to their surprise the wife became pregnant and, after a normal pregnancy and labour, gave birth to a healthy child whom the parents loved and cared for as an integral part of their family. They raised an action for damages against the Health Board on the grounds that that they had suffered loss as a result of the Board's negligence and claiming damages:

- for the physical discomfort suffered by the wife from her pregnancy, confinement and delivery (*mother's claim*); as well as
- for the financial costs of caring for and bringing up the child (*the parent's claim*—one of patrimonial loss).

1–34 At first instance, the Lord Ordinary, Lord Gill, held that:

- that normal, even if undesired, pregnancy and labour could not amount to personal injuries, or even if they could, they were injuries for which no damage was recoverable;
- that the benefits of parenthood transcended any loses which the parents might have suffered.

He also expressed sympathy with the defender's argument that public policy considerations militated against allowing such an action to be brought.

1–35 Lord Gill's views, however, were rejected by the Inner House who held that:

- the issue was not whether the effect of pregnancy/childbirth could be described as personal injury but whether or not they represented *damnum* (loss). Material prejudice suffered by a pursuer could be recognised as such a loss and was experienced by the wife;

[50] [2000] S.C.L.R. (HL) 105; 2 A.C. 59.
[51] [2000] S.C.L.R. (HL) 105; 2 A.C. 59.

- the fact that the pursuers chose to keep the child did not disrupt or break the chain of causation, namely that the defenders' negligence had caused loss;
- that the extra expenditure which the pursuers would incur in the case of the child (even if part of the normal parent/child relationship) was a loss for which they could seek compensation; and finally
- that even if the birth of a child brought about the benefits of parenthood (which could not always be said to be the case), there was no principle in Scots law that recognised that such intangible benefits had to be set off against patrimonial loss.

The decision by the Inner House was very much in line with earlier **1–36** rulings by the English Court of Appeal but it was overturned by the House of Lords on appeal. While the majority of the Law Lords accepted that under normal delictual principles there was liability, they held that the claim for maintenance costs for the child represented a claim for pure economic loss which imposed additional considerations that were not met in this case. As a result, no damages under this head could be awarded. While their decision was unanimous, the Law Lords' reasons for reaching it varied. The majority[52] based their decision on the grounds that where economic loss was concerned, a claim had to meet the test of fairness laid down in *Caparo Industries Plc v Dickman*.[53] This requires a closer link between the act and the damage than the concept of "forseeability" alone provides. For, over and above the required relationship of "neighbourhood" or "proximity" between a person owing a duty and person to whom it is owed, there exists the question of whether it is "fair, just and reasonable" for the law to impose a duty. It was held that this test had not been met in *McFarlane*. Other objections were put forward by individual judges. Lord Steyn, for example, incorporated considerations of distributive justice that indicated that the law did not permit the parents of a healthy but unwanted child to claim the cost of its upbringing from a health authority or doctor in the circumstances of the case.[54] Lord Clyde, on the other hand, expressed the view that to relieve the parents of the financial obligations of caring for their child went beyond proportionality between the wrongdoing and the loss suffered[55]; while Lord Millett was of the opinion that the law regarded the birth of a healthy, normal baby as a blessing and not as a detriment with the advantages and disadvantages of parenthood being so inextricably bound together that the benefits should be regarded as outweighing any loss.[56]

---

[52] Lord Slynn of Hadley, Lord Steyn and Lord Hope of Craighead.
[53] [1990] 2 A.C. 605.
[54] [2000] 2 A.C. 59 at 80A–E.
[55] *ibid.* at 105F–H and 106A.
[56] *ibid.* at 111D–F and 113H–114A–D.

1–37   However, since pregnancy was a type of "physical damage", the
plaintiffs were allowed to recover for all loses that flowed directly
from the pregnancy, including special damages for extra medical
expenses, clothing and loss of earnings.[57] In reaching their decision
the House of Lords rejected the argument that the claimants were
under a duty to mitigate loss by having an abortion or putting the
child up for adoption. It is noteworthy that "the mother's claim" has
never been disputed in subsequent litigation.

1–38   Other jurisdictions have not necessarily adopted the *McFarlane*
approach to the "parental" claim. In Australia, for example, in the
case of *Cattanach v Melchior*[58] a High Court of seven judges expressly
declined to follow *McFarlane* and held that a claim for maintenance
expenses for a child was competent. While the decisions in the two
cases appear to be diametrically opposed, they may be reconciled on
the basis that the common denominator in the House of Lords decision in *McFarlane* is an appeal to justice, fairness and reasonableness
based on the *Caparo* case, a case which does not feature in the
Australian jurisprudence of tort law. It is important to note that
McFarlane is a case involving damages with respect to the upkeep of
a *healthy* child.[59] Two of the Law Lords, Lord Steyn and Lord Clyde,
raised the possibility of a different outcome if the child were found to
be disabled. Subsequent case law dealing with uncovenanted pregnancy and wrongful birth has struggled to deal with the issue of how
far the ruling in *McFarlane* extends.

Wrongful Birth

1–39   How far the ruling in *McFarlane* extends is especially pertinent in
cases dealing with damages for wrongful birth where, due to the negligence of the doctor/genetic counsellor or other health carers,[60]
parents are not afforded the opportunity of aborting the fetus with
the result that a disabled child is born. What damages, if any, are
recoverable in this situation? Prior to the House of Lords decision in

---

[57] Lord Clyde, while having no difficulty in allowing the claim for *solatium* because
"the pain which she [second pursuer] suffered through the carrying of an unwanted
child seems to me to be reasonably a subject for compensation" (at 100A), nonetheless dissented from allowing a claim for loss of earnings by the mother and "for
additional costs in caring for, feeding and clothing and maintaining the child, and
the expenses of the layette" (at 106D).

[58] [2003] HCA 38.

[59] For discussion of the case see J.K. Mason, "Unwanted Pregnancy: A Case of
Retroversion?", 2000 Edin L.R. 191; J. Thomson, "Abandoning the Law of Delict?
McFarlane v Tayside Health Board in the House of Lords", 2000 S.L.T. (News) 43;
L. Sutherland, "The Blessing of the Unplanned Pregnancy—*McFarlane* in the
House of Lords", 2000 Reparation L.B. 33:5.

[60] In a substantial number of cases the error is either made within a laboratory or by
a radiographer who failed to detect evidence of abnormality during tests which are
primarily those routinely carried out as part of the ante-natal care of a pregnant
woman, although some are offered to women over a certain age or whose family
history indicates it would be appropriate.

McFarlane it appeared that damages extending to full recovery for the child's upkeep were recoverable. In *Anderson v Forth Valley Health Board*,[61] the pursuers were a married couple who had two sons born with muscular dystrophy which is a genetically inherited disease. They sued the health board for negligence on the grounds that in the light of their medical history they should have been referred to genetic counselling and if they had been, the genetic disorder would have been discovered and they would have opted for termination of the pregnancy. In the Outer House, Lord Nimmo Smith, applying the ordinary principles of delict, held that:

- there was no reason why the defenders should not have owed a duty of care to *both* pursuers in the provision of medical services;
- that the purpose of the Abortion Act was to prevent events harmful to pursuers which ought to have been within contemplation of defenders and which, if they had used reasonable care, would not have happened;
- that, in the birth of a child, the pursuers had suffered personal injuries in respect of which they could claim for *solatium* and *patrimonial* loss;
- that it cannot be said that birth of a child always outweighs any adverse consequences. Additional costs to parents associated with the children's disabilities were recoverable and did not cease on a child reaching the age of majority.[62] This was because a claim for care costs arose from the natural bond between parent and child which did not end on the child attaining majority but would continue throughout the child's life.

For these reasons the judge permitted a proof-before-answer to take **1–40** place because entitlement to damages in these circumstances was essentially a jury question. This approach to damages was followed in *McLelland v Glasgow Health Board*.[63] The pursuers in this case had a son born with Down's Syndrome. They sued the Greater Glasgow Health Board on the basis that it had negligently failed to diagnose the child's condition at a stage when the pregnancy could have been terminated. They maintained that had the condition been properly diagnosed, they would have had the pregnancy terminated and would have attempted to have had healthy children. In this case the defenders argued that:

- the father had not suffered "personal injury" and so could not recover *solatium* for his emotional distress; and that

---

[61] 1998 S.L.T. 588.
[62] Note that the parents only sought to recover the additional costs associated with the children's disability which Lord Nimmo Smith was prepared to allow in principle, provided such costs were reasonable.
[63] 1998 S.C.L.R. 1081.

- since the pursuers, in any event, would have sought to have healthy children—for whose upbringing they would have been responsible—they could not recover the ordinary costs of caring for the child, even though the defenders might be responsible for the extra cost of caring for a Down's Syndrome child.

1–41 However their arguments were unsuccessful and Lord MacFadyn in the Outer House held,

- that the mother was entitled to *solatium* covering the physical consequences to her of continuing with the pregnancy beyond the date when it would have been terminated, including the pain and suffering of the Caesarean delivery;
- that failure to provide information had caused a) severe shock and distress on discovery that the child was affected by Down's syndrome, and b) in the longer term, this failure had increased stress in bringing up and caring for the child and that for these reasons *both* pursuers were entitled to claim *solatium* for this distress[64]; and that
- the pursuers were entitled to damages in respect of expenditure which they had incurred and were likely to incur with respect to the child's future maintenance.

1–42 In this case, Lord MacFadyn did not limit damages to the extra costs associated with bringing up a disabled child, nor did he accept that the costs incurred should be offset against the costs that the pursuers would have willingly incurred with respect to a healthy child. On this issue he asked the question,

> "whether the basic cost of bringing up a handicapped child can be equated with the equivalent cost of bringing up a normal healthy child . . . it is not the amount but the nature of the expenditure, that is in issue . . . is the cost of bringing up a healthy child 'spent on an identical purpose, in pari materia with the costs of [the handicapped child]'? I find myself unable to accept that that question must be answered in the affirmative. Of course I accept that the extra costs of bringing up the handicapped child are dealt with elsewhere in the claim and are recoverable. But it does not seem to me to follow that spending money on bringing up a handicapped child who has been born as a result of the defenders' negligence is in substance the same thing as spending money on bringing up a healthy child who would have been born at some later date if the negligent omission had not taken place . . . the cost of bringing up [G] [the handcapped child] is

---

[64] This was the first time that a father was awarded damages for *solatium* on the basis of the shock and distress that he had suffered.

something which has been forced on them by the defenders' negligence. It would in my view be wrong to deny the pursuers recovery of the latter, forced, unwanted expense on the ground that, but for the negligence, they would probably have spent a similar amount of money in willingly incurring the former expense".[65]

However, by the time the case was referred to the Inner House in **1–43** 2001, the House of Lords had given their judgment in *McFarlane v Tayside Health Board*.[66] As a result of that decision, the Inner House[67] only awarded damages for *solatium*, rejecting any claim for the child's maintenance on the basis that it did not meet the *Caparo* test, that is, that it was not fair, just and reasonable to award damages even though the child had Down's syndrome.[68] Since then, there have been a number of English cases grappling with this issue which highlight significant divergences of opinion as to how to quantify the parents' claim.

Rand v East Dorset Health Authority[69]

In *Rand*, flawed ante-natal screening failed to detect that a fetus **1–44** had Down's syndrome and so the parents were denied the opportunity to terminate what had been a desired pregnancy. The claimants argued that they were now burdened with the cost of bringing up a disabled child that they would not have wanted. They sought the full costs of bringing up the child, plus additional damages to cover the special needs of the disabled child. Part of the losses claimed included loss of profit as a result of being forced to give up the family business which had had to be sold prematurely.

The court held that the existence of the Abortion Act 1967 intro- **1–45** duced a duty of care on the part of the Health Authority (defenders) to take steps to ensure the proper exercise of their duty under the Act. The very existence of the Act was sufficient to impose liability on the defenders for the financial consequences of failing to draw to the claimants' attention the fact that Mrs Rand might have been carrying a disabled child. However, the parents had suffered no personal injury and the claim was effectively for pure economic loss and as a result a claim for the full cost of the maintenance and upkeep of the child was not sustainable.[70] However, loses related to the *disability* were recoverable and were not limited in time to the child reaching the age of 18.

---

[65] 1998 S.C.L.R. 1081 at 1094.
[66] [2000] S.C.L.R. (HL) 105; 2 A.C. 59.
[67] 2001 S.L.T. 446.
[68] This was not a unanimous decision; Lord Morrison dissented.
[69] (2000) 56 BMLR 39.
[70] The judge's reasoning here was that to allow the full cost of maintenance, as was the case in *Salih v Enfield Health Authority* [1991] 3 All E.R. 400, CA, would be going too far because "It led him [the judge] to attribute no value to a handicapped life, where the facts established the contrary" (*ibid.* at 189).

So, the claim for past expenditure on therapies and equipment, and for likely future costs on these items was successful, but claims for private education and accommodation of the child failed. Mrs Rand, however, was entitled to general damages for pain and suffering and for what she had suffered during her third pregnancy,[71] and both claimants could recover damages for the loss of amenity they sustained in caring for their child, with the attendant consequences upon their private life.

1-46   Importantly, the judge distinguished "wrongful birth" cases from "wrongful pregnancy" cases on the basis that in the former the parents were committed to having a child, and that this affected not only general damages, but also what economic loss might be imposed on the defendant. As a result he found that the parents had a legally maintainable claim based upon the extended *Hedley Byrne*[72] principle for the financial consequences flowing from the child's disability, rather than from the fact of her existence. At the end of the day, Mr and Mrs Rand could only recover such losses as they had actually sustained and might reasonably sustain in the future. This included the loss of profits from the family business, suffered as a result of the claimants' giving up work to enable the mother to act as the child's primary carer. However, in determining these losses the judge held that,

> "Their [parents'] own means, as opposed to [K]'s [the handicapped child's] needs, are determinative of this issue. In my judgment this must follow as a matter of law from the categorisation of the claim as a claim for pure economic loss. I recognise that this will inevitably give rise to wealthy parents being in a position to obtain higher awards than parents of poor or modest means but this is a regular and accepted consequence in claims for damages".[73]

1-47 A similar decision was reached in *Hardman v Amin*[74] although a different approach was adopted in relation to quantum. In this case a General Practitioner failed to diagnose or test for rubella in a pregnant woman who gave birth to a very seriously disabled child, one who would never be capable of employment or of living independently and who would require constant care and supervision well into adult life. In reaching its decision the court considered the remit of

---

[71] Note: Mrs Rand had had a third child in order to prove to herself and others that she could have a normal child.

[72] *Hedley Byrne & Co v Heller & Partners Ltd* [1964] A.C. 465. This case pertains to the existence of a duty to prevent economic loss in situations where the defendant in giving advice or information was fully aware of the nature of the 'transaction' which the plaintiff had in contemplation and knew the plaintiff would rely on that advice or information in deciding whether or not to engage in a 'transaction' in contemplation.

[73] (2000) 56 BMLR 39 at 58.

[74] (2000) 59 BMLR 58.

McFarlane and concluded that it did not affect the law as it related to the wrongful birth of *disabled* children. It categorised the claim for the child's maintenance as representing one for pure economic loss which called for the adoption of the test in *Caparo*— that liability was established if damage was foreseeable, if there was a relationship of proximity, and if it was just and reasonable to make an award.[75] Having regard to the principles of distributive justice, as defined by Lord Steyn in *McFarlane*,[76] it was said,

> "if the commuters on the London Underground were asked who should bear the costs of bringing up [D] [the handicapped child] a substantial majority would say the expense should fall on the wrongdoer".[77]

In this case it was held that the requirements posed by *Caparo* were **1–48** met and it was fair, just and reasonable to make an award. However, the award would not go beyond reasonable restitution, that is, damages for extra costs associated with providing for the child's special needs and care related to his disability.[78] However, when it came to assessing quantum, this was not to be limited to the parents means but based on the child's needs on the grounds that,

> "categorisation of a claim as one for economic loss identifies the criteria to be satisfied before a duty and its scope are established, but has nothing to do with the quantification of damages once a breach of duty is shown to have resulted in loss of a type which the defendant was under a duty to avoid".[79]

He was of the view, that to limit damages to what the claimant could afford, would not provide proper compensation as the claimant would not, as far as was possible, be restored to the position she would have been in but for the breach.

Thus in cases of "wrongful birth" where parents sue for loss of **1–49** their legal right to terminate a pregnancy due to fetal abnormalities, the trial courts have adhered to the pre-*McFarlane* authorities holding the Health Authority responsible for maintenance costs. *Rand* and *Hardman* acknowledged the impact of *McFarlane* by allowing claims only for costs related to special needs. However, in the case of *Lee v Taunton and Somerset NHS Trust*,[80] the court declined

---

[75] *Caparo Industries Plc. v Dickman* [1990] 2 A.C. 605.
[76] [2000] 2 A.C. 59 at 82–83.
[77] (2000) 59 BMLR 58 at 72.
[78] The judge noted that the imposition of damages here would not be invidious or morally offensive to Daniel as the purpose of distinguishing Daniel from a healthy child was merely to quantify the additional costs caused by his disabilities (and not to question the value of his existence).
[79] (2000) 59 BMLR 58 at 74.
[80] [2001] 1 F.L.R. 419.

to limit liability to the additional costs associated with disability, which in this case involved a child being born with spina bifida due to the defendants negligent ante-natal screening. In *Lee*, when considering *McFarlane*, Toulson J. noted that,

> "[it] presents no obstacle to the present claim. I do not believe that it would be right for the law to deem the birth of a disabled child to be a blessing, in all circumstances and regardless of the extent of the child's disabilities; or to regard the responsibility for the care of such a child as so enriching in the ordinary nature of things that it would be unjust for a parent to recover the cost from a negligent doctor on whose skill that parent had properly relied to prevent the situation".[81]

1–50 As for *Rand*, he viewed the judge in that case had accepted the health authority's argument that the claimant could only recover damages in respect of such economic loss which was proved to raise from the child's disability, rather than from the fact of her existence. Toulson J. himself, however, perceived of the matter in a different light, namely that,

> "[G] [the handicapped child], was incapable of being born *other than* severely disabled. That being so, to try to separate the consequences of [G]'s existence and [G]'s disabled existence is metaphysically impossible and practically unreal. If [G]'s birth was not a deemed blessing, I cannot see a barrier to Mrs Lee recovering the full costs of his maintenance, *except for* the important fact that she was wanting to bear a healthy child. If following a termination of her pregnancy with [G], she had continued with her attempts and had been successful, she would have incurred the costs of bring up a healthy child in any event".[82]

1–51 As to the question of quantification of damages, he agreed with the decision in *Hardman* that this should be judged on the basis of the *child's* needs and not the parents' means. He took the view that,

> "if [G] were able to bring a claim, his loss would be defined by his need. But those needs are inextricably linked with Mrs Lee's needs, since she bears the burden of attempting to cater for his needs. I do not accept that her loss is defined by her means rather than by her reasonable needs".[83]

---

[81] *ibid.* at 430E–F.
[82] *ibid.* at 432B–C.
[83] *ibid.* at 433B.

Wrongful Pregnancy Resulting in Disabled Child

So far, we have been examining cases involving wrongful pregnancy **1–52** and wrongful birth but what is the position post-*McFarlane* in a combined case of wrongful pregnancy where a child is born disabled? This is the situation left open by *McFarlane* which therefore merits special attention. In *Parkinson v St James and Sea Croft University Hospital NHS Trust*[84] a doctor negligently performed a sterilisation operation on the claimant who conceived a 5th child 10 months later. She went to see a consultant at the hospital who warned her that the child might be born with a disability but she chose not to have her pregnancy terminated. The child was eventually born with disabilities—being autistic—however such disability was not immediately recognisable at birth. The judge at first instance awarded costs of providing for the child's special needs and care relating to his disability, but not for the basic costs of his maintenance. This was upheld by the Court of Appeal who held that the costs of providing for the disabled child's specialist needs and care, where the loss flowed forseeably from an unwanted conception which was caused by negligence on the part of a doctor, were recoverable. It was held that the birth of a child with congenital abnormalities was a foreseeable consequence of the surgeon's careless failure to properly carry out a sterilisation operation.[85] There was no difficulty, in principle, in accepting the proposition that the surgeon should be deemed to have assumed responsibility for the foreseeable and disastrous economic consequences of performing his services negligently where the purpose of the operation was to prevent a woman from conceiving any more children, including children with congenital abnormalities. However, damages would be limited to the special upbringing costs associated with rearing a child with a serious disability, as that would, according to Lord Justice Brooks, reflect an award that was fair, just and reasonable. In reaching his decision he noted that, if the principles of distributive justice were called in aid, ordinary people would consider it to be fair for the law to make an award in such a case, provided it was limited to the extra expenses associated with bringing up a child with a significant disability. What constituted a significant disability would have to be decided on a case-by-case basis in line with the definitions used by local authorities for the purposes of providing services under the Children Act 1989. Although it would not include minor defects or inconveniences, the expression would certainly stretch to include disabilities of the mind, including severe behavioural disabilities, as well as physical disabilities.

The reasoning underpinning Lord Justice Brooks' decision in this **1–53** case does nothing to undermine the House of Lord's decision in *McFarlane*. But Lady Justice Hale's reasoning provides an alternative

---

[84] [2001] 3 All E.R. 97.
[85] For fuller consideration of the post-*McFarlane* cases see J.K. Mason, "Wrongful Pregnancy, Wrongful Birth and Wrongful Terminology" (2002) 6 Edin L.R. 46.

perspective. Her opinion was premised on the assumption that to cause a woman to become pregnant against her will is an invasion of her bodily right to integrity.[86] She then enlarged on this, listing some of the consequences of that fundamental invasion which, because they should never have happened, remained invasive despite the fact that they derived from a natural process. They include profound physiological and psychological changes during pregnancy and for some time thereafter which are accompanied by a severe curtailment of personal autonomy so that "one's life is no longer just one's own".[87] The process of giving birth is "rightly termed labour" and the hard work does not stop after pregnancy. She observed that in this case, unlike most personal injury cases,

> "the care is provided by the very person who has been wronged and the legal obligation to provide it is the direct and foreseeable consequence of that wrong. It is, perhaps, an indication of the reluctance of the common law to recognise the cost of care to the carer that claims for wrongful conception and birth of healthy children have not previously been analysed in this way . . . the law has found it much easier to focus on the associated financial costs".[88]

1–54 Her opinion is clearly supportive of the Inner House in *McFarlane*.

In reaching her decision she pointed out that a majority of the House of Lords had accepted that, on normal principles, the McFarlanes' claim would have been allowable. The ultimately decisive concept of an equilibrium between the benefits of a child and its costs is open to challenge, and she thought it limited the damages that would otherwise have been recoverable on normal principles. This being the case, there was no reason or need to take the limitation any further than it was taken in *McFarlane* which took account of the ordinary costs of the ordinary child. This approach, she concluded, "treats a disabled child as having exactly the same worth as a non disabled child . . . It simply acknowledges that the costs are more".[89] The trouble with Lady Hale's analysis is that, as Mason and Laurie point out,[90] it can be applied almost verbatim to the wrongful pregnancy terminating in the birth of a normal child. In other words her arguments not only justify the award of damages in the event of the birth of a disabled child but it opens the way for a review of the *McFarlane* case. For in her view, the costs of bringing up a child do not amount to "pure" economic loss, but should rather be characterised as the

---

[86] [2001] 3 All E.R. 97 at 114g.
[87] *ibid.* at 116b.
[88] *ibid.* at 117e–f.
[89] *ibid.* at 123g.
[90] J.K. Mason and G. Laurie, *Law and Medical* Ethics (7th edn, LexisNexis, 2005), para.6.27.

economic loss consequent on the incursion on the woman's autonomy by becoming pregnant or remaining pregnant against her will.
Such reasoning implies that Lady Justice Hale would have concluded
such costs to be recoverable, as she points out that all of the maintenance costs are part and parcel of the caring responsibility which
flows as a direct consequence of the invasion of the women's rights,
being the conception following from the negligent medical care.

What the House of Lords would have made of such arguments has **1–55**
never been put to the test, as permission to appeal this case was
refused. Currently, therefore, *Parkinson* remains the law in this area
and the unanswered question where the child born is disabled—left
open by the House of Lords in *McFarlane*—is answered.

Wrongful Pregnancy Resulting in Disabled Parent Giving Birth to a Healthy Child

Another variant on the issue of disability arose in *Rees v Darlington* **1–56**
Memorial Hospital NHS Trust.[91] In this case the claimant was a
woman with a genetic condition which left her visually impaired and
who wished to be sterilised. The consultant to whom she was referred
knew her reasons for wanting the operation, including her belief that
her eyesight would prevent her from looking after children properly.
Unfortunately, the sterilisation operation was carried out negligently
and the claimant gave birth to a healthy child. She sued for damages.
The judge at first instance[92] ruled against the claim for damages for
the upkeep of the child, consistent with the House of Lords decision
in *McFarlane*, on the grounds that able-bodied parents could not
recover damages for the cost of bringing up a healthy child, although
the mother was entitled to damages for the pain, inconvenience and
experience of pregnancy and childbirth.

On appeal, however, the Court of Appeal held that she was entitled **1–57**
to recover the "extra" costs of bringing up her child which she would
incur as a result of her disability. The reasoning of the majority
centred on the fact that there was an important difference between
able-bodied and disabled parents. Able-bodied parents had the
capacity to care for and bring up a child themselves, but disabled
parents would need assistance in so doing.[93] Therefore, just as the

---

[91] [2003] 4 All E.R. 987 (HL).
[92] Unreported trial judgment delivered March 9, 2001.
[93] In her article entitled "Misconceptions about Wrongful Conception", 2002 M.L.R.
883, L.C.H. Hoyana attacks this reasoning, particularly Lady Justice Hale's exposi-
tion of 'deemed equilibrium' that justifies excluding the case from the remit of
McFarlane on the basis that a disabled parent 'necessarily' will have greater difficulty
in discharging her childcare responsibilities, as being discriminatory (at pp.900–901).
She points to the pitfalls of associating disability with incapacity and questions the
premise that the visually impaired cannot develop coping mechanisms but must rely
upon third parties to supply their children's care needs which, she argues, not only
perpetuates but deepens "the stigmatisation of the disabled" (at p.901).

extra costs involved in discharging parental responsibility towards a disabled child could be recovered, so also should the additional costs incurred by a disabled parent bringing up a healthy child. In receiving compensation for those extra costs, the claimant was not being over-compensated but was being put in the same position as an able-bodied person. There was nothing unfair, unjust or unreasonable in holding that a surgeon should assume a greater responsibility for the consequences of a failed sterilisation when he knows of the mother's disability and that this was the reason she wished to avoid having a child. The majority of the judges noted that in *McFarlane* their Lordships (with the possible exception of Lord Slynn) did not address the problem of the disabled child or that of a disabled mother. On this basis, they viewed *Rees* as being a legitimate extension of *Parkinson's* case and noted that disabled persons are a category of the public whom the law increasingly recognises as requiring special considerations, pointing to the Disability Discrimination Act 1995 as an important legislative landmark.

1–58   Lord Justice Waller, however, dissented from the majority opinion. He argued that on normal principles, the claim for damages for bringing up a healthy child as a result of the negligence of a surgeon would succeed.[94] It was only disallowed when the test of whether it is just, fair and reasonable was applied. He took issue with the decision in *Parkinson* on the grounds that, applying normal principles, recovery would be competent in both situations. However, in applying the just, fair and reasonable test, the court allowed recovery of the extra costs of looking after a disabled child, while disallowing recovery for the costs of looking after a healthy child. He questioned how fair it is to allow recovery, where others who would recover under normal principles are denied it. He considered an example of a lady who has four children and who does not wish to have a fifth. Having a fifth would cause a crisis in health terms, unless help in caring for the child was available. Due to *McFarlane*, she cannot recover the costs of caring for the child which might alleviate the crisis. But, he argued, the need to avoid a breakdown in her health is no different from the need of someone already with a disability and indeed her need might be greater depending on the degree of disability. He posited the question, "Does she, or ordinary people, look favourably on the law not allowing her to recover but allowing someone who is disabled to recover?"[95] For these reasons he would not have allowed recovery for the extra costs of bringing up the child incurred through the mother's disability.

1–59   When the case went on appeal to the House of Lords, it unanimously affirmed *McFarlane* on the basis that it would be improper to reverse a decision of the House within such a short period of four years. The majority of their Lordships in a court of seven judges, went on to hold that damages to cover the costs of bringing up the

---

[94] The core of his opinion is to be found at (2002) 65 BMLR 117 at [52]–[55].
[95] *ibid.* at [53].

child were not recoverable, and would not be available even though additional child-rearing costs were incurred as a result of the claimant's disability. Argument rested on whether, on the one hand, it was disability in *either* the child or the parent which dictated exceptional costs in bringing up the child—and hence attracted recompense—or whether the overriding factor was normality in the *resultant child*. It was the latter view that prevailed with the result that the appeal was successful in having the damages claim for the child's upkeep dismissed.

Nonetheless, their Lordships accepted that *McFarlane* represented **1–60** an exception to the normal rules of tort (delict), thus raising concerns that justice, at least, was not being seen to be done. Lord Bingham expressed the view:

> "I question the fairness of a rule which denies the victim of a legal wrong any recompense at all beyond an award immediately related to the unwanted pregnancy and birth."[96]

He proposed, and the majority of his colleagues supported his view, that there should be recognition that the parent of a child born after a vasectomy or sterilisation that had been performed negligently was the victim of a legal wrong. In recognition of this a conventional award of £15,000 should be made to mark the injury that had been suffered and loss of freedom to limit family size and that this award should be added to the award of damages made for pregnancy and birth in wrongful conception cases in general. It was stressed, in making this award, that it was not compensatory. This raises the question of what then it is there to represent? Mason[97] argues that it amounts to recognition of a new head of damages, that is, a breach of autonomy or interference with the right to plan one's life as one wishes.

The House of Lords judgment in *Rees* was not unanimous, there **1–61** were three dissenting judgments. Lord Steyn[98] took the view that special consideration should be given to the serious disability of a mother who wanted to avoid having a child by undergoing a sterilisation operation. In his opinion the injustice of denying such a seriously disabled mother the somewhat limited remedy of damages to cover the extra costs caused by her disability outweighed other policy consideration. He also stated that there was no United Kingdom authority to support the award of a conventional sum. Lord Hope[99] took the view that the fact that the child's parent was seriously disabled put her into a different category from able-bodied parents, and provided a ground for distinguishing the *McFarlane* case. It would be

---

[96] [2003] 75 BMLR 69 at 75.
[97] J.K. Mason, "From Dundee to Darlington: An End to the *McFarlane* Line?", 2004 Judicial Review 365 at p.385.
[98] [2003] 75 BMLR 69 at 78–87.
[99] *ibid.* at 87–94.

fair, just and reasonable to hold that such extra costs as could be attributed to the disability were within the scope of the duty of care owed by the trust, and were recoverable. He also took the view that the splitting up of the claim into two parts in order to allow recovery of one part by means of a conventional sum and deny recovery of the other was contrary to principle. Finally, in Lord Hutton's opinion,[1] the *McFarlane* case did not bar the mother from recovering damages in this case.

Legal Options

1–62   What are the legal options raised by such cases of wrongful pregnancy and wrongful birth?

- Damages should never be awarded.
- Damages should always be awarded.
- The blessing of parenthood should be offset against the economic loss and the damages adjusted accordingly.
- A distinction should be made between a healthy and disabled child.
- If such a distinction is made, damages should be recovered a) for full cost of maintaining disabled child or b) only for the extra costs associated with the child's disability.

How Law Now Stands

1–63   As the law currently stands, no damages may be awarded for the upkeep and maintenance costs of a healthy, uncovenanted child. The rule is modified in so far as a conventional award is proffered in recognition of the wrong done to a woman's autonomy by denying her the chance to exercise reproductive choice. The persistence of the Court of Appeal ruling in *Parkinson*, however, means that recompense in tort/delict is available for the excess costs imposed by any disability in the resultant child. This raises the question that if there should be another case like that of *Parkinson*, will both damages for excess upbringing costs for a disabled child *and* a conventional award be given, or will one replace the other? It remains to be seen how the law will develop.

Wrongful Life Actions—A Child's Claim

1–64   So far we have been discussing the parents' right to sue for damages in respect of "wrongful pregnancy" or "wrongful birth". We now turn to a further area which remains controversial and which concerns a child's claim for so-called "wrongful life". This is a claim by a

---

[1] *ibid.* at 94–101.

congenitally-disabled child that, through the negligence of a third party, his or her parents were not afforded the opportunity to terminate the pregnancy. The "wrongful life" claim may arise where medical tests have been negligently interpreted or carried out, resulting in failure to detect abnormalities in the fetus and where, if the parents had been properly informed, they would have sought an abortion. The conditions are, therefore, similar to those in which damages are sought for "wrongful birth"—indeed where an action for wrongful life is brought, it is customary for both to be brought together. The wrongful life action is, however, crucially different from the "wrongful birth" action in that in the latter case it is alleged that a duty was owed to the parent(s) which was not fulfilled, resulting in the unwanted birth of a child. In the "wrongful life" action, by contrast, the child him or herself brings the action (through the parents suing on the child's behalf), pleading that the defender owed a duty of care towards the child, and claiming damages on the basis that had the third party not been negligent in fulfilment of that duty, the child would not have been born at all and so forced to suffer a debilitated life. Essentially the child is saying, "I would have been better off never having existed than living this life; and but for your negligence, I would not have lived; so I deserve compensation from you."

The conceptual problems surrounding the "wrongful life" action **1–65** can be examined by looking at the leading English case of *McKay v Essex Area Health Authority*.[2] Here a pregnant woman, who had been in contact with the rubella virus, took medical advice as to whether this would have any effect on her unborn child. Through the alleged negligence of the health authority in conducting tests, she failed to receive the correct information that the fetus might well have been affected by the virus. The child was subsequently born severely handicapped. The mother initiated a number of claims including a "wrongful life" claim on behalf of the child on the basis that as a result of the health authority's negligence, the child had entered into life with highly debilitating injuries.

The Court of Appeal was not prepared to recognise the claim by **1–66** the child of damages for wrongful life.[3] The court held that a doctor clearly owes the fetus a duty not to injure it. However, in this case, the injuries which the fetus experienced were not caused by the doctor's negligence, but by the rubella virus. To uphold a duty of care in these circumstances would amount to placing the doctor under a legal obligation to abort the fetus. The court was concerned as to whether this could ever be legal. To impose such an obligation,

---

[2] [1982] 2 All E.R. 771. See also the Australian case of *Harriton v Stephens* [2004] NSWCA 93.

[3] There is of course no reason why a mother in such circumstances should not have a legal claim to damages in respect of the negligent failure to advise her that she might wish to choose an abortion discussed at para.1–28 above.

"would mean regarding the life of a handicapped child as not only less valuable than the life of a normal child, but so much less valuable that it was not worth preserving, and it would even mean that a doctor would be obliged to pay damages to a child infected with rubella before birth who was in fact born with some mercifully trivial abnormality. These are the consequences of the necessary basic assumption that a child has a right to be born whole or not at all, not to be born unless it can be born perfect or 'normal', whatever that may mean".[4]

1-67 The Court of Appeal thus held that a claim for wrongful life would be contrary to public policy as a violation of the sanctity of human life. Not only that, but it would be impossible to evaluate the damages claimed because this would necessarily involve comparing the value of existence in a physically-challenged state with non-existence.[5] Furthermore, if the medical profession were to be held liable for damages in these circumstances, doctors might in turn be encouraged to put pressure on their patients to abort in any case where there might be a risk (however small) of fetal impairment. For these reasons the court upheld the view that:

"The only way in which a child injured in the womb can be compensated in damages is by measuring what it has lost, which is the difference between the value of life as a whole and healthy normal child and the value of its life as an injured child".[6]

As the doctor and health authority were not responsible for the injury that the child in fact suffered, and as they were under no legal duty to the fetus to terminate its existence, the child's action for damages for wrongful life was dismissed.

1-68 Since the time of the facts on which the decision in *McKay* was founded, the Congenital Disabilities (Civil Liability) Act 1976 came into effect in England, and now arguably rules out any right by a child to sue for damages in respect of "wrongful life".[7] However, as the

---

[4] [1982] 2 All E.R. 771, *per* Stephenson L.J. at p.781.
[5] See Teff, "The Action for 'Wrongful Life' in England and the United States" (1985) 34 I.C.L.Q. 423 for the counter view that there is nothing to prevent us from assigning values to both life and non- existence and then calculating damages accordingly. For a rebuttal see Norrie, "Wrongful Life in Scots Law; No Right, No Remedy", 1990 J.R. 205 at pp.217–223.
[6] [1982] 2 All E.R. 771, *per* Stephenson L.J. at p.781.
[7] Under s.1(2)(b) and *per* Ackner L.J. in *McKay* [1982] 2 All E.R. 771 at 785–786. See, however, for a contrary view, Fortin, "Is The Wrongful Life Action Really Dead?" (1987) J.S.W.L. 306. Further, s.1(2A) which was inserted by s.44 of the Human Fertilisation and Embryology Act 1990 allows for an action by a disabled infant when the disability is attributable to wrongful acts or omissions. As Mason, Laurie and McCall Smith point out in *Law and Medical Ethics* (7th edn, Oxford University Press, Oxford, 2006), p.4.63, this seems indistinguishable from an action for wrongful life.

1976 Act does not apply to Scotland, here the matter is still governed by common law. In the event that an action for wrongful life should be raised in Scotland, the *McKay* case would be highly persuasive although not binding on a Scottish court. Nonetheless, given the tendency of courts on both sides of the border to follow one another's decisions in this area it is unlikely that such a claim would be successful.[8]

A different approach was adopted by the French courts which **1–69** became the first European jurisdiction to allow such an action in what is referred as the *Perruche* case.[9] As in *McKay*, a mother became infected with the rubella virus but due to her doctor's negligence she was not counselled about the risk to the fetus or the risk of a handicapped child being born. Had the mother been appraised of the risk she would have terminated the pregnancy. The parents sued for damages based on breach of contract and the court of first instance not only held both the physician and the laboratory liable for damages, but also found them liable to the child for the loss caused by his handicap.[10] On appeal, the Cour d'Appel however followed precedent and, while confirming the decision in favour of Mme Perruche, overturned the award of damages to the child. Eventually, the case was referred to full chamber of the Cour de Cassation which found in favour of the child's claim to compensation. The ruling caused a furore in France, even going so far as to prompt the medical profession to go on strike. As a result, emergency legislation was passed to rectify the situation. The law adopted by the French Senate in 2002 was to the effect that in such a situation, parents of a child born with a handicap can claim compensation for harm suffered by them but *not* for expenses attributable to the child's being handicapped (which would be covered by social services). In passing this legislation the French government considerably narrowed the scope for a damages claim by outlawing damages for the general upkeep of an uncovananted child regardless of whether s/he is healthy or disabled.[11]

---

[8] *Op cit.* above, n.21, who argues that it is inequitable that the child have no remedy in respect of, e.g. negligent genetic counselling, and suggests that one way forward may be to regard the action as one where damages are sought for 'diminished life' rather than for 'wrongful life'. Note, an action for 'wrongful life' is not admissible in Australia or Canada and only in three US States as it is usually prevented either by statute or by common law.

[9] "X c Mutuelle d'Assurance du Corps Sanitaire Francais et a" (2000) J.C.O. 2293. For discussion of the details and analysis see T. Callus, "'Wrongful Life' a la Francaise" (2001) 5 Med Law Internat 117; T. Wier, "The Unwanted Child" (2002) 6 Edin L.R. 244; A. Morris and A. Sentier, "To Be or Not To Be: Is That The Question? Wrongful Life and Misconception" (2003) 11 Med. L.R. 167.

[10] Tribunal de Grande Instance, Evry, January 13, 1992.

[11] For a full discussion of the *Perruche* case, see P. Lewis, "The necessary implications of wrongful life claims: lessons from France" (2005) 12 Euro J. Hlth Law 135.

CRIMINAL LAW AND FETAL RIGHTS

1–70 Until now we have been considering issues raised in the *civil* law of negligence relating to the unborn child. The status of the unborn child also, however, creates difficulties within the criminal law. One problem is whether causing the death of a child while it is, as yet, not a legal person can be regarded as murder or culpable homicide. In *McCluskey v HM Advocate*,[12] a man was charged with causing death by reckless driving. By his negligence he caused an accident in which a pregnant woman was injured, who then gave birth prematurely. The child was delivered alive, but died shortly thereafter. The accused defended himself on the basis that he had not caused "the death of another person" as required by s.1 of the Road Traffic Act 1972, as this could only refer to a person who was independently alive at the time that the act of reckless driving took place. Since that did not include the child who died, who was in utero at the date of the accident, the charge could not be sustained. On appeal, the High Court of Justicary rejected this interpretation of the statute, and held that "there is no authority in the law of Scotland to the effect that a relevant charge of culpable homicide would not lie"[13] where death was caused by injuries inflicted before birth, as long as that person was born alive before dying as a result of the injuries. In other words, there is no crime of killing a fetus which is never subsequently born in Scots law ("feticide"), only of murder of a legal person by infliction of injuries sustained before live birth. This approach, which protects the interests of the fetus, but only after it has been born alive and achieved legal personality, is consonant with the approach taken in the civil cases examined above. It does, however, have the perhaps paradoxical result that legally it is more culpable to injure a child in the womb so he is later born impaired, than it is to kill him prior to delivery by the mother.

1–71 The English Court of Appeal has taken a similar approach to that of the Court of Appeal in *Attorney General's Reference (No.3 of 1994)*.[14] In this case, the respondent stabbed his girlfriend, in the knowledge that she was pregnant with their child. The knife penetrated the fetus, and one month later, the girlfriend gave birth to a grossly premature daughter who subsequently died from a lung condition which was unconnected with the knife-wound, but resulted directly from the premature birth. The respondent was charged with the murder of the child but was acquitted on the grounds that there was no offence.

1–72 The Attorney-General sought a ruling from the Court of Appeal on whether murder or manslaughter could be committed where unlawful injury was deliberately inflicted on either a child in utero, or on a mother carrying a child in utero, in circumstances where the

---

[12] 1989 S.L.T. (Notes) 175.
[13] p.176.
[14] [1996] 2 All E.R. 10.

child was subsequently born alive but died thereafter, and where the injuries inflicted while in utero caused or contributed substantially to the child's death. First, the court held that causing injury to the fetus can be murder or manslaughter, provided the fetus is subsequently born; and secondly, that the statutory provision in question did not require that the person who died should be a person in being at the time the act causing the death was perpetrated.[15] Thereafter, the case went to the House of Lords which ruled out feticide absolutely.[16]

ABORTION

The cases discussed above lead us naturally to the controversial topic **1–73** of abortion and its treatment in the criminal law. Abortion can be described unemotively as the elective termination of pregnancy. In the United Kingdom, abortion is dealt with on a statutory basis in the Abortion Act 1967, as amended by s.37 of the Human Fertilisation and Embryology Act 1990 (hereafter "the HFEA 1990"). Prior to the 1967 Act, abortion was a crime at common law in Scotland, and in England under the Offences Against the Person Act of 1861, ss.58 and 59, although in both jurisdictions defences were available.[17] The Infant Life (Preservation) Act 1929 also introduced the crime (in English law only) of "child destruction", that is, causing the death of a child capable of being born alive before it has an existence independent of its mother. Prima facie, a fetus is capable of being born alive if it is 28 weeks old.[18]

The 1967 Act did not decriminalise abortion; instead what it did **1–74** was to set up the circumstances in which a termination of pregnancy would not be unlawful and provide a number of statutory defences which can be claimed by doctors to protect themselves from prosecution. Where an abortion is not carried out in a way authorised by the 1967 Act, it will still be unlawful, and the parties involved will be liable to prosecution. In practice, the effect is that the United Kingdom now enjoys a relatively liberal regime of access to lawful abortion; but nothing in the law gives a pregnant woman a *right* to an abortion, as is the case in jurisdictions such as the United States and Canada, where abortion, at least within the first trimester,[19] is

---

[15] The court also held that the requisite intent required for a charge of murder was an intention to kill or cause really serious bodily injury to the mother, since the fetus was regarded as being an integral part of the mother prior to birth, i.e. the English doctrine of 'transferred malice' applied.

[16] Note however that in England the murder of a fetus might be charged as an offence of 'child destruction' under the Infant Life (Preservation) Act 1929, if the fetus was over 28 weeks old or "capable of being born alive". For a fuller discussion of the need for an offence of feticide see *op. cit* above, n.11.

[17] See *R. v Bourne* [1939] 1 K.B. 687.

[18] 1929 Act, s.1(2).

[19] See para.1–79.

seen as part of a woman's constitutional right to "privacy" in the sense of control of her own body.[20] It is important to realise when discussing the impact of abortion law on the legal status of the fetus, that the provisions of the 1967 Act are structured neither to protect the rights of women, nor of the unborn child, but to safeguard doctors and patients from prosecution under the criminal law. However, importantly, it removed the likelihood of women seeking "back street" abortions at great risk to their mental and physical health.

The Abortion Act 1967

1–75   Under the 1967 Act, s.1(1),[21] an abortion may be carried out without breaching the criminal law if two conditions are met. First, the pregnancy must be terminated by a registered medical practitioner. Secondly, normally two registered medical practitioners must have formed the opinion, prior to termination, and in good faith, that one of four conditions laid down in s.1(1) is met.

1–76   The first ground upon which an abortion may be justified is where,

> "the continuance of the pregnancy would involve risk, greater than if the pregnancy were terminated, of injury to the physical or mental health of the pregnant woman or any existing children of her family" (s.1(1)(a)).

This involves what are often referred to as "social" conditions justifying abortion. Section 1(1)(a) is by far the most common ground under which abortion is performed in the United Kingdom. In determining whether a ground exists under s.1(1)(a), doctors may take into account the pregnant woman's "actual or reasonably foreseeable environment".[22] An abortion carried out under this ground must be performed before the pregnancy exceeds its 24th week.[23]

1–77   The other grounds for abortion found in s.1(1) are not subject to a time-limit. These are:

---

[20] See especially *Roe v Wade*, 93 S Ct 705 (1973) (United States); *R v Morgenthaler* [1988] 1 S.C.R. 30 (Canada).

[21] Which has been significantly amended by the Human Fertilisation and Embryology Act 1990, s.37.

[22] 1967 Act, s.1(2) (which, for these purposes, is unaffected by the Still-Birth (Definition) Act 1992).

[23] This time-limit was inserted by s.37(4) of the HFEA 1990 and brings Scots and English law into line on this point. S.37(4) also inserted the proviso in s.5(1) of the 1967 Act that no doctor performing a lawful abortion under the 1967 Act commits a crime under the Infant Life Preservation Act 1929. This removed the fear in England that lawfully aborting a fetus under the 1967 Act, which then proved to be capable of a live birth, might still be charged as a criminal offence under the 1929 Act. Practical problems may arise in ascertaining when a pregnancy begins. Medical practice appears to favour measuring the duration of pregnancy from the first day of the woman's last period.

- that the termination is necessary to prevent grave permanent injury to the physical or mental health of the pregnant woman[24];
- that the continuance of the pregnancy would involve risk to the life of the pregnant woman, greater than if the pregnancy were terminated[25];
- or that there is substantial risk that if the child were born it would suffer from such physical or mental abnormalities as to be seriously handicapped.[26]

Only one medical opinion is required where a registered medical practitioner is of the opinion, formed in good faith, that the termination is immediately necessary to save the life of, or to prevent grave permanent injury to the physical or mental health of a pregnant woman.[27] However, as noted above, the majority of abortions that are performed are based on the s.1(1)(a) ground to which this proviso does not apply.

In relation to all grounds, it is interesting to note that it is the **1–78** forming of the opinion in good faith by the requisite number of doctors that a s.1(1) ground exists that renders the abortion lawful—not the objective existence of the ground. It is thus extremely unlikely that a court will ever declare an abortion to have been illegally carried out in retrospect.[28] In all cases where an abortion is authorised it must be carried out in a NHS hospital or in places approved for the purpose by the Minister of Health or Secretary of State.[29] The latter proviso allows for abortions to be performed privately and for a fee.[30]

Abortion and Fetal Interests

As noted above, abortion is seen in many jurisdictions, notably the **1–79** United States and Canada, as an issue of basic legal rights where the health, welfare and wishes of the mother must be balanced with the rights and interests of the unborn child. In the United States, for example, the Supreme Court has recognised that during the first trimester the woman has a largely unfettered right to abortion. However, during the second trimester, as the fetus develops, so do its interests, and during the third trimester the state has a compelling interest to intervene and protect the life of the fetus—though not to the detriment of the life of the woman.[31] In the United Kingdom, by

---

[24] s.1(1)(b).
[25] s.1(1)(c).
[26] s.1(1)(d).
[27] s.1(4).
[28] Only one reported case seems to exist where this was held: *R. v Smith* [1973] 1 W.L.R. 1510.
[29] s.1(3).
[30] Further, the Human Fertilisation and Embryology Act 1990 introduced s.1(3A) to the 1967 Act which relaxed the location rules for 'medical' abortions—by use of antiprogesterones.
[31] See *Roe v Wade* in n.20, above.

contrast, abortion law tends to avoid the fetal/maternal rights debate by treating the whole issue as one which is primarily a matter for the medical profession, as long as they act in good faith. Just as the Abortion Act 1967 does not give a right to a woman to have an abortion, it also says nothing about the rights of the fetus. However, it is true that the issue of abortion does colour other decisions the courts make about the rights of the unborn child, since any attempt to give legal status or rights as a person to the fetus must inevitably generate conflicts with the laws that allow women access to legal abortion.[32] In some cases, third parties such as the father of the child, have sought to represent and defend the interests of the unborn child faced with abortion at the request of the mother.[33] In general, however, these attempts to extend fetal rights have been resisted by the courts.

1–80 In the leading English case of *Paton v B.P.A.S. Trustees*,[34] a woman was granted a medical certificate stating there were grounds for an abortion. Her husband applied for an injunction to restrain her from having the abortion without his consent. The court held that since an unborn child had no rights of its own, and a father had no rights at common law over a child born outside of marriage, the husband's right to apply for an injunction had to be based on his status as a husband. As the courts had never exercised jurisdiction to control personal relationships within marriage, and the husband had no right to be consulted under the 1967 Abortion Act, the court held that the husband had no rights in law, either to prevent his wife from having the abortion, or to stop the doctors from carrying it out.

1–81 The husband then took his case before the European Commission on Human Rights as *Paton v UK*,[35] on two grounds. First, that United Kingdom legislation violated the unborn child's right to life under Art.2 of the Convention of Human Rights; and secondly, that it constituted an unjustified interference with the applicant's right to respect for family life contained in Art.8.[36] Article 2 states that "Everyone's right to life shall be protected by law". The Commission ruled that this provision was subject to an implied limitation justifying termination of pregnancy in its early stages in order to protect the life and health of the woman at that stage. On this basis, it ruled that an abortion of a 10-week old fetus under British law to protect the physical or mental health of a pregnant woman was not in breach of Art.2. In its reasoning, the Commission observed that,

---

[32] As, e.g. in Ireland where abortion is, in principle, illegal because the right of the fetus to life is enshrined in the Constitution. See, for further examination of the conflicts this engenders, *Att Gen v X* (1992) 15 BMLR 104.

[33] e.g. see *Kelly v Kelly*, 1997 S.L.T. (2nd Div) 896.

[34] [1979] 1 Q.B. 276.

[35] [1981] 3 E.H.R.R. 408.

[36] For a more detailed discussion of these Articles and the Commission's interpretation of them, see Harris, O'Boyle and Warbrick, *The Law of the European Convention on Human Rights* (Butterworth, London, 1995).

"The 'life' of the fetus is intimately connected with, and cannot be regarded in isolation from, the life of the pregnant woman. If Article 2 were held to cover the fetus and its protection under this Article were, in the absence of any express limitation, seen as absolute, an abortion would have to be considered as prohibited even where the continuance of the pregnancy would involve a serious risk to the life of the pregnant woman. This would mean that the 'unborn life' of the fetus would be regarded as being of a higher value than the life of the pregnant woman".[37]

The applicant husband was no more successful in his claim that **1–82** failure to consult the father over an abortion amounted to denial of respect for family life. The Commission ruled that in so far as abortion interfered with the applicant's right to respect for family life, it was justified under Art.8(2) as being necessary for protection of the rights of the mother. It noted that,

"any interpretation of the husband's and potential father's right, under Article 8 of the Convention, to respect for his private and family life, as regards an abortion which his wife intends to have performed on her, must first of all take into account the right of the pregnant woman, being the person primarily concerned in the pregnancy and its continuation or termination, to respect for her private life . . . in the present case the Commission, having regard to the right of the pregnant woman, does not find that the husband's and potential father's right to respect for his private and family life can be interpreted so widely as to embrace such procedural rights as claimed by the applicant, i.e. a right to be consulted, or a right to make applications, about an abortion which his wife intends to have performed on her".[38]

Although the father in *Paton* was unsuccessful, the Commission in **1–83** their ruling have left open the controversial question of whether the European Convention on Human Rights affords any protection at all to the unborn child, such as a right to life subject to certain implied limitations, such as were found to exist in *Paton*.[39] What *Paton* certainly does establish is that Art.2 does not recognise an absolute right to life belonging to the unborn child.[40] It remains open for discussion

---

[37] *ibid.* at para.19, p.415.
[38] *ibid.* at para.27, pp.416–417.
[39] [1981] E.H.R.R. 408.
[40] *ibid.* at para.23, p.416.

whether the Commission would have been more interested in ascribing a (possibly limited) right to life to a more mature fetus which was, for example, "capable of being born alive".[41]

1–84   More recently in Scotland, the father in the case of *Kelly v Kelly*[42] attempted to interdict his wife from terminating her pregnancy on the ground that what was contemplated was an actionable wrong and that any wrongful action sustained by a child in utero was actionable at the instance of the child acting through his parent or guardian. His argument was that any actionable wrong was a wrong capable of prevention by interdict and that a wrong which could be interdicted was not confined to a wrong causing injury only but included a wrong resulting in the death of the child. He contended that the effect of the Abortion Act was merely to decriminalise abortion in certain circumstances and that it had no effect in regard to civil liability for abortion as a wrong. The Inner House, however, rejected his claim on the basis that while a child had a right of action in respect of an injury caused by actions before his or her birth, an injury to the fetus was not actionable before birth. The court held that,

> "The fatal flaw in the pursuer's argument was that of treating the fetus as a person with rights. In particular there was no law to the effect that the fetus had the right to remain where it was, in the womb. So long as there was an unborn fetus there was no legal persona which was separate from that of the mother; and hence no wrong done to the fetus as such".[43]

1–85   It is, however, important to note from our earlier discussions that while the fetus is not a person in law and thus has no rights, that does not mean to say that it has no legally protected interests. As our earlier discussions have shown it has been established that injury to the fetus is injury to a person if the fetus is subsequently born alive.[44] But, as Mason and Laurie observe, "this is essentially protection of the neonate"[45]; it remains the case that "recognition of the fetus *itself* has been steadfastly opposed".[46]

---

[41] See *C v S* [1987] 1 All E.R. 1230 where a father unsuccessfully argued, in circumstances similar to *Paton*, that an abortion should be prevented because the fetus was capable of being born alive and it was therefore possible that an abortion would be a crime under the Infant Life Preservation Act 1929.

[42] 1997 S.L.T. (2nd Div) 896.

[43] *ibid.* at 899K.

[44] See paras 1–16 to 1–18.

[45] Mason above, n.11 on p.3, p.5.6.

[46] *ibid.* See also the decision of the European Court of Human Rights in *Vo v France* (discussed at paras 1–09 *et seq.*) which held that there was no European Consensus on the nature and status of the embryo and/or fetus although they were beginning to receive some protection in the light of scientific progress. It noted that "At best, it may be regarded as common ground between states that the embryo/fetus belongs to the human race. The potentiality of that being and its capacity to become

OVERVIEW

As we have seen from the statute and case law examined above, the **1–86** consensus of the civil and criminal law in both Scotland and England is that the unborn child is not a legal person and has no standing in law. However if the child survives to be born alive, he or she becomes a legal person with legal rights like anyone else, and may, for example, make civil claims in negligence in respect of ante-natal injury. With regards to abortion, the unborn child is in theory given the protection of the criminal law, but in practice the decision as to whether abortion is justified and lawful under the 1967 Act is one left to the good faith of the medical profession; the 1967 Act gives neither the fetus nor the husband or partner of the mother rights to oppose or restrain the abortion.

For a brief time there did appear to be some support for fetal rights **1–87** in a number of English cases concerning pregnant women who refuse to consent to Caesarean sections. In *Re S*,[47] for example, the court exercised its inherent jurisdiction to authorise the carrying out of an emergency Caesarean section against the wishes of the mother, on the basis that the operation was vital to protect not only her own life but also that of the unborn child. The decision in *Re S* was taken on an emergency basis and was followed in two further High Court cases.[48] However, this approach was firmly quashed in the Court of Appeal decision in *Re MB*[49] where the court stressed that persons of full age and sound mind cannot be treated against their will. It made it clear that where a person is competent, that is of sound mind, s/he can refuse medical treatment for any reasons, whether rational, irrational or even on the basis of no reason at all. The only situation where non-voluntary treatment may arise, is when the patient is incapable of giving consent and when treatment is in the patient's best interests. However, where a competent pregnant woman decides to refuse treatment, there is no jurisdiction to declare medical intervention as being lawful, even although this may result in the death or serious handicap of her baby.[50]

In this particular case, the woman was declared incompetent **1–88** because it was established that it was her fear of needles which led her to refuse treatment to which she would otherwise have consented.

---

a person—enjoying protection under the civil law, moreover, in many states, such as France, in the content of inheritance and gifts and also in the United Kingdom . . . require protection in the name of human dignity, without making it a 'person' with the 'right to life' for the purposes of Article 2" (2004) 79 BMLR 71 at 106.
[47] [1992] 4 All E.R. 671
[48] See *Norfolk and Norwich Healthcare (NHS) Trust v W* [1996] 2 F.L.R. 613 and *Tameside and Glossop Acute Services Trust v CH (a patient)* (1996) 34 BMLR 175.
[49] *Re MB (an adult: medical treatment)* [1997] 38 BMLR 175.
[50] For an attempt to strengthen the legal position of the fetus through a human rights analysis of the issues see G.T. Laurie "Medical Law and Human Rights: Passing the Parcel Back to the Profession" in *Human Rights and Scots Law: Comparative Perspectives on the Incorporation of the ECHR* (Hart Publishing, Oxford, 2002).

This decision reinforced the cardinal rule in medicine that patients of full mental competence have the right to refuse consent to medical treatment, and have that refusal respected, even if that choice is not in their own welfare and may even result in their death.[51] It is only where a person is incompetent, that the court may addresses the question of whether or not treatment is in that patient's best interests, a view endorsed in a subsequent Court of Appeal decision in *St George's Healthcare NHS Trust v S (Guidelines); R v Collins, Ex p. S (No 2)*[52] that went so far as to issue guidance for healthcare professionals who are faced with deciding whether or not a patient is competent to grant consent to or refuse treatment.[53]

In the next chapter, we examine the capacity of children to enter into legal transactions, and how this affects their parents and other third parties.

---

[51] See *Re T (adult: refusal of medical treatment)* [1992] 4 All E.R. 649 and *Airedale NHS Trust v Bland* [1993] A.C. 789.

[52] [1998] 3 All E.R. 673.

[53] For discussion of the issues surrounding enforced caesareans and the case law see, H. Lim, "Caesareans and Cyborg's", 1999 Feminist Legal Studies 7 at pp.133–173; A. Morris, "Once Upon a Time in a Hospital . . . The Cautionary Tale of *St. George's Health Care NHS Trust v S.R.V. Collins and Others Ex Parte"* [1998] 3 All E.R. 673, 1999 Feminist Legal Studies 7 at pp.75–84; R. Scott, "Maternal Duties Toward the Unborn? Soundings from the Law of Tort", 2000 8 Med. L.R. 1–68.

CHAPTER 2

THE CHILD AND LEGAL CAPACITY

INTRODUCTION: PERSONALITY, RIGHT-HOLDING AND CAPACITY

As we have seen in Ch.1, a child acquires legal personality at the **2–01** moment of birth.[1] But this is just the first step towards the child's acquisition of the full legal standing of an adult. A child of, say, eight, has different rights, duties and powers than a child of 15 or one of 16; and each one is in a slightly different legal situation than an adult of normal mental capacity who, as a benchmark, has full capacity. A child, when born, may hold rights—most notably in private law, the right to own property.[2] A child may, for example, acquire property rights in the estate of a deceased as soon as he is born. A child of whatever age may also lay claim to human rights, such as the right not to be killed, the right to protection from abuse and neglect, and so forth.[3]

However, the child who has just been born can do nothing to **2–02** enforce his or her rights: he or she cannot sue the executor of the estate to hand over the portion of the estate due, nor choose to waive his or her right to that portion under the will in exchange for statutory legal rights in the estate. Although a child can own property, he or she cannot actively make contracts in respect of that property; he or she cannot, for example, buy a house with a gift of money, nor open a bank account to put it in. A child under the age of 12 cannot make a will disposing of that property in the event of death. The short way of saying this is to say that the child who has just been born does not have active *legal capacity*. Legal capacity can be defined as the power to enter legal transactions on one's own behalf.

---

[1] For discussion of the problems associated with ascribing legal personality to a fetus prior to its being born alive, see Ch.1.

[2] See Erskine, i. 6.53.

[3] See further paras 2–06 *et seq.*, and the Human Rights Act 1998, incorporating the European Convention on Human Rights (ECHR) into UK law. Until relatively recently there was very little written on the human rights of children under the ECHR; and even those who addressed the issue seemed to feel constrained to start with such apparently unnecessary statements as "Human rights are not for adults only. Children, too, are protected by human rights" (Lucy Smith, "Children, Parents and the European Human Rights Convention" in *Parenthood in Modern Society* (J. Eekelaar and P. Sarcevic (eds), Kluwer Academic Publishers, 1993)). The incorporation of human rights into UK law in the 1998 Act has, however, brought the issue of children's human rights into the foreground.

2–03   In summary, a child of any age has legal personality; a child of any age may hold or be the object of rights; but only some children, having achieved a certain age or level of maturity, have legal capacity to perform certain juridical acts. If a child does not have legal capacity to perform a certain juridical act, then as we shall see,[4] this gap will normally be filled by parents or legal representatives who are entitled to legally represent the child. In this chapter, we shall examine in more depth the legal capacity of children of different ages, before going on to look at the associated questions of children's rights and how these interact with the rights and duties of parents and other persons with parental responsibility.[5]

CONCEPTIONS OF CHILDHOOD

2–04   The idea that children are in some way a fundamentally different species to adults is not an inherent one, but one, it has been argued, which is culturally constituted. There have been different conceptions of childhood during different periods of history, in different societies, and in different groups within society. One highly influential treatise argues that in medieval European society there was no conception of childhood at all.[6] Children were merely miniature adults, and were neither separated from, nor protected from, the adult world in the way that is customary now. Significantly, there was no attempt to segregate them from adult sexual behaviour, nor to punish them differently to adult offenders. Later work has tended to re-interpret this thesis towards a conclusion that the medieval world had a *different* conception of childhood from that of contemporary society, as opposed to no differentiation between childhood and adulthood at all.[7] It is clear that it is our own peculiar conception of how children are different from adults, what differences are significant, and, consequently, how and when childhood should give way to adulthood, that informs our view of how the law should restrict, protect and empower children.[8] For example, in some non-Western cultures, play is not clearly distinguished from work, nor is work something which replaces play at a certain level of maturity. All members of the community standardly undertake some work suited to their sizes and capabilities from very early years. In Western society, there is generally a clear demarcation between work and non-work activities for children, paid work is considered inappropriate for very young children and so the hours and conditions of children's work are strictly regulated.

---

[4] See Chs 5 and 6.

[5] See Chs 4 and 5.

[6] Aries, *Centuries of Childhood* (1962).

[7] See, e.g. Archard, *Children: Rights and Childhood* (1993).

[8] Freeman, *The Rights and Wrongs of Children* (1983), Ch.1.

Nor are our conceptions of childhood fixed: they are always in a **2–05** state of evolution. As our ideas about children change, so will our ideas of what rights they should have, what legal capacity, and what protection they need. It has been suggested, for example, that as we become an increasingly computerised and media-dependent society, those differences between childhood and adulthood which are based on the attainment of literacy and education will erode.[9] In recent years, we have seen many calls to reconsider the status of children, most notably the famous statement that "the child is a person, not an object of concern".[10] As our ideas about the competency and vulnerability of children change, we will also find there is a tension between what have been perceived as the protective rights of parents or guardians in the past and the emerging independent rights of the child.

CHILDREN AND INTERNATIONAL HUMAN RIGHTS STANDARDS[11]

One of the key drivers towards a changing legal conception of chil- **2–06** dren in Scots law in the last 10 years has been the increasing regard given to international human rights standards: in particular the European Convention on Human Rights (ECHR) and the UN Convention on the Rights of the Child (UNCRC).[12] The European Convention, while not overtly "child centred" provides basic guarantees of civil and political rights for *all* citizens, including children, and has the significant advantage over the UNCRC that it is an intrinsic part of domestic law in the form of the Human Rights Act 1998, which can be freely called upon without the cumbersome need to go all the way to the European Court of Human Rights in Strasbourg for enforcement by way of individual petition.

The UNCRC, by contrast, has the status only of an ordinary inter- **2–07** national treaty, not binding in domestic law, and is enforced only by the obligation on state parties to submit reports on compliance to a central UN Committee on the Rights of the Child. The model is that

---

[9] Postman, *The Disappearance of Childhood* (1982).

[10] Butler-Sloss, The Hon. Mrs Justice, Report into the *Inquiry into Child Abuse in Cleveland*, Cm.412 (1987).

[11] See further literature on the UNCRC and ECHR from a Scottish child law angle, L. Edwards, "Incorporation of the European Convention on Human Rights: what will it mean for Scotland's children?" in *Human Rights and Scots Law* (Boyle *et al* (eds), Hart Publishing, Oxford, 2002); K. Norrie, "The Rights of Children", 2004 J.R. 55; A. Cleland and E. Sutherland, *Childrens' Rights in Scotland* (2nd edn, W.Green, Edinburgh, 2001); A. Cleland, "Children's Voices" in *Family Dynamics: Contemporary Issues in Family Law* (J. Scoular (ed.), Butterworths, 2001); K. Marshall, *Children's Rights in the Balance: the Participation-Protection Debate* (The Stationery Office, 1997); K. Tisdall, *The Children (Sc) Act 1995, Developing Policy and Law for Scotland's Children* (The Stationery Office, 1997).

[12] Adopted November 28, 1989 (28 International Legal Materials 1448), and ratified by the United Kingdom on December 16, 1991.

enforced publicity of defects in implementation will lead inevitably to reform. Yet although the UN Committee's response in 1995 to the United Kingdom's first report on implementation was trenchantly critical,[13] and the second, in 2002, was if anything even worse,[14] there have hardly been tidal waves of appalled public opinion as a result—nor is there an apparent move towards domestic incorporation of the UNCRC. The ECHR would thus seem a far better bet for making serious headway in the fields of children's rights, and indeed has already had significant domestic impact by effectively securing the abolition of corporal punishment in schools,[15] and the introduction of legal aid into the children's hearings system.[16]

2–08 Serious problems exist however with applying the ECHR to protect the rights of children. The ECHR arose out of the aftermath of World War II and the experience of living under Nazi and Stalinist totalitarian regimes.[17] As such it was primarily aimed at protecting the individual citizen's rights from arbitrary interference by the *state*. Children's rights, however, are most often infringed or restricted *not* by state interference, but by the acts of those individuals who protect, guide or represent the child—most significantly, their parents. Children, depending on their age and circumstances, lack the physical competence, and economic and social power to act on their own, and so their rights and freedoms are crucially dependent on the assistance and attitude of adults. Although traditional human rights jurisprudence extends solely to protecting the individual from the state, the case law of the European Court in Strasbourg has made it clear that states *do* have *positive* obligations to intervene where the rights of individuals are threatened by the actions of other individuals—the so-called "horizontal effect".[18] It can, for example, be a breach if a state does not restrain a father from violently punishing his child in breach of Art.3. The real problem is that ECHR jurisprudence does not yet seem to have developed an awareness of the fact that because children are dependent on adults, usually their parents, *conflicts* inevitably arise between the rights and wishes of children and their parents which need to be resolved. Since parents have more power in many ways—economic, societal, legal—than

---

[13] See comment in Grant, "Could Do Better: the Report on the United Kingdom's Compliance with the Convention on the Rights of the Child", 1995 Juridical Review 534 and K. Marshall, *Children's Rights in the Balance: the Participation-Protection Debate* (The Stationery Office, 1997), pp.28–29.

[14] See UN CRC/C/15/Add.188, October 9, 2002.

[15] See further Ch.5.

[16] See further Ch.8 and *S v Miller*, 2001 S.L.T. 531.

[17] See, e.g. A. Miller, "The European Convention on Human Rights: What does it mean for children in Scotland?" in *Children's Rights = Human Rights?* (Children in Scotland, 1988).

[18] See further, M. Hunt, "The 'Horizontal Effect' of the Human Rights Act" [1998] Public Law 423. The most cited example of a "horizontal effect" case in family law at Strasbourg is probably *A v UK* (1999) 27 E.H.R.R. 611—see further Ch.5 below.

children, one might expect parental rights to take precedence over the rights of children. And in Canada, the effect of "rights discourse" has indeed arguably been to increase concern for adult parental rights, to the sometimes detriment of both child rights and the child's welfare.[19] In the limited family-related human rights case law of Scotland, there have, as yet been no signs of this, but it remains a worry.

To take a few examples, a child's right to choose his or her own religion (guaranteed by Art.9 of the ECHR) inherently conflicts with the child's *parents'* right to insist that a child is brought up in the family creed under Art.8. In child abuse cases, the child's right to freedom from ill treatment under Art.3, may conflict with the parents' rights to respect for privacy and family life under Art.8, and the parents' due process rights under Art.6 may make investigation of the abuse almost impossible. The Convention makes little attempt to anticipate or resolve these conflicts, even where they present themselves most obviously. For example, Art.2 of the First Protocol (to which the United Kingdom is a signatory) demands respect by the state for the *parent's* right to determine how their children should be educated. There is no "exemption" clause demanding that the state balance the rights of, say, the sufficiently mature child to make their own choices in this area. **2–09**

This raises a connected problem. At the time the Convention was drafted—1950—children were still largely seen as the objects rather than the subjects of legal processes, with the main aim of the law being to protect them, rather than to award them autonomous rights. It is unsurprising therefore that children are never explicitly named as the holders of rights within the ECHR, nor is there any explicit mention of the welfare principle as a restriction on parental rights. By contrast, the UNCRC, drafted rather later—1989 rather than 1950—is self-consciously "child-centred". Unlike the ECHR, the UNCRC not only adopts as a central tenet the primacy of the child's best interests (in Art.3), but more importantly, adds to the child's right to be protected the more modern notion of the right to *participate*, and grapples with the problem of conflicts between the rights of parent and child as the child matures and develops his or her own wishes. Article 5 of the UN Convention in particular expressly provides that whilst parents have responsibility for the direction and guidance of their children, it must be provided in a manner consistent with the evolving capacity of children. Neither the ECHR itself nor its subsequent interpretative case law has yet developed this idea of the incremental growth in competence and rights of the child as he or she matures, an idea which is found in many domestic legal systems and which has pervaded English and **2–10**

---

[19] See S. Boyd, "Charting the Impact of Rights and Equality Discourse on Canadian Family Law" in *Human Rights and Scots Law* (Boyle *et al* (eds), Hart Publishing, Oxford, 2002).

Scottish child law as a break on paternalistic action ever since the case of *Gillick v West Norfolk and Wisbech Area Health Authority* reached the House of Lords.[20]

2–11 A key question is whether a system of child law which promotes the welfare of the child as paramount—such as Scots law—is compatible with an ECHR which requires in Art.8 that respect be given to the rights of parents to control their family life, and which makes no mention in its primary text of the welfare principle.[21] The Court of Session addressed this issue shortly after domestic incorporation in *White v White*[22] and found, citing the case of *Elsholtz v Elsholtz*,[23] that Strasbourg jurisprudence took the line that,

> "in [deciding a child custody case], particular importance must be attached to the best interests of the child which, *depending on their nature and seriousness may over ride those of the parent*. In particular the parent cannot be entitled under Art 8 to have such measures taken as would harm the child's health and development". [Emphasis added.]

On this basis the court found that the Scots child law system was wholly compatible with the ECHR. But this seems a tad complacent. To say that, in some circumstances, ECHR case law holds that the interests of the child may overcome the rights of the parents under the ECHR, is hardly the same as saying that in *every* case relating to parental rights and responsibilities, the welfare of the child will be regarded as *paramount*.

2–12 Finally, the ECHR, like most human rights instruments of its vintage, is only concerned with civil/political rights and not with social/economic rights. For adults, civil and political rights are central to securing the autonomy they need to shape the rest of their lives. But for children, lacking autonomy and the ability to independently amass resources, social and economic rights involving claims *to* resources, such as rights to health or leisure, rather than the rights to be left free *from* interference, which are typical of the ECHR, are arguably far more important. Again, the UNCRC stands in stark contrast to the ECHR in dealing with the full gamut of social/economic rights (though of course how far they are then implemented by states is another story).

---

[20] [1986] 1 A.C. 112.
[21] See from an English perspective, M. Woolf, "Coming of Age?—the Principle of 'the Best Interests of the Child' " [2003] E.H.R.L.R. 205, who asserts that the principle of the best interests of the child is receiving "greater reference in European human rights law" and suggest that the Strasbourg court receives guidance from the UN Committee on the Rights of the Child. It is worth noting that the "best interests of the child" does explicitly appear in the EU Charter of Rights 2000, Art.24(2).
[22] 2001 S.L.T. 485. See para.2–29, below.
[23] [2000] F.L.R. 497.

What results is a paradox. The UNCRC is well suited to advancing **2–13** the interests and rights of children but almost wholly lacks teeth in terms of domestic enforceability. The ECHR is far from the ideal starting point for pursuing the interests of children but has an excellent international enforcement mechanism and has been incorporated into United Kingdom domestic law. To misquote the well known aphorism, if one was looking to promote the rights of children in United Kingdom domestic law by the use of international human rights standards, one would not start from here.

Nonetheless, considerable headway has been made in the last 10 **2–14** years in promoting the human rights of children in Scotland. Most notably perhaps, a Children's Commissioner for Scotland was installed by statute in 2003.[24] A number of voluntary sector organisations, such as the Scottish Child Law Centre, Children Scotland, Children First and Childline Scotland, with some support from the Scottish Executive, tirelessly promote the rights and interests of children. "Child-proofing" of new legislation (scrutiny to be compliant with the UNCRC) is guaranteed, at least in theory, by the Scottish Parliament. More recently, the Scottish Executive has promoted a non-legally enforceable Children's Charter of Rights, *Protecting Children and Young People*.[25]

But the question has to be asked: how much of this rights-centered **2–15** effort is actually producing a measurable improvement in the quality of life of Scotland's children?[26] The second report of the UN Committee on the Rights of the Child in 2002[27] laid out a damning indictment of the United Kingdom's performance in implementing the guarantees of the UNCRC. Child poverty levels, and associated malnutrition, homelessness, pregnancy and suicide rates for children, were still unacceptably high. Child asylum seekers and juvenile delinquents were being detained along with adults and denied basic due process rights. Rates of exclusion of children from schools, and thus denial of education rights, though improving, were still far too high. Bullying was endemic. Family violence and sexual abuse of children within families was still of "deep concern". A third of soldiers in the United Kingdom were recruited, deliberately, from the

---

[24] Commissioner for Children and Young People (Scotland) Act 2003. The first Commissioner, Kathleen Marshall, took office in March 2004. It is noticeable however that the Commissioner's powers are basically limited to public education, investigation, and reports. She has no power to bring either ordinary or class actions in court (as is the case in Race Relations law) nor to serve enforcement notices against particular infringers of children's rights (as is the model with the Information Commissioner who polices data protection law). It is submitted that these powers are too limited to make a real sea-change to a culture of children's rights in Scotland.

[25] Available on the *www.scotland.gov.uk* website.

[26] See an assessment of the impact of the HRA 1998 on some areas of Scots law affecting children in R. Mackenzie, "Human rights act one year on" in *Journal of the Law Society of Scotland* (September 2001), p.32.

[27] See n.14, above.

ranks of the under 18s. And although corporal punishment of children in schools had been abolished, hitting of children at home was still allowed.

2–16 It is noticeable that many of these entrenched and, sometimes, appalling problems are not anything which can be fixed via private law. Indeed, within this volume we will touch only briefly on most of the problems cited above. One of the problems with writing a modern volume on child and family law is that, while traditionally a creature of private law, increasingly the "real action" in protecting and empowering children and families is in public law areas like criminal law, housing law, social security and welfare law, and immigration law. It is hoped that the rights-based focus of the Human Rights Act 1998 may lead to the development of a more holistic approach to the study of child and family law, rather than, as some fear, to the displacement of a focus on the welfare of the child, in favour of the rights of parents.

Minors and Pupils: Historical Development of Scots Law Conception of Children

2–17 In Scots law, the conception of a distinction between the capacity of adults and children is one which has been historically received from Roman law. Children are divided into *pupils* and *minors*. Pupillarity lasts from birth until the age of 12 for a girl and from birth until the age of 14 for a boy. (The distinction reflected different ages for attaining puberty.) Girls over the age of 12 but under 18, and boys over the age of 14 but under 18, are in minority.[28] Majority is now attained by statute at the age of 18.[29] The most staking feature of this categorisation of children is that it is gradated; rather than children moving from a state of incapacity to full capacity in one fell swoop, there is a recognition, albeit a fairly rough one, that the capacity of children develops slowly over time and that the progress to adulthood is cumulative rather than an arbitrary threshold to be stepped over. This historical background sharply distinguishes the development of the Scots treatment of the capacity of children from English law where, in strict principle, a child still moves straight from being an infant to an adult at the age of 18, rights and capacities under the age of 18 being conferred only by a patchwork of exceptions under statute and common law.[30] While in England the

---

[28] Erskine, i.7.1.

[29] Age of Majority (Scotland) Act 1969, s.1. Before that date, again following Roman law, minority originally lasted until the age of 25. This was reduced to 21 and then to 18.

[30] See Bainham, *Children—The Modern Law* (1993), p.19. However, this view of English children is now severely compromised by the rights of mature minors that were recognised in *Gillick v West Norfolk and Wisbech Area Health Authority* [1986] 1 A.C. 112—see paras 2–29 to 2–32.

emerging capacity of a mature minor was acknowledged only in 1986 in the *Gillick* decision, in Scotland the institution of minority has always been recognised as a halfway house between adulthood and young childhood.

At common law, the rules as to the capacity of pupils and minors **2–18** to enter various legal transactions, and especially contracts, were highly complex.[31] In general, a pupil child had no active legal capacity.[32] Instead, in all legal transactions, the guardian of the pupil, known as a tutor, acted for the child, giving any necessary legal consent. Thus, any contracts a pupil child purported to make on his or her own were void. However, as stated above, there was nothing to stop a pupil being the passive recipient of rights, so that a pupil was capable of, inter alia, owning and inheriting property. A minor child, on the other hand, had, in principle, almost the equivalent of adult legal capacity, but could only exercise it with the *concurrence* of his or her guardian, known as a curator. Thus, a contract made by a minor with the consent of the curator would be legally valid—any other contract would be void. There were numerous exceptions to this rule, by which a minor could sometimes enter legal transactions on his or her own. Furthermore, three classes of minors also had extensive capacity to act on their own without a curator: minor children who had no curator, e.g. orphans; minors who had married; and minors who had left home and taken up an independent existence (a state known as forisfamiliation).[33] For both pupils and minors, the guardian, whether known as tutor or curator, was the person with parental rights, normally the parent or parents.[34] Minors who made valid contracts either with the consent of their curators or on their own under one of the exceptional regimes, also had an advantage under the law in that they could sometimes have the contract later declared void if they had been taken advantage of due to their youth and inexperience (this was known as the remedy of minority and lesion).

The concepts of pupillarity and minority exist to this day within **2–19** Scots law but their legal consequences in relation to capacity, and particularly in relation to the formation of contracts, have been sharply reduced. The law on the capacity of children was radically transformed by the introduction of the Age of Legal Capacity (Scotland) Act 1991,[35] which introduced for most legal purposes a different categorisation of children according to whether they are above or below the age of 16. Since the older framework of pupils and minors remains in place, however, it cannot be completely forgotten and

---

[31] See, for a full account, Wilkinson and Norrie, *The Law Relating to Parent and Child in Scotland* (2nd edn, 1999) (hereafter "Wilkinson and Norrie"), Ch.1.
[32] Erskine, i.6.2, i.7.33 gives minor exceptions to this rule.
[33] Erskine, i.6.53.
[34] For the rules on who has parental responsibilities and rights, see Ch.3.
[35] Hereafter "the 1991 Act". It came into force on September 25, 1991.

when we consider the *rights* of children under 16 which are not specifically reformed or removed by the 1991 statute, as opposed to their legal capacity, the older law is still essential to a comprehensive understanding.

2–20 The 1991 Act was introduced in response to many perceived problems with the old law.[36] The law was highly complex, with more exceptions than unqualified rules.[37] It was largely drawn from the institutional writers and very old case law and was thus somewhat obscure and uncertain, and untailored to the needs of modern society. Because it was inappropriate to the modern world it was, in many respects, largely ignored. There was, in particular, a strong feeling that the ages of 12 and 14 were not especially significant for modern Scottish children and that the distinction between the sexes was not defensible. Because of the arbitrariness of the rules in modern society it was felt the law was at times over-protective and yet sometimes did not go far enough. Given all this, the Scottish Law Commission decided that comprehensive reform would be preferable to mere "tinkering with the rules".

THE AGE OF LEGAL CAPACITY (SCOTLAND) ACT 1991

2–21 The basic framework of the 1991 Act is that children under the age of 16 have, in principle, no capacity to enter into any transaction, while children over 16 have, in principle, full legal capacity.[38] A "transaction" is given a wide interpretation by s.9 of the Act to include any transaction having legal effect, which includes, notably, the making of contracts, but also expressly includes unilateral transactions, such as making a promise, giving a legal consent to medical treatment, appointing a trustee, and the raising or defending of civil proceedings in court. The age of 16 was selected as significant because it reflected "an important social reality". At 16, a child can marry; can leave school; can take up full-time employment and so become independently economically active; can embark on full-time higher education and so begin to pursue a career. To set the age of capacity, as previously, at 12 or 14 was to ignore the fact that young persons of those ages are rarely involved in significant independent legal transactions and are often still deemed to be in need of parental guidance; while to set it at 18 (the age of majority and the age at which significant public law rights arise, such as, primarily, the right to vote) was to ignore the substantial leap into the adult world which the age

---

[36] See, generally, *Report on the Legal Capacity and Responsibility of Minors and Pupils*, Scot. Law Com. No.110 (1987).

[37] For a critique of whether the 1991 Act in fact succeeded in simplifying the law, or merely introduced its own new set of complexities, see Thomson, "Minor's Rights—Some Minor Changes?", 1989 J.L.S.S. 335.

[38] s.1.

of 16 represents[39] and would have radically curtailed the existing powers of minor children without good cause. The conclusion of the Scottish Law Commission was that the age of 16 represented a realistic dividing line between those who needed special protection on account of immaturity and those who did not.

The Child Under 16

Section 1(1)(a) of the 1991 Act states that the person under 16 years **2–22** of age has no legal capacity to enter any transaction. This means that every child under 16 is, in principle, in the same position as a pupil under the old law, i.e. unable to enter any kind of transaction. Any transaction a child under 16 seeks to enter is therefore void.[40] Hence, as with the pupil under the old law, capacity must be supplied for the under-16 child by his or her parent or legal representative,[41] who performs legal functions on the child's behalf. The law on guardianship and legal representation[42] will be examined more closely elsewhere but for the moment it is enough to state that the legal representatives of a child are the persons with parental responsibilities and rights in respect of that child, which under s.3 of the Children (Scotland) Act 1995 means (i) the mother of the child, and either (ii) the father if he has been, or is, married to the mother at the time of the child's conception or subsequently, or (iii) a father who does not fit the requirements of (ii) but who is registered as the father in a United Kingdom register of births, deaths and marriages. It is possible for other parties (such as a stepfather or grandparent) to apply for parental rights including guardianship, or for a guardian to be appointed in the event of the natural parents' death.[43] However, the incapacity of under-16 children is subject to some significant exceptions.

"(1) Children under 16 have legal capacity to enter transactions 'of a kind commonly entered into by persons of his age and circumstances' so long as the terms of the transaction are 'not unreasonable' "[44]

This is the most far-reaching and also the most problematic of the **2–23** exceptions to incapacity under discussion. It is obvious that children of all ages regularly engage in a range of economic activities and

---

[39] It is interesting to observe as a very rough indicator that the publication *Basic Rights: Information for Young People in Scotland* (1993), which lists a mixture of public law and private law rights by age at which they can be exercised, has over a page of rights listed as attained at age 16 and only about a quarter of that at age 18.

[40] s.2(5).

[41] There is only one type of legal representative now for all children under 16. Tutory is abandoned as a legal phrase and curatory is abolished as an institution (see below)—1991 Act, s.5(3).

[42] The law on legal representation and guardianship was reformed shortly after the 1991 Act came into operation by the Children (Scotland) Act 1995, ss.7–10; see paras 6–10 to 6–14.

[43] Children (Scotland) Act 1995, ss.7 and 11; see also para.6–10.

[44] 1991 Act, s.2(1).

purport to enter into contracts every day (though their legal characterisation as such is not often remarked on by the parties.) For example, children buy goods such as sweets, groceries, clothes, electrical equipment, etc.; purchase services such as haircuts, cosmetic treatment and public transportation, etc.; and take out memberships in associations such as youth hostel organisations and fan clubs. Such transactions would be void under the general principle of s.1(1)(a) if no further provision was made. While this would often make little difference in a standard cash transaction, it could be crucial to securing rights under consumer protection legislation that a valid contract was made. For example, the purchaser of a defective CD player has rights in respect of quality and fitness for purpose under the Sale of Goods Act 1979 (as amended) which he would not have if the contract was void.

2–24   The aim of the provision then, is to recognise the validity of everyday, common transactions of children of differing ages and circumstances. The test is designed to be factual, rather than legally prescriptive. "Everyday" transactions, it is recognised, differ widely in different geographical areas, different social classes and at different ages. In the North of Scotland it may be common for children to buy fishing nets and bait; in urban areas it may be common for children to purchase electronic software and hardware. The provision avoids setting any normative test, such as what is a reasonable, or necessary, transaction for a child. It is also capable of changing with the times. In 1783, it was accepted that a young gentleman had capacity to buy lengths of red silk for himself for clothing but not as a gift for his lady friend, as the former but not the latter purchase was regarded as a "necessary".[45] Nowadays, probably neither contract would be regarded as a transaction "of a kind commonly entered" unless it could be subsumed into the more general transaction of purchasing clothing.

2–25   Unfortunately, although the aim of the section is clear, the drafting presents a logical impossibility. Since a child (or class of children) cannot validly enter a particular kind of transaction until he has *capacity* to enter it, how can he enter it often enough for it to become a "commonly-entered" transaction? Here we must fall back on a purposive interpretation and assume that we are talking of transactions of a kind which a child would commonly enter *if he or she had capacity to do so*. Another unsatisfactory aspect of the test is how far it deals with the needs of particular groups of children under the head of "circumstances". It is not common for all children to enter short term refuge housing, for example, but it is, arguably, common for children who have been sexually or physically abused by their parents, or have been made homeless. Are these "circumstances" which define a group in the same way as geographical or economic factors?

---

[45] *Scoffier v Read* (1783) Mor. 8936.

Finally, note that even if the transaction is of a kind commonly **2–26** entered into, it will still be void if it is entered into on *unreasonable terms*. This is intended to protect a child under 16 from making an extortionate bargain and being held to it. It is arguable that this protection could have been more simply given by extending the rights given to 16–18 year olds to set aside prejudicial transactions in s.3 of the Act (see paras 2–48 to 2–51 below) to any transactions validly entered into by children under 16.

"(2) Children at age 12 can make a valid will"[46]

This implies that any children who die before the age of 12 must die **2–27** intestate (i.e. without leaving a valid will) since it is established that no parent or guardian can make a will for a child.[47]

"(3) Children at age 12 can consent to or veto their own adoption"[48]   **2–28**

"(4) Children under 16 can consent on their own behalf to any surgical, medical or dental procedure where, in the opinion of a qualified medical practitioner, they are capable of understanding the nature and possible consequences of the procedure or treatment"

This provision, in s.2(4) of the 1991 Act, raises many highly difficult **2–29** issues, blurring as it does the distinction between the capacity and the rights of children. Prior to the 1991 Act, the right to consent to medical treatment in respect of children was most often thought of as a right accruing to parents, rather than a power of the child; and was thought of conceptually as part of the bundle of parental rights that could be exercised by parents and guardians, including their rights of custody and of guardianship, both of which continued until the child reached the age of 16.[49] The right to consent to medical treatment by parents is now best seen as an aspect of the right and responsibility to act as a legal representative of the child under the Children (Scotland) Act 1995.[50] Prior to 1991, the age at which children could give independent consent to their own treatment was uncertain, although there was some authority for the approach that a minor child, by virtue of his greater capacity and control of his own person, might be so entitled.[51] Many doctors assumed erroneously

---

[46] 1991 Act, s.2(2).
[47] *Rintoul's Trs. v Rintoul*, 1949 S.C. 297.
[48] 1991 Act, s.2(3). See further on adoption, paras 6–15 *et seq.*
[49] Until 1991, guardianship rights lasted until the child reached 18, reduced by the Age of Legal Capacity (Scotland) Act 1991, s 5(2) (but see now Children (Scotland) Act 1995, s.1(1)(b)(ii)).
[50] See further paras 5–23 to 5–34.
[51] See Norrie, "The *Gillick* Case and Parental Rights in Scots Law", 1985 S.L.T. (News) 157 for a strong argument in favour of the independent capacity of minors before *Gillick;* see Thomson for a rebuttal, "The *Gillick* Case and Parental Rights in Scots Law: Another View", 1985 S.L.T. (News) 223.

that by statute a child only had a right to consent above the age of 16; in fact, this belief derived from an English statute not applicable to Scotland.[52] The whole issue was thrown open by the landmark case of *Gillick v West Norfolk and Wisbech Area Health Authority*.[53]

2–30 Victoria Gillick applied to the English courts for determination on whether a notice issued by the Department of Health and Social Security was lawful. The notice advised doctors that while it was desirable when persons under 16 sought contraceptive advice and treatment for their parents to be informed and consulted, nevertheless, in exceptional circumstances, the doctor might treat the child alone so long as he did so in good faith and with regard to the child's best interests. Mrs Gillick argued that this advice was legally wrong, claiming (inter alia) that, in English law, a child over 16 only had a right to consent to medical treatment by virtue of statute and a child under 16 had no common law right to give such a consent. Hence it was argued that the only person who could give such a consent was the parent or guardian by virtue of their parental rights, and so a doctor would be acting illegally if he treated a child without the consent (and by implication, the knowledge) of a parent or guardian.

2–31 The Court of Appeal agreed that a child under 16 did not have the right to consent without parental approval. However, in the House of Lords by a narrow margin of three to two,[54] the decision was reversed. It was held that children under 16 could, exceptionally, consent to receiving contraceptive treatment, and, by extension, all other forms of medical procedure, *provided* they had reached a certain degree of maturity and understanding. However, the exact criteria for becoming (as it has since become known) *"Gillick*-competent" were left a matter of some controversy. Lord Fraser emphasised, along with other factors, that a doctor should only regard a child as competent if the treatment requested was in that child's best interests. Lord Scarman, on the other hand, required only that for a child to be competent he or she should not only understand the nature of the medical treatment but also have sufficient maturity to understand what was involved, including moral and family questions and the risks to health and emotional stability.

2–32 *Gillick*, while technically not of binding authority in Scotland, is highly persuasive as a decision of the House of Lords, and has also received much favourable comment from academic writers. It encapsulates a societal shift away from the belief that children are objects of property in the power of their parents—a view enshrined in many Victorian cases—to the belief that children are to be nurtured by their parents towards eventual autonomy and that parental rights exist to facilitate the welfare of the child.

---

[52] Family Law Reform Act 1969, s.8.

[53] [1986] 1 A.C. 112.

[54] It is indicative of the degree of ambivalence raised by the concept of independent rights for minor children that over the whole course of proceedings up to the House of Lords, five judges in fact found for Mrs Gillick and only four against.

It is clear that s.2(4) of the 1991 Act essentially puts the kernel of **2–33** the decision in *Gillick* on a statutory basis for Scotland. In particular, the provision appears to lean towards Lord Scarman's rather than Lord Eraser's conception of *"Gillick*-competence", speaking as it does of the "nature" and the "consequences" of the medical treatment in question. There is, deliberately, no requirement made in the section for the doctor to establish that the treatment is in the child's best interests. The Scottish Law Commission, after extensive consultation on this point, came to the conclusion that if a child was deemed to have sufficient maturity then it should not matter if the treatment was for his or her benefit or not. The implication is that if the child is found to be competent, then, like an adult, the child has a right to take risks or make wrong choices, and the willingness to take the consequences of those risks and choices. Furthermore, unlike an adult, it is still possible that the authority of the courts may be invoked to prevent the child from becoming a victim of a wrong choice made because of youth and inexperience; this is not possible in the case of an adult.[55]

In practice, the issue of the best interests of the child is not wholly **2–34** removed from the equation. In most cases, a doctor will be asked to sanction treatment which is unequivocally therapeutic. If the treatment is not unequivocally in the best interests, e.g. cosmetic surgery or tissue donation,[56] then part of the doctor's task in assessing maturity will be to consider why the child wishes to undergo this treatment and whether they have thought the risks and the advantages through. It is unlikely, for example, that a 14-year-old seeking cosmetic surgery in order to attain a more gracious nose is displaying a high level of maturity. On the other hand, a child of a similar age seeking to have his or her nose pierced arguably has a lower hurdle to surmount to prove competency since the procedure in question is less permanent and involves less risks (e.g. no general anaesthetic[57]). In the paradigm

---

[55] By application to the court under s.11 of the Children (Scotland) Act 1995, see Ch.4. At common law, an adult has the right to make a decision to refuse medical treatment even if this has fatal consequences; but see the highly exceptional case of *Re S* [1992] 4 All E.R. 671, where the Caesarean section of an adult woman was authorised by the English High Court, apparently in the interests of the fetus. See discussion in Ch.1.

[56] Particularly acute issues about non-therapeutic consent can arise when a child is asked, for good medical practice reasons, to donate, e.g. bone marrow or a kidney, to a sibling or other relative. In England the matter falls under the Family Law Reform Act 1969, s.8, and authorities on this are conflicting; the matter is addressed in Annex E of the HFEA Law and Ethics Committee Guidance on Consent to Medical Treatment, ELC (06/04).

[57] In fact, there is medical evidence that the very common practice of *ear* piercing is rather more risky than most people think: see "Ear Piercing and Children's Rights" (1994) 308 B.M.J. 1636. Oddly perhaps, Scots (and UK) law requires parental consent to tattooing under the age of 18 (Tattooing of Minors Act 1969, s.1) but has no such rule concerning other piercings of any kind: in practice however most shops seem to operate a policy of no piercing without parental consent for those under the

case of contraception, where there may be no consensus between child and parents on whether contraceptive treatment is in the child's best interests, the doctor must assess if, say, a girl of 14 has considered and balanced the health and emotional risks of under-age sexual intercourse, and the disruption to family harmony, with the advantages of contraceptive protection. In many ways, this is not dissimilar from an assessment of whether treatment is in her best interests, although it is, in principle at least, a less paternalistic approach.[58]

2–35   Section 2(4) does not just empower minor children approaching full adulthood, but reflects the gradated nature of child development. So, a very young child of perhaps five or six can give a valid consent to the school nurse bandaging his cut knee, a fairly unambivalently therapeutic procedure. The most difficult scenario, perhaps, is where a child has fluctuating capacity—able to act with full maturity on some occasions but on other occasions being rash or irresponsible. While such fluctuations in behaviour are perhaps not atypical of the adolescent child, the major difficulty is likely to arise in relation to children with mental conditions such as mood swings, or more seriously, ordinary or bipolar depression. In England, it has been established that where a child fluctuates between rational and irrational periods, then the child cannot be regarded as "*Gillick*-competent" even if during a rational period they appear able to act with sufficient maturity.[59]

> "*Gillick*-competence is a developmental concept and will not be lost or acquired on a day to day or week to week basis."[60]

2–36   Section 2(4) establishes then, that a child who meets the test of understanding may give a valid consent to a medical procedure, and by implication, following *Gillick*, that his or her parent or parents do not have a right of veto in respect of that consent, even, arguably, where the child is not acting in his or her own best interests. This, however, leaves two important questions open: first, what happens if the child *refuses* consent but the parent(s) are willing or insistent on *providing* a consent? In this case, there is a clash between the parent's right to provide a consent to medical treatment, which is an aspect of the right

---

age of 16, or sometimes 18. The Scottish Executive has consulted on this matter, in 2001 (*Regulation of Skin Piercing* (Scottish Executive, 2001)) but to no result thus far. See *Stair Encyclopaedia, Child and Family Law (Reissue)* (Butterworths, 2004), para.273.

[58] See de Cruz, "Parents, Doctors and Children: the *Gillick* Case and Beyond" (1987) J.S.W.L. 93 for a cogent argument that the "welfare" approach of Lord Eraser and the "capacity" approach of Lord Scarman are not so far removed from each other.

[59] *Re R (A Minor)* [1991] 4 All E.R. 177.

[60] *Northampton Health Authority v Official Solicitor* [1994] F.L.R. 162, *per* Sir Thomas Bingham M.R., at p.168. It is interesting to compare this with the approach traditionally taken under Scottish contract law, that a person may be *capax* during lucid intervals, even where there is fluctuating capacity.

and responsibility to act as the child's legal representative, and the capacity of the child to withhold consent. Secondly, if a child is sufficiently mature to give a competent consent, then can a *court*, rather than a parent, overrule that child's wishes and, if so, in what circumstances?

There are no answers to these questions to be found in the 1991 **2–37** Act. These are questions which are intimately concerned with the issue of whether children have autonomous rights, and how their rights interact with the rights and responsibilities of their parents and of the state. We therefore consider these issues further in Ch.4.[61]

"(5) Children under 16 may have rights to litigate independent of their parents"

In principle, the ordinary rules of the 1991 Act apply to the ques- **2–38** tion of capacity to raise and defend civil proceedings.[62] Thus, without further provision it would be the case that a person over 16 had full capacity to raise or defend actions in his own name, while a person under 16 had no capacity. In the latter case, as with other types of juridical acts, the law would assume that the parent or guardian would act for the child, raising proceedings on behalf of that child and generally acting to secure and protect their interests.

In most circumstances, this is a satisfactory state of affairs. For **2–39** example, it is routine for parents to sue for damages on behalf of their children; thus, where one parent has been killed in an accident, it is commonplace for a surviving spouse to sue for damages in respect of the death on both his or her own behalf and that of the children of the marriage.[63]

But what if the child wishes to raise an action which his or her **2–40** parent or guardian does not condone, or, more importantly, what if the child wishes to sue his or her own parent? Such actions are becoming increasingly likely, for at least two reasons. One reason is the growing appreciation of the incidence of physical and sexual abuse within families. It cannot be assumed, as it has been in the past, that the parents are always the best guardians of children's interests. The second, and connected, factor is the growth in breakdown of the traditional family. Increasingly, there are a number of options for children as to which household they should live in and who, if anyone, should have principal control of the day-to-day running of their lives. Where children have been taken into care in the form of fostering or placement for adoption, alternative family ties may have formed which they may prefer to their conventional blood ties. The converse

---

[61] See paras 4–29 to 4 37.
[62] 1991 Act, s.9, defines a "transaction" as including "the bringing or defending of, or the taking of any step in, civil proceedings".
[63] See, e.g. *Scott v Occidental Petroleum (Caledonia) Ltd*, 1990 S.L.T. 882.

may also be true.[64] Children may seek to go to court to vindicate their choices about their lifestyle: they may wish to have parental rights removed from their natural parent or parents and transferred to another relative or carer[65]; they may wish to question the decisions made about aspects of their upbringing, perhaps in relation to their healthcare, education, religion or contact with a non-resident parent.[66]

2–41 At common law, a child who did not have full capacity could nonetheless raise proceedings without the consent of his guardian where there was no guardian, or the guardian was unable to act; where there was a conflict of interest between the child and the guardian; or where the guardian refused to bring or defend proceedings.[67] In these circumstances, the court would appoint a curator *ad litem*, a special guardian who would conduct the case in the best interests of the child and owe duties to the court. These rights are preserved as an exception to the normal rule of incapacity of under-16s by the 1991 Act.[68] Furthermore, it was also thought to be possible after the 1991 Act was introduced that a child might raise an action if this was seen as a transaction "commonly undertaken by persons of his age and circumstances" (1991 Act, s.2(4), above). However, new rules relating to the child's right to litigate were introduced by the Children (Scotland) Act 1995, not least because the Scottish Legal Aid Board had proved reluctant to fund child-raised actions except in very exceptional cases. For clarity, the 1995 Act inserts two new sections into the 1991 Act.[69]

2–42 Section 2(4A) of the 1991 Act provides that persons under 16 shall have legal capacity to instruct a solicitor in any civil matter, where that person has a "general understanding of what it means to do so"; such understanding is to be presumed at age 12, but there is nothing to prevent a younger child proving they have such capacity. The new

---

[64] One of the most publicised of a number of recent English cases in which children have gone to the courts was that of an 11-year-old girl who successfully obtained a court order allowing her to live with her former foster parents *(The Times,* November 6, 1992). Conversely, in *Re T (A Minor)* [1993] 3 W.L.R. 602, a 13-year-old girl petitioned the court to allow her to remove herself from her adoptive parents and instead to grant a residence order in favour of her paternal aunt.

[65] In the media, such actions have become known colloquially as children "divorcing their parents". While an evocative phrase, it is functionally misleading since a child cannot end his relationship with his parents in several important ways—the obligation of support owed by parent to child is one implied by law and cannot be voluntarily severed *(Crozier v Crozier* [1994] 1 F.L.R. 126) nor can a child's rights to a claim on his parent's estate be waived until the child has full capacity to do so, which is acquired at age 16 (and even then might be subject to setting aside as a prejudicial transaction until the age of 21—s.3, 1991 Act).

[66] Such actions may be raised under s.11 of the Children (Scotland) Act 1995, as contemplated by s.11 (5). See Ch.4.

[67] See Maxwell, *Practice of the Court of Session*, Pt IV, Ch.3 and Macphail, *Sheriff Court Practice*, paras 4-10–4-27.

[68] 1991 Act, s.1(3)(f).

[69] 1995 Act, Sch.4, paras 53(1) and (3).

s.2(4B) of the 1991 Act goes on to add that a person who has capacity to instruct under s.2(4A) "shall also have legal capacity to sue, or to defend, in any civil proceedings". The net effect then, is that:

- children under 16 who do not meet the test of s.2(4A) capacity continue to be represented by parents or other persons qualified to act as legal representatives. If there is a conflict between them and the parent then the court may appoint them a curator *ad litem* to represent their best interests[70];
- children under 16 who *do* meet the s.2(4A) test may choose to instruct a lawyer, and raise, defend or intervene in proceedings (such as their parents' divorce) in their own name[71];
- it is still competent for parents to represent children under 16 even though the child is demonstrably s.2(4A) competent, so long as the child consents to be represented.[72] (This is an exception to the usual rule under the 1995 Act in that a parent only usually has the right to act as legal representative where the child does not have capacity to act on his own behalf.[73]);
- children over 16 can instruct a lawyer and bring and defend proceedings of any kind, except in relation to variation of trusts where they must be 18 or over.[74]

In practice, giving children capacity to sue their parents (or other **2–43** persons) is of little value unless access to legal aid by children is also ensured. The Legal Aid Board now accept that a child aged 12 or over, instructing a solicitor without parental assistance, may apply for civil legal aid or legal advice and assistance, conditional only on the solicitor instructed enclosing a letter confirming that he has satisfied himself that the child does indeed have a general understanding of what it means to instruct a solicitor (the s.2(4A) test). For a child under 12, the procedure is the same except that the Board reserves the right to query any such letter, e.g. if the child appears unreasonably young.[75]

---

[70] 1991 Act, s.1(3)(f)(iii).
[71] It remains unclear if the Scottish courts can appoint a curator *ad litem* against the wishes of a child who is competent to, and has in fact, instructed their own lawyer under s.2(4A) and 2(4B). In England, the courts have sometimes refused to allow a child to sack their guardian *ad litem*, even though they had independent capacity to hire a lawyer—see *Re S (A Minor) (Independent Representation)* [1993] 2 F.L.R. 437. In *R v Grant*, 2000 S.L.T. 372, a Scottish safeguarder case, the court expressly held that it was perfectly competent for a safeguarder to be appointed to two children even though both already had their own legal representation. However the children do not seem to have opposed this.
[72] 1995 Act, s.15(6).
[73] 1995 Act, s.15(5)(b)
[74] 1991 Act.
[75] See Scottish Legal Aid Board guidance at 1996 J.L.S.S. 83. The legal foundation of the right to apply for legal aid under the age of 16 is now to be found in the Legal Aid (Scotland) Act 1986, s.29 and the Legal Aid (Scotland) (Children) Regulations (SI 1997/ 690). Interestingly, s.29(4) of the 1986 Act does apply a welfare test, namely that "it is in the interests of the child that legal aid be made available".

2–44 It is noteworthy that s.2(4A) makes no statement about who is to undertake the job of assessing if a child has the "general under-standing" required to gain capacity to litigate. The Legal Aid Board practice note seems to assume that it is the solicitors on the "coal face" who will assess a child's capacity when they come seeking legal advice and representation, and in practice this is what does indeed happen in Scotland.[76] In England, however, where a similar law has been passed, the job of assessment of capacity has in some cases been assumed by judges, some of whom have shown hostility to the independent representation of children.[77] One issue is that in child-care cases in England, a child who claims the right to independent representation is usually still represented by a "welfare representa-tive" known as a guardian *ad litem* ('GAL') as well as their own lawyer; while any parents or carers involved may also have legal rep-resentations. Since all parties are often funded by legal aid, the potential drain on the legal aid fund of independent representation by children is seen as a serious financial threat. In Scotland, there are as yet no reported cases where judges have intervened to declare a child is not of sufficient capacity to instruct a lawyer,[78] but there are some interesting dicta in *Henderson v Henderson*,[79] a case where the sheriff was distinctly unhappy that a 10-year-old girl had joined an action for the divorce of her parents as a party minuter, repre-sented by her own lawyer. The sheriff stated that she "did not regard it as of assistance" that the child spoke on her own behalf, since (i) she held the same view as her mother (namely that her father should not exercise rights of contact) and thus the child's own appearance in court was redundant, and (ii) it would be an unnecessary drain on the legal fund if the child had her own lawyer, as both her mother and her father were already represented via legal aid. She concluded with the disapproving statement that "I would deprecate any general tendency for applications to be made for children to be party minuters and to lodge defences". Notwithstanding these

---

[76] See also the guidance to lawyers in the Law Society of Scotland's Child Protection and Representation Principles for Children's Lawyers, launched November 2005.

[77] See, e.g. *Re H* [1994] All E.R. 762.

[78] It is worth noting however *H v H*, 2000 G.W.D. 11-376, where a 13-and-a-half-year-old child with attention deficit disorder, Asperger's syndrome and Tourette's syn-drome was allowed not only to give evidence but to be sisted as a party to an action for contact raised by his step-father. The question of whether he was of an "age and maturity" to join as a party appears to have been spoken to by the bringing of evi-dence from health professionals. This appears to be the first reported civil Scottish case since the 1995 Act in which the competence of a child to give views and be a party has been assessed by anyone other than his or her solicitor and (implicitly) the presiding judge. See further also F. Raitt, "Judicial discretion and methods of ascer-taining the views of a child" (2004) 16 CFLQ 151, especially at 156.

[79] 1997 Fam. L.R. 120. See also the comments in the English case of *R. v Legal Aid Board ex parte W* [2000] 2 F.L.R. 154: "the legal aid board is not a bottomless pit and it is right that officers of the board should scrutinise very carefully cases where there may be duplication of representation".

doubts, the sheriff did not oppose the solicitor's assessment of the girl's capacity, and acknowledged that the girl had reached her views independent of her mother, even though the view was in fact the same.

The issue here is not just the multiple drains on the legal aid fund, **2–45** but also the underlying concept that where an *adult* can speak to the child's views, there is no further need to provide a lawyer to a child so he or she can present their own views via their own representative. Such an approach is inherently paternalistic in that it believes a child can only be harmed, not empowered, by contact with the civil legal process. It is submitted that such a standpoint does not give proper weight to a child's right to participate in judicial proceedings affecting their interests,[80] and to be consulted on major decisions affecting their lives, an issue discussed in full in Ch.4.

"(6) Finally, while strictly different from capacity, it is also important to note that a child under 16 retains the ability to be the passive holder of rights, although he or she may not have active capacity to enforce or proceed in relation to his or her rights"[81]

For example, a child of three may own money which is held in a **2–46** bank account in his name. However, the contract with the bank can only be made by his guardian, who supplies active capacity, and only the guardian will have capacity to make withdrawals until the child reaches competency. This principle is well illustrated by the case of *Huggins v Huggins*[82] in which it was held competent at common law to make payments of aliment direct to a pupil child, and that the tax consequences of this transaction should be determined on the basis of the child's income and exemptions, not the mother's. However, it was recognised that the administration of the money would still have to be handled by the mother since the child had no active capacity and hence the funds should be paid straight to the mother.

The Child Aged 16–18: "Young Persons"

Children over the age of 16 have full legal capacity to enter into any **2–47** legal transaction.[83] They are not subject to the control of a parent or guardian[84] as parental rights terminate when the child reaches 16.[85] They are therefore free to choose their own residence, make any

---

[80] But see *Fourman v Fourman*, 1998 Fam. L.R. 98, where the sheriff commented positively on the appropriateness of a 14-year-old child's decision to join the action as party minuter, with independent legal representation.
[81] 1991 Act, s.1(3)(e).
[82] 1981 S.L.T. 179.
[83] 1991 Act, s.1(1)(a).
[84] 1991 Act, s.5(2).
[85] *ibid.*, and Children (Scotland) Act 1995, s.2(7).

contracts they please, instigate and defend legal proceedings, pick their own religion and so forth.

2–48 However, this does not mean that children over 16 but under 18, the full age of majority, are not still regarded as in need of some degree of special care and protection. In the law's eyes, they are almost, but not quite, adults. The law recognises this in several not wholly consistent ways. For example, under the Children (Scotland) Act 1995, local authorities have extensive duties to promote the welfare of children up to the age of 18.[86] Similarly, in principle, the children's hearings system deals only with children under the age of 16 who are in need of compulsory measures of care; but if the child has already been placed under the supervision of the hearing they may stay within the system until they reach the age of 18.[87] Those who fall into this ambiguous band between age 16 and age 18 are perhaps best described as "young persons"[88] rather than children.

2–49 The 1991 Act attempts to protect young persons by providing under s.3 that any transaction entered into by a person over 16 but under 18 may be set aside if it is a "prejudicial transaction". The young person may make an application to the courts for the setting aside of such a transaction at any time until he or she reaches the age of 21. If a transaction is set aside then it is treated as void and the respective rights of the parties concerned are determined by common law principles of unjustified enrichment.

2–50 A prejudicial transaction is one which: (a) an adult, exercising reasonable prudence, would not have entered into in the circumstances of the applicant at the time of entering the transaction; and (b) has caused or is likely to cause substantial prejudice to the applicant.[89] This is an interesting test. Essentially the court is asked to consider if a particular young person in particular circumstances (a subjective test) would have entered a particular transaction if they had been a reasonable adult (an objective test). The intent is to provide a remedy in respect of transactions which are not only prejudicial but actively unreasonable or unfair. Suppose we imagine the case of a 17-year-old child who, unable to find work or receive income support, takes out a loan. It can be argued that the reasonably prudent adult in these circumstances would do the same thing—therefore the transaction will not be set aside even though the transaction is certainly prejudicial since there will be interest payments to be met. However, now suppose the loan is made at an exorbitant interest rate. We can now safely assume that the reasonably prudent adult would not enter the contract and so the application to set aside should succeed.

---

[86] 1995 Act, ss.22 and 93(2).
[87] 1995 Act, ss.54 and 93(2)(b).
[88] This is the authors' terminology and not that of the 1991 or 1995 Act.
[89] 1991 Act, s.3(2).

The effect of s.3 then, is that all transactions of young persons **2–51** are potentially voidable. It is doubtful, though, how much use will be made of these provisions. Credit transactions are often offered at ruinous rates of interest relative to the High Street standard but as a rule companies are reluctant to offer credit to persons under 18 and standard contractual terms often exclude them. More plausibly, young persons who purchase heritage and take on mortgages may well incur substantial prejudice and if badly advised, or pressurised, may be able to make a good case for setting aside either the purchase or the accompanying standard security. The possible rights of young persons to set aside transactions may make them bad risks in the eyes of potential house sellers and other contractors and so the law provides four ways in which those contracting with young persons may be protected or may seek to protect themselves.

"(i) Certain transactions are exempted from the section 3 right to apply for setting aside"[90]

In particular, a transaction made in the course of the applicant's **2–52** trade, business or profession cannot be set aside. This can be seen as a provision primarily for the benefit of the young person rather than the other party. Few adults would wish to deal on a commercial basis with someone who could turn round and disown the contract if he later decided it did not suit him.

"(ii) If the other party is induced into entering the contract by the young person's fraudulent misrepresentation as to age or any other material fact then the transaction cannot be set aside"[91]

This principle is based on the old case of *Wilkie v Dunlop*.[92] Wilkie, **2–53** a medical student aged 17, ran up a large bill during a shooting holiday with friends and then claimed that due to his age and lack of capacity (under the law at that time), the contract was void. It was held that he should not benefit from his own fraud and as he had falsely held himself out as over 18 and able to make a valid contract, he should be liable. The equivalent claim under s.3 nowadays would be for Wilkie to claim that he should be entitled to have the court set the shooting lodge bill aside as it had been a prejudicial transaction; in which case the innkeeper is entitled to respond that if he had not been defrauded into thinking Wilkie was an adult of full age, he would have declined to contract. In these circumstances, even if the contract *was* prejudicial, as a matter of public policy, Wilkie should be denied the benefit of the s.3 remedy.

---

[90] s.3(3).
[91] s.3(3)(g).
[92] (1834) 12 S. 506.

2–54   Although there has been no case law concerning this provision, it might in future raise interesting questions, given the increasing uptake by children of transactions via the Internet ("e-commerce"). Websites commonly ask those transacting to first declare that they are over 18, (or include such a requirement in their terms and conditions) but this is rarely checked in any way (the use of a credit card is often assumed to do this job but in fact there is no reason why a child could not borrow a card from an adult, with or without their knowledge). In practice it is well known that many children do transact on sites despite such age limits, and the validity of the contracts so formed is unclear. One of the drawbacks to such a false claim should be the loss of s.3(3)(g) protection. A child who holds himself out as over 18 on a website will not then be able subsequently to seek reduction of a contract on grounds of prejudice.

"(iii) The young person himself can ratify the transaction when he reaches 18"[93]

2–55   This bars him from going to court to have the transaction set aside subsequently. However, it still leaves two possible years of doubt for the other party in respect of a contract entered into by the young person on the day he becomes 16. Hence for total security:

"(iv) The young person and the other party or parties to the proposed transaction can make an application in advance to have the transaction ratified by the court"[94]

2–56   The effect again is that the transaction cannot then be set aside. The court must test any proposed transaction to see if it is a prejudicial transaction before ratifying. The court can only ratify in advance rather than retrospectively; there seems no good reason for this restriction. It is thought that very few transactions with young persons, with the possible exception of house or land purchase or sale, will be worth the cost of a court application to have them declared watertight. The lack of any reported case law on this provision since 1991 seems to bear this view out.

OTHER ASPECTS OF CAPACITY

2–57 The 1991 Act is now the principal guide to matters of capacity in private law but it is not the whole story. Other aspects of capacity remain to be determined by common law or other statutory provisions.

---

[93] s.3(3)(h).
[94] s.4.

Delictual Liability[95]

Liability in delict arises where a person, through a breach in duty, **2–58** causes harm to the person or property of another person. The most important head of delictual liability is negligence; liability in negligence arises where a person owes a duty of reasonable care to another and fails to fulfil this duty, with resulting loss or damage. In Scots law, there is a remarkable dearth of authority as to how old a child has to be before he or she can be said to be responsible for his or her own delictual acts. It seems, however, that a child of any age can be liable in delict if he or she is old enough to form an intention to do wrong or to appreciate what he or she ought not to do. The test, as Erskine says,[96] is to do with the exercise of reason, and is not based on any specific age. Since young children are rarely rich or insured against liability, few are likely to be sued directly, but Scots law has recognised in several cases that very young children can be found to have contributed through their own negligence to damage caused them by another party's fault.[97]

In most cases where damage results from the careless actions of a **2–59** child, the party damaged is likely to be more interested in suing the parents than the child, since they are more likely to have access to resources. In principle, children are not to be regarded as owned by their parents, like animals, and therefore parents are not automatically liable for the delicts of their children. However, in practice, parents or others who have physical custody or care of children may be liable in negligence if they fail to take reasonable care to supervise or attend the children. Here it seems reasonable to recall the concepts of the gradual maturing of children under the age of 16 of which we have spoken earlier. If a child is old and mature enough to be able to make independent choices, then he is also old enough to take the financial consequences of his actions. As parental rights diminish, so should parental duties of supervision. This principled argument is, however, unlikely to be of much comfort to the third party who has suffered loss.

The capacity of children to sue for damages in delict is an aspect of **2–60** capacity to litigate generally (see paras 2–38 to 2–43). Awards of damages made to children by courts are now protected by s.13 of the Children (Scotland) Act 1995, under which such order can be made relating to the payment and management of the sum for the child as the court thinks fit (see further, Ch.5). A child of any age can give an adequate discharge for damages paid to him if the court has directed under s.13(2) that the damages should be paid directly to the child and not the parent(s) or any one else (s.13(3)).

---

[95] The 1991 Act explicitly does *not* deal with delictual liability of children: s.1(3)(c).
[96] Erskine, i.1.63 and see Smith, "The Age of Innocence" (1975) 49 Tulane Law Review 311.
[97] See, e.g. *McKinnell v White*, 1971 S.L.T. (Notes) 61; *MacDonald's Tutor v Macleod*, 1995 G.W.D. 28-1498 (6-year-old guilty of contributory negligence).

Giving Evidence

2–61   There is no fixed age at which a child acquires capacity to be a witness in either civil or criminal proceedings. According to the test laid down in *Rees v Lowe*,[98] a child becomes a competent witness when a judge is satisfied that the child knows the difference between truth and lies and appreciates the duty to tell the truth. The judge should investigate to satisfy himself as to a young child's capacity and should admonish the witness to tell the truth.

2–62   The evidence of very young children may be crucial in the increasing number of cases concerning child abuse and neglect. In *Rees* itself, the witness in question was a three-year-old girl. For such witnesses, the giving of evidence in open court may be, at best, a traumatic affair and, at worst, an impossibility.[99]

2–63   In criminal proceedings, until recently, protection of the child witness was seen as an infringement on the rights of the accused to have full access to any evidence against him and to cross-examine such evidence. However, in recent years considerable attempts have been made to reduce the ordeal for children of giving evidence, and to make it possible in many cases for the child not to need to give evidence in court at all. These efforts have culminated in the Vulnerable Witnesses Act 2004, discussed below at para.2–70, which applies not just to children but to witnesses who are vulnerable due to age or infirmity, and also to those who are in danger of intimidation. Judges also still have at common law a discretion to take steps to put children at ease and may, for example, remove wigs and gowns, take evidence from children in the well of the court rather than in the witness box and permit a supportive relative to be nearby.[1]

2–64   In policy terms the best solution is still for the child not to have to appear in court at all. The problem has been in the past that, as a general principle of the Scots law of evidence, the direct evidence of a witness is preferred to a hearsay account of that evidence, such as a third-party statement, a written document, or an audio or video tape record. In both civil proceedings (including proceedings in relation to the children's hearings system) and criminal proceedings, however, statute has now allowed a much more extensive use of hearsay.

Civil Proceedings

2–65   Historically, the difficulties of the law in this area arose as a result of s.2(1) of the Civil Evidence Act 1988, which stated that any statement made by a person—which might be written, or recorded—was as admissible as direct oral evidence given in court by the same witness on the same matter. Hence, in principle, a video-taped record made of

---

[98] 1990 S.L.T. 507.

[99] See further, *Children as Witnesses* (Dent and Flin (eds), 1992) and Spencer and Flin, *The Evidence of Children: The Law and the Psychology* (2nd edn, 1993).

[1] See Lord Justice-General's Memorandum on Child Witnesses, July 26, 1990.

the testimony of a young witness to, for example, sexual abuse could be introduced instead of the witness giving direct testimony.[2] However, considerable difficulty arose in a series of subsequent cases in relation to the introduction of hearsay of a child witness whose competence had *not* been tested according to the *Rees* test; or *had* been tested subsequent to the compilation of the hearsay evidence, and the child found to be incompetent.

In *F v Kennedy (No.1)*[3] a boy, aged three at the time, gave evidence **2–66** of sexual abuse to social workers. When, later, the sheriff attempted to establish the boy's competence as a witness, the boy, intimidated by the circumstances, refused to say anything at all. The effect was that his previous statements made to social workers could not be admitted as hearsay, since direct oral evidence by the boy would not have been competent, as it had not been established that he met the *Rees* test. This was a singularly unfortunate result in child protection cases, where the object of the proceedings is to safeguard the welfare of the child, not to obtain a criminal prosecution. It meant the young child witness, even if he or she had given full evidence to social workers, still had to enter the court to have his or her competency tested, which might be just as traumatic (or impossible) as giving full testimony. Sometimes, the child was simply unable to speak to the judge to establish that the *Rees* test was met and, as a result, the case would fall due to lack of evidence, which then prejudiced the child's need for protection and the public interest in prosecuting sex offenders.[4] Despite much judicial concern, the law was left in a highly unsatisfactory state as regards the evidence of child witnesses.[5]

The Inner House finally had the chance to reconsider the matter **2–67** anew, however, in the leading case of *T v T*.[6] The Inner House seized the opportunity to sweep away all the uncertainty that surrounded this area and in order to avoid a conflict with existing restrictive precedents, convened a bench of five judges, chaired by the Lord President, Lord Rodger. The Lord President, giving the leading opinion, asserted that the approach that had been taken by the

---

[2] See further, Kearney, "The Evidence of Children: the Scottish Dimension" in Spencer (ed.), *Childrens' Evidence in Legal Proceedings* (1989).

[3] 1993 S.L.T. 1277. This was a case which was referred to the Sheriff Court from a children's hearing under s.42 of the Social Work (Scotland) Act 1968 for proof of the ground of referral, which was the sexual abuse of three children, including the witness discussed above.

[4] In *M v Kennedy*, 1993 S.C.L.R. 69 a determined sheriff spent several hours establishing the competence of a 12-year-old child who had become an elective mute through trauma subsequent to giving evidence to social workers. The point of establishing her competence was to allow her earlier statements to be admissible as hearsay. See further, Edwards, "Better Heard and Not Seen", 1994 S.L.T. (News) 9.

[5] See *L v L*, 1996 S.C.L.R. 11; *Sanderson v McManus* 1997 S.C. (H.L.) 55; *AR v Reporter for Aberdeen Local Authority*, 1999 Fam. L.R. 20.

[6] 2000 S.C.L.R. 1057. For discussion of the case see: Edwards, "Children *May* be Heard and Not Seen" (2001) Fam. L.B. 49-4.

courts since *F v Kennedy* was wrong, both in policy and in law. First, the practice which had arisen of bringing children to court to be tested for admissibility merely so their hearsay could then be admitted was both ritualistic and "somewhat disconnected . . . from reality". Secondly, applying a competence test at the time of proof rather than at the time when a statement was made was absurd and unhelpful. For example, where a witness A made a statement heard by B and subsequently A became *incapax*, there was no reason why A's hearsay should not be admitted so long as he was *capax* at the earlier date. Yet *F v Kennedy* excluded hearsay in such cases of supervening incompetence. Similarly, what if A aged 2 makes a statement heard by B aged 20, and the proof relating to these facts is heard 20 years later? Since A will now be aged 22 at the date of proof, his statements as a baby will be admissible as hearsay, even though his trustworthiness aged 2 has not been tested and may be doubted.

2–68   The Lord President went a step further, however, and re-interpreted s.2(1)(a) and (b) of the Civil Evidence Act 1988, read as a whole, to remove the test of competence at all. The Lord President found that the word "admissible" in s.2(1)(b) had two possible meanings. In the "first sense", it was to be taken to refer to the person *giving* the evidence: was the person who was called upon to give evidence competent to give that evidence?[7] This was the sense in which the Second Division had used the word in *F v Kennedy*.[8] The use of the word in that manner had to be distinguished from its use in the "second sense" however. This "second sense" concerns certain types of evidence that an admissible witness *may* give. The Lord President used the example statements given by a client to his lawyer: the lawyer would be an *admissible* witness, but unless the client waves the lawyers common law duty of confidence, those statements would be *inadmissible*.[9] With these two meanings in mind, the Lord President then turned to the provisions of the Act and it was "immediately apparent" that Parliament had used the word "admissible" in the second sense.[10] Therefore the statements of the child, or any other witness, would be inadmissible only if those *statements* were inadmissible under some rule *other* than hearsay, such as client confidentiality.

2–69   After *T v T* it was clear that, slightly paradoxically, the competence of a child witness need only be tested against the criteria set out in *Rees v Lowe*[11] in the event of the child choosing to give *direct*, oral evidence to the court. This last anomaly was, however, cleared up by the Vulnerable Witnesses Act 2004.

---

[7] 2000 S.C.L.R. 1057 at [22] (Lord President).
[8] 1993 S.L.T. 1277.
[9] 2000 S.C.L.R. 1057 at [23] (Lord President).
[10] 2000 S.C.L.R. 1057 at [24] (Lord President).
[11] 1990 S.L.T. 507. See paras 2–61 *et seq*, above.

Vulnerable Witnesses (Scotland) Act 2004[12]

Under the Act, any person under the age of 16 is regarded as a **2–70** "vulnerable witness"[13] and there are special provisions that relate specifically to child witnesses.[14] Under the Act, anyone citing a child witness must give notice to allow for appropriate arrangements to be made.[15] The notice should also indicate which of the "special measures" are likely to be the most appropriate.[16] Standard "special measures" are to be the use of live TV links, the use of a screen, and the use of a supporter for the child.[17] Other special measures which may be authorized may include the taking of evidence by a commissioner on oath, and giving evidence in chief by means of a prior statement made earlier being lodged in evidence. Notably, for such evidence, there is no need for the witness to adopt the statement or speak to it in court. In civil proceedings, a court where a child witness is to give evidence must either authorise the "special measures" or specifically make an order that these are not necessary.[18] The latter course of action should only be adopted where the risk of prejudice substantially outweighs the risk of harm to the child.[19]

This Act completes the work begun by the Inner House in *T v T*, **2–71** which had done away with the competency test for admitting hearsay evidence in civil proceedings but left the test in place where evidence was to be given directly by the child. The new law removes even that test. The law now states that evidence is not inadmissible solely because the witness does not understand the nature of the duty of a witness to give truthful evidence, or the difference between truth and lies.[20] Such matters will simply become part of the job of the judge or jury, as appropriate, to assess, when they come to decide what credence and weight to give the evidence of a child witness.

Criminal Proceedings

In general, there are stronger policy arguments to suggest that **2–72** hearsay should be excluded in criminal than in civil proceedings

---

[12] The full text of the Act is available at: *www.scotland-legislation.hmso.gov.uk/legislation/scotland/acts2004/20040003.htm*. See also "Vital voices", contributed by the Scottish Executive to March 2005, *Journal of the Law Society of Scotland*, p.14. The Act was preceded by SLC Discussion Paper No.75 and SLC Report No.125, "Evidence of Children and Other Vulnerable Witnesses" and *Vital Voices: helping Vulnerable Witnesses Give Evidence* (Scottish Executive, 2002).

[13] Other types of "vulnerable witnesses" are defined at s.11 of the 2004 Act. Here we deal only with the rules as they affect children.

[14] Vulnerable Witnesses (Scotland) Act 2004, s.11. A "child witness" is defined by s.11(1)(a) as a child under 16.

[15] Vulnerable Witnesses (Scotland) Act 2004, s.12(2).

[16] *ibid.*, s.12(2)(a).

[17] *ibid.*, s.18.

[18] *ibid.*, s.12(1).

[19] *ibid.*, s.12(4).

[20] *ibid.*, s.24.

because of the right of an accused person to a fair trial. However, as a result of piecemeal legislative reform, it was, in fact, at one point in the 1990s easier for the hearsay evidence of children to be introduced in criminal proceedings, rather than civil.[21] The law is now however to be found in the Vulnerable Witnesses (Scotland) Act 2004 which makes extensive amendments to parts of the Criminal Procedure (Scotland) Act 1995. Similar "special measures" to those available in civil proceedings are also to be available to vulnerable witnesses in the criminal courts.[22] In addition, a party intending to cite a child witness in criminal proceedings must lodge a "child witness notice" with the court 14 days before the trial diet specifying which, if any, of the special measures they consider to be appropriate.[23] There is a presumption that a child under 12 need not give evidence in person where the offence(s) charged are murder, culpable homicide, and certain sexual offences along with several other prescribed offences.[24] This presumption is only displaced if the accused can show that its operation would prejudice his case significantly and that risk of prejudice must "*significantly outweigh*" the risk of prejudice to the child's interests by presumption being rebutted.[25] There is no analogous provision in civil proceedings. As in civil proceedings, however, the need to test the competency of the child before they give direct evidence is abolished for criminal trials.[26]

Documentary Witnesses

2–73 A child cannot act as a documentary witness. A child must be over the age of 16 before he or she can competently witness a deed.[27]

Criminal Liability

2–74 Children can be held responsible for criminal acts at the age of eight.[28] However, except in the case of very serious crimes, a child under 16 will not be prosecuted in the criminal courts but will be referred to the children's hearing as in need of compulsory measures of supervision. Prosecution is only to be made on the instructions of the Lord Advocate, or at his instance.[29] The age of criminal liability in Scotland is the lowest in Europe and tolerable only because almost

---

[21] See the now amended Criminal Procedure (Scotland) Act 1995, s.259.
[22] Criminal Procedure (Scotland) Act 1995, s.271H, as inserted by the Vulnerable Witnesses (Scotland) Act 2004, s.1.
[23] *ibid.*, s.271A as inserted by the Vulnerable Witnesses (Scotland) Act 2004, s.1.
[24] *ibid.*, s.271B as inserted by the Vulnerable Witnesses (Scotland) Act 2004, s.1.
[25] *ibid.*, s.271B(3) as inserted by the Vulnerable Witnesses (Scotland) Act 2004, s.1.
[26] Vulnerable Witnesses (Scotland) Act 2004, s.24.
[27] Requirements of Writing (Scotland) Act 1995, s.3(4)(c)(ii).
[28] Criminal Procedure (Scotland) Act 1995, s.41. Criminal responsibility is specifically not affected by the 1991 Act: s.1(3)(c).
[29] Criminal Procedure (Scotland) Act 1995, s.42.

all children between 8 and 16 who commit offences are referred to the children's hearing system.[30] Nevertheless, the "Bulger" decision from the European Court of Human Rights in Strasbourg held that it was incompatible with the ECHR to prosecute two boys aged 10 in the ordinary English criminal courts for murder, notwithstanding any special measures taken to protect them.[31] This caused concern in Scotland as to whether the current age of criminal responsibility was "Convention proof". This led the Scottish Law Commission to issue a Discussion Paper[32] and subsequent Report[33] which recommended that the "gateway" age of criminal responsibility simply be abolished. Children would legally be capable of criminal behaviour at *any* age, but would only be prosecuted in the adult criminal justice system in exceptional circumstances. This would have the effect of also reversing the decision in *Merrin v S*[34] that a child had no criminal capacity below the age of eight and therefore could not be referred to the children's hearing on the basis that he had committed a criminal act, even if the act committed would have been criminal if committed by a person over the age of eight. The proposal from the Scottish Law Commission would have the practical effect of enabling a child of *any* age to be referred to the children's hearing for engaging in criminal behaviour. As yet, however, this controversial recommendation has not been implemented.

WHO IS A CHILD?

In the first chapter we posed the question, who is a legal person? In **2–75** this chapter, we have conspicuously failed to ask, or to give an answer to the question, who is a child? At the beginning of this chapter, we spoke of the idea that each society at any point in time has a different conception of the nature of childhood. A further refinement of this concept is that there are different *dimensions* of childhood—in other words, that we describe certain persons as children in certain contexts but not in others, according to social ideas of what activities are more or less reserved for adulthood.[35]

As we have seen, in terms of capacity to take part in transactions **2–76** in the sphere of private law, the law's clearest demarcation is between those under and over the age of 16. Yet, for many purposes, this clear dividing line must be compromised and, in particular, young persons within the bracket from age 16 up to age 18 live in a halfway house

---

[30] See Ch.8.
[31] *T v UK, V v UK* (1999) 30 E.H.R.R. 121.
[32] SLC Discussion Paper No.115, 2001.
[33] SLC Report No.185 (2001). Available at: *www.scotlawcom.gov.uk/downloads/rep185.pdf*.
[34] 1987 S.L.T. 193.
[35] Archard, *op. cit.* above, n.7, on p.40.

between the rights and responsibilities of full adulthood and the protection of childhood. Below the age of 16, we encounter the still less well-defined status of "mature minor" or "*Gillick*-competent" minor, a status which is of increasing importance in both case law and statute.[36]

2–77   The law often regards children as developing, immature, inexperienced or vulnerable creatures on the way to adulthood. It deals with this in diverse ways. As we have already seen, and will see, responsibilities are primarily put on parents to protect their children. Where they fail, the state may intervene. However, in addition, age limits are often imposed for particular protective purposes within various statutes.[37] A young person cannot obtain a driving licence until he or she is aged 17,[38] buy alcohol till he or she is 18,[39] nor acquire a heavy goods vehicle licence for lorries over 7.5 tonnes until he is aged 21.[40] On the other hand, the law allows children to take on a limited amount of paid employment from the age of 13.[41] These are areas where the law has not left matters to the discretion of individual parents or carers. We find more ambiguity when we look at the age up to which the law expects parents to be responsible for maintaining their children. Until recently, parents were normally under an obligation to aliment their children until the age of 18[42]; now this has for most purposes been replaced by an obligation of support which persists in principle only until the child reaches 16.[43] However, children over these ages but in full-time education or training may find they have a right to aliment up to the age of 25.[44]

2–78   It becomes obvious that we cannot simply define a child as someone under 16, or even someone who has a right to be supported by his or her parents, or to whom parents or guardians owe parental responsibilities. The ambiguity around the ambit of childhood has become ever more acute as we have entered the 21st century. Children are in many ways now indistinguishable from adults. Children regularly transact and interact via mobile phones, instant messaging and the Internet, with an independence unknown to previous generations.

---

[36] In England, the Children Act 1989 makes many important concessions to the rights of children depending on their age and understanding. In Scotland, the Children (Scotland) Act 1995 also places emphasis on giving children rights to be consulted dependent on age and maturity, but usually with a presumption this maturity is attained at age 12.

[37] The 1991 Act provides that specific statutory age limits are unaffected by the general principles of the Act—s.1(3)(d).

[38] Road Traffic Act 1988, s.101.

[39] Licensing (Scotland) Act 1976.

[40] Road Traffic Act 1988, s.101.

[41] Subject to small exceptions allowing light employment by parents at an earlier age. See *Stair Encyclopaedia*, para.269, n.6.

[42] Family Law (Scotland) Act 1985, ss.1(1)(c) and (5).

[43] Child Support Act 1991, s.55.

[44] See Family Law (Scotland) Act 1985, s.1(5) and Child Support Act 1991, s.55(1)(b) and (c). For further explanation of these complex rules see Ch.5.

They have considerable spending power, and collection of personal information relating to children is big business. Children appear on reality TV, start up dot.com businesses, and follow the latest designer trends in fashion, consumables and haircuts as avidly as their parents. Yet in other ways children are now seen as more vulnerable than ever before. The folk menace of the paedophile[45] and the Internet "sex groomer"[46] loom large; children no longer walk to school and it is seen as bad parenting in many areas to allow children to use public transport or even go outside alone. Children are again staying at home well into their twenties, due to rises in house prices, and "re-nesting" after the all too common divorce. In such a world, it is no wonder that the legal protection of children, and the conception of who is a child, presents such an unfocused and diverse aspect.

Finally, potentially the most important protections a child has may **2–79** come in the future from the international guarantees found in the ECHR and perhaps eventually even more so in the UN Convention on the Rights of the Child, which defines a child as a human being below the age of 18.[47] The most positive view, then, may be to see a child not as a person with special vulnerability but with special rights. We take this up in Chs 4 and 5. For now, though, we turn to our third crucial question: who is a parent?

---

[45] See the Protection of Children (Scotland) Act 2003 which establishes a list of suspected paedophiles who are not allowed to work with or near children.

[46] See the Protection of Children And Prevention of Sexual Offences (Scotland) Act 2005, which criminalises the preparatory "grooming" of children for under age sex via the Internet.

[47] Art.1.

CHAPTER 3

CHILDREN AND PARENTS

3–01 A child's first legal relationship is with his or her parent or parents. At one time, the law's major concern in regulating the status of children was whether their parents were married to each other. The question of illegitimacy was the first topic to be dealt with in the section of Erskine's *Institute* dealing with relationships between parent and child[1] and in the first major textbook on Scottish child law, Fraser on *Parent and Child*.[2] Nowadays, the topic of illegitimacy has virtually been expunged from Scottish family law and the law is at pains to treat all types of children equally, regardless of the marital status of their parents.[3] Instead, the focus of the law is on the legal consequences of the relationship between parent and child, how that relationship is constituted and proven and how that relationship alters with time.[4]

3–02 An essential starting point to any consideration of the law relating to children and parents is to decide who is a parent. This is no longer the relatively simple task it once was. Advances in reproductive technology have compelled us to think as a society about who should be allowed or assisted to become parents. A distinction can now be made between "natural" parents, who can conceive (in the case of the mother) or impregnate (in the case of the father) without the use of medical assistance or technology, and so-called "artificial" or "assisted" parenthood, in which the link between genetic parenthood and social or gestational parenthood may be broken. Changes in social norms, particularly the growth in cohabitation outside marriage and the increasing birth rate of children outwith marriage, compel us to think about whom we *want* to be regarded as a parent, or alternatively, what the consequences of parenthood should be. In this chapter, we will not only be categorising different types of parent,

---

[1] Erskine, VI. 2. 49.

[2] (3rd edn, 1906), p.1. Wilkinson and Norrie now take a similar approach to the text at hand in separating the issue of legitimacy from the main discussion of parentage and its effects.

[3] See Ch.5 for more detail.

[4] Hoggett and Pearl summed up this process of legal development with admirable simplicity: "Once upon a time it was the child of unmarried parents who was thought to be the problem. Now the law tries to treat the child himself just like any others but still distinguishes between different sorts of parent." (*The Family, Law and Society: Cases and Materials* (3rd edn, 1991), p.443).

but asking why these classifications have been adopted. First, in order to give this exercise a purpose, we must briefly assess the legal consequences of parenthood, especially in terms of parental responsibilities and rights.

THE LEGAL CONSEQUENCES OF PARENTHOOD

The question "who is a parent?" is an important one to ask in a **3–03** variety of circumstances. Perhaps the two most important effects of parentage from the private law point of view are:

- that parentage is an important prerequisite to establishing parental responsibilities and rights; and
- that a parent is responsible for the financial support of his or her children.

The second of these topics will be dealt with in depth in Ch.5, which **3–04** is concerned with the rights of the child. The topic of parental responsibilities and rights will be dealt with at length in Ch.4. These are not, of course, the only legal effects associated with parentage. In succession law, for example, children and parents have rights in each other's estates and so determination of parentage may be vital to establish the distribution of an estate. Children have indefeasible rights, known as legal rights, in the moveable portion of their parents' estate at common law[5]; statutory rights may also be claimed in the free estate where a parent dies in a state of total or partial intestacy.[6] Similarly, if a child dies intestate, then his parent or parents will have a claim to either all or half of the child's free estate, depending on whether the child leaves any surviving siblings.[7] The establishment of the relationship of parent and child may also be important in public law contexts, notably social security law and immigration law.

For the moment, however, we shall look at to whom Scots law **3–05** awards parental responsibilities and rights ("PRRs"). The law on this is now to be found in the Children (Scotland) Act 1995 (hereafter "the 1995 Act"). It is crucial to observe that Scots law has never drawn an automatic link between the establishment of status as a parent and

---

[5] See para.5–91.
[6] See Succession (Scotland) Act 1964, s.2(1)(a). If a parent dies intestate and leaving no surviving spouse then the combined effect of rights to *legitim* and to free estate is that the children (or issue) between them take the whole estate. The law of intestate succession is currently under review by the Scottish law Commission, as of March 2006.
[7] See Succession (Scotland) Act 1964, s.2(1)(b) and (d). If there are no siblings, the parent or parents take the whole free estate between them; if there are siblings, the siblings take half and the parents take half. For a full discussion of the modern law of intestate succession and legal rights see Meston, *The Succession (Scotland) Act 1964* (5th edn, 2002) and Macdonald, *Succession* (3rd edn, 2001), Ch.4.

the award of parental rights. This remains so today, although there is now as much emphasis on the *responsibilities* owed by parents to their children as what rights they have over them. What is included within PRRs is discussed in depth in Ch.4, but basically a parent with PRRs has all the powers necessary to promote and safeguard the welfare of the child, to provide appropriate direction and to represent the child in law.[8] All PRRs, with one exception, terminate when the child reaches 16.[9]

Automatic Parental Responsibilities and Rights ("PRRs")

3–06 According to the 1995 Act, s.3(1)(a), a child's mother automatically has PRRs in respect of her child irrespective of whether or not she is married to the child's father. By contrast, s.3(1)(b) of the 1995 Act originally gave a child's father automatic PRRs only if he was: "married to the mother at the time of the child's conception or subsequently". As we shall see below, there are now other ways for a father not married to the mother to acquire PRRs automatically. PRRs acquired by virtue of marriage subsist, however, even if the marriage is later found to be voidable.[10] If the marriage is void, but both parties believed in good faith that the purported marriage was valid (whether by error of fact or law), then the father still acquires parental rights under s.3(1)(b).[11]

3–07 So, for example, imagine that John and Jane live together for a year. Jane becomes pregnant by John and gives birth to Jimmy. The couple decide to marry. John acquires PRRs over Jimmy by virtue of, and from the moment of, the marriage, since it has occurred "subsequently" to the conception. If John and Jane now divorce, in principle John's PRRs are unaffected. If *no* award of PRRs is made by the court, then John and Jane will continue to share joint PRRs in respect of Jimmy even after their marriage has been dissolved. However, the court *may* make an order in respect of any children of the marriage which may have the effect of removing some or all of the father's (or mother's) parental rights.[12]

3–08 There is no practical difficulty about the concept that both John and Jane can exercise parental rights. By s.2(2) of the 1995 Act, where two or more persons have any parental right, either can exercise it without the consent of the other (or others). So, for example, Jane can

---

[8] 1995 Act, ss.1 and 2.

[9] 1995 Act, ss.1(2)(a) and 2(7). The exception is the duty to provide guidance to the child in s.1(1)(b)(ii) which continues until the child reaches 18.

[10] 1995 Act, s.3(2)(a). Since the only ground on which a marriage is voidable is the incurable impotence of one of the parties, there are unlikely to be many fathers taking advantage of this subsection.

[11] 1995 Act, s.3(2)(b).

[12] Though as we shall see, the court's preferred starting point will be to make no award—see Ch.4. Prior to the advent of the 1995 Act, awards of exclusive custody to the mother were made in some 90% of Scottish divorces: see Morris, Gibson and Platt, *Untying the Knot: Characteristics of Divorce in Scotland* (1993).

sign a consent form for Jimmy to be given an injection by the school nurse, as an aspect of her parental right to give a legal consent to medical procedures in respect of her child. There is no need for her to consult with John, nor does he have a right to veto her.[13] However, if John is unhappy with her decision he can apply to the court for a "specific issue order" which will allow the court to decide this particular question on the basis of the welfare of the child.[14]

Section 3(1)(b) thus leaves all other parties without automatic **3–09** PRRs. In respect of two groups, grandparents and step-parents, this has become a point of controversy. In both cases, there are arguments for and against the granting of automatic PRRs, or at least some rights, e.g. an automatic right to contact, and this is discussed further below. Parties such as step-parents, grandparents and other relatives can however acquire PRRS using a s.11 court order.

Unmarried Fathers

Historically, Scots law discouraged any legal connection between **3–10** parent and child which sprang from a relation outside marriage, so much so that an illegitimate child was said to be *filius nullius*, nobody's child, unconnected in law to both father and mother. While never an entirely true description,[15] the legislative reform of illegitimacy has removed any differences in the legal relationship of a mother to her child born within or outwith marriage.[16]

Until the Family Law Act 2006, an unmarried father had no auto- **3–11** matic parental rights under any circumstances. This was justified by the Scottish Law Commission in 1984[17] on the basis that (i) to give automatic full rights to unmarried fathers would give rights to fathers even where the child had resulted from a casual liaison or even rape; (ii) many such fathers did not have a continuing relationship with their illegitimate children; (iii) mothers who were not married to the fathers of their children might feel that they were subject to interference and harassment by fathers in the upbringing of the child, and this might cause distress or offence especially where the mother had struggled to bring up the child alone without financial support from the father; and (iv) if fathers were to have automatic rights, they

---

[13] Jane should, however, "have regard" to John's views if she is making a "major decision" concerning parental responsibilities or rights: 1995 Act, s.6(1).

[14] 1995 Act, s.11(2)(e) and (7)—see also paras 3–10 to 3–11.

[15] See Wilkinson and Norrie, para.1.39, who describe it as "inadequate, and in some degree an inept" description. For example, neither father nor mother of an illegitimate child had at common law the right to be its guardian, but the mother had the prima facie right to custody unless a court order was made in favour of someone else. Both father and mother owed the illegitimate child a duty of aliment. It was only in the field of succession that at common law the child had no relationship at all with either father or mother.

[16] See now 1995 Act, s.3(1)(a), as discussed above.

[17] *Report on Illegitimacy*, Scot. Law Com. No.82, para.2.5.

would have to be involved in proceedings relating to the child such as adoption, reception into care, etc. which might unnecessarily protract and complicate such proceedings.

3–12   However, denial of automatic PRRs to unmarried fathers became increasingly hard to justify as a result of a number of social, cultural and legal changes. The nature of child bearing outside of marriage has changed considerably since the early 1980s. Over 40% of children are now born outside wedlock,[18] and while the number of births within marriage is declining, the number outside marriage is increasing. Furthermore, of those children born out of wedlock, most were registered as the child of both parents and in a substantial majority of *these* cases the registration is not only joint, but the parents are listed as at the same address, i.e. one presumes, cohabiting.

3–13   These demographics lent support to claims by unmarried fathers to rights through the mid to late 1990s because they established that in a large number of families, children were being denied the benefit of two parents with legal responsibilities and rights simply because their parents had not entered the institution of marriage. Many children born out of wedlock were clearly not the products of a casual liaison but intended to be the joint responsibility of a settled couple. There has also been a re-assessment of the social role of the father, with a shift from "the stereotyped image of the unmarried father as a social deviant"[19] to the idea that unmarried fathers have something positive to add to the upbringing of their child, an idea reinforced generally by wider acceptance of ideals of joint parenting and shared childcare by the so-called "new father".[20] The early 2000s saw growing pressure from organisations such as Families Need Fathers for more concern to be shown for the rights and needs of fathers.

3–14   Finally, changes in the law of human rights have lent strength to the unmarried father's position. The ECHR, Art.8(1), which guarantees respect for family life, is now incorporated into United Kingdom law by virtue of the Human Rights Act 1998 and Strasbourg jurisprudence indicates a need for the state to take more positive steps to ensure rights for all fathers.[21] The steps taken under the Child Support Act 1991 to enforce the duty on unmarried fathers to pay for

---

[18] 43 % of live births to unmarried parents were registered in Scotland in 2001, 60% of these jointly registered by parents living at the same address (Registrar General for Scotland, *Annual Report* 2001, p.31).

[19] Eekelaar, "Second Thoughts on Illegitimacy Reform" (1985) 15 Family Law 261.

[20] The reality of the contribution of fathers to childcare has, however, been questioned (Bainham, "When is a Parent Not a Parent? Reflections on the Unmarried Father and his Child in English Law" (1988) 3 Int. Jnl. of Law and the Family 208), in an article that is otherwise stridently in favour of rights for unmarried fathers.

[21] Bainham, above. No specific decisions of the European Court of Human Rights have so far actually required states to give full PRRs to all unmarried fathers. However, see, inter alia, *Marckx v Belgium*, ECHR, Series A, No. 31, 18 Y.B. 248, which enjoins states to act in a manner calculated to allow ties between near relatives to develop normally; *McMichael v U.K.*, ECHR, February 24,1995, had an important influence in Scots law in encouraging the Government to have greater

the support of their children also, cynically perhaps, lead to a greater demand for corresponding rights to go with duties of maintenance. Factors such as these influenced the Scottish Law Commission in 1992 to reverse its previous position and assert that "the law discriminates against children born outside marriage by denying them a father with the normal responsibilities and rights".[22] They recommended that both parents should have automatic PRRs.[23]

Giving *all* unmarried fathers full automatic rights was however not the only, nor necessarily the optimum, solution. The demographic figures reveal that some unmarried fathers are likely to be in responsible and stable relationships; others will not be. At the furthest extreme, what the Scottish Law Commission described in 1992 as the "phantom" of the rapist father[24] cannot be dismissed lightly. Many feel that it would be immoral to give a man automatic parental rights in respect of children fathered by his rape, even if in practice he would never be in a position to exercise them.[25] Both the Scottish and English Law Commissions have in the past agreed that the attempt to distinguish "meritorious" from "unmeritorious" fathers, or cohabiting from non-cohabiting fathers, when awarding PRRs, is impractical. **3–15**

The 1995 Act, s.4 compromised by giving unmarried fathers the chance to acquire PRRs, not automatically, but as a result of agreement between the father and mother of the child, either at, or subsequent to, the child's birth. The advantage of this scheme was that rights could not be given to the father against the wishes of the mother, thus reducing the chances of interference and harassment; and, in the nature of things, such agreements were likely to be entered into only by stable couples. A similar model was adopted in contemporaneous English legislation.[26] Under s.4 of the 1995 Act, the child's mother and unmarried father may agree that, from the date of the agreement, the father shall have all the rights and responsibilities of a married father. The agreement must be made in prescribed form[27] and registered in the Books of Council and Session and, once made, is irrevocable. The agreement must be for the transfer of *all* parental rights and responsibilities: it is therefore a condition of s.4 that the mother must not have been deprived of any **3–16**

---

concern for the rights of unmarried fathers within the children's hearing system: see further Ch.8; *Soderback v Sweden* [1999] 1 F.L.R. 250 where the European Court held that the adoption of a child against the wishes of his natural father was a breach of his Art.8 right to respect for family life.

[22] *Report on Family Law*, Scot. Law Com. No.135 (1992), para.2.44.

[23] *ibid.*, para.2.50.

[24] *ibid.*, para.2.47.

[25] See Bainham above, n.20, and Thomson, "Parental Rights and Responsibilities", 1996 S.L.G. 19.

[26] See the Children Act 1989, s.4 as amended by the Adoption and Children Act 2002, s.111.

[27] A statutory form was published for making these agreements under s.4 of the 1995 Act in the Parental Responsibilities and Rights Agreements (Scotland) Regulations 1996 (SI 1996/2549).

parental rights by the courts. The problem however, is that in practice, as in England, it turns out that very few unmarried couples have chosen to avail themselves of s.4: the evidence seems to be that couples do not think to make such agreements while their relationship is still harmonious, and cannot reach agreement once it deteriorates. As a result, the Family Law (Scotland) Act 2006 ("FLSA 2006") now takes a more radical approach.

3–17   The FLSA 2006[28] amended s.3(1)(b) of the 1995 Act so that fathers also acquire automatic PRRs where, although not married to the mother, the father is registered as the child's father under any of the United Kingdom's Acts enabling registration of births, deaths and marriages. Since joint registration requires joint consent by father and mother, this has the advantage of still excluding the father whose mother is opposed to the sharing of PRRs with the father. The provision is not retrospective.[29] Some commentators have suggested that the period immediately after the birth during which the birth must be registered, is an undesirable time during which to ask a woman to decide if she wishes to share parental responsibilities with the father. She is likely to be exhausted, over-burdened, and possibly medically depressed, and it may well be difficult for her to appreciate that registering a birth jointly now has more far-reaching implications than it had in the past. However the new provision brings Scotland into line with England,[30] and it is desirable that issues of status and rights be consistent across the border. It is also possible—though perhaps unusual—for the child to be registered solely by the mother within the post-birth time limit, and the father's name added later, in which case automatic PRRs would flow from that time of registration, so long as that was after the 2006 Act amendments came into force.[31]

Section 11 Applications for Parental Responsibilities and Rights ("PRRs")

3–18   Under s.11 of the 1995 Act, any person without PRRs but claiming interest may make an application to the court for an order in relation to parental responsibilities, rights, guardianship or the administration of a child's property.[32] On such application, the court may make such order as it sees fit, but in particular it may make one of a number of orders specified in s.11(2) including a residence, contact or specific issue order. In deciding whether to grant the order applied for, the court shall: (a) regard the welfare of the child involved as a paramount

---

[28] FLSA 2006, s.23.

[29] *ibid.*, s.23(4).

[30] This provision has been the law in England since December 1, 2003. See the Children Act 1989, s.4 as amended by the Adoption and Children Act 2002.

[31] Confirmed in the Justice 1 Committee Private Briefing Paper on the Family (Scotland) Bill, supplementary note to oral hearing on March 15, 2005.

[32] As long as they have not previously been divested of parental rights. See s.11(3)(a)(i) and para.4–40.

consideration; and (b) shall not make any order unless satisfied that to do so will be better for the child than making no order at all.[33] In other words, the court must be convinced it is better to alter the status quo than to leave it alone. Before making such an order, the court is also instructed to take account of the views of the child concerned, having regard to his age and maturity; a child of 12 or more is presumed to be old enough to form a reasonable view.[34]

Section 11 can thus be used by step-parents[35] and other persons **3–19** such as unmarried fathers still lacking automatic rights[36] to apply for PRRs. It is also possible for a child's parent to prospectively transfer PRRs by nominating a person in writing as the guardian of that child, to act after the death of the nominating parent.[37] So a mother might appoint her new husband, or the unmarried father of her child, the guardian of her child after her death. The parent making the appointment must make it in writing and sign it, and must at the time of his or her death have been the legal representative of the child.

It is interesting to briefly move from the popular acceptance of **3–20** automatic rights for (at least some) unmarried fathers, to the more equivocal status of step-parents. Given the prevalence of divorce and re-marriage it is apparent that the step-family population is large and expanding. In the past, most step-families formed after the death of one parent; now most step-families are the result of re-marriage following divorce. Families may contain a mixture of children from the current relationship with children from one or more previous relationships involving either current partner. (Such families are sometimes known as "reconstituted" families.) Step-parents may informally regard their stepchildren as an integral part of their family unit, but due to their lack of a genetic link, they have no official status and no more rights in respect of these children than any other de facto carer.[38] Many worry about their lack of formal status and how they will manage if the blood parent dies first, leaving them de facto but not *de iure* in charge of children. It is of course possible for step-parents to apply for parental responsibilities under s.11. However, cases decided prior to the 1995 Act showed that the attitude of the courts in Scotland is not favourable to step-parents who attempt to compete for rights with natural parents or even natural relatives of a child. In *Bangham v Bangham*,[39] for example, a stepfather sought custody of his stepson, aged 12, who had been accepted into the

---

[33] s.11(7)(a).

[34] s.11(7)(b) and (10).

[35] Prior to the 1995 Act, such applications could be made under s.3 of the Law Reform (Parent and Child) (Scotland) Act 1986. See *Bangham v Bangham*, 1992 G.W.D. 12-96 (step-father unsuccessfully applied for custody).

[36] See, inter alia, *Sloss v Taylor*, 1989 S.C.L.R. 407 (unmarried father successfully applied for custody); *Stewart v Monaghan*, 1993 Fam. L.B. 2-5.

[37] 1995 Act, s.7. See Ch.6 for a full discussion of guardianship.

[38] See paras 6–08 to 6–09.

[39] 1992 G.W.D. 23-1296.

family on his marriage to the mother over eight years before. The mother contested custody. It was held that since the son remained in contact with his natural father, an award of custody to the stepfather was not appropriate. He was, however, allowed access.

3–21   In *Breingan v Jamieson*,[40] a stepfather was advised his case was too weak even to attempt to dispute the custody of the child of his wife by her former husband, after his wife's untimely death. Instead, custody was fought out between the former husband and the maternal relatives (who won). This categorisation of the stepfather as a poor substitute for a "real", genetic father seems particularly invidious since if a stepfather has accepted his stepchild as a "child of the family" then he is liable to aliment him in the same way as a natural parent would be.[41] Even since the 1995 Act, there seems to have been little shift in this perception of step-parents as a "poor second choice" to blood parents.[42]

3–22   Other options are available to step-parents seeking rights. The most popular option for stepfathers is probably to seek rights by adopting the stepchild jointly with the natural mother. This has problems of its own which are discussed further in Ch.6. More radically, it has been suggested that step-parents should be able to acquire rights without going to court, either through some sort of automatic sharing of rights possessed by the natural parent to whom they are married, or by agreement with the natural parent or parents.[43] Many of the same arguments can apply, as have been discussed in the context of the unmarried father. In its consultation document, *Family Matters*,[44] the SLC suggested in 2004 that step-parents might be able to make an agreement with a natural parent to share parental responsibilities and rights, in a style akin to s.4 of the 1995 Act. The details of such a scheme proved intractably difficult to resolve between all parties, however. Should the making of an agreement require the consent of the other natural parents in all cases? Should one parent who is the sole parent with PRRs (say, a mother not married to the natural father, and not jointly registered as parents) be able to confer such rights on her new partner, *without* the consent of the other natural parent? Should the agreement be terminable by mutual agreement (important given the high rate of second marriage breakdown) or should it only be revocable by a court, or should it be terminable by unilateral notice of the natural parent with PRRs? What happens in

---

[40] 1993 S.L.T. 186.
[41] Family Law (Scotland) Act 1985, s.1(1)(d). However step-parents are not liable to support their stepchildren under the scheme of the Child Support Act 1991.
[42] See evidence from Stepfamily Scotland to Justice 1 Committee Report on the Family (Scotland) Bill, paras 162 *et seq*. It was suggested however that parents can delegate (though not abdicate) PRRs to third parties under s.3(5) of the 1995 Act (though it was also acknowledged that this was little used); furthermore, as noted at para.3–19 above, a step-parent can be named as testamentary guardian by the natural parent.
[43] See Masson, "Old Families Into New: a Status for Step-parents" in *The State, the Law and the Family* (Freeman (ed.), 1984).
[44] Scottish Executive, 2004.

the event of third or fourth re-marriages? What if someone involved in such an agreement *ceases* to be a step-parent, because they divorce the natural parent or are divorced? Such manifold possibilities seemed to threaten a chaos of multiple agreements and frequent court applications. StepFamily Scotland suggested that an agreement be available only to a step-parent who had lived with the family for over two years. In the end however, the proposal was, perhaps regrettably, shelved from the Family Law (Sc) Act 2006.[45]

WHO IS A PARENT?

So far, we have established that although the law will not award 3–23 parental rights to every genetic parent, the establishment of parentage is a first prerequisite. In this section, we will first consider who is a "natural" parent and how parentage, and in particular, paternity, can be proven. The principal statute in this area is the Law Reform (Parent and Child) (Scotland) Act 1986 ("the 1986 Act"). We will go on to consider the new reproductive technologies and what problems they raise in the legal interpretation of who is a mother and who is a father.

Maternity

At common law, there was no dispute that the legal mother was the 3–24 person who gave birth to a child.[46] Motherhood was seen as certain by comparison to the possible uncertainty surrounding paternity.[47] Due to the public nature of pregnancy and birth, doubt infrequently arises which requires proof of the maternity of a child. Conceivably, mix-ups in hospital administrative arrangements may occur, in which case an action to prove maternity might be raised in the shape of a declarator of parentage under s.7 of the 1986 Act. In *Douglas v Duke of Hamilton*,[48] the pursuer sought to prove that he was the son of Lady Jane Douglas and hence the heir to substantial estates. Difficulties arose both because Lady Jane had married in secret at an age well past normal child-bearing years for the time—48 years old—and her pregnancy and delivery had been shrouded in secrecy, observed only by servants and had taken place abroad to avoid the knowledge of her brother. The mother had died before the date of the action. After evidence was brought both as to the mother's capacity to give birth at that age, and as to the gentleness and tenderness she showed her child,

---

[45] In England, however, step-parent agreements were indeed introduced by the Adoption and Children Act 2002, s.112.

[46] And this status of maternity persists even where an assigned gender of male has been adopted by a mother under the Gender Recognition Act 2004—see s.12.

[47] See the maxim from Justinian's *Digest* (D. II, 4, 5): "*mater semper certa est etiamsi vulgo conceperit*" (the mother is always certain even if the son has been conceived in promiscuity).

[48] (1769) 2 Pat. 143.

it was held the evidence established a presumption that the pursuer was her child which the defender was unable to rebut.

Paternity

3–25 Proof of paternity has always represented a problem since wherever more than one man has had sexual access to the mother during the period surrounding the date of conception there is potential uncertainty. Thus the law has developed a number of techniques to assist in establishing paternity. It is important to note that until the advent of the new reproductive techniques there was never any doubt that the father of a child was the genetic father, i.e. the person whose sperm fertilised the egg of the mother.[49] As we have seen above, someone who merely takes the social role of father such as a step-parent or new partner of the mother has not been regarded legally as a father. Because of this, until scientific tests were developed based on analysis of blood or body tissue, approaches to proving paternity had to rely on inferring proof of the genetic link from circumstantial evidence.

Proof of Paternity: Presumptions

3–26 Because of the inherent uncertainty attached to paternity, and social approval of legitimate birth, the law has always presumed certain persons to be fathers until proven otherwise. This is done by the device of legal presumptions. All legal presumptions of paternity are now found within s.5 of the 1986 Act. A person who has the benefit of such a legal presumption will be regarded in law as the father and anyone seeking to rebut this will have to prove the contrary on a balance of probabilities,[50] i.e. the normal civil standard.

Presumption Arising by Virtue of Marriage

3–27 The most important s.5 presumption is found in s.5(1)(a) and states that a man shall be presumed to be the father of a child,

> "if he was married to the mother of the child at any time in the period beginning with the conception and ending with the birth of the child".

For this purpose, a void, voidable or irregular marriage will have the same effect as a valid and regular marriage.[51]

---

[49] As in n.64 above, it should be noted that status as a father is not disturbed if that person adopts an assigned gender as a woman under the Gender Recognition Act 2004—see s.12.

[50] 1986 Act, s.5(4).

[51] *ibid.*, s.5(2). If a woman married Mr A, then bigamously went through a marriage ceremony with Mr B, then it follows logically that both Messrs A and B would have the benefit of a s.5(1)(a) presumption, since it arises from the void second marriage as well as the valid first one. In such a case, a literal reading would suggest the two presumptions would cancel each other out. One suspects that in practice the claim of the legal husband would be preferred.

This is a statutory re-enactment of the common-law presumption **3-28** that *pater est quem nuptiae demonstrant*, i.e. "the father is shown by the marriage" or the mother's husband is presumed to be the father of a child born during the marriage. Section 5(1)(a) is more extensive than the common law presumption, however, in that it presumes that a man is the father of the child if he marries the mother at any time before the child is born.[52]

The s.5(1)(a) presumption can be rebutted on the balance of prob- **3-29** abilities. This is an important alteration from the common law presumption which could only be rebutted by evidence beyond reasonable doubt. This was because a finding that the presumption was rebutted was equivalent to a finding that a married woman had had intercourse with a man not her husband, i.e. had committed adultery, which was at one time a criminal offence. A successful rebuttal of the presumption also implied that the child was illegitimate, a finding the courts have historically been reluctant to make. However, now that the legal disabilities associated with, and the whole status of, illegitimacy, have been removed from Scots law[53] there is no reason not to use the normal civil standard of proof. Given that it was virtually impossible in pre-1986 Act cases to rebut the *pater est* presumption unless the husband had had almost no possibility of access at the approximate time of conception,[54] common law cases are poor guides to the modern law on what sort of evidence is necessary to rebut the presumption on the balance of probabilities.

In any case, as we will see below, the use of scientific tests to estab- **3-30** lish paternity has now made it possible in most paternity cases to give a virtually definitive rather than probabilistic answer to who the father is. Consequently, standard of proof sufficient to rebut the presumption is no longer the major issue it once was.[55] Instead, the focus of argument has shifted to whether it is in the interests of the various parties and especially the child, to allow the use of these tests, and what inferences should be drawn from them if they are used: we will come back to these points below.[56]

---

[52] At common law, a man was not legally presumed to be the father if he married a pregnant woman, only if the child was born during the duration of the marriage. However, there was a presumption of fact (not law) that where there had been an "avowed and open courtship" of a man by a woman who subsequently fell pregnant, and he then subsequently married her, that he was the father (*Gardner v Gardner* (1876) 3 R. 695).

[53] See Ch.5.

[54] See, e.g. *Ramsay v Ramsay's Curator ad litem*, 1986 S.L.T. 590, the last case decided prior to the coming into force of the 1986 Act, in which it was stated that "nothing less than completely satisfactory evidence can be sufficient".

[55] Few paternity cases have been reported since the 1986 Act came into force which have not turned upon scientific tests, and in even fewer has evidence been lead to rebut a s.5(1)(a) presumption; see, however, *Campbell v Grossart*, 1988 G.W.D. 24-1004, where the s.5(1)(a) presumption of paternity of the husband was not rebutted by the child pursuer.

[56] See paras 3–51 to 3–56.

3–31   It is important to realise that s.5(1)(a) does not operate where a child is both conceived and born before the mother enters a marriage. Hence, where a couple cohabit and the woman has a child, the male partner will not be presumed father under s.5(1)(a) even if they subsequently marry. No legal presumption arises simply because a man is cohabiting or associating with a woman at a time when she conceives or gives birth.

Presumption Arising by Acknowledgment and Registration

3–32   However, the law does implicitly pay some recognition to the type of case where the father of a child, although not married to the mother, can be clearly identified from the circumstances of the parents.

3–33   Section 5(1)(b) of the 1986 Act provides that a man shall be presumed to be the father of a child if: (i) both he and the mother have acknowledged that he is the father; and (ii) he has been registered as such in the appropriate Register of Births, Deaths and Marriages.[57] Normally, both of these requirements will be combined in one in the shape of the declarations the parents must make before a man who is not the husband can be registered as the father of a child. It is, of course, possible for these steps to be taken at a time when the mother is still legally married to another man. In such a case, where a man already has the benefit of the s.5(1)(a) presumption, s.5(1)(b) does not operate; hence, in such a situation the only man who gains the benefit of a presumption of paternity is the husband (or ex-husband) and there is no possibility of conflict.

3–34   Section 5(1)(b) is clearly intended to extend the benefit of the presumption of parentage to cohabiting couples but it is important to note that legally its scope is quite different. The presumption is based not on evidence of co-residence but on joint acknowledgment and registration. Generally, an unmarried father can only be registered as such if he makes a joint request with the mother, which requires her assent and his presence at the registry office.[58] Thus, even if a couple are cohabiting, the father may not be registered through the mother's hostility to the idea, his indifference or general inconvenience. Contrarily, 60 per cent of extra-marital births are registered jointly by parents who live at the same address.[59]

3–35   As with s.5(1)(a), this presumption can be rebutted by evidence on the balance of probabilities.

---

[57] Note that this is in line with the familiar rule that a man's name on the birth certificate does not prove he is father, but there is *a presumption* that he is father.

[58] Registration of Births, Deaths and Marriages (Scotland) Act 1965, s.18. It is possible for either a mother or father acting alone to register the child born out of wedlock as the child of a particular father by taking along statutory declarations by both the mother and the man in question that he is the father of the child; but in practice such types of registration are numerically small.

[59] Registrar General for Scotland, Annual Report, 2001, p.31.

Presumption from Prior Decree of Declarator of Parentage

If a judicial finding that X is the father of a particular child is made **3–36** in an action for decree of declarator of parentage,[60] then it gives rise to a legal presumption that X is father whenever the issue is raised in the future.[61] This presumption takes precedence over any other presumption arising from marriage or registration or a prior court decree.

Proof of Paternity: Scientific and Other Evidence

If the presumptions above do not apply or if the facts of paternity **3–37** are nonetheless disputed, then the matter must be resolved by evidence. The question of paternity may be resolved by raising an action for decree of declarator of parentage or non-parentage (under s.7 of the 1986 Act) or may arise as an incidental question within other proceedings such as an action for divorce, aliment, or parental rights or responsibilities.[62] The standard of proof in proceedings to establish or deny parentage is the normal civil standard of the balance of probabilities.

Scientific Tests: Blood Groups and DNA Profiles

The most useful evidence in modern paternity proceedings is **3–38** undoubtedly that gathered from scientific tests, such as blood tests or "DNA profiling". These tests attempt to discern if a man, or one of several men, is the genetic father of the child in question. Originally, the attitude of Scots law to the use of blood tests was hostile. Blood tests work on the well-known basis that a person's blood has characteristics which distinguish it from the blood of other people. Typically, blood types fall into the groups O, A, B or AB, although there are many more subtle classifications. Since the genes responsible for these blood types are inherited from parents, an analysis can be done comparing the blood of the child and both parents. Such a blood group analysis is not well suited to establishing paternity, however, because in principle it provides only an exclusionary result, i.e. it can establish that a man could *not* be the father but not conclusively that he must be (since there are many persons who share a single blood group typing). Thus, the consequence of blood group testing in a paternity

---

[60] Under s.7.

[61] s.5(3).

[62] 1986 Act, s.7(5). Only declarators of parentage or non-parentage can be sought; decorators of legitimacy, illegitimacy and legitimation were abolished by the Family Law (Scotland) Act 2006, s.21(2). The declarator can be raised in the Sheriff Court or Court of Session if any of the child or alleged or presumed parent was domiciled in Scotland, or habitually resident for one year or born in Scotland or the sheriffdom, as appropriate. A "presumed" parent is one with the benefit of a presumption of parentage under s.5 of the 1986 Act. Declarator can be asked for independently or as an ancillary order in other relevant proceedings (s.7(5)). It is possible to seek declarator after the child has died: s.7(2)(c).

case may be that a child is proven to have no known father, and if a presumption of paternity of the husband is rebutted, then the child may also be rendered illegitimate. Given these factors, and also the fact that early blood tests were invasive and relatively unreliable, the Scottish courts took the view early on that no-one should be compellable by the courts to undergo tests, or to give consent for anyone else to do so.[63] It was held in *Whitehall v Whitehall*[64] that to subject a person to a blood test against their will would be to force them to undergo a surgical operation against their will, albeit a minor one, and so would constitute an "unwarrantable invasion of private rights".

3–39   As blood testing became more refined, however, the lack of a power to order the taking the blood samples became less justifiable. Judicial opposition to the use of blood tests had declined[65] but courts were still constrained by the principle in *Whitehall*. The debate was brought to a head by the commercial availability of a new type of scientific test known as DNA testing or DNA finger-printing. DNA is genetic material found in all human body tissue, not just blood. A sample of body tissue from a human body can be processed to produce a DNA profile, which is a pattern of bands resembling the bar-code found widely on supermarket goods. A DNA profile is highly individual, unlike a blood group, hence the comparison to fingerprints. By comparing DNA profiles from a child, the mother and one or more possible fathers, it is possible to say with an extremely high degree of probability—verging on certainty[66]—that a certain person positively is the father of a particular child. Thus, a positive as opposed to an exclusionary result can be derived. Since DNA tests can be done using any bodily tissue, such as hair or nails, rather than just blood, they are a less invasive procedure than blood tests, particularly for young children.

3–40   Clearly, DNA evidence, freely available in paternity cases, could contribute a great deal in terms of a speedy, reliable and cheap means to determine the action. However, initially it remained open to the parties to refuse to give a sample. In *Torrie v Turner*[67] the Inner House held that the principle in *Whitehall* applied to DNA testing. Lord Mayfield reluctantly conceded that the law had not changed because of the advent of a conclusive method of testing such as DNA testing. The matter might have gone to the House of Lords had legislation not intervened.

---

[63] We refer here, of course, to civil proceedings only.

[64] 1958 S.C. 252. See also *Imre v Mitchell*, 1958 S.C. 439.

[65] See, e.g. *Docherty v McGlynn*, 1983 S.L.T. 645; *Allardyce v Johnston*, 1979 S.L.T. (Sh. Ct.) 54.

[66] It was said in *Torrie v Turner*, 1990 S.L.T. 718 that DNA evidence as to paternity was "beyond statistical doubt" (Lord Mayfield, at p.719L). However, in criminal proceedings where a prosecution will fail if a reasonable doubt as to guilt is raised, there have been attempts to rebut the accuracy of particular instances of DNA testing: see MacDonald, "DNA profiling—Less Than the Whole Truth?", 1990 S.L.T. (News) 285.

[67] 1990 S.L.T. 718.

The Law Reform (Miscellaneous Provisions) (Scotland) Act 1990, **3–41** s.70(1)(a) now makes it plain that in any civil proceedings, the court may request a party[68] to proceedings to provide a sample of blood, or other body fluid, or of body tissue, for the purpose of blood or DNA tests. The use of the word "may" makes it clear that the court has a discretion whether to choose to make such a request and will not do so in every paternity case. The court may make this request either on the application of one of the parties, or of their own volition.

However, the civil liberties argument, which was so strong in the **3–42** early history of blood test cases, has not been entirely abandoned. If a request is made, and the party it is addressed to does not comply, then they will not under the present law be physically compelled to undergo tests, nor be rendered in contempt of court, which could result in imprisonment pending compliance, as both of these were felt to be unacceptable sanctions in civil proceedings.[69] Instead, following the model of parallel English legislation,[70] if a party to whom a request has been made does not comply, then the court may draw such adverse inference, if any, as seems appropriate, taking into account the subject matter of the proceedings.[71]

Consent on Behalf of a Child

Section 70 also deals with the case where consent to the taking of **3–43** a sample must be given on behalf of a child. As we saw in Ch.2, a child under 16 has no capacity in theory to give a consent to any legal transaction,[72] including a consent to the taking of a blood or body tissue sample for the purpose of paternity tests. However by s.2(4) of the Age of Legal Capacity (Scotland) Act 1991, a child may have capacity to consent to giving a sample if they are "capable of understanding the nature and possible consequences of the procedure", in the opinion of a qualified medical practitioner. There will, therefore, be two classes of children: those who are capable of understanding

---

[68] A party under s.70 includes an executor, even if this is someone other than a relative, such as a solicitor (*Mackay v Murphy*, 1995 S.L.T. (Sh. Ct.) 30, in which the sheriff commented "It may be difficult but one should eventually be able to get blood out of a solicitor"). It does not however include a curator *ad litem* appointed to an adult incapax defender in a paternity action—see *Cameron v Carr*, 1997 S.C.L.R. (Notes) 1165. However the sheriff in that case ingeniously suggested that instead, in such a case, the court could supply consent to the taking of a sample under s.6(3) of the Law Reform (Parent and Child) (Scotland) Act 1986 (see para.3–45 below.)

[69] See *Blood Group Tests, DNA and Related Matters*, Scot. Law Com. Discussion Paper No.80 (1988) and subsequent report (Scot. Law Com. No.120 (1989)).

[70] Family Law Reform Act 1987, Pt III; prior to this legislative change English law also forbade the court to order a person to undergo blood tests (*S v S* [1972] A.C. 24).

[71] 1990 Act, s.70(2). This resolves doubt as to whether the court had power to draw adverse inferences at common law—see *Docherty v McGlynn* above (n.84); *cf.* Lord Mayfield in *Torrie v Turner*, 1990 S.L.T. 718 who felt such a power had to be provided by Parliament.

[72] Age of Legal Capacity (Scotland) Act 1991, ss.1(1)(a) and 9(d). See Ch.2 for a fuller discussion of children's capacity.

the nature and consequences of giving a blood or DNA sample for the purpose of determining parentage; and those who are not. Under s.70(1)(a), a request may be made to a child in the first class to provide a sample if they are a party to the proceedings.[73] It is hard to see though what adverse inference can usefully be drawn if a child refuses to give a sample, as he may be as much in the dark about his origins as anyone else.

3–44 However, if it is desired to take a sample from a child in the second class, i.e. a non-competent child, then legal consent must be given by a person who has power to supply that consent. If such a person is unwilling to assist by providing consent to taking a sample, then under s.70(1)(b) of the Law Reform (Miscellaneous Provisions) (Scotland) Act 1990 the court can request them to do so.[74] As with any other s.70 request, if consent is not then given, an adverse inference may be drawn if appropriate.

3–45 Who then has power to give a legal consent to the taking of a sample on behalf of an incompetent child? By s.6(2) of the Law Reform (Parent and Child) (Scotland) Act 1986, any person having parental responsibility for a child under 16, or care and control of such a child, may give consent.[75] If no such person exists, or if such a person exists but it is not reasonably practicable to obtain a consent from him, or he is unwilling to accept the responsibility of giving or withholding consent, then the court may give that consent.[76] If the court supplies a consent in one of these circumstances, then it must first be satisfied that the taking of the sample would not be detrimental to the child's health; it is very unlikely this will be the case with modern DNA testing, which need not involve the collection of blood. Note that there is no inherent overriding power in the court to give a consent on behalf of a child just because the person with parental responsibility does not *wish* to supply this evidence. Instead, the correct procedure when consent is refused is to ask the court to make a s.70(1)(b) request, and if this is refused, to draw the appropriate adverse inference.

3–46 A difficult chicken-and-egg problem arises where presumptive fathers enter actions to assert or deny their own paternity. A married man is presumed to be the father of his child by s.5(1)(a) (so long as the child was either conceived or born during the course of the marriage) and is also therefore presumed to have parental responsibility

---

[73] They may well not be. For the child's right to be given notice of proceedings concerning him or her, see para.4–58.

[74] Again, so long as they are a party to the proceedings.

[75] This is probably an extension of the common law position prior to the 1986 Act under which the right to give a legal consent to the taking of a sample was an aspect of the parental right of guardianship only. A curator *ad litem* appointed to safeguard the interests of a child in paternity litigation cannot give consent on behalf of the child: *Docherty v McGlynn*, 1983 S.L.T. 645 at 647.

[76] s.6(3).

and rights by virtue of s.3(1)(b) of the 1995 Act. Should such a presumptive father be able to give a consent for a sample to be taken from the child in question, if his own paternity is what is actually in dispute?

This problem arose in the leading Inner House case of *Docherty v McGlynn*.[77] Here, the mother of a child had died before the action was raised. At the date of her child's conception and birth, the mother was married to McGlynn, who was therefore the presumptive father by virtue of marriage. However, the mother had left the father and taken up living with her lover, Docherty, before the birth of the child. Docherty raised an action of declarator to establish that he was the father of her child and not McGlynn. He had de facto care of the child, and he had also been registered as the child's father at its birth. McGlynn sought to defend his paternity using blood test evidence. The principal issue in the case was whether McGlynn, as the presumptive father had the right to give a legal consent to the taking of a sample for blood tests from the child. If not, this evidence would be unavailable. **3–47**

It was held that the presumptive father retained the right to give a legal consent in respect of a child unless and until that presumption was rebutted by contrary proof. A mere challenge to that paternity did not in any way deprive such a father of the right to exercise his rights and powers. In fact, a presumptive father is required to go on fulfilling his parental responsibilities unless and until the presumption of paternity is rebutted. **3–48**

In *Docherty*, the presumptive father was attempting to uphold his own presumed paternity. But what if (as will more often be the case) he had been attempting to *disprove* it? It was suggested obiter by Lord Emslie in *Docherty*,[78] commenting on the case of *Imre v Mitchell*,[79] that a husband seeking to deny the paternity of a child born to his wife, cannot rely on his own right to consent to the taking of blood samples from that child. Lord Cameron was concerned, that the child's interests might be prejudiced, since the effect of a successful challenge by a husband denying paternity would be to render the child illegitimate, which was still a stigma that might cause pain and distress. It has been argued forcefully[80] since *Docherty* that the legislative and social stigmata of illegitimacy have been so reduced since 1983 that it is no longer a justification for restricting access to blood tests. However, the matter remains unresolved and there has been recent support for Lord Cameron's views on the remaining stigma of illegitimacy, notwithstanding the changes in the law, in *Smith v Greenhill*.[81] It can only be definitively **3–49**

---

[77] 1983 S.L.T. 645.
[78] At p.647.
[79] 1958 S.L.T. 57.
[80] See Thomson (4th edn, 2002), p.180.
[81] 1993 S.C.L.R. 776, *per* Sheriff Craik at p.777C.

said that *Docherty* stands as authority for the proposition that a presumptive father has a right to give a consent to blood or DNA tests on his child, so long as he is seeking to uphold not deny his paternity.[82] Now that the status of illegitimacy has been entirely abolished however,[83] it is hard to see a court taking this line of reasoning seriously.

3–50 It is submitted in any case that the question of how the outcome of blood or DNA tests may affect the welfare of the child is one that should be considered only after the question has been settled of whether a legal consent to the taking of the sample exists. There is no requirement under s.6 that a person with parental responsibilities must take into account the welfare of the child when deciding whether to give or withhold consent, let alone regard it as paramount. Such a requirement would be unworkable since the interests of adult parties involved in actions either to deny or affirm parentage are very different from the interests of the children involved. The paradigm paternity action, for example, is probably one in which a man denies he is the father of a particular child in order to avoid financial responsibility. The father's interest is not in the welfare of the child but in his own financial affairs. A paternity action is not an action relating to parental responsibilities or rights[84] (although decisions about parental rights may flow from it) and so the welfare of the child is not the paramount consideration. On the other hand, the court does and should maintain an interest in the welfare of the child in paternity proceedings. They have an undoubted power in the exercise of their protective jurisdiction to exclude evidence derived from blood or DNA tests where to admit it would be against the interests of the child.[85] However, this power is separable from the issue of who can give a legal consent. It is in essence a question of discretionary exclusion of evidence.

Making a s.70 Request

3–51 Two further questions arise from the 1990 legislation. First, given the court has a discretion to make a request to a party to provide a DNA sample under s.70, when will they exercise that discretion? Secondly, if a request is made and the party refuses to comply, what "adverse inferences", if any, are likely to be drawn? Similar issues of policy are raised in both cases.

---

[82] In *Petrie v Petrie*, 1993 S.C.L.R. 392 (discussed below at para.3–52) a husband, seeking to rebut the presumption of paternity, asked the court to make a s.70 request to his wife to give her consent to the taking of a sample from the third child of their marriage. If there was certainty that a presumptive father could give such a consent to *disprove* his own paternity, there would have been no reason for him to make such a request.

[83] Family Law (Scotland) Act 2006, s.21.

[84] See *Soutar v Kilroe*, 1994 S.C.L.R. 757.

[85] See *Docherty v McGlynn*, 1983 S.L.T. 645, especially *per* Lord Cameron at p.650.

In Petrie v Petrie[86] a husband sought to deny paternity of the third **3–52** child of his wife in the course of their divorce proceedings. He asked the court to request his wife to consent to the taking of a sample of blood from their daughter under s.70. The wife argued that no request should be made, on the grounds, inter alia, that: (i) the request if granted might result in the child being found to be illegitimate; and (ii) the husband should not be allowed to seek to rebut his own presumed paternity on grounds of "mere suspicion". Rejecting the wife's arguments, the court held that if it were to refuse to make a request for a DNA sample, it would be blinding itself to a clear and relevant piece of evidence. The father already had doubts about paternity and it was better for these to be resolved than for the presumption of paternity to be preserved artificially. It would always be in the interests of the parties and usually in the interests of the child for the truth to be ascertained.

The argument in *Petrie* is fundamentally about whether it is always **3–53** best for the truth about parentage to be known or whether there are circumstances in which it may be best for it not to be revealed, or at least, not explored. In *Docherty*[87] the First Division were conscious that a "difficult and delicate" balance had to be struck between the desirability of achieving truth through litigation, which requires that the best evidence should be available, and the preservation of the interests of the child. On the whole though, they were convinced that the interests of the child are usually best met by establishing certainty rather than by withholding the truth.[88] Lord Emslie remarked that "The very worst that could happen to this child is that she may be left in a state of uncertainty upon a matter of vital importance in her life".

But what if there is good reason to believe that the child's interests **3–54** will not be best met by revealing the truth? Thomson suggests that it is no longer a good enough reason to obstruct the truth about paternity emerging that a child who was presumed legitimate may be rendered illegitimate. On the other hand, he suggests that exceptional circumstances might justify this, such as that the child might be revealed as the product of an incestuous relationship.[89] In ordinary life, what seems of great concern is not revelations about the history of the child's origins but how the disclosure of paternity is likely to affect their present day-to-day care. In *Docherty*, however the facts about paternity turned out, the child was guaranteed a loving father. In *Petrie*, the parents were in any case already at the divorce courts. In *Smith v Greenhill*,[90] however, disclosures about paternity threatened the child's security within an established family unit. In this case,

---

[86] 1993 S.C.L.R. 391.
[87] At this time the court had no statutory power to request blood or DNA samples.
[88] In constructing this balance the First Division drew upon the English House of Lords case of *S v S* [1972] A.C. 24.
[89] Thomson (4th edn, 2002), p.180.
[90] 1993 S.C.L.R. 944.

Mrs Greenhill had had an affair of uncertain length with Smith, but had throughout the affair remained living with and (it was proven) having sexual relations with her husband, by whom she already had two children. Mrs Greenhill conceived another child who was registered as the child of her husband, who was also the presumptive father by s.5(1)(a) of the 1986 Act. Smith sought to establish his paternity of the child so he could apply for access rights. The wife wanted nothing to do with Smith by this stage. The court agreed to make a request for a DNA sample to be taken from Mrs Greenhill but she refused to comply. The question then arose as to what adverse inference should be drawn by the court. The court chose *only* to infer that Mrs Greenhill had not been telling the whole truth about the extent and duration of her relationship with Smith. This, on the facts, was not enough to rebut the husband's presumption of paternity and so Smith lost the case. On appeal, the decision was upheld but it was admitted that if there had been no husband in the picture with a presumption of paternity, a more damning inference might have been drawn.

3–55   *Smith* resembles the English Court of Appeal case of *Re F*[91] in which the facts were very similar. The child in that case was being brought up as the child of the mother and her husband and the court agreed that it would do the child no good to allow the mother's former lover access to DNA tests to prove his paternity. Balcombe L.J. said that,

> "Anything that may disturb . . . the stability of that family unit within which [the child] has lived since her birth is likely to be detrimental to [her] welfare".

But this, again, is not the whole story. In recent years, the need of a child to know the truth about his or her genetic origins and if necessary, to explore them, has been stressed in the adoption context.[92] If such a psychological need exists, it should apply equally here. Knowing who one's true father is does not *necessarily* mean that the relationship with a social father need be prejudiced.[93] If the child's welfare is to be explored when deciding whether to make a s.70 request, or what adverse inferences should be drawn, then the long-term psychological welfare as well as the short-term material welfare should be considered.[94]

3–56   *Smith* also establishes that the court is not bound to draw any adverse inference when a s.70 request is not complied with if it feels it is not appropriate to do so.[95] This might arise, for example, where a person refuses to give a sample of blood, because of religious scru-

---

[91] [1993] F.L.R. 598.

[92] See Tresiliotis, *In Search of Origins: the Experience of Adopted People* (1973) and para.6.70. The need to know one's genetic heritage is also recognised to a limited extent in relation to children born via egg or sperm donation: see paras 3.97–3.98.

[93] Of course it may do: see, e.g. *Watson v Watson*, 1994 S.C.L.R. 1097.

[94] See further, pursuing this argument Fortin, "*Re F*: the Gooseberry Bush Approach" (1994) 57 M.L.R. 296.

[95] *Smith v Greenhill*, 1993 S.C.L.R. 944, *per* Sheriff Principal Nicholson at p.948B.

ples, fear of contracting HIV infection or needle phobia. Since DNA tests do not usually require the taking of blood, however, these are unlikely scenarios.

Other Evidence

If, for some reason, DNA or blood test evidence is not available **3–57** then it may still be necessary to use other types of more circumstantial evidence to try to establish paternity. In the past, evidence was often lead to try to establish that the pursuer could not have been the father because around the estimated date of conception he did not have sexual access to the mother of the child. These claims are based on establishing that if the pursuer had been the father, then given his dates of access, the gestation period of the child would have been either abnormally short or abnormally long. Because of the very high standard of proof required in the past to rebut the presumption of paternity, the courts have allowed some extremely unlikely periods of gestation as possible. In *Preston-Jones v Preston-Jones*,[96] for example, the court was willing to believe that a child was the legitimate child of the husband even though this implied a gestation period of either 360 days or 186 days and the child had the appearance of an ordinary full-term baby. It is unlikely a modern court would accept such a story given the change to proof on the balance of probabilities.[97]

Many other facts will be relevant evidence in a paternity dispute. In **3–58** the past, evidence has been lead as to the mother's opportunity to have sexual relations with other men, her actings around the time of conception, the opinions of friends and relatives, and so forth. The naming of a father on the birth certificate of a child is of evidential use but is in no way conclusive as the certificate is a record of birth not parentage. It is not significant where a woman has an equal chance of conceiving by either of two men that one is her regular boyfriend or partner.[98]

ASSISTED PARENTHOOD

We turn now to the question of assisted parenthood and the law. It is **3–59** useful here to survey briefly what types of treatments for infertility are available and what kind of major legal issues arise.[99] We will then

---

96 1951 A.C. 391. See also *Currie v Currie*, 1950 S.C. 10.

97 A modern case in which abnormal gestation period evidence was used is *Wilson v Currie*, 1991 G.W.D. 14-872; 300 days accepted as not impossibly long.

98 *Robertson v Hutchison*, 1935 S.C. 708, where the mother had sex in one night with both her boyfriend and another man. No finding of paternity could be made. Of course if one had been her husband, then because of the presumption of paternity he would have been found to be the father.

99 There is a vast literature about the legal and ethical implications of the new reproductive techniques. As an introduction see Mason and McCall-Smith, *Law and Medical Ethics* (7th edn, 2005); Douglas, *Law, Fertility and Reproduction* (1991); *Legal Issues in Human Reproduction* (Maclean (ed.), 1989); *Law Reform and Human*

examine three general issues: how do the new techniques affect the definitions of who is a legal parent; what kinds of person should have access to parentage via these treatments; and what rights do children produced by these techniques have to discover their genetic origins?

Artificial Insemination

3–60 Artificial insemination involves the injection into a woman of sperm collected from a male donor. A woman may be artificially inseminated with the sperm of her husband or partner as a treatment where, for example, infertility derives from the man's low sperm count. This type of treatment (known as artificial insemination by husband[1] or AIH) is merely a mechanical variation on natural insemination and as such has few legal implications.[2] On the other hand, if a man cannot produce sperm or if his sperm cannot successfully fertilise his wife or partner, then artificial insemination by donor (AID[3]) may be the answer.[4] AID was originally a controversial method of treatment in the context of use by, primarily, married couples, since the use of third-party donor semen was seen as akin to adultery. However, it was established in *MacLennan v MacLennan*[5] that AID could not be regarded as adultery since that required a sexual act involving penetration of the female by the male organ. The use of AID by a married woman without the consent of her husband will however probably constitute unreasonable behaviour and therefore be grounds for divorce.[6]

3–61 AID has been available as an NHS treatment since 1968 and since that time has become morally uncontroversial but has nevertheless remained shrouded in secrecy. Male infertility has been regarded as a stigma and something to be hidden. Sperm donations have traditionally been made by anonymous donors (though this is changing—see below) and in many or most cases in the past, the husband or other "social" father has been falsely registered as the father on the birth certificate rather than the genetic donor (for obvious reasons it is hard

---

Reproduction (Maclean (ed.), 1992). For a feminist perspective especially; see the essays in *Reproductive Technologies: Gender, Motherhood and Medicine* (Stanworth (ed.), 1987).

[1] Artificial insemination treatment may be sought by unmarried couples but the acronym is a useful one.

[2] AIH can raise issues when it is used as a means to try and select in advance the sex of a child. Such approaches are currently not wholly perfected but already raise issues of eugenics, medical ethics and abortion as family planning. See Mason and McCall-Smith above (n.99), p.75.

[3] An increasingly common alternative term for this is DI (Donor Insemination) which avoids confusion with Auto Immune Deficiency Syndrome (AIDS).

[4] Couples may hedge their bets by attempting treatment using insemination with sperm from husband and donor (AIHD). This may be regarded for legal purposes as equivalent to AID.

[5] 1958 S.C. 105.

[6] Divorce (Scotland) Act 1976, s.1(2)(b).

to give statistics). The main legal problem arising out of AID is who should be regarded as the father of the child—the "social" father or the sperm donor? This problem is now addressed in the Human Fertilisation and Embryology Act 1990 (hereafter "the HFEA 1990") discussed below.

In vitro Fertilisation

AID is a relatively cheap and painless technique and has been in use **3–62** since at least 1884. Treatment for female infertility is generally more difficult and has arrived much more recently on the scene. *In vitro* fertilisation (IVF) is a form of treatment for female infertility in which the human egg (or ovum) is fertilised outside of the womb, in a petri dish, and then re-implanted. Where a woman has blocked fallopian tubes, for example, the removal of one of her own eggs, fertilising it with her husband's sperm, and implanting it back into the womb will be a way to avoid the physical blockage. This is akin to AIH in creating no real problems as to legal parentage.[7] On the other hand, it may be that the woman cannot produce eggs to be implanted, or that her ovaries have been removed as cancerous. In cases like these, egg or ovum donation from another woman may be the answer. The egg donated may be fertilised with sperm of the husband or regular partner of the woman who is being treated, and the fertilised egg or embryo created re-implanted into the infertile woman's womb. The result of this ovum donation is that the woman who bears the child—the "gestational mother"—is a different person from the woman who supplied the genetic material—the "genetic mother". It is possible in this kind of scenario that the husband or partner of the woman undergoing treatment may also be infertile, in which case ovum donation may be combined with the use of third-party donated sperm. Here the embryo implanted is composed of genetic material entirely from donors other than the couple seeking to have a baby at the end of the day. (This is sometimes known as embryo donation or transfer.) In this case we effectively combine the problems of parentage of AID with those of ovum donation.[8]

IVF, unlike AID, has never been regarded at any stage of its devel- **3–63** opment as an inherently immoral or stigmatised practice. However, as we shall see below, the legal regulation of IVF is affected by the social context in which it is used.

Surrogacy is in many ways an odd companion to the two techniques **3–64** discussed above, since it is neither a medical technique to combat physical infertility, nor does it require any kind of essential technology, nor is it particularly new. However, the perceived need to regulate surrogacy arrangements has had an important inter-relationship with

---

[7] This was the treatment used to create the original "test tube baby", Louise Brown, in 1978.
[8] This may sound like a remote possibility. However, it has been estimated this might apply to as many as one in every 100 marriages where children are sought.

the regulation of other infertility techniques. Surrogacy is as old as the Bible, which furnishes a good example of its use. When Rachel could not give Jacob, her husband, a child, he had intercourse with her hand-maid and by that means acquired two sons.[9] Jacob had no option but to resort to natural intercourse, but the techniques of AID, and, in particular, ovum donation, have made surrogacy a much more attractive option in the last decade or so.

3–65 If a couple (the "commissioning parents") wish to commission a child from a surrogate mother, then it is possible that the surrogate may be inseminated by the commissioning husband using AID, thus avoiding natural intercourse. It is also possible for the commissioning mother to donate an egg, which can be fertilised with the sperm of the commissioning husband, and the resulting embryo implanted into the surrogate mother. Such an exercise in total surrogacy has been evocatively labelled "womb-leasing" and though it is medically identical as a technique to embryo donation discussed above, it raises very different issues of policy, since it is not the gestating mother but the commissioning mother who intends to be the social parent.

3–66 Both these enhancements to old-fashioned surrogacy have made it a growth area, especially in the USA. However, even in the United Kingdom, reportedly 157 children had been born as of 1996 via surrogacy with the help of one non-commercial surrogacy agency, Childlessness Overcome Through Surrogacy (COTS). Surrogacy can be seen as an effective treatment for the infertility of women who cannot bear a child to term, e.g. because they have had a hysterectomy. In the United Kingdom, however, the governmental attitude to surrogacy has oscillated between panic, hostility and indifference. There are a great many complicated arguments surrounding the morality or otherwise of surrogacy.[10] Surrogacy is seen as ethically dubious because it tends to involve a commercial relationship between would-be parents and the mother of a child. Surrogacy is sometimes seen as akin to adoption, and a commercial surrogacy contract as akin to baby-selling, which is outlawed in most countries out of concern for the welfare of the child. Looking at the welfare of the surrogate mother, surrogacy is seen as exploitative, especially as research reveals that many surrogates are on low incomes or unemployed.[11]

3–67 On the other hand, surrogacy can be seen as empowering women by giving them an alternative wage-earning capacity. In many ways, these arguments parallel the debate about female prostitution. Finally, when surrogacy agreements go wrong the practical difficulties can be enormous. In the nature of such agreements there is a

---

[9] Genesis 30:1–6.

[10] There is another body of literature focusing specifically on surrogacy. In addition to the sources above, see especially the Warnock Report which laid the ground work for the HFEA 1990: Report of the Committee of Inquiry into Human Fertilisation and Embryology Cmnd.9314 (1984), Ch.8.

[11] Parker, "Motivation of Surrogate Mothers: Initial Findings" (1983) 140 American Journal of Psychiatry 117.

risk that the surrogate will decide to keep the child (or try to) and then issues such as parentage, parental rights and responsibility and financial support will have to be adjudicated in the court.

In the United Kingdom, legislation was passed to prohibit the **3–68** arrangement of a surrogacy contract on a commercial basis in the Surrogacy Arrangements Act 1985,[12] long before other infertility techniques were dealt with in the HFEA 1990. This was an emergency measure resulting from a "moral panic" following Britain's first widely publicised court case involving a surrogate mother and a commissioning couple.[13] Non-commercial surrogacy, however, remains legal. Since then it is fair to say that the government has chosen to maintain a rather distrustful distance from surrogacy which it has neither encouraged nor totally suppressed. Recent years have, however, perhaps seen institutional opposition to surrogacy services softening and in 1998, surrogacy was reportedly available for free in one third of NHS clinics.[14] The HFEA 1990, s.36, substituting s.1A into the 1985 Act, tidied up one problem left unattended to by the 1985 Act by declaring that a surrogacy contract should be unenforceable. Thus there is no possibility that commissioning parents can seek a remedy in contract to force an unwilling surrogate to hand a baby over. On the other hand, it means that neither contracting party can rely on the terms of the agreement they have entered into, which may not be to the benefit of anybody, including the child. It has been suggested that,

> "surrogacy is better policed by a scheme in which the legal system recognises and enforces surrogacy contracts, rather than one in which they are left limbo-dancing in the twilight of social disapproval and legal vacillation."[15]

One solution might be some system whereby the courts must approve a surrogacy contract before it is entered into, rather like their vetting of an arranged adoption before making an adoption order. Certainly surrogate motherhood and any associated contractual obligations will always be a minefield, as most recently demonstrated in the United Kingdom by the "Internet Twins" case, where a broken contract left two new born babies in a protracted legal limbo between the United Kingdom and California, to much public disquiet.[16]

---

[12] The Act expressly provides that the surrogate mother herself and the commissioning parents do not commit a criminal offence; e.g. it is the agency, lawyer or doctor who specifically make money from arranging or assisting in surrogacy that the Act criminalises.

[13] *Re C (a minor)* [1985] F.L.R. 846 (perhaps better known as the "Kim Cotton" case.) The moral outrage was caused not only by the fact of surrogate motherhood and the fact that the surrogacy was arranged by a branch of a commercial US agency, but by Ms Cotton's intention to sell her story for money.

[14] See Brazier report, 1998, below, n.17. HFEA Code of Practice (6th edn, 2003), para.3.17 explicitly allows surrogacy in HFEA licensed clinics.

[15] Morgan, "Who to Be or Not to Be: the Surrogacy Story" (1985) 49 M.L.R. 358.

[16] *W v H (child abduction: surrogacy)* [2002] 2 F.L.R. 252.

3–69 In 1998, Professor Margaret Brazier conducted a comprehensive review of United Kingdom surrogacy regulation.[17] The main conclusions were: first, that payments to surrogate mothers should cover only "genuine expenses" associated with pregnancy. "Additional" payments would be prohibited and courts would lose the power to authorise questionable expenses retrospectively; secondly, surrogacy clinics would be required to register with an agency run by the relevant Department of Health and would, like HFEA clinics, be subject to a Code of Practice; thirdly, the non-enforceability of surrogacy contracts (s.1A of the 1985 Act) and the ban on advertising surrogacy services introduced in the 1985 Act should continue. It may be asked however if there is a point to encouraging people to negotiate in advance as to what items of expenditure will be payable expenses, if the agreement reached cannot subsequently be enforced? Finally, the report recommended the creation of a new consolidated Surrogacy Act. These recommendations are largely rubber-stamped in the comprehensive HFEA 1990 review commenced in 2005, discussed below at para.3.93.

Maternity

3–70 Earlier we noted that at common law there was no difficulty in assuming that the genetic mother was also the person who gave birth to the child. However, ovum and embryo donation techniques open up a choice as to who is the "true" mother between the gestational mother and the genetic mother. The Warnock Committee, considering this issue, consciously based their recommendation as to who should be the legal mother on a model based on egg donation to a woman who wished to bear and bring up a child, rather than on egg donation to a surrogate mother.[18] They therefore recommended that when a child is born to a woman following the placing in her of an egg or embryo, then the woman giving birth should be treated for all purposes as the mother of that child. This is implemented in s.27(1) of the HFEA.[19] This conclusive preference for the gestational mother as the legal mother can be justified on the basis that the bonding which takes place during nine months of pregnancy is the essential basis of motherhood. However, it is a radical diversion from the previous default assumption for genetic parenthood.[20]

Section 29(1) provides that a person who is to be regarded as the mother under s.27(1) is to be treated as such "for all purposes".

---

[17] M. Brazier, *Surrogacy: Review of Current Arrangements for Payment and Regulation*, Cm.4068 (1998).

[18] See Warnock Report above (n.10), para.8.19.

[19] See also s.29(1).

[20] Nor is it an uncontroversial or universal choice. In California, e.g. the Supreme Court has gone the other way and the genetic mother has been recognised as legal mother on the basis that she had the *intention* to become the parent, unlike the surrogate (see *Johnson v Calvert* (1993) 5 Cal 4th 84). This opens up the intriguing prospect of an international private law of parentage.

However, this provision does not apply to any title, coat of arms, honour or dignity transmissible on death.[21] For these rather limited purposes, genetic parenthood is all that counts.

Paternity

As discussed above, the new techniques open up a choice as to who **3–71** should be father as well as mother. At common law, in cases of AID, or AID combined with IVF, the genetic father, i.e. the sperm donor, was the legal father. This meant that although invariably of unknown identity, he could theoretically be held liable for maintenance of any children (and there might be several) who had been produced using his sperm. On the other hand, the person who intended, and was indeed often desperate, to play the role of the father was the husband or partner of the woman who had been inseminated. As we have seen, he would often be willing to perjure himself to register the child falsely as his own genetic child. The Warnock Committee, considering the paradigm case of a married couple undergoing AID treatment[22] to conceive a child, were unanimously agreed that the AID child should be treated in law as the child of the mother and her husband where they had both consented to treatment.

The HFEA 1990 goes further than the Warnock proposals in **3–72** extending this deemed paternity not only to husbands but also to unmarried partners undergoing AID or associated treatment together. Section 28(2) is the basic provision. It provides that a husband, whose wife conceives after the donation of sperm, or implantation of an embryo created with donated sperm, then her husband is to be treated as the father of the child *unless* it is shown that he did not consent to the treatment. In other words, there is a rebuttable presumption that the husband consents. The husband is to be treated as the father for all purposes except for minor exceptions relating to succession to titles, coats of arms, etc.[23] This solves the problem of false birth registration as "all purposes" must surely imply the right to register as the legal father.[24] The presumption of the husband's consent is reasonable given that it is routine in clinics to secure the consent of the husband before embarking on treatment.

Section 28(3) extends deemed paternity to the case where an **3–73** unmarried couple are being treated together. This achieves the result that a man who is not married to his partner and is not the genetic father of her child is nonetheless conclusively deemed to be its father.

---

[21] s.29(4).

[22] Warnock Report, para.4.17.

[23] s.29(1) and (5).

[24] Although when this provision was being debated in the House of Lords, Lord Denning remarked that he was unhappy about the statutory encouragement of perjury. It is still possible under the Act for a child to discover something about his or her true genetic heritage—see paras 3–97 to 3–98.

This at the time of the passing of the HFEA was a surprisingly strong vindication of social parenthood; it can now be seen as in line with recent moves towards extending the rights attached to marital status to cohabiting couples *mutatis mutandum*. Of course, since he is unmarried the father will still not have any parental rights over the child unless he is jointly registered as the father of the child (s.3(1)(b) of the Children (Scotland) Act 1995), or makes an agreement under s.4 of the 1995 Act, or seeks a court order.

3–74   On the other hand, the sperm donor is removed from the legal picture entirely. By s.28(6) he is not to be treated as the father of the child.[25] Thus, the genetic link is broken entirely, at least as long as the sperm donor has given an effective written consent to bring him within the regulatory framework of the Act.[26] If the mother has been treated without the consent of a male partner, therefore the resulting child will be legally fatherless. If the sperm donation was made on a "DIY" basis, however,[27] s.28(6) does not apply and the sperm donor will remain the legal father. This is intended to discourage informal sperm donation outwith the licensing controls of the Human Fertilisation and Embryology Authority (hereafter "the HFEA"), which licenses and supervises all clinics that provide infertility treatment under the Act.

3–75   What if a husband avoids the deeming provision of s.28(2) by proving that he did *not* consent to the treatment of his wife by AID? It seems logical that the normal presumption of genetic paternity by virtue of *marriage* under s.5(1) (a) of the 1986 Act would still persist.[28] So a husband will normally be presumed the father under this provision even if he had refused to consent to the treatment. However, it will not be hard for the husband to rebut the presumption in this situation as he will be able to lead the evidence of artificial insemination and prior infertility, which will prima facie disprove the genetic link.[29]

Receiving "treatment services . . . together"

3–76   As noted above, s.28(3) was intended to extend the deemed paternity provisions of s.28(2) to unmarried couples entering treatment for infertility together. The phraseology used has, however, given rise to considerable difficulty. First, can "treatment services" be said to be "provided for her [the mother] and a man together" where the man plays no actual physical role in the fertilisation process at all? This is

---

[25] See also s.28(4) which provides that if a husband or partner is deemed father under s.28(2) or (3) then no-one else is to be treated as the father of the child.

[26] Sch.3, para.5.

[27] e.g. where a male friend is recruited to assist a lesbian or lesbian couple to conceive outwith any clinic or doctor's surgery.

[28] This seems the best reading of the rather unclear provision in s.28(5)(b) of the HFEA 1990.

[29] He might also use DNA testing as discussed above to rebut the s.5(1)(a) presumption.

true of any case where the sperm of a donor is used for either AID or the creation of an embryo which is then implanted in the woman. In *Re Q (Parental Order)*[30] an English court found that s.28(3) did not extend to cases of this nature. Fortunately this was overruled in *U v W*[31] where the court found that if a doctor was responding to a request for treatment from a woman and a man as a couple, then on the facts, they might still qualify under s.28(3) even though there was no actual physical participation by the man. Secondly, what if an unmarried couple begin fertility treatment together, but by the time of actual conception or birth they have split up? This was the scenario in the English House of Lords case of *Re R (A Child) (IVF: Paternity of Child)*.[32] B, the intended mother, entered treatment services with her partner D, who signed the required consent form for treatment. D and B then split up, but B continued treatment without him, unknown to D and the hospital. With some difficulty, their Lordships held that although the couple had indeed been receiving treatment together at the time of the original consent, they were not by the time of the eventual birth, and so D was not deemed the father by s.28(3). Clearly though, this decision was to some extent influenced by the court's dislike of B's deception.

Finally, and perhaps most perplexingly, have a couple consented to **3–77** "treatment services . . . together" where there is a major mix up in the treatment (and hence the baby) delivered? In the remarkable case of *Leeds Teaching Hospitals NHS Trust v Mr and Mrs A*[33] Mr and Mrs A, a white couple, went to the fertility clinic for IVF treatment having spent years unsuccessfully trying for a baby. So, unfortunately, at the same time did Mr and Mrs B, who were black. When twin babies were born to Mrs A, she noticed they were clearly of mixed race. It became apparent after DNA tests that Mr B's sperm had been injected by mistake into Mrs A's egg, which, when fertilised, had been re-implanted into Mrs A's uterus. The legal question, then, was who was the father? The court accepted that s.28(2) could not operate to deem Mr A the legal father, even though he was married to Mrs A, because he had not consented to a "treatment" of Mrs A being impregnated by Mr B. Fundamental error had vitiated his consent. This left the outside possibility of invoking s.28(3) to make Mr A the legal father. However, the same error also, the court held, "vitiate[d] the whole concept of 'treatment together' for the purposes of the 1990 Act." Accordingly, s.28(3) cannot operate to deem a man the father if his consent to being treated together with the mother is void through fundamental error.[34]

---

[30] [1996] 1 F.L.R. 369.

[31] [1997] 2 F.L.R. 282.

[32] [2005] 2 A.C. 621.

[33] [2003] EWHC 259 (QB).

[34] Interestingly, the court nonetheless were prepared to contemplate awarding parental rights of residence to Mr and Mrs A, the intended "social" parents, even though the genetic and legal father of the child remained Mr B, as s.28(6) also did not operate to remove the paternity of the "sperm donor" in these circumstances of error. See further Norrie, "Paternity and Reproductive Technology", 2002 S.L.P.Q. 232.

The Surrogacy Dimension

3–78   We have seen above that the status provisions of the HFEA 1990
were drafted in an attempt to solve the problems of maternity and
paternity associated with AID and IVF. In particular, it was assumed
that the couple receiving infertility treatment were the couple who
intended to become parents and bring up the child. However, in the
surrogacy situation, these assumptions are false. In a case of total surrogacy, applying the HFEA 1990, the legal mother of the child is
deemed to be the surrogate mother, as she is the one who bears the
child and gives birth (s.27) and if the surrogate mother is married at
the date of treatment, then her husband will be deemed to be the legal
father of the child (s.28(2)) unless he can prove that he did not consent
to the insemination or to the IVF treatment. In many cases of surrogacy it will be impossible for him to prove this lack of consent, or he
may well have actually consented.

3–79   These are not the results one would expect.[35] They are only explicable if regarded as a way other than criminal sanctions by which the
law attempts to discourage people from entering non-commercial
surrogacy agreements. After all, the whole aim of surrogacy is that
the commissioning parents should have their own legal child at the
end of the day. Potential surrogate parents may think twice when they
are advised they will not automatically be treated as the legal parents
of their surrogate offspring. To add insult to injury, the commissioning father who (assuming he is the sperm donor) would have been,
prior to the HFEA 1990, the legal as well as the genetic father, entirely
loses his legal status as father as a result of s.28(6) of the HFEA 1990.

3–80   There are, nonetheless, approaches surrogate parents can take to
try to obtain parental responsibilities and rights, and at best, full
status as legal parents in relation to their surrogate children. It is
possible, for example, to apply for a residence order under s.11 of the
1995 Act. However, such an application will, of course, be regulated
by the welfare of the child. In the few reported United Kingdom
cases on residence disputes between surrogate mothers and commissioning parents, the courts have generally inclined towards the
view that a child is better off with the natural, gestational parent
where a maternal bond has already formed. In *Re P*,[36] for example,
the surrogate mother declined to hand over twin babies to a married
professional couple, having been inseminated by the husband; she
subsequently won custody. The court, significantly, placed a higher
value on the preservation of the maternal bond that had formed
than on the material advantages the commissioning couple could
offer.

---

[35] These undesirable results in the surrogacy situation were pointed out in an early
  paper: Montgomery, "Assisted Reproduction after the Family Law Reform Act
  1987" (1988) Family Law 23.
[36] [1987] 2 F.L.R. 421.

On the other hand, in the only Scottish surrogate mother case to **3–81** date, *C v S*,[37] the sheriff awarded custody to the commissioning parents rather than the gestational mother, principally on the grounds that the year-old child had (pursuant to the contract) been living with the commissioning parents since birth and was a near stranger to the natural mother. The Inner House reversed the sheriff by making an adoption order rather than a custody order, but still found it in the child's welfare to reside permanently with the commissioning parents. It is hard to imagine a case in which the United Kingdom courts would prefer the claim of the commissioning couple to that of a surrogate mother who had retained possession of her child after birth.

Even where both commissioning parents and surrogate mother **3–82** agree that the arrangement should go ahead as planned, merely awarding parental responsibilities and rights to the commissioning couple is not the ideal solution. For one thing, parental rights terminate at 16; furthermore, the rights extend to upbringing but the rights holder is still not a legal *parent*, which has legal consequences for, inter alia, succession, nationality and domicile.

If commissioning parents wish to become full legal parents, the **3–83** obvious legal avenue is adoption. However, this option is even more difficult than acquiring parental rights. Adoption not only requires a court order but will usually involve the commissioning parents to undertake the lengthy process of vetting that all prospective adoptive parents must pass through. Furthermore the question of whether a surrogacy arrangement is equivalent to baby-buying may rear its head. Section 51 of the Adoption (Scotland) Act 1978 prohibits adoptive parents from making any payment in consideration for the adoption of a child, although such a payment is licit if for reasonable expenses or if authorised by the court under s.51(3). In *Re an Adoption Application (Surrogacy)*,[38] the commissioning parents Mr and Mrs A made a payment of £5,000 (cut down from an original agreement for £10,000) to a surrogate mother who gave up her job to have the child. When Mr and Mrs A applied for an adoption order, the court had to consider whether this payment contravened the law. Latey J. held that the mother had not been primarily motivated by financial considerations and that there was nothing commercial about this adoption.

It seems that payments for loss of earnings and expenses can **3–84** safely be made to a surrogate, and then retrospectively authorised by the court, but anything on top akin to a fee will risk prejudicing any adoption. What exactly can be got away with as "expenses"

---

[37] 1996 S.L.T. 1387.
[38] [1987] 2 All E.R. 826. The case concerned the equivalent provision in the English Adoption Act 1976.

remains controversial.[39] In *C v S*, discussed above, the commissioning parents were refused an adoption order at first instance, because they had paid the surrogate £8,000. The sheriff regarded this as far more than could truly be justified as expenses, since the surrogate was unemployed with no prospect of work. On appeal to the Inner House, however, the Lord President found that even if the money was an illegal payment, it had been made to secure a parental order under s.30 of the HFEA 1990, not as consideration for an *adoption*. There was therefore no contravention of s.51. This seems an artificial distinction justifiable only on the facts of the case.

Parental Orders

3–85 A tailor-made option for commissioning parents seeking legal status is now to be found in s.30 of the HFEA 1990, which allows such parents to apply within six months of the surrogate child's birth for a *parental order*. The effect of a parental order is that the child shall be treated for all legal purposes as the child of the applicant parties. It is effectively equivalent to an adoption order without the need to go through the adoption process.[40] Numerous conditions must be satisfied before a court can grant a s.30 order. Only married parties who are both over the age of 18 can apply. The child must have a home with them at the date of the application. The surrogate mother must consent freely to the making of the order; so must her husband or partner if he is the legal father of the child by virtue of s.28(2) or (3) of the HFEA 1990. Most importantly, the court must be satisfied that no money has changed hands other than expenses reasonably incurred.[41]

3–86 Section 30 was introduced at the last minute into the HFEA 1990 in response to a well-publicised case going though the courts at that time, *Re W (minors)*,[42] which involved a surrogate mother bearing a child conceived by means of embryo transfer, that is, a child who had no genetic relation to the surrogate at all. Although there was no dispute between the surrogate and the commissioning parents, the local authority intervened and sought guidance from the courts as to who was the legal mother.[43] The case brought to public notice the difficulties of commissioning parents seeking to become legal parents

---

[39] In adoption cases, sums of £8,000 or more paid to the child's natural mother have been authorised while sums as low as £1,000 have been declared illegal, depending on the circumstances.

[40] See further the Parental Orders (Human Fertilisation and Embryology) (Scotland) Regulations (SI 1994/2804).

[41] HFEA 1990, s.30(7). However, as in adoption, a payment made can be retrospectively authorised by the court: see *Re Q (Parental Order)* [1996] 1 F.L.R. 369.

[42] [1991] 1 F.L.R. 385.

[43] Since this was prior to the passing of the HFEA 1990 in Parliament, s.27 had of course not yet cleared this point up.

of their surrogate children.[44] Montgomery has commented that s.30 "demonstrates the worst features of a legislative system which allows anecdotal evidence to determine the shape of reform"[45] and it is true that the conditions for making a s.30 application are modelled closely on the *Re W* parents.

There seems no good reason why parental orders should be limited to married couples, especially given that the HFEA 1990 status provisions generally extend the same rights to unmarried heterosexual partners as to spouses. One might go further and assert that following the Civil Partnership Act 2004, there is no reason why it should not extend also to same-sex couples, thus allowing a lesbian couple for the first time to become true co-parents in law.[46] Furthermore, s.30 lacks the consideration of comparable adoption legislation. For example, there is no provision akin to that found in the Adoption (Sc) Act 1978 by which the consent of the surrogate mother can be dispensed with if she is withholding consent unreasonably.[47] More subtly, s.30 is philosophically at odds with the rest of the Act in which it is embedded in that it positively encourages couples to commission surrogate children. **3–87**

"Intentional" Parentage

A different approach than that of treating surrogacy as a kind of post-natal adoption is possible. In the case *of Johnson v Calvert*,[48] the Californian Supreme Court was asked to rule on whether a genetic commissioning mother or a surrogate gestational mother was the legal mother. The court decided in favour of the genetic mother, but not for that reason. Instead, they held that it was the woman who *intended* to bring about the birth of a child she intended to raise as her own who should be treated as the legal mother. This concept of "intentional" parentage would produce what might be called the "right" result in both surrogacy and conventional assisted reproduction cases. However, it is a radical approach which is unlikely to be adopted by United Kingdom courts or legislatures. **3–88**

---

[44] In fact, due to difficulties with birth registration procedure, it took another four years before the *Re W* parents could apply for a s.30 order (s.30 came into force on November 1, 1994).

[45] Montgomery, "Rights, Restraints and Pragmatism: the Human Fertilisation and Embryology Act 1990" (1991) 54 M.L.R. 524 at p.530.

[46] Sheldon, in S. Sheldon, "Fragmenting Fatherhood: the Regulation of Reproductive Technologies" (2005) 68 M.L.R. 523, makes this point in relation to s.28(3) of the 1990 Act and its non-application to same-sex couples, as well as to s.30 (p.553).

[47] *cf.* s.16(2) of the 1978 Act. For this reason, the commissioning parents in *C v S* (above at para.3–81) were unable to seek a parental order, their original plan, and had to revert to seeking an adoption order.

[48] (1993) 5 Cal 4th 84.

Regulating Access to Assisted Reproduction

3–89   In most Western democratic countries there are no legal obstacles
to becoming a parent by natural means. If natural parents fail to look
after their children adequately they may be removed by the state; but
concepts such as the licensing of natural parents, or restrictions for
the sake of population control,[49] are regarded as an unwarranted
intrusion into personal privacy. When children are born as a result of
reproductive technology, however, the ground shifts. On the one
hand, here is an opportunity to regulate access to parentage without
the need for an abhorrent invasion and monitoring of ordinary family
life and sexual relations. On the other hand, it can be asked why infertile would-be parents should be regulated when any other person,
however unfit for parenting, can have a child without passing tests.
The debate turns on whether assisted reproduction is seen more as
akin to natural childbirth or to adoption, but is complicated by the
fact that artificial procreation is in general a considerably more expensive business than the natural kind. If the state is putting resources
into assisted reproduction then arguably it has a stake financially in
making sure the children are born to adequate homes, so that it does
not end up meeting the costs of their care—in addition, of course, to
its protective interest in the welfare of future children.

3–90   One type of restriction on access to IVF treatment which undoubtedly already operates is economic. Not all NHS clinics offer IVF and
without NHS support, such treatment is prohibitively expensive for
many couples, particularly as the success rate (i.e. the live birth rate)
is low and therefore multiple attempts are not unusual. Plans do exist
to offer three free cycles of IVF on the NHS to all who wish it,[50] but
this is still likely to take some years, and to exclude various groups,
e.g. would-be mothers over a certain age (see further below). The
costs of surrogacy are less easy to quantify[51] but empirical evidence
shows it is often a way for infertile middle-class couples to acquire
babies carried to term by working-class or unemployed women.

3–91   An obvious goal of regulation is to protect the welfare of as yet
unconceived children. What criteria for suitable parents this indicates
is highly controversial. Clinics providing treatment under the HFEA
1990 are licensed by the Human Fertilisation and Embryology
Authority and as a condition of that license must comply with guidelines provided in a Code of Practice. Section 13(5) of the HFEA 1990
provides that a woman shall not be provided with infertility treatment
including AID and IVF unless account has been taken of the welfare

---

[49] China's one-family one-child policy is probably the best known example of this kind
of regulation.
[50] See Mason and McCall Smith, *Law and Medical Ethics* (7th edn, 2005), Ch.4, n.105
(and n.34, para.3–77, of this chapter on current state of play as at March 2006).
[51] According to press reports in April 1996, the first NHS-funded birth to a surrogate
mother via ovum donation occurred in 1994. The cost to the public was around
£5,000.

of any child that may be born as a result of the treatment. While the HFEA 1990 was going through Parliament, strenuous attempts were made to limit access to treatment to married, or at least stable heterosexual couples, to the exclusion of single women and lesbians. Although these amendments were largely defeated, what remains is a codicil to s.13(5) to the effect that the welfare of the child includes its need for a father. In the HFEA Code of Practice, centres are enjoined to have regard to the child's need for a father but may also consider if there is someone within the mother's family or social circle who is willing to share responsibility for the child's needs.[52] This perhaps surprisingly liberal interpretation of s.13(5) does not affect the reality that few clinics are prepared to offer services leading to (wrongly) so-called "virgin births".[53] The comprehensive HFEA review of 2005[54] has sought advice on whether s.13(5) should be entirely removed from the law, or amended.[55]

Other factors which may be taken into account include the age, **3–92** medical history, and motivation of the parents and whether there is a possibility of risk to any children born.[56] Motivation may include the desire to be able to pre-select the sex of the child: the HFEA has found itself in difficulties here in the past. In principle, sex selection for social reasons only is discouraged by the HFEA, but where sex selection is essential for the birth of a healthy child, e.g. where a genetic disease is transmissible only to male children), or for the creation of a healthy "saviour sibling" (a child who can, e.g. donate tissue to cure a sibling with an inherited genetic disease) the HFEA, and on judicial review, the courts, have seemed willing to allow it in very limited circumstances.[57] In jurisdictions abroad, both the birth of children to post-menopausal women and the treatment of black women with eggs donated by white donors, for social reasons, have stirred controversy. The HFEA's current Code of Practice does not place a limit in theory on the age up to which treatment services may be provided, although it does suggest that women over 35 and men over 45 should be counselled as to the implications of their age for success in treatment.[58] Clients are also advised that they will not be supplied with gametes from a donor with "different physical

---

[52] (6th edn, 2003), Pt 3, especially paras 3.13–3.15.
[53] The "virgin birth" media outcry of 1991 is interestingly dissected in Cooper and Herman, "Getting The Family Right: Legislating Heterosexuality" (1991) 10 Canadian Journal of Family Law.
[54] Below at n.64.
[55] *ibid.*, Annex B, question 17.
[56] HFEA Code of Practice (6th edn, 2003), paras 3.1–3.25.
[57] See further discussion in the *Hashmi* case—*R (on application of Quintavelle on behalf of Comment on Reproductive Ethics) v HFEA Authority* [2003] 2 All E.R. 105; [2003] 3 All E.R. 257 (on appeal). But *cf* the *Masterton* case cited by Mason and McCall-Smith, (7th edn, 2005), at p.95 where the HFEA refused permission to a couple to select for a girl expressly, because an earlier daughter had died.
[58] HFEA Code of Practice (6th edn, 2003), para.3.7.

characteristics" than the intended parent(s) unless there are "compelling reasons" for doing so.[59]

Assisted Reproduction after Death of, or Separation from, Partner

3–93   Yet another set of difficult questions revolve around whether the state should assist, or even allow, a woman to have children by their partner even after his death. This issue was raised to great public concern by the difficult case of Mrs Diane Blood. Mrs Blood obtained a sample of her husband's sperm while he was on his deathbed, in a coma, and thus without his consent. Although there was anecdotal evidence that the two had always planned to have children, there was no written consent to storage of Mr Blood's gametes prior to insemination, as required by the HFEA 1990. In the end Mrs Blood won her case, but only under EC law on freedom of movement of goods and services, which required the United Kingdom clinic to allow the transmission of the sperm sample to a foreign clinic which was prepared to carry out the post-death insemination treatment.[60] It remains the law, notwithstanding Mrs Blood's court battles, that a donor *may* still give permission for his sperm to be used after his death, but if this consent cannot be proven, then such post-death insemination is illegal in the United Kingdom.[61]

3–94   The situation was perhaps even more difficult in *Evans*. This case concerned a woman who had created stored embryos with her male partner via treatment in HFEA clinics, but who had then separated from the partner, who in turn had then withdrawn consent to storage and subsequent uses of the embryos. The principle of the law here is that in essence a man cannot be forced to become a father against his will. In Evans' case however this was a particularly hard case as she subsequently had cancer and lost any other chance of having children. Her argument that the HFEA rules were thus in breach of her right to respect for family life under Art.8 of the ECHR, was, however, rightly, if harshly, rejected by the United Kingdom courts[62] and eventually, by the European Court of Human Rights.[63]

3–95   Many of the most controversial issues touched on above—the use of stored embryos after the death of one or more of the original gamete donors, sex selection of embryos, pre-implantation diagnosis,

---

[59] *ibid.*, para.3.19.

[60] [1997] 2 All E.R. 687. In the end Mrs Blood had two children posthumously using the sperm of Mr Blood, both conceived via fertility treatment in Belgium.

[61] Domestic UK law was however slightly changed by the Human Fertilisation (Deceased Fathers) Act 2003, s.1, so that a child resulting from post-death insemination or egg or embryo implantation *can* be recorded as the child of the deceased father, so long as that father's written consent to the procedure exists.

[62] *Evans v Amicus Health Care Ltd* [2004] 3 All E.R. 1025; [2004] EWCA (Civ) 727. See further S.A.M. McLean, "Creating postmortem pregnancies: A UK perspective" [1999] Juridical Rev 323.

[63] *Evans v UK*, European Court of Human Rights, App. No.6339/05, March 7, 2006.

and the general area of the creation of "designer embryos"—are ventilated in the wholesale review of the HFEA 1990 and the HFEA which the government launched in 2005.[64] It seems likely that we will see major legal changes in the framework for the control of fertility and assisted reproduction in the near future, as both law and society struggle to keep up with the pace of scientific advances in this area.

Section 13(5) and the Code of Practice provide some central reg- **3–96** ulation but also leave clinics (and their ethical committees) with a great deal of discretion as to which infertile persons they choose to treat. Can an applicant turned down for treatment seek review by the courts? In the case of *R v Ethical Committee of St Mary's Hospital ex parte Harriott*,[65] a woman sought judicial review of the decision of the hospital ethical committee and consultant not to accept her for IVF treatment. She had in fact been rejected because of her criminal record for prostitution and brothel-keeping. Significantly, her (unsuccessful) application for review was based on the claim that the hospital had treated her unfairly by not revealing they had already rejected her as an unfit parent for some 14 months. Her counsel made no attempt to attack the substantive policies of the hospital concerning IVF candidates. Such an attack would only seem possible if the hospital selection policy was discriminatory to a group, not an individual, e.g. if a clinic refused to treat any black or Jewish patients.

Children and their Genetic Heritage

As noted above, AID has in the past been typically a procedure **3–97** cloaked in secrecy. Egg donors are also usually anonymous unless they are family members. Although donors involved in licensed treatment can no longer be held financially responsible for their offspring[66] there are other reasons why anonymity is desirable. The Warnock Report took the view that anonymity of third-party donors was not only a matter of good practice but protected all concerned from emotional difficulties and, crucially, ensured a plentiful supply of donors.[67] However, occasions may arise where some knowledge of genetic history is desirable for medical reasons, e.g. where a couple plan to marry and fear that they may be incestuously related, or where they wish to check against the possibility of reinforcement of a genetically transmitted disease. Section 31 of the HFEA 1990 thus provided that a child born as a result of treatment services might, on

---

[64] *Review of the Human Fertilisation and Embryology Act—a Public Consultation* (2005), available at *www.dh.gov.uk/Consultations/ClosedConsultations*.

[65] (1988) 18 Fam. Law 165.

[66] See para.3–74.

[67] Para.3.03. A survey in 1994 of sperm donors found that 63% would not have donated sperm if their identity was to be made available to resulting children when they reached 18 (HFEA 3rd Annual Report (1994), para.6.1).

attaining 18, seek non-identifying information of this type from a register kept by the HFEA to be prescribed by regulations. A person under 18 but over 16 who is about to marry may also apply for information relating to the marriage.

3–98   In the adoption context there has been general acknowledgment that children who have been removed from their birth families may feel a need to know something about their heritage. The adoption legislation now facilitates this need.[68] If the children of AID and IVF feel the same need to investigate their origins, they have in the past probably been frustrated by what they can obtain from the register, which usually provides access only to basic medical and genetic information, and not the names or personal identifying details of donors unless they choose to supply these. Mason and McCall-Smith have argued in the past[69] that the children of assisted reproduction, unlike adopted children, need never question their maternity nor their paternity, since there will be nothing to indicate anyone other than their parents was involved in their conception judging by the birth certificate or circumstances of birth. However this view has not won the day. In *Rose v Secretary of State for Health,*[70] s.31 was successfully challenged as insufficient on the ground that it potentially infringed the right to identity, which forms part of Art.8 of the ECHR. Accordingly, new regulations were passed which will in future ensure that the children of donated eggs and/or sperm will be able to find out the name, date and place of birth, appearance and last known address of their genetic parents.[71] It appears, however, that, as predicted, this provision has caused the supply of donors to dry up, with harmful affects for the entire infertility treatment programme.

CONCLUSIONS

3–99 This chapter has shown us that the question "who is a parent?" is not a simple one, just as in the last chapter we similarly found there was no glib definition of a child. There are a multiplicity of different types of parents in the modern world—genetic or "natural" parents, "assisted" parents, surrogate parents, step-parents and social parents—but the law attempts to sort them out by rigid rules into two simple classes: parents and non-parents. As we have seen, these rules are often, inevitably, inconsistent: for example, "licensed" sperm donors are genetic parents but not legal parents, while the husband

---

[68] Adoption (Scotland) Act 1978, s.45.
[69] See Mason and McCall-Smith (7th edn, 2005), above n.50, pp.86–87.
[70] *R. (on the application of Rose and another) v Secretary of State for Health* [2002] 2 F.L.R. 962; (2002) 69 BMLR 83.
[71] HFEA (Disclosure of Donor Information) Regulations 2004 (SI 2004/1511). These regulation are prospective only and so will only apply to children who reach 18 in 2023, i.e. 18 years after the Regulationss came into force on April 1, 2005.

of a woman receiving AID treatment is a legal parent, though not a genetic one. Even when the parents have been separated from the non-parents, there is an apparent further sub-division into "first-class" parents, with automatic responsibilities and rights, and "second-class" parents who must (if they wish to) somehow acquire these. The next three chapters look at how the law describes the legal relationship between, respectively, "parents", "non-parents", and the children they care for.

CHAPTER 4

PARENTAL RESPONSIBILITIES AND CHILDREN'S RIGHTS I

4–01 In the last two chapters we spoke of the relationship between a child and his or her parents as the first legal relationship in which a child partakes. We have looked at how the law decides who is a child, and who is a parent, for various legal purposes. We have seen to which parents the law gives automatic parental responsibility and rights ("PRRs"), and which are excluded. In this chapter we will discuss the different ways in which the law describes the *relationship* between parents and children: how the law deals with conflict between the rights of parents and the wishes of children, and how the courts resolve disputes about the parent–child relationship. Here, we are at the heartland of the law of parent and child and must explore some highly controversial questions: how can children move from being objects of concern or outright property to autonomous individuals with their own rights and duties?; should parents be free to bring up their children as they please?; what criteria should courts use to assess good and bad parenting? In this chapter we will be looking in detail at Pt 1 of the 1995 Act.[1] In the next chapter, specific aspects of parental responsibility and children's rights in Scots law will be examined. Any discussion of parental responsibility must start with some appreciation of the different models for the relationship between parent and child which have been dominant at different stages of the development of Scots family law.[2]

PARENTAL POWER

4–02 In Roman law, the father of the household or *paterfamilias* had absolute power over his children, whom he could deal with as he wished, even having the power of life or death. This idea of *patria potestas* in somewhat diminished form was received into Scots law and was still found in Stair's time as can be seen from this quote from his Institutes: "The obligation of children towards their parents consists mainly in their obedience to them".[3]

---

[1] Pt 1 of the 1995 Act came into force on November 1, 1996.
[2] For a comparable study of the development of English law, see the seminal article, Eekelaar, "The Emergence of Children's Rights" (1986) 6 O.J.L.S. 161.
[3] *Stair Encyclopaedia*, i. 5.8.

However, by the latter part of the nineteenth century it was clear **4–03** that the *patria potestas* was subject in some circumstances to the control and intervention by the courts. Fraser wrote that where the court was satisfied that,

> "the government of a father is vicious or immoral, or calculated to engender irreligious or atheistical opinions, or that the treatment of the child is cruel, harsh and oppressive, they have an undoubted jurisdiction to interfere for the benefit of the child".[4]

It has been argued that what was being protected at the time was not so much the interests of the child as of society. For example, the protection of children from harsh or oppressive treatment may have been aimed at maximising the labour pool at a time of frantic industrialisation. The protection of the child from "atheistical" fathers may have been intended to safeguard the dominant religious attitudes of the day.[5] Nonetheless, these kinds of decisions by courts to intervene in the custodial rights of fathers are clearly the end of absolute parental rights, and the beginning of what is today enshrined as the "welfare principle".

PARENTAL RIGHTS AND THE WELFARE PRINCIPLE

It is one of the fundamental tenets of modern child law that parents **4–04** do not have absolute rights but are only entitled to exercise their rights in the interests of the child. This idea first entered the statute book in 1866,[6] when the courts were instructed when dealing with issues of custody or access to have regard to the welfare of the child concerned. In 1925,[7] the welfare of the child was declared to be the paramount consideration in these kind of disputes. In 1986, the Law Reform (Parent and Child) (Scotland) Act declared with great generality that in any proceedings relating to parental rights, the court should regard the welfare of the child as paramount, a provision now restated in similar terms in the Children (Scotland) Act 1995, s.11(7). Furthermore, s.2(1) of the 1995 Act enacts, for the first time explicitly, that parents only have rights in order to fulfil their parental responsibilities.[8] Responsibilities must be carried out in the interests of the child, so far as this is practicable.[9]

---

[4] Fraser on *Parent and Child* (2nd edn, 1866).
[5] See on this Eekelaar, *op. cit.* above n.2, at pp.162–163.
[6] Guardianship of Infants Act 1886.
[7] Guardianship of Infants Act 1925.
[8] For a more detailed historical sketch see *Stair Encyclopaedia*, Vol.10, paras 1274–1280.
[9] 1995 Act, s.1(1).

4–05　　Even laws, which seem on the face of them not wholly at one with the welfare principle, can be reconstructed to fit this mould. For example, Scots parents historically had the right to "reasonably chastise" their children.[10] In more modern terms this was interpreted to mean that parents have the right to hit their children, but only to the extent that the punishment is in the children's best interests and fulfils a parental responsibility, e.g. to provide direction and guidance to the child.[11] If a dispute arose as to whether the parents were mis-applying discipline, the court had to decide if the parents were putting the welfare of the child first in making their child-rearing decisions.[12] This illustrates one of the biggest problems that arise when one tries to apply the "best interests" standard: who should decide what it means? The parent (who will maintain that the child needs to learn certain correct behaviour)? The child (who will almost certainly not want to be hit)? The courts (who may feel by "average" societal standards these particular parents are over-strict disciplinarians)? And is the welfare principle really the only appropriate standard here? Should parents have the right to discipline children only to fulfil their parental responsibilities, or because it fulfils some of their own needs (e.g. a bit of hush), or because they feel entitled as parents to bring up their children how they like?

4–06　　The "welfare principle" protects children from parental excess or caprice but it leaves them subject to what Freeman has called "liberal paternalism".[13] This is basically the once uncontroversial idea that parents know better than children do what is good for the latter. If parents are supposed to exercise their rights in the interests of the child, this usually translates as the parents deciding what choices are best for the child concerned. An alternative approach is what has been called "substituted judgment". The parents, when deciding what is best for the welfare of the child, do not decide on the basis of what *they* think is good for the child, but consider what the *child* would have felt to be best for him *if he were an adult*. (In both cases, where a parent or parents' judgment is dubious or clearly contrary to the child's welfare, it can be called into question in court, or as a last resort the state can take the child out of the parent's care or impose criminal sanctions on the parent for child-neglect or abuse.)

4–07　　In reality, choices parents make for their children tend to be examined only when they come under the scrutiny of the courts, usually at the instigation of a third party such as social work or the police. In *Re D (Sterilisation)*,[14] for example, an educational psychologist

---

[10] Children and Young Persons (Scotland) Act 1937, s.12(7).

[11] 1995 Act, s.1(1)(b).

[12] The law has now further restricted any right of reasonable chastisement following significant case law in the European Court of Human Rights: see further below and para.5–11.

[13] Freeman, *The Rights and Wrongs of Children* (1983).

[14] (1976) Fam. 185.

brought to the attention of the English courts the planned sterilisation of an 11-year-old mentally handicapped girl. Since the right to consent to medical procedures is an aspect of parental rights, and the child's mother had consented, the operation appeared prima facie to be legitimate. However, Heilbron J. held that the procedure was not in the girl's best interests. Sterilisation should not be undertaken lightly since it would irrevocably remove the girl's basic right to reproduce. On the particular facts of this case, the girl was likely at some future date to be able to make an informed choice about whether sterilisation was appropriate, and might have the intellectual capacity to marry. The mother had consented to the operation because she herself was afraid her daughter would become pregnant and have an abnormal child; these were her own fears rather than a true consideration of the child's own future welfare and wishes. Since Heilbron J. specially noted that the child might one day look back and feel frustration and resentment that she was sterilised without her consent at such a young age, it is fair to consider this a case where "substituted judgment" was employed.

In *Re B (A Minor) (Wardship: Sterilisation)*,[15] by contrast, no **4–08** such consideration of the childs future capacity to choose was possible. Here, the court was asked to decide if the sterilisation of "Jeannette", a 17-year-old mentally handicapped girl with very limited intellectual development, was legitimate. Again, both her mother and the doctors concerned supported the operation. Jeannette was of far more limited mental capacity than the girl in *Re D*. Although she was sexually aware, it was unlikely she would ever be able to make a causal link between sexual intercourse and pregnancy. She could not be placed on any effective contraceptive regime. If she became pregnant, all options of termination, natural or Caesarean delivery would be extremely traumatic and possibly dangerous for her, and she was unlikely to be able to care for or enjoy looking after the child. In these circumstances, the House of Lords found sterilisation was in her best interests. Lord Templeman in particular emphasised that this decision was not for the social good but was exclusively made as in Jeannette's own interests:

> "I desire to emphasise once again that this case is not about sterilisation for social purposes; it is not about eugenics; it is not about the convenience of those whose task it is to care for the ward or the anxieties of her family; and it involves no general principle of public policy. It is about what is in the best interests of this unfortunate young woman and how best she can be given the protection which is essential to her future well-being so that she may lead as full a life as her intellectual capacity allows".[16]

---

[15] [1988] 1 A.C. 199.
[16] *ibid., per* Lord Templeman at p.212-C.

Note that in determining Jeanette's welfare, Lord Templeman's emphasis was wholly on what was necessary to *protect* her; there is no reference to what she might have wanted had she had the mental capacity to express her views now or in the future.

4–09   In both these cases, although the legal issue was whether the parent was giving a consent to treatment that was in the welfare of the child, the final decision was truly made by the court. In fact one of the dicta made by the House of Lords in *Re B* was that in future all such decisions to sterilise mentally-handicapped children must be confirmed by the courts.[17] The welfare principle implicitly restricts parental autonomy, and it is one of the continuing tensions in child law how far parents—or families—should be entitled to bring up their children as they see fit, and how far they should be restricted by the state and by societal standards to which they may not personally accede.

4–10   These tensions can be seen very clearly in a Scottish medical consent case, *Finlayson Petr*.[18] Here, a child of nine suffered from severe haemophilia. His parents refused to consent to the child receiving transfusions of the blood product "Factor VIII", partly because of fear he would contract AIDS and partly because they preferred homeopathic remedies. The case was referred to the Children's Hearing who found that although the parents were genuinely concerned for the child's well-being, they were not objectively acting in the best interests of the child. This enabled a finding to be made that the child was in need of compulsory measures of care due to lack of parental care,[19] and allowed the Hearing to impose conditions relating to the child's treatment. Effectively, the parents' view of correct parenting was overturned. Similarly, parental refusal to consent to treatment for their children on conscientious religious grounds has been overridden by the courts.[20]

4–11   Clearly, the greatest damage is done to parental autonomy, and the bitterest conflicts caused, when children are forcibly removed into care. The degree of autonomy given to parents tends to be as much a

---

[17] *Practice Note, Official Solicitor Sterilisation* [1993] 3 All E.R. 222. See, e.g. *Re F* [1990] 2 A.C. 1. In Scotland, power has been granted by the court to a tutor-dative to consent to the sterilisation of a mentally-handicapped adult on the best interests principle—*L v L's Curator ad Litem*, 1997 S.L.T. 167.

[18] 1989 S.C.L.R. 601.

[19] Social Work (Scotland) Act 1968, s.32(2)(c); now see s.52(1)(c) of 1995 Act.

[20] e.g. *Re E (A Minor) (Wardship: Medical Treatment)* [1993] 1 F.L.R. 386. At levels of life or death however, religious views often remain involved if not decisive in controversial cases. See, e.g. *NHS Trust v MB* [2000] EWHC 507 (Fam) in which the court upheld the decision of parents taken on conscientious religious grounds that the life of their infant child (who was born severely physically handicapped, but not in a coma or persistent vegetative state) should be preserved by medical intervention such as ventilation, even though the view of doctors was that the child's quality of life was so poor he should be allowed to die. The decision was taken exclusively on a "best interests of the child" analysis, not on the basis of any argument based on right to respect for family and private life under Art.8 of the ECHR.

political as a moral choice.[21] Following a number of recent child abuse scandals[22] in which social work authorities were seen as exercising unreasonable power to the detriment of both parents and children, extensive changes have been made to childcare legislation both in Scotland and England,[23] in a bid to restate the balance between parental autonomy and state power to intervene. We consider this further in Chs 7 and 8.

If parental rights are always subject to the welfare principle, can **4–12** they really be called "rights" at all? They are certainly not rights in the same sense as rights to property, or contractual rights, which impose correlative duties on a defined person or persons, and sanctions if those duties are not met.[24] In *F v Wirral Metropolitan Borough Council*,[25] a mother voluntarily placed her two children in the care of the local authority. Some months later, the local authority decided to compulsorily assume parental rights over the children with a view to placing them for adoption. All this was done legitimately in accordance with the statutory childcare code. The mother, lacking any other remedy, sued the local authority for damages for their interference with her parental right to enjoy the company of her children. The Court of Appeal rejected her claim. Parental rights were not absolute rights but more akin to privileges or claims, derived from parental duty and existing only for the protection of the child.[26] Since the local authority had statutory duties imposed on it to protect the welfare of children, it might well have to interfere with the privilege or right of a parent to the society of his or her child. It would be inconsistent with both the welfare principle and childcare legislation if the authority were found to be liable in damages in a civil action for fulfilling its statutory duties. Hence no common law action lay for interference with parental rights.[27]

This does not mean that parents have no remedies at all. If, for **4–13** example, their wishes concerning the medical treatment of their young child were being ignored, they could apply to the courts for, say, a specific issue order under s.11 of the 1995 Act.[28] But such an

---

[21] See Adler, *Taking Juvenile Justice Seriously* (1985), Ch.3.

[22] See, inter alia, *Report of the Inquiry into Child Abuse in Cleveland* ("the Butler-Sloss Report"), Cm.412; *Report of the Inquiry into the Removal of Children from Orkney in February 1991* ("the Clyde Report"); *Report of the Inquiry into Child Care Policies in Fife* ("the Kearney Report").

[23] Children (Scotland) Act 1995, Pt II; Children Act 1989.

[24] In Hohfeldian terms, parental "rights" are not claim-rights but more akin to privileges or even duties. See for discussion of this Eekelaar, "What Are Parental Rights?" (1973) 89 L.Q.R. 210; Dickens, "The Modern Function and Limits of Parental Rights" (1981) 97 L.Q.R. 462.

[25] [1991] Fam. 69.

[26] The authority for this proposition at the time was the speech of Lord Fraser in *Gillick* [1986] A.C. 112 at 183.

[27] A Scottish Outer House case, *McKeen v Chief Constable, Lothian and Borders Police*, 1994 S.L.T. 93 appears implicitly to follow the same reasoning as *Wirral*.

[28] See para.4–48, below.

order, like their "right" itself, would be conditional on the parent's preferred choice of medical treatment being in the child's welfare.

Another important way in which parental rights differ from conventional property rights is that they cannot voluntarily be relinquished, sold or abdicated (1995 Act, s.3(5)). However, it is legitimate to arrange to *delegate* responsibility to someone else, e.g. a friend, relative or baby-sitter,[29] although liability for failure of duty will still lie with the parent or parents.[30]

PARENTAL RESPONSIBILITY

4–14 If parental rights, as we have seen, exist only to enable parents to fulfil their parental responsibilities, then the whole concept of rights becomes subservient to, if not quite subsumed by, the idea of *responsibility*. This is very much the approach taken by the 1995 Act, which for the first time in Scots legislative history lay out a list of parental duties in its first section.

4–15   Parents have in relation to their children the responsibility:

(a) to safeguard and promote the child's health, development and welfare;
(b) to provide, in a manner appropriate to the stage of development of the child—
  (i) direction;
  (ii) guidance
  to the child;
(c) if the child is not living with the parent, to maintain personal relations and direct contact with the child on a regular basis; and
(d) to act as the child's legal representative.[31]

4–16 These responsibilities last until the child reaches 16, with the exception of s.1(1)(b)(ii) which persists until the child is 18.[32] A parent now has the right:

(a) to have the child living with him or otherwise to regulate the child's residence;
(b) to control, direct or guide, in a manner appropriate to the stage of development of the child, the child's upbringing;

---

[29] See *Scott v Occidental Petroleum (Caledonia) Ltd*, 1990 S.L.T. 882 (decided at common law) where it was agreed a mother's responsibility for administering a child's property could be delegated to a judicial factor but not completely transferred to trustees.
[30] 1995 Act, s.3(6).
[31] *ibid.*, s.1. References hereafter are to the 1995 Act unless otherwise stated.
[32] s.1(2).

    (c) if the child is not living with him, to maintain personal relations
        and contact with the child on a regular basis; and
    (d) to act as the child's legal representative.[33]

It is evident that the new responsibilities of s.1 are intimately related
to the rights of s.2. This is only natural as the rights are endowed to
enable parents to fulfil their duties. The duty on the non-residential
parent to maintain personal relations and regular contact with his
child in s.1(1)(c), for example, is enabled by the *right* to contact in
s.2(1)(c).

The list of rights in s.2 is comprehensive, superseding any analo- **4–17**
gous rights previously enjoyed by parents at common law.[34] What was
known as the right of "custody" prior to the 1995 Act has been split
neatly into its two aspects: first, the right to regulate the physical residence of the child; and secondly, the more general right to determine
every aspect of the child's upbringing. This will include such matters
as the right to determine how and where the child is educated, what
religion the child is raised in, how the child's leisure time is spent, what
clothes the child wears, with whom he or she associates and a myriad
other matters. Not every aspect of "upbringing" however may be
regarded as a matter of parental right.[35]

If a parent does not share a home with his or her child then he or
she has the right to maintain contact with that child, a right known
prior to the 1995 Act as "access". Such a right might be exercised by
visits to, or at, the main place of residence of the child or elsewhere,
or by periods in which the child temporarily resides with the non-
residential parent, e.g. weekends, school holidays. The right to act as
the child's legal representative covers acts such as the giving of a legal
consent, the representation of the child in litigation and the administration of the child's property, all of which were previously seen as
elements of the parental rights of guardianship. Since a legal consent
may be required for a wide range of activities such as having a surgical procedure or joining a club or association, there may well be some
overlap between the right to direct the child's upbringing and the right
of legal representation. We consider some of these aspects of parental
responsibility in more detail at paras 5–23 *et seq.*

All parental *rights* terminate at age 16.[36] This is consistent with the
view taken by the Age of Legal Capacity (Scotland) Act 1991 that
children attain full legal capacity at the age of 16.[37] Yet, even young

---

[33] s.2(1).
[34] 1995 Act, s.2(5). *Statutory* rights given to parents, e.g. the right to register the name of the child at birth, are unaffected.
[35] e.g. in *Flett v Flett*, 1994 S.C.L.R. 189 it was originally held in Scots law that the giving of children's surnames was not a matter of PRRs but merely custom and practice. This was later reconsidered: see Ch.5, para.5.22.
[36] s.2(7).
[37] 1991 Act, s.1. See Ch.2.

persons over 16 may benefit during the transient stage between childhood and adulthood of 16–18 from parental *guidance* as opposed to control. For this reason, parents are still legally *responsible* for the guidance of their children to the age of 18 although they have no formal right to make choices for them.[38]

4–18   Does the move from talk of parental rights to responsibility signify a real sea-change in Scots law towards child-centeredness or just a change of terminology? The 1995 Act attempts to give the concept of responsibility teeth by making it plain that children have title to sue parents who fail to fulfil their parental duties.[39] Furthermore, children need no longer be represented by their parents in such litigation, nor by a curator *ad litem* whose principal duty is to the court, but are recognised as having independent capacity to instruct solicitors so long as they are capable of understanding the nature and consequences of such an act.[40] Although doubtless Parliament did not envisage this would cause gangs of disgruntled children to rush out and serve writs on their slovenly parents, it is a valuable remedy. Children might, for example, sue errant divorced fathers who failed to exercise their duty of contact regularly (although it is doubtful how useful a remedy the court could provide). More seriously, they might sue parents for damages in respect of sexual or physical abuse. However, the courts will probably be unwilling to find a parent negligently rather than deliberately in breach of parental duties. Consider comments recently made by the Court of Appeal in the English case of *Surtees v Kingston-Upon-Thames Borough Council*[41] in which foster parents were sued for negligently allowing a child in their care to be scalded while bathing:

> "There are very real public policy considerations to be taken into account if the conflicts inherent in legal proceedings are to be brought into family relationships . . . We should be slow to characterise as negligent the care which ordinary loving and careful mothers are able to give to individual children, given the rough-and-tumble of home life".

Having said all this, one might go further and ask why the parental responsibilities of s.1 are not turned round and listed as the rights of children. To answer this requires more consideration of what is meant by "children's rights".

---

[38] See *Report on Family Law*, Scot. Law Com. No.135 (1992), paras 2.7–2.13. It was also suggested that persons under 18 were owed such guidance in terms of the UNCRC which defines children as persons under 18.

[39] 1995 Act, s.1(3) but see also cases cited at para.4–42.

[40] 1991 Act, s.4A, inserted by 1995 Act, Sch.1, para.44. See further on a child's capacity to litigate independently, paras 2–38 to 2–43.

[41] [1991] 2 F.L.R. 559.

CHILDREN'S RIGHTS[42]

The 1995 Act is arguably not concerned with children's rights. As we **4-19** have seen, it clearly states that parental rights exist only in order to further the interests of children and not the interests of parents. However, this is not the same as saying the Act gives *children* rights. An example helps to illustrate this. In the case of *Finlayson Petr*, discussed above, the parents' view of how best to fulfil their parental duties was rejected by the courts in the interest of the child involved. Essentially, the parental right to decide was replaced by the right of the courts to decide. At no point in the case was the opinion of the child himself, a 9-year-old boy, canvassed as to whether he supported his parents' views on medical treatment; and whatever his wishes were, they would not legally have decided the issue (though they might have contributed to the court's view of what his best interests were). He had no *right* to decide his medical treatment but was subject to the desire of his parents, themselves subject to the restraint of the welfare principle.

Similarly, in divorce cases, where there is disagreement between **4-20** parents as to post-divorce arrangements for children, the court is instructed to decide which parent shall have the child living with them, and any issue of contact, on the basis that the welfare of the child is paramount but *having regard* to the views of the child.[43] In such cases, it is not unusual for the court to hear the wishes of the child but equally usual for these wishes not to be automatically respected. The justification is that children, depending on their age and maturity, do not always know what is best for them. In *Fowler v Fowler*,[44] for example, a pre-1995 Act custody case where the views of the child concerned were put forward in evidence, Lord Stott had this to say:

> "I am fully conscious of the fact that that while in questions of custody the interest of the child is the paramount consideration it cannot be assumed that a child's interests necessarily coincide with her wishes."

He subsequently went on to consider if the child's views had been extracted by pressure from one or both parents, or brainwashing,

---

[42] There is a large body of literature on the nature of children's rights which it is outwith the scope of this book to deal with in detail, A useful recent collection is *The Ideologies of Children's Rights* (Freeman and Veerman (eds), 1992); see also the essays in 5 *International Journal of Law and the Family* (1991), and *Children's Rights in Scotland* (Cleland and Sutherland (eds), 2nd edn, 2001). See also the extensive discussion on the inter-relationship of children's rights in domestic law and international human rights standards below and at paras 2–06 *et seq.* above.

[43] 1995 Act, s.11(7)(a) and (b).

[44] 1981 S.L.T. (Notes) 9. See also *Russell v Russell*, 1991 S.C.L.R. 429; *Joffre v Joffre*, 1992 G.W.D. 27-1522, and para.4–87 below.

before accepting them as valid and the child as reasonably intelligent. This paternalistic attitude is perfectly acceptable in accord with the welfare principle under the 1995 Act but does not accord children *rights* in the divorce process.[45]

4-21   There are many definitions of rights but what they tend to have in common is the idea that a right must be respected by those against whom it can be said to operate. If the right is flouted then the rightholder can use the rules and agents of the legal system to protect and assert it. Feinberg states that:

> "Rights are not mere gifts or favours, motivated by love or pity, for which gratitude is the sole fitting response. A right is something a man can stand on, something that can be demanded and insisted upon without embarrassment or shame."[46]

Adults can vindicate their right to ownership of their own property in the courts. They can ask a court to restore their right to freedom if they are imprisoned for no legal cause. Children may be able to sue their parents to fulfil their PRRs under the 1995 Act but they cannot, within that Act's schema, ask the court to uphold their right, say, to live with their father rather than their mother *unless* they can convince the court this is in their best interests. Effectively, this means, in the strict sense, the child does not have the right of freedom of residence in the same sense as an adult does. Of course a child may simply refuse to stay with the allotted parent and run away; he or she retains de facto power, depending on age. But this is not the same as having legal rights.[47]

Domestic Children's Rights and the Influence of International Human Rights Standards

4-22   In recent years, however, as discussed above at paras 2–05 *et seq.*, the landscape of children's rights has shifted radically as a result of greater awareness of international human rights standards, both in the form of general human rights instruments and those tailored directly for children. In Ch.2, we discussed how the incorporation of the European Convention on Human Rights (the "ECHR") into United Kingdom domestic law in the Human Rights Act 1998 provides basic guarantees of fundamental civil and political rights to all United Kingdom citizens, which are now directly enforceable in *all* United Kingdom courts (not just final courts of appeal after exhaustion of

---

[45] For further consideration of the wishes of the child in residence and contact orders see para.4–87.

[46] Feinberg, *Social Philosophy* (1973), pp.58–59.

[47] Kathleen Marshall makes this point strongly, stating that if children's rights in decision making are not recognised, they will subvert parental attempts to control them (Marshall, "Rights and Responsibilities in the Family", unpublished paper available from Scottish Child Law Centre, 1993).

other remedies, or at the European Court of Human Rights in Strasbourg). For the first time therefore, children (although not mentioned as a particular subset of citizens empowered by the ECHR) can at least in theory make claims for enforcement of their private law rights in United Kingdom domestic courts, without necessarily having those claims mediated by the "best interests" principle. (Perhaps, more unfortunately, the same is also true for claims made by parents in respect of their rights *over* children.[48]) This has the potential to revolutionise the effectiveness of child rights, and we have already seen considerable change in the law as a direct result of challenges made under the ECHR. Corporal punishment of children, for example, was banned from local authority schools as a result of a Strasbourg ECHR case, *Campbell and Cosans v UK*[49] and more recently, the parental "right of chastisement" discussed at para.4.05 above was abolished as a result of the Strasbourg case of *A v UK*.[50] Parental rights to discipline children physically remain, but in extremely attenuated form and it will probably not be too long before international pressure demands abolition of "smacking" altogether. For right or wrong, this has been a clear victory for children's rights.

The UN Convention on the Rights of Children ("UNCRC"), **4–23** arguably the most influential and authoritative source of rights for children in modern law as discussed in Ch.2, is, meanwhile, not a source of Scots or United Kingdom law, having not yet been incorporated. It is thus merely persuasive in Scots courts. However it is often cited in Scottish child law cases and was one of the leading influences on the drafting of the 1995 Act. Furthermore the Government of the United Kingdom is under an international obligation to bring its domestic law into line with the minimum standards set by the Convention and must periodically supply reports on its progress in meeting this obligation.

One right asserted in the UN Convention has particular significance for private law rights and is implementable without the need for comprehensive economic programmes: the right of the child to be consulted in Art.12.

Article 12 states that: **4–24**

> "1. States parties shall assure to the child who is capable of forming his or her own views the right to express those views freely in all matters affecting the child, the views of the child being given due weight in accordance with the age and maturity of the child.

---

[48] However the Scottish courts have so far successfully attempted to resist incursion into the welfare principle by the "rights based discourse" of the ECHR. See para.2–06 above discussing *White v White*, 2001 S.L.T. 485, and Ch.2 generally on adoption and human rights.

[49] 1982 4 E.H.R.R. 293.

[50] [1998] EHRLR 82; [1999] 27 E.H.R.R. 611. See further Ch.5 at paras 5–11 *et seq.*

2. For this purpose, the child shall, in particular, be provided the opportunity to be heard in any judicial or administrative proceedings affecting the child, either directly or through a representative or an appropriate body, in a manner consistent with the procedural rules of national law".

It is this right, the right to be heard and thus to participate in decisions, rather than to actually make or take control of decisions, which is unequivocally protected and recognised by the Children (Scotland) Act. Section 11(7)(b) of the 1995 Act provides that when a court is making any order relevant to parental responsibilities or rights then it shall have regard so far as practicable to the views (if he or she wishes to express them) of the child concerned, taking account of his or her age and maturity. Furthermore, a child aged 12 or more is presumed to be sufficiently mature to form a view (s.11(10)). Although this is newly stated in statute, it is nothing very novel in the law of Scotland. As we have seen above in *Fowler*, the courts have always been prepared to consider the views of the child concerned as one of the factors relevant to making a decision about custody or access (now residence and contact). However, this has never compelled them to accept the views of children as decisive and s.11(7)(b) does nothing to alter this.

4–25   What is more radical is the provision in s.6(1) of the 1995 Act that where *any person* makes a "major decision" relating to parental responsibility or rights then they shall have regard as far as practicable to the views of the child.[51] Again, this is subject to the child's age and maturity and a 12-year-old child is presumed sufficiently mature to form a view. In theory, this affects every serious decision made by a parent. For example, parents who are divorcing often execute minutes of agreements which make detailed arrangements as to with whom the children should reside and what contact arrangements should be made for the non-residential parent. Such agreements are subject to the scrutiny of the court during the divorce process to see whether they are in the welfare of the child, but are usually rubber stamped. Parents must in theory consult their children of sufficient age and maturity before making such agreements. What sanctions are there for non consultation? Presumably the court could refuse to accept the provisions of the minute if there was inadequate evidence of consultation. In most parental decisions however, the courts are not directly involved, e.g. if parents choose to move the household, without consultation, from Edinburgh to Lerwick, and in such circumstances it is hard to see what legal damages there could be even if the children went so far as to sue the parents for their failure in duty of consultation. The Act also specifically provides that lack of consultation cannot be grounds for challenging a transaction entered

---

[51] They should also take account of the views of any other person with parental responsibilities and rights.

into by a third party in good faith, e.g. if a parent acting as legal representative sold a 12-year-old child's house to a bona fide third party without the child's knowledge or consent then the child could not have that sale reduced.[52] There was considerable scepticism at the time that s.6 was passed that its effect would be symbolic only, and 10 years on it is still unclear if parental consultation is embedded in practice as well as theory. A pilot study by the Scottish Executive in 2002 found that there were still problems with respect to hearing the "voice of the child": social barriers to child representation and participation in legal proceedings still remained (see also C.2); children have difficulties accessing the information necessary to participate (though the Internet may have partly ameliorated this since); and gender differences exist, with boys finding it less easy than girls to talk to their families. More training for legal and other professionals would also help children to participate in decisions.[53]

Can it be said then that the 1995 Act does not only protect children **4–26** but also gives them significant rights? The right of consultation found in ss.11 and 6 is a far cry from the kind of children's rights espoused by radical child liberationists. Writers such as Richard Parson and John Holt have argued for the equal treatment of children under the law, which they take to mean having equal rights like adults to work for money, vote and take a full part in political affairs, travel and live away from home, control (or abandon) their own education, handle their own financial affairs, engage in sexual relations legal between consenting adults and generally run their own lives in a self-determining fashion. They argue that age is as suspect and discriminatory a reason to withhold rights as race or gender once were, that some children exceed some adults in cognitive ability, and that in any case, adults are not tested on their cognitive capacities before they are allowed to vote, work, etc. As Parson has put it, "The only people in our society who are incarcerated against their will are criminals, the mentally ill and children in schools".[54]

There is little sympathy for this kind of extreme advocacy of chil- **4–27** dren's rights in Scots law and for good reason. The corollary of rights is responsibility, and if we are to give children these kind of rights of self-determination then we are also logically giving them responsibility for their own survival,[55] and the power not only to run but also to wreck their own lives. Freeman, for example, justifies compulsory education of children and restrictions on child employment, because if children are not forcibly given the opportunity to

---

[52] s.6(2).
[53] See Marshall, Tisdall, Cleland at al., *"Voice of the Child" Under the Children (Scotland) Act 1995: Giving Due Regard to Children's Views In All Matters That Affect Them, Parts 1 and 2* (Scottish Executive Central Research Unit, 2002).
[54] Parson, *Birthrights* (1978), p.96.
[55] Bainham, e.g. points out that if children are emancipated from parental rights and responsibility, it seems hard to justify why parents should be under an obligation to pay maintenance (1994 J.S.W.L. 552).

gain an education then they will not be able to maximise their future development and realise their potential for a future as a rationally autonomous person. He argues persuasively that the ideas of child rights and child protection are not so opposed as has been presented thus far, and that respect for the personality of children can be expressed by protection consonant with their age and maturity, as well as respect for their independent capacity.[56] Another way to say this perhaps is that one of the rights of children should be a right to a childhood.[57]

4–28   The right to consultation can be regarded in this context then as a kind of compromise between child protection and child autonomy: it gives children the chance to participate in and influence decisions affecting them, but it does not allow them through immaturity or inexperience to jeopardise their own future. While parents and children have roughly harmonious goals, this seems a viable solution. But we must turn now to examining how serious conflict between the wishes of parents, and children as they approach adulthood, is handled by the law.

Conflict between Children and Parents

4–29 In the discussion so far we have talked, for simplicity, of children as if they were all of the same kind. But it is of course apparent that children vary considerably in their maturity and capacity to understand and thus to make their own choices. In particular, adolescent children approaching the age of 16 and full capacity have a special claim to have their choices given weight. They are also more likely to find themselves in conflict with parents than younger children as an inevitable part of the process of growing up, and particularly, reaching sexual maturity. Above, we noted that by s.2(7) of the 1995 Act, parental rights extend until the child reaches 16. Thus it seemed that children to this age have no independent rights to make their own choices, but are subject to the rights of parents, who are themselves responsible for exercising these rights in accordance with the welfare principle.

4–30   This model does not fit well with the current international appreciation for the rights of children, nor with the idea that children are of steadily growing capacity throughout their childhood. Scots law historically recognised the emerging capacity of older children by dividing persons below the age of majority into pupils, who had little or no active legal capacity, and minors, who were still subject to the control of their parents or guardians in relation to their property, but were free to make their own decisions concerning their person. However, this distinction was more or less swept away by the Age of

---

[56] Freeman above (n.11), Ch.2.
[57] *ibid.* at p.3.

Legal Capacity (Scotland) Act 1991, which states in s.1 that children under 16 in principle have no legal capacity to enter any juristic transaction (subject to some important exceptions) while children over 16 have essentially full adult legal capacity.[58]

However, this is not the end of the story for children under 16. In **4-31** Ch.2, we considered in detail the case of *Gillick v West Norfolk and Wisbech Area Health Authority*,[59] an English case but one which has been accepted as highly influential in Scots law. Here the House of Lords held that, exceptionally, children under 16 have the right to give their own consent to medical treatment, provided they have attained a degree of maturity and understanding sufficient to appreciate the risks and advantages of the treatment proposed; a standard that has since become known as *"Gillick*-competence". There was, however, dissention between Lords Fraser and Scarman as to whether a child could only be regarded as *"Gillick*-competent" if he or she were acting in his or her best interests. Lord Scarman held, correctly in the view of this writer, that competence involves only "sufficient understanding and intelligence" which would mean competent children would be free, like adults, to make mistakes as well as wise choices in their own welfare.

It is clearly the ratio of *Gillick* that if a child is found to be *Gillick*- **4-32** competent, not only does he or she have the right to consent, but also a parent cannot exercise any right of veto. So a girl of 15 who is found to be *Gillick*-competent can go on the Pill without having to get the consent of her parent, and even if the parent finds out and opposes this course, this will have no legal effect.[60] Lord Scarman in a key dictum put it this way:

> "parental right *yields* to the child's right to make his own decisions where he reaches a sufficient understanding and intelligence to be capable of making up his own mind on the matter requiring decision".[61] [Emphasis added.]

On the face of it, this seems to imply quite plainly that where a child is competent to consent, parental rights terminate. Thus, if a competent child refused to consent, the parent's right to consent would have terminated and so no-one could consent to the procedure: hence the child would have an effective right to refuse any procedure.

However, English cases subsequent to *Gillick* have interpreted it **4-33** quite differently. In *Re R (A Minor)*[62] a girl aged 15 years and 10 months suffered from severe mental health problems including psychotic episodes. The question arose as to whether the local authority,

---

[58] Discussed in detail in Ch.2.
[59] [1985] 3 All E.R. 402. See paras 2–29 to 2–32.
[60] However, it must be noted that both Lords Scarman and Fraser felt that a doctor was under a duty to try *to persuade* the child to consult with parents.
[61] Lord Scarman, at p.422a.
[62] [1991] 4 All E.R. 177. See also *Re W* [1992] 4 All E.R. 62.

who had assumed parental rights from her natural parents, could consent to psychiatric treatment, including the administration of drugs, even if R herself *refused* to consent. R was found in the course of proceedings not to be *"Gillick-*competent" due to the fluctuating nature of her mental capacity, but Lord Donaldson chose anyway to discuss how the issue would have been resolved, if she had been so competent. He found that even if R had the right to consent, the *parent's* right to consent did not totally disappear but was simply no longer able to defeat any consent given by the child. Thus, even if the child *refused* to give a consent, there was nothing to stop the parent supplying it. Lord Donaldson chose to regard both the child and the parents as "keyholders": both parents and child hold a "key"—the right to consent to treatment—but if one does not choose to "unlock the door", that is, give consent, this did not mean another keyholder cannot. Thus, even if R refused to take anti-psychotic drugs, the local authority could still give consent for them to be given.

4–34   In Scotland, as we saw in Ch.2, the kernel of *Gillick* was put on a statutory basis in s.2(4) of the 1991 Act, which provides that children under 16 can consent on their own behalf to any surgical, medical or dental procedure where, in the opinion of a qualified medical practitioner, they are capable of understanding the nature and possible consequences of the procedure or treatment. No Scottish case has yet authoritatively decided if the right to "consent" of s.2(4) includes the right to refuse consent[63] and in this absence of authority *Re R* must thus be regarded as persuasive. This would be bad news indeed for children's rights in Scotland, as it appears to sanction the possibility of mature and competent children being subjected against their wishes to drug treatment, compulsory hospitalisation, and possibly even abortion or surgical procedures such as the removal of organs for donation. In *Houston*[64] Sheriff McGowan found that a mother did not have the right to give a consent to detention of her 15-year-old son, when the son himself, who, it was conceded, was competent under s.2(4), was refusing consent. In his view,

> "the patient [was] competent and entitled to decide not to accept the medical treatment prescribed for him. That refusal is not overridden by the consent given by the mother".

These remarks, though strongly asserted, do however, appear to be obiter and therefore not binding on future courts.

---

[63] In *V v F*, 1991 S.C.L.R. 225, Sheriff Poole found parents had the right to consent to the treatment of a 15-year-old girl for depression, even in spite of her own refusal to accept treatment (hospitalisation). However, the case was decided prior to s.2(4) coming into force, and it is difficult to tell from the report if the girl in question was regarded as *"Gillick-*competent" or without legal capacity to consent; hence it is of little value as a precedent.

[64] 1996 S.C.L.R. 943.

Most Scottish commentators, such as Wilkinson and Norrie, have **4–35** however taken the view that *Re R* and *Re W* do not represent the law of Scotland and that the right to consent does include the right to refuse consent.[65] Current NHS guidance notes to doctors in Scotland also recommend that the refusal of treatment by "competent young people" under 16 "must be respected".[66]

This leaves one final concern: do the *courts* have the right to over- **4–36** ride the wishes of the *Gillick*-competent child? To this the answer is almost certainly yes,[67] so long as the child is under the age of 16 the court retains the right to make an order "in relation to (a) parental responsibilities [and] (b) parental rights" (s.11(1) of the 1995 Act).[68] We examine the criteria the courts will apply when deciding whether to make a s.11 order in the next section.

Section 2(4) of the 1991 Act deals only with medical treatment, as **4–37** does the *ratio of Gillick*. However, there seems no good policy reason why mature minors approaching the age of 16 should not be able to make their own choices in other areas which would previously have been dealt with solely by parents by virtue of their parental rights. For example, children who are mature enough to understand the nature and consequences of their choices should be able to make their own choice of religion, even if it is not clearly in their welfare, e.g. a religion which encourages the giving away of all one's property, or forbids the use of modern medicine, despite parental opposition. Similarly competent children should be able to determine their own residence. These were rights which once accrued to a Scots child at a pre-determined age of minority (12 for a girl, 14 for a boy) but which are better seen now as arising from a certain degree of cognitive capacity and emotional maturity rather than mere attainment of age. As with the right to consent to medical treatment, if a child is competent to consent then the parent's right to determine the issue should terminate.

---

[65] See Wilkinson and Norrie (2nd edn), para.8.50; L. Edwards, "The right to consent and the right to refuse" [1993] Jur Rev 52.

[66] *A Guide to Consent to Examination, Investigation, Treatment or Operation* (NHS in Scotland, 1992), para.14. These notes are currently under review at time of writing (April 2006). The new version suggests: "Occasionally, there may be a difference of opinion between the young person and the parent. Dealing with the situation professionally and tactfully may help reach an agreement. However, where the child has the capacity to make the healthcare decision in question, then the child's decision must be respected even if it differs from the parents' views or yours".

[67] In England, it was established in *Re W* (above) that the courts could override the wishes of a child until the age of 18 by virtue of their inherent protective jurisdiction. In Scotland, it seems highly unlikely the child over 16 but under 18 could be subjected to the authority of the court, even via the *nobile officium*, since the whole scheme of modern child law is that the child over 16 is *sui juris. Sed quaere* Lord Hope's comments in *Law Hospital NHS Trust v Lord Advocate*, 1996 S.L.T. 848.

[68] Logically, it could be asserted that once the child is competent, the issue is no longer one of *parental* rights and therefore the court has no jurisdiction. However, the court is likely to regard the issue as one falling into their competence since parental rights and responsibilities under ss.1 and 2 last prima facie until the child is 16.

COURT ORDERS

4–38 The courts may become involved with the relationship between children and parents for a number of reasons. As we have seen, outside agencies, such as hospitals, may apply to the courts to establish if parents are exercising their rights in the welfare of the child concerned. Children themselves may invoke the jurisdiction of the court in order to assert their own rights or to challenge parental discretion. And as we saw in Ch.3, it is not uncommon for a person with no PRRs, such as an unmarried father, step-parent or grandparent to apply to the court for full PRRs or some aspect thereof (e.g. rights of contact with the child). Most commonly, however, the courts will be invoked because of a conflict of wishes between two persons who both have PRRs. This conflict most frequently arises in the context of divorce.

Applications for Parental Responsibility and Rights

4–39 Under s.11 of the 1995 Act, an application can be made to the court in relation to parental responsibilities, parental rights, guardianship or the administration of the child's property. Such an application can be made by:

(a) persons who already have parental responsibilities or rights, such as, typically, married parents;
(b) persons who have never had parental responsibilities or rights but claim an "interest"[69]; and
(c) the child[70] him or herself.

Who qualifies as a person who "claims an interest" in relation to s.11? Obvious candidates include unmarried fathers without automatic PRRs, grandparents and siblings of the child concerned, who may be seeking contact, perhaps if the child has been adopted by new parents who have no desire to maintain contact between the newly adopted child and the natural relatives.[71] In *F v F*,[72] Lord Hope took a general liberal approach to the question of interest. His attitude was that the requirement of a claim of interest "was not intended to restrict the category of [applicants] with results which could in some cases be contrary to the best interests of the child". It would seem that not only blood relatives and carers, but also anyone with a connection to, or interest in, the welfare of the child, such as

---

[69] s.11(3)(a)(i) and (ii).
[70] 1995 Act, s.11(5). For a child's right to instruct a solicitor and raise an action in his or her own name, see paras 2–38 to 2–43.
[71] A sister in this position was held to have "interest" in *AB v M*, 1988 S.L.T. 652 (decided in relation to s.3 of the Law Reform (Parent and Child) (Scotland) Act 1986).
[72] 1991 S.L.T. 357 (again, decided in relation to s.3 of the 1986 Act).

a friend, teacher, doctor, health visitor, etc. can claim the requisite
"interest".[73]

However, persons who have been deprived of parental responsibil- **4–40**
ities and rights as a result of their child being adopted, freed for adoption, compulsorily taken into care by the local authority by virtue of
a parental responsibilities order[74] or made the subject of a parental
order,[75] are currently *barred* from using s.11 to re-acquire rights.[76] The
policy behind the law here is that since these persons will either have
been deprived of PRRs for good reasons, or have consented to the
removal of PRRs, they should not be allowed to return to the courts,
possibly repeatedly, to attempt to recover some or all rights, as this
would not be in the interests of the welfare and stability of the child,
(and, where applicable, the new adoptive family).

Potential problems arise however with the strictness of this rule. For **4–41**
example, a birth mother, who consented to the making of an adoption
order during a period of illness or drug addiction, might later be reha-
bilitated and seek, not the return of her child, but a limited right, such
as contact, and this might be seen in an older child adoption as in the
interests of all concerned. It has in fact been declared to be a breach
of Art.8 of the ECHR for a parent whose rights were removed by a
freeing for adoption order to have no right thereafter to seek contact
rights, within certain contexts such as "open" adoption.[77] As a result,
it is likely that both parental responsibilities orders (PROs) and
freeing for adoption orders will shortly be replaced by "permanency
orders" in the Adoption (Scotland) Act 2006, and that under that law,
even after PRRs are removed from parents by a permanency order, it
will still be possible for those persons to seek PRRs, albeit only with
the leave of the court.[78] Hopefully this will strike a balance between
allowing repetitive litigation in hopeless cases which could nonetheless
prejudice the stability and welfare of the child in question, and giving
genuinely meritorious cases a chance to explore the substance of their

---

[73] A restrictive approach to title and "interest" was however applied to a same-sex
partner in *X v Y* (2002) Fam. L.R. 58 (see para.4–76 below). It is submitted this case
was wrongly decided.

[74] Under s.86 of the 1995 Act—see paras 7–59 to 7–62.

[75] Under s.30 of the HFEA 1990—see paras 3–85 to 3–87.

[76] 1995 Act, s.11(3)(a)(iii) and (4) (extending the House of Lords decision in *D v
Grampian Regional Council*, 1995 S.L.T. 519, which was made in relation to s.11's
predecessor, s.3 of the Law Reform (Parent and Child) (Scotland) Act 1986).

[77] See *Midlothian Council v W*, 2005 S.L.T. 146. (But note obiter dicta in *West Lothian
Council v McG*, 2000 S.C. 411, which clearly indicate not every freeing case will
involve a breach of Art.8.) Freeing for adoptionn has to be distinguished from the
making of an ordinary adoption order, where the court is allowed to make a contact
order at the same time as allowing the adoption. Accordingly, the s.11 bar on birth
parents seeking contact after adoption was, by contrast, held *not* to be contrary to
Art.8 in *Dundee City Council v GK and the Scottish Ministers*, December 22, 2005,
noted in (2006) Fam. L.B. 79-5. For discussion of freeing for adoption, its replacement by permanency orders, and "open" adoption, see Ch.6.

[78] See further, Ch.6.

claims in court. Local authorities are also barred from using s.11[79] as in principle if they wish to acquire rights over children, or deprive natural parents of responsibility, they should use the "public law" provisions of the adoption and childcare statutes, which contain detailed procedures designed to safeguard the interests of those parents as well as the welfare of the child. Interestingly, however, it has been held possible for local authorities to *defend* s.11 actions, and to enter them as party minuters.[80]

4–42   Controversy has also arisen in relation to title to sue in s.11 applications for contact by children under 16. As noted above, s.11(5) clearly contemplates that s.11 applications might be made by children themselves, as well as their parents, or other holders of PRRs, so long as they could claim "interest". Yet in *D v H*,[80a] it was held by Sheriff Principal Bowen, on rather technical grounds,[81] that a 15-and-a-half-year-old boy was not entitled to seek an order under s.11(2)(d) for contact with his 14-year-old sister. The policy argument underlying is that since parental rights are given to persons to further the exercise of parental responsibilities, the Act did not contemplate parental rights being granted to persons under 16 who cannot fulfil such responsibilities. Not only does this run against the longstanding policy of Scots law that a liberal attitude to title to sue in family actions should be adopted (see para.4–40 above) but it also seems to fly in the face of the 1995 Act's general empowering attitude towards children's rights in general, and children's rights of independent litigation in particular. *D v H* was distinguished (though not over-ruled) in the Dundee Sheriff Court case of *E v E*.[82] The key distinction asserted was that the pursuer in *E v E* had a better case on the merits than the boy in *D v H* and therefore should not be denied the opportunity to pursue his case. The sheriff took note also however of the rights of the child under both the ECHR and the UNCRC and declared that s.11 should not be interpreted restrictively but to accord with these instruments.

4–43   It is worth noting that if a child sought contact with an *adult*, the problem could be avoided if the court was craved to impose a parental *responsibility* on the adult in question, rather than a parental *right* on the child pursuer.[83] However this seems a rather artificial solution to an artificial problem.

---

[79] 1995 Act, s.11(5). There was dissent over whether this prohibition existed in relation to s.3 of the 1986 Act: see *M v Dumfries and Galloway*, 1991 S.C.L.R. 481, not followed in *City of Edinburgh DC v M*, 1996 S.L.T. 112.

[80] *McLean v Dornan*, 2001 Fam. L.R. 58; 2001 S.L.T. (Sh Ct) 97.

[80a] 2004 S.L.T. (Sh Ct) 73.

[81] The basic argument is that s.11(2)(b) of the 1995 Act only allows the court to impose responsibilities and rights n persons who are "at least 16 years of age" (or a parent of the child in question.) Section 11(2)(d) which allows the making specifically of a contact order has no such restriction. The order in *D v H* was sought under s.11(2)(d) exclusively, but the Sheriff Principal accepted that contact orders are all sub-sets of orders imposing PRRs made under s.11(2)(b).

[82] 2004 Fam. L.R. 115.

[83] See s.11(2)(b)(i).

An application can be made under s.11 either as an independent **4-44** action, or as an ancillary issue to divorce proceedings.[84] The action can be raised in the Sheriff Court or the Court of Session. In independent applications, the Court of Session has jurisdiction if the child is habitually resident in Scotland at the date of the application, or is present in Scotland and not habitually resident in any other part of the United Kingdom.[85] It also has an emergency jurisdiction to hear the case if the child is present in Scotland and at the date of the application it is necessary for the protection of the child to make an order immediately.[86] The appropriate Sheriff Court has concurrent jurisdiction on the same basis with the additional proviso that the child be habitually resident, or present (as appropriate) in the sheriffdom.[87] In relation to s.11 applications specifically relating to the administration of the child's property, the Court of Session has jurisdiction if the child's property is situated in Scotland or the child is habitually resident in Scotland; the Sheriff Court has jurisdiction if the property is situated, or the child is habitually resident in, the sheriffdom.[88] Where a s.11 application is made relating to the guardianship of the child, jurisdiction is based on the child's habitual residence in Scotland or as appropriate, the sheriffdom.[89]

All the above is now, perhaps unfortunately, subject to mandatory **4-45** European rules of jurisdiction, known as Brussels II *bis*,[90] governing all Member States of the EU. These rules take precedence over the 1986 Act in all cases to which the Regulation applies.[91] Brussels II *bis* determines which part of the United Kingdom hears a case relating to parental responsibility—Scotland, England and Wales, Northern Ireland, etc.—but does not determine which *courts*, e.g. Glasgow or Dundee Sheriff Court, hear a particular case *within* a part of the United Kingdom.[92] That decision thus still falls under the rules of the Family Law Act 1986. In most domestic cases involving parents and children exclusively Scottish habitually resident, the new rules are

---

[84] 1995 Act, s.11(1) and (1A). See Ch.14 for background to the divorce process and ancillary actions, and jurisdiction to raise such.

[85] Family Law Act 1986, ss.9(a) and 10(a).

[86] *ibid.*, s.12.

[87] Family Law Act 1986, ss.9(b), 10(b) and 12.

[88] 1995 Act, s.14(1) and (2).

[89] Family Law Act 1986, s.16.

[90] EC Council Regulation No 2201/2003 which came into force with direct effect in the UK (and throughout the EU) on March 1, 2005. It repealed the previous Brussels II Regulation No 1347/2000. For clarity, Brussels II *bis* is also incorporated into Scots law by the European Communities (Matrimonial and Parental Responsibility Jurisdiction and Judgments) (Scotland) Regulations (SSI 2005/42). Reg.5 of the 2005 Regulations expressly applies the EC rules to ss.9, 11 and 13 of the Children (Scotland) Act 1995. The amendments only apply to actions commenced after March 1, 2005.

[91] Children (Scotland) Act 1995, s.14(5), inserted by SSI 2005/42, above; Family Law Act 1986, s.17A, inserted by *ibid.*

[92] See further, *Butterworths Family Law Service*, paras C602 *et seq.*

likely to make little difference. But in cases involving a foreign element, these rules may be very significant.

4–46 The Regulation covers cases involving "parental responsibility" whether or not the action is connected to an action of divorce, judicial separation or nullity. So actions for say, contact or residence, in relation to children of an unmarried couple, or stepchildren, are included.[93] "Parental responsibility" includes rights of custody and access, guardianship, actions to do with the child's person or property, fostering and the protection of the child. It does not however cover parentage, adoption, the name of the child, maintenance (aliment), trusts or succession.[94] In general, under Art.8 of Brussels II *bis*, the courts of a Member State have jurisdiction if the child is habitually resident[95] in that Member State at the time the court is seised. However under Art.9, if the child moves lawfully[96] (i.e. not by means of abduction or retention) to another EU Member State, the courts of his former habitual residence retain jurisdiction in relation only to variation of access or contact rights for three months. (This rule applies only if the holder of access/contact rights remains in the former state and there is no agreement ("prorogation") for a new jurisdiction to be in charge of the matter.) Parties can agree on a new jurisdiction to hear disputes relating to parental responsibility so long as this is in the welfare of the child.[97] If a court cannot be identified from the above rules to hear an action for parental responsibility, the court where the child is present shall have jurisdiction.[98] This also applies to refugee and internationally-displaced children. In exceptional cases, a court can transfer a child case to a court it regards as better placed to hear the case.[99]

4–47 In actions for divorce, judicial separation or declarator of nullity of marriage, the court not only has jurisdiction but also the obligation to consider whether it is necessary for them to make a s.11 order in relation to any child of the family under the age of 16.[1] In other

---

[93] Art.1(1), Brussels II *bis*.

[94] Art.1(2) and (3), *ibid*.

[95] "Habitual residence" is not defined in the Regulation. Instead, it is to be interpreted according to the case law of the court where the matter arises (Art.66). Accordingly in Scotland, existing Scottish case law on "habitual residence" is relevant.

[96] If the child moves *unlawfully*, i.e. as a result of removal or retention in breach of custody rights acquired by law or by court order or by agreement, then the rules as to when the court may accept jurisdiction are different, and somewhat similar to those in the Hague Convention on the International Abduction of Children 1980, though stricter—see Arts 2(11) and 10 and 11. However Brussels II *bis* takes precedence over Hague for EU Member States—see Art.66. The question of child abduction, and the problems it rises in relation to jurisdiction, recognition and enforcement of judgments relating to parental responsibilities and rights, are beyond the scope of this text.

[97] Art.12, Brussels II *bis*.

[98] Art.13, *ibid*.

[99] Art.15, *ibid*.

[1] 1995 Act, s.12(1) and (3). A "child of the family" includes any child of *both* the parties getting divorced, or any other child who has been *treated by both parties* as

words, if the court felt it necessary it might, for example, make an order that a child reside with a third party, if neither parent seemed a suitable carer given the evidence presented during the divorce hearing. In exceptional cases, the court can postpone granting the decree of divorce (or other decree) until it has given further consideration to the case, if it feels this is desirable in the interests of the child.[2] It might wish to seek more information in the form of independent reports on the welfare of the child, or hear evidence from the child him- or herself.[3] The court's other option in such cases is to refer the child to the children's hearings system, specifying that a particular ground of referral has been found to be established. In such circumstances, the Principal Reporter retains a discretion to decide if a hearing should be convened, depending on whether he feels the child is in need of compulsory measures of supervision.[4]

Types of s.11 Order

Section 11(1) provides that the court can be asked to make any **4–48** order it thinks fit in relation to parental responsibilities or rights, guardianship or the administration of the child's property. As well as this general power, some particular "named" s.11 orders can be sought. These include:

A *residence order*,[5] which regulates with whom a child under 16 is to live. A parent with a residence order may thus choose to look after the child at home, or decide the child should live elsewhere, e.g. with a relative during the holidays. The order can specify that a child resides with different people during specified periods. For example, the child might live with the mother during term and the father during school holidays. A contact order (see below) could regulate each parent's right to contact during their non-residential period;

A *contact order*,[6] which regulates the arrangements for maintaining personal relations and direct contact with a child under 16. The order can specify that contact be exercised by personal contact at a supervised venue such as a local authority contact centre, at the home of the non-residential parent, or elsewhere; or via letter, telephone, e-mail, etc. It might also make provisions as to time periods or that leave that to agreement[7];

---

a child of their family (other than a foster child placed by a local authority or a voluntary organisation): s.12(4).

[2] 1995 Act, s.12(2).

[3] See below, paras 4–55 to 4–59.

[4] 1995 Act, ss.12(1) and 54. See further, Ch.8.

[5] s.11(2)(c).

[6] s.11(2)(d).

[7] There is clearly a cross-over between applying for a residence order and applying for a contact order which involves a certain amount of residence, e.g. overnight stays. *McBain v McIntyre*, 1996 S.C.L.R. (Notes) 181 illustrates how seeking the wrong order can cause problems and gives some guidance.

A *specific issue order*,[8] which regulates any specific issue which has arisen, or may arise, in relation to parental responsibility, rights, guardianship or the administration of a child's property. A typical example where this may be useful is where, after divorce, the parents continue to share parental responsibility and rights but the child lives with the mother, who gives consent to the school nurse to vaccinate the child for rubella. Since either parent can exercise a parental right without the consent of the other,[9] legally only a court order can interfere with a decision of the mother. The father can dispute the mother's decision, by asking the court to resolve this specific issue. Similar applications might be made in respect of one parent's decision about the child's education, religious upbringing, residence in the United Kingdom or leisure. In *G v G*[10] the mother sought a specific issue order that the daughter attend a private fee-paying boarding school at the father's alimentary expense. On appeal the father successfully defeated the claim, on the grounds that there was no reason as yet to disturb the status quo under which the girl was attending an excellent day school. An alternative order in such circumstances would be—

- An *interdict prohibiting the taking of a particular step*[11] in fulfilment of parental responsibility or rights. Taking the scenario above again, the father could dispute the mother's decision to consent to vaccination by asking the court to interdict the step she had taken. In such cases, the decision of the court will primarily rest on the welfare principle, not the wishes of either parent;
- An order *depriving* a parent of parental responsibility or rights.[12] This would be the appropriate order to seek if, for example, it was desired to entirely remove a parent's rights, e.g. the right of a father to deal with a child's property where he had proved financially corrupt or incompetent;
- An order *imposing* upon a person parental rights or responsibilities.[13] This would most typically be used where a person *without* automatic responsibility and rights, such as a grandparent, sought rights in relation to a child. As discussed in para.4-42, such orders cannot be imposed on a person under 16 unless they are the parent of the child in question;
- An order appointing or removing a person as a *guardian* of the child.[14]

Section 11 also contemplates the making of a number of orders specifically relating to the management of a child's property, which

---

[8] s.11(2)(e).
[9] s.2(2).
[10] 2000 (59) Fam. L.B. 5.
[11] s.11(2)(f).
[12] s.11(2)(a).
[13] s.11(2)(b).
[14] s.11(2)(h). See below, Ch.6.

are discussed in more detail at paras 5–30 to 5–32. Any reference in s.11 to an order includes a reference to an interim order, or any order varying or discharging an order.[15]

Criteria for Making a s.11 Order

There are three basic principles under s.11(7) which the court is **4–49** instructed to bear in mind when making any s.11 order.

The Welfare of the Child is Paramount

The welfare or "best interests" principle has been the paramount **4–50** consideration of the court in cases relating to parental rights (and now, responsibility) since the Guardianship of Infants Act 1925. What is meant by the "welfare of the child" is a classic problem of linguistic open texture. Hundreds if not thousands of reported cases have turned on the interpretation of this phrase. Below we will discuss how the welfare principle has been construed in existing case law.

The Court Should Not Make Any Order Unless It Considers It Better Than Making No Order at All

This has been called the *minimum intervention principle*,[16] and imple- **4–51** ments an important part of the general philosophy of the Children (Scotland) Act, namely that courts should not interfere unnecessarily with the arrangements reached by a parent, or parents. (As we will see in Ch.7, courts are instructed to take a similar approach in relation to the making of orders taking children into local authority care.) Prior to the 1995 Act, it was common and indeed often virtually automatic for courts to award sole custody to one or other parent, whether this was by the agreement of the parents or, less frequently, after a disputed proof.[17] Although custody was only one of several parental rights held jointly by married parents, such a sole custody award was often perceived as effectively removing the non-custodial parent from any involvement with, or responsibility for, the child's life. Divorce was seen as a carve-up, in which the winner gained custody, and the loser, if they were lucky, took access rights as a consolation prize.

The SLC recognised this as an unsatisfactory state of affairs, and **4–52** preferred when reconsidering the law to reinforce the notion that "a child will continue to have two parents after separation or divorce who share responsibility for his/her upbringing".[18] Under the 1995 Act, not only is the terminology of sole custody dispensed with, but joint responsibility is actively promoted. Since married parents

---

[15] s.11(13).

[16] Nome, *Children (Scotland) Act 1995* (2nd edn, 2004).

[17] In 90% of ordinary divorce actions involving children in 1991, an award of sole custody to one or other parent was made (92% to mother, 7% to father): Morris, Gibson and Platts, *Untying the Knot: Characteristics of Divorce in Scotland* (1993).

[18] *Report on Family Law*, Scot. Law Com. No.135 (1992), para.2.29.

automatically share PRRs prior to divorce, the minimum intervention principle implies that an award of sole PRRs to one parent on divorce—the nearest equivalent of the former "sole custody" award—must be positively justified by the party seeking it as better than no award. The Act thus effectively implements a presumption that joint parental responsibility will be the norm after divorce. If parents are seen as owing responsibilities to their children, rather than as having rights, then it should rarely be in the interests of the child to deprive one parent unnecessarily of such responsibility.[19]

4–53   The less desirable flip side of the minimum intervention principle, it was thought for some time after the passing of the 1995 Act, was that it discouraged the award by the courts of shared PRRs to unmarried couples whether cohabiting or not. Unmarried fathers with no automatic parental rights, it was thought, had the onus of proof against them and thus had to show the court by positive evidence of some kind that it was better to make an order in their favour than to leave the legal status quo as it stands. In a number of post-1995 Act cases, argument on this point dominated the case more than the actual merits. The perceived difficulties raised for unmarried fathers would, in any case, have been severely diminished by the granting of automatic PRRs to many or most unmarried fathers by the Family law (Scotland) Act 2006 (see para.3–18). However since these provisions are not retrospective, it is fortunate the courts have also chosen to clarify the issue. The notion of an onus of proof for parties without existing PRRs was dispelled in the Inner House case of *White v White*.[20] In a stirring judgment, Lord McCluskey[21] made it plain that,

> "Nowhere in the 1995 Act do I find a provision that, in arriving at a decision in relation to contact between a father and his daughter, the paramount consideration shall be the onus of proof".[22]

Lord Rodger further clarified the law. If onus was no longer an issue, then on what basis was the court to make a s.11 order? Quite simply the court must "consider all the relevant material and decide what would be conducive to the child's welfare." Or even more simply, the decision in *White* returns the law to the basic principle that the welfare of the child is paramount and should be assessed on the balance of probabilities, on what evidence is available, independent of any question of presumptions and onuses.

---

[19] A notable pre-1995 Act case in which the sheriff accepted this argument and thus refused to make any order for custody for either party is *Potter v Potter*, 1993 S.L.T. (Sh. Ct.) 51. See also *Ross v Ross*, 1997 S.L.T. (Sh Ct) 51 (decided under pre 1995 Act rules), but *cf McNeill v McNeill* (1997) Fam. L.B. 30-7.

[20] 2001 S.L.T. 485 (IH).

[21] Effectively also therefore, on this point, reversing the decision from which he had previously dissented in the Inner House in *Sanderson v McManus*, 1995 S.C.L.R. 902 (I.H.), discussed below at paras 4–93 to 4–94.

[22] At 493L–494A.

Along with the minimum intervention principle, comes the idea **4–54** that any order made under s.11 should have the *minimum effect necessary* to achieve its purpose. Section 11(11) states that any order shall have the effect of depriving a parent of rights and responsibilities only so far as expressly stated and only to the extent necessary to give effect to the order. This has important implications again for post divorce or separation arrangements. If during divorce proceedings, one parent applies for and gets a residence order in relation to a child, then, unless expressly stated to do so, this order should not deprive the other parent of any of his or her rights and responsibilities under ss.1 and 2 (except, obviously, the right to determine the child's residence).[23] Thus, it is not in any way equivalent to the "carve-up" described above which was the common result of the old law. Where one parent truly wishes to remove the other parent from having any involvement with or responsibility for the child's life, they will have to seek an order explicitly depriving that parent of all rights and responsibilities. The court will then have to decide if such an order is appropriate on the basis of the s.11 criteria. In the pre-1995 Act case of *Clayton v Clayton,*[24] the father of the child was a 72-year-old professor of genetics and the mother, with whom the child lived, a Ph.D. student some 30 years his junior. The father, who was notably cantankerous and strong-willed, sought constantly by virtue of his joint parental rights to question and undermine the mother's decisions about the child, in relation to health and leisure as well as education. The court agreed to award sole custody to the mother on the grounds that the father's constant interference was undermining her confidence as a single parent, and this was not in the welfare of the child. It is submitted that a similar decision would now be made to award PRRs solely to the mother.

The Court Shall, as far as is Practicable, have regard to the Views of the Child, Taking Account of the Child's Age and Maturity

A child aged 12 or more is presumed to be sufficiently mature to **4–55** form a view, without prejudice to the possibility of a child under that age being sufficiently mature.[25] As discussed above, this provision formally meets the requirements of Art.12 of the UNCRC which states that children have a right to be heard in any judicial proceedings affecting them. It is necessary to consider however: (i) how children are to be given an opportunity to indicate they wish to express their views; and (ii) by what method they can then effectively communicate their views.

---

[23] Note, however, that if the person in favour of whom a residence order is made does not have all the parental rights and responsibilities of ss.1 and 2 then they shall have them all while the order is in force (s.11(12)).

[24] 1996 G.W.D. 18-1000.

[25] s.11(10).

4–56 Prior to the 1995 Act, disputes as to parental rights, especially in the context of divorce, were largely seen as disputes between adults in which children were the objects of the process, not participants. Parents, not children, were the parties to the action.[26] The vast majority of divorces are undefended and involve only affidavit evidence, and even in those that are defended on issues relating to parental rights, only a very small fraction involve the hearing of oral evidence.[27] Furthermore, in around a quarter of divorces, disputes between parties, including disputes over the children, are settled by means of a joint minute of agreement negotiated between parties and presented to the courts very much as *a fait accompli*.[28] Thus, it is illusory to imagine that the courts frequently hear direct evidence of the views of children. A more realistic summary is that the courts usually accept the arrangements of parents unless these are the subject of dispute, or there is other evidence at hand, from parties such as a social worker, psychologist or advocate, which attracts more detailed inspection. Moreover, the courts increasingly attempt to encourage parents to agree on arrangements for their children, if necessary by referring them to mediation.[29] There are no guarantees that children will be given a voice in mediation, nor that their interests will be paramount. Children are also sometimes seen as too vulnerable to be involved in the brutality of divorce mediation. However attempts are being made by mediation practitioners to involve children more in such mediation, as required by their right of consultation under s.6 of the 1995 Act.[30]

4–57 The views of children are thus most often supplied to the courts indirectly via affidavit evidence supplied by the competing parties, via partisan expert witnesses such as educational psychologists, or at best

---

[26] A child could, in theory, join the action as a party minuter. However, in practice this was virtually unheard of.

[27] In 1991, 79% of ordinary divorce actions were undefended and proved be means of affidavit evidence only, and 19% were defended and proved by affidavit only. Only 2% of actions involved the hearing of oral evidence. See Morris, Gibson and Platts, *Untying the Knot: Characteristics of Divorce in Scotland* (1993).

[28] See Wasoff, McGucken and Edwards, *Mutual Consent: Written Agreements in Family Law* (Scottish Office, Central Research Unit, 1997). "Joint minutes of agreement" are agreements lodged with the court to which the court interpones its authority. In 1990 they featured in 20% of ordinary Scottish divorce actions. Separating parents also often make "minutes of agreement" which are simple contracts about the separation arrangements not forming part of a court process. Around 70% of minutes and joint minutes made by parties with children contain arrangements between parties as to who the children should live with. Minutes would be presented as part of the documentary evidence the court sees, and would rarely be questioned in an undefended divorce. See further, Ch.15.

[29] See Ordinary Cause Rules 1993 (hereafter "OCR"), 33.22.

[30] It is difficult to find out how many children actively participate in the mediation of their parent's divorce or separation. The Family Mediation Scotland Annual Review 2005 gives no clues, but does indicate that 71% of the children "involved in" their mediations are under 12 and therefore do not prima facie have s.6 rights. The website of CALM, the association of solicitor-mediators in Scotland, gives no such figures.

via independent reports. The court has the power to order an independent report, usually compiled by a solicitor, advocate or social worker,[31] and a sheriff may choose to hear direct oral evidence from a child, although, again, in the past this has been the exception rather than the rule. The Rules of Court governing procedure in family actions were reformed after the 1995 Act[32] in an attempt to give children a better opportunity to participate in legal processes affecting their welfare—in particular, the divorce of their parents.

First, in any action affecting a child under 16, that child must **4–58** receive intimation of the action, via a form written in "child-friendly" language, which provides brief details of the action and invites the child to inform the sheriff if he or she has views he or she wishes to express.[33] The sheriff has discretion to postpone or dispense with intimation, e.g. where the child is too young to understand the issues. Secondly, the sheriff is given a wide discretion to take such steps as he or she sees necessary to ascertain the views of the child.[34] This attempts to meet difficult problems associated with asking children to give evidence in court. Children are easily intimidated by the prospect of giving oral evidence in a courtroom, yet sheriffs have felt uneasy in the past about speaking to children in their chambers, as such private communications do not have the status of proven evidence.[35] Furthermore, children will often be unwilling to publicly give evidence preferring one parent to the other. An important provision in the rules allows a sheriff to record the views of a child, as expressed by the child him or herself or a third party, or in writing supplied by the child, and seal those views as confidential in the court process.[36] Sheriffs may however *choose* not to seal evidence as confidential for reasons discussed in the next paragraph.

One of the main problems for children expressing their views is **4–59** acknowledged to be that without guarantees of confidentiality they may not be able to speak freely, either directly to a court as party[37] or witness, via affidavits, or through a third party such as a curator *ad*

---

[31] The court can order such reports either under common-law powers or by virtue of the Matrimonial Proceedings (Children) Act 1958, s.11.

[32] Act of Sederunt (Family Proceedings in the Sheriff Court) 1996 (SI 1996/2167).

[33] OCR 33.7 (as amended) and Form F9. Rules of the Court of Session 1994 (hereafter "RCS"), 49.23. If the child concerned is too young to understand or might be upset or traumatised by being told about the action then as an alternative, r.33.33(7) provides that the pursuer can crave that intimation be dispensed with, and averments justifying dispensation must be included in the initial writ along with the crave. If neither intimation nor crave for dispensation is included in the writ then it is faulty: see *Gallacher v Gallacher*, 1997 S.C.L.R. (Notes) 174.

[34] OCR 33.19(2). RCS 33.27A.

[35] *MacDonald v MacDonald*, 1985 S.L.T. 244.

[36] OCR 33.20.

[37] See for example *Henderson v Henderson*, 1997 Fam. L.R. 120, discussed above at para.2–43. Although the child in question, a 10-year-old girl, did successfully win the right to join the case as a party with her own independent representation, she was unable to speak in confidence to the judge about her father having contact with herself.

litem. Children, especially younger and more vulnerable children, often do not wish to be seen as taking the side of one parent against the other. Sometimes children will be afraid of admitting what they feel or know if there is a risk of a parent finding out afterwards, e.g. where they are making allegations of physical or sexual abuse. They may be physically scared of one or other parent. For this reason, it is often said that confidentiality is an essential part of giving children a voice in legal proceedings.

4–60   In *Dosoo v Dosoo*[38] two children, aged 14 and 12, were interviewed by the sheriff and contributed their views on contact to a report which was made up. This report partially contributed to the father being denied contact. The children asked that their views remain confidential. The father asked for disclosure of the children's views (asking, in fact, for the envelope to be unsealed) and arguing that to refuse to do so would be a breach of his rights to a fair hearing and respect for his right of family life, under Arts 6 and 8 of the ECHR. The Sheriff however held that she was *not* required to reveal the record to the father. The children were clearly afraid of the repercussions if their father read what they had said. The sheriff went on to observe as a general rule,

> "that for a child to be able to express his views 'freely' he must be able to feel confident in privacy if he so wishes, and the court should respect that privacy except in very compelling circumstances."

This approach also respected the children's rights to a voice in proceedings under Art.12 of the UNCRC.

4–61   *Dosoo* was reconsidered in *McGrath v McGrath*.[39] In *McGrath* the child wished to express her views to the sheriff via her curator *ad litem* but for them not to be revealed to her parents. The father asked for disclosure, but lost at first instance. On appeal, the Sheriff Principal attempted to balance the interest of the father, in disclosure of the case against him as part of natural justice, with the interest of the child in confidentiality and free expression, drawing on the English House of Lords case of *Re D*[40] and the European Court of Human Rights case of *McMichael v UK*.[41] In *Re D*, the House of Lords had declared that to decide such issues the court must go through a three-part test:

i.   determine whether disclosure of the material would involve a real possibility of significant harm to the child;
ii. if it *would* involve such a risk, consider whether the overall interests of the child would benefit from non disclosure; and

---

[38] 1999 S.L.T. (Sh Ct) 86; 1999 S.C.L.R. (Notes) 905.
[39] 1999 S.L.T. (Sh Ct) 90; 1999 S.C.L.R. (Notes) 1121.
[40] [1995] 4 All E.R. 385.
[41] [1995] 20 E.H.R.R. 205.

iii. finally, if satisfied the interests of the child pointed to non-disclosure, then that consideration had to be *weighed against* the interests of the parent or other party in disclosure.

The outcome was that, unlike in *Dosoo*, in *McGrath* the father won a rehearing. Sheriff Principal Bowen noted ruefully that,

> "The practicalities involved in reconciling the right to a fair hearing and a child's right to express his views are thus of immense difficulty. They can best be resolved in my view by having regard to the principles set out by Lord Mustill [in *Re D*, above]".

One point not canvassed in *Dosoo* and *McGrath* is that a child just as **4–62** much as a parent can make an "ECHR" argument, on top of the "Art.12, UN Convention" argument. Children *too* have rights to a fair hearing under Art.6 of the ECHR, which, it could be argued, are prejudiced if confidentiality of submissions cannot be guaranteed. But since *McGrath*, the matter of confidentiality seems to have reached an uneasy solution and there has been little further litigation on this point.[42] It may still be desirable to put in place some sort of procedure such as now exists in the children's hearings system, where a party can be excluded from the hearing while a child speaks, but is then on re-admittance guaranteed the right to be told the substance though not the letter of what has occurred while he was excluded.[43]

RESIDENCE ORDERS

The Welfare Principle

When making a residence order, the paramount concern of the **4–63** court is the welfare of the child. Innumerable factors can be taken as affecting the child's welfare, amongst which only the most prominent are the physical and emotional welfare of the child, the age and sex of the child, the characteristics of the parents or other applicants including their moral, material, spiritual and sexual nature, the relationship of the child with others sharing a proposed residential household, the psychological security of the child and so forth. Interpreting the welfare principle has been described rather fuzzily in the House of Lords as,

> "a process whereby, when all the relevant facts, relationships, claims and wishes of parents, risks, choices and other circum-

---

[42] Although see *Johnston v Johnston*, 2000 Fam. L.B. 47-7; *Grant v Grant*, 2000 G.W.D. 5-177; and *Oyeneyin v Oyeneyin*, 1999 G.W.D. 38-1836.
[43] 1995 Act, s.46(2).

stances are taken into account and weighed, the course to be followed will be that which is most in the interests of the child's welfare as that term now has to be understood."[44]

4–64 In England, courts are assisted by a statutory checklist of factors to take into account when making an order under the Children Act 1989. No such checklist occurs in the 1995 Act, but considerable help can be found in the copious case law relating to applications for custody and access prior to the 1995 Act. However, this authority must be treated with caution for a number of reasons. First, these decisions were based solely on the welfare principle, while s.11 applications must also be decided with reference to the minimum intervention principle and the wishes of the child concerned, and so a different balancing of factors may ensue. Secondly, and more importantly, however, a decision on custody prior to 1995 was, as we have seen, factually if not legally, often equivalent to a comprehensive disposal of the child to one parent, not simply a decision on where the child should reside. Thus many factors which the court has sometimes regarded as extremely significant in deciding custody, such as the child's moral welfare or one parent's sexuality, may be regarded as less so when making a residence order, where the non-residential parent continues in law to play an important role in the child's life.

4–65 Another caveat that is true of all authority in this area is that each case is not properly a precedent but simply an example. No case turning on the welfare principle can ever have a truly determinate outcome, at least within a conventional doctrinal analysis.[45] The welfare principle ideally demands a comprehensive approach in which all the disparate factors that may be relevant are identified, studied and balanced. The courts have thus firmly declared that there is no pre-eminent right of a mother to be the "natural custodier" of her child. Even to suggest so would be to subvert the proper test of the child's best interests.[46] Nor is there a pre-eminent right of a natural or biological parent (of any gender) to be preferred to a non-parent if the latter can provide overall the better environment.[47] Similarly, a foreign decree can never simply be accepted by a Scottish court as determining the issue of residence even if it has been issued by a court of competent jurisdiction who have

---

[44] *per* Lord MacDermott in *J v C* [1970] A.C. 668 at 710–711.

[45] See Lord Jauncey in *Brixey v Lynas*, 1996 S.L.T. 908 which was concerned with whether a maternal preference exists in respect of a child of tender years: "[This case] raises no question of legal principle and is devoid of merit" (at p.909B). For a discussion of how decisions about children based on the welfare principle can be made potentially predictable by reference to a non-doctrinal feminist analysis, see Edwards, "Modelling Law Using a Feminist Theoretical Perspective" (1995) 4 Law, Computers and Artificial Intelligence 95.

[46] See *Dance v Archibald*, 1989 G.W.D. 13-535 *per* Lord Cameron of Lochbroom; *Mooney v Mooney*, 1987 G.W.D. 3-80; *Whitecross v Whitecross*, 1977 S.L.T. 225.

[47] *Breingan v Jamieson*, 1993 S.L.T. 186, although *cf.* Lord Morison's comments in *Clark v Clark*, 1987 G.W.D. 35-1240.

conducted a satisfactory enquiry into the facts.[48] The welfare principle must be the court's first concern, and the order of the foreign court, though deserving of "grave consideration", cannot prevent the domestic court from reaching a different conclusion if necessary.[49] Finally, it is clearly a breach of the welfare principle to prefer the "innocent" party in a divorce to the "guilty" one,[50] (at least if on that ground alone) and in any case this distinction is now meaningless in divorces granted on grounds of non-cohabitation.

Status quo Principle

One way of short-cutting the Herculean task of balancing all the **4–66** factors in a case is to adopt a shorthand method. The Scottish courts have developed such an approach in their use of what has become known as the status quo principle. When a couple with children split up, there is often a reasonable space of time before any (non-interim) application relating to parental rights and responsibility is adjudicated by the courts. This is obviously particularly true in the context of no-fault divorce. During this time, some settled arrangement will usually arise for the care of the child; in the majority of cases, for example, de facto care is assumed by the mother. The courts will often actively choose to preserve this existing arrangement, known as the status quo, since it can be relatively easily ascertained if the existing situation is in the child's welfare or not. It is more difficult for the courts to guess on inadequate evidence what other arrangement might be better for the child. Thus a working, if not necessarily optimum, arrangement can be safely rubber-stamped by the court. In addition, there is psychological evidence that continuity of relationships is important to children post-divorce, which the courts appear to have implicitly adopted judging from their frequent references to stability as a major positive aspect of childcare arrangements.[51]

---

[48] *Sinclair v Sinclair*, 1988 S.L.T. 87; *Campins v Campins*, 1978 S.L.T. (Notes) 41. Although this principle is now rather undermined in the interests of expediency by the Hague and Europe Conventions on Child Abduction (see note below).

[49] The prospects for undeterred forum shopping this seems to open up are restricted by the provisions of the Child Abduction and Custody Act 1985, which implements two international conventions on child abduction for the UK. Although outwith the scope of this book, the net effect is, broadly, that cases arriving in the Scottish courts and involving children habitually resident in a Convention signatory country are not investigated on the merits and instead the child is returned to that country for the case to be adjudicated, unless there are very good reasons not to return the child. See also *Calleja v Calleja*, 1996 S.C.L.R. (Notes) 963 in which the Inner House applied broadly these same rules to a case concerning a country not signatory to these conventions (Malta).

[50] *Hume v Hume*, 1926 S.C. 1008, in which the court asserted a presumption still existed in favour of the spouse innocent of matrimonial fault, is now universally understood to be overruled.

[51] Goldstein, Freud and Solnit, *Beyond the Best Interests of the Child* (1973) is regarded as the most influential text promoting this theory. See also Wallerstein and Kelly, *Surviving the Break-Up: How Children and Parents Cope With Divorce* (1980).

4-67 In *Breingan v Jamieson*[52] the mother of a seven-year-old girl tragically died young. The daughter's custody[53] was subsequently disputed by, on the one hand, her father, who had lost custody of the child some years earlier on his divorce from the mother, and on the other, the maternal aunt, who had looked after the child since the mother's death along with other maternal relatives. Lord MacLean found that although the child had a good relationship with her father and his new wife, and there was no reason they could not supply her with a home, nevertheless, to remove her "to a totally different environment would be disruptive of her settled, happy life and detrimental to her best interests". This trumped the claim of the father which was "based effectively upon his role as the child's natural or biological parent".

4-68 In recent years, the Scottish courts have rarely reversed an existing status quo. Although the principle can only ever assist in interpreting the welfare principle, and cannot replace it, it can fairly be said that there is a presumption that the preservation of the status quo is in the child's best interests.[54] This is true even when it is arrived at by means other than consensus. In *Black v Black*,[55] a wife left her husband, along with the two sons of the marriage, because of his "social drinking" and went to stay with her father in England. Later, the husband took the sons back to the former family home in Scotland on an access visit and refused to return them. About a year later, he sued for custody. At first instance, custody was awarded to the mother. On appeal to the sheriff-principal it was held that, despite the disadvantages of the father's lifestyle—which included excessive encouragement of football to the detriment of traditional education, as well as habitual imbibing—the welfare of the boys was favoured by "the security of the life which they have with their father in familiar surroundings, with friends and at a school they know and like".[56] The sheriff-principal went on to add, in response to the claim that the status quo was being given undue weight, that "the fact that the status quo is not a paramount consideration does not mean that it is an unimportant one".[57] In the remarkable case of *Sherwin v Trumayne*[58] an unmarried father abducted his very young son from the mother, in breach of the Irish custody order she held, and cared for him alone for over a year before applying for custody in Scotland. Despite the circumstances, the judge was not prepared to

---

[52] 1993 S.L.T. 186.
[53] The words "custody" and "access" are used in relation to cases heard prior to November 1, 1996 when the Children (Scotland) Act 1995, Pt I, came into force, although, under that Act those words have been rendered meaningless.
[54] See *Hannah v Hannah*, 1971 S.L.T. (Notes) 42, *Breingan* above (n.47), *Brixey v Lynas* above (n.45), and cases discussed, below.
[55] 1990 S.L.T. (Sh. Ct.) 42.
[56] 1990 S.L.T. (Sh. Ct.) 42, at 46I.
[57] *ibid.* at 46J.
[58] 1992 G.W.D. 29-1681.

reverse the status quo and rejected claims that his decision was a "kidnapper's charter". The test was the welfare of the child, not that of either competing party.[59]

It appears then that some fairly negative factor or combination of factors is required before the courts will reverse an otherwise apparently stable and beneficial status quo situation. In *Kyle v Stewart*,[60] for example, a mother entrusted her child to her sister shortly before taking a fatal overdose. Although the sister then looked after the child, the natural father was subsequently awarded custody. The main negative factors seem to have been the sister's immaturity and the fact that she was already herself an unmarried mother.[61] Many of the cases cited below turn, explicitly or otherwise, on whether some negative aspect of the status quo is sufficient to persuade the courts to make an award altering it.

Parental care, Behaviour and Lifestyle

Since a parent with residence will be the primary carer for a child, **4–69** it is of vital importance that an order should not be made in favour of a parent who will do damage to the child's mental or physical welfare. Violent behaviour, aggression and bad temper,[62] severe drunkenness and alcoholism,[63] or a history of child neglect on the part of a parent will thus, as one might imagine, be negative indicators, unless they are past problems which are highly unlikely to revive.[64] A residential parent must be able to supply the child with the essentials of life including food, clothes, lodging and emotional sustenance.[65] Either poverty, unemployment, or physical or mental disability may impede a parent in his or her ability to supply some or all of these, but frequently such disadvantages can be ameliorated by the availability of welfare benefits and social work support. In the past, the Scottish courts have generally taken the approach that disparities in financial means between two competing parents can be settled by an appropriate award of aliment, and that consequently, the emotional support and stability a household can offer should be regarded

---

[59] See also *Basinski v Basinski*, 1993 G.W.D. 8-533. The court will not usually, however, decide on the merits if a child has been abducted in breach of a court order from a foreign country, or in breach of foreign custody rights—see further above.

[60] 1989 G.W.D. 14-580.

[61] See also *Hastie v Hastie*, 1985 S.L.T. 146.

[62] *Geddes v Geddes*, 1987 G.W.D. 11-349

[63] In *Shearer v Shearer*, 2004 G.W.D. 38-773, the court granted residence to a working father in preference to the mother, who though a full-time carer, had a history of drinking.

[64] In *Early v Early*, 1989 S.L.T. 114; 1990 S.L.T. 221, the father had two prior convictions for child neglect and had drunk heavily in the past, but was now seen as a reformed character and was awarded custody (albeit in competition with a lesbian mother).

[65] In *Shishodia v Shishodia*, 1995 G.W.D. 17-926 a father lost custody, inter alia, because he sent a boy child out on several occasions wearing female clothing.

as more important than material advantages.[66] An unemployed father who can be a full-time carer might therefore be preferred to a working mother.[67] However, since the advent of the Child Support Act 1991, aliment for children is no longer at the discretion of the court assessing residence, and child support is quantified using a standard inflexible formula in all but exceptional cases.[68] This may have made it more acceptable to the courts to take cognisance of financial matters. In *Brixey v Lynas*,[69] the dispute was between a father from an affluent middle-class background and a mother from a discernibly less privileged background. The sheriff in awarding custody to the father commented that "I have . . . come to the view that I should not deprive the child of the advantages which the accident of her paternity make available to her".[70] Although his award was later reversed, on this point he was expressly affirmed by the Inner House, who found that the advantages of background and environment were relevant. On the other hand, those advantages could not be decisive, and other considerations such as the long-term future of the child and her emotional security should hold sway.

Abuse

4–70   A particular problem in Scottish society is the prevalence of domestic violence, particularly by men against female partners. It can be argued in theory that violence against a *partner* does not necessarily impact upon any *child* of the household, but empirical evidence has shown that the indirect effects on children of growing up in a climate of domestic abuse are deleterious even where the child is not physically harmed.[71] Furthermore violence against a partner is often a sign that children of the household are also being abused or potentially at risk.

4–71   How should such violence be taken into account when making a s.11 order? On the one hand it can be argued that a violent partner may still be a loving and non-violent father (say). On the other hand, the welfare of the child is, research shows, most closely connected to

---

[66] *Geddes v Geddes*, 1987 G.W.D. 11-349.

[67] *Sloss v Taylor*, 1989 S.C.L.R. 407.

[68] See Ch.5. It should be noted, however, that an award of financial provision under s.9(1)(c) of the Family Law (Scotland) Act 1985 can be made in order to share fairly the economic burden of caring for a child after divorce between the parents. Such an award can be made in the form of a periodical allowance. A similar award can now be made under the Family Law (Scotland) Act 2006 where unmarried parents separate, and under the Civil Partnership Act 2004, where same sex partners terminate their civil partnership.

[69] 1994 S.L.T. 847, appealed to House of Lords, 1996 S.L.T. 908. This point was not, however, argued on appeal.

[70] 1994 S.L.T. 847 at 849. Both father and mother were unemployed.

[71] See M. Hester, "Domestic violence and child contact arrangements in England and Denmark 1996" and M. Kaye, "Domestic Violence, residence and contact" (1996) 8 Child and Family Law Quarterly 285.

the welfare of the primary carer, for whom an award of contact with a violent ex-partner may mean continuing risk of abuse and terror. In countries like New Zealand, rules have been adopted that if there is evidence of domestic violence which seems to affect the child, there is a presumption of no contact between the violent parent and the child. In Scotland a "softer" solution was adopted in the Family Law (Scotland) Act 2006[72]: the court ,when making any s.11 order, must have regard to the need to protect a child from abuse or the risk of abuse which affects or might affect the child; and also to the ability of the abuser to care for or meet the needs of the child. The court must also consider the effect any abuse might have on the primary carer. "Abuse" is defined widely to include violence, harassment, threatening conduct and any other conduct giving rise to physical or mental injury, fear, alarm or distress.[73] Psychological as well as physical abuse is thus clearly included. Abuse may also be aimed at a parent or other person, e.g. a sibling, as well as at the child, and includes "domestic abuse". "Conduct" includes both speech, and presence in a specified place or area.[74] So simply coming up to a mother in a shopping centre, or outside a school, given a history of abuse, could, it seems, be regarded as "abuse" if it caused that mother fear or distress.

Finally, it is provided in s.11(7D) of the 1995 Act that the court **4–72** shall also decide if it would be appropriate to make a s.11 order where that order involves two or more relevant parties having to co-operate with each other.[75] "Relevant parties" here includes anyone with PRRs and any parent of the child.[76] So, for example, if a father with a history of violence sought joint PRRs, or overnight contact two days a week (say), this would involve co-operation with the mother, and the court would have to take into account how feasible this was, given the background of abuse.

Arguably these rules add little new to Scots law. Courts have generally regarded evidence of domestic abuse or violence as relevant in the past,[77] and the minimum intervention principle should already have operated to cause the court to stop and think before making any s.11 order that would be unworkable due to non-cooperation. However the symbolic aim of the provisions, to highlight the need to think about the indirect and direct effects of domestic abuse in residence and contact disputes, is laudable. Time will tell if more stringent rules such as a presumption of no contact where violence exists are still needed.

---

[72] FLSA 2006, s.24 inserting s.11(7A)–(7B) into the Children (Scotland) Act 1995.

[73] *ibid.*, inserting s.11(7C) into the 1995 Act.

[74] *ibid.*

[75] Actually, in theory, cooperation is never needed in the exercise of any parental right according to s.2(2) of the 1995 Act. However, the non-pedantic meaning of the new sub-section is clear.

[76] FLSA 2006, s.24 inserting s.11(7D)–(7E) into the 1995 Act.

[77] See, e.g. *Haggerty v Woodrow*, 2005 G.W.D. 35-654, a pre-FLSA 2006 case.

Sexuality

4–73   The thorniest problems perhaps arise in relation to parental sexuality. The liberal and pluralistic values which generally prevail in
current Scottish society in strict theory indicate that the courts
should only be interested in the sexual preferences of parents in so
far as they affect the child's welfare, e.g. if a parent has paedophile
tendencies. In practice, however, the courts have in the past seemed
willing to listen to evidence that it may in some indirect way be bad
for the child to be brought up by a lesbian or homosexual parent,
most notably the argument that such a child may be stigmatised in
their peer group by having gay parent(s). In the first Scottish case on
gay parenting, *Early v Early*,[78] the mother, who had recently begun
cohabiting in a lesbian relationship, sought custody of her third
child, a boy aged 10. Although the mother had the benefit of the
status quo, custody was given to the father. Lord Davidson accepted
expert testimony that the lack of a male role model in the child's life
might lead to long-term problems, that there could be problems with
teasing at school (stigmatisation), and, in general, there might be
"unusual difficulties". This approach was affirmed by the Inner
House. What is clearly objectionable about this decision is not that it
implicitly prefers an upbringing in a heterosexual household to a
homosexual one—which is at root a value-oriented stance which can
neither be approved nor vilified on an objective basis[79]—but that the
court overtly based its judgement on stereotyped expert evidence
about the risks for any child of growing up in any lesbian household[80] rather than on a consideration of the happiness and future of
this particular child.

Following *Early*, a number of Scottish cases took a more favourable,
or at least less stereotyped judicial approach towards gay and lesbian
parenting, including *Meredith v Meredith*,[81] and *Hill v Hill*.[82]

---

[78] 1989 S.L.T. 114, affirmed by Inner House at 1990 S.L.T. 221.

[79] The English Court of Appeal, e.g. took it as unnecessary to prove that a heterosexual household is better for a child than a homosexual one in *C v C* [1991] F.L.R. 223.
Glidewell L.J. stating: "I regard it as axiomatic that the ideal environment for the
upbringing of a child is the home of loving and sensible parents, her father and her
mother. When the marriage between father and mother is at an end that ideal cannot
be attained. When the court is called upon to decide which of the two possible alternatives is then preferable for the child's welfare, its task is to choose the alternative
which comes closest to that ideal." See comment in Boyd, "What Is a Normal
Family?" (1992) 55 M.L.R. 269.

[80] In *Early*, the mother's sexuality was not public knowledge, and therefore the risks
of peer-group hostility low, but this factor seems to have been disregarded. Generic
evidence could as well have been introduced denying that risks exist for children
raised in lesbian households: see, e.g. Tasker and Golombok, "Children Raised By
Lesbian Mothers", 1991 Family Law 184, whose research found no discernible stigmatisation of children of lesbian mothers compared to a sample of children of
single heterosexual mothers.

[81] 1994 G.W.D. 19-1150.

[82] 1991 S.L.T. 189.

Radical change came however in 1997 in the shape of *T Petr.*,[83] an   **4–74**
adoption case, in which the Inner House found that there was no reason in *principle* why an adoption order should not be made in favour of
an unmarried homosexual applicant, who in practice would bring up
the child along with his long-standing male partner. At first instance,
Lord Gill refused to grant the adoption order, even though the couple
had been fostering the child for some 18 months, the social work
department supported the petition, and the mother did not object. His
reason was that the risks of gay parenting had not been properly
explored, ironically because all parties involved in the litigation felt the
arrangements were in the welfare of the child. However, Lord Hope in
the Inner House made it plain that nothing in the adoption legislation,
with its emphasis on the welfare principle, suggested that it was a "fundamental objection to an adoption" that the applicant was living in a
homosexual relationship. It would be wrong to adopt any "hard and
fast" rule,[84] or generalisation as to the attitude the courts should adopt
towards homosexuals, as this in itself would be contrary to the assessment based on all circumstances demanded by the welfare principle.
Although these comments were made in the context of adoption, they
have proven very influential in areas such as residence and contact.[85]

Gay parenting is an area which has perhaps transformed less as   **4–75**
a result of shifting views in Scotland, and more as a result of international human rights pressures against discrimination. In particular,
the ECHR has had a deciding influence, both pre- and post-incorpo-
ration. Since the English House of Lords case of *Fitzpatrick v
Sterling House Association*[86] it has been generally accepted that gay
partners can claim the benefit of the right to respect for their family
life under Art.8 of the ECHR, as well as the right not to be discriminated against. But of course, such rights have to be balanced against
other considerations and it cannot be predicted how any particular
case concerning gay parenting or gay rights in general, will be
addressed by the courts. In *Grant v South West Trains Ltd*,[87] for
example, a case about an employee's gay partner's rights, the
European Court of Justice found the other way, opining that,

> "stable relationships between two persons of the same sex are
> not regarded as equivalent to marriages of stable relationships
> outside marriage between persons of the same sex."

---

[83] 1997 S.L.T. 724. *T Petr* was also followed in England in *In Re W (a Minor)
(Adoption: Homosexual Adopter)* [1997] 3 All E.R. 620, a case dealing with an
adoption application by a lesbian woman cohabiting with another lesbian.

[84] These comments were adopted with approval from the speech of Lord Kilbrandon
in the English House of Lords case of *Re D (Adoption: Parent's Consent)* [1977]
A.C. 602 at 641g–642b.

[85] See further Ch. 6, and Norrie, 1996 S.L.T. (News) 321.

[86] [2001] A.C. 27. This case actually concerned whether the gay partner of a deceased
had the right to succeed to his tenancy under statute as a member of his family.

[87] 1998 ICR 449 (ECJ Case C-249/96).

Notwithstanding this uncertainty, commentators such as Norrie[88] have declared that the ECHR has made discrimination in child law against a parent on grounds of sexuality illegal forthwith,[89] and that *Early* is unequivocally overruled. Norrie rests his case most proximately on the ECHR case of *da Silva Mouta v Portugal*[90] in which the Strasbourg court held that discrimination based on a person's sexual orientation may constitute a breach of Art.14. The facts of the case were that a homosexual married father had his claim for a residence order rejected by the Portuguese courts on the basis that a homosexual relationship did not provide a healthy environment for the social and moral development of the child. The European Court held that there had been no reasonable proportionality between the objective of the court order (to uphold the welfare of the child) and the means used to achieve it (discrimination on grounds of sexual orientation) and thus the father's rights had been violated.

4–76 However much influence the ECHR has, problematic decisions are still likely to arise in Scotland. The recent case of *X v Y*[91] raised a number of controversial issues. A Glaswegian lesbian couple, M and C, wanted to have a baby. After various unsuccessful experiments, they recruited F, who was himself a homosexual and in a gay relationship with D. F was not a conventional sperm donor. He claimed he had been assured he would have "heaps of contact" when the child was born, not only for himself, but also for his partner, and his side of the family, e.g. his mother. He took an active part in the pregnancy, visiting the prospective mother, attending an ultrasound scan, etc. and was named on the birth certificate as father of the child, A, and bought many gifts for the child. Shortly after the birth, however, M and C apparently joined forces in a desire to shut the father out of the life of the child. F raised an action for contact in November 2000. M defended, and C, her lesbian partner, also joined the action to seek PRRs for herself.

4–77 The sheriff held that the father should be granted parental rights and responsibilities, as he was "as the starting point . . . the known and chosen biological father". Furthermore, he could supplement M and C's "narrow and somewhat claustrophobic perspective" when the child wanted to know more about its origins. The sheriff's second finding was that the father had a right to respect for family

---

[88] Norrie, 2000 5(2) S.P.L.Q. 169.

[89] But see *per contra* the ECHR case of *Frette v France* [2003] 2 F.L.R. 9, noted briefly at (2002) Fam. L.B. 58-6. See also Hogg, "Attitudes to Sexual Identity and Practice" in *Human Rights and Scots Law* (Boyle *et al* (eds), Hart Publishing, Oxford, 2003); Dempsey, "Same Sex Couples in Scots Law, Part 1" (SCOLAG, October 2002), pp.181–183.

[90] 2001 Fam. L.R. 2.

[91] (2002) Fam. L.R. 58. And see L. Edwards, "Glasgow Kisses and Parental Wishes: *X v Y*" (2003) 7 Edin. L.R. 101.

life between him and the child A under Art.8 of the ECHR.[92] By contrast, the lesbian couple, M and C, with A, were *not* a "family unit" and as such C did *not* have a right to respect for her family life in respect of A, despite the fact she, not M, had been A's full time carer since M returned to work. As a result, C also did not have the right to seek PRRs since she did not have the relevant "interest" (see para.4–39 above). This seems out of step with previous Scottish cases on title which have not tied the claim of "interest" to the more intensive claim of "family life". In the past, actions for PRRs have been brought by an aunt (no blood tie but *in loco parentis*[93]), a step-parent (arguably the heterosexual equivalent to C[94] (a s.3 case)) and many heterosexual cohabitees. There is no apparent need or reason to tie the broad requirement of "interest" to the much narrower category of people who have "family life" with the child, except in this case to exclude C from a decision on the merits.

X v Y is however likely to be an anomalous case.[95] Given the arrival **4–78** of the Civil Partnership Act 2004,[96] which gives same sex partners who choose to enter civil partnerships rights almost identical to married persons, and the new Adoption (Scotland) Bill 2006, which explicitly allows a gay couple, for the first time, the right to adopt as a couple, it seems that Scots law is well on the way to purging itself of discrimination on grounds of sexuality.

Other types of parental sexual conduct, such as adultery or promis- **4–79** cuity, will rarely now be seen as affecting the welfare of the child, and it is irrelevant if they have formed the basis for the breakdown of the marriage. What the courts are pragmatically more concerned with tends to be not pre-divorce recriminations but post-divorce relationships: they are responsive to evidence that a parent has formed a new partnership, especially where the child has a good relationship with the new partner, or alternatively that a new support network has been formed which can provide back-up for a lone parent. This is particularly true for fathers, as the Scottish courts sometimes seem unwilling to believe that a single man can care for a child without the

---

[92] The ECHR case of *M v Netherlands* App. No.16944/90, 74 D.R. 120, February 8, 1993, which had held that an anonymous sperm donor did *not* have "family life" with a child who was born to a lesbian couple by AID, was distinguished on the grounds that F was not anonymous but had played a major role in the child's life. (It should also be noted that if the insemination had been carried out in a licensed NHS clinic, under the Human Fertilisation and Embryology Act 1990, s.28(6), the pursuer would not have been the legal father.)

[93] *Breingan v Jamieson*, 1993 S.L.T. 186—see para.4–66.

[94] See, e.g. *Bangham v Bangham*, 1992 G.W.D. 12-96.

[95] Indeed, only a few weeks after *X v Y* hit the press, a similar case (unreported, but see *Scotland on Sunday*, April 7, 2002) was decided in Edinburgh Sheriff Court. A lesbian couple both sought parental rights and responsibilities in respect of each other's biological child. Sheriff McPartlin granted this decree, which was supported by the natural father of one of the children. There seems to have been no issue raised concerning title to sue.

[96] See further Ch.9.

support of a good woman, be it mother, sister, cohabitee, nanny or new wife.[97] It can be significant that one parent is willing to keep all the children of a family together,[98] though this need not always hold, for example, if the children themselves wish to live with different parents or, because of age or separation, have never developed relationships *inter se*.[99] The courts will not generally look favourably on a parent who continues to have such an embittered relationship with a former partner that he or she will not contemplate allowing that partner contact should they be granted residence: under the 1995 Act contact is now a responsibility of each parent, for the benefit of the child, and not a privilege which can be casually restricted. Of course in some exceptional circumstances, such as emigration to a new and prosperous future, it may be in the child's welfare to reside with one parent, even though this effectively cuts off contact with the other parent.[1]

Religion

4–80   The courts will look not only at sexual behaviour but at other aspects of the moral environment in which the parent proposes to raise the child. Traditionally it was said that the Scottish courts were interested in children being exposed to some kind of religious upbringing, as opposed to a wholly atheist upbringing, but were unconcerned about the merits of one religion over another.[2] In modern times this view has been based on two cases from the 1950s: *McClements v McClements*[3] and *McKay v McKay*.[4] In *McClements*, a father who was a convinced atheist was denied custody on the grounds that the child ought not to be denied the opportunity of being brought up in a religious faith. In *McKay*, the father was not only a self-admitted atheist but also a communist. He was granted custody, but only on condition that his own mother, who shared childcare duties, undertook to bring the child up with a religious education. Lord Clyde, awarding custody to the father in these circumstances, made the much-quoted remark that,

> "Since the paramount consideration in custody cases is the welfare of the child, it would be almost impossible for a court in

---

[97] In *Hogarth v Hogarth*, 1991 G.W.D. 30-1771, custody turned on the respective merits of the nannies employed by the father and the mother. In *Brixey v Lynas*, 1996 S.L.T. 908, the sheriff made it clear his award was as much to the father's family as the father himself.

[98] *Early v Early*, 1989 S.L.T. 114; 1990 S.L.T. 221.

[99] *Johnson v Johnson*, 1972 S.L.T. (Notes) 15. See also *Aberdeenshire Council Petrs*, 2004 G.W.D. 23-495 (an adoption case involving separation of siblings).

[1] *Johnson v Francis*, 1982 S.L.T. 285. See further paras 4–84 *et seq.* below.

[2] *McNaught v McNaught*, 1955 S.L.T. (Sh. Ct.) 9. See also Thomson, *Family Law* (4th edn, 2002), p.227.

[3] 1958 S.C. 286.

[4] 1957 S.L.T. (Notes) 17.

Scotland to award the custody to an atheist . . . For atheism and the child's welfare are almost mutually exclusive".[5]

In today's increasingly secular society these comments have rightly **4–81** been criticised. In practice, however, in almost all modern cases, religion is not argued as a determining factor and the court does not inquire into it before granting decree of divorce.[6] Hence, even if these opinions still have any force of authority they have largely been bypassed. Wilkinson and Norrie argue persuasively that these cases never laid down a rule of law as such and that exposure to a narrow bigoted religious view may be as detrimental to the child's welfare as a militant and uncompromising atheism.[7] Certainly, recent cases in both Scotland and England have been more concerned with the potentially harmful effects of some non-mainstream religions than with the benefits of a religious upbringing. In *McKechnie v McKechnie*,[8] the court refused to award joint PRRs to the father of a child who was a Jehovah's Witness, because, inter alia, this would have given the father parental rights in respect of the child's medical treatment, whose welfare might be prejudiced should he need medical treatment such as a blood transfusion.[9] In modern English cases, courts have expressed concern about the effects of fringe or cult-like religions such as the Church of Scientology ("immoral and socially obnoxious"[10]) and the Exclusive Brethren ("harsh and restrictive"[11]).

It is submitted that except in the most extreme and obvious cases, **4–82** neither the religious beliefs nor the sexual practices of a parent should affect the court in determining whether to make a residence order. In both cases, neither a religion nor a lifestyle should be presumed to be harmful to the welfare of the child without evidence. Furthermore religious freedom, it must be remembered, is guaranteed by the ECHR.[12] In almost all cases, as we have seen, a residence order will leave the responsibilities and rights of the other parent untouched and he or she will therefore be fully able, and indeed obligated, to bring to the child an opportunity to know of and participate in lifestyles and credos other than those practised by the residential parent. Furthermore, the non-residential parent will have as much right as the caring parent to "control, direct and guide"[13] the child's upbringing, including his or her religion and

---

[5] 1957 S.L.T. (Notes) 17.

[6] A relatively recent exception was *Baretdji v Baretdji*, 1985 S.L.T. 126.

[7] See Wilkinson and Norrie, paras 10.31 *et seq.*

[8] 1990 S.L.T. (Sh. Ct.) 75.

[9] This reasoning is in fact hard to understand since even if the father refused consent to treatment, the mother would be able to supply it: 1995 Act, s.2(2).

[10] *per* Latey J. in *Re B and G (Minors)* [1985] F.L.R. 134 at 157.

[11] *Hewison v Hewison* (1977) 7 Family Law 207. See also *Re R (A Minor) (Residence: Religion)* [1993] 2 F.L.R. 163.

[12] See Art.9 of the ECHR and *Hoffman v Austria* (1994) 17 E.H.R.R. 293.

[13] 1995 Act, s.2(1)(b).

education, and to give legal consent to medical treatment if this is necessary. If conflict does arise, it can better be settled by recourse to a specific issue order under s.11 of the 1995 Act[14] at that time, rather than by pre-judging the issue in the context of an application for residence.

Race

4–83   The first reported case in the Scottish courts on the factor of race in relation to residence orders was *Osborne v Matthan*.[15] The child in question, F, was raised for her first eighteen months by her black Jamaican mother, Matthan, in Jamaica. Matthan then came to live in London where she worked as a dealer in illegal drugs. Her daughter was often looked after by her next door neighbour, Osborne, a white woman. Eventually Matthan was convicted of drug dealing and jailed for three years. During this time she asked Osborne rather than any of her own family to look after F temporarily. On her release from jail in late 1996, Osborne petitioned for custody[16] of the child. Matthan, who faced deportation to Jamaica, was permitted to stay in the country to defend. Sheriff Wheatley, surveying the mother's history of unrepentant criminal activity came to a first conclusion that,

> "there could be no reason whatsoever in this case for supporting the defender's claim to have custody of her child returned to her but for the question of race. The pursuer and her family are white; the defender and her children are black."

He then accepted expert evidence that ideally,

> "[a child] should be brought up within its own racial and cultural identity, with pride in its identity and the appropriate and consequent measure of self esteem. To deprive a child of this was to risk serious advantage."

Racism was endemic in British culture and a child estranged from its cultural roots was likely to have an inability to deal with racial prejudice when encountered. However in the circumstances of this case, the choice was between making a trans-racial placement or uprooting the child from what was "undoubtedly" a warm and loving environment. Furthermore as the mother was to be deported to Jamaica, F would simultaneously be removed from her familiar home and from the only country and culture she had ever known to one wholly alien.

---

[14] See above, para.4–48.
[15] 1997 S.L.T. 811 (Sheriff Court); 1998 S.C. 682; 1998 S.L.T. 1264 (Inner House). See also *AH and PH, Petitioners*, 1997 Fam. L.R. 84, an adoption case involving a trans-racial placement; *Perendes v Sim*, 1998 S.L.T. (Notes) (Scottish woman and Greek Cypriot father).
[16] This was a case based on pre-1995 Act law.

Custody was granted to Osborne but with three caveats designed to secure the child's future welfare. The defender mother was to continue to be allowed to play as major a part in Fiona's life as circumstances would permit. Fiona was to be given every assistance in future to visit or even to go to live with her mother eventually. In the meantime, Osborne was to comply with advice and guidance from social work authorities, etc. on how the child's ethnic and cultural identity might appropriately be secured. The decision was upheld on appeal to the Inner House.

Emigration and Residence/Contact

Another problem that has become pressing in modern times is how **4–84** to deal with the situation where the parent with primary care wishes to emigrate, and the other parent argues this will mean he (or she) will be unable to maintain contact. Section 2(3) of the Children (Scotland) Act 1995 provides that no person is allowed to remove a child from its habitual residence in the United Kingdom without the consent of any other party with rights (whether or not a parent). Hence emigration issues often come to the courts either in residence disputes and/or as specific issue orders. Should the wishes of the caring parent be sacrificed to the welfare of the child? Indeed can the welfare of the child be separated from the welfare of the primary carer? What if *both* parents care for the child? Can the courts achieve any sort of compromise? Traditionally, the courts have allowed the parent who is the primary carer to emigrate with their children.[17] However in *Fourman v Fourman*[18] things were more complicated. An Australian born woman had married a Scottish man, but following their separation, she now wished to return to Australia to be near her own family and retrain as an aromatherapist, along with the three children of the marriage aged 14, 10 and 6. The father, an academic, did not wish to move to Australia, but could plausibly obtain employment there. The case was also unusual in that it was accepted that since the separation, there had been true shared and equal care of the children by both parents separately: the children spent seven days with the father and seven with the mother.

The sheriff found that it was not in the best interests of the children that they should move to Australia, and that they should continue to spend an equal amount of time with both parents, and to remain together. A clear contrast was drawn between what was in the welfare of the *mother* and what was in the welfare of the *children*, the sheriff obviously feeling that the mother's desire to return to Australia was mainly for her own benefit, not the children's. This case was however clearly unusual in that the children's welfare was dependent on the care and presence of both parents.

---

[17] See, e.g. *Borland v Borland*, 1990 G.W.D. 33-1883 (mother taking children to Crete with new Greek partner, father remaining in Scotland).
[18] 1998 Fam. L.R. 98.

Another important factor in recent emigration cases is the views of the child(ren) involved. In *Fourman*, the eldest child, a boy of 10, joined the action as party minuter to express his wish to go on seeing both his parents and for the children to stay together, and his views and those of his siblings were clearly influential. In *Shields v Shields*[19] (discussed further at para.4.88) the views of the nine-year-old boy in question, once elicited, proved decisive in preventing his mother from seeking leave to emigrate. In *M v M*,[20] however, emigration was allowed, at least partly because the oldest of three children, age 12, supported her mother's desire to move to the USA.

Even if the court allows emigration, the other parent can seek an order to maintain contact by phone calls, letters and visits, including residential contact.[21]

The Child's Age and Sex

4–85   Children of different ages have different needs, particularly at two stages—infancy and adolescence—and this may be a factor which the court finds relevant. At one time the Scottish courts probably acceded to a doctrine that children of "tender years" were better placed with their mother than their father.[22] Until recently it was thought, *pace* the odd judicial comment,[23] that no such presumption now existed in Scots law. However, in *Brixey v Lynas*,[24] the House of Lords found that custody of a female child who was 14 months at the date of the original proof but nearly four years old by the time the case reached the Lords, should be awarded to her mother. On the facts this was an understandable decision on the familiar status quo principle, since by that time the child had been in the care of the mother for around three and a half years, while the father had only had sole care for the two or three months prior to that period. However, the decision of the Inner House, who reversed the original award to the father made at sheriff-court level, was explicitly made on the basis that "during his or her infancy, the child's need for the mother is stronger than the need for a father".[25] This appeared to raise the ghost of the rule of maternal preference. The House of Lords affirmed the decision, but were at pains to stress that they were in no way laying down any type of legal principle or presumption.[26]

---

[19] 2002 S.L.T. 579.

[20] 2000 Fam. L.R. 84.

[21] See *Borland v Borland*, above.

[22] *McLean v McLean*, 1947 S.C. 79.

[23] e.g. "In general it is in the best interests of a female child of tender years to be in the custody of her own mother", *per* Lord Marnoch in *Lewis v Lewis*, 1992 G.W.D. 27-1524.

[24] 1996 S.L.T. 908.

[25] 1994 S.L.T. 847 at 849, Lord Morison having quoted from Wilkinson and Norrie (1st edn), p.211.

[26] 1996 S.L.T. 908.

This begs the question: when is a presumption not a presumption? **4–86** According to Lord Jauncey,

> "Nature has endowed men and women with very different attributes and it so happens that mothers are generally better fitted than fathers to provide for the needs of very young children. This is no more discriminatory than the fact that only women can give birth."[27]

And later:

> "the advantage to a very young child of being with its mother is a consideration which *must* be taken into account in deciding where lie its best interests in custody proceedings."[28]

These look remarkably like assertions that unless there is evidence to the contrary, a mother will be deemed better at caring for a young child than a father: something that is commonly known in law as a presumption. It is of course still open to fathers to prove on the facts of a particular case, that the best interests of the child lie with them, and this will be particularly plausible if they are already satisfactorily caring for the child and have established a status quo.[29] On the other hand, a mother of a young child with the status quo will find her position doubly strengthened. This result has been criticised as sexually discriminatory[30]: but it also contains an indubitable kernel of common sense.[31] It is disappointing though, to see a decision, like *Early*,[32] on an individual child made on the basis of a general stereotype.

It has been suggested that when approaching adolescence a male child needs the care of his father if there is no male figure within the household and that this may be a relevant consideration for residence.[33] There seems no reason, however, why a male role-model or mentor cannot be found outside the residential household, e.g. through contact with the father.

---

[27] *ibid.* at p.911E–E

[28] *ibid.* at p.911K–L.

[29] This was the case in *Whitecross v Whitecross*, 1977 S.L.T. 225 (boy aged almost two); *Sherwin v Trumayne*, 1992 G.W.D. 29-1681 (girl aged two); and *Cowen v Brown*, 1991 G.W.D. 29-1718 (girl aged three). In all three cases the father retained custody.

[30] Sutherland, "Mother Knows Best", 1994 S.L.T. (News) 375; her criticism was vigorously rejected by Lord Jauncey in the House of Lords. See further, Edwards, "Mother Still Knows Best", 1996 Fam. L.B. 23-5.

[31] French, *Guardian*, July 8, 1996, suggests that a presumption in favour of the mother is justified since statistically, most physical and sexual abuse of children is male-perpetrated. This, of course, sets up a contrary stereotype.

[32] 1989 S.L.T. 114; 1990 S.L.T. 221.

[33] *ibid.*

The Views of the Child

4–87　　The courts are now explicitly instructed to have regard to the views of the child.[34] In pre-1995 Act case law, as discussed above, children did not have any right to be heard, but the courts, when presented with the views of children, would give them some regard, especially where the child had reached minority. Under the 1995 Act, s.11(7)b), the courts must actively give children an opportunity to express their views and will presume a child over the age of 12 to be mature enough to do so.[35] However the courts' paramount concern remains the welfare of the child. Historically, the Scottish courts have taken the attitude that children do not always know what is best for them: in the words of Lord Stott quoted above, "it cannot by any means be assumed that a child's interests necessarily coincide with her wishes".[36] The evidence of children has also been regarded with some suspicion, since young children may be "coached" or pressurised into speaking for or against a parent. Awareness of the UNCRC and particularly Art.12 and its promotion of the "voice of the child" has however more recently lead to considerable weight being placed on the views of children, especially, though not exclusively, mature children aged 12 or over. In *Smith v Woodhead*,[37] for example, a 12-year-old boy's wish to live with his grandmother rather than his mother was held to be of "considerable" and eventually, decisive, significance, even though it was based on the erroneous belief that his mother no longer wanted him.

4–88　　*Shields v Shields*[38] goes further by emphasising that it is not just the right of children to speak, but also the *duty of the court* to *hear* them. The dispute concerned a mother who wished to take her son, D, to Australia, against the wishes of her ex-husband. At the beginning of the case, D was aged seven and a half. The parties and sheriff agreed that intimation to D should be dispensed with. By the time the sheriff issued decree, in favour of the mother, the child was aged over nine. The father appealed unsuccessfully to the sheriff principal, who in refusing the appeal nevertheless noted his surprise that the child had never been asked what *his* views were on going to Australia. The father appealed again to the Inner House, this time successfully. A number of points were emphasised. First, even if everyone had initially agreed to dispense with the views of the child, that did not

---

[34] 1995 Act, s.11(7).

[35] Children under 12 frequently do however give evidence of their views. Younger children can have their views presented effectively by being interviewed by the sheriff in court or in chambers, by writing notes, or via a curator *ad litem*. In *Fairbairn v Fairbairn*, 1998 G.W.D. 23-1148 the views of children as young as seven and five, elicited by a curator, contributed towards a decision to transfer residence from the father to the mother.

[36] *Fowler v Fowler*, 1981 S.L.T. (Notes) 9.

[37] 1996 G.W.D. 10-533.

[38] 2002 S.L.T. 579.

exonerate the court from its duty to provide the child with the opportunity to speak. Secondly, that duty was *continuing*, so even if the child was too young to consult at the start of proceedings, he should still have been asked if he wanted to state views later on. Indeed, the sheriff had a duty to ascertain the wishes of the child *at the time the order was made*, according to the wording of s.11(7). At that time, the child was nine and should definitely have been consulted. In general, Lord Marnoch stated,

> "so far as according a child the opportunity to make known his views, the only proper and relevant test is one of practicability".

In *Shields* itself, when it became plain the boy would express unwillingness to move to Australia, rather than restart the case with a new Sheriff Court hearing, the mother abandoned the case.[39]

Contact Orders

Contact is an increasingly fraught issue, for a number of reasons. **4–89** First, it should be remembered that in most divorces, the mother of a child, and the father who is or has been married to that mother, already have both the responsibility and the right of contact under ss.1 and 2 of the 1995 Act, if they do not have the child living with them. After the FLSA 2006 comes into force, most unmarried fathers too will have automatic rights of contact. These rights are not in principle terminated on divorce. It is likely, therefore, that an application for a court order for contact will only be made where the parents are actively hostile to each other, often with a history of the parent with interim care impeding contact, since the details of contact can otherwise be settled by agreement.[40] Secondly, the parent seeking the contact order may well have decided to do so because he (and it usually will be he) knows that he would have had little chance of winning if he had sought a residence order. This contributed to the perception prior to the 1995 Act that access, as it then was, was a default consolation prize for losers of custody battles. Thirdly, applicants for contact orders thus disproportionately involve what might be called "sub-standard" parents such as drug

---

[39] There may have been some retrenchment from the high standard of duty demanded of the court in *Shields:* see *G v G*, 2003 Fam. L.R. (Notes) 118 and *C v McM*, 2005 Fam. L.R. 21 (where *Shields* was distinguished by the Sheriff Principal, on the grounds that the child in question had been given two opportunities to speak in the past, via interviews with social workers acting as reporters to the court. There was said to be no obligation on the court to give the child an opportunity to express a view more than once.)

[40] An award of access was made in only 15% of ordinary divorce actions in 1991: Morris, Gibson and Platts, *Untying the Knot* (Scottish Office, CRU, 1993); compare to a figure of around 90% for custody orders. Of course some applications for access will have been made outside divorce actions, e.g. by unmarried fathers.

addicts, inmates of jail[41] and parents of non-standard sexuality. Fourthly, contact is often as much a bargaining counter in a dispute between separating parents over a number of areas, such as pension rights, the matrimonial home, child support and the residence of the child, as it is something of independent value.[42] The 1995 Act seeks to promote contact as primarily a responsibility owed by a parent to the child. In practice though, parents may well think of contact as their own "right", an aspect of their due as parents, and therefore something that can be traded in against other rights, such as property rights. It is possible that the incorporation of the ECHR and its "right to respect for family life" under Art.8 may also have added to this perception.

4-90 All of these factors have meant that the relatively few contested applications for contact (or access, prior to November 1996) tend to be hard-fought, embittered and increasingly legally complex. As a result, the even fewer reported cases around which discussion about contact tends to be structured in legal textbooks, are only the thinnest, least representative and most pathological end of the wedge, involving couples who have intransigently refused to reach agreement, and fathers who often have specific problems in gaining contact because of, e.g. their violent relationship with the mother. To these cases, the courts will, undoubtedly, apply the s.11 criteria. Many of the reported cases cited above in relation to residence will be applicable *mutatis mutandis* in discerning what is in the welfare of the child. However, it must be remembered that for most of the children of divorce and separation in Scotland, contact will be settled by agreement rather than in court, and in such cases it is hard to know if the s.11 criteria are being applied. Similar issues may arise when contact disputes are referred to mediation.

4-91 In reported cases in recent years, the most bitter disputes have centred around the question of whether a father has an inherent right to maintain contact with his child, or whether it is necessary for him to prove to a court that his contact with the child will positively be of benefit to him or her. Until the case of *Porchetta v Porchetta*,[43] it was largely assumed in the courts that contact with a biological father was inherently desirable[44] unless strong evidence was produced to the contrary, e.g. the father was violent towards the child, or might abduct the child if given the opportunity.[45] In *Porchetta*, however, Lord

---

[41] The courts are not keen on granting contact orders compelling jail visits by children: see *Guillar v Scott*, 1994 G.W.D. 33-1932 and *Morrow v Morrow*, 1989 G.W.D. 13-533 but cf. *A v M*, 1999 Fam. L.R. 42 (postal contact allowed); *Harvey v Duff*, 1995 G.W.D. 5-229 (contact after jail sentence terminated allowed).

[42] See generally Wasoff, Dobash and Harcus, *The Impact of the Family Law (Scotland) Act 1985 on Solicitor's Divorce Practice* (Scottish Office, CRU, 1990).

[43] 1986 S.L.T. 105.

[44] See, e.g. *Blance v Blance*, 1978 S.L.T. 74; *Brannigan v Brannigan*, 1979 S.L.T. (Notes) 73.

[45] *Puddinu v Puddinu*, 1987 G.W.D. 4-105.

Dunpark recognised that, given the paramount interest of the welfare of the child, a father cannot have an absolute right to contact. The father in *Porchetta* had had virtually no contact with his 18-month-old son since his birth, and the mother was adamantly opposed to the resumption of contact. In the circumstances, there was "not a shred of evidence"[46] to suggest that this would be in the best interests of the child. The court made no award of access.

In *Russell v Russell*,[47] Sheriff Gordon identified the *Porchetta* approach as demanding that "it is for the parent seeking access to show, and indeed satisfy the court, that it will be in the interests of the child."[48] The onus in seeking contact lies with the applicant, then, to prove he or she has something positive to bring to the child, that is, something more than the simple fact of a biological link to the child. So, where a father has little or no relationship with his child, or where his contact causes great distress to the child, he will find this onus impossible to shift.

The *Porchetta* approach was, arguably, implemented by the 1995 **4–92** Act in the form of the minimum intervention principle, which states that a s.11 order should not be made unless it is better that an order be made than that no order be made at all. This appeared at first blush to put the onus on an applicant father to bring some evidence, of some kind, to justify the making of a contact order by proving it is in the best interests of the child. Where this proved most controversial was in the borderline cases, often involving fathers not married to the mother of the child, who may have had little or no contact with the child, and who had little positive evidence they were a beneficial presence in the life of the child other than the sheer fact that they were the genetic or natural father of the child. How much weight should the courts give to this blood connection *per se*?

In the leading case of *Sanderson v McManus*,[49] a natural father, **4–93** without PRRs, sought access. There was disputed hearsay evidence that the father had once assaulted his child on a contact visit. Against this was asserted the intrinsic value of the natural parent-child relationship. The father had made weekly visits to the child at a contact centre until these were terminated by the sheriff. The Inner House by a 2:1 majority found that a parent had no "right" to access and that the onus of proof to demonstrate access was in the welfare of the child was on the father, an onus he had not in the circumstances discharged. He was therefore denied access. More notable than the decision of the majority, however, is the ferociously dissenting judgement of Lord McCluskey, who declared that the courts should preserve contact between a natural father and his child

---

46 1986 S.L.T. 105 at 106.
47 1991 S.C.L.R. (Notes) 429; see also the English House of Lords case of *Re KD (A Minor)* [1988] 1 All E.R. 577, denying any absolute right of a *mother* to access.
48 1991 S.C.L.R. (Notes) 429 at 430F.
49 1996 S.L.T. 745; 1995 S.C.L.R. 902.

unless there were very strong reasons to the contrary: essentially endorsing the *pre-Porchetta* state of affairs. This was because the parent-child link was,

> "a natural link, the importance of which is felt instinctively; it is a deep and abiding theme in literature, both sacred and profane, and in social and political history. It is a link which is properly understood to have value quite independently of any supposed 'right' in a parent to obtain from a court of law an order allowing 'access' to his or her child".[50]

4–94 Lord McCluskey's worries were taken account of in the subsequent Inner House decision in *White v White*.[51] As noted earlier, the Inner House in *White* swept away any belief that a person without existing parental rights had any special onus to overcome in seeking them. Instead it reinstated the welfare principle, correctly, as the paramount concern of the court. On the matter of the value to be given to Lord McCluskey's "natural link", Lord Rodger, giving the lead judgement, firstly approved the much quoted statement of Lord Hope in *Sanderson v McManus* in the House of Lords that "it may normally be assumed that the child will benefit from continued contact with the natural parent". This was true in all cases involving fathers, whether they had existing PRRs or not. This was not, he went on to say, any kind of "presumption" or "assumption" but merely "a working hypothesis born of human experience". Thus the court is entitled to take account of the value of a child having contact with his father, without any need for this to be proven in evidence, e.g. by bringing the evidence of a child psychologist. However there remains, it seems, no "presumption" that a father should have contact with his child, though the courts will lean towards assuming this is usually a good thing.

Contact Orders and the Child's Wishes

4–95 In disputes over contact, it is almost impossible to disentangle the question of respect for the wishes of the child from the issues of objective welfare and father's rights. In the not atypical event of hostility and bitterness between the parents after they break up, it is difficult to separate out the true attitude of the child towards contact from the feelings of both the warring parents. A parent with residence may influence the child to reject the other parent or to accept a new cohabitee as a replacement. Most likely, the child will not be certain of his or her own wishes. The practice of the Scottish courts is similarly variable. At one time, they were prepared to grant

---

[50] *Sanderson v McManus*, 1996 S.L.T. 750 at 752 D-E. Affirmed House of Lords, 1997 S.L.T. 629.
[51] See para.4–53, above.

a father an order for contact even if the children had expressed a wish not to see him, if it seemed that the child's attitude was being mediated by the hostility or new arrangements of the mother. In *Cosh v Cosh*,[52] for example, it was said that the unwillingness of the children to see their father was neither "genuine" nor "reasonable". In *Blance v Blance*,[53] it was even said to be the duty of the parent with residence to encourage and persuade the child to comply with the court order for contact, by all means short of physical compulsion.[54] However, in cases like *Russell*,[55] above, the court has become more willing to recognise that if a child becomes distressed and upset whenever contact is attempted then it can not be in his or her best interests to enforce it against the child's will, even where distress is partly inspired by the attitude of the residential parent.[56] The problem here is that the statute gives the courts no guidance on whether they are to prefer the current or future welfare of the child, the latter of which may be better met by continuing contact even at the cost of current tears. It must be doubted furthermore if approaches such as those in *Blance*[57] square with the duty of the court under s.11 to have regard, as far as practicable, to the wishes of the child. It is often said that contact decisions in difficult cases like these are better made using mediation services rather than in a courtroom; yet as we have pointed out above, mediation may not be the best place for the child's wishes to be heard, nor does it tend to be effective in long-running embedded disputes.[58]

Enforcement

Finally, what if a parent obtains a contact order but the parent with residence will not comply?[59] In that case, as a final resort, the frustrated parent can enrol a motion that the party with residence be   **4–96**

---

[52] 1979 S.L.T. (Notes) 72.

[53] 1978 S.L.T. 74.

[54] See also *Brannigan*, 1979 S.L.T. (Notes) 73; *Joffre v Joffre*, 1992 G.W.D. 27-1522; *Collins v Collins*, 1993 G.W.D. 5-245.

[55] 1991 S.C.L.R. (Notes) 429.

[56] See also *Cower v Cower*, 1969 S.L.T. (Notes) 78; *Cuthbertson v Cuthbertson*, 1993 G.W.D. 32-2020.

[57] *per* Lord Stewart: "The best interests of the child may inevitably involve some temporary upset and the whole purpose of the court awarding access would be frustrated if the effective decision were to be handed over to the child" (1978 S.L.T. 74 at p.75).

[58] One survey found that around 70% of disputes on contact resolved through mediation terminated with agreement of some kind: Jones, *Family Conciliation in Scotland* (Scottish Office, 1990). But this does not take into account the fact that between two-thirds and four-fifths of parties who bring a dispute to mediation do not find it is appropriate or practicable and withdraw from mediation.

[59] As discussed at para.4–45, international child abduction disputes arising from abuse of contact rights are outwith the scope of this book. Note, however, that the UK government may in future join the Council of Europe Convention on Contact Concerning Children (see Consultation Paper, Scottish Executive, 2005).

declared in contempt of court, a common law offence which can be punished by fine or imprisonment. This can also be used as a sanction where the party with the contact order breaches it, e.g. by repeatedly returning the child after the prescribed time.[60] The problem, with such a "stick" is that it will rarely be in the child's best interests for the primary carer to be sent to jail.[61] An alternative canvassed in *G v G*[62] is to reverse the award in force and, say, give residence to the father away from an obstructive mother. Of course this approach, too, does not necessarily place the child's interests first.

THE WELFARE PRINCIPLE: FINAL THOUGHTS

4–97 Much of this chapter has been taken up with consideration of the nature of the welfare principle and how Scots law uses it both as a check on parental power, and as a criterion for dealing with disputes between parents which arrive at the courts. It is worth considering though, if the best interests of the child *are*, or *should*, always be the paramount consideration. We have already noted several times the potential and actual clashes between parents claiming rights under the ECHR, especially Art.8 which governs right to respect for family and private life, and the welfare principle. There are also areas of domestic law clearly affecting the vital interests of children where the welfare of the child is not paramount.

4–98 When making an exclusion order under the Matrimonial Homes Act 1981, for example, the child's welfare is relevant but in no way overriding,[63] even though children are profoundly affected by domestic violence taking place in their household. Instead, the balance the court is instructed to strike is primarily between the property rights of the entitled spouse and the risk to the health of the non-entitled spouse. Similarly, when the court considers whether to return a child to its place of habitual residence under the child abduction conventions, the welfare principle does not apply, since otherwise the purpose of the legislation would be defeated[64]: instead the courts are only concerned if return will bring a "grave risk" to the child, or in limited cases, where the mature child objects to removal.[65] The failure of the Hague Convention on International

---

[60] *Johnston v Johnston*, 1996 S.L.T. 499. Since contempt of court is a criminal offence, proof of allegations must be beyond reasonable doubt.

[61] Although jail may not be necessary—see *Hunter v Hunter*, 1998 Fam. L.B. 33-5, where the mother refused access by the father to his daughter and was fined £100 for contempt.

[62] 1999 Fam. L.R. 30.

[63] Matrimonial Homes (Family Protection) (Scotland) Act 1981, s.4(2). See further Ch.11.

[64] See *Dickson v Dickson*, 1990 S.C.L.R. 692.

[65] See further Anton, *Private International Law* (3rd edn, 1990).

Child Abduction 1980 to take adequate account of the rights of the child as well as of parents is one reason why this instrument is currently under review.[66]

Perhaps the most important example comes from the Child Support Act 1991, considered in the next chapter, where a child support officer need only have "regard" to the welfare of the child when making a maintenance assessment.[67] Such assessments can be made even when the overall effect is negative for the child, for example, where an absent father is no longer financially able to visit the child, or to provide unofficial financial support to top up state-provided benefit.

There is also an argument that the welfare principle does not **4–99** truly govern child residence and contact cases because it is so indeterminate that it can be imputed with whatever values a particular judge wishes to uphold.[68] At least one Australian judge has admitted that,

> "the best interests approach depends upon the value system of the decision-maker . . . [and] simply creates an unexaminable discretion in the repository of the power".[69]

Many feminist writers have argued that the courts interpret the welfare principle in residence and contact cases in ways which reinforce stereotypes of women as "natural mothers" or "home-makers", or allow male partners to continue to exercise control even after breakdown of the relationship.[70]

It is radically unlikely that Scots law will ever abandon the paramountcy of the welfare principle because it is so deeply entrenched;

---

[66] The Hague Convention is to be reviewed in late 2006. And see also the abduction provisions of EC Regulation Brussels II *bis*, No 2201/2003 which came directly into force in the UK on March 1, 2005 and applies in abduction/retention disputes involving parties from Member States of the EU. Art.11(4) of Brussels II *bis* narrows the "grave risk" defence to return under Hague even further. S.11(2) does however require that courts *must* give the child to be returned a right to be heard, but does not make the child's welfare paramount or even, it seems, a significant factor. The assumption is that the child's welfare is best met by the case being returned to the courts of his or her habitual residence for local adjudication.

[67] Child Support Act 1991, s.2. It has been cynically suggested that the White Paper preceding the introduction of the 1991 Act, *Children Come First*, Cm.1263 (1990) might have been better titled *Taxpayer Comes First*.

[68] See Mnookin, "Child Custody Adjudication: Judicial Functions in the Face of Indeterminacy" (1975) 39 Law and Contemporary Problems 226.

[69] Brennan J. in *Secretary, Dept. of Health and Community Services v JWB and SMB*, F.L.C. 92-3 at 79 and 191(1992), quoted in Parker, "The Best Interests of the Child—Principles and Problems" in Alston, *The Best Interests of the Child* (1994).

[70] See, e.g. essays in Smart and Sevenhuijsen, *Child Custody and the Politics of Gender* (1989).

because there is no viable alternative; and not least, because it would be in breach of the UNCRC (though not, perhaps, the ECHR). However, more sophisticated statutory guidance (as we now have in relation to domestic abuse) or a non-exhaustive "checklist" of factors to be given attention may yet be needed by the Scottish courts when making s.11 orders.

CHAPTER 5

PARENTAL RESPONSIBILITIES AND CHILDREN'S RIGHTS II

In the last chapter we looked at the basic framework of in Pt 1 of the **5–01** Children (Scotland) Act 1995 and examined the principles to be applied by the Scottish Courts in making "contact" and "residence" orders in cases of parental dispute. In this chapter, we will look in more detail at some key examples of parental responsibilities and rights, and children's rights, including a child's right to financial support under the Child Support Act 1991. It should be stressed that this coverage cannot be comprehensive.

PARENTAL RESPONSIBILITIES AND RIGHTS

As we saw in Ch.4, under s.1 of the 1995 Act, a parent now has the **5–02** responsibility:

(a) to safeguard and promote the child's health, development and welfare;
(b) to provide, in a manner appropriate to the stage of development of the child—
    (i) direction, and
    (ii) guidance to the child;
(c) if the child is not living with the parent, to maintain personal relations and direct contact with the child on a regular basis; and
(d) to act as the child's legal representative.[1]

Under s.2 of the Act, parents are given correlative rights in order to **5–03** allow them to fulfil these responsibilities. These include the right to regulate the child's residence; the right to "control, direct or guide" the child's upbringing in a way appropriate to that child's stage of development; the right to maintain contact with the child if not living in the same household; and the right to act as legal representative. As seen in the last chapter, these rights are not absolute, like property rights, but instead can only be exercised if to do so is in the interests of the child[2]; and if necessary, the courts can be invoked to

---

[1] 1995 Act, ss.1(1) and 2(1).
[2] See above, paras 4–39 *et seq.*

clarify what the child's best interests involve by means of a s.11 order.

5–04　The parental rights and responsibilities contained within the 1995 Act do not easily map onto the well-grooved categories of parental rights described in textbooks before 1995. Without attempting to be exhaustive, parents will now be legally responsible for: choices relating to the child's health, education, training, and discipline; moral, physical, psychological and spiritual development; as well as the administration of the child's property and litigation on behalf of the child.

Health and Welfare

5–05　A parent has a duty to "safeguard and promote" a child's health. This duty is enabled by the right of a parent as legal representative to give the consent which is required by law for any medical treatment.[3] The right to make choices about a child's healthcare is thus primarily an aspect of the right of legal representation.

5–06　This right is controlled in two ways. First, a parent cannot give consent to treatment on behalf of a child unless to do so would be in the child's best interest. We discussed this in detail at paras 4–07 to 4–10. Secondly, the law now recognises that a child of sufficient maturity has the right to give a medical consent on his or her own behalf.[4] As we saw in Ch.4, this generates thorny issues as to whether the right of the child to consent should supplant or merely run in parallel to the right of the parent. It is submitted that in Scots law, once a child is deemed competent to consent under s.2(4) of the Age of Legal Capacity (Scotland) Act 1991, the right of the parent to consent flies away. Thus if a child is competent, a parent cannot give a consent even if the child is refusing consent to treatment which might be objectively in his or her best interests.[5]

5–07　How can a parent's duty to promote health and physical welfare be enforced? As we have seen, children have title to sue parents in respect of their parental responsibilities.[6] However, neglected or abused children are rarely in the best position to initiate legal proceedings, or may simply be too young. Children can, of course, sue their parents in delict for breach of duty when they have reached adulthood: but since such cases must be raised within three years of either the cause of the action, or of the date at which the child ceases to be under legal disability by reason of non-age[7] (whichever is later),

---

[3] Except in limited circumstances, e.g. where the patient is unconscious and treatment is necessary: see Mason and McCall-Smith, pp.218 *et seq.*

[4] Age of Legal Capacity (Scotland) Act 1991, s.2(4).

[5] See the full discussion at paras 4–29 *et seq.*

[6] 1995 Act, s.1(3), *Young v Rankine*, 1934 S.C. 499.

[7] Prescription and Limitation (Scotland) Act 1973, s.17(2) and (3). It is submitted that all children have three years to sue from attaining the age of 16 (Age of Legal

the action may well be time-barred, unless the court is willing to extend the triennium period on equitable grounds.[8] Limitation of actions is a particularly difficult issue in relation to actions in respect of child abuse, especially sexual abuse, where the child may not have been conscious that there was legal redress for the harm, or indeed that they had been abused at all, until many years later. Memories of abuse are often buried or repressed, and may only resurface in therapy. In *Stubbings v Webb*,[9] an English case, the Court of Appeal was prepared to count the triennium as running from the date when the plaintiff, aged 30, became *aware* that there was a causal link between her long-term emotional problems and the abuse she had suffered as a child. However, on appeal the House of Lords reversed this decision, Lord Griffiths stating that he "would have the greatest difficulty in accepting that a woman who knows that she has been raped does not know that she has suffered a significant injury".[10] This restrictive approach, which is not supported by much research into the long-term effects of childhood abuse,[11] now seems however to have also been adopted in Scots law.[12] It should be noted however that the Scots authority concerned *prescription*, which extinguishes a right of action entirely as opposed to *limitation* which merely cuts off the right to sue.

The Scottish courts have a discretion to extend the triennium **5–08** under s.19A of the Prescriptions and Limitation (Scotland) Act 1973, but this discretion is used fairly sparingly. The most difficult problem, perhaps, in persuading a court to exercise its discretion, is that encountered in the "Nazareth House" litigation; whether it is better to allow the victims of abuse, now grown up, to have their day in court, or whether old memories should be left to settle. In *S or B (AP) v M*,[13] a victim of abuse in institutions run by nuns in the 1950s–1970s, sued in 2000 for injuries sustained to him no later than 1959. His argument was that until there had been nation-wide publicity about the abuse inflicted in these homes, the pursuer had suppressed his memories of the traumatic events and there-fore the limitation period should be waived on equitable grounds.

Capacity (Scotland) Act 1991, s.1(1)), notwithstanding the exception in the new s.2(4B) inserted by the Children (Scotland) Act 1995, Sch.4, para.53, which allows a child to raise civil proceedings in his or her own name as soon as he or she has sufficient understanding. See concession to this effect by all sides in *Cameron v Stenhouse*, 1998 G.W.D. 24-1230.

[8] 1973 Act, s.19A.

[9] [1991] 3 All E.R. 949 (C.A.); [1993] 2 W.L.R. 120 (H.L.).

[10] [1993] 2 W.L.R. 120 at 126.

[11] See further, Neeb and Harper, *Civil Action for Childhood Sexual Abuse* (1994), Ch.7.

[12] See opinion of Temporary Judge T J Coutts in *S and Ors v Murray and others*, O.H. August 20, 2004, at *www.scotcourts.gov.uk/opinions/a119100.html* at paras 54–59; see also *Kelly v Gilmartin's Excx*, 2002 S.C. 602.

[13] [2005] CSOH 70.

Lord Drummond Young refused to exercise his s 19A discretion, declaring:

> "It was clear during their evidence that the raising of these actions has caused considerable distress to all three pursuers . . . it is clearly most upsetting for anyone to have to think in detail about unhappy memories of childhood. I cannot think that it is genuinely in the pursuers' interests to rake over those memories."[14]

It is submitted that such paternalism is perhaps more appropriate to (some) children than to adults. *If* the probative hurdles of the time lapse since the abuse could be surmounted, and without prejudice to the defenders (a major problem in itself), the victims should have been allowed a chance to prove their case.

5–09 Problems of limitation are also found in relation to claims for criminal injuries compensation for child abuse.[15]

5–10 The major aim of the law, however, must be to prevent abuse, not award compensation after it has happened. The state enforces parental duty in various ways. Neglect, ill-treatment or the infliction of unnecessary suffering or injury to the health of a child meet with criminal sanctions.[16] More commonly, a child who appears to be in need of care, or suffering from abuse will be referred to the Children's Hearings' System as in need of compulsory measures of supervision.[17] If a ground of referral is proven or accepted, then the child can be made the subject of a supervision order within the parental home, or if absolutely necessary, removed into care on a transient or permanent basis.[18]

Physical Punishment of Children

5–11 In most cases of neglect or abuse, if the facts are proven, the parents will have no defence. However, one major area of controversy concerns the traditional right of the parent (or parent-substitute, such as a school teacher) to discipline or chastise the child. Scots law traditionally allowed parents the right to discipline their children by hitting them, so long as the punishment remained "reasonable"; however, where the punishment was unreasonable, disproportionate to the child's age and unruliness, or appeared to have simply been

---

[14] *ibid.*, para.143.
[15] Criminal Injuries Compensation Act 1995, 1996 Scheme, para.17 reduced the time-limit for claims under this regime to two years. But this may be waived, where considered reasonable and in the interests of justice. See *Dyet v CICB*, 1999 S.C.L.R. 1066 (OH).
[16] See para.5–11 below.
[17] See 1995 Act, s.52(2). It is a ground of referral, e.g. that a child is likely to suffer unnecessarily due to lack of parental care (s.52(2)(c)(i)).
[18] See further Chs 7 and 8, below.

dealt out as retribution for bad behaviour without any "educational" element, then it became an abuse of parental responsibility, and could still be sanctioned, either by criminal[19] or child protection[20] routes.

Considerable pressure was placed on the government from groups **5–12** such as EPOCH (End Physical Punishment of Children) to make all physical punishment of children automatically illegal. Many European countries, in line with Art.19(1) of the UNCRC, which requires Member States to protect children from all forms of physical violence, have already completely banned corporal punishment of children.[21] In *Campbell and Cosans v United Kingdom*,[22] the European Court of Human Rights found that corporal punishment of a child in school was not necessarily either "inhuman" or "degrading" treatment and so was not contrary to Art.3 of the ECHR. However the Strasbourg court did find that individual parents had a right to require the school not to hit their children as part of their right to have their children educated according to their religious and philosophical convictions.[23] Faced with a scenario in which some children in a school could be caned while others could not, the government gave in and banned corporal punishment in schools entirely.[24]

This still left the major question of whether parents themselves **5–13** were allowed to hit their kids. The Scottish Law Commission proposed as far back as 1992 that parents should not have the right to hit a child with an object, such as a stick or belt, or to hit a child in a way that would cause injury or to cause discomfort lasting more than a very short time.[25] These proposals however remained politically impossible to implement until matters were brought to a head by an English ECHR case, *A v UK*.[26] In this case, a child was viciously beaten by his stepfather acting *in loco parentis*. The case was prosecuted as criminal assault, but the defence of reasonable chastisement was accepted by a jury. When taken to the European Court of Human Rights, the United Kingdom was found guilty of a violation of Art.3 of the ECHR ("no one shall be subjected to torture or to inhuman or degrading treatment or punishment") and

---

[19] Under s.12 of the Children and Young Persons (Scotland) Act 1937, now repealed. See *Peebles v Macphail*, 1989 S.C.C.R. 410 (incensed mother slapped two-year-old child once, knocking him over); cf. *Guest v Annan*, 1988 S.C.C.R. 275 (father smacking eight-year-old in fit of anger found to have no criminal *mens rea*); *G v Templeton*, 1998 S.C.L.R. 180; *D v Irvine*, 2005 Fam. L.R. 94.

[20] *B v Harris*, 1990 S.L.T. 208; *Kennedy v A*, 1993 S.L.T. 1134.

[21] e.g. Sweden, Finland, Denmark, Norway, Austria and Cyprus.

[22] (1982) 4 E.H.R.R. 293.

[23] See Art.2 of First Protocol to ECHR.

[24] See now the Standards in Scotland's Schools Etc (Scotland) Act, s.16. The ban was initially only in the public sector but was extended to schools in the private sector in 1998 by the Education (Scotland) Act 1980, s.48A(1A) as amended by Education Act 1983, ss.293 and 294, which explicitly banned "inhuman or degrading treatment".

[25] *Report on Family Law*, Scot. Law Com. No.135 (1992), paras 2.67 *et seq.*

[26] [1998] EHRLR 82; [1999] 27 E.H.R.R. 611.

placed under a duty to reform its law of assault so that such cases could not recur.

5–14   Consultation took place in both England and Scotland[27] and the result for Scotland were not exceptionally major changes ushered in by the Criminal Justice (Scotland) Act 2003, s.51. "Smacking" is still not banned entirely, even, as suggested in draft, in relation to very young children. The defence of reasonable chastisement is also retained even if the words *per se* are removed from the legal vocabulary,[28] and replaced by a detailed checklist which strongly resembles the SLC's 1992 proposals, only ten years on. In deciding if corporal punishment was justified as an aspect of "parental right", or if not, was a criminal assault, a court must have regard to the nature of the punishment, its duration and frequency, any effect on the child, and the child's age and personal characteristics. Blows to the head, shaking and hitting using an implement are rebuttably presumed to be non-justifiable assaults.

Religious Upbringing

5–15   A parent has the right to determine in what religion a child should be brought up as part of the right to "control, direct and guide" the child's upbringing under s.1. Where there is disagreement between parents about the religious upbringing of the child, the court may be asked to adjudicate, e.g. if asked to consider religion as a factor when making a residence, contact, specific issue or other s.11 order. As we saw in Ch.4, the courts' concern will be the objective welfare of the child, not the relative spiritual merits of different religions.[29]

5–16   The law may also, occasionally, have to intervene in the religious upbringing of a child even where there is no inter-parental conflict. In extreme circumstances, religious practices which are regarded as harmful to children may be treated as criminal.[30] In lesser circumstances, it is also possible that the child may be referred to the Children's Hearings System,[31] or otherwise taken under the protection of the local social work department.

---

[27] See for Scotland, the Consultation Paper *Physical Punishment of Children in Scotland* (Scottish Executive, February 2000). See also research carried out by the Central Research Unit, Anderson, Murray and Brownlie, *Disciplining Children: Research with Parents* (Scottish Executive, 2002).

[28] Children and Young Persons (Scotland) Act 1937, s.12(7), is repealed; however note that s.12(1) concerning child neglect continues. See, e.g. *L v Stott*, 2002 G.W.D. 35-1163.

[29] See recently *M v C*, 2002 S.L.T. (Sh Ct) 82 (father objecting to Roman Catholic mother sending child to catechism classes after school).

[30] Female circumcision is the main example: Prohibition of Female Circumcision Act 1985; see also discussion of criminal sanctions for child abuse and neglect, para.5.11, above. Circumcision of male infants, a recognised practice in the Jewish and other faiths, is regarded as comparatively minor and has no special regulation.

[31] *Finlayson, Petr*, 1989 S.C.L.R. 601.

If a child does come under the care or supervision of the local **5–17** authority as a "looked after" child[32] then the authority must have regard to the child's religious persuasion, racial origin and cultural and linguistic background when making any decision about the child.[33] In particular, if it is decided to apply for an adoption order in respect of the child, then, even if the consent of the parent or parents has been dispensed with, courts and adoption agencies must still have regard for, inter alia, the child's religious persuasion.[34] It could, for example, be made the condition of an adoption order that the child be brought up in or at least be informed about, say, the Muslim religion.[35] It should be noted that the statutory duty is to have regard to the *child's* religion not the *parent's*. It is submitted that following *Gillick*, a child of sufficient maturity and understanding has the right to choose his or her own religion and this right should be respected by a local authority.[36] All education authorities are under a duty to provide for religious instruction and religious observance in schools.[37] The syllabus, according to guidelines laid down by the Scottish Office Department of Education, should focus on Christianity as the main religious tradition in Scotland but should also take account of the teachings of other religions. However, s.9 of the Education (Scotland) Act 1980 provides a "conscience" clause which allows any parent to withdraw a child from religious instruction or observance at school if they so desire.

An interesting recent point raised in the House of Lords case *R.* **5–18** *(on the application of Williamson) v Secretary of State for Education and Employment*[38] is how far parents can exercise their rights of religious freedom and expression under Art.9 of the ECHR if these rights appear to contravene the rights of their children or the common consensus of society as expressed in laws. As noted above, since 1998, corporal punishment has been banned in all schools in the United Kingdom, public and private. The appellants sought the right to use corporal punishment in four independent schools as part of their religious beliefs. The House of Lords unanimously rejected their claims. In a pluralist society a balance had to be held between freedom to practice one's own beliefs and the interests of others

---

[32] See Ch.7.
[33] 1995 Act, s.17(4)(c).
[34] Adoption (Scotland) Act 1978, s.6(1)(b)(ii), as amended by the 1995 Act. s.95.
[35] Under s.12(6), 1978 Act. A similar condition was made in *H and H, Petrs*, unreported, O.H., March 10, 1995.
[36] See paras 4–31 *et seq.*, above. Under s.6(2) of the 1978 Act, a child is presumed old enough at the age of 12 to form a view to which a court or adoption agency should have regard. It is submitted that these bodies should also presumptively have regard to a child's views on his or her own religious upbringing at the same age.
[37] Unless a majority of local voters decide to remove this requirement: Education (Scotland) Act 1980, s.8.
[38] [2005] UKHL 15.

affected by those practices. The ban on corporal punishment in schools pursued a legitimate aim in protecting the rights and dignity of children. Prohibiting only punishments which might breach Art.3 or Art.9 would be impossible to enforce.

Education[39]

5–19   Parents have both a duty to provide suitable education for their children of school age[40] and a right to determine how their child should be educated.[41] These can be seen as aspects of their general rights and duties as parents under ss.1 and 2 of the 1995 Act, but are more commonly looked at as statutory rights under the distinct Acts dealing with education.[42] The parental right to have children educated according to their religious or philosophical convictions is also guaranteed by Art.2 of the First Protocol to the ECHR.

5–20   *Children* were, for the first time in Scots legal history, given a statutory right to education under s.1 of the Standards in Scotland's Schools Etc (Scotland) Act 2000 (the "2000 Act"). Education law is in something of a transitional state from an area largely dominated by parental rights versus the state (particularly in relation to allocation of resources), to an area where children also have a voice, particularly since the incorporation of the ECHR. As Barnes points out, although parents must have regard to the wishes of children when making major decisions about education,[43] children have very few positive rights in domestic education law. While parents have a number of useful statutory rights when seeking to oppose education authority decisions, e.g. to make a placing request for a particular school, or to view the child's school records, the child has almost none. One important exception is that a child now has the right to oppose their own exclusion from school.[44]

---

[39] This section is not intended to be a comprehensive guide to this specialised area. See further, *Butterworths Family Law Service*, Education section; Barnes, "The right to education in Scotland" (2001) J.L.S.S. July, p.23.

[40] Education (Scotland) Act 1980, s.30(1). This duty can be met "by other means" than by enforcing regular attendance at a school, e.g. by educating the child at home.

[41] *ibid.*, ss.28(1) and 28A–H (substituted by the Education (Scotland) Act 1981).

[42] A "parent" under the Education (Scotland) Act 1980, as amended, is defined as including a guardian, any person who has parental responsibilities in relation to the child, has care of the child or is liable to maintain the child. This latter category brings in the father of a child, even if lacking parental rights and not a carer: see Child Support Act 1991, s.4.

[43] See Children (Scotland) Act 1995, s.6. Note also the 2000 Act, s.2(2) which obliges an education authority to take account of the views of the child or young person when fulfilling its duty to educate. This could, e.g. empower a mature child to seek a placement to a different school than that chosen by his or her parents. See further s.2(1) of the 2000 Act, which, in wording drawn from Art.29 of the UNCRC, also obligates the education authority to secure education which "is directed to the development of the child's personality, talents and mental and physical abilities to their fullest potential". While beyond the scope of this book, this may have considerable implications for the education rights of gifted and special needs children.

[44] 2000 Act, s.41. See, e.g. *S v City of Glasgow Council*, 2004 S.L.T. (Sh Ct) 128.

Disputes between parents about how their child should be edu- **5–21**
cated, as we have seen, can be resolved via a s.11 specific issue order.[45]
Failure to meet the statutory duty to educate one's children is an
offence.[46] Despite the general political emphasis on strengthening
parental choice in education, in reality, parental choice, at least for
those who do not wish to or cannot afford to enter the private sector,
is limited by a number of factors including geographical catchment,
denominational issues and, most importantly, the financial resources
of the authority. In *Harvey v Strathclyde Regional Council*,[47] a mother
sought to enforce her wish that her child be sent to a local non-
denominational school which the education authority planned to
close as part of a general rationalisation scheme. Her claim was that
the Regional Council had breached its duty to her under s.28 of the
Education (Scotland) Act 1980 by planning to close the school of her
choice. Despite evidence that the majority of people in the relevant
area opposed the closure plan, the House of Lords eventually held
that the region had only to give "regard" to the general principle of
parental choice, and that the decision of the authority was an administrative one which could not be faulted unless it was so unreasonable
that judicial review would be appropriate. In the wake of *Harvey*, s.28
has been said to place education authorities under "an unenforceable
duty".[48]

Names

It appears that parental responsibilities and rights include the legal **5–22**
right and duty to give the child a surname. In *M v C*,[49] a mother, Mrs
C, changed her name to her maiden name (McC) following her
divorce and at the same time unilaterally changed the name of
her son to match. The father opposed the change in court.
Distinguishing the pre-1995 Act case of *Flett v Flett*,[50] the sheriff
held that providing a name was an aspect of the parental duties
implied by s.1(1)(a) of the 1995 Act, and the decision was not therefore simply one for the parent with residence but should be based on
the welfare of the child. In this case, it was more in the child's interests to preserve the surname he had known all his life until very
recently, that of his father—a standard status quo decision. The
sheriff was unconvinced by English authority that a child may be
stigmatised if he lives in a family where he has a different name than

---

[45] See para.4–48, above. See also *Lavelle v Lavelle*, 2001 G.W.D. 4-144, which involved
    a child bringing an action to enforce payment of her preferred educational option.
[46] Education (Scotland) Act 1980, s.35(1) and see *O'Hagan v Rea*, 2001 S.L.T. (Sh Ct)
    30. Truancy is also a ground for referral to the Children's Hearing.
[47] 1989 S.L.T. 612.
[48] Logie, "Parental Choice and the Courts", 1989 S.L.T. (News) 417. See also *Dundee
    City Council, Petrs*, 1999 Fam. L.R. 130.
[49] 2002 S.L.T. (Sh Ct) 82.
[50] 1995 S.C.L.R. 189.

his mother (and/or her new partner). In *D v D*[51] a similar decision was reached. The mother's long-term aim was to exclude the father from the child's life; retaining the child's paternal surname would be a "constant reminder" that the father had a right to play an equal role in the child's life.

Legal Representation

5–23 Legal representation embraces the administration of any property belonging to the child, the giving of any legal consent which the child him- or herself is incapable of giving, and acting in any transaction the child is incapable of entering into alone.[52] "Transaction" is widely defined and includes legal contracts, unilateral promises and the bringing and defending of civil proceedings.[53] Litigation was dealt with in Ch.2, paras 2–38 *et seq.*, and we have looked at the issues surrounding the giving of a legal consent in relation to medical treatment in Ch.4, paras 4–29 *et seq.* Here we will principally focus on the administration of a child's property and the making of contracts in relation to that property.

The Child's Property

5–24 Typically, the mother and father (if he has automatic or acquired PRRs) will be the joint legal representatives of the child.[54] Any other person may also apply under s.11 to be granted this responsibility and right. In litigation, the court may appoint a special type of limited legal representative known as a curator *ad litem* to represent the child's interests to the court for the duration of those proceedings only. It is also possible for a parent-substitute known as a "guardian" to be appointed by will[55] who has all the rights and responsibilities of the appointing parent, but whose role is, in practice, often restricted to legal representation. Each parent or other person can act without the consent of the other[56] and disputes over legal representation can be resolved by the court as specific issues under s.11 (para.4.48, above). A third party can thus rely on any one legal representative being entitled to act for the child. There is no need for a majority of representatives to agree, as is the case with trustees administering trust property.

5–25 The right to act as legal representative is restricted in two ways. First, the representative must act, as usual, in the interests of the child.[57] Secondly, the representative only has the right to administer

---

[51] 2005 G.W.D. 9-128.

[52] 1995 Act, s.15(5)(a).

[53] Age of Legal Capacity (Scotland) Act 1991, s.9.

[54] 1995 Act, s.3.

[55] See paras 6–10 *et seq.*

[56] 1995 Act, ss.2(2) and 7(5).

[57] 1995 Act, s.1(1).

the child's property, or to give a consent or enter any transaction on behalf of the child where the child is incapable of acting for him- or herself.[58] Whether a child has capacity depends on the rules of the Age of Legal Capacity (Scotland) Act 1991.[59]

Example: a boy aged 15 seeks consent from his mother or father to **5–26** sign a contract for Saturday employment. The parents have the right as legal representatives to refuse to enter the contract on behalf of the child. But if the transaction is seen as one which is commonly entered into by children of that age and in those circumstances, and the terms are not unreasonable, then, under s.2(1) of the 1991 Act, the child will have capacity to enter into the contract himself. In that case, the parents' rights in connection with the contract terminate, so they cannot veto it.

Administration of the Child's Property

Parents have the right and responsibility as legal representatives to **5–27** administer a child's property. At common law, parents were restricted in what they could do with the property of their children, with a duty to be conservative in investment and to preserve the child's heritage. Under s.10(1)(b) of the 1995 Act, however, all such restrictions are relaxed and legal representatives are entitled to do anything in relation to that property which the child could do if of he or she was of full age and capacity. Parents can thus pass a good title to assets owned by the child, sell heritage as well as moveable property, donate the child's funds, use the capital as well as the income out of a legacy, and invest in risky as well as safe investments.

What then is to stop parents maladministering their children's **5–28** property, e.g. selling the property of a child and putting the proceeds to their own benefit, rather than that of the child? Or putting money bequeathed to a child into their own bank account and refusing to pass it on to the child when he or she is old enough to administer the money himself?

Before the 1995 Act, the situation was highly unsatisfactory.[60] In **5–29** theory, parents and guardians were regulated in two ways. First, they were subject to the supervision of the Accountant of Court in their administration of a child's property.[61] Secondly, under the Trusts Acts 1921 and 1961, parents were defined as a type of trustee, and trust law applied to their transactions on behalf of the child. Parents were thus, inter alia, forbidden from acting in their own cause (*auctor in rem suam*) and could be called on to account for their transactions with the child's property. In practice, however, this protection was little-known, obscure in detail and largely illusory.

---

[58] 1995 Act, s.15(5).
[59] See paras 2–21 *et seq*.
[60] For a full account, see Wilkinson and Nome, para.15–34.
[61] Judicial Factors Act 1849, ss.10 and 25(2).

5–30   The 1995 Act introduces an entirely new scheme in ss.9 and 10 of the 1995 Act.[62] Parents (and guardians) are no longer to be regarded as trustees under the Trusts Acts.[63] Instead the Act attempts to identify and regulate occasions where the child comes into ownership of reasonably large amounts of property.[64] A child most commonly acquires substantial assets via trust, inheritance or an award of damages. In these three cases, the child's property will usually be passed to the parents for future administration, by, respectively, a trustee, an executor or a court. The strategy of the Act then is to focus on these occasions when the property is held at an interim stage by someone other than a parent, and to consider at that time if supervision may be desirable *before* the money reaches the parents. Section 9 sets out a number of rules *requiring* trustees, executors and other persons holding property worth £20,000 or more for the child, to seek directions from the Accountant of Court as to how the property should be administered, before they pass the property to the parents for administration. Such persons *may* also seek directions voluntarily if they hold property worth between £5,000 and £20,000. When directions are sought, the Accountant of Court may direct that:

- a judicial factor be appointed to administer the property. This is usually a solicitor or accountant who is appointed by court to look after the property of a person incapable of doing so, and who is supervised by the Accountant of Court.[65] This might also be a way of placing parents under judicial scrutiny; or
- all or part of the property should be transferred to himself; or
- all or part of the property should be transferred without further ado to the parent or guardian who will administer it on behalf of the child.[66] If there is any dubiety about how the parents will handle the money, conditions may be attached before the property is transferred to the parents, e.g. that there shall be no capital expenditure without the permission of the court.[67]

5–31   Similar provisions apply under s.13 when a court makes an award of damages to a child. When money becomes payable to a child in court proceedings, i.e. damages or settlement, the court may make such order as it thinks fit. *I v Argyll and Clyde Health Board*,[68]

---

[62] See guidance approved by the Professional Practice and Civil Procedure Committees of the Law Society of Scotland, for solicitors taking instructions from a child's legal representative or guardian in relation to a money claim on behalf of the child; reprinted at (2004) J.L.S.S. August, p.38.

[63] Sch.4, para.2, amending Judicial Factors Act 1849, and para.6, amending Trusts Act 1921, s.2.

[64] See *Report on Family Law*, Scot. Law Com. No.135 (1992), Pt IV.

[65] Judicial Factors Act 1849.

[66] s.9(5).

[67] s.9(6)(a).

[68] 2003 S.L.T. 231.

provided some useful guidance here. First, s.13 takes precedence over s.9. So even if the sum of damages is over £20,000 it is not mandatory to ask the court or Accountant of Court for directions, though it may be desirable. Secondly, the person who owes the damages—in *I*'s case, the Health Board—is not "the protector of the child" and need not seek directions either from the court or the Accountant of Court. That job should fall to the legal representative—in *I*'s case, his parents. Thirdly, in general it was emphasised that s.13 was more flexible than the pre-1995 Act common law: in particular there was no duty to appoint an expensive judicial factor unless there was some reason to believe the payment to the child's parents could not be secured by some other simpler means, e.g. a reporting condition.

The Act also protects children by imposing a duty in s.10 on any **5–32** person administering a child's property as legal representative to act as a reasonable and prudent person would act on his or her own behalf (the standard of care required of a trustee). What remedies does the child have for breach of this duty? A legal representative who fails to meet the s.10 standard can be called on to account for his or her intromissions.[69] No liability is incurred if he or she has expended the child's funds in proper discharge of the parental duty to safeguard and promote child's health, development and welfare.[70] However, a child can only require the legal representative to account when he or she has ceased so to act, which will usually not be until the child has reached the age of 16.[71] The child however has the right to sue for damages arising out of the parent's failure in fiduciary duty as soon as he or she has capacity to instruct proceedings, which will usually be earlier.[72] Furthermore, an application could be made to the court at any time under s.11, to remove the parent as legal representative, or to replace him with a judicial factor.

Can a child have a contract, which a parent made on his or her **5–33** behalf, set aside if the parent did not act in the child's interests, as required by s.1(1)? For example, if a parent might sell a painting, bequeathed to the child, to a friend for a knockdown price. Although the Act does not say so expressly, by analogy with the law of trusts such transactions should be voidable if the parent has acted in his or her own interests and not those of the child.[73]

On the other hand, a child does not have the right to reduce a con- **5–34** tract made by a parent just because he or she did not agree with it. Under s.6(1), a child has a right to be consulted in any major decision

---

[69] 1995 Act, s.10(1). This is a remedy derived from the law of trusts. For full details, see Wilson and Duncan, *Trusts, Trustees and Executors* (2nd edn, 1995), pp.451 *et seq.*

[70] s.10(2).

[71] s.2(1)(d) and (7).

[72] An action of accounting is a separate remedy from an action for breach of fiduciary duty. See Walker, *Civil Remedies* (1974), Chs 17 and 58.

[73] See Wilkinson and Nome, para.15–47.

taken by parents in the exercise of parental responsibility.[74] The sale of important assets belonging to a child, such as a house, may well fall into this category. However, even if the child has not been consulted, or if due regard has not been given to his or her views, this does not give the child, or any other person, a right to reduce a transaction entered into with a third party, as long as that party acted in good faith.[75]

CHILDREN'S RIGHTS

5–35 Children share with adults many rights which are generally regarded as being part of public law or the law of civil liberties, such as the right to be housed or the right to freedom of speech. In this chapter, however, we shall restrict ourselves to looking at the key private law rights for children: the right not to be discriminated against on grounds of the lack of marital status of one's parents; the right to support during life from one's parents; and the right to support on death under the rules of succession.

The Right not to be Discriminated Against Because of Parents' Marital Status

5–36 Children born to unmarried parents were historically described as "illegitimate" and suffered serious legal discrimination as a result. As noted in Ch.3, however, discrimination against illegitimate children became steadily less tenable from the late 1970s on, for a number of reasons. In terms of sheer numbers, more and more children are born outside wedlock each year, with the percentage now over 40 per cent of all births. Attitudes towards sexual morality have changed and there is an increasing tendency for children to be born to stable cohabiting couples. In terms of both public ideas of fairness and international human rights standards, legislation providing equal rights for illegitimate children became essential by the early 1980s.[76] This became especially clear after the European Court of Human Rights found, in the case of *Marckx v Belgium*, that rules discriminating against an illegitimate child in relation to succession rights were in breach of the ECHR.[77] Reform was at first accomplished on a piecemeal basis,[78] but in 1986, the Law Reform (Parent and Child)

---

[74] A child of 12 or over is presumed old and mature enough to express a view to which parents should have regard.

[75] s.6(2).

[76] The UK became a signatory to the European Convention on the Legal Status of Children Born out of Wedlock in 1981.

[77] Under Arts 8 and 14; (1979) 2 E.H.R.R. 330.

[78] Notably by the Law Reform (Miscellaneous Provisions) (Scotland) Act 1968 and the 1985 Act.

(Scotland) Act, s.1(1) laid down the general principle, with some exceptions, that the fact that one's parents were married or not was to have no differential legal effect.

The Family Law (Scotland) Act 2006, s.21 took this process one **5–37** step further and amended s.1 of the 1986 Act to abolish completely the status of legitimacy and illegitimacy in Scotland henceforth. No person whose status is governed by Scots law is now to be known as illegitimate, and declarators of legitimacy, legitimation and illegitimacy are abolished. A few connected problems are also tidied up by the 2006 Act. The domicile of a child, once dependent on the marital status of the parents, is now determined by s.22 of the 2006 Act as follows. If the parents of a child are domiciled in the same country as each other, and the child has a home with one or both, the child is domiciled in the same country as the parents. If these conditions do not apply, the child is deemed to be domiciled in the country with which he or she for the time being has the closest connection.

Minor Exceptions

Deeds executed before, or, indeed, after the commencement of the **5–38** 2006 Act may still refer expressly to "illegitimate" children, but given the lack of meaning now attached to the term, this is now extremely unlikely to happen. In respect of all deeds executed since the Law Reform (Miscellaneous Provisions) (Scotland) Act 1968,[79] a reference to children will be interpreted as presumptively referring to *all* children whether their parents were married or not. Only for deeds executed before that, does the presumption go the other way.[80] If despite the presumption, there is clearly a reference that needs interpretation according to the old law of legitimacy, then and only then will that law need to be consulted.

Similarly, statutes which were enacted before the 2006 Act came **5–39** into force, are also in theory not subject to the abolition of illegitimacy.[81] However, in practice, most statutes affecting children have been amended either by the 1986 Act, or subsequently, to reflect a position of legal equality of all children and to remove offensive terminology.

Finally, nothing in the 1986 or 2006 Act affects the rules relating **5–40** to the transmission of titles, coats of arms, honours and dignities, and, for these purposes only, declarators of legitimacy, illegitimacy and legitimation are retained.[82] If any question about the effect of a parent's marriage on the status of a person arises as a matter of

---

[79] 1986 Act, s.1(4)(b) and 1968 Act, s.5.
[80] *Mitchell's Trs v Cable* (1893) 1 S.L.T. 156. For the actual rules on legitimacy and legitimation, see Wilkinson and Norrie, Ch.1, or the first edition of this text.
[81] 1986 Act, s.1(4)(a).
[82] 1986 Act, s.9(1)(c) as amended by 2006 Act.

international private law, then the question shall be determined by the law of the country in which the person is domiciled when the question arises.[83]

The Child's Right to Financial Support

5–41   It is a fundamental tenet of the law of both Scotland and England that a child has a right to financial support from both of his or her parents, whether or not they are or have been married and whether or not they live together or apart. The Family Law (Scotland) Act 1985 (hereafter "the 1985 Act") sets out the principles for determining what support is owed by parents to their children ("aliment"). In practice, however, the provisions of the 1985 Act are rarely invoked where the parents share a household with each other and the child, and in cases where the parents live apart, the 1985 Act rules on aliment have largely been eclipsed by the Child Support Act 1991 as amended (hereafter "the 1991 Act") which has introduced wide-ranging changes throughout the United Kingdom in relation to the child's right to support.

5–42   The 1985 Act provides in s.1 that an obligation of aliment is owed by a father and mother to his or her child[84] and by any person to a child who has been "accepted" as part of their family,[85] except where the child has been boarded out as a foster child by the local authority or a voluntary organisation. For the purposes of the 1985 Act, a child is generally defined as a person aged under 18, but may also include a person over the age of 18 but under the age of 25 who is "reasonably and appropriately undergoing instruction at an educational establishment, or training for employment or for a trade, profession or vocation".[86] As we will see later in this chapter, these provisions of the 1985 Act extending alimentary liability beyond genetic or adoptive family are potentially undermined by the rather different provisions of the 1991 Act under which parents only have a duty to support their *legal* children.[87]

---

[83] 2006 Act, s.41.

[84] 1985 Act, s.1(1)(c).

[85] 1985 Act, s.1(1)(d). A child whom a father once treated as his own child but subsequently discovers to have been fathered by another man has not been "accepted" by him as a child of the family, i.e. ss.1(1)(c) and 1(1)(d) are mutually exclusive: *Watson v Watson*, 1994 S.C.L.R. 1097.

[86] 1985 Act, s.1(5). Since *Macdonald v Macdonald*, 2000 Fam. L.B. 46-4, a number of enterprising students have used or attempted to use this section to support them during their studies, often when they have become estranged from a well-off parent during parental divorce. In quantifying aliment in these cases (see para.5–45 below), a student loan will be regarded as part of the child's own resources: *Park v Park*, 2000 S.L.T. (Sh Ct) 65. Students will not necessarily be penalised because they do not obtain a part-time job (*Watson v McLay*, 2002 G.W.D. 2-73) or a loan where this might lead to unreasonable debt (*Hay v Hay*, 2000 Fam. L.B. 46-4).

[87] 1991 Act, s.1(1) states that each parent of a qualifying child is responsible for maintaining him or her, and s.54 then defines "parent" in relation to any child as meaning

The child's right to support from a parent's estate after death are **5–43** dealt with in the law of succession, considered below at paras 5–91 *et seq*. Leaving aside questions relating to the death of one or both parents then, there are three main scenarios when discussing a child's rights to support in Scotland:

(1) where the child is living with both parents;
(2) where the child is living apart from both parents;
(3) where the child is living with one parent and the other lives elsewhere.

Before we go on to consider each of these broad positions in more **5–44** detail, it should be noted that although the duty of aliment is owed to the child, it is generally the person with care of the child who receives any money that is payable for the aliment of the child. As we have seen in previous chapters, if the child has limited legal capacity this means that financial support owed to a child will usually be administered by a parent or other adult.

Where the Child is living with Both Parents

Here, the position is regulated by the 1985 Act. As discussed in **5–45** para.5–41, both parents are bound to aliment their child and if they fail to do so either the child, or a person acting on behalf of the child, such as a parent, guardian or person with whom the child lives or who is seeking a residence order, can sue to enforce the obligation.[88] An obligation of aliment may also be owed by a person who has accepted the child as a member of his family. In such circumstances, there is no order of liability but any person who is sued for aliment may ask the court to take account of the obligations of aliment owed by other parties.[89]

In determining the amount of aliment to award under the 1985 **5–46** Act, the court must have regard to the factors in s.4(1),[90] namely the needs and resources of the parties,[91] the earning capacity of the parties, and, generally, all the circumstances of the case. The court can have regard as it wishes to any support given by the defender to

---

any person who is in law the mother or father of the child. For legal definitions of "parent", see Ch.3: broadly this includes genetic and adoptive parents and persons who are to be treated for all purposes as parents under the Human Fertilisation and Embryology Act 1990.

[88] 1985 Act, s.2(4).

[89] 1985 Act, s.4(2). See, e.g. *Inglis v Inglis*, 1987 S.C.L.R. 608, where a father asked for the alimentary obligation of the aunt and uncle of the child, who were looking after him and had "accepted" him, to be taken into account.

[90] These are also the factors used to assess spousal aliment claims. They are examined in detail in Ch.10, as is the rest of the 1985 Act regime relating to awards of aliment.

[91] This can include the resources of the child him- or herself: see *Wilson v Wilson*, 1987 G.W.D. 4-106.

any person whom he or she maintains as a dependant in his or her household, whether or not there is a legal requirement to maintain that person.[92] Conduct is only relevant if it is manifestly inequitable to leave it out of account.[93] The court when making an order for aliment will usually make an order for periodical payments for a definite or indefinite period[94] but can also exceptionally make orders for lump-sum payments, e.g. for educational expenses.[95]

5–47   However, where a child is living as part of a family with both parents, the parental obligation to aliment is usually fulfilled by their provision for the child's everyday needs.[96] It is a defence to an action for aliment that the defender is already fulfilling the obligation of aliment, and intends to continue doing so.[97] Generally speaking, the issue of failure to adequately aliment a child within the household arises more frequently in the context of child protection law and the criminal law of neglect or abuse than in the private law of aliment.[98]

5–48   An order for aliment once made can be varied or recalled by the courts on a "material change of circumstances".[99] This is subject, however, to the jurisdiction of the Child Support Agency, discussed below, at paras 5–61 *et seq.*

Where the Child is living Apart from Both Parents

5–49   It is not uncommon for children to live with neither of their parents either because the parents have chosen to place them else-where, e.g. at a boarding school, or because the children have been abandoned or removed from the parents under the rules of child protection law. In these circumstances, the duties of the parents to aliment in principle persist. If the local authority looks after a child under the provisions of Pt II of the 1995 Act, then in general the parents retain their obligation to aliment the child. However, if the local authority removes parental responsibilities and rights from the parents by an order made under s.86 of the 1995 Act (or in future, a permanency order: see Ch.6), then the parents cease to have a duty of aliment.[1] Where children are living apart from their birth

---

[92] s.4(3)(a). Support given a *claimant* for aliment by other parties, whether or not legally obligated, can also be taken into account under the head of "resources" in s.4 — see, e.g. *Ritchie v Ritchie*, 1989 S.C.L.R. (Notes) 768.

[93] 1985 Act, s.4(3)(b).

[94] *ibid.*, s.3(1)(a).

[95] *ibid.*, s.3(1)(b).

[96] *ibid.*, s.2 (6).

[97] *ibid.*

[98] See Chs 7 and 8.

[99] 1985 Act, s.5.

[1] 1995 Act, s.86 is silent on this point. However s.78 of the Social Work (Scotland) Act 1968 provides that "contributions" in respect of a child under 16 who is "looked after" by the local authority (see 1995 Act, s.17(6) and para.7–24) are payable *only* by any natural person who has parental responsibilities as defined under s.1(3) of the 1995 Act. This seems to imply that there is no such obligation on parents whose responsibilities have been removed. See Ch.7.

parents because they have been adopted, the duties of the birth parents, including the duty to aliment, are transferred to the adoptive parents.[2] Where the child is living with local authority foster parents, they have no alimentary obligations beyond those agreed in the fostering arrangements.[3] Foster parents are reimbursed by the state for the care of foster children through allowances made under regulations.[4] Finally, where there is no parent or other person who can be identified as having a duty to aliment a child, the child has the right to support from the State. The 1995 Act provides that local authorities have a duty to provide accommodation for a child who has no parent or other person with parental responsibilities or whose parent or guardian cannot provide the child with suitable accommodation or care.[5]

Where Children are Living With One Parent

The rules on financial support of children living with one parent **5–50** have been fundamentally altered by the implementation of the 1991 Act. The Act radically reformed the system of child maintenance in four main ways:

- it removed decisions about maintenance from the jurisdiction of the court in most cases and created a Child Support Agency within the social security system to administer the Act;
- it provided that decisions about levels of child support were to be made by the application of a rigid formula in nearly all cases, thus altering the position from that which previously existed under the 1985 Act, where the court had a wide discretion in setting the level of aliment;
- it provided that parents' private agreements as to maintenance could always be overridden in the event of the parent with care claiming state benefits, or of either parent applying to the Child Support Agency for a maintenance assessment (as long as the Agency has jurisdiction under the transitional provisions to process the application). Thus parents cannot oust the interest of the state that as much child maintenance as possible should be recovered from the liable parent(s);
- the welfare of the child is not paramount under the 1991 Act, as is traditional in Scots law in any matter relating to children. Instead the child's interest is only to be given "regard" when reaching decisions on child support.[6]

---

[2] Adoption (Scotland) Act 1978, s.12(1); 1991 Act, s.54.
[3] Foster parents with whom the child is boarded out are especially excluded from the duty of aliment under the 1985 Act, s.1(1)(d).
[4] See Fostering of Children (Scotland) Regulations 1996 (SI 1996/3263).
[5] 1995 Act, s.25. See paras 7–14 *et seq.*
[6] s.2 of the 1991 Act requires that a child support officer "shall have regard to the welfare of any child likely to be affected by his decision".

Background to the Child Support Act 1991

5–51 Traditionally in Scots law, a child's right to support from his or her parents after family breakdown was governed by the private system of family law. Lone parents caring for their children in the absence of the other parent could apply to the courts for aliment and the question of whether any aliment was due from the non-resident parent, as well as amounts payable, were determined by the court. Parents were also free to reach their own agreements on aliment and indeed, to waive their right to aliment altogether and choose instead to depend on their own earnings or state support.

5–52 The increasing frequency of divorce, as well as the recognition that many non-resident parents were unable or unwilling to contribute to the financial support of their children, led to the need to extend state-provided child (and child-carer) maintenance. Eligibility for supplementary benefits (now income support) was extended first to lone mothers, and in 1975, to male lone parents. All lone parents thus became entitled to receive benefits whether or not they were available for work, a privileged position in the social security system shared only with other special groups, e.g. those over retirement age and those with disabilities. At the same time as extending state benefits for lone parenthood, the Department of Health and Social Security (now Department of Social Security or "DSS") began to recover child maintenance from the non-resident parents of children whose caring parent was in receipt of supplementary benefit. These non-residential parents were known as "liable relatives"[7] since the state was taking on the obligation of support which these non-paying parents were legally liable to fulfil. The State thus began to attempt to enforce the private law alimentary obligations of non-resident parents in order to reduce its own expanding social security bill. Until the Social Security Act 1986, non-resident parents were required to pay maintenance at a rate equivalent to the relevant supplementary benefit scales for children. When supplementary benefit was replaced by income support in 1988, the maintenance obligation of non-resident parents was increased to include the amount equivalent to the family and lone parent premiums on top of the allowance for children.[8]

5–53 In many cases, however, no attempt was made to recover payment, and in many others only a minimal amount was recovered. In 1988, the DSS's savings from maintenance recovery amounted to £126 million, but this was a decrease in real terms of 9 per cent since 1981/1982 when the amount recovered in maintenance payments was £103 million. The percentage of income support expenditure

---

[7] Under the Supplementary Benefits Act 1976, s.17 (now repealed).
[8] See the Finer Report, Report of the Committee on One-Parent Families, Cmnd.5629 (1974) for the formula used by the DSS under the supplementary benefit system to calculate the liability of absent fathers.

recovered almost halved from 13 per cent to 7 per cent during this period. In 1988/1989, the cost of social security to lone parents was reported by the DSS as £3.2 billion, compared with £1.4 billion in 1981/82.[9]

As the number of lone parent families rose, the legal arrangements **5–54** for child maintenance were increasingly criticised. First, the parallel provisions in the private and public law systems were seen as incoherent: while the DSS was concerned to ensure that as many fathers as possible contributed to the financial support of their children after divorce or separation, meanwhile the courts were absolving some fathers from the payment of their alimentary obligations on the grounds that the DSS were supporting their children, and that having to pay aliment for the children of a previous relationship would create financial hardship for the absent parent.

Secondly, research began to show that even where aliment for chil- **5–55** dren from non-resident parents was ordered by the court, the amounts ordered tended to be small. Moreover, in a large number of cases aliment was never paid, and in a further proportion of cases in which payments *were* made, aliment was paid erratically. For example, in 1980, awards for aliment of children were made in less than half (44 per cent) of the 2,500 Scottish divorce actions involving dependent children. The median amount of aliment per family was £10. In the same year, one-third of all awards for aliment or periodical allowance were never paid at all, while of the remainder over half (54 per cent) were no longer being paid three years later.[10] Later research showed that by 1991, awards for aliment featured in only 40 per cent of Scottish divorces involving children, and that the median amount per week was £23.[11]

Thirdly, there was increasing evidence that children of lone **5–56** parents were likely to be living in poverty both because of the failure of the private maintenance system to provide realistic support and because lone parent families depend heavily on means-tested social security benefits,[12] with consequently low standards of living.

---

[9] Committee of Public Accounts, *DSS: Support for Lone-Parent Families* (1993). See, e.g. *Delaney v Delaney* [1990] 2 F.L.R. 457.

[10] Dobash and Wasoff, "Financial Awards in Divorce and Prospects for Payment", in *Socio-legal Research in the Courts* (Adler and Millar (eds), Central Research Unit Papers), Vol.1. See also, for similar findings in England and Wales, Eekelaar and Maclean, *Maintenance after Divorce* (1986), and Bradshaw and Millar, *Lone Parent Families in the U.K.* (1991), DSS Research Report No.6.

[11] Morris, Gibson and Platts, *Untying the Knot: Characteristics of Divorce in Scotland* (1993).

[12] Figures from DSS (*Social Security Statistics 1993*, Department of Social Security (1994)) show that nearly 75% of lone mothers receive income support, 15% receive family credit (an in-work benefit for lower paid workers) and less than 1% receive Disability Working Allowance (similar to family credit for those with disabilities).

5–57   By the end of the 1980s, all these factors had led to social security spending on lone parent families being targeted as an area in which savings could be made by reinforcing the principle that parents have an inescapable obligation to support their children.[13] The result was the Child Support Act 1991. However, since implementation of the Act on April 5, 1993, the legislation has attracted an alarming amount of censure. The Child Support Agency has been criticised for both incompetence and inability to deliver its objectives.[14] Some of the provisions of the 1991 Act have now been substantially modified, particularly those relating to the formulae for determining maintenance due, and to the scope of the Agency's remit. These changes have been detailed in a series of statutory instruments, the Child Support Act 1995 and, most significantly, the Child Support, Pensions and Social Security Act 2000. We will now examine the details of the scheme of maintenance provided by the 1991 Act as amended.

The Child Support Act 1991

5–58   The 1991 Act cuts across the existing arrangements for the aliment of children in both private law and the social security system,[15] taking priority over the 1985 Act, and effectively removing child support from the private law arena. The CSA has jurisdiction over children (i) under 16; (ii) in full-time education which is not advanced education,[16] and under the age of 19; or (iii) under 18 and either available for work or youth training while the parent is still claiming child support in respect of the child. This contrasts with the wider ambit of the 1985 Act, in which children could qualify for aliment from their parents up until the age of 25 in certain circumstances including "advanced" education, and from non-parents who have "accepted" them as a child of the family (see para.5–42). While both the non-resident parent and parent with care owe duties of support towards the child, the non-resident parent must meet his or her obligation of support by making periodical payments of maintenance as determined by the 1991 Act formulae.[17] The extent

---

[13] For commentary on the policy background to the original 1991 Act, see Maclean, "The Making of the Child Support Act of 1991: Policy Making at the Intersection of Law and Social Policy" (1994) 21 Journal of Law and Society 505.

[14] See House of Commons Social Security Committee, *The Operation of the Child Support Act* (1993–1994 HC 69); House of Commons Social Security Committee, *The Operation of the Child Support Act: Proposals for Change* (1994–1995 HC 470); National Audit Office Memorandum on the Child Support Agency, June 1995; Ombudsman report, *Investigation of Complaints against the Child Support Agency* (1994–1995 HC 135).

[15] For a concise summary of the 1991 Act as originally enacted from a Scots lawyer's perspective see Wilson, 1991 S.L.T. (News) 417.

[16] See ss.3 and 55 of the 1991 Act as amended. Basically what is covered by this is education up to, but not including, the tertiary stage, i.e. university or college. But see para.5–42 for possible claims beyond that point under the Family (Scotland) Act 1985.

[17] 1991 Act, s.1(2).

of the non-resident parent's obligation to provide support as worked out by the Child Support Agency is his or her "maintenance calculation" which can be enforced under the Act.[18]

Almost all disputes about maintenance arise in cases where the **5–59** child lives with one parent. There are just over 950,000 dependent children aged under 18 in Scotland. Of these, nearly one fifth (190,000 or 18 per cent) live in a lone-parent family. Lone-parent families form 16 per cent of families in Scotland.[19] In addition, lone parenthood has traditionally been the preserve of mothers: 95 per cent of all lone parents in the United Kingdom are mothers.[20] Given these figures, it would make a great deal of sense to refer to parents with care as "mothers" and non-resident parents as "fathers"; the provisions of the child support legislation, however, are expressed in gender-neutral language. The 1991 Act removes these controversial issues from private agreement, supervised only by the courts, to the public sphere and the stewardship of the Secretary of State for Social Security.[21] Private agreements can still be made, but these can always be overridden by either a mandatory or voluntary application for a maintenance assessment to the Agency[22]. The 1991 Act follows recent social security law in that its substance is largely left to be filled out through delegated legislation. In outlining the 1991 Act and its subsequent regulations and reforms, we will draw upon the key elements at para.5–50 above: namely the effect of the Act on the jurisdiction of the courts; the formula approach; restrictions on private agreements; and the implications of the legislation for the welfare of the child.

The present system, which applies to all applications after March **5–60** 3, 2003, abandons the traditional rule that each parent is liable to maintain the child. Only the income of the non-resident parent ("NRP") is taken into account, no matter what the income or resources of the person with care ("PWC") may be. This important change to the original 1991 scheme was brought in by the Child Support, Pensions and Social Security Act 2000.

---

[18] 1991 Act, s.1(3), see below at para.5–68.
[19] Data contained in reports from the General Register Office for Scotland on the 1991 Census 10% sample.
[20] OPCS, *General Household Survey 1991* (1993).
[21] 1991 Act, s.8.
[22] The question of the status of registered minutes of agreement has caused difficulty. The issue is discussed in *Woodhouse v Wright Johnston & McKenzie*, 2004 S.L.T. 911. Temporary Judge TG Coutts referred to the "*Isles* Decision" (CSCS/5/97) as "plainly wrong" and confirmed that a registered Minute of Agreement could not be regarded as a Court Order within the meaning of the 1991 Act. Accordingly, neither party nor the child is precluded from making an application to the Agency by reason alone that there is in existence a Minute of Agreement in relation to aliment. The Agency has taken the contrary view and has refused to make calculations of Child Support in cases where the parties have entered into a written agreement. Sooner or later an action will come before the courts so the matter may eventually be made clear.

Applying to the Child Support Agency

5–61   Application to the Agency for a maintenance assessment can be made by the PWC, the NRP[23] (whether or not either is on benefit[24]), or the child him- or herself if over the age of 12.[25] From the coming into force of the 1991 Act, on April 5, 1993, all parents in receipt of specified state benefits[26] have been *obliged*[27] to co-operate with DSS officials in seeking a maintenance assessment from the Child Support Agency, under s.6 of the 1991 Act. Since only a small minority of all lone parents are *not* in receipt of at least one of the four means-tested benefits which make applications to the Agency compulsory,[28] in practice this is the key provision in the 1991 Act, and the main reason for its enactment.

5–62   Where the PWC is on income support and the amount of child support payable is *less* than the amount received in benefit, the PWC continues to receive benefit, and any sums recovered from the NRP go towards the expenses of the Child Support Agency and towards reimbursing income support. There is no financial gain for the lone parent on Income Support or Income Based Jobseeker's Allowance other than the Child Maintenance Premium, which allows the PWC to receiver the first £10 per week paid by the NRP.

5–63   Where child support *exceeds* income support entitlement, then the PWC is no longer eligible for the benefit, and child support payments due from the absent parent are either paid directly or via arrangements made by the Agency when making the maintenance assessment.[29] Where the PWC is in receipt of family credit or disability working allowance, which are similar benefits for low-paid employees, then any child support payable is taken into account when benefit entitlement is calculated. £15 of child support is disregarded for this purpose. Benefit calculations for family credit and disability working allowance are made six-monthly, and benefit amounts are fixed during each six-month period regardless of any changes in financial circumstances, whether these are advantageous to the parent with care or not.

---

[23] 1991 Act, s.4.

[24] Subject to the transitional provisions discussed below at para.5–64.

[25] Only if the child is habitually resident in Scotland and if no application has already been made by a parent with care or absent parent: 1991 Act, s.7.

[26] To date, these are income support, income-based jobseeker's allowance family credit and disability working allowance.

[27] 1991 Act, s.6. See however s.6(2) which provides that the parent with care will not be required to authorise the recovery of child support if either the requirement or the authorisation would entail "a risk of her, or of any child living with her, suffering harm or undue distress as a result".

[28] See para.5–59 above. For a fuller account of the implications of the 1991 Act for lone mothers, see Wasoff and Morris, "The Child Support Act: A Victory for Women?" in Jones and Millar (eds), *The Politics of the Family* (1996).

[29] 1991 Act, s.29(3).

Jurisdiction of the Courts

The 1991 Act removes the determination of child maintenance in **5–64** most circumstances from the courts. Section 8 of the 1991 Act provides that where a child support officer has[30] jurisdiction to make a maintenance assessment with respect to a qualifying child, then the court is barred from making, varying or reviving an order for aliment in respect of that child. Thus, in principle, where the Agency has jurisdiction, the courts do not.

In practice however, the Agency was at the time of implementa- **5–65** tion, and remains to this date, unable to take on the full workload of all the mandatory and voluntary applications for assessment which it would potentially receive. Transitional provisions were therefore enacted to allow the courts to continue temporarily to make and vary[31] aliment awards in cases where the PWC was *not* in receipt of income support, family credit or disability working allowance,[32] *and* where either (i) the PWC had obtained a court order for aliment before April 5, 1993, or (ii) had made a written agreement relating to aliment with the NRP before April 5, 1993.[33] This allowed the Agency to devote its first efforts to processing "new" cases, where a PWC, who had no existing court order or agreement for aliment in place, sought state benefit. The original intention was to have phased in the excluded cases into the ambit of the Child Support Agency by the end of the 1996/97 tax year, but this has now been postponed indefinitely, or at least until a final date is set for the end of the transitional period.[34]

Furthermore, it has now been provided that even if parents did *not* **5–66** make an agreement before April 5, 1993, they can still ask the court to make a maintenance order which is in all material respects in the same terms as a written agreement entered into by the parties *after* that date.[35] Such a court order if obtained will indefinitely postpone the intervention of the Child Support Agency in relation to that child until the transitional period ends.[36]

---

[30] It does not matter if the Agency has or would have made an assessment or not, so long as it had capacity to do so: s.8(2).

[31] It appears a court will not *revoke* an order for aliment even where it has jurisdiction to do so simply in order to allow the parent with care to apply to the Child Support Agency: *B v M* [1994] 1 F.L.R. 342. The correct ground for variation or revocation of an aliment order (or for termination of an agreement for aliment) is that since the date of the decree or the making of the agreement, there has been a "material change of circumstances" (1985 Act, ss.5 and 7). (It is specifically provided that the making of a maintenance assessment is a "material change of circumstances" (1985 Act, ss.5(1A) and 7(1A).)

[32] Such parents would thus be applying to the agency as "voluntary" cases under s.4 rather than as compulsory cases under s.6.

[33] These provisions were originally found in statutory instruments. See now 1991 Act, s.4(10).

[34] Child Support Act 1995, s.18(8).

[35] 1991 Act, s.8(5).

[36] Child Support Act 1995, s.18.

5–67   Some residual jurisdiction, other than that arising due to transitional provisions, remains with the courts in respect of awards of aliment. This principally arises:

(i)   where maintenance is sought for children who are aged over 16 (or over 19 if in full-time non-advanced education and the court has jurisdiction under the 1985 Act)[37];

(ii)   where an additional or "top-up" aliment award is sought on top of the amount set by child support officers using the ordinary 1991 Act formula.[38] This will be relevant only where the NRP is a very high-income earner;

(iii)   where the NRP lives abroad[39];

(iv)   where support is sought from a non-parent, e.g. a step-parent, who has "accepted" the child as a member of his family.[40] This is possible under the 1985 Act, but not the 1991 Act;

(v)   where support is sought for a child with a disability[41];

(vi)   where the action is raised for educational expense such as school fees.[42]

In these circumstances, the rules of the 1985 Act discussed above at paras 5–49 *et seq.* will apply to any claim.

The Formula Approach: Quantification of Maintenance

5–68   The 1991 Act provides that the maintenance assessment owed by an absent parent was to be determined by the application of a formula, or more precisely, a set of formulae.[43]

5–69   The government published a Green Paper, *Children First: A new approach to child support*[44] which proposed a radical simplification of the much vilified child support formula. The aim was to reduce the amount of time the Child Support Agency spent working out assessments (and getting them wrong) so that they could spend more time and money on collection, reducing errors and reducing their backlog.

5–70   The new Child Support Maintenance formula, which was adopted in the 2000 Act, is much simpler than its predecessor. Instead of a very complex algebraic calculation we now have a superficially simple system, leaving out of account some of the factors which made the "old" system so cumbersome and unwieldy. On the other hand, the

---

[37]   See para.5–58 above on the age limits on qualifying children under the 1991 and 1985 Acts.

[38]   1991 Act, Sch.1, para.10(3)

[39]   1991 Act, s.44.

[40]   1985 Act, s.1(1)(d). See para.5–42 above.

[41]   1991 Act, s.8(8) and (9)

[42]   1991 Act, as amended, s.8(7).

[43]   See 1991 Act, Sch.1 and associated regulations. For a concise account of how the formula operated on commencement of the 1991 Act, see Wasoff, "The New Child Support Formula: Algebra for Lawyers", 1992 S.L.T. (News) 389.

[44]   Cm.3992, July 1998.

new system leaves out some factors which could be broadly seen as supporting equity between the parents. It could be said that the new system took Child Support from Byzantine complexity to brutal simplicity, bypassing fairness on the way.

The concept of the Maintenance Requirement, a lynchpin of the **5–71** original formula, is abolished. Now the liability for maintenance will be calculated by reference to the NRP's income, together with consideration of any other children living with the NRP, and also any element of shared care, i.e. residential contact. The Basic Rate applies to those NRP who have a net income of £200 or more per week. The Reduced Rate applies to an NRP if he has a net income of between £100 and £200 per week. The Flat Rate applies to the NRP with a net income of less than £100.[45] The Nil rate applies to a number of specific cases, such as students in full-time education, 16 and 17 year olds in receipt of Income Support and prisoners.[46]

To calculate the liability of the NRP at the Basic Rate, first we must **5–72** establish his net income. For Child Support purposes this is his gross income under deduction of:

(i) liability to income tax;
(ii) liability for National Insurance Contributions; and
(iii) all pension contributions.[47]

Secondly, we look at how many children, if any, are living with the **5–73** NRP and being maintained by him. If there is only one of these "relevant other children" then the NRP's net income is notionally reduced by 15 per cent. If there are two, the net income is reduced by a notional 20 per cent, and if there are three or more, the figure is reduced by a notional 25 per cent. It is important to remember that this reduction applies to the net income of the NRP before any other calculation.[48]

Thirdly, we look at the number of Qualifying Children, that is, chil- **5–74** dren of the NRP who are living with the PWC. If there is only one, the NRP pays 15 per cent of his net income in child support maintenance. If there are two, he pays 20 per cent; and if there are three or more, he pays 25 per cent of his net income, all after taking into account any diminution of his net income as a result of having "relevant other children" living with him.

Finally, we look at the number of nights per week on average the **5–75** qualifying child or children spend with the NRP. Non-residential

---

[45] 1991 Act as amended, Sch.1, paras 3 and 4 and Child Support (Maintenance Calculation and Special Cases) Regulations 2000 (SI 2001/155), regs 3 and 4.

[46] For the full list, see the 1991 Act, Sch.1, Pt I, para.5 and Child Support (Maintenance, Calculation and Special Cases) Regulations 2000 (SI 2001/155), reg.5.

[47] Schedule to the Child Support (Maintenance, Calculation and Special Cases) Regulations 2000 (SI 2001/155) paras 3–6 and Child Support Act 1991 as amended, Sch.1, para.2(1).

[48] 1991 Act, as amended, Sch.1, para.2(2).

contact does not count for theses purposes. The amount of child support maintenance paid by the NRP is reduced by the proportion shown below. If the NRP does not have any of the qualifying children staying with him for at least one night per week on average then there is no diminution in his liability.[49]

Reviews and Appeals

5–76   Where decisions made by child support officers are contested, they can be internally reviewed by the Agency.[50] The most appropriate review that will usually be sought by an aggrieved PWC or NRP is that provided by s.18 of the 1991 Act. If the s.18 review is unsuccessful, the case may be appealed to the Child Support Appeals Tribunal ("the CSAT"), which forms part of the Independent Tribunal Service.[51] Where the assessment made by a child support officer is deemed to be faulty, the CSAT does not substitute its own assessment, but instead will resubmit the case for fresh calculations to another child support officer. An appeal then lies from the CSAT to the Child Support Commissioners,[52] with the permission of either the tribunal chairman or the Commissioners themselves, and from there to the "appropriate court",[53] but only with the leave of the Commissioners or the appropriate court, and only if a point of law is at issue. The "appropriate court" is the English Court of Appeal,[54] even if the appeal comes from Scotland, unless the Child Support Commissioners choose to refer a case to the Court of Session on the grounds that to do so would be more convenient in the circumstances of the case.[55] It should be noted that as is usual for tribunals, no legal aid is available to complainants at any stage up to arrival at the "appropriate court", despite the complexity of the child support legislation. Financial aid for legal advice and assistance is available to those who wish help with Child Support law problems, and with negotiating with the Agency, but cover is not available for attendance at, nor even for, preparation for the Tribunal diet itself.

Enforcement

5–77   The 1991 Act contains provisions requiring the disclosure of financial information in order to make child support calculations.[56] These provisions are subject to regulation but extend considerable powers of entry, examination and enquiry in relation to child support

---

[49] 1991 Act, Sch.1, paras 7 and 8, and Child Support (Maintenance, Calculation and Special Cases) Regulations 2000 (SI 2001/155).
[50] 1991 Act, ss.16–19.
[51] *ibid.*, s.21 and Sch.3.
[52] *ibid.*, s.24.
[53] *ibid.*, s.25.
[54] For a bemused response to this not atypical feature of social security appeal structures, see Wilson, 1991 S.L.T. (News) 417.
[55] 1991 Act. s.25(3A).
[56] *ibid.*, ss.14, 14A and 15.

calculations to the Agency.[57] The 1991 Act includes effective penalties for both PWCs and NRPs who refuse to co-operate with the Child Support Agency. Where a PWC in receipt of one of the relevant state benefits refuses without reason[58] to name the father of her child(ren), she may be subject to a direction that her benefit be reduced.[59] These "reduced benefit directions" were initially little used, and involved a relatively minor docking of benefit for a restricted period: however, a woman's personal benefit may now be reduced by a more draconian 40 per cent for an initial three years which can be extended for as long as she continues not to co-operate in revealing the father.[60] A reduced benefit direction can be appealed to a CSAT.[61] The child's welfare is a factor when a reduced benefit direction is made *but is not paramount.*[62]

Once a maintenance calculation has been made, two special orders **5–78** are available in order to enforce it, namely, *liability orders* and *deductions from earnings orders.*[63] The Secretary of State as part of his powers to arrange for the collection and enforcement of maintenance calculations can make deductions from earnings orders which require employers of a NRP to make deductions against the NRP's wages, and pay them directly to the Child Support Agency. Such an order can be applied for even if the NRP is not in arrears, and takes priority over ordinary diligence by creditors against the wages of the absent parent.

If a deduction from earnings order is not practical, e.g. because **5–79** the NRP has no steady employer or is self-employed, then the Agency also has the power to apply to the Sheriff Court for a liability order against an NRP, but only after at least one child maintenance payment has been missed. This order can then be enforced by the ordinary types of diligence available to creditors such as poinding, inhibition and adjudication, but not by arrestment of earnings.[64] "Time to pay" directions cannot competently be attached to liability orders made under the Child Support Act. The most draconian sanctions for failing to make the maintenance payments ordered by the Agency are Disqualification from Driving and

---

[57] 1991 Act, ss.14 and 15.
[58] 1991 Act, s.46(3) states that the parent must have reasonable grounds for believing that if she were required to reveal the information there would be a risk of her or one of her children suffering harm or undue distress. Child support officers follow DSS guidelines as to what purported reasons shall be accepted in such cases. It is not a good reason for non-disclosure, e.g. that the father of the child is married to someone other than the parent with care. See further House of Commons Social Security Committee 4th Report, *Child Support: Good Cause and the Benefit Penalty* (1995–1996 HC 440).
[59] s.46(5).
[60] SI 1996/1945.
[61] s.46(7).
[62] 1991 Act, s.2.
[63] *ibid.*, s.31 (deductions from earnings orders); s.33 (liability orders).
[64] *ibid.*, s.38.

imprisonment. It is clear that these latter penalties should be used only in cases of wilful refusal or culpable neglect on the part of the liable person.[65] An NRP who thinks that he would prefer to spend the maximum period of six weeks in prison rather than pay any of his Child Support debt should remember that, unlike an ordinary fine, a Child Support liability for which he serves a period in prison remains to be enforced on his release; and he can be imprisoned again for the same debt.

Variations

5–80   The original 1991 Act Child Support system was a particularly inflexible one, leaving little room for the different vicissitudes of modern life nor for the alleviation of the hardships caused by the rigorous application of an algebraic formula to people's lives and the lives of their children. The Child Support Act 1995 introduced a "Departures" system which was meant to allow a more realistic and elastic application of the principles of Child Support law. The softening of the rigid formula was certainly very limited, but it did, at last, permit a party to point out some of the obvious injustices which frequently occurred under the old 1991 Act. This system of departures was further refined in the 2000 Act which replaced the departures system with "variations".[66]

5–81   There are three possible grounds for a variation. These are as follows.

Special Expenses[67]

5–82   Under this head, an NRP can apply to have certain special expenses taken into account in the calculation of maintenance. There are five types of Special Expenses which may allow a variation under this ground:

(a) contact costs;
(b) costs arising from the long-term illness of a relevant other child[68];
(c) prior debts;
(d) boarding school fees[69];

---

[65] 1991 Act as amended, ss.40A and 40B. See also Waite J. in *R. v Luton Magistrates Court ex parte Sullivan* [1992] 2 F.L.R. 196 at 201, in which he stressed that the sanction of imprisonment was an extreme sanction for extreme circumstances; indeed "a power of extreme severity. Indeed it might be argued that the existence of such a power in a society which long ago closed the Marshalsea prison and abandoned imprisonment as a remedy for the enforcement of debts, is anomalous".
[66] The new rules are to be found in 1991 Act, as amended, Sch.4B.
[67] 1991 Act, Sch.4B, para.2.
[68] *ibid.*, Sch.1, para.10C(2).
[69] It may be necessary to distinguish between the part of the fees which relate solely to education, and the part which relates to the costs of boarding as such.

(e) payments in respect of certain mortgages, loans or insurance policies.[70]

Contact costs are expenses incurred to allow the NRP to exercise direct contact with his child or children if these costs are unusually large. They can even include the cost of overnight accommodation, but not if the accommodation is for residential contact. Prior debts may be relevant if they were incurred before the NRP became an NRP, and were incurred for the benefit of both parents, for the qualifying child or for the benefit of another child falling within prescribed criteria.

Pre-April 1993 Property or Capital Transfers[71]

If an NRP transferred property or capital prior to April 1993 **5–83** partly or wholly in lieu of Child Maintenance (or aliment), then a reduction may be allowed. Plainly there are not many applications under this ground, and the incidence of such applications must inevitably decline and disappear.

Additional Cases[72]

There are four relevant heads here: **5–84**

(a) the PWC may seek a variation because the NRP has assets in excess of a prescribed limit, currently £65,000 excluding, e.g. his normal home and excluding any asset used in the course of trade or business[73];
(b) a variation may be possible if the NRP has income in excess of £100 per week which would *not* normally be taken into account for the purposes of the calculation of net income, e.g. unearned income, rental income, share dividends, etc.[74];
(c) a PWC may seek a variation if the NRP's lifestyle is inconsistent with his declared net income for the purposes of a calculation under Pat 1 of Sch.1 of the 1991 Act. Evidence in support of a variation under this Special Case can refer to motor cars and houses owned by the NRP, holidays taken and other forms of conspicuous (and not so conspicuous) consumption. Significantly, the NRP will have a complete defence to such a variation application if he can show that the lifestyle referred to is funded by a new partner.
(d) the PWC may seek a variation by showing that the NRP has deliberately and unreasonably reduced the amount of his income for the purposes of the maintenance calculation.

---

[70] 1991 Act, Sch.4B, para.2(3(e).
[71] *ibid.*, Sch.4B, para.3.
[72] *ibid.*, Sch.4B, para.4.
[73] The Child Support (Variations) Regulations 2000 (SI 2001/156), reg.18.
[74] *ibid.*, reg.19, and 1991 Act, Sch.1, paras 4(1)(b) and 5(a).

Conclusion

5–85   The Child Support Act 1991 introduced radical changes in the rules relating to child maintenance. First, responsibility for this area of law was transferred from the private to the public sphere and from a judicial to an administrative forum. Secondly, an obligation that was previously part of the discretionary family law system was separated from other family matters and is now governed almost exclusively by rigid formulae embodied in regulations and assessed by civil servants.

5–86   How successful has it been? The 1991 Act and its attendant regulations have had a chequered history. The legislation itself was enacted very speedily: the initial announcement of intention to resort to legislation on this issue was made by Thatcher during a public lecture in 1990. The proposal to legislate on this issue was generally welcomed: the proposition that all parents should support their children financially regardless of whether they live together or not attracted a high level of consensus. Nevertheless, the actual proposals were the subject of much disquiet and parliamentary lobbying and debate. Despite criticisms of the White Paper and Child Support Bill, the Act was passed in June 1991 with implementation to begin in April 1993.

5–87   Analyses of the outcomes for lone-parent families after implementation of the 1991 legislation showed that very few lone-parent families would ever benefit from the new provisions. It was argued that even where the Act had potential to raise the standards of living for some children living apart from one parent (those who were already in the most advantaged financial positions), the problems of implementation were likely to negate these possible gains.[75] PWCs would also suffer by having their freedom either to make private agreements with the father of their child, or to cut all ties with such fathers, removed. NRPs, too, would suffer inequity in some cases due to the inability of the system to consider their individual financial and personal circumstances.

5–88   Such pessimistic predictions have come all too true. The Child Support Agency has proved unable to cope with its workload and the targets set for assessment, collection and enforcement of child maintenance have been consistently missed. Many of the Agency's assessments are wrong; by mid-1995, £525 million was owed in outstanding maintenance; and the running costs are high: nearly £200 million per year.[76] Plans to bring all cases in which child maintenance is an issue within the ambit of the Agency have seemingly

---

[75] See Millar, "Poor Mothers and Absent Fathers: Support for Lone Parents in Comparative Perspective" and Wasoff and Morris, "The Child Support Act: a victory for women?", both in Jones and Millar (eds), *The Politics of the Family* (1996).

[76] See the Memorandum by the Comptroller and Auditor General, *Child Support Agency* (National Audit Office, June 1995).

been abandoned. In short, the new policy and legislation for the maintenance of children has been an abject and highly public failure. By 2006, the Agency admitted that there were outstanding arrears of child support maintenance amounting to £3 billion, a figure which was increasing by £30 million per month. Radical change to the Agency and its work seems inevitable although the *raison d'etre* of the Agency, the collection of a tax on parenthood, will not change.

What does this mean for the child's right to support? Quite simply, **5–89** it means that the recognised financial disadvantages accruing to children living in lone-parent families have remained unchanged by the removal of the determination of aliment from the courts to the Child Support Agency. In some cases, their financial position has worsened. Worse, it means that in some cases the requirement to seek child maintenance from non-resident parents has had an adverse effect on the child's relationship with that parent, and in some cases, on the child's relationship with its parent with care.[77]

While it is not yet clear how the removal of aliment from the scope **5–90** of family law has affected the private agreements made between parents on separation and divorce, it seems likely that property transfers, in particular of the matrimonial home, may no longer be so often made in favour of the parent with care. In brief, this means that children are more likely to be uprooted from the former matrimonial home on separation or divorce. For children already having to cope with the stress of parental separation, the poverty of lone-parent family life, and the changing relationships with parents, this would involve yet another unhappy consequence of 1991 Act.

The Child's Right to Support on Death of Parents: Succession[78]

Children have indefeasible common law rights to a portion of the **5–91** moveable estate of both their parents. These rights are known as "legal rights", or sometimes *legitim*, and occur in both testate and intestate succession. In other words, parents in Scotland cannot cut their children out of their will. The *legitim* right is to one third of the moveable estate if there is also a surviving spouse of the deceased, or one half otherwise. (Identical rights go to the surviving spouse of the deceased, if any.) This fund is then divided equally on a *per capita* basis between all the surviving children of the deceased, without any discrimination as to children born outwith marriage[79] or adopted children.[80] However, a blood child of a deceased who has been made the subject of an adoption order or freeing for adoption order, has no

---

[77] See, e.g. Clarke, Craig and Glendinning, *Children Come First?* (1994) and *Losing Support* (1993).
[78] See further, Wills and Succession, Vol.25, *Stair Encyclopedia*.
[79] See paras 5–36 *et seq.* above.
[80] 1964 Act, s.23.

claim on the deceased's estate. Any child who has predeceased the parent can be represented by his or her issue.[81] Normally in such circumstances distribution will be on a *per stirpes* basis,[82] unless all claimants are of the same generation in which case distribution is *per capita*.[83]

5–92 *Example 1:* X dies, leaving £90,000 in moveable estate. He leaves a surviving spouse and two surviving children, A and B. One child, C, died six months before X, but left two children D and E. The *legitim* fund is £30,000 (one third of moveables), and is divided up £10,000 each to A and B, and £5,000 each to D and E (sharing the £10,000 C would have got if he had survived).

5–93 *Example 2:* same facts as above except that A, B, and C *all* predecease X. A leaves one child, B leaves seven children and C leaves two children, as above. All 10 children share equally in the *legitim* fund as they are all in the same degree of relationship to the deceased, taking £3,000 each.

5–94 Where the deceased parent has made a will and left in it a legacy to a child, that child must choose between taking legal rights or taking the legacy. This election can, it seems, only be made by the child when he or she acquires full legal capacity at the age of 16[84]; if that election is made while the child is between the ages of 16 and 18, it can potentially be set aside as a prejudicial transaction under s.3 of the Age of Legal Capacity (Scotland) Act at any time until the child reaches the age of 21.[85] It is not settled if a parent has the right to make this election for the child as an aspect of legal representation.[86] Lifetime advances by the deceased parent towards the child of a non-alimentary nature can nominally be collated into the *legitim* fund, so as to enhance the share of the other children and diminish the share of the child who had received lifetime monies. However, if a child disclaims legal rights, advances towards that child cannot be collated.[87]

5–95 When a parent dies without making a will, then the child may have rights in intestacy on top of legal rights. Under the Succession (Scotland) Act 1964, on intestacy, "prior rights" which go to any surviving spouse of the deceased are first taken off the estate.[88] These

---

[81] Succession (Scotland) Act 1964, s.11. "Issue" includes descendants "however remote": s.36.

[82] *ibid.*, s.11(2)(b).

[83] *ibid.*, s.11(2)(a).

[84] Age of Legal Capacity (Scotland) Act 1991, s.1.

[85] See further, Edwards and Barr, "The Age of Legal Capacity: Further Pitfalls—Part 1", 1992 S.L.T (News) 77.

[86] In current executry practice, executors are advised to retain sufficient funds when distributing an estate to provide for an election for legal rights by the child when he or she reaches 16. But see now Children (Scotland) Act 1995, s.15(5)(b) and 1991 Act, s.9.

[87] *Coat's Trs*, 1914 S.C. 744.

[88] 1964 Act, ss.8 and 9. See further, Ch.10.

often exhaust the estate, but if assets remain, legal rights are then exigible. Finally, if anything is left after legal rights, and there are surviving children or issue of the deceased, that free estate is divided between them in the same proportions as the *legitim* fund was divided.[89] In effect, this means that if a parent dies intestate, and without leaving a surviving spouse, then the children or remoter issue take the whole estate.

The succession rights discussed above can be claimed by children **5–96** under 16 and adult children, without distinction, even if the child has not been in contact with the parent for many years. It can be argued that succession rights, like alimentary rights, should be based on need—especially legal rights which infringe on freedom of testation—and should thus cease at 16 in the same way as aliment and support rights. On the other hand, historically legal rights, and free estate rights, were granted not to meet the needs of dependent children but to keep a certain percentage of family property within the blood-related family. Longstanding reform proposals[90] (which may well be replaced by new research promised by the Scottish Executive) would strengthen the position of the surviving spouse in both intestacy and testacy at the expense of the children, at least for medium-sized[91] estates.

---

[89] 1964 Act, *ss*.2(1)(a), 5(1) and 6.
[90] *Report on Succession*, Scot. Law Com. No.124 (1990).
[91] Under the Scottish Law Commission (SLC) 1990 proposals, in testate succession, children would not have a right to claim legal rights out of the first £100,000 of estate; and in intestacy, the surviving spouse would take outright the first £100,000 of estate and split any excess 50:50 with the children. It is likely that if these proposals were ever implemented, the figures would be updated for inflation.

CHAPTER 6

CHILDREN AND NON-PARENTS

6–01 When looking at the law relating to children thus far, we have stressed the central position granted to the relationship between legal parents and the child. As we saw in Ch.3, the law defines a legal parent principally as a genetic parent, with some amendment to take account of phenomena such as assisted reproductive techniques. However, many children also enjoy close and significant relationships with persons who are not their parents but who may assist or sometimes even replace parents in the caring role. These persons may include siblings, grandparents, step-parents and new, unmarried partners of one or both parents, as well as temporary carers such as babysitters and child-minders. As will be seen in greater detail in the following chapters on marriage and divorce, it is now not uncommon for families to be established or reconstituted in many permutations other than the classic nuclear family, due to the prevalence of divorce and re-marriage, and the increasing level of cohabitation between both heterosexual and homosexual partners. Furthermore, the majority of women of working age are now in full- or part-time employment and so it is likely that children will at some point be cared for at least part-time by persons other than natural parents. In consequence, it is important to look at the rights and duties given by the law to non-parents in relation to children. The rights (or lack of them) of unmarried fathers and step-parents have already been discussed in Ch.3 (see paras 3–12 and 3–20, above).

6–02 Sometimes a child cannot be brought up by either or both natural parents, whether through inability, choice, death of the parent, or abandonment of the child. In those cases, the law intervenes to provide alternative care. The law relating to the duties of local authorities to provide care for children is now principally to be found in Pt II of the Children (Scotland) Act 1995 (see Chs 7 and 8). However, it is often regarded as the best solution where permanent alternative care is necessary for *a parent-substitute* to be found for the child. There are two main ways in which this can be achieved: first, the appointment of a guardian, an event which is relatively infrequent in modern times; or secondly, much more commonly, the adoption of the child. We will look in detail at the processes whereby substitute parents are provided below.

NON-PARENTS

Persons other than parents do not have automatic PRRs under ss.1 **6–03** and 2 of the Children (Scotland) Act 1995. However, they may be able to gain PRRs by making an appropriate application under s.11 of that Act. As discussed in Ch.4, anyone claiming "interest" (see para.4–39) has title to make such an application.[1] However, it has not always been easy for a non-parent to win an application for residence in competition with a natural parent, although the paramount criterion will as always be the welfare of the child. In *Kyle v Stewart*,[2] for example, the mother of children took a fatal overdose and left a note asking her sister to take over the care of the children, which she did. In a subsequent custody dispute between the father of the children and the mother's sister, the father won, despite the sister having the benefit of the status quo. Lord Caplan expressed the opinion that the father should not be deprived of his right to care for his children unless some other course would plainly be materially better for the child. Similarly in *Clark v Clark*,[3] a custody dispute between grandparents and the natural parents, it was said that the parents had a "pre-eminent right to custody".

However, in *Breingan v Jamieson*,[4] the court was quite willing to **6–04** accept that the child in question was well settled with her maternal aunt and grandparents and the status quo should not be disrupted in order to return her to her natural father (and his new wife), with whom she had not lived for some years.[5]

Step-parents, who have a purely social, not blood, connection to **6–05** the child, may have even greater difficulties in convincing a court that their relationship is one which should be supported in law[6] and for many step-parents in a continuing relationship with the natural parent of the child, the simplest and most attractive option is to adopt the child. This solution raises problems of its own, however, which are discussed later in this chapter at paras 6–25 *et seq.* Any non-parent

---

[1] Children (Scotland) Act 1995, s.11(3)(a)(i). It is no longer necessary for an applicant for PRRs who is not a parent or guardian of the child either to prove they have special grounds for their application, or to notify the local authority (1995 Act, Sch.4, para.26, repealing ss.47–49 of the Children Act 1975). If a court has any dubiety about a non-parental application for, e.g. residence, it can refuse to make an order on general welfare grounds, substitute whatever s.11 order it thinks fit (s.11(2)), or refer the child to the children's hearing (s.54).

[2] 1989 G.W.D. 14-580.

[3] 1987 G.W.D. 35-1240.

[4] 1993 S.L.T. 186. See also para.4–67.

[5] See also *Smith v Woodhead*, 1996 G.W.D. 10-533, where a 12-year-old boy's wish to remain with his grandmother in preference to going back to stay with his mother was respected by the court; and *W v B*, Aberdeenshire Sheriff Court, 2000 G.W.D. 30-1165. where a deceased mother's wish for her child to go to her sister and brother (who had the status quo) rather than the unmarried father of the child was accepted by the court as in the child's best interests.

[6] See para.3–20.

who succeeds in obtaining a residence order is given not just the right to regulate residence but also all the parental responsibilities and rights that a mother or married father living with the child would have, for as long as the order remains in force.[7] Thus, a grandparent with a residence order can also consent to the vaccination of the child or deal with that child's property.

6–06 Grandparents are perhaps the class of relatives most discriminated against under the current case law on the welfare of the child and s.11 orders. Two particular situations recur again and again. One is where the mother, often unmarried, has been unable to care adequately for her child for whatever reason (age, lack of money, physical or mental problems) and her own mother has stepped into the breach and partly or entirely brought the child up. In such cases, the maternal grandparents often have a great deal to offer the child but have no rights of contact, etc. if circumstances change, e.g. the mother finds a new partner, or moves away. Another common scenario is where the parents separate, the mother has de facto or perhaps *de iure* sole care of the child, and wishes to exclude the father from her life, or, alternately, the father has little interest in pursuing his right and responsibility to maintain contact. In such circumstances, again, it is often the paternal grandparents who are as, or more, keen than the father to maintain contact, which will often be opposed by the mother seeking to make a new life for herself, especially in the all too common domestic abuse scenario.

6–07 To deal with these kinds of problems, the possibility of grandparents having automatic limited rights of contact was canvassed during the period prior to the FLSA 2006. However this proposal did not gain popular support and was not implemented—in this writer's view, a missed opportunity. This leaves grandparents with the simple option of persuading a court that it is in the best interests of the child that they should have contact (or residence). In scenario 1, above, this is sometimes possible,[8] especially if an appeal can be made to the status quo principle (discussed in Ch.4 at para.4.66), although difficulties may arise concerning the age and potential infirmity of the grandparents if full residence is sought.[9] But in scenario 2, the odds are stacked against the paternal grandparents. They are unlikely to have the benefit of the status quo and the mother is likely to be the primary carer, and hostile to contact. Furthermore, allowing contact with the grandparents may also open up the possibility of contact with the father, unfortunate if he has been excluded from the child's life because of a history of violence or criminality. In such cases the courts will rarely make an

---

[7] 1995 Act, s.11(12).

[8] See, e.g. *Wright v Wright*, 1999 G.W.D. 3-115; *A v M*, 1999 Fam. L.R. 42; *C v K*, 2004 G.W.D. 40-813.

[9] But see *Senna-Cheribbo v Wood and Masterton*, 1999 Fam. L.B. 38-4; 1999 G.W.D. 4-162.

order in the grandparents' favour, however much they objectively have to give to the child[10].It would be helpful perhaps if the courts had some guidance as to how are they supposed to balance current against future welfare of the child.

Many non-parents caring for children on a temporary basis will **6–08** not wish to seek a residence or any other court order. However, it may still sometimes be important for a person with temporary care, such as a child-minder or baby-sitter, legally to be able to take decisions relating to the child, e.g. to take a child for treatment if he has suffered a minor injury. Section 5 of the 1995 Act makes it plain that any person who has care or control of a child under 16[11] can do what is reasonable in all circumstances to safeguard the child's health, development and welfare. In particular, consent can be given to any medical procedure, but only as long as: (i) the child him- or herself does not object, if that child has capacity to give consent on his or her own behalf; and (ii) the parent of the child has not already indicated that he or she would refuse consent. So, for example, a private foster parent could probably consent to a child being assessed by a local authority doctor for child abuse; but not if the mother or father had previously forbidden the foster parent from allowing the local authority near the child. Furthermore, a parent with responsibilities and rights can expressly or impliedly delegate power to any other person.[12]

As we saw in the last chapter, the obligation to maintain a child **6–09** applies primarily between a legal parent and the child. However, it should not be forgotten that under s.1(1)(d) of the 1985 Act, any person owes aliment to a child whom they have "accepted" as a child of their family.

GUARDIANS

A guardian is someone *other* than a parent who takes on the role of **6–10** parent-substitute.[13] Guardianship is now primarily regulated by ss.7 and 8 of the 1995 Act. A guardian has all the same responsibilities

---

[10] See, e.g. *Muirhead v Ness*, 1996 G.W.D. 30-1784; *Rashid v Rashid*, 1999 Fam. L.R. 91; 1998 G.W.D. 25-1241; *Black v McLeod*, 1999 G.W.D. 1219; *N v L and Fife Council*, 2004 G.W.D. 37-750.

[11] Except teachers (s.5(2)) who are given powers to deal with children under the Education (Scotland) Act 1980.

[12] 1995 Act, s.3(5). However, such delegation does not reduce the parent's own duties so that parent could still be sued for failure in duty if, for example, a baby-sitter chosen by the parent mistreated the child: 1995 Act, s.3(6)

[13] Compare the former law under the Law Reform (Parent and Child) (Scotland) Act 1986, where a "guardian" *included* a parent with parental rights (embracing tutor and curator prior to the Age of Legal Capacity (Scotland) Act 1991). "Guardian" was a confusing term since it was also differently defined in various statutory contexts: see *Report on Family Law*, Scot. Law Com. No.135 (1992), Pt III.

and rights as a parent has under ss.1 and 2 of the 1995 Act,[14] subject to any court order, including the right to act as legal representative, but has historically been appointed mainly in connection with the administration of the child's property, and possibly civil litigation. A guardian is most commonly appointed by a parent in his or her will to act after that parents' death, as a so-called "testamentary guardian".[15] A guardian can now also appoint someone to act in turn as guardian after his or her own death.[16] An appointment as guardian must be in writing and signed by the appointing parent or guardian.[17] A parent or guardian cannot appoint someone as guardian if they were not themselves entitled to act as legal representative at their date of death,[18] e.g. because the local authority had removed parental responsibilities by court order. The guardian appointed must accept the post, either expressly or impliedly by acts which are not consistent with any other intention, e.g. by organising the sale of an asset belonging to the child.[19] It is also possible for any person claiming interest to apply to be appointed as a child's guardian by the court.[20] If one parent appoints a testamentary guardian, then after that parent dies the other surviving parent will retain parental responsibilities and rights and *act jointly* with the guardian.[21] Disputes between them can be resolved by the courts if necessary.

6–11 *Example:* H and W have a child C, aged 3. H dies, and appoints X as testamentary guardian. X wishes to sell investments belonging to C to Y. W disagrees. W and X are joint legal representatives and either can act without the other (s.2(2)). W cannot stop X making a valid contract to sell to Y; her remedy is to apply to the court under s.11(2)(f) asking the court to interdict this step on the grounds that it is not in the best interests of the child (s.11(7)(a)). Note that if child C had been older, and especially if aged 12 or older, the court would also have to have regard to the child's views on the sale (s.11(7)(b)) as would W and X (s.6(1)).

6–12 The appointment of a guardian is specifically defined as a "major decision" under s.6(1) of the 1995 Act.[22] Thus mature children (presumptively of age 12 or older) should be consulted about who might become their guardian, as should any other person with parental responsibilities and rights. Guardianship terminates on the death of the guardian, or the child, or when the child reaches 18, unless the

---

[14] 1995 Act, s.7(5).
[15] *ibid.*, s.7(1).
[16] *ibid.*, s.7(2).
[17] *ibid.*, s.7(1) and 7(2).
[18] Or would have been so entitled if the child is born posthumously.
[19] 1995 Act, s.7(3).
[20] *ibid.*, s.11(2)(h).
[21] *ibid.*, s.7(1)(b).
[22] *ibid.*, s.7(6).

deed of appointment otherwise specifies.[23] However, once the child reaches the age of 16, the guardian, like a natural parent, will have only the *responsibility* to provide guidance to the child,[24] and no rights. It is also possible for a guardian, again like a natural parent, to have his or her rights removed by court order, e.g. for bad behaviour or incompetence.[25]

Guardians are subject, when administering property for children, **6–13** to the same duties of care as natural parents, as laid out in s.10 of the 1995 Act. We considered these duties in detail in Ch.5.[26]

Guardianship, at least in the sense of appointing a person to look **6–14** after the property interests of the child, is a dwindling phenomenon. It is very rare in modern times for children under 16 to be orphaned. Even should this occur, substantial property left to a child without parents is most often tied up in trust and administered by trustees. The physical and emotional care of a child after the death of a parent or parents is by far the more important issue and is much more likely to be resolved by a general application by a relative for parental responsibilities and rights, or a residence order: or, if there are no interested relatives, by the intervention of the state, which is under a duty to provide care in the form of adoptive or fostering parents or residential placement. Guardians are traditionally appointed by will, but many Scottish parents do not make wills at all, let alone put in a guardianship clause. If there genuinely is a specific need to appoint someone to look after the child's property, this may well be best met by the appointment of a judicial factor who will be subject to court supervision.

ADOPTIVE PARENTS

Adoption[27] is the process by which the legal relationship between a **6–15** child and his or her birth parents is severed and a new legal relationship between that child and his adoptive parents is created. Adoption differs crucially from a simple award of parental responsibilities and rights in that the adoption order operates, in principle, for the duration of the life of the child, whereas parental rights terminate when the child reaches 16. In 1972, the Houghton Committee Report[28]—which fundamentally shaped current adoption law—defined adoption as "the permanent legal transfer of parental rights and responsibilities".

---

[23] 1995 Act, s.8(5)(a) and (b).
[24] *ibid.*, ss.1(1)(b)(ii), 2(7) and 7(5).
[25] *ibid.*, ss.11(2)(h) and 8(5)(c).
[26] paras 5–24 *et seq.*
[27] See further Wilkinson and Norrie (2nd edn, 1999), Chs 4 and 5, and McNeill, *Adoption of Children in Scotland* (3rd edn, 1998).
[28] Report of the Departmental Committee on the Adoption of Children, Cmnd.5107 (1972).

6–16   More recently, adoption law has been reviewed in both England and Wales[29] and Scotland.[30] Although a number of significant changes were recommended in both jurisdictions, the basic model for adoption remains the same. In this chapter we have represented Scots law as it existed at June 2006, before the passing of the Adoption and Children (Scotland) Bill 2006: we have, however, attempted to anticipate the Bill's broad provision, where this is a significant change from existing law. The Bill was introduced in March 2006 and is expected to come into force in 2008, at which point it will repeal and replace the 1978 Act.

6–17   Adoption provides a substitute parent or parents for the child where the birth parents are unable, unwilling or unfit to care for the child, and thus the making of an adoption order meets a very much wider set of needs than the appointment of a guardian, which is used almost exclusively to deal with the death of one or both parents. The public perception of adoption is still on the whole a process whereby infants are placed with childless couples who are unrelated to the child. In fact, the demographics of modern adoption are very different, with important implications for the development of the law since the last major consolidation in this area in the Adoption (Scotland) Act 1978.[31] Since the 1970s, the number of new adoptions has fallen each year as the supply of young healthy children who can be placed for adoption has declined, for reasons to do with the falling birth rate, changes in sexual morality, universally available contraception and abortion, etc. Over the 20 years leading up to 2003, adoption applications fell by two-thirds—there were almost three times as many adoption applications in 1983 as 2003, when only 373 applications were made.[32] Over a longer period the decline is even more apparent: in 1975, 1,800 adoption orders were made while 30 years later the figure was about 400.[33] Nowadays, non-relative adoptions of children under the age of four account for only around 10 per cent of all adoptions in that age range, and while there were 280 adoptions of children under the age of one year in 1983—one-quarter of all applications in that year—there were only 20 in 2003, representing a steady decrease in infant adoptions. The majority of applications for adoption of children are made by relatives *not* strangers: some 45 per cent of all

---

[29]   *Adoption: A New Approach* (2000, Department of Health) leading to the Adoption and Children Act 2002.

[30]   *Adoption Policy Review Group—Report on Phase 1* (Scottish Executive, 2002) and *Report on Phase 2* (Scottish Executive, 2005). The Scottish Executive largely adopted the proposals of the Review Group into the Adoption and Children Bill, as first published March 2006.

[31]   Important changes were made to the 1978 Act by the Children (Scotland) Act 1995. At the time of writing, the 2006 Bill is yet to go through all of the parliamentary process and the Bill is reported as of end June 2006.

[32]   These and other statistics, except where otherwise stated, are taken from *Adoption Statistics 2003* (Scottish Executive National Statistics Publications, 2004).

[33]   See *Civil Judicial Statistics* (1975) and above.

applications for adoption were made by a birth parent together with a new step-parent in 1989, which rose to 63 per cent in 2003. However the total number of applications by relatives in respect of, especially, children under four, is declining; most of the decline in applications since the mid-1990s can be explained by a reduction in relative adoptions, while non-relative adoption numbers have remained relatively stable. As we will see below, the procedure required for adoption is significantly different in non-relative adoptions, which usually involve an adoption agency, than in step-parent adoptions, where the child is almost invariably not placed by an agency.

The development which has attracted most attention over the last **6–18** 20 years has been the increase in numbers in adoption of children originally termed "hard to place", and now often referred to as "special needs" children. These children tend to be older than average, or have physical or mental disabilities, or emotional or behavioural difficulties, often related to poor early care or in some cases neglect or abuse. As it has become harder to find healthy infants to adopt, the percentage of these adoptions has risen consequentially. In 1992, over a third of adoptions arranged by local authority adoption agencies concerned children aged five or over. It is now regarded as preferable in almost all circumstances for older children who cannot be cared for by their birth families to live in private homes, with either foster or adoptive parents, rather than to enter long-term residential care. Ideally, adoptive care, with all the benefits of permanency, should be sought rather than foster care. Adoption is therefore increasingly being seen by local authorities as another option in the range of approaches it may take towards planning a permanent future for children whose natural families cannot meet the child's needs (discussed further in Ch.7, below). This is a far cry from the original aims of the adoption legislation as introduced in 1930, when adoption was principally seen as a remedy for childless couples, a way to make provision for children whose parents had died, or a means to legitimate children after the re-marriage of one parent.

The adoption of older children has, in particular, opened up a **6–19** debate about "open adoption" (discussed further below, at para.6.65): children adopted later than infancy will remember and may retain attachments to their birth families (including siblings and other relatives as well as mothers and fathers). It is currently a highly controversial issue whether these links should be maintained or severed, especially given that "special needs" adoptions have a much higher rate of breakdown[34] than conventional "baby" adoptions.

Finally, it should be noted that as it has become ever harder to adopt **6–20** healthy infant children from the United Kingdom, prospective adopters have increasingly begun to explore the possibility of adopting

---

[34] Research suggests that almost 40% of placements of children aged 9–11 years at placement break down. See Fratter, *Permanent Family Placement: A Decade of Experience* (1991).

such children from other countries, notably in recent years, from Eastern Europe.[35] These inter-country adoptions may involve removing children from their birth culture, language and sometimes ethnic group as well as family, and have aroused much debate. They are also legally complex. We consider the legal arrangements for such adoptions in more detail at para.6.80.

We will now consider the law regulating the adoption process.

GENERAL DUTIES AND PRINCIPLES: ADOPTION AGENCIES, COURTS AND CHILDREN

6–21 The two key institutions in the adoption process are the courts, to whom application must be made for an adoption order, and the adoption agency, who, except in certain cases discussed below, must place the child for adoption and will vet the suitability of prospective adopters. An adoption agency is either a local authority or an approved adoption society[36] including corresponding institutions in England and Wales.[37] Approved adoption societies are often run by voluntary or religious bodies. Approval to be an adoption society is sought from the Scottish Ministers under s.3 and lasts for three years. Approval can be withdrawn for ineffectiveness or failure to comply with requirements to provide information to the Secretary of state.[38] Adoption agencies are regulated by Pt 1 of the 1978 Act and the Adoption Agencies (Scotland) Regulations 1996.

6–22 According to s.6(1)(a) of the 1978 Act,[39] both a court and an adoption agency, when reaching any decision relating to the adoption of a child, must regard the need to safeguard and promote the welfare of the child concerned throughout his or her life as the paramount consideration. This formulation was introduced by the Children (Scotland) Act 1995. Before 1995, the welfare of the child in adoption was only *the first* rather than the paramount consideration. This was intended to preserve a balance between the interests of the child and the right of a natural parent not to have his or her child removed without very good cause. However, it is inconsistent both with modern child law and the UNCRC not to endorse the paramountcy principle wherever possible. Note also that the court or agency are enjoined to look at the child's welfare *throughout his or her life*, not just childhood. This should be compared to s.11(7) of the 1995 Act, dealing with court actions for parental rights, which makes no such requirement. Adoption, as we have seen above, is regarded as a status

---

[35] In 2003, Scottish Office statistics recorded 15 adoptions of children from overseas, 4% of all adoptions in that year.

[36] 1978 Act, s.1(4).

[37] *ibid.*, s.65(1).

[38] *ibid.*, s.4.

[39] As substituted by s.95 of the Children (Scotland) Act 1995.

for life and it must therefore enhance the child's welfare not only now but for the foreseeable future.

Courts and agencies are also under a duty to have regard to the **6–23** views of the child when making any decision, taking account of the child's age and maturity, as well as to the religious persuasion, racial origin and cultural and linguistic background of the child (s.6(1)(b)). An agency in placing the child must also have regard to any wishes of the child's parents or guardians as to religious upbringing.[40] A child is deemed mature enough to express a view at the age of 12.[41] A child over the age of 12 also has an absolute right to veto either his or her own adoption[42] or his or her freeing for adoption.[43] Agencies have a duty to consider alternatives to adoption,[44] while courts are required to consider whether it would be better for a child to make an adoption order or not[45] (discussed below in relation to step-parent adoptions).

Who can Adopt?

At present, an application to adopt can, in principle, only be made **6–24** by a single person, or a married couple. Applicants must be either domiciled or habitually resident for one year preceding the application in any part of the United Kingdom, or the Channel Islands or Isle of Man. Where the application is made by a married couple, both must be 21 or over,[46] unless one applicant is already the natural parent of the child, in which case that parent need only be 18.[47] Where the application is made by a single applicant, he or she must be over 21 and either not married, or, if married, the court must be satisfied that his or her spouse cannot be found, or is incapable of making the application through mental or physical ill-health, or the spouses have separated or are living apart and the separation is likely to be permanent.[48] It is thus currently impossible for a cohabiting couple to apply to adopt together, although in practice of course one partner can apply as a single person. The existence of the cohabiting relationship and its stability would then be relevant to the adoption agency and the court. The Adoption Policy Review Group ("APRG") recommended, however, that unmarried couples, including same sex couples, should be able to adopt jointly.[49] This proposal was accepted

---

[40] 1978 Act, s.7.
[41] s.6(2).
[42] 1995 Act, s.12(8).
[43] *ibid.*, s.18(8).
[44] 1978 Act, s.6A.
[45] *ibid.*, s.24(3)
[46] *ibid.*, s.14(1A).
[47] *ibid.*, s.14(1B).
[48] *ibid.*, s.15.
[49] Consultation paper on Scottish Executive proposals in response to phase two of the Adoption Policy Review, Scottish Executive, June 30, 2005 (hereafter "APRG 2"), para.3.2 (available at *www.scotland.gov.uk/*).

by the Scottish Executive and included in the Adoption and Children Bill. If enacted, joint adoption will be extended to married couples, civil partners and those living together as if a married couple or as if civil partners in an enduring family relationship.[50]

Step-Parent Adoptions

6–25   Either of the child's birth parents can apply to adopt the child alone, but since this would have the effect of severing the legal link between the other birth parent and the child, it must be shown that there is some reason justifying the exclusion of the other parent, e.g. that he or she is dead or cannot be found.[51] In practice, birth parents rarely if ever have reason to adopt their own children, except in conjunction with a new step-parent. In that case, it is possible for a step-parent to apply on his or her own to adopt the child of their spouse.[52] This has the advantage over a joint application by the couple that the natural parent does not have to become an adoptive parent, and thus can continue to appear as a birth parent on the child's birth certificate. The effect of such an adoption is that the child is deemed to be the child of the natural parent and step-parent applicant from his or her date of birth.[53]

6–26   As noted earlier, around 60 per cent of all adoption applications are adoptions by relatives. Step-parents often wish to adopt the children of their new spouse in order to acquire parental rights and generally take equal responsibility, but such an adoption has the significant disadvantage of severing the legal link not only between the child and the other birth parent, but also with any relatives on that side of the family. If a mother divorces the father of her child, remarries, and her new husband adopts the child, the natural father not only loses his right and duty to maintain contact with the child, but also loses title to apply for contact in the courts subsequent to the making of the order.[54] The child also loses all succession[55] and alimentary[56] rights in respect of the birth father. This is particularly unfortunate given the high incidence of breakdown of second marriages: the child may lose one family without really gaining another. For these reasons, prior to the Children (Scotland) Act 1995, the courts were required specifically to consider when making an

---

[50] For the position in England and Wales see Adoption and Children Act 2002, s.144(4) and (5) as amended by the Civil Partnership Act 2004.

[51] *ibid.*, s.15(3).

[52] *ibid.*, s.15(1)(aa), inserted by 1995 Act, s.97.

[53] Even if the marriage between parent and step-parent took place after the birth of the child: s.39 as substituted by 1995 Act, s.97.

[54] 1978 Act, s.11(3) and (4). These provisions are likely to be replaced by a restriction on a natural parent who has lost PRRs through adoption being allowed to seek a s.11 order, but only with the leave of court. See discussion at Ch.4 and para.6–65.

[55] Succession (Scotland) Act 1964, s.23(1).

[56] 1978 Act, s.12(3)(b).

adoption order in step-parent cases if it would better promote the child's welfare to make a custody order.[57] This has now been replaced by the more general requirement that a court should not make an adoption order unless it considers that it is better to do so than not to.[58] This, combined with the general duty on the court to make the welfare of the child its paramount consideration, should lead a court to consider whether it is necessary to take the extreme step of making an adoption order, or whether some lesser alternative, e.g. a residence order, might suffice.

Many step-parent adoptions are undertaken to achieve ends which **6–27** can be met by procedures less final than adoption, e.g. the child's surname can be changed on his or her birth certificate to match that of a new step-parent simply by application to the Registrar of Births, Deaths and Marriages.[59] There is also a complementary duty on adoption agencies to consider alternatives to adoption before making arrangements for the adoption of a child.[60] This might extend, for example, to investigating the possibility of a member of the extended family seeking a residence order, rather than placing the child for adoption.

Birth parents (other than a father who has no PRRs[61]) who wish **6–28** to oppose the adoption of their child by the new spouse of the other birth parent, have the right to withhold consent to the adoption (discussed further below at paras 6–42 *et seq.*), in which case an adoption order cannot be made unless the court is willing to dispense with their consent.[62] In *Re B*,[63] the English courts considered whether a natural father was unreasonably withholding agreement in refusing to consent to the adoption of his child. Gumming Brace, J. stated that:

> "It is quite wrong to use the adoption law to extinguish the relationship between the protesting father and the child, unless there is some really serious factor which justifies the use of the statutory guillotine. The courts should not encourage the idea that after divorce the children of the family can be reshuffled and dealt out like a pack of cards in a second rubber of bridge".[64]

---

[57] Formerly in s.53 of the Children Act 1975, repealed by the 1995 Act, Sch.5.

[58] 1978 Act, s.24(3) as substituted by 1995 Act, Sch.2, para.16.

[59] Registration of Births, Deaths and Marriages (Scotland) Act 1965, s.20. Note also that a parent can also, later in the child's life, seek a s.11 order to change a child's surname as an aspect of PRRs (see Ch.4) (although this will be dependent on what is in the child's welfare).

[60] 1978 Act, s.6A, as inserted by 1995 Act, s.96.

[61] The effect of s.23 of the FLSA 2006 will be that the number of fathers in this situation will diminish.

[62] 1978 Act, ss.16 and 16(2).

[63] [1975] Fam. 127.

[64] [1975] Fam. 127 at p.143.

6–29 These comments were affirmed in the Scots case of *A v B*[65] and are all the more true given the emphasis placed by the Children (Scotland) Act 1995 on maintaining contact between the child and both parents after parents split up. In principle, these kinds of issues are more properly dealt with in the original divorce rather than via a later adoption petition. However, it is clear that most step-parent adoptions are not in practice disputed either by the court or the natural parent whose rights are removed.

Criteria for Adopters

6–30 No criteria for adopters other than age, residence or domicile and marital status are laid down in the primary legislation. Agencies, like courts, are under a general duty to have regard to the child's welfare throughout his or her life as the paramount consideration when making any decision to place a child for adoption; and must specifically have regard to the child's own wishes, and to his or her religious persuasion, racial origin and cultural and linguistic background.[66] This does not mean that, for example, an Asian child cannot be placed with white adoptive parents. In *AH and PH, Petrs*,[67] such an adoption was allowed by the courts, with the caveat that the adopters should use their best endeavours to ensure that the child was brought up to be aware of his black identity and ethnic origins and traditions.[68] In practice, adoption agencies operate detailed criteria for prospective adopters, which they are required under the Adoption Agency Regulations[69] to make available in written form. These criteria are implemented by the adoption panels which each adoption agency is required to establish and whose function, inter alia, is to consider whether prospective adopters are suitable to be adoptive parents, whether adoption is in the best interests of the particular child in question, and to match the child available for adoption to the proposed adoptive parents. An adoption panel must be composed of both men and women and the numbers, qualifications and experience

---

[65] 1987 S.L.T. (Sh. Ct.) 121. Also see the Inner House case of *HQ and LQ v CG*, unreported, October 16, 1992. In both these cases, the court refused to dispense with the consent of natural fathers and thus refused to make an adoption order.

[66] 1978 Act, s.6 as substituted by 1995 Act, s.95; see paras 6–21 *et seq.* above.

[67] Unreported, Outer House, March 10, 1995.

[68] This requirement was added as a condition to the adoption order under s.12(6). Such trans-racial adoptions are not uncommon, partly because it is sometimes difficult to recruit adoptive parents from ethnic groups whose culture does not embrace adoption of children from outside the extended family. They do, however, remain controversial: see, e.g. Hayes, "The Ideological Attack on Trans-Racial Adoption in the USA and Britain" (1995) 9 I.J.L.F. 1.

[69] Adoption Agencies (Scotland) Regulations 1996 (SI 1996/3266), reg.10. Typical criteria include matters such as the age of applicants, the length of relationship where the prospective adopters are a couple, or whether the prospective adopter has recently undergone fertility treatment.

of its members must be sufficient to enable it to discharge its functions effectively. The panel must under the regulations receive information about the child to be adopted and the prospective adopters, including a detailed case history of the child and a home study report on the applicant(s) prepared by a qualified social worker.

The 1996 Regulations prescribe a timescale as well as the process **6–31** which requires to be undertaken prior to an agency placement or application for a freeing order. In recent years, it has become more common in contested cases for failures to comply with these regulations to be relied upon as a defense in freeing and adoption applications. In *Dundee City Council v M*,[70] the Inner House expressed general disapproval of refusing applications on this kind of procedural point. In that case, the sheriff had dismissed a freeing application on the ground that the parent had not been invited to attend the meeting of the adoption panel. The sheriff thought that this breached the procedural requirement of Art.8 of the European Convention on Human Rights (ECHR). The Inner House did not agree.[71]

Gay Adoption

Even after prospective adopters have been successfully vetted and **6–32** the child placed with them for adoption, it is still open to the court, when the application for an adoption order is made, to consider whether it is in the welfare of the child to make an order in favour of the proposed adopters.[72] One question which has been considered in Scotland is whether a homosexual applicant should be barred in principle from adopting. In *T Petr*,[73] the Inner House found that given the primacy of the welfare principle, there could be no fundamental objection *in principle* to adoption by a single male adopter living with another man in a stable homosexual relationship. The decision in each case should be made on its own facts. As noted above, once the Adoption and Children (Scotland) Bill has passed, it will for the first time become legitimate for a same-sex couple to adopt as *joint* parents.

---

[70] 2004 S.L.T. 640.

[71] This requirement ensures that parents are involved in the decision making process to the extent necessary to protect their interests: see *W v United Kingdom* (1988) 10 E.H.R.R. 29. A breach of procedure does not always require that the adoption order granted must be declared invalid however: in *Re T (A Minor) (Adoption: Validity of Order)* [1986] 1 All E.R. 817, an adoption agency failed to notify the birth parent of its decision that adoption was in the best interests of the child. The English Court of Appeal held that the failure did not affect the validity of the adoption order subsequently granted.

[72] 1978 Act, s.6.

[73] 1997 S.L.T. 724; 1996 S.C.L.R. 897. See further the discussion of gay parenting at paras 4–73 *et seq.*

Who can be Adopted?

6–33   An adoption order can only be made in respect of a child who was under 18 at the date the adoption application was made.[74] A child who is or has been married cannot be adopted.[75] An adopted child can be re-adopted.[76]

6–34   In most cases, the child must be at least 19 weeks old at the date the adoption order is made, and must have had his or her home with the applicant adoptive parents for the preceding 13 weeks.[77]

THE ADOPTION PROCESS

6–35   There are fundamentally two types of adoption: those in which the child is placed with prospective adopters by an adoption agency, and those where the child is not placed by an agency and is a relative of the adopters.[78] The underlying principle is that children should not be disposed of by their parents, nor acquired by would-be parents on some kind of open market, without the supervision of the state. Thus, private placement is only legal where the child to be adopted is a relative of the adopters (s.11(1)). Anyone who privately arranges the adoption of a child in contravention of s.11(1) is guilty of a criminal offence.[79] The prohibitions against private placement do not have extra-territorial effect[80] and thus it is not a crime under Scots law to travel to collect a child in, say, Romania, and then to bring him or her back to Scotland where an adoption order can be sought in the Scottish courts. Nor is it necessarily the case that if an offence under s.11(1) is committed, then an adoption order cannot be made.[81]

---

[74] 1978 Act, s.12(1). See *Cameron v Gibson*, 2005 Fam. L.R. 108, which held the age bar to be an absolute bar to validity.

[75] 1978 Act, s.12(5).

[76] *ibid.*, s.12(7).

[77] *ibid.*, s.13. This applies to all adoptions where the child is placed by an adoption agency and to adoptions by step-parents, parents or relatives. In all other cases, e.g. children brought from abroad, no order is to be made until the child is one year old during which period the applicant must have had his or her home at all times with the applicants.

[78] 1978 Act, s.11. There are a small number of situations which do not fall within this classification, namely, inter-country adoptions which are discussed at para.6.80 below; and where a child has been placed on a non-adoptive basis, e.g. with a local authority foster carer, and the care then lodges an application to adopt the child without the agreement of the agency.

[79] 1978 Act, s.11(3).

[80] *Re A (Adoption: Placement)* [1988] 1 W.L.R. 229. A crime may of course have been committed under the law of the country where the child originally lived: see the *Mooney* case, reported in *Guardian*, October 15, 1994, in which a British couple, attempting to remove a child from Romania, were jailed for breach of Romanian criminal law.

[81] See obiter comments in *D&D v F*, 1994 S.C.L.R. 417.

Trafficking in children for money is forbidden in Scots (and United **6–36** Kingdom) law. It is an offence to pay for the adoption of a child, or for any consent to adoption (s.51). Not only that, but in such circumstances, the court may feel that as a matter of public policy no adoption order should be made.[82] The court's duty in considering whether to make an adoption order is to balance the interest the child has in being adopted against the need to discourage illegal fees and baby-buying. In *C v S*[83] an infertile couple commissioned a surrogate mother to bear a child for them and made a payment of some £8,000 to her, supposedly as "expenses". The child was conceived using sperm donated by the prospective father and came to live with the commissioning couple shortly after birth. The couple sought an adoption order. The Inner House held that no illegal payment had been made, since although the money far exceeded the true expenses of the birth, it had been paid to secure a parental order[84] not an adoption order, and was thus not struck at by s.51; but even if it had been, the need to safeguard the child's welfare by allowing an adoption order would have outweighed the public policy objection.

There is one major exception to the rule on payments in consider- **6–37** ation for adoption. Foster parents are often paid allowances in respect of the care they give to the children they foster. If such foster parents seek to adopt the child they foster, which is often desirable to provide "hard to place" children with a permanent and secure home, the termination of foster payments may be a disincentive to adoption. Section 51A[85] thus now provides that all adoption agencies are required to establish their own "adoption allowances" schemes so that payments can be made, inter alia, to those such as foster carers in this situation. Such allowances may also be paid, e.g. in recognition of the costs associated with adopting a sibling group. These payments do not constitute illegal fees.[86]

Where the child has been placed by an adoption agency, the child **6–38** must live with the applicants for 13 weeks before application can be made for an adoption order, and the adoption agency must be allowed sufficient opportunity to see the child with the applicant(s) in the home environment, otherwise an order cannot be made. If the child is living with a parent, step-parent or relative, the same rule applies and the local authority must be given adequate access.[87] In a non-agency adoption, notice must be given to the local authority at least three months before the adoption order is made so that they can

---

[82] 1978 Act, s.24 as amended by 1995 Act. Sch.2, para.16 now makes it clear that the court has a *discretion* whether or not to make an order in such a case.
[83] 1997 S.L.T. 1387. This case also establishes that in Scotland, as in England, an illegal payment can be retrospectively authorised by the court.
[84] Under s.30 of the Human Fertilisation and Embryology Act 1990. See para.3–85.
[85] The Adoption Allowance (Scotland) Regulations 1996 (SI 1996/3257) generally prescribe the shape of these schemes.
[86] 1978 Act, s.51(3).
[87] *ibid.*, s.13.

investigate the suitability of the applicants and whether the adoption was in breach of the rules about private placements.[88] A child is often placed with applicants for some considerable time before an adoption order can be obtained due to court delays. And until an adoption order is made the natural parents retain their parental rights.[89] In such cases it would be contrary to the welfare of the child if the natural parents could simply change their minds about adoption and remove the child. Section 27[90] thus provides that if consent has been given by the natural parent(s) to the placement of the child with the prospective adopters, then the parent(s) cannot remove the child without the leave either of the adoption agency or the court.

Application to the Court for Adoption Order

6–39   Application may be made for an adoption order to the Court of Session, or the Sheriff Court for the sheriffdom where the child resides with the prospective adoptive parents. All adoption proceedings are private.[91] Thus, the identities of the child and the petitioners are not made public, proceedings are generally conducted *in camera*, and after the order has been made the process is sealed and access allowed only to exceptional persons, such as the child him- or herself on reaching the age of 16.[92] These unusual features of adoption procedure mean that it is almost impossible to combine an adoption hearing with another action. This may create difficulties where, for example, a grand-parent seeks a residence order in respect of a child whom the adoption agency have placed with other parties for adoption.[93]

Information about the Application

6–40   When an application is made for an adoption order, the court must appoint a curator *ad litem* to safeguard the interests of the child, and provide a report to this effect to the court. A reporting officer whose role is to obtain and witness any consents to adoption required from the parent(s) of the child will also be appointed.[94] These two functions are often performed by the same person. Furthermore, the adoption agency who placed the child,[95] or in a non-agency case, the local authority,[96] is required to submit to the court a report on the suitability

---

[88] 1978 Act, s.22.

[89] Unless the child is also subject to a supervision order of the children's hearing, or parental responsibilities and rights have already been removed from the natural parents by a court order (see below at para.6–74).

[90] The form in which such consent must be given is prescribed in the Adoption Agency Regulations, above, n.69, regs 14 and 15 and Schs 6 and 7.

[91] 1978 Act, s.57.

[92] See the 1978 Act, s.45(5).

[93] See *F v F*, 1991 S.L.T. 357; *A v B*, 1955 S.C. 378.

[94] 1978 Act, s.58.

[95] *ibid.*, s.22.

[96] *ibid.*, s.23.

of the applicants and the welfare of the child. Great stress is laid on the reports obtained from the agency or authority and curator *ad litem* or reporting officer.[97] If the court has reservations about either making or refusing an order outright, it has the discretion to postpone determination of the issue for up to two years, during which probationary period an order for parental responsibilities and rights in favour of the applicants can be made instead.[98] In addition, if the court making the adoption order is worried that the child may be in need of compulsory measures of supervision, then it can find a ground of referral established and refer the child to the children's hearing.[99]

Some children who are placed for adoption, will already have been **6–41** found to be in need of compulsory measures of supervision, and will be subject to a supervision requirement made by a children's hearing.[1] This will usually be the case in relation to children placed by agencies. Adoption provides a long-term solution for children, whereas the hearing is more concerned with short-term solutions to immediate problems, and is furthermore required, like any person other than an adoption agency, to not become involved in "arranging" an adoption.[2] The 1995 Act made it clear, however, that the hearing did have a role to play in the adoption process. When an adoption agency decides to make a freeing application, places a child for adoption or is aware that an application is to be made to adopt a child who is subject to a supervision requirement, the hearing must now be asked to review the child's case, and provide advice for the court hearing the application.[3] If the court goes on to make an adoption order (or freeing for adoption order), then it can discharge the supervision requirement if it sees fit.[4]

The Requirement of Agreement

It is a key requirement in Scots adoption law that a court should **6–42** not make an adoption order unless satisfied that each parent or guardian of the child freely, and with full understanding of what is involved, gives consent to the adoption.[5]

---

[97] *Central Regional Council v M*, 1991 S.C.L.R. 300; *Petition of AB and CB to Adopt X and Y*, 1990 S.C.L.R. (Notes) 809.

[98] 1978 Act, s.25. APRG 2 recommended that interim adoption be abolished. This recommendation is included in the 2006 Bill.

[99] 1995 Act, s.54.

[1] See generally, Ch.8.

[2] *A v Children's Hearing for the Tayside Region*, 1987 S.L.T. (Sh. Ct.) 126. There is reason to doubt whether this decision remains good law since the 1995 Act. The 2006 Bill resolves this difficulty by making it clear that placing a child with prospective adopters by way of the adding of a condition to a supervision requirement, is not to be regarded as the making of an adoption arrangement.

[3] 1995 Act, s.73 and 1978 Act, s.22A (in relation to approved adoption societies rather than agencies). APRG 2, para.9.12, recommended that similar notification continues to be made in future, but at an earlier stage.

[4] 1978 Act ss.12(9) and 18(9) inserted by 1995 Act, Sch.2, paras 7(d) and 11(d).

[5] *ibid.*, s.16(1). Subject to the rules on freeing for adoption, discussed below at para.6–74.

6–43   A "parent" is defined as:

(i) the mother of the child, whether married or unmarried[6]; and
(ii) the father *but only* if he has parental responsibilities or rights under ss.1(3) and 2(4) of the 1995 Act in respect of the child.[7]

6–44 A father who has never been married to the mother does not have automatic parental responsibilities and rights under the 1995 Act.[8] While it remains the case that an unmarried father will not automatically acquire PRRs, by virtue of the FLSA 2006, he will acquire PRRs if acknowledged as the father of the child on registration of the birth.[9] Thus unless he has acquired PRRs, either by this provision, via a s.11 court order, or via s.4 agreement,[10] his consent to the adoption is not needed. Although not required to consent, a father without PRRs should not however be automatically shut out of the adoption process. He may be able to claim a right to respect for his family life with the child under Art.8 of the ECHR.[11] A father without PRRs may thus still be entitled to appear in the freeing or adoption process and oppose the application on the question of whether the order is in the best interests of the child.[12] A father who has acquired one particular parental responsibility or right—who, for example, has applied successfully for an award of contact under s.11 of the 1995 Act—probably also qualifies as a "parent".[13]

6–45   A guardian is any person appointed by deed or will or by a court to act as guardian (see para.6–10 above).

6–46   What happens if a person who is required to consent opposes the adoption? In that case, the court has a discretion to dispense with that person's consent, but only if one or more of the grounds in s.16(2) is found to be established. At present, these are that the parent or guardian:

(a) is not known, cannot be found, or is incapable of giving agreement;
(b) is withholding agreement unreasonably;

---

[6] A mother cannot give a valid consent until six weeks after the child's birth.
[7] 1978 Act, s.65(1).
[8] 1995 Act, s.3(1)(b).
[9] 2006 Act s.23. Note this section does not operate retrospectively.
[10] These are sections of the 1995 Act. See further paras 4–39 and 3–19, above.
[11] See *Keegan v Ireland* [1994] ECHR 18 (May 26, 1994). *Cf.* the older Scottish position in *A and B v C*, 1987 S.C.L.R. 514.
[12] Note also the duty on agencies to consider notifying natural fathers of decisions (1996 Regulations, above, n.69, reg.12(3)). It is suggested that agencies should presumptively notify fathers of such decisions standing the requirement in the Human Rights Act 1998 for public bodies to act in a manner consistent with ECHR rights.
[13] This was not an issue prior to the 1995 Act, as such a father qualified as a "guardian" which was defined in s.65(1) to include a father who had the right of guardianship, custody, access or any other parental right. This part of the definition was repealed by 1995 Act, Sch.2, para.29, but it is asserted that these provisions are implicitly subsumed into the new definition of "parent" quoted above.

(c) has persistently failed, without reasonable cause, to fulfil one or other of his or her parental responsibilities in relation to the child. If the parent in question is living with the child, then that responsibility is to safeguard and promote the child's health, development and welfare. Otherwise, the responsibility is to maintain personal relations and direct contact with the child on a regular basis; or

(d) has seriously ill-treated the child, whose reintegration into the same household as the parent or guardian is, because of the serious ill-treatment, or for other reasons, unlikely.

One of the most significant reforms recommended by the Adoption **6–47** Policy Review Group prior to the drafting of the 2006 Bill was that the grounds for dispensing with consent should be simplified.[14] This recommendation was taken up in the Bill, which provides for consent to be dispensed with solely on the grounds that the parent cannot be found or is unable to give consent, or that the child's welfare requires that the consent should be dispensed with.[15]

Dispensing with Consent: The 1978 Act and the 2006 Reforms

It is clear that dispensing with consent is a two-stage process[16]: **6–48**

(1) the court must establish that a ground in s.16(2) does exist, based on the facts to hand (primarily the various reports); and

(2) the court must *then* decide if, given the existence of a ground, it *should* dispense with consent.

One of the most controversial issues here has been how far the welfare **6–49** of the child should influence each of these two stages. By virtue of s.6, the court must regard the welfare of the child as paramount when reaching any decision relating to the adoption of the child. Nonetheless, it has been suggested that the welfare principle is, or should, only be a relevant consideration at stage (2) of the dispensation process. In fact, things are not as clear-cut as this, particularly when looking, as we will do below, at the s.16(2)(b) ground for dispensing with consent that a parent is unreasonably withholding consent. It is axiomatic that as a matter of basic human rights, natural parents have an interest in retaining legal links to their child.[17] Thus the adoption legislation does not give the courts a simple

---

[14] APRG 2, paras 3.20–3.25.

[15] This reflects the position in England and Wales: Adoption and Children Act 2002, s.52(1).

[16] *Lothian Regional Council v A*, 1992 S.L.T. 858; also *L v Central Regional Council*, 1990 S.L.T. 818.

[17] See, e.g. Lord Guest in *A v B and C*, 1971 S.C. (H.L.) 129 at 143: "It has been said more than once that, other things being equal, it is in the best interests of a child to be with its natural parents".

unfettered discretion to dispense with the consent of a parent where this seems to them to be in the interests of the child.[18] Commentators such as Thomson argue that stage (1), establishing a ground, must be gone through "strictly" without "direct"[19] reference to the welfare principle, before turning to stage (2), considering whether an adoption order should be made. This is because if the welfare principle were to be allowed to colour the conclusion whether a ground exists, which the judge must draw from the evidence he has to hand, then there would be no fundamental safeguard left to prevent a court from effectively having an open power to dispense with consent, whenever it sees it as necessary given the best interests of the child. The possible doomsday scenario arising from such an approach would be that any parent who did not offer the *best possible* care for their child, rather than obviously inadequate care, might be in danger of having their parental rights removed. It is clear that this is not the intention or function of the adoption legislation, which, as has been stated many times, demands that a balance be struck between the interests of the child, the natural parents and the adoptive parents.[20]

6–50 Given the terms of the proposed reform to the grounds for dispensing with consent, the question arises: will this represents a weakening of the rights of birth parents? Will the new simplified grounds move us towards the doomsday scenario noted above? The answer is, probably not. First, as noted below, welfare considerations have always had some part to play in the first part of the two-stage test, particularly in relation to the unreasonably withholding consent ground. Secondly, a two-stage test is still proposed. The court will be asked first, not to determine whether adoption is in the *best interests* of the child; but whether the best interests of the child require the consent of the parent to be dispensed with. It is suggested that the courts will be well able to determine a threshold for dispensing with such consent which is set at a level significantly higher than the view that adoption is the "best bet" for the child. In *White v White*[21] the Lord President noted that the question of welfare was always approached with certain assumptions in mind. Among these will be that the natural bond between child and parent should not be severed without pressing reasons. As the Inner House has noted in the context of making a freeing order:

> "It is difficult to imagine a more drastic intervention by the state in family life than the termination of the legal relationship between parent and child".[22]

---

[18] It did, in fact, at an earlier stage of Scottish legal history: see Adoption (Scotland) Act 1930.

[19] Words derived from the dictum of Lord President Hope in *Lothian Regional Council v A*, 1992 S.L.T. 858, cited by Thomson, p.251.

[20] See as *locus classicus* the speech of Lord Reid in *A v B and C*, 1971 S.C. (H.L.) 129, discussed at para.6–30.

[21] 2001 S.L.T. 485 (IH).

[22] *West Lothian Council v M*, 2002 S.L.T. 1155, *per* Lord Reed at 1165.

This approach is also reinforced by the restrictive attitude taken by **6–51** the European Court of Human Rights towards adoption without parental agreement. In a series of decisions[23] the Strasbourg court has held that adoption without parental consent constitutes a prima facie breach of the right to respect for family life, which can only be allowed if substantially justified under Art.8(2) of the ECHR. In *Johansen v Norway*,[24] the Court went as far as to hold that adoption contrary to the wishes of the parent could be justified only by "exceptional circumstances relating to the best interests of the child". The influence of ECHR considerations can be seen in the adoption of the language of "necessity" in the proposed new ground. It is suggested that if the simplified ground is enacted, Parliament will not be presumed to have lowered the threshold for dispensing with parental consent.

Returning to current law, establishing a s.16(2) ground is, by and **6–52** large, a question of fact and degree.[25] It may seem difficult to understand how considerations of the child's welfare can or cannot influence whether a ground is found to be established. For example, it is a simple question of fact whether a parent is not known, or cannot be found.[26] Persistent failure without reasonable cause to fulfil a parental responsibility involves a more complicated assessment of the different factors but is still essentially an objective assessment from the facts drawn to the judge's attention. The most thorny problems arise, however, when considering the ground in s.16(2)(b), that the parent or guardian has unreasonably withheld consent.

Any natural parent who wishes to oppose an adoption petition, **6–53** whether he is, for example, a divorced father who has made no effort to see his child for many years, or a young single mother who has few resources with which to care for her child, can assert on a subjective basis that they are reasonably withholding consent to the adoption. It is thus self-evident that the decision must be taken by a court on an objective basis if every adoption petition brought on this basis is not to be denied, and the welfare of the child put in jeopardy. Lord Reid in the leading House of Lords case of *A v B and C*,[27] put it this way:

> "The test is an objective test—would a reasonable parent have withheld consent? I think that a reasonable parent, or indeed any other reasonable person, would have in mind the interests or claims of all three parties concerned—the child whose adoption is in question, the natural parents and the adopting family. No doubt the child's interests come first, and in some cases they may

---

[23] *Johansen v Norway* (1997) 23 E.H.R.R. 33; *Soderback v Sweden* [1999] 1 F.L.R. 250; *K and T v Finland* [2000] 2 F.L.R. 79 (April 27, 2000).
[24] Above.
[25] *Lothian Regional Council v A*, 1992 S.L.T. 858 at 862E-F.
[26] 1978 Act, s.16(2)(a).
[27] 1971 S.C. (H.L.) 129 at 141.

be paramount. But I see no reason why the claims of the natural parent should be ignored . . . And the adopting family cannot be ignored either . . . So to balance these claims is no easy task. Often no ideal solution is possible. We are dealing largely with future probabilities for the decision once made is irrevocable. So we cannot be certain what will be the child's interests in the long run. That seems to me to be an additional reason for giving considerable weight in proper cases to the claims of the natural parents and the adopting parents."

6–54 But if the test is an objective test then what must be considered is not whether the decision the parent actually made was reasonable, in the light of his or her own subjective concerns, but whether *a reasonable parent* would have made such a decision to refuse to give consent.[28] And clearly one of the factors a reasonable parent would take into account in reaching their decision is whether it is in the best interests of the child to be adopted. As Lord Justice-Clerk Ross succinctly put it in *Petition of AB and CB to adopt X and Y,*

> "In our opinion if the respondent was acting reasonably, he would put the welfare of the children first, and if he did that, he would not withhold consent."[29]

6–55 Clearly, however, the welfare of the child is not the only factor the reasonable parent would take into account in reaching his decision, nor is it necessarily true that it must be his *paramount* consideration.[30] It is the *courts* (and adoption agencies) who are enjoined by s.6 to make the welfare of the child their paramount consideration in any decision relating to adoption; not the parent, nor even the "reasonable parent". And it is also clear that the court's function in assessing whether consent is being unreasonably withheld is not to substitute their judgement for that of the parent, but rather to assess whether the parent's decision to withhold consent falls within a band of possible reasonable decisions. As Lord Hailsham of St Marylebone said in *Re W*[31]:

> "The question in any case is whether a parental veto comes within the band of possible reasonable decisions and not whether it is right or mistaken. Not every reasonable exercise of judgment is right, and not every mistaken exercise of judgement is unreasonable. There is a band of decisions within which no court should seek to replace the individual's judgement with his own".

---

[28] See *D v F*, 1994 S.C.L.R. 417 at 423.
[29] 1990 S.C.L.R. 809 at 813.
[30] *P v Lothian Regional Council*, 1989 S.L.T. 739.
[31] [1971] A.C. 682 at 700.

The parent is thus not required to make the "right" decision, nor the **6–56** one that is "best" for the child. This, as we have already suggested, would require the reasonable parent to give up their child if they believed there plausibly existed prospective adoptive parents who could do better for the child than themselves. Rather, what is implied by s.16(2)(b) is that the decision to withhold consent can be regarded as objectively unreasonable if "no reasonable parent, in all the circumstances, would withhold agreement to the making of an adoption order".[32] Thus, only a certain minimum, not optimal, expectation is made of the reasonable parent: objectively, he must feel that he does not fall below a certain minimum threshold demanded of reasonable parenting.[33]

The welfare of the child is therefore clearly relevant to the estab- **6–57** lishment of the s.16(2)(b) ground, but only to the extent that a reasonable parent would take it into account.[34]

What factors should the reasonable parent take into account when **6–58** considering the welfare of the child in relation to their decision whether to give or withhold consent? It has been held that an alcoholic mother who had failed to give up drinking,[35] a homosexual father[36] and a mother with a chronic personality disorder which led her periodically to exhibit bizarre and self-destructive behaviour,[37] would, if placing themselves in the role of reasonable parent, find that they were unreasonably withholding consent. Considerations of welfare are not restricted to the material welfare of the child, so, for example, an unmarried 15-year-old mother can reasonably choose to withhold consent if objectively she is mature enough to cope satisfactorily with the duties of motherhood, even though if she agreed to give consent, her child would be placed with adoptive parents who would provide a higher material standard of living.[38]

The most difficult cases are perhaps those where the parent once **6–59** agreed to have the child placed for adoption, but now at some later date has withdrawn consent, either because his or her circumstances have changed for the better, or simply because of a change of mind. In such circumstances, the child may well have become settled in the adoptive placement and it may seem in the welfare of the child not to disturb the new arrangement. In *A v B and C*[39] itself, an unmarried

---

[32] *per* Lord President Hope in *Lothian Regional Council v A*, 1992 S.L.T. 858 at 862.
[33] See comments of Lord President Emslie in *A and B v C*, 1977 S.C. 27 at 31: "the ultimate decision must be a balanced decision which can never be reached by considering only whether life with the proposed adopters would be a 'better bet' for the child than life with his own parent".
[34] *Re W, per* Lord Hailsham at p.699; affirmed in *Lothian Regional Council v A* (n.21 above), at p.863.
[35] *R v Lothian Council*, 1987 S.C.L.R. 362.
[36] *Re D* [1977] 1 All E.R. 145.
[37] *Lothian Regional Council v A*, 1992 S.L.T. 858.
[38] See *A and B v C*, 1977 S.C. 27.
[39] 1977 S.C. 27

woman had a child by a married man with whom she was having an affair, and agreed that the child be placed with adoptive parents. Subsequently, the father was divorced by his wife, and married the mother, at which point both parties withdrew their consent to the adoption. It was held, with some regret by the court, that although the married parents could now provide an adequate home for the child together, their consent had been unreasonably withheld since the facts showed that both parents were unstable, the father's attitude to mother and child was selfish and ambivalent and by contrast the child would be happy and well cared for in the adoptive home. In *D v F*,[40] a young Irish mother placed her child privately, and possibly illegally, with a Scottish adoptive couple; when she later had a change of heart about the adoption it was held that she was unreasonably withholding consent. One of the principal contributing factors to this decision was that she herself had, without external pressure, chosen to place her child with these adopters.

6–60　　What constitutes "persistent failure without reasonable cause" to fulfil parental responsibilities? It was held in *Central Regional Council v B*[41] that this must be defined in an objective, not a subjective, fashion. In that case, a mother had failed to care adequately for her children with the result that they had been in the care of the local authority for over three years. The mother claimed she had a reasonable excuse for her failings as a parent in that she had experienced poor health and been ill-treated by her husband. This claim was rejected; the question was whether, applying the standard of the reasonable parent, there was a reasonable cause for the persistent failure in duty. It is thus clear that a parent need not intend to neglect his or her duty to the child: what matters is whether on the facts there *was* neglect without an objectively reasonable cause. An example of reasonable cause might be where a father fails in his duty to maintain contact with his children because he works abroad or has no money to travel to visit his children.

6–61　　How long must failure on duty go on to become "persistent"? It seems that it must endure over a substantial period of time, but need not be permanent.[42]

6–62　　As noted above, the parental duty required of a parent by s.16(2)(c) varies according to whether the parent lives with the child in question or not. The ground will most often be invoked to deal with cases where a parent has disappeared from the child's life for some time, e.g. where the parent is clearly unable to care for the child but is still unwilling to permit adoption.

6–63　　Finally, under s.16(2)(d), it is a ground for dispensing with consent that the parent has seriously ill-treated the child and the

---

[40] 1994 S.C.L.R. 417.

[41] 1985 S.L.T. 413. This was a case concerning the identical ground for assumption of parental rights and responsibilities from a parent.

[42] *Strathclyde Regional Council v F*, 1995 Fam. L.B. 17-6 affirming statement in Wilkinson and Norrie (1st edn), p.542.

child's reintegration into the same household as that parent is unlikely. This may be for reasons unconnected to the parent's ill-treatment of the child, e.g. because the other parent has remarried. However, more often the likelihood of reintegration will be related to the seriousness of the ill-treatment.

The Adoption Order

Once the court is satisfied that any required consent has been given, **6–64** or that a ground for dispensing with consent exists, or that the child has been freed for adoption and that order has not been revoked, it can proceed to decide whether in the welfare of the child an adoption order should be made.[43] Any condition can be attached to the order under s.12(6).[44] The order vests parental rights and responsibilities under ss.1(3) and 2(4) of the 1995 Act in the adopters[45] and extinguishes the corresponding rights and duties which any parent or guardian held immediately before the order was made.[46] The obligation of the parent to pay aliment to the child is also ended.[47] Although the adoption order effectively severs the legal link between natural parent and child, some legal connections remain. A child remains related to his or her natural parents for the purpose of determining prohibited degrees of relationship and incestuous relationship.[48] Marital and sexual relations with the adoptive parents (though not adoptive siblings) are struck at in addition.[49] An adopted child remains the child of his natural parents for any determination of immigration or nationality status.[50] For succession purposes, an adopted child is generally treated as the child of the adopters and not of the natural parents[51] but adoptive status may still affect the rights in succession of a child in executries governed by the law before September 10, 1964.[52]

OPEN ADOPTION

As discussed at the start of this chapter, it is a controversial issue in **6–65** modern adoption law and practice whether adoption should, as now, be in essence a legal guillotine, severing all connection between natural family and adopted child, or whether some connections can

---

[43] s.16(1).
[44] On conditions of contact with the natural parent, see below at paras 6.65 *et seq.*
[45] ss.12(1) and 65(1).
[46] s.12(3).
[47] s.12(3)(b).
[48] s.41(1).
[49] See Ch.9.
[50] s.41(2).
[51] Succession (Scotland) Act 1964, s.23(1).
[52] i.e. when the above section came into force. See further, Wilkinson and Norrie, p.522–3.

or should be maintained.[53] This is a particularly acute issue where an older child is adopted, who still has real links to his birth parents and relatives. As we have seen above, the making of an adoption order has a drastic effect on the relationship of the natural parent(s) to the child. Given this, it is unsurprising that in *D v Grampian Regional Council*,[54] the House of Lords took the view that "it is perfectly clear that the whole [adoption] procedure is intended to produce a permanent result for the adopted child".[55] As a result, they held that if parental rights were removed from a natural parent by an adoption order, or freeing for adoption order, then that parent should be divested not only of their rights, but also of their title to go to the courts and ask the court to make an order for, inter alia, contact or residence in their favour. To allow birth parents to seek s.11 orders post-adoption would undermine the permanency of adoption and involve "driving a coach and four through the procedure for adoption".[56] This rule was then codified in statute as s.11(3) and (4) of the 1995 Act.

6–66   In practical terms, this meant that if a parent wished to retain legal rights of contact with their natural child after an adoption or freeing for adoption order was made, then they had to seek a condition of contact, to be attached to the adoption order at the time it was made (s.12(6), 1978 Act). Despite initial dubiety in Scotland whether such conditions were legitimate,[57] since the decision in *B v C*,[58] it has become clear that such a condition is competent.

6–67   Such a condition should not, however, be made simply to meet the parent's desire to stay in touch with the child, since it is the welfare of the child, not the adult, which is the paramount concern. In any case, the safeguard for the adult's wishes is the requirement of consent to adoption. In *K Petrs.*,[59] a condition of access was made in favour of a natural mother, not for her benefit, but so that the child might understand, in time, the nature of her relationship to the natural mother and why she was adopted. In *B v C*,[60] a six-year-old child was placed with adoptive parents not because of any fault on the part of

---

[53] See, inter alia, McWhinnie and Smith, *Current Human Dilemmas in Adoption* (1994); Adcock, Kaniuk and White, *Exploring Openness in Adoption* (1993); Paterson and Hill, *Opening and Reopening Adoption: Views from Adoptive Families* (1994).

[54] 1995 S.L.T. 519.

[55] *per* Lord Jauncey at p.521.

[56] *ibid.* at p.522.

[57] See *A v B*, 1987 S.L.T. (Sh. Ct) 121, *per* Sheriff Stewart who remarked obiter that "it would appear, one would have thought, inconsistent with the creation of a new relationship between adoptive parents and an adoptive child . . . if a condition were attached to an adoption order whereby the natural father retained access to the child".

[58] 1996 S.L.T. 1370. The Inner House followed the decision of the House of Lords in the English case of *Re C (A Minor) (Adoption Order: Conditions)* [1989] A.C. 1.

[59] 1994 Fam. L.B. 8-2.

[60] 1996 S.L.T. 1370.

the birth parents but because both were suffering from an incurable and progressive degenerative illness. The Inner House agreed that the child would benefit from supervised contact with the parents which could vary from time to time, especially as the child herself was likely to inherit the disease and would benefit from understanding its nature and effects. Since it would be necessary to vary the contact as the disease progressed, the court made it a condition of the order that either party might apply to vary the access condition until the child reached the age of 16. Although the facts of the case were unusual, the broader principle that a child might benefit from continuing contact even though all other circumstances pointed to the advantages of adoption in securing a permanent substitute family, are of wider application. The Court, however, emphasised that it regarded the case as an exceptional one:

> "The guiding principle is that adoption provides complete security to the child by making the child part of the adopting parents' family. Conditions expressed in favour of third parties, which might make it necessary for the court to become involved in the making of further orders with a view to the child's welfare, will not be appropriate except in the very rare cases where the child's welfare might be prejudiced if a condition to that effect were not to be made. As Lord Ackner observed in *Re C*, in normal circumstances it is desirable that there should be a complete break from the child's natural family".[61]

Thus, even after *B v C*, the Scottish courts continue to support the **6–68** "clean break" model of adoption in the main.[62] In *West Lothian v M*, Lord Reed noted the lack of judicial attention even in the face of an apparent shift in practice towards more open adoption; he referred to one study showing 52 per cent of placements with some level of direct contact.[63] In England and Wales the appellate Courts have given greater consideration to open adoption. In *Re T (Adopted Children: Contact)*,[64] for example, the Court of Appeal considered whether it was appropriate to make an adoption order given acceptance that continuing contact would be in the best interests of the child. The Court held that such an order should not ordinarily be made, but in doing do was able to rely on the ability of a birth parent in England and Wales to seek a contact order after adoption, with the leave of the Court. In Scotland, as discussed above, this is not possible because of the statutory bar on birth

---

[61] 1996 S.L.T. 1370 at 1377.
[62] But see positive dicta in *McCreight v City of Edinburgh*, 2003 S.L.T. (Sh Ct) 45.
[63] 2002 S.L.T. 1155, discussed also below at para.6–78. The survey referred to is an English one, Lowe and Murch, *Supporting Adoption* (BAAF, 1999). It is difficult to determine how prevalent continuing contact is in Scotland. No relevant statistics are published.
[64] [1995] 2 F.L.R. 251.

parents seeking s.11 orders after a court order has removed their PRRs. The 2006 Adoption Bill will however replace this bar with the more lenient rule that a birth parent should obtain the leave of the court where their child had been adopted before being allowed to seek a contact or other s.11 order. This should allow both courts and birth parents a wider opportunity to consider the merits of post-adoption contact.

6–69 What remains absent from the Scottish cases to date is any serious judicial consideration of when continuing direct contact after adoption will be consistent with the welfare of the child.[65] The APRG recommended that principles governing decisions in this area should be set out in guidance by the Scottish Ministers, e.g. that the contact should be for the benefit of the child and serve some purpose such as reassuring the child of the wellbeing of the birth family. At present, decisions at first instance seem to be largely guided by expert evidence, rather than by judicial principles.

6–70 "Open adoption" is not just about whether birth parents, or other relatives, should retain rights to see their children after adoption. It is also about whether contact should be maintained in many other more indirect ways, e.g. by the exchange of letters and photographs, or the making of progress reports by the adoptive parents to the birth parents. Such strategies are increasingly common. More generally, "open adoption" is about whether adoption should be a secret event, or whether adopted children should have rights to know their history and trace their genetic parents. Since the 1970s there has been a general acknowledgement that adopted children sometimes exhibit a need to know about their origins and should be given assistance in this area when they have reached adulthood.[66] As already noted, adoption proceedings are private, and the court process which would contain details of help to a child searching for birth parents, is sealed to the public. Section 45 of the 1978 Act thus specifically provides that adopted persons should have access to an Adopted Children Register at the age of 16, which allows them to access their original birth certificate with the name of a birth parent on it. When this kind of information is sought from the Registrar General, adoption agencies have a duty to provide appropriate counselling to the person seeking information.[67] Adoption agencies also come under duties to provide adopted persons aged 16 or over with access to the case records relating to their adoption, which are otherwise confidential.[68]

---

[65] One expert who has been frequently involved as an expert witness in adoption cases in Scotland, Prof. J. Triseliotis, has produced an extensive body of work on the issue, including a helpful framework for considering whether post-adoption contact is in the best interests of the child.

[66] See especially Triseliotis, *In Search of Origins* (1973).

[67] s.45(6) and (6A).

[68] Adoption Agencies (Scotland) Regulations 1996, para.25.

Scotland is still at an early stage in coming to grips with the full **6–71** ramifications of "open adoption" compared to other jurisdictions.[69] It has been argued, for example, that adopted children have inadequate rights to track down their genetic inheritance, e.g. when suspecting genetically transmitted disease.[70] Furthermore, there is little to no legal concern for the interests of post-adoption birth parents, as opposed to adopted children.[71] A birth parent who wishes to find his or her natural child once that child has grown up has no legal right to do so, and in Scotland can only rely on the assistance of voluntary bodies who offer a registration service for parents searching for children.[72]

Perhaps most fundamentally of all, a child has no right to know if **6–72** he or she is adopted, or, if under 12, is to be adopted. In *C Petrs*,[73] a mother sought to adopt her own child, age six, in conjunction with her husband who was, unknown to the child, not his natural father. The local authority were unable to question the child as to his views on the adoption because the applicants wished the child's true parentage kept a secret from him. Sheriff Gow held that, despite general experience that a child's interest lies with knowing the truth about his or her status, there was no hard and fast rule that a child of six had to be told he was to be adopted, and he did not feel it was contrary to the child's welfare to make the adoption order. If the child had been of age 12 or more, then he could not have been kept in ignorance as his consent would have had to have been obtained.[74]

It is fair to say that in Scotland the jury is still out on open adop- **6–73** tion. This is both because the term is used to refer to very disparate ideas, as we have seen; and because different types of adopted children have very different needs. As discussed above, there are clear distinctions to be drawn between step-parent adoptions, baby adoptions and "special needs" children adoptions, and different approaches to "open-ness" are justified in relation to each group. The cautious approach of the Adoption Law Review,[75] whose conclusion in 1993 was that "it would be clearly wrong to introduce widespread changes in adoption law to facilitate 'open adoption' without proper research",

---

[69] In countries such as New Zealand, birth parents not only often continue to have contact with the child after adoption, but regularly assist in the process of choosing the adoptive parents. This is beginning to occur in Scottish adoption practice. See the discussion of what constitutes "open adoption" in Paterson and Hill, *Opening and Reopening Adoption: Views from Adoptive Families* (Central Research Unit Papers, 1994), Ch.2.

[70] Turnpenny, "The Dilemmas of Sharing Genetic Information" in *Current Human Dilemmas in Adoption*.

[71] It is the duty of the local authority to provide counselling support for birth parents: 1978 Act. s.1(1)(b).

[72] In Scotland, the only organisation offering this kind of help is BirthLink, the Adoption Contact Register—see *www.birthlink.org.uk/*. In England there are a number of contact registers including one run by the Registrar General.

[73] 1993 S.C.L.R. 14.

[74] s.12(8).

[75] *The Future of Adoption* (1993).

has moved on to an acceptance by the APRG in 2005 that "it may be in the best interests of some adoptees to allow a degree of contact between the child and the birth family". Reform of the law in the 2006 Bill should at last allow this to happen with greater ease.

FREEING FOR ADOPTION

6–74 As we have seen, establishing a ground for dispensing with consent in contested cases is not always straightforward. In the end, only a very small number of adoption applications made to the court are refused because consent is refused and not dispensed with. But the effect of refusal can be to cause enormous delay in the adoption process. This causes particular difficulty if the child has been placed with, and become settled with, the prospective adopters for some time, on a basis of informal consent from the natural parent or parents. If that consent is subsequently withdrawn when the formal adoption application is made, then lengthy proceedings may need to be initiated for dispensation with parental consent. In the meantime the child is in legal limbo, with the birth parents retaining all rights.

6–75 To prevent this difficulty, the Houghton Committee in 1972 recommended a new procedure known as "freeing for adoption", which was introduced in the Children Act 1975.[76] A freeing for adoption order is sought on the same conditions as an adoption order, but, ideally, can be obtained before the child is placed with prospective adopters. The effect is to transfer PRRs not to adoptive parents, but to the adoption agency.[77] A child who is freed for adoption can thus be placed with prospective adopters without fear that the placement will be disrupted by a change of heart by the natural parent(s).[78] Freeing for adoption has been criticised on the basis that it can leave a child with no parent other than the local authority. However it is increasingly used in difficult contested cases, in part due to the requirement that a freeing application be made in agency cases where parental consent has been refused.[79] The number of freeing application peaked in 2000 at 113. By way of comparison, in the same year, 405 adoption applications were made.[80]

"Freeing Orders"

6–76 Application for a "freeing order" is made by an adoption agency.[81] Such an application cannot be made unless each parent or guardian of the child has given consent to adoption, as discussed above, or the

---

[76] See now 1978 Act, ss.18–21.
[77] s.18(5).
[78] A freeing order cannot be made unless the child has been placed for adoption or is likely to be placed for adoption: see s.18(3).
[79] 1996 Regulations, regs 17 and 18.
[80] *Adoption Statistics 2003* (Scottish Executive, 2004).
[81] 1978 Act, s.18(1).

adoption agency is actively applying for such consent to be dispensed with.[82] As with an ordinary adoption application, consent need not be sought from a father who is not married to the mother and does not have parental responsibilities and rights. However, the court before making a freeing order must satisfy itself that such a father has no intention of applying for an order under s.11 of the 1995 Act, or of entering a s.4 agreement with the mother of the child. If it is established that the father does have such an intention, then no freeing order can be made unless the court feels it is likely the s.11 order or s.4 agreement will not be made.[83] Since a freeing order itself requires either consent or possible dispensation of consent, it may, like an adoption order application, involve protracted proceedings. To try to deal with this, s.25A of the 1978 Act provided that in contested dispensation cases, the court should draw up a timetable for steps in the proceedings and give directions to ensure this is adhered to. Delay has continued to be a cause for concern in contested freeing and adoption proceedings. To address this problem, each of the Sheriffs Principal has issued a practice note on adoption procedure.[84]

If a freeing order is made, the natural parent can declare that he or **6–77** she does not wish to be further involved with the adoption proceedings.[85] Any parent who does not make such a declaration is entitled to be told by the adoption agency when and if an adoption placement has been made, and if it such a placement has broken down.[86] If no adoption has taken place within 12 months of the freeing order and the child no longer has a home with the prospective adopters, then the former parent can apply to have the freeing order revoked.[87] If the order is revoked, then the court must make a s.11 order concerning who is to have parental responsibilities and rights in respect of the child.[88] Thus, the child need not be returned to the natural parents; instead, for example, the court might make a residence order in favour of a relative, or foster parents.

More recently, freeing orders have become less commonly used, **6–78** mainly because of concerns over their compliance with the ECHR rights of birth families, particularly where there was continuing direct contact with the child in question. The court cannot under current law ensure continuing contact by attaching a condition to the freeing for adoption, the statute having no such provision. In

---

[82] s.18(2)(b).

[83] s.18(7).

[84] These practice notes are available at *www.scotcourts.gov.uk*.

[85] 1978 Act, s.18(6).

[86] 1978 Act, s.19. Note that there is no duty to tell the birth parents if the adoptive placement has broken down *after* the final adoption order has been made.

[87] 1978 Act, s.20. The agency can also now apply for revocation of a freeing order (s.20(1A)). The criterion for whether the order should be revoked is, of course, the welfare of the child under s.6. Revocation applications are rare. Adoption statistics record only two between 1993 and 2003.

[88] s.20(3).

West Lothian Council v M,[89] this was confirmed, the court holding there was no provision in relation to freeing for adoption as there is under s.12(6) of the Adoption (Scotland) Act 1978 to make such conditions relating to an adoption order, as the court "thinks fit". And as discussed at para.6–65 above, the birth parent is also barred after PRRs are removed from applying for a s.11 order for contact.[90] In *West Lothian Council*, the sheriff was asked to grant freeing orders in respect of two children who had continued to have direct contact with their respective birth fathers. The fathers argued that the granting of the orders breached their rights under Art.8 of the ECHR. The court did not in fact have to determine this important issue, as the case began prior to the commencement of the Human Rights Act 1998. The subsequent case of *Dundee City Council v K*[91] was, however, decided under the 1998 Act. Here, the sheriff had granted a freeing order where the father wished to re-establish contact with his child. The father appealed, raising the Art.8 issues canvassed in the *West Lothian* case. The court held that the statutory bar, while sometimes unfortunate for some families and parents, did not of itself make Scots law in breach of Art.8. Each case had to be considered on its own facts. In the case in question, the sheriff had made a specific finding that contact between the child and her father was *not* in her best interests. The situation might have been different if this finding had been reversed, in which case the sheriff might have been obliged not to make the freeing order. The statutory framework has thus in principle been confirmed as Convention compliant, while recognising that an order might not be granted where family life demands that contact is maintained with a birth parent.

6–79   The 2006 Adoption Bill suggests that freeing orders be replaced by a new "permanence order", performing the same basic function, but to which a condition enabling consent after freeing (or a condition adding any other parental right or responsibility) can be attached. These will be known as "ancillary provisions". The test for such provisions will be the best interests of the child. The making of a permanence order, like an adoption order, will under the 2006 Bill, require either consent of the birth parent(s), or dispensing with that consent; and the grounds for this will also be the new simplified grounds, i.e. that the parent or guardian cannot be found or is incapable of giving consent; or that the welfare of the child requires the consent to be dispensed with. These changes should resolve the human rights problems described above. The order will also replace parental responsibilities orders (PROs) under s.86 of the 1995 Act (see further Ch.8).

---

[89] Above, n.63.
[90] See 1995 Act, s.11(3)(a)(iii) for the bar on application after a freeing order is made.
[91] 2005 CSIH 90; 2006 S.L.T. 63.

INTERCOUNTRY ADOPTION

Intercountry adoption (ICA) is a complex area of law and social **6–80** welfare policy and practice. The information here is merely a brief outline of the legal provisions for ICA in Scotland. Welfare and policy issues are covered in a range of publications.[92] ICA is a term used by social work and legal professionals, adoption agencies, central government and adopters. It is adoption where the adopters reside in the United Kingdom; the child resides in a country outside the United Kingdom (the state of origin); and the adopters either bring the child into the United Kingdom for the purposes of adoption, or adopt the child in his or her state of origin, with that order being recognised as adoption in United Kingdom law.

Other adoptions may involve international issues without being **6–81** ICAs. Examples of these include adoptions of stepchildren from overseas now living in the United Kingdom; or by adopters who have returned to live in the United Kingdom after working abroad, where they adopted children but the adoptions are not recognised in the United Kingdom. These are domestic adoptions with international aspects.

The current primary legislation for ICA in Scotland is the 1978 Act **6–82** as amended and added to by the Adoption (Intercountry Aspects) Act 1999. The Adoption and Children Act 2002 has further ICA amendments for Scotland, but these have not yet been brought into force. The primary legislation is restated in the Adoption and Children (Scotland) Bill 2006. The details of the system are in secondary legislation, regulations and court rules.[93]

ICA in the United Kingdom was formerly governed by informal **6–83** good practice procedures. Prospective ICA adopters were expected to be assessed, with a home study, in the same way as domestic adopters. Papers were processed through the "Central Authority" (central government) and the Home Office for immigration clearance. Adopters then arranged their adoption abroad. However, this system had no statutory basis and there were increasing concerns about abuses. In addition, it was necessary to legislate to enable the United Kingdom

---

[92] See, e.g. Peter Selman, *Intercountry Adoption: Developments, Trends and Perspectives* (BAAF, 2000), an anthology about ICA; and Sutton and Hudson, *A better deal* (BAAF, 2005), a training resource for Scottish social work practitioners.

[93] The Adoption of Children from Overseas (Scotland) Regulations 2001 (SSI 2001/236), cover all intercountry adoptions which are not from Convention countries. The Intercountry Adoption (Hague Convention) (Scotland) Regulations 2003 (SSI 2003/19), cover adoptions from Convention countries. The Act of Sederunt (Child Care and Maintenance Rules) Amendment (1993 Hague Convention Adoption) 2003 (SSI 2003/4), amends the Sheriff Court rules for Convention adoptions orders. The Act of Sederunt (Rules of the Court of Session Amendments) (Miscellaneous) 2004 (SSI 2004/52) includes amendments to the RCS for Convention adoptions orders.

to ratify the 1993 Hague Convention on Protection of Children and Co-operation in Respect of Intercountry Adoption. The 1999 Act and the Adoption (Intercountry Aspects) Act (Northern Ireland) 2001 were passed to achieve these aims.

6–84 The 1999 Act is applicable to all the United Kingdom except Northern Ireland, which has its 2001 Order. The 1999 Act provides a regulatory system for ICA in Scotland, with provision for regulations and court rules.[94]

6–85 There are three different types of countries of origin for children adopted under the ICA rules. There are differences in the rules for each of the three groups of countries, although the underlying assessment processes are the same. The different types also affect whether there has to be an adoption application in the United Kingdom after the child comes here. The three types are Convention countries, designated countries and non-convention/non-designated countries. Convention countries have implemented the 1993 Convention. Designated countries are those on the designated list, whose adoption orders are recognised in the United Kingdom. Countries which are neither Convention nor designated list ones are referred to as non-Convention/non-designated countries. An up-to-date list of Convention and designated countries is available on the website for the Department for Education and Science (DfES), which is responsible for adoption matters in England.[95]

6–86 For all three types of countries, prospective adopters must have an assessment, a home study, prepared by an adoption agency, assessing them as ICA adopters. This should be for adoption from a specific country. After assessment, the agency takes the prospective adopters to its adoption panel, and then the agency decision-maker either approves them as ICA adopters for the specific country; or does not approve them. When there is approval, the papers are sent by the agency to the Scottish Executive.

6–87 If the proposed adoption is from a Convention country, the Scottish Executive is the Central Authority. If they agree that an application should go ahead, the papers are passed to the Home Office for immigration clearance. After this, the Scottish Executive as Central Authority pass the papers to the Central Authority for the state of origin and the prospective adopters make arrangements there. If the proposed adoption is from a designated or non-convention/non-designated country, the process is the same, except the Central Authority is the DfES. The Scottish Executive pass the papers to the DfES and then on to the Home Office. After completion of arrangements in the state of origin, adopters may bring the child into the

---

[94] *ibid.*
[95] The DfES website, *www.dfes.gov.uk*, provides useful general information about different countries. The *Frequently Asked Questions* include a list of Convention and designated countries. However, the legal information on the site is for England only and should be treated with care.

United Kingdom. If they have not gone through these processes, then they may be guilty of an offence.[96]

When a child enters the United Kingdom, she or he will be in one **6–88** of four situations. The child will have been:

(1) adopted in a Convention country; or
(2) brought in from a Convention country for adoption here; or
(3) adopted in a designated list country; or
(4) brought in from a non-convention/non-designated country for adoption in the United Kingdom.

In the first or third situations, there is no court application in **6–89** Scotland, as both types of adoption are recognized in United Kingdom law. In the second or fourth situations, there has to be an adoption application in Scotland. In the latter two situations, adopters must contact their local authority to advise that the child is living with them, to give notice of a private fostering arrangement under the Foster Children (Scotland) Act 1984; and also of their intention to adopt.[97]

If a child is brought in for adoption from a convention country, a **6–90** Convention adoption order application is made under s.17 of the 1978 Act,[98] in the Sheriff Court or the Court of Session. Rules for both courts include provision for Convention adoption order applications.[99]

If the child is brought in for adoption from a non-convention/non- **6–91** designated country, the case is treated similarly to a domestic application, under s.12 of the 1978 Act and the appropriate court rules.

---

[96] See s.50A of the 1978 Act, inserted by s.14 of the 1999 Act.
[97] Notice is given under s.22 of the 1978 Act, in non-agency adoptions.
[98] The original s.17 of the 1978 Act was replaced by a new s.17 by 1999 Act, s.3.
[99] The Act of Sederunt (Child Care and Maintenance Rules) Amendment (1993 Hague Convention Adoption) 2003 (SSI 2003/4), amends the Sheriff Court rules for Convention adoptions orders. The Act of Sederunt (Rules of the Court of Session Amendments) (Miscellaneous) 2004 (SSI 2004/52) includes amendments to the RCS for Convention adoptions orders.

CHAPTER 7

THE CHILD IN NEED OF CARE

INTRODUCTION

7–01 At 7am on Wednesday, February 27, 1991, social workers and police made a planned and synchronised "dawn raid" on six households in South Ronaldsay, Orkney.[1] Nine children aged from 8–15 years from four families were removed by the use of place of safety orders obtained from a sheriff, and flown to undisclosed locations on the Scottish mainland. Neither children nor parents received warning of the planned social work action. The children were removed from their homes because the social work department feared they were at risk, following allegations made by seven children from another family, W, that organised ritual child abuse and satanic practices were taking place on the island. The Orkney children were separated from each other and from their parents and were not allowed to take with them toys and objects from home: one child was housed in a school for young offenders due to an unproven belief he was an abuser as well as a victim. A minimum of contact with parents was allowed, and the children were interviewed intensively by social workers, the police and child experts from the RSPCC. The place of safety orders, which authorised the detention of the children, were upheld at children's hearings which the children themselves were not allowed to attend. In April 1991, some five weeks later, the children were returned home after Sheriff Kelbie declared that the proceedings were "fatally flawed" because of procedural irregularities.[2] As a result, the evidence of abuse was never heard or tested and, subsequently, the police investigation of the parents and others for criminal offences relating to abuse was dropped. In June 1991, Lord Clyde conducted an extensive inquiry into what had gone wrong in Orkney.[3] His remit was explicitly not to explore whether sexual abuse *had* occurred in Orkney, but

---

[1] Further details of the Orkney case can be found from a number of sources, e.g. Asquith, *Protecting Children—Cleveland to Orkney: More Lessons To Learn* (1993); Reid, *Suffer The Little Children* (1992).

[2] Kirkwall Sheriff Court, April 4, 1991. Further legal points arising out of the removal were decided in *Sloan v B*, 1991 S.L.T. 530.

[3] *Report of the Inquiry into the Removal of Children from Orkney* (1992) ("the Clyde Report").

rather to look at how such allegations should be investigated and how children in such circumstances should be protected and questioned. The terms of reference of the inquiry related to the way in which the children had been removed; how they had been detained and, in particular, how they had been interviewed and cared for; and what proceedings should have followed upon the children's removal. In March 1996, the Orkney Islands Council reached an out of court settlement with the four South Ronaldsay families to pay each child £10,000 and each parent £5,000 in damages.[4]

The facts of the Orkney case, it must be stressed, are idiosyn- **7–02** cratic—the allegations of abuse were extremely complex and hard to prove, and the setting for events was isolated and lacking in full professional support—but they illustrate vividly how difficult the work of child protection can be. They also raise many of the fundamental questions which the Scottish legislation governing this area attempts to address. These are questions like:

- what level of risk must be suspected, and what facts must be proven, before a child should be removed from the family home?;
- what rights should parents have to maintain contact with a child who has been removed from the home?;
- what rights should the local authority have to investigate suspected abuse?;
- how far should the state be able to make decisions about a child in opposition to the wishes of the parents? To put it another way, what is the correct balance between family autonomy and protection of the welfare of the child?;
- what rights should parents have to oppose the intervention of the state in the *courts*?;
- does removal of a child replace parental with administrative abuse? Would it be better if a suspected abuser was removed from the home, rather than the child?;
- how should the wishes of the *child* concerned be regarded by the state and the courts, as separate from the interests of his parents or family?

The Orkney facts also make it plain that in child protection cases a **7–03** number of different legal aims may conflict. The primary aim of the state agencies should be to protect and help the child. But the state also has an interest in prosecuting wrongdoers under the criminal law. The children themselves (and, in Orkney, the parents) may wish to invoke the civil law of delict to seek compensation in damages for harm they have suffered[5]; alternatively they may wish to explore criminal injuries

---

[4] *The Scotsman*, March 5, 1996. See also Edwards, "Suing Local Authorities for Failure in Statutory Duty: Orkney Reconsidered after *X v Bedfordshire*" (1996) 1 Edin. L. Rev. 115.

[5] See further paras 5–08 *et seq.*

compensation.[6] These are both important remedies; but in this chapter, and the next, our principal focus will be to look at how the state can intervene to help in circumstances in which children appear to be in need of care or protection from outwith their family. Child abuse—both sexual and physical—is one of the most visible phenomena in this area but is by no means all that social workers and courts are concerned with. Children may be in need of support or protection because of poverty or deprivation, because parents may be disabled or mentally ill, or otherwise unable to cope with the demands of parenting, or because parents have died, disappeared or been sent to jail. Children may also, as we shall see, be perceived as in need because they have begun to commit criminal offences, or play truant from school, or because they are themselves physically or mentally ill or otherwise have special needs, e.g. for educational assistance.

7–04   In such circumstances, state agencies have a number of options. In Orkney, the immediate remedy chosen in response to suspected abuse was to remove the children from their homes as a form of emergency protection. But in many other, more ordinary, circumstances of need, the first line of state intervention is to provide more resources to the child and the family, which might take the form of financial assistance, support from social workers, day care, added home help *et al*. As we shall see, one of the general tenets of the Children (Scotland) Act 1995, Pt II is that it is better for the state to intervene as little as possible in the care that is given by families to their children. In some circumstances, parents may decide with the social work department that it is better if the children are accommodated by the local authority for some while. In others, parents will be deeply opposed to their children being removed from home and if this seems necessary in the welfare of the child, the local authority will have to obtain legal authority to accomplish it. They will have to decide if, as in Orkney, emergency protection seems necessary, or whether there is no imminent risk of significant harm. Some children move in and out of local authority care, or remain accommodated by the local authority, for considerable time. In such cases, the social work department must consider if a permanent solution for the child's care and upbringing away from his natural family is necessary. We have already considered such a permanent solution in the last chapter, when looking at adoption.

7–05   In this chapter we will be looking in detail at the options for action by the state outlined above. The law governing childcare and protection was radically reformed by, and is now principally to be found in Pt II of the Children (Scotland) Act 1995[7]; some sections of the Social Work (Scotland) Act 1968 ("the 1968 Act") are also still relevant. It is undoubtedly true that the Orkney crisis described above, and the succeeding Clyde Report, have been catalysts for change; but they have by

---

[6] See Criminal Injuries Compensation Act 1995.
[7] Pt II came into force on April 1, 1997. References in this chapter are to the 1995 Act unless otherwise stated.

no means been the only contributors to the major sea-changes taking place in Scots law. Other influences have been the Review of Child Care Law in Scotland which led in 1993 to the White Paper, *Scotland's Children*[8]; the Kearney Report on childcare policy in Fife[9]; the Skinner Report on residential childcare[10]; the Scottish Law Commission *Report on Family Law*[11] which shaped Pt I of the 1995 Act; and the Children Act 1989 which, like the 1995 Act after it, brought sweeping reform to the English law of child protection, and was at least partially a response to an earlier controversial multiple child abuse case in Cleveland in 1987.[12] As in other parts of the law relating to children, the UNCRC and the ECHR have also been taken into consideration.

Finally, it must be noted that there are three main institutions in **7–06** Scotland which are involved where children are in need of care and protection. As will be seen, the local authority has both duties and powers in relation to children, which are usually exercised by its social work department. The courts also have a significant role in preventing the local authority from taking unfettered action and giving children and parents a right to judicial hearing. The third major institution is the children's hearings system. The hearings system was introduced in 1971 under the Social Work (Scotland) Act 1968 as a system whereby both children who were seen as "delinquent", and those who were seen as in need of care and protection, could be given the measures of care that they needed. The hearing is neither a court nor a department of the local authority but an independent tribunal. It is, however, serviced by the local authority in that they are responsible for implementing its disposals, which most commonly take the form of requirements of compulsory supervision. Its function is to decide in partnership with children and parents what steps should be taken to fulfil the best interests of the children who are referred to it. Children who appear to be in need of help can be referred by any person to an official known as the reporter, whose decision it then is whether there are grounds for convening a hearing to consider the child's case ("grounds of referral"). Disposals of the hearing can be appealed to the courts. The children's panel, as it is sometimes known, has a key role in Scottish childcare law, which will be explored in detail in Ch.8.

General Principles: Courts and Children's Hearings

Section 16 of the Act sets out three important principles which **7–07** apply whenever a court or children's hearing determines any matter relating to a child (subject to exceptions noted below). As can be seen,

---

[8] Cm.2286 (1993).
[9] *Report of the Inquiries into Child Care Policies in Fife* (1992–1993 HC 191).
[10] *Another Kind of Home: A Review of Residential Child Care* (1992).
[11] Scot. Law Com. No.135 (1992).
[12] The Cleveland Inquiry commenced in August 1987 and culminated in the Butler-Sloss Report in June 1988 (*Report of the Inquiry into Child Abuse in Cleveland in 1987*).

they parallel the provisions in s.11 in Pt 1 of the 1995 Act laying down the criteria for when an order relating to parental responsibilities and rights should be made[13]:

1. *The child's welfare is paramount.*[14] However, where the court or hearing consider there is a risk of serious harm to the public (whether physical or not) a decision inconsistent with the welfare principle can be made.[15] This could, for example, allow a children's hearing or sheriff to make a supervision requirement placing a child in a residential school for young offenders on the basis of public protection rather than on welfare needs[16];

2. *The child's views, taking account of the age and maturity of the child, are to be given regard as far as practicable.* Children must be given an opportunity to express their views. Children of 12 years or older are presumed mature enough to express a view but such maturity can be shown at a younger age.[17] Children can of course not only now express a view, but instruct their own lawyers to represent them in proceedings.[18] A curator *ad litem* may also be appointed by the court to represent the best interests of the child and at a hearing, or any appeal to the courts from the hearing, an official known as a safeguarder may be appointed to the child for similar purposes[19];

3. *Neither the court nor the hearing is to make any requirement or order with respect to the child unless it considers that it would be better for the child that the requirement or order be made, than that none should be made at all.*[20] This "no order" or "minimum intervention" principle applies to a very wide range of decisions, including decisions of the children's hearing when making or reviewing supervision requirements, or confirming emergency protection measures[21]; and decisions by the sheriff when hearing appeals from a children's hearing,[22] or when granting emergency

---

[13] See paras 4–49 *et seq.*

[14] s.16(1).

[15] s.16(5).

[16] A child may be placed in secure accommodation as a disposal of the hearing but there are further safeguards to this in the form of the criteria in s.70(10)—see further Ch.8.

[17] s.16(2).

[18] See further paras 2–38 *et seq.*

[19] 1968 Act, s.34A (introduced by the Children Act 1975, s.66). A safeguarder need not be a lawyer but often is. The expanded rights of independent representation for children under the 1995 Act raise the possibility of clashes between lawyers acting in the "best interests" of the child and those representing the child's own wishes. See further Cleland, Ch.10, in Cleland and Sutherland, *Children's Rights in Scotland* (2nd edn, 2001).

[20] s.16(3).

[21] s.16(4)(a).

[22] 1995 Act, s.16(4)(b)(iv) and (4)(c). This includes substituting his own judgment for that of the hearing under s.51(5)(c)(iii).

protection orders,[23] or parental responsibilities orders.[24] It does *not*, however, apply to the case where a sheriff considers whether to make a child protection order, nor does it apply to the deliberations of the children's hearing when deciding whether to continue and confirm the child protection order.[25] The duty to consult the child discussed above also does not apply to these decisions.[26]

In practice, this means there is a statutory presumption that neither **7-08** the hearing nor the sheriff should intervene unless it is clearly the best measure to secure the child's welfare. The appropriateness of this provision in the context of child protection has been questioned. In the private law context, as we saw in Ch.4, the "minimum intervention" principle most often operates to preserve the rights and responsibilities of both parents towards the child even if they have divorced. There is clear evidence this is better for the child than to remove the responsibility of one parent on a routine basis, as was common prior to the 1995 Act.

However, in Pt II cases, as Thomson has argued,[27] it is likely there **7-09** is already a prima facie case for intervention if the child has come to the attention of the local authority or been referred to the hearing. By definition, these are cases that have already been investigated by the social work department or the reporter as likely to require intervention and so the "minimum intervention" principle may well be inappropriate and not in the interests of the child. Minimum intervention can be justified on the ideological basis that families know best what to do for their children and should be left alone as much as possible by the state.[28] It can be regarded as a principle resetting the balance between families and the state after what was seen as the overzealous intervention of social workers in cases in the 80s and early 90s. However, a minimum intervention principle is also a useful means by which the financial resources devoted to childcare and protection can be rationed and globally restricted. It is clear that the social work resources that are needed to deal with children in need have risen since 1995. This means that a "laissez faire" approach to intervention in the welfare of the child may allow the state to save money, or at least to target resources towards cases where crisis has

---

[23] 1995 Act, s.16(4)(b)(i)–(iii). This includes a decision to make, vary or discharge a child assessment order or exclusion order; or grant a warrant; or vary or discharge a child protection order. These are all forms of emergency protection discussed below.

[24] s.16(4)(b)(i).

[25] s.16(3) and (4).

[26] s.16(2) and (4).

[27] Thomson, "The Welfare Principle—Under Attack or Strengthened?", 1996 S.L.T. (News) 115.

[28] Thomson himself has argued that "family autonomy may be regarded as a hallmark of a democratic society": Thomson (4th edn), p.289.

already arisen, rather than towards the more long-lasting and expensive activity of crisis prevention.[29]

Local Authority Powers and Duties

7–10   The 1995 Act, Pt II, in conjunction with what remains of the 1968 Act, attempts to set out a new framework to support children and their families in the community, emphasising partnership between parents and local authorities. The local authority is generally under a duty to promote social welfare by making available advice, guidance and assistance to persons in the area for which they are responsible (s.12 of the 1968 Act). This assistance can take the form of cash, but only in exceptional circumstances,[30] assistance in kind,[31] the provision of residential nursing accommodation,[32] home helps or laundry facilities.[33] Assistance under s.12 is restricted to persons aged 18 or over.[34] This is because the 1995 Act now gives local authorities special duties in relation to children in need.

7–11   In particular, s.22 provides that local authorities have duties to promote and safeguard the welfare of children in their area who are "in need". This phrase is broadly defined[35] to include:

  (i) children who are unlikely to achieve or maintain a reasonable standard of health or development without local authority assistance;
  (ii) children whose health or development is likely to be significantly impaired without such assistance;
  (iii) disabled children; and
  (iv) children affected by the disability of another member of the family.

7–12 Local authorities have powers to assist children who fit this broad definition, and the families of those children, with the aim of improving things for the child *without* removing him from the home environment. Indeed, the authority is expressly charged with promoting the upbringing of such children by their family.[36] Although this section *enables* action by the authority, it can thus be seen as working hand in hand with the minimum intervention principle for courts and children's hearings discussed above.

---

[29] See Waterhouse and McGhee, "Justice and welfare—has the Children (Scotland) Act 1995 shifted the balance?" (1998) 20 J.S.W.L. 49.
[30] See s.12(3) and (4). The assumption is that a person in need of cash should approach the social security authorities first.
[31] s.12(1).
[32] s.13A.
[33] s.14.
[34] 1968 Act, s.12(2) as amended by 1995 Act, Sch.4, para.15(11).
[35] s.93(4)(a).
[36] s.22(1)(b).

One of the major proposals of the White Paper *Scotland's* **7–13**
Children was that local authorities should adopt strategic planning
in order to improve the services they could deliver, better utilise
resources, facilitate inter-agency co-operation and achieve consistency between different areas. As a result local authorities were
placed under a duty to publish plans relating to services for children
("in need" or otherwise).[37] Local authorities also come under specific
duties to co-operate in the provision of services to children with
other agencies and authorities such as health boards[38]; to provide
day care facilities for pre-school children under five[39]; towards disabled children[40]; and to provide after-care assistance for children
who are leaving care and who are over 16 but under 19.[41] Local
authorities are also given a discretion, though not a duty, similarly
to assist children leaving care who are aged 19–21.[42] This help can
take the form of the provision of cash, or in kind. Provision of
accommodation to children and young persons is dealt with below.
However, it should be noted that s.38 introduces a framework for the
provision of short stay refuges for children under 18 who appear to
be at risk of harm and at their own request seek such accommodation. The stay in such refuges will be limited to seven days, or in
exceptional circumstances, 14 days.[43]

Accommodating Children

In certain circumstances, parents may agree with the local author- **7–14**
ity that it is best that the child be cared for by someone other than the
family, usually on a temporary basis, perhaps because one or both
parents are ill, hospitalised, pregnant or suffering an episode of
depression. Such care is often anecdotally referred to as "respite" or
"voluntary" care. Under s.25, local authorities have a *duty* to provide
accommodation for children under the age of 18[44] in their area
(whether residing there or simply found there) in any of the following
circumstances:

(a) no-one has parental responsibility for the child;
(b) the child is lost or abandoned; or
(c) the person caring for him is prevented, whether or not perma-
     nently and for whatever reason, from providing him with suitable
     accommodation or care.[45]

---

[37] s.19.
[38] s.21.
[39] s.27.
[40] ss.23, 24.
[41] s.29.
[42] s.29(2).
[43] s.38(5).
[44] See definition of "child" in s.93(2)(a).
[45] s.25(1).

7–15 Local authorities may provide accommodation in a family—that is, with foster carers—with a relative of the child, with another suitable person, in a residential setting or make other appropriate arrangements making use of services available to children cared for by their own families. These may be in England and Wales or Northern Ireland.[46]

7–16 Local authorities also have the *power* to provide accommodation for children in their area if this would safeguard and promote their welfare.[47] This power extends to young people who are over 18 years but under 21 years.[48]

7–17 The value of s.25 is that it enables local authorities to offer accommodation to children where this seems appropriate without the need to take more drastic steps such as removing parental rights from the parents or referring the child to the children's hearing. In principle, parents of a child who is being accommodated under s.25 lose none of their parental responsibilities or rights (hereafter "PRRs"). A key requirement of s.25 then is that the authority must obtain parental agreement before receiving the child into their accommodation. The local authority cannot provide a child with accommodation if anyone with *both* parental responsibilities *and* the right to regulate the child's residence and control, direct and guide the child's upbringing,[49] objects, provided that that person is also willing to accommodate or arrange for the provision of accommodation to the child (s.25(6)). A child of 16 years or over can give his own consent to be accommodated despite parental objection.[50] While these provisions preserve parental rights to control the residence of the child,[51] they may be, in some cases, problematic.

7–18 *Example:* Husband (H) and wife (W) have separated and their child (C) is living with W; H has taken little interest in C. W is going into hospital and wants the child accommodated by the local authority. H objects and proposes his home as alternative accommodation. As a married father, he has all parental responsibilities and rights unless removed by court order. In terms of s.25(6), the local authority cannot provide s.25 accommodation even if they suspect the husband's care will be inadequate. Nothing within the section provides that the alternative accommodation arranged by H must be suitable or safe. However, if W has obtained, or obtains, a *residence order*,[52] then she can agree to the child being accommodated despite the objection of H.[53] If the non-objecting parent did not or could

---

[46] s.26.

[47] s.25(2).

[48] s.25(3).

[49] Under s.2(1)(a) and (b) 1995 Act, as amended by Family Law (Scotland) Act 2006.

[50] s.25(7)(a). This is consonant with the rule that a child is of full legal capacity at age 16 (Age of Legal Capacity (Scotland) Act 1991, s.1).

[51] s.2(1)(a).

[52] Under s.11(2)(c).

[53] s.25(7)(b).

not obtain a residence order, and respite care still seemed desirable, then the authority would have to consider some other option, such as referral to the children's hearing.

Before providing a child with accommodation, the local authority, **7–19** so far as is practicable, must ascertain the child's views, taking account of the age and maturity of the child. A child of 12 years or more is presumed able to form a view.[54] This overcomes, to some extent, the objections made against the corresponding provisions under the 1968 Act that "voluntary care" was voluntary for the parents, but not for the child.

Accommodated Children and Parental Rights of Return

As we have seen, parents of a child who is being accommodated **7–20** under s.25 lose none of their parental responsibilities or rights. As the statute makes crystal clear, a person with parental responsibilities may thus remove the child from the accommodation provided by the local authority *at any time*.[55] However, if the child has been in the accommodation for a continuous period of at least six months,[56] 14 days' notice in writing must be given before the child can be removed.[57] This allows the authority some time in which to consider whether they need to take legal action to retain the child.

Can a local authority *refuse* immediately to return a child accom- **7–21** modated under s.25 of the Act before the six months are up if they fear that to do so is not in the welfare of the child? One thing the authority certainly cannot do is apply to the court for a residence order in respect of the child under s.11 of the 1995 Act, since s.11(5) specifically forbids local authorities from doing this. However, s.11(5) does not prevent an authority from *defending* a s.11 action. In a pre-1995 Act case, *M v Dumfries and Galloway Regional Council*,[58] a local authority refused to return a child who had been voluntarily placed in its accommodation in its care under the equivalent provision of the Social Work (Scotland) Act 1968. The child had been in care for more than six months but the parents had given the required written notice.[59] The child made allegations of sexual abuse against the father after which the authority refused to return him. The parents raised an action for delivery of the child which the local authority successfully opposed by arguing that the action related to parental rights and was therefore governed by the welfare principle, and that it was not in the child's best interests to return home. It appears possible to similarly defend the child by inaction under the 1995 Act.[60]

---

[54] s.25(5).
[55] s.25(6)(b).
[56] This can be accommodation provided by more than one local authority.
[57] s.25(7).
[58] 1991 S.C.L.R. 481.
[59] Then, 28 days: see 1968 Act, s.15.
[60] See *M v D and Dumfries and Galloway Council*, 2001 Fam. L.R. 58, and para.4.41, above.

7–22   This is not, however, the best solution. If the local authority wished to prevent the removal of the child from its care, it could more properly refer the child to the reporter to the children's panel[61] or apply to the court for a Child Protection Order, if there was a risk of immediate significant harm to the child if returned (see paras 7–28 *et seq.* below).

7–23   Similar considerations apply to restriction of contact rights. The parents, so long as they have PRRs, retain the right to maintain contact with the child[62] and the authority cannot restrict this without seeking some legal warrant for their action.[63]

"Looked after" Children: s.17

7–24   Children in s.25 accommodation are described in the Act as "looked after" by the local authority, and this means the authority has significant duties towards them. Other groups of children also fall into this category, including:

- children subject to a supervision requirement imposed by a children's hearing;
- children under warrants, orders or authorisations, including child protection orders, child assessment orders or parental responsibilities orders[64];
- children towards whom the authority has responsibilities who are subject to orders analogous to those described above made in other parts of the United Kingdom.[65]

7–25 Around 12,000 children in Scotland are "looked after" children.[66]
Local authority duties towards "looked after" children are set out in s.17[67] and include:

- (a) the duty to safeguard and promote the welfare of the child as their paramount concern;
- (b) the duty to make reasonably available to such children, services which are supplied to children cared for by their own parents[68];

---

[61] But this would require clear evidence for at least one condition set out in s.52(2): see Ch.8.

[62] s.2(1)(c).

[63] In fact, the authority comes under a duty to *promote* contact between the accommodated child and his parents, subject, however, to the welfare principle—see s.17(1)(c), discussed at para.7–25 below.

[64] Discussed below at paras 7–28 *et seq.*

[65] s.17(6).

[66] *Children's Social Work Statistics 2004–2005* (Scottish Executive).

[67] Protecting the public from "serious harm" may allow a local authority to override these duties (s.17(5)).

[68] Notably, schooling. There has been considerable concern about the poor educational experiences and outcomes of children looked after away from home: see Maclean and Gunion "Learning With Care: The Education of Children Looked After Away from Home by Local Authorities in Scotland" (2003) 27(2) Adoption and Fostering 20.

(c) the duty to take such steps as are both practicable and appropriate to promote, on a regular basis, personal relations and direct contact between the child and any person with parental responsibilities, having regard to the welfare principle[69];

(d) the duty to provide advice and assistance, with a view to preparing the child for when he or she is no longer looked after by a local authority[70];

(e) the duty, as far as is practicable, to ascertain the views of the child, his or her parent(s) or any other person who has parental rights in relation to the child, or any person whose views are seen as relevant, before making any decision about the child.[71] The authority must then give due regard to these wishes. Account must be taken of the child's age and maturity.[72]

(f) the duty when making decisions relating to the child to take account of the child's religious persuasion, racial origin, cultural and linguistic background.[73]

Parents come under a duty in relation to "looked after" children to advise the local authority of any change of address without unreasonable delay. Breach is a criminal offence.[74]

Emergency Protection of Children

If the local authority feels that the child is imminently at risk in the **7–26** family home then they must consider what emergency action should be taken. There are basically three options: removing and accommodating the child under s.25 with the agreement of the parents or person with residence order; removing the child against the wishes of the parents using a child protection order; or seeking an alternative to emergency removal of the child which nonetheless safeguards the child. (A child might also of course make the decision on his or her own to leave the family home.) A range of orders to effect these options are found in Ch.3 of Pt 2 of the 1995 Act, several of which parallel similar orders found in the Children Act 1989 which is in operation in England and Wales.

Prior to the 1995 Act, children could be removed from parents in **7–27** emergency situations by use of place of safety orders, which could be obtained very speedily from a sheriff or a justice of the peace. These empowered the local authority to remove the child to an

---

[69] s.17(1)(a)–(c).
[70] s.17(2).
[71] s.17(3).
[72] s.17(4). Oddly, there is no presumption of maturity at 12 or over as is usual in the 1995 Act.
[73] s.17(4)(c).
[74] Unless the move was to an address where the other parent was resident and the first parent genuinely believed the other had informed the authority (s.18).

undefined "place of safety".[75] Such orders were used to remove the Orkney children and were subjected to detailed criticism by Lord Clyde in his report.[76] The main flaws identified in the old scheme were that:

(i) children were not always removed *only* in circumstances when they were actually in imminent danger or risk of harm if not removed. For example, in Orkney, the removal of the children was planned some two weeks in advance. Were they really in danger of harm if their removal could be delayed for so long? Since removal from home is a traumatic event, it should only be "absolutely justified where the alternative is the certain exposure to harm"[77];

(ii) there were *insufficient alternatives* to the drastic step of removal of the child. For example, in many cases, immediate removal was unnecessary when what would suffice was a power to gain access to the child to examine him or her for evidence of abuse.

(iii) the *parents* were not given adequate rights in the process. When children were removed by place of safety orders, the parents did not have a chance to oppose the removal for up to a week, and then only at a meeting of the children's hearing. It was felt that parents should be entitled to make an immediate challenge, and to a sheriff rather than the hearing.

(iv) the *rights of the child* were insufficiently guarded in the process. When a child was taken into care via a place of safety order, the precise rights, duties and powers of those involved with the child were not clear. Nor was the status of the parents, e.g. whether they retained rights to maintain contact with the child.

Removal of the Child: Child Protection Orders

7–28 The 1995 Act attempts to implement the Clyde recommendations by replacing the place of safety order of the 1968 Act with the child protection order (hereafter "CPO") laid out in ss.57–60. Application for a CPO can be made to the sheriff by "any person",[78] or specifically, by a local authority.[79] Under s.57(1) the sheriff has a discretion to grant the CPO if:

---

[75] Under s.37 of the 1968 Act, now repealed. For a full discussion of the 1968 Act system of emergency protection, see Wilkinson and Norrie, pp.457–462.

[76] See Ch.16 of the Clyde Report; also Lord Clyde, "Lessons from the Orkney Inquiry" in Asquith, *Protecting Children* (NCB, 1993). It should be noted that problems with place of safety orders had been identified as early as the *Review of Child Care Law 1990* (1993), Pt 14.

[77] Lord Clyde, "Lessons from the Orkney Inquiry", p.21.

[78] 1995 Act, s.57(1). If the application is made by someone other than a local authority, e.g. a policeman or health worker, notice must be given to the relevant authority: s.57(5).

[79] 1995 Act, s.57(2). On territorial jurisdiction, see *Fife Council, Applicant* (2003) Fam. L.B. 63-5.

(a) he is satisfied that there are reasonable grounds to believe that—
   (i) the child is being so treated[80] that he is suffering significant harm, *or*
   (ii) will suffer such harm if he is not removed to, and kept in, a place of safety.
   As an alternative, ground (ii) can be established if the child is already being accommodated[81] by the local authority and he will suffer harm if not *kept* there; and
(b) an order is *necessary* to protect the child from such harm (or further harm).

When the application is made by the local authority under s.57, a CPO can be made if they establish that: **7–29**

(i) they have reasonable grounds to suspect the child is being, or will be, so treated (or neglected) that he is suffering, or will suffer, significant harm; *and*
(ii) they are making inquiries to decide if any action to safeguard the child is needed; *and*
(iii) those inquiries are being unreasonably frustrated by denial of access to the child, which the authority reasonably feel is required as a matter of urgency.[82]

The emphasis in both cases is on the current existence or future risk **7–30** of *"significant harm"*, a key phrase which recurs when we come to look (below) at child assessment orders and exclusion orders. It would seem in line with the provisions of the Clyde Report that harm which has occurred in the *past*, but which is not causing the child to suffer either now or in the foreseeable future, should not form grounds for a child protection order. In such circumstances, the correct action (if any) should be to refer the child to the children's hearing. A different interpretation has however been reached in England and Wales where the same phrase is used in the emergency protection provisions of the Children Act 1989.[83] It remains to be seen how the Scottish courts will interpret "significant harm": Norrie suggests that it should mean harm of a "not minor, transient or superficial nature".[84]

A key problem that has arisen in both Scotland and England **7–31** is whether a CPO can be taken immediately on, or even before, the birth of a child, where the mother or family has a long history of

---

[80] "Treated" includes "neglected".
[81] Presumably this refers to accommodation under s.25.
[82] s.57(1).
[83] See *Re M (A Minor) (Care Order) (Threshold Conditions)* [1994] 2 F.L.R. 577; also *In Re O (Minors) (Care: Preliminary Hearing)* [2003] UKHL 18. However, the context of English child protection law is so different (and even the wording subtly different) that these cases cannot be regarded as binding or even necessarily persuasive.
[84] Norrie, *Children (Scotland) Act 1995* (2nd edn, 2004).

involvement with social work and there are fears of the safety of the newborn infant. In Scotland, a CPO can clearly not be taken in respect of a fetus: a fetus is not a legal person[85] and therefore not "a child" as the Act demands. Furthermore to apply a CPO to a fetus would seriously impinge on the autonomy and human rights of the mother. The Strasbourg court has expressed grave reservations about the practice of taking children into care at birth as an infringement of the rights under Art.8 of the mother and family.[86] They have also been uneasy about the instant removal of children from families who do not at that time have legal representation or advice.[87] In Scotland there is conflicting authority as to whether parents or families in this situation have a right to legal representation before a child can be removed at birth.[88] Lord McCluskey took the view in *K and F Applicants*[89] that "in the case of a child not yet born, the need for urgency is far from obvious" and confirmed to the ECHR-friendly view that the sheriff should receive legal representations in such cases before removal. This is probably the safest course to follow except in extreme emergency. Emergency protection orders have, in any case, been less and less used since the Orkney debacle: research by Francis and McGhee[90] found a downward trend in the use of emergency protection orders overall since the introduction of the 1995 Act, and hypothesised that this was partly due: (i) to the greater judicial scrutiny of CPOs than place of safety orders, leading to greater reluctance to seek them to attention; (ii) to the "minimum intervention" principle; and (iii) to the principle of working in partnership with parents. It is not impossible however that the number of emergency orders sought may rise again, given the rising number of children on the child protection register and public concern about, especially, children born to addict parents.[91]

Making a CPO: Terms, Conditions and Directions

7–32   The CPO must identify the applicant and as far as is practicable, the child concerned. It should state the grounds on which the application was made and be accompanied by supporting evidence.[92] The sheriff, when making the CPO, should be guided by the welfare principle as the paramount consideration.[93] He or she is not, however,

---

[85] *Hamilton v Fife Health Board*, 1993 S.L.T. 624.
[86] See, e.g. *K and T v Finland* [2001] 2 F.L.R. 707.
[87] See *P, C and S v UK* (2003) 38 E.H.R.R. 28.
[88] *C Petr.* (2001) Fam. L.R. 42 *cf. K and F Applicants*, 2002 S.L.T. (Sh Ct) 38 and (2001) Fam. L.R. 44.
[89] Above.
[90] Francis and McGhee, *Child Protection and Social Work Practice: Exploring the Impact of the Children (Scotland) Act 1995* (Dept of Social Work, University of Edinburgh, 2000).
[91] See further, para.8–22.
[92] s.57(3).
[93] s.16(1).

subject to the duty to consult the child, nor to the principle of "minimum intervention" discussed above.[94] However, if a CPO is granted, the applicant should subsequently implement it only to the extent necessary to safeguard the welfare of the child.[95] The sheriff when making the CPO can make it subject to such terms and conditions as seem appropriate.[96] He or she can, in particular, require any person to produce the child; authorise the removal of the child by the applicant to a place of safety, and the keeping of the child at that place; authorise the prevention of the removal of the child from any place where the child is accommodated; and provide that the location of the child once removed to a place of safety should not be disclosed.

It should be stressed that the applicant—who will usually, but not **7-33** invariably be a local authority—is only empowered to do what is specifically authorised by the sheriff in the CPO. The parental responsibilities and rights of the parent or carer of the child are not removed, nor are they transferred to the applicant. (The local authority does, however, owe duties to the child who has been removed by CPO as a child "looked after" by the authority.[97]) In principle, therefore, the applicant—say, an authority—has no parental rights to, for example, consent to the medical or psychiatric assessment of the child who has been removed for suspected abuse.[98] Nor do they have the power to restrict the parent's contact with the child (unless they have been authorised to keep the child's location a secret) since in principle the parents retain the right and responsibility to maintain contact.[99]

To deal with this, s.58 provides a general power and discretion to **7-34** the sheriff when making a CPO to make whatever *directions* seem necessary to promote and safeguard the welfare of the child. Such directions must relate to the exercise or fulfilment of parental responsibilities or rights in relation to the child.[1] Particular provision is made for directions about contact and medical treatment. The sheriff may give directions as to contact between the child and (a) any parent of the child; (b) any person with parental responsibilities in relation to that child; and (c) any other specified person or class of persons.[2] He may also make a direction *prohibiting* contact between the child and any person, or add conditions, e.g. that contact be supervised by a social worker.[3] In relation to medical consent, s.58(5) specifically

---

[94] See nn.25 and 26 above.
[95] s.57(6).
[96] s.57(4).
[97] s.17, discussed at paras 7–25 et seq.
[98] This point was controversial in relation to place of safety orders under the 1968 Act: see Thomson, 1991 S.L.T. (News) 379.
[99] s.1(1)(c) and 2(1)(c).
[1] 1995 Act, s.58(4). Such directions can be made by the sheriff on application or *ex proprio motu* (s.58(4) and (6)) and may be subject to appropriate conditions.
[2] s.58(1).
[3] s.58(2).

provides that "a direction may be sought in relation to" any physical or mental examination of the child, any other assessment or interview of the child, or any treatment of the child arising out of such examination or assessment.

7–35 The intent of s.58 is that the parent's refusal to co-operate with medical assessment of the child need not fatally hamper the social work investigation of the abuse. But what if the child *him- or herself is* competent to give a medical consent? Under s.2(4) of the Age of Legal Capacity (Scotland) Act 1991, a child is able to give a valid consent to medical treatment if in the opinion of a qualified medical practitioner, the child is of an age to understand the proposed treatment and its possible consequences.[4] If a child is so competent then by s.90 of the 1995 Act, that child's consent must be sought and the local authority cannot, it seems, override it by asking the sheriff to add a direction to this effect. Thus *a parent's* refusal of consent can be overcome but the child's, apparently, cannot.[5] This is consonant with the view of the Clyde Report that a child has a right to refuse treatment or assessment even if misguided.[6]

Recall, Variation and Duration of CPOs

7–36 As we have seen above, it was one of the major recommendations of the Clyde Report that if children had been removed from the home by emergency action, then parents should have an opportunity as soon as possible to challenge this action before a sheriff. To this end, there are detailed provisions which allow for recall and variation of CPOs. It is important to note that once the CPO is granted, it must be implemented within 24 hours or it will lapse.[7] The intention of the legislation again here is to prevent authorities from applying for CPOs as insurance where there is no actual or imminent threat to the child.

7–37 The reporter to the Children's Panel (the Principal Reporter) must be told forthwith of the implementation of the CPO, and can subsequently decide to liberate the child if circumstances have changed, or further information indicates the conditions for making the CPO are no longer satisfied.[8] If the child is not liberated, the reporter must arrange a children's hearing on the second working day after the implementation of the CPO.[9] This hearing's role is to consider whether the CPO and any directions should be continued or varied.[10] It is sometimes known as an "initial" hearing.[11] If the CPO is continued by the

---

[4] See further paras 2–29 *et seq.*
[5] The same conclusion is reached explicitly in the parallel English provisions: see Children Act 1989, s.38(6).
[6] Clyde Report, para.17.42.
[7] s.60(1).
[8] s.60(3).
[9] s.59(2), (3).
[10] s.59(4).
[11] Norrie, *Children (Scotland) Act 1995* (2nd edn, 2004).

initial hearing, and compulsory measures of supervision are seen to be necessary, then grounds of referral[12] must be put to a further hearing on the eighth working day[13] after the CPO was implemented.[14]

Thus, if the parents do not successfully challenge the CPO at any **7–38** earlier stage, the CPO must at latest come to an end on the eighth working day after it was taken, when the hearing meets to decide whether grounds of referral exist.[15] However, parents have an opportunity to challenge the CPO in the courts, at two earlier stages:

Stage 1 challenge: After a CPO has been made by the sheriff under **7–39** s.57(1) or (2), application to a sheriff to set aside or vary the CPO (and/or directions made under s.58) is possible before the commencement of the "initial hearing".[16] Such an application must be determined within three working days. The reporter can arrange a hearing to give advice to the sheriff in relation to the CPO.[17] If the sheriff determines that the conditions for making the CPO are *not* satisfied, he or she must recall the order and cancel any directions under s.58.[18] If satisfied the conditions for granting the CPO *are* met, the order and any directions granted under s.58 should be confirmed or varied, new directions can be granted, and the order continued in force until the full children's hearing on the eighth working day.[19]

If a "stage 1" challenge is made, there is no "initial" hearing, and **7–40** if the CPO is confirmed by the sheriff, the child will be kept in the place of safety with any directions made about contact, etc. maintained, until the eighth working day hearing.[20] At that stage, the normal procedure in relation to children's hearings comes into play.[21]

Stage 2 challenge: If *no* "stage 1" challenge is made prior to the **7–41** "initial" hearing then there is a second chance to make an application to recall the CPO within two working days of the "initial" hearing.[22] The options available to the sheriff are the same as in the "stage 1" application for recall, except that an advice hearing need not be convened.[23] If the CPO is continued (with or without variation of the order and/or directions) a full hearing is held on the eighth working day from the implementation of the original CPO as above.[24]

---

[12] At least one ground of referral to the hearing system must be admitted by both child and parents or proven before a sheriff before the hearing can go on to dispose of the child's case. See further s.52 and Ch.8.

[13] "Working day" does not include weekends, January 1 and 2, and December 25 and 26: s.93(1).

[14] s.65(2).

[15] s.60(6)(e).

[16] s.60(8).

[17] s.60(10).

[18] s.60(13).

[19] s.60(12).

[20] s.60(12)(d).

[21] See Ch.8.

[22] s.60(8)(b).

[23] s.60(10).

[24] s.65(2).

7–42   A stage 1 or 2 challenge may be made by the child, a person with parental responsibilities or rights in relation to the child, a person who ordinarily has charge of the child, anyone who by regulation was notified of the application for the order, and the applicant for the order.[25] There is no further appeal from a sheriff granting, refusing or continuing a CPO, to the sheriff principal or Inner House.[26] This is appropriate given the emergency and time-limited nature of the order.

7–43   This is a highly complex procedure with many tight time limits which can perhaps best be grasped in the form of a flowchart (see Figure 1 overleaf).

7–44   If it is not "practicable" to make an application to a sheriff for a CPO, emergency authorisation for removal can be made by a Justice of the Peace.[27] This would most likely be used only in rural or remote areas or perhaps on public holidays. However, application would then have to be made for a "proper" CPO within 24 hours.[28] A police constable also retains the power to remove a child to a place of safety, but again, only for 24 hours.[29]

Alternatives to Removal of the Child

Child Assessment Orders

7–45   Removing the child via a CPO is a drastic step both for the child and the family. In line with the general principle of minimum intervention and the recommendations of the Clyde Report, the 1995 Act provides two other orders which are less invasive for the child. The child assessment order introduced by s.55 (hereafter "CAO") is tailored to deal with emergency situations where there are concerns about the child's safety, and the authority is being denied access to the child to find out if their concerns are legitimate and whether further action is necessary. For example, the school may report that a young child had a black eye and bruising, that no explanation had been given by the mother, and that neither the social worker nor the doctor had been allowed to see the child. In such circumstances, it may be possible to clear up the issue by examination of the child without the need to remove the child from the home.

7–46   The local authority (and no other person) can apply to a sheriff for a CAO where it has reasonable cause to suspect that the child is being treated or neglected in such a way that he "is suffering, or is likely to suffer significant harm". The authority must show that the assessment is *required* in order to find out if there is neglect or ill treatment, and is unlikely to be carried out, or performed satisfactorily, unless

---

[25] s.60(7).
[26] s.51(15).
[27] s.61.
[28] s.61(4).
[29] s.61(5) and (6).

FIGURE 1

*Child Protection Orders Sections 57–62**
Application to Sheriff by "any person" *s.57(1)*/by local authority *s.57(2)*

Application Refused	OR	Application granted in terms of *s.57(1)* or *(2)* with/without conditions *s.58*—falls if not implemented by end 24 hours (*s.60(1)*)

Reporter can liberate child (*s.60(3)*) **but** not if "initial" CH commenced under *s.59(2)* or application made to sheriff to set aside CPO/directions commenced under *s.60(7)* (*s.60(3)*)	OR	*s.60(7)*—before "initial" CH, "Stage 1 Challenge" to sheriff to recall order etc. This must be determined within 3 working days (*s.60(8)*) (Reporter can arrange a CH (*s.60(10)*) to give advice to sheriff.)	OR	"Initial" CH on 2nd working day after implementation of the CPO to decide if the order (and/or any directions under *s.58*) should continue/be varied *s.59(2)(3)(4)*

Recall order *s.60(13)* and cancel any directions under *s.58* (*s.60(12)*)	OR	Confirm order in force and/or vary order, directions (*s. 60(12)*)

CPO not continued by CH, ceases to have effect (*s.60(6)(a)*)	OR	CPO continued

"Stage 2 Challenge" Application to sheriff to recall order, etc., within 2 working days of the "initial" CH (*s.60(8)(b)*). Application to be determined within 3 working days (*s.60(8)*)	OR	(if no challenge)

Recall order (*s. 60(13)*) and cancel any directions under *s.58*	OR	Confirm order in force and/or vary order, directions *s.60(12)*. Until

Full hearing with grounds
(On 8th working day after
implementation of the CPO)
➤ (*s.65(2)*) ◄

---

*In this flowchart CH = Children's Hearing; CPO = Child Protection

the order is made.[30] The order can only last seven days, with the sheriff specifying the commencement and duration of the assessment period.[31] In some circumstances, examination of the child at home will be impractical and so a CAO can also provide authorisation for the child to be taken to "any place", e.g. a hospital, surgery or clinic, for the purpose of assessment and to be kept there for a period of time specified by the sheriff.[32] If the child is to be kept away from home, then the sheriff can make directions about contact between the child, his parents and others.[33]

7–47   There is little difference between the threshold criteria required for making a CAO and a CPO and there will be a temptation for the local authority to seek the more all-encompassing remedy on the grounds of expediency—it will be much easier to arrange the assessment of a child removed into their temporary care, as well as easier generally to safeguard his or her welfare. Indeed, s.55(2) expressly states that if the sheriff considers when hearing the application for a CAO that the conditions for making a CPO are met, he *shall* make a CPO rather than a CAO—a mandatory not discretionary provision. This provision has been castigated as sloppy drafting,[34] since even when application is made for a CPO *ab initio* the sheriff has a discretion whether or not to grant it, but it may also be an intended recognition of the fact that in England and Wales, where equivalent provisions have been available for some time, the evidence is that a CAO is not much used when a CPO[35] can be applied for. A similar pattern of little use of CAOs in Scotland was observed by Francis and McGhee.[36]

7–48   Another issue raised by the drafting of s.55 is what happens if the parent refuses to comply with the CAO. Section 55(3) merely provides that the CAO may "require any person...to permit [the authority or its agent] to carry out an assessment in accordance with the order". "Person" here obviously includes a parent with responsibilities, who would normally have the right to give or withhold consent to medical or other assessment. The section does not transfer parental rights to the authority, it merely places an obligation on the person who does have such rights. What happens if the parent refuses to produce the child or give consent to assessment? Presumably such a stubborn parent could be held in contempt of court, but this would not immediately assist in the main point of the exercise, namely, assessment of

---

[30] s.55(1).

[31] s.55(3).

[32] s.55(4).

[33] s.55(5).

[34] See Norrie, *Children (Scotland) Act 1995* (2nd edn, 2004).

[35] See Dickens, "Assessment and the Control of Social Work: An Analysis of the Reasons for Non-Use of the Child Assessment Order", 3 J.S.W.L. 88. The English equivalent of a CPO is an "emergency protection order" or EPO. See Children Act 1989, s.44.

[36] Above, n.90.

the child.[37] One solution may be for the sheriff to cast his requirement in the form of a s.11 order awarding the appropriate right to the authority on an interim basis.[38] As with CPOs, the child's own capacity, if sufficiently mature to give or withhold consent to medical treatment, is preserved.[39]

Exclusion Orders

Where there is a basis for concern about a child's safety within a **7–49** household, prior to the 1995 Act the only option was to remove the child from that household unless the suspected abuser would leave voluntarily. The exclusion order (hereafter "EO") allows the suspected abuser to be removed from the household instead. Such an order is in line with the tenet that the child's needs should take precedence over those of the adults involved. However, what the legislation attempts to do rather than provide to the court an unfettered discretion to exclude, is to require the sheriff to balance the interests of the child and the adult involved using multiple tests. In this sense, the provisions of ss.76–80 have many similarities to the provisions of the Matrimonial Homes (Family Protection) (Scotland) Act 1981 which allow the court a discretion to make an order excluding one spouse or cohabitee for the protection of the other.[40]

Only a local authority can apply for an exclusion order, and appli- **7–50** cation must be made to the sheriff. The grounds on which the sheriff may choose to make an EO are laid out in s.76(2):

1. the child[41] must have suffered or be likely to suffer "significant harm" as a result of the conduct or threatened or reasonably apprehended conduct of the "named person" who is to be excluded.[42] This is the same test as when a sheriff is asked to make a CPO, appropriately, as the alternative to an EO would be to remove the child via a CPO; *and*
2. the making of the order must be *necessary* for the protection of the child *and* would better safeguard the child's welfare than removing the child from the family home.[43] Obviously if this test

---

[37] Compare the English law provisions relating to child assessment orders in s.43 of the Children Act 1989. S.43(7) gives the local authority clear authority to carry out the assessment named in the CAO *which is supplemented* by the duty placed on the parent.

[38] It is clear that a sheriff has jurisdiction to make s.11 orders *ex proprio motu*.

[39] 1995 Act, s.90. This applies even though not explicitly referred to in s.55.

[40] See Ch.11.

[41] "Child" means a child under 16 or a child aged 16–18 who is under a supervision requirement of the children's hearing or who has been referred to the hearing: s.93(2)(b).

[42] For an example of the kind of facts involved, see the first reported cases on EOs, *Russell v W*, 1998 Fam. L.R. 25.

[43] "Family home" is defined very widely—see s.76(12). The main thrust of the definition is that it is a family residence where the child ordinarily resides with the parent(s) or other carer(s).

is not met but there *is* a risk of significant harm, the local authority should seek a CPO, or possibly a CAO. Even if it does not do so the sheriff can choose *ex proprio motu* to grant a CPO rather than an EO[44]; *and*

3. before an EO can be made, there must be a person left in the family home who is capable of caring for the child and any other member of the family, and who will go on residing in the family home.

7–51 On top of these requirements, the sheriff *shall not* make an exclusion order if it appears to him to be "unjustifiable or unreasonable" to do so.[45] The sheriff is to have regard to all the circumstances of the case, when considering if an EO would be unjustifiable or unreasonable, but in particular[46] to the conduct of members of the child's family, the respective needs and financial resources of members of the family, and the extent to which the family home or any item in it, is used in connection with a trade or profession.[47] It may well be asked how the making of an EO could ever be unreasonable, given the paramountcy of the welfare of the child[48] if tests 1 and 2 above have been met, but what this part of s.76 clearly seems to contemplate is a balancing exercise between the potential trauma to the child of removal and the proprietary/ occupancy rights of a resident alleged abuser—rather as the Matrimonial Homes (Family Protection) (Scotland) Act 1981 seeks to strike a balance between protection of the abused spouse or cohabitant, and the occupancy and property rights of the allegedly violent or threatening spouse. It would seem viable, then, for a suspected abusive father to put up as defence to an EO that the mother has enough money to move out with the child(ren) instead— although this does not seem prima facie to be the best option for the child. Such a father has further backing from the principle of minimum intervention, as discussed above, which also applies to a decision to make an EO.[49]

7–52 The sheriff in deciding whether to make, vary or discharge an EO must so far as practicable have regard to the views of the child concerned taking account of its age and maturity.[50]

---

[44] s.76(8).

[45] s.76(9).

[46] s.76(9) and (10).

[47] In particular, the sheriff must consider if residence in the family home is required as a condition of employment, and the consequences for the family of breaking such a condition, e.g. eviction of the whole family—s.76(9)–(11). An example might be where the named person has lodgings in a pub as a condition of the job, or is a live-in caretaker or janitor.

[48] s.16(1).

[49] s.16(3) and (4)(b)(i).

[50] s.16(2) and (4)(b)(i).

Procedure, Effect and Duration

Before a sheriff can make an EO, the "named person" must be given **7–53** a chance to be heard or represented before the sheriff.[51] However, in emergency circumstances an interim EO can be made forthwith having the same effect as an EO, without hearing the person to be excluded, so long as the sheriff is satisfied the test in s.76(2) is met.[52] A full hearing at which the named father has a right to present his case must then be held within three working days.[53] At this hearing the sheriff can either make a final order or confirm, vary or recall the interim order.[54] It appears that the obligation to consult the child applies to interim EOs in the same terms as it does to ordinary EOs.[55] But since that obligation is only to consult the child "so far as practicable", in many cases there will probably be deemed insufficient time to notify and consult the child.

The effect of the EO is to suspend the named person's rights of **7–54** occupancy (if any), and to prevent him entering the home without the permission of the local authority.[56] Thus permission to re-enter from the excluded person's spouse or partner, even if they own the home, is ineffective, and such entry would be a breach of the order. Without further provision, breach of an EO would have to be enforced by application to a civil court. But as with the Matrimonial Homes Act, 1981, an EO can be given extra "teeth" by the addition of an interdict to prevent the named person entering the house, backed up by the attachment to the interdict of a power of arrest for breach.[57] This power of arrest, which must be notified to the excluded person to be effective,[58] enables a police constable to arrest without warrant the excluded person if he has reasonable cause to suspect that person is in breach of the interdict.[59] After such arrest, the excluded person can either be liberated if the police are satisfied there is no further likelihood of breach of the interdict, or they can detain him until he is brought to court for the offence of criminal breach of the interdict.[60] In such circumstances, the court appearance must take place on the first day after the arrest, excluding

---

[51] 1995 Act, s.76(3). The sheriff must also consider the views of any person who under Rules of Court must be notified that the EO has been made. This includes the person who will continue to care for the child within the family home.

[52] s.76(4).

[53] Act of Sederunt (Child Care and Maintenance Rules) 1997, r.3.36.

[54] 1995 Act, s.76(5). An interim EO can also only last a maximum of six months: *Glasgow City Council v H*, 2003 S.L.T. 948 .

[55] s.76(12).

[56] s.77(1).

[57] 1995 Act, ss.77 and 78. Application to attach the interdict to the EO is made under s.77(2) and (3). Application for the power of arrest can be made *only* by the local authority (not, e.g. the resident spouse) "at any time while an exclusion order has effect": s.78(2).

[58] s.78(3).

[59] s.78(6).

[60] s.78(7), (10)–(14).

weekends and court holidays[61]; the procurator-fiscal can also decide not to take any criminal proceedings.[62] If it appears to the sheriff that the interdict was broken and there is a substantial risk of violence by the excluded person against any member of the family, or any other appropriate person, then the excluded person can be detained for up to two days.[63] All this applies to interim EOs in the same terms.[64]

7–55   As well as an interdict prohibiting entry to the home, a sheriff can also attach to an EO a warrant for summary ejection, an interdict prohibiting the removal of named items from the home, e.g. the children's clothes or school books, an interdict prohibiting the excluded person from entering or remaining in a specified area in the vicinity of the home, and an interdict prohibiting the excluded person from taking any specified step in relation to the child.[65]

7–56   What if the local authority wishes to exclude the father not only from the family home but from coming into contact with the child at all, perhaps at school or a part-time workplace?[66] In principle, beyond the authority of the exclusion order itself, the authority has no right to restrict a father's contact with the child as the order has no effect on his PRRs including the right (and duty) to maintain contact.[67] One solution might be to ask the sheriff to add an interdict prohibiting the named person from "entering or remaining in a specified area *in the vicinity of the* home".[68] But this would depend on whether the school, for example, fell within that "vicinity".[69] Visiting the child at school might be classified as "taking any step" in relation to the child and an interdict could possibly be sought on that basis.[70] Another alternative might be to ask the sheriff to make an "order regulating the contact between the child and the named person".[71] Such an "order" would override a married father's automatic right to contact with his child while not living with him or her, and if necessary, a power of arrest could be obtained and attached for enforcement purposes.[72]

---

[61] s.78(11).

[62] s.78(10)(b).

[63] Not including weekends and court holidays: s.78(13)—a father caught trying violently to break into the family home on the Thursday night before a public holiday weekend might therefore be committed to jail until the following Wednesday.

[64] s.76(12).

[65] s.77(2).

[66] The child may not be in danger of abuse in a public place but he could be threatened or upset by contact and the authority might also wish to prevent the father intimidating the child not to give evidence in court or to a children's hearing.

[67] Unless, e.g. a children's hearing had made a supervision order with condition relating to contact—see Ch.8.

[68] s.77(3)(d).

[69] Similar problems of interpretation have arisen in the past in relation to Matrimonial Homes Act interdicts and exclusion orders. See Ch.11.

[70] 1995 Act, s.77(3)(e). This subsection does *not* require that the specified step taken be one taken "in the fulfilment of parental responsibilities or exercise of parental rights": *cf.* s.11(2)(f).

[71] s.77(3)(f).

[72] s.78(1).

An EO lasts for a maximum of six months.[73] However a second or **7–57**
subsequent EO may be sought immediately, and on the same set of
facts.[74] A sheriff can direct that it terminates earlier, or it may be
varied or recalled.[75] This time limit is only intended to allow the local
authority and the family a breathing space to consider how best to
secure the child's welfare permanently, e.g. by voluntary exclusion.
Application can be made to the sheriff to have the EO varied or
recalled by the authority, the excluded person, the non-excluded
spouse or partner[76] or any other person left in the family home caring
for the child(ren). The statute makes no explicit reference to appeals
from an EO but it has been held that appeal lies to the Sheriff
Principal[77]

Exclusion Orders and Sale of the Family Home

One response by a person who is named in an application for com- **7–58**
pulsory exclusion under s.76 may be to threaten to sell the family
home, if they are sole or co-owner. In the Matrimonial Homes
(Family Protection)(Scotland) Act 1981 ("the 1981 Act"), prejudice
to the occupancy rights of the non-entitled spouse who has excluded
an entitled spouse is avoided by means of conveyancing devices:
specifically, a third party who buys the house in question or part of
the house cannot enter and prejudice the occupancy of the non-
entitled spouse, and the existence of a non-entitled spouse must be
declared when missives are entered for sale of the house.[78] Sections
76–80 of the 1995 Act contain no equivalent provisions, probably
because it was envisaged that the 1981 Act protection would cover the
situation. However, this may still leave some problems, e.g. if the child
is left living with someone who does not qualify for protection under
the 1981 Act, such as an elder sibling or grandmother, in which case
the house is still vulnerable to sale.

Permanency Planning for Children: Parental Responsibilities Orders

A parental responsibilities order (hereafter "PRO") is sought by a **7–59**
local authority as part of long-term planning to safeguard the future
of a child when it seems that reintegration of that child into the family
home is unlikely and undesirable. A local authority may apply to a
sheriff for a PRO. Other options may be adoption, or freeing for
adoption.[79] The provisions relating to PROs in ss.86–89 effectively
replace the procedure formerly found in ss.16–18A of the Social Work

---

[73] s.79(1).
[74] *Glasgow City Council v H*, 2003 S.L.T. 948.
[75] s.79(2)(a) and (b).
[76] "Partners" are persons who live together in a family home as if they were husband
and wife (s.79(4)).
[77] *Glasgow City Council v H*, 2003 S.L.T. 948.
[78] See further Ch.11.
[79] See Ch.6.

(Scotland) Act 1968. It is likely that both PROs and freeing for adoption orders will be replaced by a single "permanency order" under the Adoption (Scotland) Bill 2006. These new orders are discussed more fully in Ch.6.

7–60   Under the 1968 Act, a local authority could remove parental rights from parents by an administrative resolution, leaving it to the parents to oppose their action in the courts. This was heavily criticised as placing an unfair burden on parents, particularly as the parents concerned were likely to be those least able to harness the legal system to their advantage. Under the 1995 Act, s.86, the local authority must take the initiative to apply to the sheriff for a PRO. The sheriff then has a discretion whether to make an order transferring parental responsibilities and rights from the parents to the authority, if he is satisfied that *each* "relevant person" has either unconditionally consented to the making of the order, or that one or more grounds are established in respect of that "relevant person".[80] These grounds are that the "relevant person":

   (i) is not known, cannot be found or is incapable of consenting; or
  (ii) is withholding agreement unreasonably; or
 (iii) has persistently failed without reasonable cause to fulfil one or more of certain parental responsibilities. For a parent who is living with the child, these are the duties to safeguard and promote the child's health, development and welfare. For a parent not living with the child, this means the duty to maintain regular contact with the child; or
 (iv) has seriously ill-treated the child and their reintegration into the same household as that person is unlikely.[81]

7–61   These grounds are identical to those for the making of an adoption or freeing for adoption order, which is appropriate as both are long-term solutions for children involving transfer of PRRs from natural parents to other persons.[82] A "relevant person" is a person who is a parent *or* who for the time being has parental rights in relation to a child.[83] However, "parent" is not defined in Pt II of the 1995 Act. For consistency with the adoption legislation, it should mean only a parent who holds parental responsibilities[84]; however, this will need to be established by the courts. Note that consent or an alternative ground has to be established in respect of *each* relevant person.

---

[80] s.86(2).
[81] s.86(2)(b).
[82] See discussion of the case law relating to these grounds in paras 6.42 *et seq*. At least some of the grounds for assumption of parental rights under the 1968 Act were far more morally accusatory and therefore more controversial than the current grounds.
[83] s.86(4).
[84] Adoption (Scotland) Act 1978, s.65(1) as amended by 1995 Act, Sch.2, para.29. Norrie, *Children (Scotland) Act 1995*, (W. Green, 2nd edn, 2005) supports this view.

In deciding if a ground is met, the sheriff will have to have regard to **7–62** the usual three over-arching principles, i.e. the paramountcy of the child's welfare, the need not to make an order unless it is better to do so than to make none and the need to have due regard for the wishes of the sufficiently mature child.[85] Since a PRO is a relatively extreme order in its effect, it has been suggested that the minimum intervention principle should lead the sheriff to consider if some less drastic option, e.g. making a residence order in favour of a foster carer or relative, might not suffice. A sheriff always has the option of making a s.11 order as he or she thinks fit even if it has not been applied for by a contesting party.[86] If the local authority intends to apply for a PRO in respect of a child who is under a supervision order, then they must ask the hearing to make a report to the court hearing the application.[87]

Effect and Conditions

The effect of the PRO is to transfer all PRRs[88] over the child to the **7–63** local authority; and although it is not actually stated as such, this must presumably remove them from the "relevant persons" in respect of whom grounds have been established.[89] The only explicit exception is that parents retain the right to give or withhold consent to the adoption or freeing for adoption of their child.[90] The natural parents thus lose all rights including the right to have the child living with them, the right to consent to medical treatment and the right to contact with their child.

Furthermore, parents whose rights have been removed by a PRO **7–64** are also stripped of title to apply to the courts for residence or contact under the ordinary provisions of s.11.[91] This has been regarded in recent years as unreasonable given the right to respect or family life under Art.8 of the ECHR; this is one of the reasons why PROs are to be replaced by permanency orders.[92] While PROs still operate, however, the sheriff can impose a condition of contact at the time it is made if he sees it as appropriate.[93] Furthermore, under s.88, the local authority comes under a *duty* to presumptively allow reasonable contact between the child and any "relevant person" or person who used to have a residence or contact order prior to the making of the

---

[85] 1995 Act, s.16.

[86] s.11(2).

[87] s.73(4).

[88] Probably as defined in ss.1(3) and 2(4). It is not clear from s.86 if the parental duty to aliment the child, which is not a duty listed in s.1 of the 1995 Act, is removed by the PRO. However, parents who do not have parental responsibilities under the 1995 Act are not expected to contribute to the care of the child by the local authority under s.78 of the Social Work (Scotland) Act 1968. See Ch.5.

[89] s.86(1).

[90] s.86(3).

[91] s.11(3)(a)(iii) and (4)(d), extending decision in *D v Grampian*, 1996 S.L.T. 519 (H.L.).

[92] See Ch.4, para.4–41.

[93] s.86(5).

PRO, subject, of course, to their paramount duty to safeguard the child's welfare. Also, under the special title given by s.86(3), an application can be made by a person with interest for the sheriff to regulate contact, at any time *during* the duration of the PRO. It is also worth noting that nothing has affected the *child's* right to apply for contact to *the parent* under s.11(5).[94] In any application to make, vary or discharge a PRO, or a s.88 contact order, the normal three overarching principles will apply.[95]

7–65 Application can be made by the parent, the local authority or the child to vary or discharge the PRO at any time.[96] Unless the PRO is earlier discharged, or the child is adopted or freed for adoption, the order terminates when the child reaches 18: this may seem odd given that the child is usually *sui juris* at 16, but it should be remembered that the local authority, like any other "parent", will cease to have *rights* over the child at age 16 and will only continue to have the duty to provide guidance to the child until he or she reaches 18.[97]

Assessment of Local Authority Powers and Duties under Pt II

7–66 The powers and duties discussed above and laid down by the 1995 Act are more comprehensive, more detailed and more hedged about with safeguards and threshold criteria than was ever the case under the 1968 Act. The 1995 Act for the first time laid out the duties owed towards children looked after by the local authority in one place in primary legislation. The accommodation and emergency protection provisions try hard to meet the injunction of Lord Clyde that "removal of a child in a case of alleged abuse is not a remedy of first resort but rather a remedy to be adopted after all other courses have been considered and found to be inadequate".[98] The exclusion order in particular is an ingenious and yet obvious concept. The 1995 Act also tried to ensure that the provisions for taking children into long-term state care conformed to the basic requirements of natural justice. Parental responsibility orders, like freeing for adoption orders, have however been found to be unsatisfactory in terms of respect for the Art.8 rights of birth parents and families, and are likely soon to be replaced by more Strasbourg-confirm "permanency orders".

7–67 However, certain points should be made. First, it is all very well to impose statutory duties on local authorities, but it remains unclear if these duties can be enforced in court by members of the public. The leading English House of Lords judgment of *X v Bedfordshire County Council* in 1995 made it seem extremely unlikely that any child, or

---

[94] This is particularly so as s.88(1) is actually phrased to emphasise that contact is the right of the *child*, not the parent. But see also the problems highlighted about under-16 applications for parental rights in para.4–42.

[95] s.16.

[96] s.86(5).

[97] s.1(b)(ii), 1(2) and 2(7).

[98] Clyde Report, para.16.9.

indeed parent, could ever claim damages for the fail... authority to fulfil a public statutory duty. An effective immun... action was given to public authorities performing statutory duties. There are good reasons of policy, which clearly informed this judgment, why it is undesirable that aggrieved members of the public should be able, *e.g.* to sue an authority for failing to remove a child in need into care. Social workers are limited by lack of resources from being able to perform their duties to 100 per cent perfection; they are also in the unfortunate position of being "damned if they do" remove a child from home and "damned if they don't", as in several child abuse scandals where children were left with deficient parents and suffered as a result. But the blanket immunity given local authorities performing social welfare functions by *X v Beds*, was controversial in discounting any accountability of social services to parents and children at all, even where there had been plain negligence. *X v Beds* was subsequently challenged in the European Court of Human Rights on the grounds that by denying title to sue, it breached Art.6 of the ECHR, which guarantees access to justice and a fair hearing in court. However, to many experts' surprise, the view of the English courts appeared to be vindicated, with some caveats, by the Strasbourg court.[1] The position is still highly complex,[2] and, in Scotland remains to be tested.

Secondly, the overwhelming detail and complexity of the provisions relating to emergency protection, and particularly CPOs, in Pt II of the 1995 Act, may be difficult for its users to understand; it is, perhaps, overkill. In England, reportedly very little use has been made of the analogous rights given to parents by the Children Act 1989 to apply for immediate setting aside of emergency protection orders. In Scotland, parents may well also be choosing to ignore the complex procedure for opposing CPOs and simply wait to deny the grounds of referral when the case reaches the children's hearing eight days later. This is very much the picture which Francis and McGhee found in their study of CPOs and CAOs taken by local authorities in Scotland between 1995 and 2000.[3]   **7–68**

Thirdly, s.76 exclusion orders also seem to have been under-used in the 10 years since the 1995 Act came into force. There have only been, to this author's knowledge, two reported cases on EOs in the last 10 years. Total numbers obtained will of course be different, but Francis and McGhee reported only 25 being obtained between 1997 and   **7–69**

---

[99] For a full account see Edwards, (1996) 1 Edin. L. Rev. 115.

[1] *Z v UK* and *TP and LM v UK*, Apps No 29392/95 and 28945/95.

[2] e.g. some claims against local authorities as vicariously liable for the personal negligence of their servants remain possible: so do actions against local authorities in respect of breach of common law, not statutory, duties, e.g. when education authorities are negligent by allowing bullying at school—see, e.g. *Scott v Lothian Regional Council*, 1999 Rep. L.R. 15.

[3] See n.94, above.

displaying the same reluctance to
...r own property which was seen in the
...al Homes Act.[4] On the other hand it may
, and the enforcement of an exclusion order
...-excluded spouse or partner does not wish to
...ten be the case). A gap of six months may also
...in practice to make any real changes to the family

7–, ...y, the task of balancing the public duty to intervene in
...s of the child, with private rights to autonomy remains
ex...narily hard. The intervention of human rights law since the
1998 ...ct, which in its nature tends to be "on the side of" the parents
or birth family, and "against" the state, may perhaps make the task
even harder.

---

[4] See Ch.11.

CHAPTER 8

NEEDS NOT DEEDS? THE CHILDREN'S HEARINGS SYSTEM AND BEYOND

In the last chapter we outlined the legal framework within which **8–01** Scots law attempts to provide for children in need of resources, care or protection. The focus of discussion was on the powers and duties of local authorities, how these interact with the rights of the child and the family concerned, and the role of the courts in ensuring accountability for the acts of local authorities. In this chapter, we will look beyond the local authority to consider the role of the children's hearings system. The hearings system, as discussed below, deals with both children in need of care, and children who have committed offences. It is thus not only a crucial part of the Scottish childcare regime, but also by far the most significant component of the juvenile criminal justice system. In the last 10 years, the hearings system's role in both arenas has been increasingly questioned, perhaps especially in relation to juvenile crime. New initiatives to reduce juvenile crime, with a distinctly punitive flavour, as opposed to the hearing's welfarist philosophy, have been introduced: notably the Antisocial Behaviour Orders ("ASBOs") ushered in, in this jurisdiction, by the Antisocial Behavior etc. (Scotland) Act 2004. Other innovations, such as parenting orders, have for the first time in the juvenile justice system, tried to impose responsibilities, not just on young offenders, but on those who may be deemed to be responsible for their behaviour. It is of some concern whether these approaches can be harmoniously integrated into the Scottish welfare-based system. We shall attempt, at the end of the chapter, to formulate some conclusions as to whether the children's hearing can survive, and if so, in what form.

BACKGROUND[1]

The children's hearings system was created by the Social Work **8–02** (Scotland) Act 1968 (hereafter "the 1968 Act"), following the report

---

[1] See further for historical background, Martin *et al*, *Children Out of Court* (1981), Martin and Murray, *The Scottish Juvenile Justice System* (1982) and *Juvenile Justice in Scotland: Twenty Five Years of the Welfare Approach* (Lockyear and Stone (eds), T & T Clark, 1998). For up-to-date facts and statistics, see the Scottish Executive website, the website of the Scottish Children's Reporter Administration ("SCRA"),

of the Kilbrandon Committee[2] which was set up in 1961 with the remit:

> "To consider the provisions of the law of Scotland relating to the treatment of juvenile delinquents and juveniles in need of care and protection or beyond parental control, and, in particular, the constitution, powers, and procedure of the courts dealing with such juveniles, and to report".

8–03 From the very outset, then, the Kilbrandon Committee was charged with considering together two groups of children until then regarded as quite separate: those who were labelled as juvenile offenders or truants, and those who were perceived as being in need of care and protection. The conclusions of the Kilbrandon report were radical. First, the distinction usually drawn between juvenile offenders and children in need of care and protection was seen as being meaningless and unhelpful. Both were "children in trouble".[3] Juvenile delinquency was perceived as a symptom of underlying social or psychological problems, of the child having needs which were not being met by the family or the educational system. The aim of the juvenile justice system, then, should be to meet the needs of such a child, not to punish him or her.

8–04 Secondly, following on from the concept that children who offend, and children in need, should be treated in a uniform way, came the idea that such children should be dealt with not in the ordinary courts, but in a special tribunal where proceedings would be informal and where the welfare of the child would be the paramount concern in making a decision, or "disposal", relating to that child.

8–05 Thirdly, the Committee recommended that these new tribunals (to be known as "children's panels") should be staffed by lay persons rather than by legally trained judges, and should be fora in which the panel members, the child, the parents and involved social workers would be able to talk freely, unrestricted by the rules of legal procedure and evidence which are normally required in a judicial forum. Ideally, lawyers would be unnecessary. Where facts were disputed, e.g. whether a child had actually committed an offence, these should be legally

---

www.scra.gov.uk and www.childrenshearingsscotland.gov.uk. Statistics about the hearings system are now published annually in the *Annual Report of the SCRA*, available online. The two standard legal texts are Kearney, *Children's Hearing and the Sheriff Court* (2nd edn, Butterworths, 2000) and more recently Norrie, *Children's Hearings in Scotland* (2nd edn, W.Green, 2005). An excellent review of the political, historical and criminological background to the hearings system as part of the juvenile justice system in Scotland can be found in McAra, "The Scottish Juvenile Justice System: Policy and Practice" in *Juvenile Justice Systems: International Perspectives* (J. Winterdyk (ed.) (2nd edn, Canadian Scholars Press, 2002)).

[2] *Report of the Committee on Children and Young Persons*, Cmnd.2306 (1964) (hereafter, the "Kilbrandon Report").

[3] This phrase is taken from Kelly, *Introduction to the Scottish Children's Panel* (1996).

established in the courts, where the safeguards of due process would be fully retained, rather than in the welfare-centred tribunal. However, crucially, the court's role would be restricted to proof, and judges would play no part in assessing the needs of the child and making the final disposal. The spheres of *justice*, as found in the courts, and *welfare*, predominant at the children's panel, would therefore be kept separate. The panel, being interested in meeting the child's needs for care and supervision, not in retribution or "justice", would have no powers to punish in the conventional sense, e.g. to fine either child or parents, or to imprison, but only to impose compulsory measures of supervision.

The Kilbrandon Report was published in 1964 and following a **8–06** Government White Paper in 1966,[4] most of the proposals made were accepted and implemented in the 1968 Act. The child tribunal became known as the "children's hearing". Minor changes to the system, such as the introduction of safeguarders,[5] were made by the Children Act 1975. However, the Children (Scotland) Act 1995 recodified and, in several ways, radically altered the scheme of the 1968 Act, following recommendations in, inter alia, the Review of Child Care Law in Scotland, the Clyde Report on Orkney, the White Paper *Scotland's Children*[6] and the Finlayson Report in 1992.[7] Only very minor changes were made by the Family Law (Scotland) Act 2006. As we shall discuss later, the entire system is now under its most far-reaching review since its inception.[8] In contrast to its early years when there was little empirical evidence to back up points of principle, the hearings system has been subject to detailed empirical scrutiny in recent years: both major reviews across the whole system,[9] and individual reports on particularly important parts of the hearing, e.g. home supervision,[10] or reports on piloted innovations, e.g. "fast track" hearings.[11]

Most of the law relating to the hearings' system is now to be found **8–07** in Pt II of the 1995 Act with a few provisions still remaining in the

---

[4] *Social Work and the Community*, Cmnd.3065 (1966).

[5] See para.8–30 below.

[6] Cm.2286 (1993).

[7] Finlayson, *Reporters to Children's Panels: Their Role, Function and Accountability* (1992).

[8] The Scottish Executive launched Phase 1 of its comprehensive review of the children's hearings, *Getting It Right For Every Child*, in 2004. A *Report on Responses* by Stevenson and Brotchie was then released in 2004. In June 2005, *Getting It Right: Proposal for Action* (although limited in scope) was issued. Phase 2 of the consultation is expected in 2006.

[9] Notably Hallett, Murray, Jamieson and Veitch, *The Evaluation of the Children's Hearings in Scotland, Vols 1–4* (Scottish Office Central Research Unit, 1998); and the Edinburgh Study of Youth Transitions and Crime, lead by McAra and Smith, publications available at *www.law.ed.ac.uk/cls/esytc*. See also the external review by the NCH in Scotland, *Where's Kilbrandon Now?* (NCH, 2004)

[10] See Murray, Hallett *et al*, *Home Supervision* (Scottish Executive, 2002).

[11] See the *Fast Track Hearings Research: Interim Report November 2003* (Scottish Executive, 2003) and *Fast Track Children's Hearings Pilot: Final Report of the Evaluation of the Pilot* (2005).

1968 Act. References in this chapter are to the 1995 Act unless otherwise stated.

THE CHILDREN'S HEARINGS SYSTEM: PERSONNEL AND PROCEDURE

The Child

8–08   The children's hearings system deals principally with children up to the age of 16. However, children over 16 but under 18 in respect of whom a supervision requirement remains in force may also come before a hearing.[12] Young persons under 18 who have been prosecuted for offences in the criminal courts may also be remitted to the hearing for disposal, rather than being sentenced by the court; the court may also simply seek the advice of the hearing relating to the disposal of such a case.[13]

Personnel

8–09   The key personnel of the children's hearings system are the members of the children's panel, and an official known as the reporter. Every local government area is under a duty to establish a children's panel whose function is to hear cases referred to the children's hearings system.[14] A children's hearing consists of a chairman (or woman) and two other members, and must include both a man and a woman.[15] The members of the children's panel are theoretically appointed at the discretion of the Secretary of State for Scotland, but in practice appointments are made on the recommendation of the Children's Panel Advisory Committee ("CPAC") established in each local government area.[16] The CPAC is also responsible for the recruitment and training of potential panel members.[17] Panel members are supposed to be lay representatives of their community with some interest in or experience of children and their problems, and are unpaid, although expenses are met.[18] However, they do receive extensive training in relevant areas of law, social work and child psychology.

8–10   The reporter is an official whose primary role is to decide which children should come before a children's hearing. Although a reporter acts on behalf of a single local authority area, since the introduction of the Local Government etc. (Scotland) Act 1994, all reporters have

---

[12] 1995 Act, s.93(2)(b). Supervision requirements are discussed below at paras 8–48 *et seq.*

[13] Criminal Procedure (Scotland) Act 1995, s.49(1).

[14] s.39.

[15] s.39(5).

[16] Sch.1, paras 1 and 3. Small authorities can set up joint CPACs if the Secretary of State agrees (para.8).

[17] Sch.1, para.9.

[18] Sch.1. para.11.

been employed by a national umbrella organisation known as the Scottish Children's Reporter Administration ("SCRA") since April 1, 1996 and not by local authorities.[19] The SCRA was introduced following local government reorganisation, but is also designed to minimise differences in practice between reporters. The SCRA is headed by a Principal Reporter for Scotland. The reporter need not be legally qualified, and may instead draw, for example, on a background in social work or education.[20]

The reporter's role in the hearings system is crucial. His or her function is to receive reports on children who may be in need of compulsory measures of supervision, from sources such as the police, procurators fiscal, social work departments, schools and members of the public[21] and then to investigate to decide if these children should be referred to a hearing.[22] The reporter also provides legal advice where this is required at the hearing itself, and makes applications to the sheriff to have a ground of referral established if this becomes necessary.[23] The reporter should only refer a child to, and arrange for,[24] a hearing if satisfied that: **8–11**

(i) at least one of the "grounds of referral" under s.52(2) (discussed below) is satisfied in respect of the child; *and*
(ii) the child is in need of compulsory measures of supervision.[25] "Supervision" includes measures for the protection, guidance or control of the child.[26]

If the reporter does *not* choose to refer the child to a hearing, he or she may either decide no action is necessary, in which case the child and parents must be informed of this, or refer the case to the local authority, which may then wish to consider if there is a case for action on its part, e.g. an offer to accommodate the child under s.25, or to provide assistance under s.22.[27] In over half of all cases, the reporter decides that no action is either desirable or justified, and in 2003/2004, only 10 per cent of all cases referred ever reached a hearing.[28] Once the reporter **8–12**

---

[19] s.40(2).
[20] s.40(1).
[21] Although anyone may make a referral, in practice around 75–85% of referrals come from the police.
[22] s.56.
[23] See paras 8–44 to 8–45.
[24] The 1995 Act is silent on the territorial jurisdiction of the hearing but to date it has been interpreted as extending to any child habitually or ordinarily resident in Scotland, or not so resident but subject to an existing supervision requirement of the hearing. It is not wholly clear if jurisdiction can be founded on mere presence (as where a non-Scottish habitual resident commits a crime in Scotland during a brief visit). See *Mitchell v S*, 2000 S.L.T. 524, *cf. Walker v C (No.1)*, 2003 S.L.T. 31.
[25] ss.56(6), and 65(1).
[26] s.52(2).
[27] 1995 Act, s.56(4). See further, Ch.7 above.
[28] See *SCRA Annual Report 2003/2004*.

has decided no action is necessary, no hearing can subsequently be arranged based solely on the same set of investigated facts.[29]

8–13   The reporter thus has complete discretion to divert a child out of the children's hearings system if he or she feels that that child is not in need of compulsory supervision or would suffer more than gain by becoming involved in the legal process.[30] This discretion is based on the child's welfare rather than the extent of any alleged offence. For example, it might be clear on the facts that a child has committed an offence of joyriding, once, for a prank; but if the subsequent investigation revealed that the child's family were well able to deal with the situation and no need for intervention was disclosed, then the case would not be pursued. Alternatively, a report of a very minor crime, such as the theft of a carton of milk, might on investigation disclose a family in need of help to control the child, or a child who is not being properly cared for. The reporter's discretion cannot be appealed or reviewed, otherwise than by the public law remedy of judicial review of administrative action. What is clear from the statistics is that the reporter's discretion serves to divert a high percentage of young offenders from becoming involved with the juvenile justice system. In 1994, only 30 per cent of cases referred to the reporter on "offence" grounds were subsequently taken to a hearing. By 2003/2004, this was down to 12.5 per cent—one eighth of those referred. Given continuing empirical findings that minor criminal behaviour is a transient stage that many and perhaps most young persons go through,[31] and grow out of, with interventions and contact with the adult criminal justice system as likely to have a negative effect as a positive one, the reporter plays a crucial diversionary role in filtering off and protecting such young persons from needless stigmatisation and exposure to more experienced offenders.

8–14   It should be noted that although most juvenile offenders will be referred to the children's hearings system, in some very serious cases, children over the age of eight[32] may still be prosecuted in the criminal courts.[33] Such prosecution can be undertaken only on the instructions

---

[29] s.56(5).

[30] Note that the police must report all children they have arrested and detained, who are *not* to be charged with criminal offences in the ordinary courts, to the Principal Reporter. However, the reporter then has a discretion to release the child if he or she does not feel the child is in need of compulsory measures of supervision in which case no hearing will be held (s.63).

[31] Anderson and Kinsey found in a self-reporting study that over two thirds of young persons reported committing at least one offence in the previous nine months and one third reported a moderately serious offence (*Cautionary Tales, A Study of Young People and Crime in Edinburgh* (Scottish Office, Criminal Research Unit, 1993)).

[32] Criminal Procedure (Scotland) Act 1995, s.41.

[33] However a child may still quite validly be referred to the hearing on offence ground, and a proof of that ground undertaken in the Sheriff Court, in respect of a crime which can only be *prosecuted* in the High Court of Justiciary: see *Walker v C (No.2)*, 2003 S.L.T. 293 (rape as offence ground).

of the Lord Advocate or at his instance, and may be brought only in the High Court of Justiciary or the Sheriff Court.[34] In practice, such prosecutions are restricted to serious crimes, such as murder or rape, or those involving a penalty of disqualification from driving.[35]

The Grounds of Referral

The grounds of referral in s.52(2)[36] represent a set of threshold cri- **8–15** teria which must be proven to exist, or be agreed to, by both the child and the parents,[37] before a children's hearing can begin to consider if compulsory measures of supervision are necessary. These grounds are that the child:

(a) is beyond the control of any relevant person;
(b) is falling into bad associations or is exposed to moral danger;
(c) is likely—
    (i) to suffer unnecessarily; or
    (ii) to be impaired seriously in his health and development, due to a lack of parental care;
(d) is a child in respect of whom any of the offences mentioned in Schedule 1 to the Criminal Procedure (Scotland) Act 1995 have been committed;
(e) is, or is likely to become, a member of the same household as a child in respect of whom any of the offences referred to in paragraph (d) above have been committed;
(f) is, or is likely to become, a member of the same household as a person who has committed any of the offences referred to in paragraph (d) above;
(g) is, or is likely to become, a member of the same household as a person in respect of whom an offence under sections 1 to 3 of the Criminal Law (Consolidation) (Scotland) Act 1995 (incest and intercourse with a child by a step-parent or person in position of trust) has been committed by a member of that household;
(h) has failed to attend school regularly without reasonable excuse;
(i) has committed an offence;
(j) has misused alcohol or any drug, whether or not a controlled drug within the meaning of the Misuse of Drugs Act 1971;
(k) has misused a volatile substance by deliberately inhaling its vapour, other than for medicinal purposes (the "glue-sniffing" ground);
(l) is being provided with accommodation by a local authority under section 25, or is the subject of a parental responsibilities order obtained under section 86, of this Act and, in either case,

---

[34] Criminal Procedure (Scotland) Act 1995, s.42.
[35] See Lord Advocate's instructions of August 3, 1987.
[36] Grounds (d) and (g) in s.52(2) were amended by the Criminal Procedure (Consequential Provisions) (Scotland) Act 1995, Sch.4, para.97.
[37] See para.8–40 below.

his behaviour is such that special measures are necessary for his adequate supervision in his interest or the interest of others.

(m) has been referred after an Antisocial Behaviour Order was made in respect of the child (see para.8–65, below).

8–16 The vast majority of referrals to the reporter are on grounds (a) (child beyond parental control), (c) (lack of parental care), (d) (child is a victim of an offence), (h) (truancy), and (i) (child has committed an offence). The grounds of referral are frequently grouped into two classes: "offence" (ground (i)) and "non-offence" grounds (all other grounds). In the early days of the hearings system, the vast majority of referrals to the reporter were on "offence" grounds. In 1994, this was still true: there were 25,735 offence referrals (60 per cent) as compared to 17,189 non-offence referrals (40 per cent). Ten years later, according to the 2003/2004 statistics, the position is exactly reversed, with about 60 per cent referrals on non-offence grounds as against 40 per cent on offence grounds. The number of "offence" referrals as a percentage of total referrals to the reporter declined steadily from the inception of the hearings system till about 1988, since which time it has been fairly stable. By contrast, the percentage of non-offence referrals to the reporter has steadily increased, rising by 156 per cent between 1984 and 1994 and doubling again between 1994 and 2003/2004. This increase is mainly attributed to increased societal sensitivity to, belief in, and investigation of, physical, sexual and emotional child abuse and neglect. The picture overall is of a system which has shifted from being predominantly a forum for dealing with juvenile delinquency, to one which is increasingly dominated, in a way never anticipated by the Kilbrandon reformers, by how to protect children, mainly from their own families.[38]

8–17 At the same time, though, the problem has grown of "persistent" young offenders, who seem to be immune to, or at least hard to rehabilitate using, traditional Kilbrandon methodology and disposals. The *SCRA Annual Report for 2003/4* illustrates this with figures that show the percentage of children re-referred to the reporter on offence grounds steadily rising over the last 5 years: from 33 per cent in 2000/2001 to 37 per cent in 2003/2004. This hard core of repeat or persistent offenders, who do not seem to leave the hearings system save to move to the adult criminal justice regime, has become a key source of governmental and public concern, and reducing the rate of youth re-offending is now one of the explicit aims of the hearings system.

8–18 Some of the grounds of referral have been the subject of significant judicial interpretation.

---

[38] In 2005, in 80% of cases of children identified as at risk, where the source of the abuse or risk was known, that source was one or both of the child's birth parents (*Children's Social Work Statistics 2004–2005* (Scottish Executive)).

Child is Offender (Ground (i))

Since an offence can only be committed by a child aged eight or **8–19** over, ground (i) can only be established in respect of children aged eight or over.[39] An offence by a child must be proven beyond reasonable doubt if either the child or a "relevant person" disputes the accusation.[40]

Child Victim of Sch.1 Offence (Ground (d))

For this ground to be fulfilled, technically the child must be a victim **8–20** of one of the offences listed in Sch.1 to the Criminal Procedure (Scotland) Act 1995. These offences are mainly to do with physical or sexual assault and neglect of children but are limited to crimes committed under Scots criminal law, which is territorial in extent. The courts, however, have been willing to recognise crimes committed under a foreign law, but analogous to a Scottish offence, as founding the ground of referral, since the purpose of the ground is not to prosecute the offender but to protect the child.[41] However, despite the emphasis on protection of the child, a crime cannot be established as committed unless any required element of *mens rea* (criminal intention) is demonstrated to exist, even if it is clear that the *actus reus* (criminal act) has occurred and the child has suffered as a result.[42] Ground (d) can be established even if the offender's crime has become "spent" under the Rehabilitation of Offenders Act.[43]

Child is falling into Bad Association or is exposed to Moral Danger (Ground (b))

Where a child has been referred to the panel under this ground as **8–21** a result of an offence allegedly committed by himself, it remains possible to find that the child has been exposed to "moral danger" although the conduct was that of the child. In *Costanda v M*[44] the only evidence of this ground was that the child had himself committed an offence, namely lewd and libidinous behaviour with his 10-year-old cousin. On appeal to the Inner House, Lord Coulsfield made two points:

(i) as the whole basis of the ground raised was the commission of an offence by the child, proof must be not only of "moral danger" but whether the child has committed the offence (s.52(2)(i)), and as a result it had to be beyond reasonable doubt and by corroborated evidence;

---

[39] *Merrin v S*, 1987 S.L.T. 193.
[40] See below, paras 8–44 *et seq.*
[41] *E v Kennedy*, 1992 G.W.D. 25-1400 and *S v Kennedy*, 1996 S.L.T. 1087.
[42] *Kennedy v A*, 1993 S.L.T. 1134.
[43] *Kennedy v M*, 1992 G.W.D. 39 2283.
[44] 1997 S.L.T. 1396; 1997 G.W.D. 16-704.

(ii) if the offence was proven, it would be possible to find "exposure to moral danger" notwithstanding the only behaviour proven was that of the child. A practical approach had to be taken and the "moral danger" ground did not necessarily imply that there had to be an *external* corrupting factor proven.

Lack of Parental Care (Ground (c))

8–22   Since this ground requires only that the child is "likely" to suffer unnecessarily due to lack of parental care, it can be established even where suffering has not yet occurred, for example, in the most extreme case, where a baby has just been born, and is in the care of a parent who is known to be incapable of adequate childcare due, for example, to drug or alcohol addiction.[45] "Parental care" is undefined but must be related to the duties of parents now detailed in s.1 of the 1995 Act, to promote the child's health, development and welfare. The test of whether parental care is adequate or not is an objective one: thus a parent cannot, for example, argue that they were acting in the child's welfare by refusing to allow that child medical treatment on religious or conscientious grounds, if objectively the child is suffering due to the lack of medical care.[46] However, the objective standard does not require parents to meet some ideal level of care which might be provided by some other parent; only to provide the care which would be expected of parents by a reasonable person.[47] Since there is no proviso that the lack of parental care be "without reason", it appears there is no defence if parents are unavoidably prevented, e.g. by lack of money, or ill health, from providing adequate care for the child.

Child Member of Same Household as Child Victim, or Perpetrator, of Offence (grounds (e), (f) and (g))

8–23   In all these grounds, issues arise as to what constitutes membership of a household. It is clearly established that a "household" does not

---

[45] *cf.* the English House of Lords case of *D v Berkshire County Council* [1987] 1 All E.R. 20 where a child was made a ward of court immediately after birth on care and protection grounds; also *McGregor v L*, 1981 S.L.T. 194. The Scottish Executive announced plans in May 2006 (*Hidden Harm—Next Steps: Supporting Children and Working with Parents* (Scottish Executive)) for immediate and in some cases drastic intervention when children were exposed to risk from drug dependent parents: see previously *Hidden Harm: Responding to the Needs of Children of Problem Drug Users* (Scottish Executive, June 2003) and Scottish Executive response thereto, October 2004. It is clear that removal of children from seriously addicted parents is promoted: Justice Minister Cathy Jamieson said: "Everyone accepts that taking a child away from its parents is a heart wrenching decision to make. It is a step that should never be taken lightly. But I am convinced that where a child is placed in serious danger by parents who are addicted to drugs, it is the safety of the child that must always come first".

[46] *Finlayson, Petr*, 1989 S.C.L.R. 601.

[47] *D v Sinclair*, 1995 G.W.D. 19-1053.

just refer to a simple house or geographical location. In *McGregor v H*, Lord President Emslie defined a household as:

> "a family unit or something akin to a family unit—a group of persons, held together by a particular kind of tie who normally live together, even if individual members of the group may be temporarily separated from it".[48]

This dictum has been interpreted as follows:

(i) child A continues to be a member of the same household as child B, who has been the *victim* of an offence, even if B has left the household temporarily, e.g. to live with foster parents, and no longer inhabits the family home he previously used to share with child A[49];

(ii) child A continues to be a member of the same household as child B, even if child B died some time before the date at which the ground is to be established.[50] This extends the dictum in *McGregor v H* to cover *permanent* absence from the household, and would also apply where child B did not die but permanently left the household, e.g. to live with adoptive parents[51];

(iii) child A continues to be a member of the same household as the *perpetrator* of an offence, even if that person moves out to live elsewhere, for so long as there is reason to believe that person still has links to, or contact with, child A or other members of the household.[52]

In all these cases, it would avoid the purpose of the grounds of refer- **8–24** ral in s.52(2)(e), (f) and (g), if the ground could be defeated by moving either the offender or the victim physically out of the household for a short while. According to the Inner House, therefore, neither the passage of time, comings and goings (temporary or permanent) in the household nor the gender of the occupants has any crucial impact on the identity of the household.[53] What matters is the purposive question of whether the household is still held together by "ties of affection and regular contact",[54] so that there is cause to fear that a child within that household is at risk of abuse or corruption from another member of the household.[55]

---

[48] 1983 S.L.T. 626 at 628.
[49] *McGregor v H*, 1983 S.L.T. 626.
[50] *A v Kennedy*, 1993 S.C.L.R. 107, where child B had in fact died several years before child A was born.
[51] As in *Cunningham v M*, 2004 S.L.T. (Sh Ct) 73.
[52] *Kennedy v R's Curator ad Litem*, 1993 S.L.T. 295.
[53] *A v Kennedy*, above.
[54] Cited also in *Cunningham v M*, above, n.51.
[55] See Lord President Hope at p.300 in *Kennedy v R 's Curator ad Litem*, above.

PROCEDURE AT THE CHILDREN'S HEARING

Attendance

8–25   If the reporter feels that ground(s) of referral exist in respect of a child and that the child is in need of compulsory measures of supervision, then he or she should arrange for a hearing to be convened. Prior to the hearing, the reporter may arrange for a "business meeting" to be held in order to discuss any aspects of procedure which need to be settled before the hearing proper begins,[56] e.g. who is entitled to attend the hearing or should be allowed to attend at the discretion of the hearing chairman. The hearing meets in private, and no persons other than those strictly necessary for the proper consideration of the case should be present.[57] The child who is the subject of the hearing now has both the duty, and an absolute *right* to attend at all stages of the procedure, even if he or she is too young to understand the full import of the proceedings or may suffer from hearing some of the evidence.[58] However, the child's *duty* to attend can be dispensed with by the hearing (or a business meeting) if the child has been referred as the victim of an offence, or in any case if it would be detrimental to the interests of the child to attend: this provision is likely to be used routinely in the case of very young children.[59]

8–26   Where the child fails to attend the hearing, either the hearing or the Principal Reporter can issue a warrant to compel him or her to attend on cause shown that it is necessary, in which case the child once found will be taken to a place of safety.[60] A hearing must then be convened to consider the child's case on the next working day where practicable.[61] The child can only be kept in the place of safety by virtue of the warrant for seven days, or until the hearing is first convened to consider the case if this is earlier.[62] If the hearing needs to be continued, and there is a fear the child will abscond, or the child needs to be kept in a place of safety for his or her own protection, then the hearing can grant a warrant to keep the child in a place of safety for up to 22 days.[63] Conditions can be attached to the warrant, including a condition that the child be kept in secure accommodation.[64] The reporter

---

[56] s.64.

[57] s.43.

[58] 1995 Act, s.45(1)(a) and (b). This clears up the controversy existing prior to the 1995 Act as to whether a child could be excluded from his or her own hearing, e.g. on welfare grounds. See *Sloan v B*, 1991 S.L.T. 530 and Norrie, "Excluding Children From Children's Hearings", 1993 S.L.T. (News) 67. Note that a business meeting is *not* a stage of the hearing: s.93(1).

[59] s.45(2). This is a matter that will normally be considered at a "business meeting"—see above.

[60] s.45(3)–(6).

[61] s.45(7).

[62] s.45(6).

[63] s.66(1)–(3).

[64] ss.66(6) and 70(10).

can apply to the hearing to extend the warrant for a further 22 days on cause shown, with or without variation of any condition imposed, and this such application can be made more than once.[65] However, the child can only be detained by warrant for a maximum of 66 days[66] unless a warrant for further detention is sought from a sheriff.[67] The sheriff has an unlimited discretion as to how long the warrant should last.[68] Any warrant imposed by a hearing can be appealed to the sheriff, and then to the Inner House, or to the sheriff principal and thence by his leave to the Inner House.[69]

In some cases, a hearing will have been convened as a legal require- **8–27** ment because a child has been removed to a place of safety by virtue of a CPO obtained by a local authority or some other person. Once a child has been removed under a CPO, then unless it is subsequently recalled by the sheriff, or the child liberated by the reporter, a hearing must be convened to consider the child's case by the eighth working day after the day on which the CPO was implemented.[70] We considered the complex procedural steps following a CPO in detail in Ch.7, at paras 7.36 *et seq.* A hearing may also be convened where an ASBO or interim ASBO has been made in respect of a child: see para.8.65 below. In such a case, a special ground of referral is regarded as already having been established, and there is no need either for proof or acceptance of a ground of referral,[71] so the hearing can proceed straight to merits and disposal.

Apart from the child him or herself, the other parties with a right **8–28** to attend the hearing are members of the press,[72] representatives of the Council on Tribunals[73] and any "relevant persons", who also have a duty to attend unless it would be unreasonable to require their attendance.[74] "Relevant persons" include any persons with parental responsibilities or rights in respect of the child under Pt I of the 1995 Act, and any person who ordinarily has charge of, or control over, the child.[75] This automatically includes the mother of the child,[76] the father who is or has been married to the mother[77] and the cohabiting

---

[65] s.66(5).

[66] s.66(8).

[67] s.67.

[68] s.67(2).

[69] 1995 Act, s.51. The appeal to the sheriff from the hearing imposing the warrant must be heard within 3 days or the warrant ceases to have effect: s.51(8).

[70] s.65(2).

[71] Antisocial Behaviour etc. (Scotland) Act 2004, s.12(1) and s.12(3) and (4) amending s.52(2) and s.65(1) of the 1995 Act.

[72] 1995 Act, s.43(3)(b). They can, however, be excluded if this is necessary in the interests of the child or they are causing significant distress to the child (s.43(4)). See also para.8–31.

[73] s.43(3)(a).

[74] 1995 Act, s.45(8). Attendance can be enforced by fines.

[75] 1995 Act, s.93(2)(b). See *S v Lynch*, 1997 S.L.T. 1377.

[76] s.3(1)(a).

[77] s.3(1)(b).

unmarried father, step-parent, relative or, indeed, any other person who takes everyday care of the child. This definition has also been held to include (at least some) foster parents.[78] But it excludes the unmarried father without automatic PRRs, or any other relative who does not care regularly for the child. Any person can, however, be allowed to attend at the discretion of the chairman of the hearing.[79] Normally, social workers associated with the case will be allowed to attend under this discretion.

8–29 What, if anything, can a relative do, if they wish to put their views to the hearing but the chairperson does not choose to extend an invitation to attend? In a number of cases,[80] unmarried fathers without PRRs sought to obtain rights to, variously, attend the hearing, be appointed as a "guardian" and be declared a "relevant person" by virtue of an application under s.11 for parental rights and responsibilities. These attempts have however largely been repelled, on the sensible grounds that: (i) the rights sought are largely for the benefit of the adult, not the child; and (ii) that a s.11 order should not be used as a back-door method to undermine the right of the hearing chairperson to decide who was allowed to attend the hearing. It is likely that most of the problems in this area will in practice be resolved with the granting of automatic PRRs to unmarried fathers who are registered as the child's father after the coming into force of the FLSA 2006.

Representation and Legal Aid

8–30 To meet the child's needs, the hearing must consider in every case whether it is necessary to appoint a safeguarder,[81] an official who has a function similar to that of a curator *ad litem* in ordinary court proceedings and who is often, though not necessarily, a lawyer. The safeguarder's role is to discover and represent the best interests of the child to the court, but not to represent the *wishes* of the child, which may diverge. It was originally necessary for there to be a conflict of interest between parent and child before a safeguarder could be appointed, but this is no longer the case. Safeguarders were

---

[78] *S v N*, 2002 S.L.T. 589, which affirmed the approach that had applied under s.93's predecessor in the Social Work (Scotland) Act 1968 as was set out in *Kennedy v H*, 1988 S.L.T. 586 and *C v Kennedy*, 1991 S.C. 68. A short-term foster carer might not however be regarded as "ordinarily" having control of the child. Note that if *X v Y* (2002) Fam. L.R. 58 (discussed at para.4–82) was to be followed, it would seem to imply that a same-sex partner, even if a cohabiting co-carer, would not be treated as a "relevant person". This interpretation is doubted by the author. There appears, perhaps oddly, to be no special provision making a same-sex civil partner under the Civil Partnership Act 2004 a "relevant person" in respect of the child of their partner.

[79] Children's Hearings Rules 1996, r.13.

[80] See *L v H*, 1996 S.C.L.R. 285; *G v H*, 1999 G.W.D. 24-1124; *P v P*, 1999 S.C.L.R. 679; *T v A*, 2001 S.C.L.R. 647.

[81] 1995 Act, s.41(1). Safeguarders cannot, however, be appointed in applications for child protection orders—s.41(2).

introduced into the hearings system in 1985,[82] but at least initially relatively little use was made of them.[83] As discussed at para.8.35 below, the role of some legally-trained safeguarders has now been substantially expanded to provide access to legal representation for children at some, though not all, hearings.

Both parents and the child are allowed to bring along one person **8–31** to accompany them to the hearing.[84] This may be a supportive person such as a friend, but may equally well be a lawyer. As we saw in Ch.2, a child of sufficient capacity may instruct a lawyer independently of his parents.[85] Apart from this very limited window of opportunity, the Kilbrandon vision, as earlier discussed, was that the hearing would benefit from being a relatively informal tribunal, without the involvement of lawyers for children or parents, or judges, or prosecutors. Accordingly, in principle (and as is normal with other tribunals, such as employment tribunals) legal aid was not made available for representation at the hearing, but only if the case was appealed to the Sheriff Court or the Inner House. Limited aid is available for non-representational legal advice and assistance, e.g. advice before the hearing; and some lawyers chose to provide their services free or *pro bono* to children or families; but, largely, this prohibition ensured that lawyers were absent from the actual hearing.

The blanket non-availability of legal aid for representation of the **8–32** child was found to be contrary to Art.6(1) of the European Convention on Human Rights ("ECHR") in the leading case of *S v Miller*.[86] This was the first major human rights challenge to the legality of the hearings system after the coming into force of the Human Rights Act 1998. The Inner House (First Division, comprising of the Lord President (Rodger), Lord Penrose and Lord Macfadyen) first held that the children's hearings were a civil, as opposed to a criminal, tribunal. There was thus no absolute entitlement to legal aid for every child appearing before the hearing, as would have been required if the hearing in question had fallen under Art.6(3). Nor was there

---

[82] By the Children Act 1975, s.66 (now repealed).

[83] In 1994, 421 safeguarders were appointed in approximately 5% of all children's hearings. By 2000, there were about 200 appointed across Scotland who handled between four and 12 cases per year. The main bottleneck in use of safeguarders appeared to be poor recruitment levels due to inadequate renumeration. The proportion of cases with a safeguarder however grew from less than 1% at inception to more than 9% in 1999/2000 (Hill, Lockyer, Morton, Batchelor and Scott, *Scotland's Children: Children (Scotland) Act 1995 Research Findings No.1, The Role of Safeguarders in Scotland* (Scottish Executive)).

[84] Children's Hearings Rules 1996, r.11.

[85] Paras 2–38 *et seq.*

[86] 2001 S.L.T. 531. See further Edwards, "*S v Miller:* The End of the Childrens' Hearings System As We Know It?", 2001 S.L.T. (News) 187. See for other human rights challenges to the hearings' system thus far, *C v Miller*, 2003 (October) SCOLAG 185, in which minor procedural errors were not held to imply a breach of Art.6, and *Martin v N*, 2004 S.C. 358, discussed below at para.8–33.

such a right even for every child appearing on an *offense* ground of referral. Lord Penrose remarked that,

> "the sole purpose of the hearing is to find a solution to the child's problems which best suits the child's needs on a proper application of the welfare principle".

8–33 The proceedings as a whole, therefore, were not characterised as criminal proceedings, even where the ground of referral was (as in S's case) based on an offence committed by the child.[87]

Was legal aid required even if the hearings fell only within the requirements of Art.6(1)? It was already clear from the jurisprudence of the European Court of Human Rights in Strasbourg in *Airey*'s case, that an absolute bar on legal aid could be seen as unfair, and thus a breach of Art.6(1).[88] The Scottish Executive argued strongly that the reason legal aid was not available was to maintain the informality and child-orientated approach of the hearings system. These arguments were, however, rejected. Without access to legal aid, and hence legal representation, it could not be guaranteed that "[no] child would ever be unable to conduct his own case effectively before the hearing". Furthermore, the Lord President pointed out, lawyers were already appearing on a sporadic basis without any apparent destabilising of the system. In such circumstances, it was better to put legal representation on an equal footing rather than leaving it largely available only to those with the means to pay. The Inner House also held that the defect in process was not cured by the availability of legal aid at an appeal stage, since by that time prejudice to the child might have already become embedded. Accordingly, as matters stood, there was a breach of Art.6(1).[89]

8–34 If access to free legal representation was essential in *some* hearings, then which hearings would those be? Clearly allowing legal aid for every child at every hearing would not only be expensive to the public purse, but potentially catastrophic for the character of the hearings system which might be suddenly flooded by lawyers. The Inner House

---

[87] 2001 S.L.T. 531 at [50]. On determining whether the hearings were criminal or civil in nature, see also Lord President at [10]–[24] and Lord Macfadyen at [10]–[50]. See also para.8–44 below.

[88] *Airey v Ireland*, Series A No.32 (1979). See also *Benhan v UK*, Reports, 1996—III 738

[89] However the lack of availability of legal representation in the past does not mean that the disposals made by all hearings before *S v Miller* are retrospectively invalidated, unless there is proof of actual unfairness leading to actual prejudice which had not been corrected by review or appeal remedies available : *M v Caldwell*, 2001 S.L.T. (Sh Ct) 106. In *S v Miller (No.2)*, 2001 S.L.T. 1304, it was held that *S v Miller* itself did not require the court to make a formal declaration of incompatibility with the ECHR as the legal aid point was to be addressed by regulations. See also Jamieson, "*S v Miller*: Should A Declaration of Incompatibility be Made?", 2001 S.L.T. (News) 137.

offered some guidance as to which cases should be afforded free representation[90] including:

1) hearings where there might be a deprivation of liberty, e.g. those potentially leading to the making of a supervision requirement with a condition of secure accommodation;
2) hearings involving very young children[91] or those of "limited intelligence or limited social skills";
3) hearings involving difficult issues of law, e.g. defences such as provocation or self-defence, or where there are complicated documents and reports to consider;
4) generally, any case of such "complexity" that legal aid is demanded, bearing in mind the *Airey* requirement that the child must have *effective* access to justice.[92]

The Lord President also made the point that the need for legal aid may arise at either the "grounds of referral" stage or the "disposal" stage.

In response to *S v Miller*, the Children's Hearings (Legal **8–35** Representation) (Scotland) Rules 2002[93] were introduced.[94] The 2002 Rules provide for children to be represented for free, *not* by ordinary solicitors, but only by "legal representatives" who are drawn from the panels of safeguarders and curators *ad litem* created more or less simultaneously.[95] "Legal representatives" must be both a member of one of these panels and hold a current solicitor's practicing certificate.[96] It would appear that it remains competent for an "ordinary" solicitor to represent children at the hearings under r.11 of the Children's Hearings (Scotland) Rules 1996.[97] Appointment of a "legal representative" will not preclude appointment of an ordinary safeguarder. The test to determine whether a "legal representative" should be appointed is taken straight from *S v Miller*, namely: is it required to allow the child to "effectively participate" or is there a possibility the child may be placed in secure accommodation?[98] The

---

[90] See Lord Macfadyen at [62] and Lord Penrose at [74].

[91] Although note that this will not include the cases of children too young to accept or deny the grounds of referral as these will transmit automatically to the Sheriff Court for proof, where legal aid is already available. The age group envisaged in *S v Miller* thus seems to be roughly 5–12.

[92] The bar on legal aid and possible infringement of Art.6 was not addressed by the Court in *S v Miller*.

[93] SSI 2002/63, hereinafter "the 2002 Rules".

[94] These came into effect on February 23, 2002. At the time, the Scottish Executive indicated that these would be a stop-gap solution, with a more permanent solution to follow. The 2005 *Getting it Right* consultation review paper (see n.8) notes only the intention to place a duty on the SCRA to "ensure the provision of legal representation for children, where this is necessary".

[95] See: SSI 2001 Nos. 476 and 477 respectively.

[96] r.5.

[97] See para.8–31, above.

[98] r.3(1).

decision to appoint a "legal representative" can be taken at either the s.64 business meeting[99] or later by the children's panel itself.[1] This flexibility in appointment is necessary as it may not always be apparent from the outset that there will be any particularly difficult matters at a hearing.

8–36   The creation of "legal safeguarders" is not the solution to end all problems after *S v Miller*. First, safeguarders (and curators), as noted above, are supposed to represent the best interests, not the wishes, of the child. Legal representatives, it might be argued, should follow the child's wishes and agenda, even where they are not in his or her welfare. This change in mandate may make it difficult for some safeguarders to adapt to their new role. Secondly, even though legal representation is now available to children at the hearing, an Art.6(1) challenge would still seem possible from "relevant persons", who may also be unable to present their case "effectively" at the hearing without legal aid. It might be said that the disposal of the hearing does not affect the relevant person but the child, hence the relevant person cannot be prejudiced by an "unfair" hearing: but it is obvious that, in substance, a parent whose child is taken into foster care as a result of an adverse hearing has as much to lose as the child. (An ECHR Art.8 right to respect for family life claim might also seem appropriate.) One possible suggestion is that the Art.6 rights of all at the hearing, *including* relevant persons, might be better guaranteed by the introduction of legally-trained reporters acting in a judge-like capacity, or by the use of legal assessors in "complicated" cases, or even by introducing legally-trained panellists. None of these ideas, however, have attracted popular support,[2] nor the idea of a "family hearing", where the needs of siblings and parents would be considered alongside those of the child referred (see the responses[3] to the Executive's 2005 *Getting It Right For Every Child* consultation).

8–37   Finally, another ground of possible challenge to the hearings system, raised in *S v Miller*, is whether the children's panels are an "independent tribunal" as required by Art.6 of the ECHR. Panellists are appointed "for such period as specified by the Secretary of State" and can be removed by the Secretary of State at any time.[4] In *Starrs v Ruxton,*[5] the case which abolished temporary sheriffs, the Inner House held that a court or hearing may not be compliant with Art.6 if it is not "independent and impartial". Elements in determining independence

---

[99] See para.8–25 *et seq.*
[1] r.4.
[2] Although see support from Elaine Sutherland in Nicholson "Hearing a New Tale" (2004) J.L.S.S. (June) 16, a discussion by experts of the future options for reform of the hearings system.
[3] See Stevenson and Brotchie, *Report on the Responses to the Phase One Consultation on the Review of the Children's Hearings System* (Scottish Executive, 2004).
[4] Children (Scotland) Act 1995, Sch.1, para.2.
[5] 2000 J.C. 208; 2000 S.L.T. 42.

and impartiality included the manner of appointment and term of office, guarantees against outside pressures, appearance of independence, freedom from subjective bias, and from legitimate objective doubt as to bias. In fact, however, the evidence was that, in practice, panellists were appointed for five years and were routinely eligible for re-appointment, sometimes after some degree of re-training. There was no evidence at all that any panellist had ever been removed for any reason except refusal to take part in necessary training and no suggestion that any panel had actually been biased in favour of the Scottish Executive or Ministers because of fears of lack of tenure; nor was the issue of personal future preferment relevant here (as it had been with temporary sheriffs). Looking at the practice rather than the form then, the hearing was, it was held, an independent and impartial tribunal.

Exclusion and Confidentiality

In some circumstances, it may be very difficult for a child to speak **8–38** freely to the panel members if one or both parents are present. Parents will usually be entitled to be present as "relevant persons", but under s.46(1), the hearing has the right to exclude any relevant person (and any representative of theirs) for so long as is necessary either to obtain the child's views, or to avoid causing the child significant distress. However, the child cannot be guaranteed confidentiality even after exclusion, because the excluded person must be informed by the hearing chairman of the substance of what has taken place in his or her absence.[6]

Confidentiality is, in general, a problem within the hearings sys- **8–39** tem. On the one hand, parents who face the possible imposition of measures of compulsory supervision have basic rights as a matter of procedural justice (under Art.6 of the ECHR, and also at common law) to know what the case is against them or their children. On that basis, all information that is given to panel members should be shared with the parents. On the other hand, cases will sometimes involve sensitive information which neither the hearing nor, sometimes, one or more of the parties may wish disclosed to all other parties. For example, one parent might discover that the other is adulterous, or has a history of violence. Most importantly, given full disclosure, the hearing cannot guarantee that views expressed by a child about his or her parent(s) will remain private. Despite these difficulties, following the European Court of Human Rights case of *McMichael v UK*,[7] the Principal Reporter became obliged[8] to make available to each parent[9] a copy of any report made available to the children's hearing. This still left the children themselves without a

---

[6] s.46(2).
[7] [1995] Fam. Law 478; ECHR, February 24, 1995.
[8] Children's Hearings (Scotland) Rules 1996, r.5(3). Reports prepared before this date in the expectation of non-disclosure to parents will be replaced by composite reports.
[9] See r.5(3)(b).

statutory right to access to reports concerning their own case, a position conceded in *S v Miller* (above) to be contrary to Art.6 of the ECHR. As a result, guidance was issued by the Principal Reporter under which children over 12 are sent the same documents as are panel members and relevant persons, although information may be withheld if likely to cause significant distress or harm to the child, a relevant person or other persons, or if it is likely to impede prevention or detection of crime.[10]

Process

8–40   As we saw in Ch.7, any decision or determination made by a children's hearing must be informed by the basic three principles of the 1995 Act:

1. the child's welfare is paramount[11];
2. the child must be given an opportunity to express a view and regard must then be given to those views as far as is practicable having regard to the age of maturity of the child.[12] Competence to express a view is presumed at 12 or over;
3. the hearing should not make any requirement unless it feels it is better to do so than to do nothing (the "minimum intervention" principle).[13]

8–41 These principles were discussed in depth at Ch.7, para.7–07. It is important to note, however, that a hearing can make a disposal or decision which is inconsistent with the child's welfare where they consider there is a risk of serious harm to the public.[14] So, for example, a child might be committed by the hearing to a secure unit[15] for the protection of the public even if this did not best meet the needs of that child. Such a disposal is however difficult to square with the original Kilbrandon philosophy.

8–42   The procedure of the hearing is primarily laid down in the Children's Hearings (Scotland) Rules 1996 and is intended to foster informal discussion between the child, parents, and hearing members.[16] The first task of the chairman of the hearing is to explain the ground or grounds under which the child was referred to the hearing as in need of compulsory measures of supervision, and then to establish if these ground(s) are accepted by both the child and any "relevant person".[17] If any of these persons refuses to accept any of

---

[10] See *SCRA Practice Guidance Note 24*.
[11] s.16(1).
[12] s.16(2).
[13] s.16(3).
[14] s.16(5).
[15] See below, para.8–53.
[16] SI 1996/3261. See Rose, "Proceedings in Children's Hearings", 1994 S.L.T. (News) 137.
[17] s.65(4).

the grounds, then the reporter must make an application to the Sheriff Court under s.68 for the sheriff to establish as proven the ground(s) that are disputed, unless the hearing is willing to discharge the referral on the grounds that the child no longer seems to be in need of compulsory measures of supervision.[18] The sheriff must hear the s.68 application within 28 days of it being lodged.[19]

If a "relevant person" does not appear at the hearing, then it is not **8–43** necessary to secure his or her acceptance of the ground(s).[20] However, if the *child* does not attend, his or her acceptance cannot be dispensed with, and either the referral must be discharged, or an application made to the sheriff for proof.[21] This is true even if the hearing has already agreed at a business meeting to release the child from his or her obligation to attend the hearing[22]—hence it will often be desirable for the child to attend at least long enough to listen to the explanation of the grounds, and have a chance to accept some or all of them. If the child concerned is incapable of understanding the grounds of referral, because of age or otherwise, then an application must be made to the sheriff for proof, or else the referral must be discharged.[23] If one or more, but not all, of the grounds are accepted, then the hearing may either move on to dispose of the case under s.69 with respect to those grounds which *are* accepted, or if they feel this is inappropriate, they can await the determination of the sheriff who is charged with establishing the disputed grounds before moving on to the disposal stage.[24]

Establishing the Grounds of Referral—s.68 Proofs

Proceedings before a sheriff under s.68 are held in chambers.[25] The **8–44** application to have the ground(s) of referral established is presented by the reporter, and legal aid is available for representation of both parents and child.[26] The need for the appointment of a safeguarder must be considered by the court.[27] All grounds of referral must be established on the balance of probabilities, i.e. the civil standard of proof, except ground (i), that the child has committed an offence, which must be established beyond reasonable doubt.[28] Grounds (d),

---

[18] s.65(7).
[19] s.68(2).
[20] s.65(10).
[21] s.65(4).
[22] 1995 Act, s.45(2) is explicitly made subject to s.65(4). This safeguards the child's right to dispute the grounds of referral.
[23] s.65(9).
[24] s.64(6).
[25] s.93(5).
[26] Both the child and any "relevant person" may also be represented by a non-legally qualified person: s.68(4).
[27] s.41.
[28] 1995 Act, s.68(3)(b). See also *Costanda v M*, 1997 S.L.T. 1396; 1997 G.W.D. 16-704, noted above at para.8–21.

(e), (f) and (g), all of which may require proof of an offence being committed by someone *other* than the child, can be established on the usual civil standard.[29] Thus, it is not at all anomalous that an alleged abuser of a child might be found not guilty of the crime in the criminal courts, but then be proven to be the abuser in a s.68 proof. As Lord Justice-Clerk Ross said in *Harris v F*:

> "The purpose of a ground of referral such as [this] is to advance the welfare of the child and to protect the child...Protection of a child is in my opinion a justification for applying a lower standard of proof in applications under s 42 [now s.68] and it is still a justification even if the person concerned is ultimately acquitted of the offence in the criminal courts".[30]

A proof that a child has been the victim of an offence can proceed even if a criminal prosecution is pending, although this is undesirable because of the potential prejudice to the accused in criminal proceedings.[31] The basic rules of evidence and procedure are observed at a s.68 proof but there are various judicial dicta that proceedings are neither civil nor criminal but uniquely *sui generis*,[32] and in *W v Kennedy*,[33] Lord Sutherland went so far as to say that,

> "it would be quite wrong for [the interests of the child] to be thwarted by the application of rigid rules of evidence or procedure just because such rigidity may be appropriate in other types of proceedings".

Nonetheless, in recent years, proofs have become increasingly adversarial, especially when allegations of abuse are introduced, and strict attention has been paid to certain evidential rules of hearsay and evidence,[34] even where the effect has been to exclude crucial evidence of children and, as a result, arguably to impede child protection.[35] It is likely that Art.6 of the ECHR may in future lead to even more "legalisation" of the hearing and proof process. As at the hearing stage, the child has a right and a duty to attend but can be released from this

---

[29] *McGregor v D*, 1977 S.L.T. 182; *B v Kennedy*, 1987 S.L.T. 765; *Harris v F*, 1991 S.L.T. 242.

[30] At p.246. See also *Kennedy v B*, 1992 S.C.L.R. 55.

[31] *P v Kennedy*, 1995 S.L.T. 476.

[32] *McGregor v D*, 1977 S.L.T. 182; *A v Kennedy*, 1992 S.C.L.R. 387.

[33] 1988 S.C.L.R. 236.

[34] e.g. the rules on admission of hearsay under the Civil Evidence (Scotland) Act 1988, under which proceedings relating to proof of grounds of referral are categorised as civil proceedings: 1988 Act, s.9. See also ss.68A and B introduced into the 1995 Act by the Vulnerable Witnesses Act 2004 (see para.2.70 above) which restrict the use of certain types of evidence relating to sexual experience at the hearing (as is also the case in criminal trials).

[35] See further paras 2–65 *et seq.*

obligation by the sheriff[36] and parents have a right to attend but can be excluded in the interests of the child by the sheriff.[37]

If the ground(s) for referral are established or accepted, the sheriff **8–45** remits the case back to the children's hearing to consider and dispose of the case.[38] If none of the grounds are found to be proven, then the sheriff must dismiss the application and discharge the referral and any warrant by means of which the child has been detained.[39]

The child, a relevant person, or the reporter can appeal the sheriff's **8–46** decision on the grounds to the Inner House[40] or to the sheriff principal and thence, with his leave, to the Inner House.[41] The appeal is by way of stated case either on point of law or in respect of any irregularity in the conduct of the case. If the appeal is upheld by either the sheriff principal or the Inner House then the case is remitted back to the sheriff for disposal in accordance with such instruction as the appeal court gives.[42]

New Evidence

In some cases, a ground of referral may be properly established as **8–47** proven at the date of the hearing, but subsequently new evidence may arise which requires the court to reconsider. For example, it may be established that a child was the victim of sexual abuse on the basis of evidence given by that child, but later it may emerge that that testimony was produced by pressurised interrogation techniques.[43] Section 85 provides that application for review of a ground of referral may be made by either the child or a "relevant person" where:

(i)   there is new evidence which would materially have affected the original determination;
(ii) the new evidence is credible,[44] reliable and admissible;
(iii) there is a reasonable explanation for failure to lead the evidence at the original hearing.

If the sheriff quashes the ground, then the options are either to terminate the supervision requirement, immediately, or as at some future

---

[36] s.68(4) and (5).
[37] Act of Sederunt (Child Care and Maintenance Rules) 1997, r.3.47(6).
[38] s.68(10).
[39] s.68(9).
[40] s.51(11)(b).
[41] s.51(11)(a)(ii) and (b).
[42] s.51(14).
[43] See *L, Petrs (No.1)*, 1993 S.L.T. 1310 and *L, Petrs (No.2)*, 1993 S.L.T. 1342 (the "Ayrshire case"). In this case, which arose prior to the introduction of s.85, review was achieved by application to the *nobile officium*.
[44] *cf. R v Kennedy*, 1993 S.L.T. 910, where review was not allowed but the only new evidence was that a girl who was not a reliable witness had changed the details of her account of sexual abuse.

date, or if some ground of referral may still be made out, then the case may be remitted to the reporter to arrange a new hearing.[45]

Disposal of the Case: Supervision Requirements

8–48   Once the grounds of referral have been either accepted or established in court, the case is remitted back to the children's hearing who can either continue the case to gather further relevant information, discharge the referral or make a supervision requirement under s.70 if they feel this is necessary in respect of the child.[46] Where a child has been referred to the hearing from "relevant proceedings" under s.54, then the ground will already have been established and the hearing can proceed straight to disposal.[47] If a supervision requirement is imposed by the hearing, then the local authority has the responsibility of implementing it, e.g. placing the child with foster parents to meet a residential requirement.[48] One of the key problems in the hearings system which emerged in the responses[49] to the *Getting It Right* consultation was the lack of any ability by the reporter or the panel to compel the local authority to implement a supervision requirement. Given a global lack of resources in social services, this was a serious issue in the panel achieving effective results, particularly in relation to persistent offender cases. Accordingly, s.71A of the 1995 Act[50] for the first time empowers the Principal Reporter to apply to the sheriff to have him order the local authority to implement a hearing requirement. Given the current emphasis on agencies working in partnership for the good of the child, however, it is likely this power will only be exercised as a "backstop option".[51]

8–49   In making a disposal, the hearing is not restricted to consideration merely of the facts that have been proven as part of the grounds of referral. Rather, proof of any ground is the key that unlocks the door to consideration of *all* the circumstances of the case, proven or unproven.[52] Thus, even evidence which was inadmissible at a s.68 proof, e.g. hearsay statements made by a child who was not a competent witness, might be used by the hearing to formulate their disposal. However, any fact which was specifically *disproven* at proof cannot be relied upon by the hearing at the disposal stage.[53] While

---

[45] ss.85(7) and 68(10).

[46] s.69(1).

[47] These "relevant proceedings" are most often likely to be divorce proceedings or independent applications under s.11 relating to parental responsibilities and rights. See further para.4–47.

[48] s.71.

[49] Above, n.8.

[50] Inserted by s.136 of the Antisocial Behaviour (Scotland) Act 2004. See also new s.70(3A)–(3E) and s.71(1A).

[51] Alan Miller, former Principal Reporter for Scotland, quoted in Nicholson, "Hearing a New Tale" (2004) J.L.S.S. (June) 16.

[52] *O v Rae*, 1993 S.L.T. 570.

[53] *M v Kennedy*, 1993 S.L.T. 431.

this approach can be criticised as contrary to natural justice, it is in line with the conception of the hearing as a child-centred forum whose paramount concern is welfare not justice. The hearing is of course bound by the minimum intervention principle and the welfare principle to make no disposal and discharge the case if it seems to them this meets the needs of the child as well as making a requirement would.

Review of Supervision Requirements

As a fundamental principle, a child should be subject to a supervision requirement no longer than is necessary to secure his or her welfare.[54] Any requirement can last no longer than a year unless continued by a review hearing,[55] which can also choose to terminate or vary the requirement.[56] This ensures that a child's case is regularly reconsidered. As well as the mandatory annual review, a review *must* be requested by the local authority if: **8–50**

1. they are satisfied the requirement is no longer needed; or
2. a condition in the requirement is not being complied with by the child; or
3. the authority intends to apply for an adoption, freeing for adoption or parental responsibilities order in respect of the child.[57] In this case, the hearing's role at review is to provide advice to any future court who may deal with application for the order in question.

Furthermore, the child or any relevant person may require a review at any time at least three months after the original hearing or last review hearing.[58] Finally, the hearing making the requirement may itself set a date for the next review.[59] **8–51**

It is also now possible under the Antisocial Behaviour (Scotland) Act 2004, s.12(5)[60] that if a child comes before a court which makes an ASBO or interim ASBO in respect of a child, and that child is already subject to a supervision requirement, then the court may require the reporter to convene a hearing to review the supervision requirement. This is the first time that the court has had any part in ordering a review.[61] **8–52**

---

[54] s.73(1).
[55] s.73(2).
[56] s.73(9).
[57] s.73(4).
[58] s.73(6).
[59] s.70(7).
[60] Amending 1995 Act, s.73(8).
[61] See further para.8–65 below.

Conditions and Effect of Supervision Requirements

8-53   The hearing may attach such conditions to a supervision requirement as they see fit,[62] including a requirement that the child must
reside at any place. Effectively, there are two main types of supervision requirements: those where the child is required to live outside the
family home (hereafter "residential supervision requirements") and
those where the child is supervised by social workers within the family
setting ("home supervision requirements").[63] Children under residential supervision requirements may live in local authority residential homes, or with foster parents. The panel can order that the
address of a child under a supervision requirement should not be disclosed to any specified person, e.g. an abusing father or mother.[64] In
exceptional circumstances, the hearing may require that a child,
usually though not invariably one referred as an offender, should
reside in secure accommodation. The hearing must be satisfied that
such a requirement is necessary and that *either:*

(i) the child has previously absconded or is likely to abscond again
and in that event the physical, mental or moral welfare of the
child would be at risk; or
(ii) the child is likely to injure himself or some other person unless
kept in such accommodation.[65]

8-54 Children under a secure accommodation condition are effectively
subject to an unlimited sentence of detention which can potentially
last until the age of 18, albeit subject to review within three months of
the condition first being made.[66] It is hard to reconcile this either with
the welfare aims of the hearings system or the requirements of natural
justice.[67] However it was held in *S v Miller*[68] that a secure accommodation condition was not a breach of Art.5 of the ECHR, because
although it *was* a "deprivation of liberty", it was excuseable as made
"for the...educational supervision" of a minor child. Drawing on the
Strasbourg case of *Koniarska v UK,*[69] the court held that:

---

[62] s.70(3).
[63] Most supervision requirements made are home supervision requirements: of
"looked after" children as at 2005 (almost all of whom are "looked after" by virtue
of supervision requirements) 57% were looked after at home, 29% were with foster
carers or prospective\adopters, and 13% were in residential care. Furthermore, the
percentage of residential supervision requirements is declining (24% in 1984 to 13%
in 1994) (*Children's Social Work Statistics, 2004–2005*).
[64] ss.70(6) and 73(11).
[65] s.70(9) and (10). 120 new secure accommodation conditions were made in 1994.
[66] See the Secure Accommodation (Scotland) Regulations 1996 (SI 1996/3255), r.11(1).
[67] Harris and Timms describe the equivalent English regime as "punishment disguised
as care". (Harris and Timms, *Secure Accommodation in Child Care: Between
Hospital and Prison or Thereabouts?* (1993), p.50).
[68] Above, para.8–32.
[69] ECHR, 12 October 2000.

"the words 'educational supervision' must not be equated rigidly with the notion of classroom teaching. In particular in the present context of a young person in local authority care, educational supervision must embrace many aspects of the exercise, by the local authority, of parental rights for the benefit and protection of the person concerned".

As noted above,[70] a child now has a right to a free legal representative **8–55** at any hearing where a secure accommodation condition is made or likely to be made. However if there is no time to provide such a representative, and a condition or warrant is made, the procedural deficit can be fixed if the legality of any such condition or warrant for secure accommodation made is "speedily" reviewed by a judicial authority, with a legal representative available to the child.[71]

A possible alternative to secure accommodation is for the hearing **8–56** to make a condition restricting movement, or an "electronic tagging" order.[72] This will involve intensive support and monitoring services (monitoring is facilitated by an electronic "tag") where the young person is restricted to, or away from, a particular place. The electronic tag must be supported by a full package of intensive measures to help the young person change their behaviour. The conditions for the making of an electronic tagging order are the same as for secure accommodation, and the implication is clearly that this may be an effective way to deal with persistent young offenders without actually locking them up. In this sense it can be seen as a welfarist initiative. Cleland[73] notes however that given an emergent climate of treating persistent child offenders "differently", this order could be abused if it was mainly used to preserve public safety (as ASBOs are used, in fact) rather than where the *child's* needs demand it. The English experience of tagging of youth offenders (which has been in place since 2001) certainly seems to show that the human element of intense supervision in the tagging regime remains as vital as the technology itself.[74]

Contact

The hearing, in particular, *must* consider whether to attach a condition **8–57** regulating contact with the child.[75] Contact is an issue where dispute will often arise when a child is subjected to a residential supervision requirement. What rights do parents have if the hearing

---

[70] See para.8–35.

[71] *Martin v N*, 2004 S.C. 358.

[72] Antisocial Behaviour etc. (Scotland) Act 2004, s,135 amending s.70 of the 1995 Act. See the Intensive Support and Monitoring (Scotland) Regulation 2005 (SSI 2005/129).

[73] Cleland, "The Antisocial Behaviour etc. (Scotland) Act 2004: Exposing the Punitive Fault Line Below the Children's Hearings System" (2005) 9 Edin L.R. 439.

[74] Moore, "The Use of Electronic and Human Surveillance in a Multi Modal Programme" (2005) 5 Youth Justice 17.

[75] s.70(2).

adds as a condition to such a requirement that contact with their child is to be limited or terminated? The effect of the supervision requirement, and any condition, is not to *remove* the statutory rights and duties a parent would normally be able to exercise under ss.1 and 2, but to "suspend" them for the duration of the requirement. Thus, the parent cannot exercise his or her parental rights in any way incompatible with the terms of the supervision requirement.[76] A condition restricting contact therefore takes precedence over the parent's ordinary right to maintain contact. Even if the panel do not place particular restrictions on contact, they can legitimately provide that it be at the discretion of the local authority, in which case the authority has the right to restrict contact as it sees fit.[77] However, since a child under a supervision requirement is a "looked after" child under s.17, the local authority should at least start from a presumption that contact with the parents is desirable.[78] The authority's paramount concern, however, will still be the welfare of the child.

8–58 If parents are denied contact, either by the specific terms of the requirement of the hearing, or by the decision of the local authority, can they mount a challenge? In *D v Strathclyde*,[79] the Inner House found that the effect of a condition of contact in a supervision requirement was not only to suppress the parental rights of contact, but to remove from the parent title to sue for contact in the courts. This was because any award by the court would interfere with the obligations of the local authority to implement the supervision requirement. As the court asserted in *D v Strathclyde*, "a collision would always be on the cards".[80] This had the unfortunate effect, however, that for parties who were not "relevant persons", they had neither the right to attend the hearing and argue their view on contact there (the "public law" remedy), nor the right to raise the matter in the ordinary civil courts (the "private law" remedy). This was particularly unfortunate for unmarried fathers without PRRs who nonetheless wished to stay in touch with their child, sometimes against the wishes of the mother and/or the reporter.

8–59 In *P v P*[81] however, a situation arose where a "collision" was *not* inevitable. A two-year-old girl was subject to a supervision requirement, which included a condition that she reside with her grandmother. There was no condition as to access, which meant it was left to be regulated by the local authority in accordance with their duties under s.17 in respect of a "looked after" child. The natural mother

---

[76] 1995 Act, s.3(4) implementing the pre-1995 Act case of *Aitken v Aitken*, 1978 S.C. 297; 1978 S.L.T. 183.

[77] *Kennedy v M*, 1995 S.C.L.R. 88. Note that the hearing cannot restrict contact merely to facilitate the adoption of the child as they are not an adoption agency and would be acting ultra vires: *M v Children's Hearing for Strathclyde*, 1988 S.C.L.R. 592.

[78] 1995 Act, s.17(1)(a), (c) and (3). See further, Ch.7.

[79] 1985 S.L.T. 114. Affirmed in *A v G*, 1996 S.C.L.R. 186 (Updates).

[80] *ibid.* at 116.

[81] 2000 S.L.T. 781.

had dropped out of the picture but the natural father wanted to apply for contact. The grandmother raised an action under s.11 for a residence order. Her intention was to make sure she had power to do all things necessary for the child's welfare in relation to third parties, e.g. deal with her education, which was not a power the hearing could give her.[82] The Inner House held, in these circumstances, that they had power to grant the residence order sought.

Perhaps more surprisingly, the court also allowed an application **8–60** for contact from the natural (unmarried) father. *D v Strathclyde* was distinguished on the basis that, in that case, there was an explicit condition as to access, with which an access order by the court would inevitably be "in collision"; whereas in *P v P* there was *no* explicit condition as to access. Furthermore the local authority would be intimated of any s.11 action if the child was subject to a supervision requirement, and could then join the action to defend the child's welfare and the child protection plan if necessary.

Medical Consent

The hearing also has the right to attach a condition requiring the **8–61** child to submit to medical examination or treatment.[83] Again, a parent cannot exercise any parental right in a way which is incompatible with the terms of the supervision requirement. So a mother cannot veto a medical examination ordered by the hearing by virtue of her rights as legal representative. However, the rights of some children *themselves* to give or receive consent must be taken into account. The Age of Legal Capacity (Scotland) Act 1991, s.2(4) provides that a child can give a valid consent to treatment if he or she is capable, in the opinion of a medical practitioner, of understanding the nature and possible consequences of the procedure or treatment. Such a competent child also has the right to *refuse* treatment.[84] Under s.90 of the 1995 Act, a child of sufficient maturity retains these rights even if required to submit by a supervision requirement.

Duration

A supervision requirement terminates: **8–62**

(i) when the child reaches 18[85]; or
(ii) after a year if not renewed by a review hearing (see above).

---

[82] She might also have anticipated a possible termination of the supervision requirement, which would have left the natural mother the only person with PRRs. Note that s.11(12) provides that a person with no prior rights who gains a residence order can exercise all PRRs.

[83] s.70(5).

[84] For the full argument supporting this point, see paras 4–29 *et seq.*

[85] s.73(3).

Appeals Against Disposal

8–63   Either the child or any "relevant person" may appeal the disposal of the hearing to the sheriff within three weeks.[86] The sheriff receives the same reports that were available to the hearing but may also hear oral evidence from the reporter, the appellant(s) and any other party. If the sheriff is not satisfied that the hearing's disposal was justified in all the circumstances of the case, then he or she must allow the appeal, in which case there are three options:

  (i) remit the case back to the hearing for reconsideration along with the reasons for the decision;
 (ii) discharge the child from any further hearing or proceedings; or
(iii) *substitute* his or her own disposal for that of the children's hearing (s.51(5)(c)(iii)). The sheriff can only make a disposal which could have been made by the hearing under s.70, i.e. a supervision requirement with or without conditions.[87]

The third of these options was introduced by the 1995 Act and has been heavily criticised as breaking down the separation of functions fundamental to the original Kilbrandon scheme under which the courts are responsible only for establishing facts as proven, while the hearing is responsible for deciding what should be done in the welfare of the child.[88]

8–64   A further appeal against the disposal (including a substituted disposal by a sheriff under (iii) above) lies from the sheriff to the sheriff principal and thence to the Inner House (with the leave of the sheriff principal),[89] or directly to the Inner House.[90] There is no appeal to the House of Lords. As with appeals against a finding that grounds are proven, the basis of appeal is either point of law or procedural irregularity.[91] In relation to the latter ground, as Sheriff Mowat stated in *D v Sinclair*,[92] a sheriff should not alter the disposal of the hearing merely because he disagrees with it, but only where there has been some flaw in the procedure adopted by the hearing, or where proper consideration has not been given to some factor in the case.

ANTISOCIAL BEHAVIOUR ORDERS AND PARENTING ORDERS

8–65   As we noted at the start of this chapter, since around 1995 there has been an increased emphasis in both Scotland and England on what can

---

[86] s.51(1).
[87] s.51(5).
[88] See, e.g. Kelly, *Introduction to the Scottish Children's Panel*, pp.50–51; McGhee, Waterhouse and Whyte, "Children's Hearings and Children in Trouble" in Asquith, *Children and Young People in Conflict with the Law* (1996).
[89] s.51(11)(a)(i) and (b).
[90] s.51(11)(b).
[91] s.51(11).
[92] 1973 S.L.T. (Sh. Ct.) 47.

be done to control the perceived increase in youth crime and offensive behaviour, and, in particular, persistent offending. The Antisocial Behaviour etc. (Scotland) Act 2004 (the "2004 Act") introduced into Scotland, for children, the antisocial behaviour orders ("ASBOs"), which had already arrived in England and Wales somewhat earlier via the Crime and Disorder Act 1998. The 2004 Act applies to children in Scotland over 12 but under 16.[93] (ASBOs for adults in Scotland were also introduced by the 1998 Act.) It was argued during the passing of the 2004 Act that ASBOs were unnecessary for under 16s, since there was already in place a wide range of diversionary measures to keep offending young people out of the criminal courts, including the children's hearings, early intervention projects and restorative justice projects. However the government insisted that a small number of persistently antisocial young people existed for whom no current measures were effective.[94] In Scotland, this has meant that, in addition to the welfare-centred hearings system, we now have, sitting rather oddly in conjunction with the Kilbrandon model, an alternate means of controlling the behaviour of delinquent children via the courts. While 1,169 ASBOs had been made in respect of children in England by March 2004,[95] in Scotland, however, interestingly, only two child ASBOs were made in the first year of operation.[96]

ASBOs, rather like interdicts, are court orders, made in the civil **8–66** Sheriff Court, which constrain persons not to commit certain types of antisocial behaviour, usually in specified locations. Examples might be hanging round in front of a specified cashpoint, or building exit, or inside a supermarket, or shopping mall; making undue noise in domestic areas; littering; fly-posting; or spray-painting. The court will make an ASBO if satisfied that a person over 12 has engaged in antisocial behaviour, and that the ASBO is necessary to protect other persons from further antisocial behaviour.[97] Antisocial behaviour is defined as acting in a manner that causes, or is likely to cause alarm or distress; or a course of conduct[98] that causes, or is likely to cause, alarm or distress to at least one person who is not part of the household of the person served with the ASBO. Local authorities and registered social landlords may apply for

---

[93] At the time of writing, suggestions have been made to extend ASBOs to children under 10 in England and Wales—so-called "baby ASBOs".

[94] See *Guidance on Antisocial Behaviour Orders: Antisocial Behaviour etc. (Scotland) Act 2004* (Scottish Executive, 2004), para.20.

[95] See "Youth Justice News" (2005) 4(3) Youth Justice 222.

[96] (2005) J.L.S.S. (November) News. This low number of ASBOs was "blamed" on the difficulty of getting the children's hearing to adapt to the new system. In the same year period, no parenting orders were made (see below). By January 2006 ((2006) J.L.S.S. (January) News), councils in general were reported to be making up to 60% more ASBOs compared to a year earlier, indicating a more smoothly operating system, but still only four child ASBOs had been made.

[97] 2004 Act, s.4(1) and (2).

[98] i.e. at least 2 occasions of conduct. Conduct includes speech (2004 Act, s.143(2)).

ASBOs; they cannot be sought by the police, procurator fiscals or the Crown. An ASBO is an order sought in the civil courts under civil procedure.[99] It is not proof of a criminal conviction, and does not form part of a criminal record. Accordingly it was expected that ASBOs would be established on the civil standard of the balance of probabilities. In England, however, the House of Lords have held that although ASBOs *are* civil orders, the criminal standard of proof may be applicable to proving past conduct.[1] It is not yet known if this reasoning will be followed in Scotland.[2] However *breach* of an ASBO is a criminal offence,[3] punishable by fine, or by imprisonment (although detention is not allowed for children under 16[4]).

8–67 The relationship between the hearings system and the "ASBO system" is complex. Before deciding to apply for an ASBO for a child, the guidance suggests that a multi-agency approach should be taken, with the local authority consulting with other agencies who have already been involved with the child, including the SCRA.[5] Where an ASBO is sought in relation to a 12–15 year old, the court *must* ask the reporter to arrange an advice hearing before determining the application.[6] However although "regard" must be given to the advice of the hearing, it need not be followed. Notably, the court, unlike the hearing in Pt II of the 1995 Act, is under no obligation to regard the child's welfare as paramount. In determining an *interim* ASBO, or an application for variation or revocation of an ASBO, the sheriff must similarly take account of the reporter's views[7]. If either a full or interim ASBO is made, the court *may* require the reporter to bring the child before a hearing,[8] which will then decide whether to impose a supervision requirement (or, more likely, if an existing one should be varied). If there is no existing supervision requirement in place, there is no need to prove, or have a ground of referral accepted: a ground of referral is deemed to have already been established, and the hearing can proceed straight to disposal.[9] Similarly, the court may refer the child to the hearing to have his or her supervision requirement reviewed, without any need for the reporter to exercise their usual discretion whether to seek review.[10] Effectively in both these cases, the will of the court trumps the discretion of the reporter.

---

[99] 2004 Act, s.4(1) and Scottish *Guidance on ASBOs*, above n.94, para.33.

[1] *R. (on the application of McCann) v Manchester Crown Court* [2003] 1 A.C. 787. See discussion in Guthrie, "Antisocial Behaviour", 2005 S.L.T. (News) 145.

[2] The Scottish *Guidance on ASBOs* refers to a "quasi-criminal standard" of proof: see para.36.

[3] 2004 Act, s.9.

[4] *ibid.*, s.10.

[5] Scottish *Guidance on ASBOs*, paras 67 *et seq.*

[6] 2004 Act, s.4(4).

[7] *ibid.*, ss.7(3) and 5(2).

[8] *ibid.*, s.12.

[9] *ibid.*, s.2(4).

[10] *ibid.*, s.12(5).

The mooted alternative to extending the courts-based "ASBO **8–68** system" to embrace children, was to give the children's hearing the power to impose an ASBO as part of its panoply of disposals. However it was felt that the hearing system was mainly designed to act in the welfare of the child, while—reading between the lines— ASBOs were mainly designed to be punitive if breached.[11] The introduction of ASBOs to the hearing would also probably have required the extension of full legal representation to all children at the hearing, with concomitant issues for procedure and the legal aid purse. A halfway house would have seemed possible under which an ASBO could still have been obtained from the courts but only on the request of, or perhaps with the consent of, the Principal Reporter.[12] Indeed, it seems odd that the Principal Reporter is not empowered to seek an ASBO on his own. All these options, one assumes, were deemed politically unacceptable. It also seems strange that when an ASBO is made in respect of a child, as noted above, the court *may*, but does not *have to*, refer the child to a hearing, even if they are not already known to the hearing system (unlikely but possible). ASBOs are theoretically not limited in time; while supervision requirements made by the hearing must be reviewed at lest annually. Given the acknowledgement that "most if not all under 16s subject to an ASBO will need a package of intensive support"[13] it would seem imperative to make sure the "ASBO child" is under mandatory regular review.

It is too early to deliver a verdict on whether ASBOs can be sought **8–69** and tailored to work harmoniously with the existing Scottish juvenile justice and hearings system, especially given the low numbers obtained thus far. Many commentators have expressed worries that ASBOs are an extremely blunt instrument with which to retrain delinquent behaviour which may be as much a product of deprivation, environment and peer group, as individual guilt or fault. One children's rights worker, for example, has expressed the view that:

> "Anecdotally, it seems children on ASBOs are predominantly working class, living with lone parents and excluded from school. ASBOs further degrade the very children that have already had to put up with a disproportionate amount of humiliation and aggression".[14]

---

[11] The Scottish *Guidance on ASBOs* (above n.94), para.66 admits that "ASBOS for under 16s [are] intended as a deterrent".

[12] Consent by the reporter is clearly not required: but *Guidance*, para.65, does suggest there should be "a *level* of agreement with other interested parties...including the Principal Reporter that an ASBO is the most appropriate intervention in the circumstances". [Emphasis added.]

[13] Scottish *Guidance on ASBOs*, above, para.115.

[14] Willow, "ASBOs: Not meeting children's needs" (2005) 23 Howard League Magazine 7.

Guthrie[15] has also observed that as a significant number of children in respect of whom ASBOs might be sought, are also likely to already be "looked after" children under s.17 of the 1995 Act.[16] If this is the case, there is a patent conflict between the local authority's duties to safeguard and promote the welfare of the child, and the main purpose of ASBOs which is to protect the external community. Such a conflict, could, as Guthrie suggests, be explored by an action for judicial review of the local authority.

Parenting Orders

8–70   The 2004 Act also introduced radical new orders to alter the conduct of the *parents* of children and young persons.[17] If a child[18] has engaged in antisocial behaviour, or offended, then the local authority in whose area the child lives, or the Principal Reporter, can apply to the sheriff (under summary procedure) to make a parenting order for up to a year[19]. The Principal Reporter can also seek a parenting order solely on the ground that the order is desirable in the interests of the child.[20] The reporter and the local authority are required to consult before making an application for a parenting order.[21] The court can also be asked to consider if a parenting order should be made in certain proceedings,[22] e.g. if an ASBO is made in respect of a child.[23]

8–71   The parenting order will require the parent to comply "during a specified period…not exceeding twelve months…with such requirements as are specified".[24] As Sutherland says, this is a "breathtakingly broad" phrase.[25] In practice this is likely to mean that parents are required to attend counselling, or guidance sessions for a particular period. A "parent" is defined to be the same as a "relevant person" under s.93(2)(b) of the 1995 Act.[26] Unlike with ASBOs, the paramount consideration in making a parenting order is the welfare of the

---

[15]   Above, n.1.

[16]   See above, paras 7–18 *et seq.*

[17]   See generally Pt 9 of the 2004 Act and *Guidance on Parenting Orders: Antisocial Behaviour (Scotland) Act 2004* (Scottish Executive, April 2005). These orders are still in a "pilot" phase till April 2008.

[18]   Defined for these purposes as a person under 16: see 2004 Act, s.117.

[19]   2004 Act, s.102.

[20]   *ibid.*, s.102(3).

[21]   *ibid.*, s.102(9).

[22]   *ibid.*, s.114. In any relevant proceedings, e.g. a divorce, the court may require the Principal Reporter to consider whether to apply for a parenting order. It is not clear if these are restricted to civil proceedings.

[23]   2004 Act, s.13. The sheriff must be satisfied that making the order is desirable in the interests of preventing antisocial behaviour by the child *or* protecting their welfare.

[24]   2004 Act, s.103.

[25]   Sutherland, "Parenting Orders: A Culturally Alien Response of Qustionable Efficacy?", 2004 Jur Rev 105 at p.117.

[26]   See para.8–28 above.

child.[27] As with ASBOs, although a parenting order is a civil order obtained in the civil Sheriff Court, breach of a parenting order (without reasonably excuse) is a criminal offence[28] punishable by a fine, and eventually jail if the fine is not paid.

Interestingly, a hearing can now *require* the reporter to go to court **8–72** to seek a parenting order.[29] If obtained, this is the first time the hearing has been able to (albeit indirectly) exert compulsory powers over the behaviour of the parents it sees, rather than just the child.[30] Some commentators see this as a major step forward for the effectiveness of the hearing. Sutherland on the other hand argues that (unlike in the United States, from which legal system parenting orders have been borrowed) we have no tradition of compulsion of parents in the interests of the child in Scotland, and that parenting orders are a culturally alien transplant which are unlikely to work. She points to evidence that even in the United States, which has a long tradition of holding parents legally responsible for their children in both civil and criminal law, parental compulsory education has been regarded as, in the main, a failure. Effective or not, it also seems plausible that parenting orders might at some point be subject to human rights challenges, either under Art.7 of the ECHR which prohibits the imposition of penalties for conduct which is not a crime, or under Art.8 which guarantees non-interference with family life.

ASSESSMENT OF THE HEARINGS SYSTEM

Since its inception in 1971, the Scottish children's hearings system has **8–73** been regarded as a major step forward both in juvenile justice and in child protection when compared to the court-based system which existed before that time.[31] The Kilbrandon philosophy, which attempts to protect children already in need from being further traumatised by the courts system, and which places the needs and the voice of the child at centre stage, has been applauded and studied throughout the world. Yet, for a number of reasons it would not be false to say that the hearings system is currently in crisis.[32] As a result,

---

[27] 2004 Act, s.109(1). The court also has to have regard to the views of the child, with, as usual, a child of 12 presumed mature enough to express a view (ss.109(2) and 108(6)).

[28] 2004 Act, s.107.

[29] *ibid.*, s.116, inserting s.75A into the 1995 Act.

[30] Supervision requirements made by the hearing prior to the 2004 Act (and any conditions attached) affected only the behaviour of the *child*: see 1995 Act, s.70(3) and (5).

[31] See further McAra, "The Scottish Juvenile Justice System: Policy and Practice" in *Juvenile Justice Systems: International Perspectives* (J. Winterdyk (ed.), 2nd edn, Canadian Scholars Press, 2002).

[32] See the forum of experts commenting on the future of the children's hearings system at Nicholson (2004) J.L.S.S. (June) 16. See also Edwards, "*S v Miller*: the End of the Hearings System As We Know It?", 2001 S.L.T. (News) 159; also the *Getting It Right For Every Child* consultation, above n.8.

the hearings system is currently going through its most root and branch review since its inception, the outcomes of which may change some of the fundamental characteristics of the system.[33]

8–74   In the 35 years since it first began operating, the children's hearings system has had to meet a number of unforeseen challenges. These can be loosely categorised as the challenge of the rise in awareness of child abuse and neglect; the perceived threat of the "persistent young offender"; and the creeping "legalisation" of the hearings, particularly in the wake of human rights legislation.

8–75   First, when conceived by Kilbrandon, children's hearings were primarily seen as a replacement for juvenile courts. In their first year of operation, some 87 per cent of children were referred to the hearings system on the ground that they had committed an offence.[34] Since then, however, the percentage of children referred on care and protection grounds, e.g. sexual abuse, has steadily risen until, in 2003/2004, around 60 per cent of referrals came to the hearing on care grounds as opposed to 40 per cent on offence grounds. Furthermore, there is a greater tendency for children referred on grounds such as abuse or parental neglect to be placed under supervision requirements and for those requirements to be renewed on review, while children referred as offenders are often discharged or removed from supervision on review: it has been estimated that around 80 per cent of children on supervision at any time originally came before the hearing on care and protection grounds.[35] Arguably, the children's hearings system was not created to deal with the legal and evidential complexity, inter-family conflict and controversial nature of abuse cases, and is struggling to deal with these issues.

8–76   Secondly, even what used to be thought of as the more "straightforward" child offender cases are now enmeshed in governmental concern. As public anxiety about youth crime and unruliness has grown in the last 5–10 years, it has increasingly been felt that the disposals available to the hearing may be insufficiently punitive to discourage a hard core of young delinquents, who re-offend with regularity until they move on to the adult justice system.[36] The hearings system has been subject to a barrage of journalistic criticism, accused of being a "soft option" by sheriffs, and held complicit in the

---

[33] See *Getting it Right For Every Child*, and its sequelae, above.

[34] See Martin *et al, Children out of Court* (1981), at p.36.

[35] Table 15c, *Social Work Statistics, 1994*. Unfortunately, more recent editions of these statistics do not report this figure in a comparable way.

[36] See McAra, above n.1, at p.272 of this chapter, who compares the period 1968–1985, cited as the "high point of welfarism in juvenile justice in Scotland" to 1995–2000, which she characterises as a period of "protective tutelage" when "issues of juvenile justice have become increasingly caught up in the new Labour Government's social inclusion and social crime prevention agendas". See also McDiarmid, "Welfare, Offending and the Scottish Children's Hearings System" (2005) 27 J.S.W.L. 31; McAra (2006), "Welfare in Crisis? Youth Justice in Scotland" in *Comparative Youth Justice* (B. Goldson and J. Muncie (eds), Sage, 2006).

(false) perception of an explosion of juvenile criminality. The original Kilbrandon Report rested on the belief that "delinquent conduct was often symptomatic, a reflection of some maladjustment or failure of development".[37] If the child was given help, e.g. exposed to social education, then the criminal behaviour would disappear. The stance was "paternalistic not punitive".[38] A child offender, in the eyes of Kilbrandon, could only suffer from contact with the conventional court-based justice system.

Since then, we have seen a major public change in attitude towards **8–77** the whole concept of juvenile delinquency. Increasingly, public opinion desires that young persons be accountable for their crimes, and that as much attention be given to the needs of the victim as of the offender.[39] It is clear that some young offenders are resistant to rehabilitation, and will continue to offend until they pass out of the hearings system and into the courts. Mid-adolescence is the peak age group for offending, and a substantial percentage of those appearing in the adult criminal justice system are young persons aged 16 and 17.[40] This poses three questions: first, do the disposals currently available to the hearing discourage persistent offending? Secondly, if not, how can the hearing deal with these children better? Thirdly, and most controversially, could persistent young offenders be better dealt with by the courts, either wholly or partially?

The first question was addressed in 2002 by the setting of a target **8–78** of a 10 per cent reduction in persistent young offenders by 2006.[41] This was not an easy goal, given that between 1998/1999 and 1999/2000 there was a 20 per cent increase in the number of young people referred to the Reporter for 10 or more offences.[42] Since that time the figures both on offenders and recidivists have been variable, although there has been (as discussed at para.8.16 above) a clear steady rise in the number of children re-referred to the hearing on *offence* grounds, with re-referrals constituting over 37 per cent of all offence referrals as at 2003/2004. In an attempt to achieve this target, the hearing has been experimenting with "fast track hearings", hearings with substantial extra resources targeted at persistent offenders, defined as children who had been referred to the reporter on five or more occasions within a six-month period. The aim was

---

[37] Martin *et al, op. cit.*, above, n.53, at p.7.

[38] *ibid.*, p.313.

[39] One approach to this is *restorative justice*, where the offender is encouraged or required to make amends to his or her victim, such as repairing damaged property or offering compensation or apologies. Restorative justice schemes are now operating in conjunction with the hearings system in various local authority areas in Scotland : see *SCRA Annual Report, 2003–2004*, p.12. See further Brookes, "Restorative justice in Scotland's youth justice system" in McGhee, Mellon and Whyte (eds), *Meeting needs, addressing deeds—working with young people who offend* (NCH for Scotland, 2004).

[40] See Graham and Bowling, *Young People and Crime* (1995).

[41] *National Standards for Scotland's Youth Justice Services* (Scottish Executive, 2002).

[42] McDiarmid, above, citing the *SCRA Annual Report for 2001.*

to reduce re-offending rates, not only by reducing the time for a case to be processed, but by targeting significant amounts of social services resources at these cases, so that hearings requirements of assessment and direct work with the children were guaranteed implementation.[43]

8–79　　Although the "Fast Track" approach did "capture the hearts and minds of those engaged in implementing it" and seems to have been a success for the children and social workers involved, it did not, significantly, reduce crime rates or young offender re-offending rates in Fast Track areas compared to comparison areas. Given the large amount of expenditure involved, and the fact that this could be seen as diverting resources away from other referral groups which also have pressing needs, e.g. serious rather than persistent offenders, the fast-track approach has to be regarded as "not proven with regard to impact on offending".[44]

8–80　　So what of the third question, whether to reintroduce elements of court-adjudicated punitive justice into the youth crime field? This approach can be seen in the recent legislation on ASBOs, discussed above, and in the piloting of a youth court in Hamilton for 16–17 year olds, and some 15 year olds.[45] These can both be seen as developments to deal with incorrigible young persons where the hearing has run out of options. Advocates of the hearings system maintain strongly however that these new additions are incompatible with the welfare- and child-centred focus of the traditional hearing and are regressive in moving back towards a juvenile courts model of criminal justice, which has been increasingly discredited in reducing crime in England and elsewhere for decades.[46] In the end, these debates are intensely political and it is as hard to predict how they will turn out as it is to predict the winner of the next General Election. It is hoped however that the empirical evidence emerging from studies like the Edinburgh Youth Transitions and Crime project will be used to the fullest in working out what options actually do reduce crime and

---

[43] Significant failures to implement the supervision requirements of hearings in "ordinary" offender cases were noted by the Audit Scotland report: *Dealing with offending by young people* (2002), paras 147–148. See also Cleland, "The Antisocial Behaviour etc. (Scotland) Act 2004: Exposing the Punitive Fault Line below the Children's hearings System" (2005) 9 Edin L.R. 439, commenting on the *Fast Track Hearings Research: Interim Report November 2003* (Scottish Executive, 2003). According to the *Fast Track Children's Hearings Pilot: Final Report of the Evaluation of the Pilot* (2005), around £13,000 was spent per "fast track" case during the pilot period. Much of this may, however, have been expended on setting up infrastructure at the start of the pilot rather than individual cases.

[44] Quotes from *Fast Track Children's Hearings Pilot: Final Report of the Evaluation of the Pilot* (2005).

[45] See McIver *et al*, *The Hamilton Sheriff Youth Court Pilot: The First Six Months* (Scottish Executive, July 2004).

[46] See most recently the Howard League for Penal Reform report: *Out For Good?* (2006) which reports that almost 70% of England and Wales young offenders are reconvicted within two years of their release from custody.

recidivism, as opposed to which are most appealing to an electorate at any given time.

Thirdly, the hearing, originally conceived as a lay tribunal, more **8–81** child-centred than a court, and comparatively unfettered by deference to rules of procedure and evidence, has become subject to increasing "legalisation". Case of abuse and neglect in the family have always fitted badly within the hearings model of discussion and consensus, because in these cases there is a clear conflict of interests between the family and the hearing as to what is best for the child and will satisfy the parents. To this, we have now added the major problem of how to adapt the hearings system, based on the supremacy of the welfare of the child, to the demands of the ECHR, which upholds the individual due process rights of both the child and other parties, as implicitly superior to the needs of the child. As discussed above, the ECHR has already demanded major adjustments to the former Kilbrandon stance that legal representation should be discouraged, and it is possible we may still see further challenges under Art.6 to, e.g. the lack of legal aid for "relevant persons" and the non-independent role of the reporter. One result of that issue, which has already been acknowledged as problematic by the former Principal Reporter,[47] may be the introduction of legally-trained chairpersons, or even some kind of assessor/judge.

Combining all three of the above problems seems to demand a **8–82** major reassessment of how the hearing works, and perhaps even its abandonment. In the Scottish Executive consultative review of the hearing, *Getting It Right for Every Child*, the executive asked if the basic tenets of the Kilbrandon system should be retained. This received a warm response from the overwhelming majority of respondents to the consultation[48] who also supported the idea that the central focus of the hearings system should remain on the *child*'s welfare, rather than balancing their interests with the needs of the family, or the protection of the community. This seems to recognise, at least for now, that it would be a retrograde step to retreat from the hearings model to a court-based system for dealing with children who offend. An only slightly less radical approach than abolition, however, would be to abandon the Kilbrandon ideal of treating children in need, and children who offend, within an identical regime, as both "children in trouble" and to introduce separate systems of "welfare" and "offence" hearings. The argument here, which was strongly promoted by the government in 2004,[49-50] is that these are two groups of children with quite different problems, and

---

[47] Alan Miller, in Nicholson (2004) J.L.S.S. (June) 16.
[48] Stevenson and Brotchie, *Summary Responses to the Phase One Consultation on the Review of the Children's Hearings System* (Scottish Executive, 2004).
[49-50] McDiarmid, above, at p.35.

that any system dealing with them needs different powers of disposal and/or treatment to respond effectively. Yet, empirical research, like that of the Edinburgh Youth Transitions study,[51] has gone a long way towards proving that child victims have far more in common with child offenders than might be thought at first blush, indeed that being a victim of some kind of abuse, bullying or criminal activity is one of the most likely indicators of becoming an offender[52]; and thus it seems likely that we can understand and tackle youth crime and recidivism most effectively by retaining the Kilbrandon ethos and treating these two groups as one. The *Getting It Right* consultation also received little support for a separation of hearings into two camps, or the creation of specialised hearings, and the government has now, it seems, retreated from this aspiration.[53]

8–83 The hearings system clearly has serious issues to deal with as it moves towards its 40th birthday. But it should be remembered that no evidence has yet disproved the Kilbrandon ethos of welfarism over punitiveness, and that much empirical evidence emerging supports it. It is true also that the hearings system grapples with two of the most intractable problems in modern society: the prevalence of domestic abuse and the tendency of young people to pass through a delinquent phase. The strength of the hearings system is that it does provide some kind of transitional forum through which young offenders can pass before being exposed to the full rigours of the adult criminal justice system. It also provides a crisis alert system by which resources can be targeted towards children and young persons who need them before they face the world as unassisted adults. But it cannot perform these functions without adequate resourcing, and sympathetic partnership with both the criminal justice authorities, and social services through whom it must work. In particular the hearing system cannot be criticised if the disposals it recommends are not carried out, or carried out too late, or inadequately, because of its dependence on implementations by agencies external to itself. As Cleland notes, one respondent tellingly commented on the "fast track hearings" pilot discussed above, that

---

[51] See Smith, *The Links Between Victimisation and Offending* (Edinburgh Study of Youth Transitions and Crime, Number 5, 2004). Smith found that delinquency rates were seven times as high among those who had self-reported as victims of five types of crime as those who had not been victims of any. The types of crime measured included being threatened or hurt, being kicked, punched or hit, having objects stolen, being hurt with a weapon, etc.

[52] See also the smaller SCRA *Study on Youth Offending in Glasgow* (2003) and Waterhouse *et al* study discussed in Waterhouse, McGhee and Loucks, "Disentangling offenders and non-offenders in the Scottish children's hearings: a clear divide" (2004) 43(2) Howard Journal 164. McDiarmid, above, cites both studies as evidence that "the Kilbrandon justification for mixing the deprived and the depraved holds good" (at 38).

[53] McDiarmid, at 35.

"if operated properly, this was the way the children's hearings system was meant to be".[54]

For the rest of this book, we will be looking at how the law regulates the status and relationships of children when they have emerged as adults, and left both the safeguards and the restrictions of child status behind.

[54] Cleland, above n.73, at p.446.

CHAPTER 9

FAMILIES, MARRIAGE AND CIVIL PARTNERSHIP

9–01

Families take many forms in Scotland today. They include lone-parent households, cohabiting heterosexual and same-sex couples with or without children, as well as marital relationships. Individuals may enter into a number of these forms in their lifetime as they move *from* marriage to lone-parenthood on to a cohabiting relationship, or from cohabitation to marriage. The changing dynamics of family life create a challenge for Scots family law in its approach to the recognition and enforcement of legal rights and duties among family members. What constitutes a "family" for legal purposes may be at odds with social perceptions of what makes a family unit. This has led to changes in Scots law embracing the Civil Partnership Act 2004, the Gender Recognition Act 2004 and the Family Law

9–02 (Scotland) Act 2006.[1]

Here are some data on contemporary families and households:

- 43 per cent of live births were to unmarried parents but over 60 per cent of these were jointly registered by parents living at the same address[2];
- at the time of the 2001 Census, there were 163,434 "cohabiting couple" family households in Scotland. Of these, 62,443 had one or more dependent children[3];
- there were 32,154 marriages in Scotland in 2004, of these over a quarter represented people who had previously been married[4];

---

[1] The changes implemented by the Family Law (Scotland) Act 2006 represent ongoing debate over the years on the subject of reform outlined in *Report on Family Law*, Scot. Law Com. No.135 (1992); *Improving Scottish Family Law* (Scottish Office, 1999); *Parents and Children* (Scottish Executive White Paper, 2000); *Family Matters: Improving Family Law in Scotland* (Scottish Executive, 2004).

[2] Registrar General for Scotland ("RGS"), *Annual Review of Demographic Trends 2001*, p.20. Available at *www.gro-scotland.govuk/statistics/library/annrep/annrep/index.html*.

[3] RGS, *Mid 2003 Population Estimates for Localities in Scotland* (Table 4). Available at *www.gro-scotland.gov.uk/statistics/library/poptest/mid-2003-population-estimates-for-localities.html*.

[4] RGS, *Annual Review of Demographic Trends* 2004. Available at *www.gro-scotland.gov.uk/ files/2004-rg-review.pdf*. The RGS marriage records show that the number of marriages have decreased steadily since 1971: Ch.1 p.36.

- there were 11,277 divorces in Scotland in 2004[5];
- 49 per cent of children adopted in Scotland in 2000 were adopted by a step-parent or relative of the child[6];
- a quarter of non-married adults aged 16–59 in Great Britain were cohabiting in 2000/2001[7] and the number is projected to rise considerably from 2 million in 2003 to 3.8 million in 2031. The cohabiting population is also projected to become much older[8];
- the number of married couple families declined from over half of the families in Scotland in 1991 to 43 per cent in 2001. In contrast, the proportion of cohabiting couples, ungrouped individuals and lone-parent families in Scotland rose between 1991 and 2001[9];
- the presence of dependent children in the family still has a major effect on the economic activity of women. In spring 2002, 52 per cent of women whose youngest dependent child was under 5 years of age were working either part-time or full-time (36 per cent and 17 per cent respectively). Seventy per cent of women whose youngest dependent child was aged 5–10 were working (26 per cent full time and 44 per cent part time)[10];
- on separation or divorce, mothers with children experience on average a 20 per cent drop in income[11];
- although child income poverty has fallen since 1997, it is still the case that almost 1 in 3 children in the United Kingdom remain in income poverty[12];
- in 2001 a quarter of dependent children in Scotland were living in a lone-parent family, usually with the female parent[13];
- children in lone parent families, children of couples where the parents work only part time or are unemployed, those in families with 3 or more children, or with a mother under 30 were all at higher risk of low income than other groups of children[14];

---

[5] RGS, *ibid.*, p.10. While there was a marked increase in the number of divorces in Scotland up to the early 1980s, since then the numbers have fluctuated. Increasing levels of cohabitation may be related to the recent decline in divorces as the breakdown of cohabiting relationships is not subject to divorce proceedings.

[6] *Op.cit.* above, n.2, p.47. This number has fallen to 33% in 2004: see RGS above, n.4, at p.11. Approximately one in eight children are estimated to experience life in a step-family. See *For Scotland's Children* Report (Scottish Executive, 2000).

[7] National Statistics, *Social Trends* No.33 (Stationery Office, London, 2003), p.45.

[8] National Statistics, *Population Trends Autumn.* No.121 (2005), p.80. Available at *www.statistics.gov.uk/downloads/theme_population/PT121_V1.pdf*.

[9] Taken from Scottish Census Data in 2001 discussed in A. Morrison, D. Headrick, F. Wasoff, and S. Morton, *Family formation and dissolution: Trends and attitudes among the Scottish Population* (Research Finding 43/2002), p.3.

[10] *Op.cit.* above, n.7, p.158.

[11] *Poverty, Issue 11* (Winter 2002), p.3.

[12] J.Flaherty, J.Veit-Wilson and P. Dorman, *Poverty: the Facts* (5th edn, Child Poverty Action Group, 2004), p.145.

[13] *Op.cit.*, above n.9, p.3.

[14] *National Statistics Online*, published October 2005, downloaded from *www.statistics.gov.uk/CCI/nscl.asp?ID=7672*, Low Income: Fewer children in poverty in recent years, p.1. For details on low income families see J.H. McKendrick,

- over the last thirty years there has been an increase in the proportion of one person households[15];
- the first statistics on Civil Partnerships published by the General Register Office for Scotland on June 22, 2006 show that since the Civil Partnership Act came into force on December 5, 2006, 343 partnerships have been registered in Scotland. 220 male partnerships and 123 female.

CHANGING APPROACHES TO DEFINING FAMILIES IN TERMS OF MARRIAGE

9–03

Traditionally, marriage has had a central role in family law, but growing recognition and acceptance of other types of non-marital family units has led to changes in the way that law deals with them. Thus, Scots law no longer discriminates against children on the basis of whether or not their parents were married.[16] In *Fitzpatrick v Sterling Housing Association*,[17] the House of Lords held in an English case, that a same-sex partner was capable of being a member of the original tenant's "family" for the purposes of succeeding to his deceased partner's tenancy.[18] Statutory provision for this interpretation to take effect in Scotland has been made under s.108 the Housing (Scotland) Act 2001.[19] Recognition of same-sex partnerships by the

---

S. Cunningham-Burley and K. Backett Milburn, *Life in Low Income Families in Scotland: A Review of the Literature* (Scottish Executive Social Research, Edinburgh, 2003). According to G. Palmer, J. Carr and P. Kenway, *Monitoring Poverty and Social Exclusion in Scotland 2004* (Joseph Rowntree Foundation, 2004), "the proportion of people in low income households in Scotland is very similar to the average for Great Britain as a whole", at p.9.

[15] *Op. cit.* above, n.7, p.43.

[16] Law Reform (Parent and Child) (Scotland) Act 1986, s.1(1) gave legal equality to children regardless of the marital status of their parents. This has been amended by the Family Law (Scotland) Act 2006 so that s.1(1) of the 1986 Act abolishes the status of illegitimacy in Scots law.

[17] [1999] 4 E.R. 705 (HL). Majority noted that such a person would have to establish the characteristics of "family", namely "a mutual degree of inter-dependence, of the sharing of lives, of caring and love, and commitment and support" (at 714).

[18] In the Court of Appeal [1997] 4 All E.R. 991 (whose judgment was overturned by the House of Lords), Lord Justice Ward, who dissented from the majority opinion, was prepared to go even further and view the surviving partner as a "spouse" of the deceased based on the functions he fulfilled (at 1022). The House of Lords, however, rejected this interpretation on appeal. However, in *Ghaidan v Godin-Mendoza* [2002] 4 All E.R. 1162 the Court of Appeal held that in order to render the Rent Act 1977 compatible with the Human Rights Act 1998 and Art.8, the words "as his or her wife" were to be read to mean "as if they were his or her wife or husband". This new construction would enable a same-sex partner to be treated as if he or she were a spouse and thus entitled to succeed to the tenancy.

[19] For a an overview of the way in which same-sex couples were treated in Scots law up to 2002 see B. Dempsey, "Same-Sex Couples in Scots Law—Part 1" (2002) SCOLAG No.300, 181 and "Same-Sex Couples in Scots Law—Part 2" (2002) SCOLAG No.301, 201.

Civil Partnership Act 2004 and the Family Law (Scotland) Act 2006, which gives increased rights and protection to *cohabiting* same-sex couples, illustrates that Scots law is sensitive to developments taking place in the broader European and International community of which it forms part. Such developments include international conventions such as the United Nations Convention on the Rights of the Child and the European Convention on Human Rights and Fundamental Freedoms, to which the United Kingdom is a signatory. The latter has now been partially incorporated into United Kingdom law by the Human Rights Act 1998 and has brought about change as decisions of the European Court of Human Rights (ECtHR) at Strasbourg may now be directly founded upon by United Kingdom citizens along with rights under the Convention.

HUMAN RIGHTS ACT 1998

9–04

The Human Rights Act does not provide in a straightforward way that the Convention shall have effect as part of United Kingdom law, but seeks instead to give effect to what it defines as "the Convention Rights"[20] in a number of different ways. First, it establishes a "rule of interpretation". Legislation is to be "read and given effect" in a way which is compatible with "Convention rights"[21]; and the Act provides that courts must, in determining questions relating to such rights, "take into account" the jurisprudence established by the Strasbourg Commission and Court.[22] This is so even where the decision would be at odds with an earlier decision of a United Kingdom court. Secondly, the Act provides that it is unlawful for a "public authority" to act in a way which is incompatible with a Convention right[23]; and s.7 gives "victims" of any such unlawful act the right either to rely on the Convention right in any legal proceedings or to institute legal proceedings against the relevant authority. Thirdly, the Act, whilst recognising the ultimate sovereignty of the Westminster Parliament, provides in s.4 a controversial procedure whereby a court may make a declaration that a statutory provision is incompatible with a Convention right. If it does so, then a Minister may adopt the special procedure laid down by the Act and make an order effecting the necessary changes rather than bringing new legislation before Parliament in the usual way.[24]

---

[20] s.1.
[21] s.3.
[22] s.2.
[23] s.6.
[24] HRA 1998, s.10. Note discussion of this declaration of incompatibility in *S v Miller (No.2) (1st Div)*, 2001 S.L.T. 1304, where the court declined to make such a finding on the basis that it was now agreed that Scottish Ministers had power under existing legislation to make regulations to provide for representation before a children's hearing.

This is only possible where the Minister believes there exist "compelling reasons" for adopting such procedure and it is necessary to **9–05** remove the incompatibility.

Of key interest in family law are: Art.8 dealing with the right to respect for private and family life[25]; Art.12, dealing with the right to marry; Art.14, dealing with the right not to be discriminated against; and Art.6 dealing with the rights to a fair and public hearing in proceedings determining an individual's civil rights and obligations. Over the years the European Court of Human Rights (hereafter "ECHR") has expounded on the concept of what constitutes a "family" together with the range of persons that fall within its ambit and the rights accorded to them. In *Marckx v Belgium*,[26] the European Court held that the notion of family life under Art.8 is not confined to marriage-based relationships but may encompass other de facto ties[27] such as those existing between an unmarried mother and her child. In *Christine Goodwin v UK*,[28] the Court held that the failure to allow a transsexual to marry a person of the sex opposite to their re-assigned gender was not only a breach of Art.12, but a failure to respect the applicant's right to private life in breach of Art.8. In *da Silva Mouta v Portugal*,[29] the Court held that there had been discrimination in violation of Art.14 as well as a breach of Art.8 when a Portuguese court recalled a residence order in favour of a father, on the basis of his sexual orientation as a gay person. In *P, C and S v UK*,[30] the Court held that a mother's rights under Articles 8 and 6 had been breached by the removal of her son straight after birth, without providing her with relevant and sufficient reasons for their action and without affording her the opportunity to have legal representation.[31]

---

[25] Immigration is an area where recent cases have alleged human rights violations under Art.8. See *Ahmed v SS for Home Department* [2002] I.N.L.R. 345; *Akhtar v SS for Home Department*, 2002 S.L.T 1239 (OH); *Saini v SS for Home Department*, 2001 S.C. 951 (OH).

[26] (1979–1980) 2 E.H.R.R. 330.

[27] See also *X, Y and Z v UK, Application No.25680/94*, European Commission on Human Rights, Information Note No. 129, 6 where the Commission found the UK in violation of Art.8, in respect of family life, where the Registrar General refused to allow a post-operative female-to-male transsexual in a stable relationship to be registered as the father of a child born as a result of artificial insemination because only a biological man could be regarded as the father for the purposes of registration.

[28] (28957/95) [2002] I.R.L.R. 664. Note, that while no judgment of the ECHR has yet found that homosexual partners had a right to marry under Art.12 as this matter falls within the "margin of appreciation" of the Member State that allows that State to make its own decision as to whether or not same sex marriages are permissible. However, in *S v UK* (1986) 47 D. & R. 271 the Commission held that even though a stable homosexual cohabiting relationship did not fall within the definition of "family life", such a relationship might still be a matter affecting *private life*.

[29] 2001 31 E.H.R.R. 47.

[30] 2002 Fam. L.B. 59–7.

[31] In this case the mother had a previous conviction in America for harming one of her children and had been diagnosed with Munchausen's syndrome by proxy. The local authority found out her prior history and took out an order allowing them to

In some cases, however, discrimination in relation to substantive **9–06** rights contained in the Convention, including the right to respect for family life, may be permitted where a state can show that it has a legitimate aim, and there is a reasonable relationship of proportionality between the legitimate aim and the means employed to achieve it. So, for example, in *McMichael v UK*[32] an unmarried father took his case to the European Court on the basis that he had no domestic legal right to obtain custody of his son or to participate in care and adoption proceedings before a children's hearing involving his son. He argued that this infringed his right to respect for "family life" under Art.8 in a discriminatory manner that was contrary to Art.14. His action was unsuccessful. Further, while the European Court in *Marcks v Belgium*[33] held that family life is not confined to marriage-based relationships but may encompass other de facto ties, it ruled that there had been no violation of Arts 8 and 14 in *McMichael's* case. This was because the Government was able to appeal to the proviso contained in Art.8(2) which enables any interference with family life to be justified on the basis that it is in accordance with the law and necessary to achieve a legitimate aim in a democratic society. In taking account of this the European Court allows what is known as a "margin of appreciation" to Member States, taking on board the political climate at the given time.

In *McMichael v UK* the Court accepted the United Kingdom **9–07** Government's explanation that the aim of the relevant legislation was to provide a mechanism for identifying "meritorious" fathers who might be accorded parental rights, thereby protecting the interests of the child and the mother. For discrimination to occur under Art.14 the treatment of an individual or disposal in a case must have "no objective and reasonable justification", as occurs when it does not pursue a "legitimate aim" or there is not a "reasonable relationship of proportionality between the means employed and the aim sought to be realised".[34] The Court ruled that in *McMichael* the Government's aim was legitimate and that the conditions imposed on natural fathers for obtaining recognition of their parental role respected the principle of proportionality. There was thus an objective and reasonable justification for the difference of treatment complained of.[35] Following on from *McMichael*, the court in *B v UK*[36] revisited the issue of whether unmarried fathers were discriminated against given

---

remove her son hours after his birth. A care order followed and within a year the child had been freed for adoption. See also *S v Miller*, 2001 S.L.T. 531 on childrens' rights to legal representation before a children's hearing.

[32] (1995) 20 E.H.R.R. 205.
[33] (1979–1980) 2 E.H.R.R. 330.
[34] See *Marckx v Belgium* (1979–80) 2 E.H.R.R. 330 at para.33.
[35] *McMichael v UK* (1995) 20 E.H.R.R. 205 at para.98.
[36] [2000] 1 F.L.R. 1.

that their rights were not protected in the same way as those of a married father under English law. It reached the conclusion that the Children Act 1989 did not violate an unmarried father's rights, as, following on from *McMichael*,

> "there exists an objective and reasonable justification for the difference in treatment between married and unmarried fathers with regard to the automatic acquisition of parental rights."[37]

Since these cases, there have been moves to minimise these distinctions[38] and legislation has been enacted in England to confer parental responsibilities and rights on fathers whose names were jointly registered on the birth certificate with the mother.[39] Scotland has followed suit and conferred parental responsibilities and rights on unmarried fathers where they have jointly registered the birth with the mother.[40]

MARRIAGE

9–08 It is clear that families and marriage need not go together. At one time, under the common law, marriage had substantial consequences for spouses but a series of statutes has limited its legal consequences. Nonetheless, marriage still has important legal consequences for family members, e.g. concerning rights to property and support, parenthood, financial provisions on the termination of a relationship and for rights to intestate succession on the death of one of the spouses. The Civil Partnership Act 2004 has conferred similar rights on same-sex couples who are registered yet, despite the reforms brought about by the Family Law (Scotland) Act 2006, heterosexual and same-sex cohabiting couples still experience differential treatment.

Who Can Marry?

9–09 The law dealing with marriage is set out in the Marriage (Scotland) Act 1977 (as amended by the Marriage (Prohibited Degrees of Relationship) Act 1986 and the Family Law (Scotland) Act 2006). It provides that parties are free to marry provided they do not fall within the legal impediments to marriage set out in s.5(4) of the 1977 Act. The following constitute a legal impediment to a marriage where:

---

[37] *B v UK* [2000] 1 F.L.R. 1 at 5.

[38] See *Re H: Re G (Adoption: Consultation of Unmarried Fathers)* [2001] 1 F.L.R. 646 (Fam Div) where the court recognised that a father may have a right to respect for his family life even if he was unaware of the child's existence.

[39] Under s.4 of the Children Act 1989 (as amended by s.111 of the Adoption and Children Act 2002).

[40] Family Law (Scotland) Act 2006, s.23.

- the parties fall within the forbidden degrees of relationship[41];
- one of the parties is, or both are, married[42];
- one or both parties will be under the age of 16 on the date of the solemnisation of the intended marriage[43];
- one of the parties is, or both are, incapable of understanding the nature of a marriage ceremony or of consenting to marriage[44];
- both parties are of the same sex[45]; or
- one of the parties is, or both are, not domiciled in Scotland and the marriage would be void according to the law of the domicile of the party or parties.[46]

Marriage (Scotland) Act 1977

The Marriage (Scotland) Act 1977[47] regulates the conditions **9–10** under which individuals may marry in Scotland. These conditions underpin a framework for marriage which is Christian, heterosexual, and monogamous. Lord Penzance's famous nineteenth-century observation that,

> "marriage as understood in Christendom may be defined as the voluntary union for life of one man and one woman to the exclusion of all others"[48]

still serves to characterise the legal model of marriage today, albeit with some modifications. According to this model, certain types of marriage, including homosexual and polygamous marriage, cannot be contracted in Scotland. The English law of marriage has also enacted these exclusions.[49] In both Scotland and England, however, recognition is in principle accorded to such marriages where they have been validly entered into according to *both* the law of the place where the marriage was celebrated, and the domicile laws of both

---

[41] Marriage (Scotland) Act 1977, s.5(4)(a). These are relationships based on consanguinity and affinity as set out in s.2 and Sch.1.

[42] s.5(4)(b).

[43] Marriage (Scotland) Act 1977, s.5(4)(c). Note that where such a marriage takes place (which is most unlikely given the fact that birth certificates must be submitted to the registrar) it will be void under s.1.

[44] Marriage (Scotland) Act 1977, s.5(4)(d). Lack of capacity to understand or consent to marriage may involve mental incapacity or error (but only as to the identity of the person or the nature of the ceremony and not as to its effects); fraud (but only in so far as it produces the appearance without the reality of consent); marriages entered into under force and fear or duress, and sham marriages (discussed below).

[45] s.5(4)(e).

[46] Marriage (Scotland) Act 1977, s.5(4)(f). For more detailed information on marriage see Edwards and Grififths, *Family Law* (1997), pp.246–262.

[47] As amended by the Marriage (Prohibited Degrees of Relationship) Act 1986.

[48] *Hyde v Hyde* (1866) L.R. 1 P. &D. 130 at 133.

[49] Under the Marriage Acts 1949–1986. For a commentary on these Acts see Hale, Pearl, Cooke and Bates, *The Family, Law & Society: Cases and Materials* (5th edn, 2002), pp.57–70.

parties to the marriage.[50] Parties who have validly married abroad may seek matrimonial remedies, such as divorce and financial provision, from the Scottish (and English) courts, provided they have an adequate jurisdictional connection with that court.[51] Jurisdiction in respect of most matrimonial cases is now governed by Council Regulation No.2201/2003 (commonly known as Brussels II *bis* or the Revised Brussels II Regulation).[52]

Restrictions on Marriage

9–11 We turn now to the conditions and restrictions imposed on marriage.

FORBIDDEN DEGREES OF RELATIONSHIP: CONSANGUINITY, AFFINITY AND ADOPTIVE RELATIONSHIPS

9–12 All societies have marriage prohibitions of some kind. These vary from culture to culture. In Scotland (as is the pattern for the rest of the United Kingdom) the prohibitions are based on consanguinity (blood), affinity (marriage) and adoption.[53] The form they take derives from Christian morals and values embedded in canon law. So, for example, marriage with affinal relations was struck down on the basis of the Augustinian doctrine that when a man and a woman married they become of one flesh rendering the blood relations of one the blood relations of the other and thus ineligible for marriage.[54] All provisions concerning prohibited degrees are now to be found in the Marriage (Scotland) Act 1977.

9–13 Section 2 of, and Sch.1 to, the 1977 Act represent the end result of cumulative efforts over the years to reform and pare down the

---

[50] In general, the law of the place of celebration governs the formalities of the marriage and the law of domicile governs susbstantive validity. It is beyond the scope of this book to enter into discussion concerning conflict of laws. For further details see Morris, *The Conflict of Laws* by D. McClean and K. Beevers (6th edn, Sweet & Maxwell, London, 2005) paras 9.021–9.024. See also K. Norrie, *Would Scots Law Recognise a Dutch Same-Sex Marriage?*, 2003 Edin L.R. Vol.7(1), pp.147–173.

[51] See Domicile and Matrimonial Proceedings Act 1973, ss.7 and 8 and Matrimonial Proceedings (Polygamous Marriages) Act 1972, s.2, as amended by the Schedule to the Private International Law (Miscellaneous Provisions) Act 1995 (see paras 14–36 to 14–38 and 14–42 to 14–47 below).

[52] This regulation came into force on March 1, 2005. It contains a set of rules applicable in all member states except Denmark ("The European rules") but allows national law to apply in certain cases. For details see Morris, *The Conflict of Laws* (6th edn), above n.50, paras 10–003—10–005. See para. 14–39.

[53] They are detailed in the 1977 Act, s.2 and Sch.1.

[54] It has been observed that at one stage in Scottish history this doctrine, taken to its extreme, gave rise to a situation where it "was surprising that any valid marriage could have taken place in Scotland at all": Clive and Wilson, *The Law of Husband and Wife in Scotland* (W. Green for the Scottish Universities Law Institute, Edinburgh, 1974), p.88.

restrictions on marriage. Relationships which fall within the prohibited degrees are definitively listed, so that where a relationship is
not expressly struck at by the Act, the parties know they are free to
marry (barring some other type of impediment).

What are the Relationships Struck at?

The prohibited relationships are set out in the columns to Sch.1 **9–14**
detailed below.

1 Relationships by consanguinity

Column 1	*Column 2*
Mother	Father
Daughter	Son
Father's mother	Father's father
Mother's mother	Mother's father
Son's daughter	Son's son
Daughter's daughter	Daughter's son
Sister	Brother
Father's sister	Father's brother
Mother's sister	Mother's brother
Brother's daughter	Brother's son
Sister's daughter	Sister's son
Father's father's mother	Father's father's father
Father's mother's mother	Father's mother's father
Mother's father's mother	Mother's father's father
Mother's mother's mother	Mother's mother's father
Son's son's daughter	Son's son's son
Son's daughter's daughter	Son's daughter's son
Daughter's son's daughter	Daughter's son's son
Daughter's daughter's daughter	Daughter's daughter's son

2 Relationships by affinity

Daughter of former wife	Son of former husband
Former wife of father	Former husband of mother
Former wife of father's father	Former husband of father's mother
Former wife of mother's father	Former husband of mother's mother
Daughter of son of former wife	Son of son of former husband
Daughter of daughter of former wife	Son of daughter of former husband

2A Relationships by affinity (repealed by the Family Law (Scotland) Act 2006)

Mother of former wife	Father of former husband
Former wife of son	Former husband of daughter

3 Relationships by adoption

Adoptive mother or former adoptive mother	Adoptive father or former adoptive father
Adopted daughter or former adopted daughter	Adopted son or former adopted son

These restrictions in 1 to 3 above apply if either (i) the marriage is solemnised in Scotland or (ii) either party is domiciled in Scotland at the time of the ceremony.

Consanguinity

9–15   Consanguinity refers to restrictions based on a blood relationship. This means that a person cannot marry his or her parent, grandparent, or great-grandparent; child, grandchild or great-grandchild; brother or sister; uncle, aunt, nephew or niece.

9–16   For the purposes of determining consanguinity, relationships of the half blood are treated as being of the same order as relationships of the full blood[55] and for these purposes marriage is irrelevant.[56] So, for example, a half brother and sister (who share only one parent in common), are prohibited from marriage in just the same way as a brother and sister who share both parents in common, whether or not the parents in either case were married to each other.

Affinity

9–17   By contrast, affinal relationships are those based on marriage rather than blood connections. In the past there was a wide-ranging ban on such relationships, even where these were in the second or third degree. A man could not marry his deceased wife's sister until 1907.[57] Since then, there has been a gradual relaxation of these restrictions[58] until it is now the case that a person is only restricted from marrying his former spouse's child, grandchild or parent.[59]

9–18   However, even in these cases the law has been relaxed by the Marriage (Prohibited Degrees of Relationship) Act 1986, which amended the 1977 Act to allow marriage between step-relations in certain instances. Section 2(1A) of the 1977 Act[60] now provides that:

(1) Parties who are related within the degrees of affinity set out in Schedule 1, paragraph 2, may marry provided that they have:

---

[55] s.2(2)(a).

[56] See para.17, Sch.1 to the Law Reform (Parent and Child) (Scotland) Act 1986 which inserts s.2(4) into the Marriage Act 1977.

[57] Deceased Wife's Sister's Marriage Act 1907.

[58] See the Deceased Brother's Widow's Marriage Act 1921 and the Marriage (Prohibited Degrees of Relationship) Act 1931.

[59] See s.2 of, and Sch.1 to, the Marriage (Scotland) Act 1977.

[60] As inserted by para.2(b) of Sch.2 to the Marriage (Prohibited Degrees of Relationship) Act 1986.

(i) both attained the age of 21 at the time of the marriage, and
(ii) the younger party has not at any time before attaining the age of 18 lived in the same household as the other party and been treated by the other party as a child of the family.

So, for example, a woman may now marry her mother's former husband provided both are over the age of 21, *and*, if she is the younger party, she has not lived in the same household as her step-father, and been treated by him as a child of the family, before she reached the age of 18. The aim here is to allow parties to marry who have never assumed a parent and child type of relationship, even although they would fall within the technical restrictions of affinity.

Provision has also been made for former in-laws to marry so that a **9–19** woman can marry the father of her former husband or the former husband of her daughter, and a man can marry the mother of his former wife or the former wife of his son. The stringent conditions regulating marriage in these circumstances, formerly set out in s.2(1B) of the 1977 and in para.2A of Sch.1 (that required both parties to be over 21 and that both former spouses of the parties be dead), have now been abolished by s.1 of the Family Law (Scotland) Act 2006.[61]

Should there be a difference between permitted sexual relationships **9–20** for marriage and criminal law purposes? Not all relationships within the prohibited degrees for marriage are criminalised as incestuous. Under the Criminal Law (Consolidation) (Scotland) Act 1995,[62] sexual intercourse between people related only through marriage is, as a general rule, not treated as incest. It has been suggested that the prohibited degrees of relationships for marriage should be brought into line with the less restrictive approach taken by the criminal law.[63] On the other hand, it can be argued that sexual relations with a step-parent or person who has adopted a parental role are abusive even if consensual, and should rightly be stigmatised by the criminal as well as the civil law. The 1995 Act deals with this by creating a new statu-tory offence of sexual intercourse with a stepchild or former stepchild where that person is under the age of 21 or has at any time before attaining the age of 18 lived in the same household and been treated as a child of his or her family.[64]

Adoptive and Other Relationships

Another set of restrictions on marriage based on social rather than **9–21** biological links is to be found in the context of adoption. A person cannot marry their adoptive parent or former adoptive parent, or

---

[61] This implemented Recommendation 46, p.71 of the *Report on Family Law*, Scot. Law Com. No.135 (1992).
[62] Criminal Law (Consolidation) (Scotland) Act 1995, s.1. These provisions were for-merly found in the Incest and Related Offences (Scotland) Act 1986.
[63] See Norrie, *Incest and Forbidden Degrees of Marriage in Scots Law*, 1992 J.L.S.S. 216.
[64] s.2.

their adopted child or former adopted child.[65] As these are the only express prohibitions based on adoption, anyone can marry their brother or sister by adoption, provided no other prohibition applies. Although adoption severs all legal ties between biological parent and offspring, marriage between a child and his or her parent is struck at under the rules relating to consanguinity.[66] These rules also prohibit an adopted child from marrying his or her genetic brother or sister.

Policies Behind Prohibition

9–22   There are anomalies in the treatment of who may and may not marry on the basis of consanguinity, affinity, and adoption. For example, first cousins, adoptive siblings, and stepbrothers and stepsisters are free to marry in our legal system, while other cultures consider these relationships too close. When it comes to considering reform in this area, it is necessary to question the underlying basis upon which such restrictions are founded. There are a number of different theories which are put forward, focusing on in-breeding, socialisation, the family, social and cultural systems, revulsion and demographic factors. In the past, a division was made between what were considered scientific theories, covering biological determinism and prognoses about in-breeding and genetic revulsion, and those theories which were social and cultural in origin. Today this division is highly contested as it is argued that all knowledge (including science) is shaped by social and cultural considerations.[67]

9–23   It is clear that social and cultural considerations as well as the fear of bearing children with genetic defects affect the legal restrictions on marriage. One argument is that prohibitions on sex and marriage are intended to uphold the relations of power and authority within the family unit. To allow unregulated sexual competition between family members is to open up the family to disruption, thereby undermining the stability of the unit. Thus, we Wnd it acceptable that those who, in genealogical terms, stand in step-relation to one another as parent and child should be permitted to marry, provided they have never, in fact, taken on the roles of parent and child in a particular household.

Prior Subsisting Marriage

9–24   Parties who are already married may not enter into another marriage until the prior marriage has been dissolved by death or divorce.[68]

---

[65] Marriage (Scotland) Act 1977, s.2 and Sch.1, para.3.

[66] See s.41 of the Adoption (Scotland) Act 1978 which provides that the rules in s.39 of the Act, which terminate the relationship between the adopted child and his or her genetic parents, do not apply in determining the forbidden degrees of consanguinity and affinity relating to the law of marriage.

[67] See Kuhn, *The Structure of Scientific Revolutions* (University of Chicago Press, Chicago, 1962) and Mendelssohn, *The Social Production of Scientific Knowledge* (D.Reidel Pub. Co, Dordrecht, 1977).

[68] *Burke v Burke*, 1983 S.L.T. 331.

Communities exist in Britain whose traditions embrace polygamy, and here the requirement of monogamous marriage causes concern. Polygamous marriages are in fact very rare amongst the immigrant community in the United Kingdom. However, it has always been the case in United Kingdom law that a marriage has been regarded as "polygamous" if it was entered into under a law which *permitted* polygamy, e.g. Islamic law.[69] Polygamous marriages have historically been accorded recognition by United Kingdom courts for some purposes, but not all. It was not until 1972, for example, that parties to a polygamous marriage, whether actually or potentially polygamous, could seek a divorce in the United Kingdom courts.[70] According to Morris, "it is now clear that English law does recognise valid polygamous marriages unless there is some strong reason to the contrary".[71]

Age

In Scotland, a person may not marry until he or she is 16 years **9–25** old.[72] Once that age is reached, however, an individual is free to marry without parental consent (provided other restrictions do not apply). The age of 16 is also the age at which the law recognises the right of individuals to enter into sexual relations with one another without incurring criminal sanctions,[73] including male homosexual relationships, as the age of consent is now also 16.[74] These age limits reflect a concern to protect children from exploitation while at the same time recognising an age at which young persons become sufficiently mature to make their own decisions. The age of 16 for marriage is in line with other provisions of modern Scots law regulating the capacity of children.[75] While 18 remains the official age at which the transition of status in the life cycle from child to adult is finally accomplished,[76] full legal capacity is now achieved at the age of 16 under the Age of Legal Capacity (Scotland) Act 1991.[77]

---

[69] *Lee v Lau* [1967] P. 44; but see the policy-motivated decision in *Hussain v Hussain* [1982] 3 W.L.R. 679, where the marriage was characterised as monogamous although entered into under a law which permitted polygamy, because neither party had capacity under their domicile law to take more than one spouse.

[70] Matrimonial Proceedings (Polygamous Marriages) Act 1972, s.2(2). This section has now been amended by the Schedule to the Private International Law (Miscellaneous Provisions) Act 1995.

[71] Above, n.50, p.228. See also: Private International Law (Miscellaneous Provisions) Act 1995, s.7.

[72] 1977 Act, s.1.

[73] Criminal Law (Consolidation) (Scotland) Act 1995, s.5.

[74] *ibid.*, s.13.

[75] In the past, Scots law recognised that girls could marry at 12 and boys at 14. These were the respective ages at which the sexes acquired the status of minor. However, the age limit for marriage was raised to 16 for both sexes by the Age of Marriage Act 1929. At that time it was, and remains, the lowest age at which parties may marry in Europe without parental consent.

[76] Under the Age of Majority (Scotland) Act 1969.

[77] See details in Ch.2.

Lack of True Consent

9–26   Marriage in Scotland must be a voluntary union. Capacity to understand and the giving of true consent are therefore vital. Under s.5(4)(d) of the 1977 Act, there is a legal impediment to marriage where this understanding is lacking. The emphasis that Scots law places on consent may be traced back as far as the Institutional writers and Stair's observation that marriage "is, and ought to be, of the most free consent".[78] This meant that, in the past, even where *a form* of marriage ceremony had taken place, a marriage might nonetheless be declared invalid if it could be established that there was no real and proper exchange of consent to the marriage. In "sham" marriages it was claimed that *both* parties withheld matrimonial consent,[79] whilst in marriages which were claimed to be entered into due to force or fear, one of the parties argued that his or her will had been overcome so that there could be no true consent to marriage.[80] In the past, both situations rendered such marriages void. However, the Scottish Law Commission recognised in 1992 that as far as sham marriages were concerned they should no longer be open to a claim of invalidity due only to a "mental reservation" of one or more of the parties at the time of the ceremony.[81] Their recommendation has been implemented by s.2 of the Family Law (Scotland) Act 2006 which inserts s.20A into the Marriage (Scotland) Act 1977 setting out the grounds on which a marriage is void and expressly providing that,

> "If a party to a marriage gave consent to the marriage other than by reason of duress or error, the marriage shall not be void by reason only of that party's having tacitly withheld consent to the marriage at the time when it was solemnised".

Mental Incapacity

9–27   Where an individual suffers from mental illness or impairment of some kind, the question is whether he or she is "capable of understanding the marriage and giving consent thereto"[82] at the time that the marriage takes place. In *Long v Long*,[83] it was held that although a young woman had been subject to supervision in an institution for long periods of time due to her mental state, she was nonetheless capable of understanding the nature of marriage and of giving her consent at the time that she participated in a marriage ceremony. Mental incapacity will only render a marriage void where a party to

---

[78] Stair, i.4.1.

[79] e.g. *Orlandi v Castelli*, 1961 S.C. 113; *Mahmud v Mahmud*, 1977 S.L.T. (Notes) 17; *Akram v Akram*, 1979 S.L.T. (Notes) 87; *Ebrahem v Ebrahem*, 1989 S.L.T. 808

[80] e.g. *Mahmood v Mahmood*, 1993 S.L.T. 589. See paras 9–32 and 9–34 below.

[81] See *Report on Family Law*, Scot. Law Com. No.135 (1992), para.8.20, Recommendation 48(6).

[82] *Long v Long*, 1950 S.L.T. (Notes) 32.

[83] *ibid.*

the marriage "was incapable of understanding the nature of marriage or consenting to the marriage".[84]

Error and Fraud

Scots law takes a very restricted view of the grounds on which **9–28** consent to marriage may be vitiated through error and/or fraud. In the leading case of *Lang v Lang*,[85] a man was induced to marry a pregnant woman in the belief that he was the father of her child. When it became clear that he could not be the father, due to the very short gestational period that would have been involved, he sought to have the marriage annulled on the basis of essential error and fraudulent misrepresentation. However, a court of seven judges held that a marriage could be annulled for error only if it related to the identity of the person, or the nature of the ceremony. In the case of the former, this involves actual mistaken identity, as, for example, where A thinks that he or she is marrying B, but is in fact marrying C.[86] It does not cover error as to the attributes (such as sterility) or qualities (such as lack of chastity) of the person. In respect of the ceremony, the error must concern the nature of the ceremony itself and not merely its effects. The definition of "error" has now been embodied in statutory form as,

> "(a) error as to the nature of the ceremony or (b) a mistaken belief held by a person ('A') that the other party at the ceremony with whom A purported to enter into a marriage was the person whom A had agreed to marry".[87]

On the issue of fraudulent misrepresentation, the court in *Lang* held **9–29** that fraud could only found an action of nullity of marriage where the fraud produced the appearance without the reality of consent. This is so unlikely in relation to modern formal marriage that in Clive's view "fraud . . . is not a ground of nullity in Scots law".[88] However, other jurisdictions, such as England, take a broader approach to nullity for error and allow a marriage to be annulled on the basis that, at the time of the marriage, one party suffered from "communicable venereal disease"[89] or that the wife was pregnant by a man other than her petitioning husband.[90]

---

[84] Marriage (Scotland) Act 1977, s.20A, as inserted by s.2 of the Family Law (Scotland) Act 2006.

[85] 1921 S.C. 44.

[86] A biblical example of this kind of situation is provided by the story of Jacob who was deceived into marrying Leah, thinking that he was, in fact, marrying her sister Rachel. Genesis 29.

[87] Marriage (Scotland) Act 1977, s.20A, inserted by s.2 of the Family Law (Scotland) Act 2006.

[88] E.M. Clive, *The Law of Husband and Wife in Scotland* (4th edn, W.Green, Edinburgh, 1997), para.7.036.

[89] Matrimonial Causes Act 1973, s.12(e).

[90] *ibid.*, s.12(f)

Duress/Force and Fear Marriages

9–30   Under the ordinary law of contract in Scotland it is recognised that a person may enter a contract in circumstances which clearly show the act is not voluntary. If it may successfully be shown that the contract or deed was agreed as a result of force and fear (rather than fraud or undue influence) than such a contract or deed entered into is void, rather than merely voidable.[91] It is not enough in the context of marriage that one party, while uttering words of consent, has mental reservations about the marriage for, as in the ordinary law of contract, to allow this kind of subjective approach to consent would be unreasonable to the other party entering into the agreement. Instead, it must be shown that the will of the party raising the plea was genuinely overcome by external pressure.

9–31   In *Buckland v Buckland*,[92] a man was falsely accused of sexually corrupting a young woman in another country. He was faced with the choice of marrying the young woman or going to court. If he chose the latter, his solicitor advised him that he would almost certainly be found guilty and face a prison sentence. Faced with these choices, he married the woman. Later, he returned to England where he successfully had the marriage annulled on the basis that his consent to marriage had been vitiated by fear. What is interesting is that there are dicta in the case to the effect that if he had been *guilty* of the charges laid against him the English court would not have granted the declarator. This is in one sense an odd approach to take, for if the issue is whether or not there is true or overborne consent, it should not matter whether or not the fear is *justly* imposed; instead, what is crucial is that it does in fact operate to overcome the party's will. However, in the general law of contract it is recognised that certain forms of *legitimate* pressure, e.g. to threaten to sue for a lawful debt, will not allow a plea of force and fear to be raised.[93]

9–32   Arranged marriages in Scots law have subjected this difficult area of law to scrutiny. In *Mahmood v Mahmood*[94] and *Mahmud v Mahmud*[95] the petitioners, a woman and a man respectively, sought to have their marriages annulled on the basis of force and fear in the form of familial pressure. In *Mahmood*, the marriage was arranged between the two families in 1983 without the woman's knowledge. She was informed of the arrangement in March 1988 and pressure was put on her to consent to the marriage. It was alleged that her parents had threatened to disown her, to stop supporting her financially and to send her to live in Pakistan if she refused to go through with the marriage. In addition, she was informed that her

---

[91] McBryde, *The Law of Contract in Scotland* (2nd edn, W.Green, Edinburgh, 2001), para.17.02.
[92] [1968] P. 296.
[93] See, e.g. *Hunter v Bradford Property Trust Ltd*, 1977 S.L.T. (Notes) 33.
[94] 1993 S.L.T. 589.
[95] 1994 S.L.T. 599.

failure to consent to the marriage would bring disgrace not only on herself, but on the Pakistani community in Edinburgh. Aged 21, aware that her elder brother and sister had been disowned by her family for this reason, and given the fact that she worked in her parents' shop and was totally dependent on them financially, she went through with the marriage ceremony in April 1988, although she had informed her prospective husband that she did not want to marry him. The parties lived together for only three months (until the end of July) during which time they rarely spoke to each other and had sexual intercourse only twice. At the end of that time the woman raised an action to have the marriage annulled on the basis of her lack of consent.

The husband argued that the threats were not of such gravity as to **9–33** sway or overcome the will of an ordinary person. Previous case law had established that threats must be sufficient to cause fear of immediate danger to life, limb or liberty.[96] Lord Sutherland, however, held that the specific threats averred would support a plea of force and fear if they exceeded the limits of proper parental influence. It was not sufficient for the pursuer simply to claim that her will had been overcome by fear of her parents' or community's disapproval. Nonetheless, the whole circumstances leading up to the marriage ceremony, combined with evidence of what happened after the ceremony, might demonstrate that her consent was not genuine and was made under duress.[97] This approach was later followed in *Mahmud*.

In *Mahmood*, Lord Sutherland had allowed the matter to proceed **9–34** to a proof before answer because of the averment of specific threats which, if proved, could be said to exceed the limits of proper parental influence. He observed that it would not have been sufficient for the woman to claim that her will had been overcome by fear of her parents' or her community's disapproval but held that it was necessary to explore the circumstances leading up to the threats being made and what had happened after the marriage ceremony in order to see whether her consent was genuine. This approach found approval in the *Mahmud* case.

In *Mahmud*, the male petitioner was 31 years old. As in the previ- **9–35** ous case, a marriage had been arranged on his behalf many years earlier with a woman in Pakistan. In 1992, he found himself under pressure to marry this woman on the basis that, as the youngest son in a Muslim culture, it was his duty to provide a wife to look after his ailing mother, and that failure to follow through on the marriage would bring dishonour to his family in the Pakistani community in Scotland and Pakistan. At this time he was living with another woman in Scotland and they were expecting their first child. Bowing to family pressure, he went through a ceremony of marriage with the woman from Pakistan. However, he did not see this woman before

---

[96] See *Szechter v Szechter* [1971] P. 286.
[97] This was the term used by Lord Sutherland, 1993 S.L.T. 589 at 592.

the marriage ceremony, which took place in a registry office on his way to work, or after the event. The woman was subsequently deported back to her home in Pakistan. In this case, Lord Prosser held that the sustained pressure from the man's family had destroyed the reality of his consent to the marriage and overborne his will.

9–36   It is important to stress that these cases do not establish a general ruling that arranged marriages are invalid because they represent an inherently forceful imposition of the parents' will. Each case depends on its own particular facts and depends on establishing that the apparent exchange of consent is vitiated by proof of duress or force and fear.[98] As s.20A(4) of the 1977 Act makes clear, consent obtained through duress will still render a marriage void.

Same-Sex

9–37   One of the fundamental requirements for marriage is that it takes place between a man and a woman. Under s.5(4)(e) of the 1977 Act, there is a legal impediment to marriage where parties are of the same sex. This restriction is based on Judaeo-Christian approaches to marriage which regard capacity to procreate as crucial.[99] Over time, ideas about the relationship between marriage, procreation and property have changed[1] along with the reasons for why people marry.[2] Much emphasis has been placed on the development during the twentieth century of companionate marriage, that is marriage for reasons of affection and sentiment.[3] Yet if the predominant view of marriage is one of individual choice, for companionship, then why should parties of the same sex be denied access to marriage simply on the basis of inability to procreate, if they meet all the other requirements?

---

[98]   The Scottish Executive recently joined with the UK Government to undertake a consultation on forced marriages entitled, *Forced Marriage: A Wrong Not a Right*. The consultation closed on December 5, 2005. See *www.scotland.gov.uk/Topics/People/Equality/18500/Forced*. See also the case of *Sohrab v Khan*, 2002 S.C. 382 where the judge granted a decree of nullity finding, inter alia, that whatever semblance of consent was exchanged at the marriage ceremony was vitiated by the duress placed upon the bride by her parents.

[99]   See the comments of J. Ormrod in *Corbett v Corbett* [1971] P. 83 at 105: "sex is clearly an essential of the relationship called marriage, because it is and always has been recognised as that of man and woman. It is the institution on which the family is built and in which the capacity for natural heterosexual intercourse is an essential element".

[1]   See M. A. Glendon, *The New Family and the New Property* (Butterworths, Toronto, 1981), pp.64–137.

[2]   See D. Gittins, *The Family in Question: Changing Households & Familiar Ideologies* (2nd edn, MacMillan, Basingstoke, 1985).

[3]   Alternatively, Marxists and feminists continue to propose different models of marriage based on the family as an economic unit. See Delphy and Leonard, *Familiar Exploitation: A New Analysis of Marriage in Contemporary Western Societies* (Polity, Cambridge, 1992) and Smart, *The Ties that Bind: Law, Marriage and the Reproduction of Patriarchal Relation* (Routledge & Kegan Paul, London, 1984).

Legal challenges to the exclusion of same-sex marriages have **9–38**
mainly taken the form of cases concerning transsexuals.[4] The leading
case in this area is *Corbett v Corbett*[5] which established that the criteria for identifying a person's sex are determined at birth according to
certain immutable biological features.[6] In *Corbett* one of the parties
who was born a male at birth underwent sexual realignment surgery
and thereafter lived as a woman known as April Ashley. April, who
had a passport issued in that name and who was accepted as a woman
for national insurance purposes, took part in a marriage ceremony
with a man. The relationship did not work out and the man raised an
action to have the marriage annulled on the basis that April was not
a woman for the purposes of marriage.[7]

The judge set out four main criteria for determination of sex, being: **9–39**

- the chromosomal make up of the person;
- the presence or absence of gonads (ovaries or testicles);
- the structure of the genitals; and
- the person's psychological orientation.

The first three criteria, which carried the greatest weight, were to be
assessed according to the position at birth. While the judge's interpretation of the medical evidence has been criticised,[8] it is clear that
a broader psychological approach based on perceptions of gender,
rather than on the attribution of biological sex, was rejected. As a
result, until the passing of the Gender Recognition Act 2004, a man
who perceived of himself as a woman and who adopted that gender
role, could not be considered a woman for the purposes of marriage,
whether or not he has had sex-change surgery. The same was true for
a woman who adopts a male gender (as in the case of *Rees v UK*[9]).

Although *Corbett* is an English case, it appears to be in line with **9–40**
Scots authority. In *X Petr*,[10] it was held that the entry as to sex at birth
made in a person's birth certificate may be altered only if a genuine
mistake in registration was made at that time. While attempts have

---

4 But note the decision of a trial court in the US state of Hawaii: *Baehr v Miike*, Civil
   Case No. 91 1394 (First Circuit Court Hawaii, December 3, 1996), that the state had
   no reason to deny a marriage licence to a male homosexual couple. In expectation
   of this judgment, the US Congress passed the Defence of Marriage Act 1996 which
   provides that any other US state need not recognise such a marriage.
5 [1971] P. 83.
6 For a different approach see the Australian case of *Att-Gen (Cth) v Kevin and
   Jennifer* [2003] FamCA 94 (February 21, 2003) where the full bench of the Family
   Court declined to follow *Corbett*, finding that post-operative transsexuals will normally be members of their reassigned sex.
7 He alternatively sought to have the marriage annulled on the basis of wilful non-
   consummation.
8 See J. K. Mason, *Medico Legal Aspects of Reproduction and Parenthood* (Aldershot:
   Dartmouth Publishing, 1990), p.8.
9 [1987] 2 F.L.R. 111.
10 1957 S.L.T. (Sh. Ct.) 61.

been made to challenge the criteria for the determination of sexual identity these have not, as yet, been successful.[11] Where, however, someone is born whose sex is indeterminate at birth, so that he or she is intersex, then a choice must be made taking into account not only the preponderance of biological criteria but that person's medical history and development.[12] If later developments, including psychological factors, suggest that the original assessment of the child's sex was wrong, then it can be changed.[13]

Human Rights Challenges

9–41 Attempts were made to challenge United Kingdom law on same-sex marriage on another front, on the basis that it discriminates against Art.8 (right to respect for private and family life) and Art.12 (right to marry). Initial challenges were unsuccessful,[14] which meant that, prior to the decision in *Christine Goodwin v UK*,[15] the United Kingdom was not obliged to change the birth certificates of post-operative transsexuals to reflect new sexual identities. The court had reached these earlier decisions having regard to the lack of any shared approach among contracting states towards the complex issues raised by transsexualism and on the basis that individual states were entitled to rely on a margin of appreciation to defend a refusal to grant new legal gender status to post-operative transexxuals. However, it did note that the United Kingdom had not kept the need for appropriate legal measures in this area under review and reiterated that all the contracting states should do so.

---

[11] *Re P and G (Transexuals)* [1996] 2 F.L.R. 90. This case attempted to challenge *Corbett* on the basis of advances made in scientific thinking on the subject. While the applicants were unsuccessful in getting their entries in the Register of Births altered, the court's judgment indicates that the registrar's decision could have been set aside if he had used indicators of sexual identity which had clearly been superseded by scientific advances of which he ought to have been aware. In *Bellinger v Bellinger* the Court of Appeal ([2002] 1 All E.R. 311) accepted that recent research in the field of Gender Identity Disorder was leading to the view that the criteria for designating a person as male or female were complex and probably not simply an outcome of the first 3 criteria laid down in *Corbett*, but that such research had not yet gained sufficient recognition to amount to an advance in medical science that would overturn the ruling in *Corbett*. The House of Lords affirmed the court's decision ([2003] 2 All E.R. 593).

[12] *W v W (Gender: Nullity)* [2001] 1 F.L.R. 324. In this case the woman had been registered as a boy by her parents and she had been brought up as such by her adoptive parents. However, it would appear that while the woman's chromosomal and gonadal sex was male, the appearance of her external genitalia was ambiguous so that she was neither a normal man nor woman, and her general appearance from early teens, plus her gender orientation was female. The court held that the biological test in *Corbett* was not satisfied, that there had been an error in registering the respondent as a boy, and that she was a female for the purposes of marriage.

[13] *ibid.*

[14] See *Rees v UK* (1986) 9 E.H.R.R. 56; *Cossey v UK* [1991] 13 E.H.R.R. 622; *Sheffield v UK* [1998] 2 F.L.R. 928.

[15] [2002] I.R.L.R. 664.

By the time the case of *Christine Goodwin v UK* was raised, the **9–42** Court had changed its position and held that the United Kingdom was in breach of Arts 8 and 12. It did so because it argued, that while the Court should not depart from precedents laid down in previous cases without good reason, the Convention is first and foremost a system for the protection of human rights, therefore the Court must have regard to the changing conditions within the respondent state and within contracting states generally as well as responding to any evolving convergence as to the standards to be achieved. It found the current position of transsexuals in the United Kingdom to be unsatisfactory and unsustainable. It found that the right of transsexuals under Art.8, to personal development and to physical and moral security in the full sense enjoyed by others in society, could no longer be regarded as a matter of controversy requiring the lapse of time to cast clearer light on the issues involved. It rejected the Government's claim that the matter fell within their margin on appreciation (except with respect to the appropriate *means* of achieving recognition of the right protected under the Convention), and found that there were no significant factors of public interest to weigh against the interest of the applicant in obtaining legal recognition of her gender re-assignment.

With regard to Art.12, the Court considered whether the allocation **9–43** of sex in national law to that registered at birth was a limitation impairing the very essence of the right to marry in this case. It found that it was artificial to assert that post-operative transsexuals have not been deprived of the right to marry as, according to law, they remain able to marry a person of their former opposite sex. The Court observed that while fewer countries permit the marriage of transsexuals in their assigned gender than recognise the change of gender itself,[16] it was not persuaded that this supported an argument for leaving the matter entirely to the contracting states as being within their margin of appreciation. The Court said to do so would be tantamount to finding that the range of options open to a contracting state included an effective bar on any exercise of the right to marry. The margin of appreciation could not extend so far, and barring a transsexual from enjoying the rights to marry under any circumstances amounted to a breach of Art.12 in the present case. In order to bring law in the United Kingdom into line with the Court's findings in *Goodwin*, legislation in the form of the Gender Recognition Act 2004 was introduced. The ruling in *Goodwin* does not, however, affect the position of same-sex couples who continue to be excluded from marriage in the United Kingdom.[17]

---

[16] The Court noted that 54% of contracting states, including Austria, Belgium, Denmark, Finland and the Netherlands, permit post-operative transsexuals to marry a person of sex opposite to their acquired gender.

[17] While same-sex couples are not yet permitted to marry they may enter into a civil partnership which will endow them with virtually all the same rights that are accorded to married couples.

9–44   Legalising transsexual marriage means that a person who is genetically male, and was once socially male, becomes entitled to marry another genetic male (or the equivalent for genetic females). It is, therefore, legally indistinguishable from legalising homosexual marriage.[18] However, the former is often seen as a reasonable legal development while the latter is perceived as considerably more radical. Why is this? Perhaps the answer lies in the fact that transsexual marriage does not seek to challenge the fundamental institutional basis of marriage as a union of persons of opposite *gender*. Transsexual partners who wish to marry intend to take on the roles of a man and a woman. With homosexuals, this is not the case. While some European jurisdictions, such as the Netherlands and Belgium, permit same-sex marriage,[19] others such as such as Sweden,[20] Denmark,[21] the Netherlands,[22] and France,[23] allow partners of the same sex to enter into registered partnerships, or legally enforceable cohabitation contracts. To bring Scotland and the United Kingdom into line with these developments, the Civil Partnership Act 2004 was introduced in order to provide same-sex couples with the same type of legal rights that apply to married couples in the form of a civil partnership.[24]

The Gender Recognition Act 2004[25]

9–45   The purpose of the Gender Recognition Act 2004 is to provide transsexual people with legal recognition in their acquired gender. This is achieved through the issue of a full gender recognition certificate by a Gender Recognition Panel. To be eligible for this the panel must be satisfied that the applicant (who must be at least 18)[26]:

---

[18] The Scottish Law Commission is unwilling to extend support for marriage for transsexuals for these reasons. See *Report on Family Law*, Scot. Law Com. No.135 (1992), p.68.

[19] See also a decision in the US case *Goodwin & Others v Department of Public Health*, 440 Mass 309 798 N.E. 2cd 941 where the Supreme Court of Massachusetts held that restricting marriage to partners of the opposite sex violated constitutional protections.

[20] See the Registered Partnership (Family Law) Act 1994.

[21] Registration of Partnership Act 1989. See Nielson, *Family Rights and the "Registered Partnership" in Denmark* (1990) 4 I.J.L.F. 297, at pp.297–307.

[22] Marriage for same-sex couples was introduced in 2001. For details see K. Waaldijk, "How the Road to Same Sex Marriage Got Paved in the Netherlands" (Ch.23) in *Legal Recognition of Same-Sex Partnership. A study of National and International Law* (R. Wintemute and Mads Andenas (eds), 2001).

[23] Du Pact Civil de Solidarité et du Concubinage (PACS) which has been added to the French Civil Code devoted to marriage. This allows two persons, whether of a different or the same sex, to enter into a registered partnership. For details see E. Steiner, "The Spirit of the new French registered partnership law—promoting autonomy and pluralism or weakening marriage?" C.R.L.Q. Vol.12(1), pp.1–14.

[24] See paras 9–60 to 9–70 below. Application for civil partnership has been possible since December 5, 2005.

[25] Fully in force since April 4, 2005.

[26] 2004 Act, s.1.

- has or has had gender dysporia. This is defined by s.25 as meaning "the disorder variously referred to as gender dysphoria, gender identity disorder and transsexualism"; and
- has lived in the acquired gender throughout the preceding two years; and
- intends to continue to live in the acquired gender until death.[27]

The applicant must include in his or her application:

- a statutory declaration as to whether or not the applicant is married; and
- any other information or evidence required by an order made by the Secretary of State; and
- any other information or evidence which the panel determines the application may require (including any other information or evidence which the applicant wishes to include).[28]

Where an application is successful, the panel must grant a full gender recognition certificate if the applicant is unmarried[29] or where married, an interim gender recognition certificate.[30] Where a court ends a marriage on the ground that an interim recognition certificate has been issued to one party, it must also issue a full gender recognition certificate.[31] However, if the marriage is dissolved or annulled on some other ground, in proceedings started within six months of the grant of an interim gender recognition certificate, or if the spouse of the person to whom an interim certificate has been issued dies within this period, the person with the interim certificate may apply again to the panel within six months of the date on which the marriage comes to an end. The panel must issue a full certificate if satisfied that the applicant is no longer married. Where an application is rejected, applicants may appeal on a point of law to the Court of Session.[32]

On issuing a full gender recognition certificate, the Secretary of **9–46** State must send a copy to the Registrar General for Scotland where the applicant is entered in the United Kingdom birth register so that

---

[27] 2004 Act, s.2. This is to be established through the medical evidence of the type laid down in s.3. This includes a report from a registered medical practitioner, or a chartered psychologist, either of whom must be practicing in the field of gender dysphoria. This report must include details of diagnosis. The second report need not be from a medical professional practicing in the field of gender dysphoria, but could be from any registered medical practitioner. At least one of the reports must include details of any treatment that the applicant has undergone, is undergoing or that is prescribed or planned, for the purposes of modifying sexual characteristics.

[28] s.3(6).

[29] s.4(2).

[30] s.4(3).

[31] s.5(1).

[32] s.8(1).

a new entry may be created to reflect the acquired gender.[33] As a result the applicant will be entitled to a new birth certificate reflecting the acquired gender. In practical terms this means that if the acquired gender is the male gender, the person's sex becomes that of a man and, if it is the female gender, the person's sex becomes that of a woman.[34] This does not however,

> "affect things done, or events occurring, before the certificate is issued; but it does operate for the interpretation of enactments passed, and instruments and other documents made, before the certificate is issued (as well as those passed or made afterwards)".[35]

As far as marriage is concerned this means that once the acquired gender has been legally recognised it will operate to allow a person to marry someone of the opposite gender to his or her acquired gender. However, restrictions will continue to cover relationships flowing from any previous marriage in the birth gender.[36]

9–47   There are some other important consequences that flow from the registration of a gender recognition certificate. Although the general rule is that the person's gender will be that of the acquired gender, s.12 provides that where parenthood is concerned, although a person is regarded as being of the acquired gender, s/he will retain their original status as either the father or mother of a child in order to ensure the continuity of parental responsibilities and rights. Similarly, when it comes to dealing with criminal law, many definitions of sexual offences remain gender-specific and hence refer specifically to acts committed by a man upon a woman. Section 20 ensures that where criminal liability would exist, but for the fact that a person—either the victim or the perpetrator—has subsequent to the offence changed gender, then criminal liability will exist regardless of the gender change. On the other hand, when it comes to succession, s.15 establishes that the

---

[33] 2004 Act, s.10(4) brings Sch.3 dealing with registration into effect. Under Pt 2 of Sch.3 that deals with Scotland, the Registrar General is to maintain, in the General Register Office of Births, Deaths and Marriages in Scotland, a Gender Recognition Register ("GRR"). This register will not be open to public inspection or search. Where a full gender recognition certificate is issued the Registrar General must make an entry in the GRR and mark the original entry referring to the birth (or adoption) of the transsexual person to show that the original entry has been superceded. This will ensure that caution is exercised when an application is received for a certificate from the original birth (or adoption) record. If applicants for a birth certificate provide details of the name recorded on the birth certificate, they will be issued with a certificate from the birth record. If they supply details recorded on the GRR, they will receive a certificate complied from the entry in the GRR. The mark linking the two entries will be chosen carefully to ensure that the fact that an entry is contained in the GRR is not apparent. The mark will not be included in any certificate compiled from the entries on the register.

[34] s.9(1).

[35] s.9(2).

[36] 2004 Act, s.11 and Sch.4, Pt 2.

general principles stated in s.9(1) apply; that is, if a will refers to the "eldest daughter" and a person who was previously a son becomes the "eldest daughter" following recognition in the acquired gender, that person (subject to s.18)[37] will inherit as the "eldest daughter".

Likewise, s.13 establishes that persons are to be treated in their **9–48** acquired gender for the purposes of acquiring state benefits, [38] especially where these include survivor's benefits such as Widowed Mother's Allowance,[39] Widow's Pension,[40] Invalidity Pension[41] and Category A retirement pension.[42] As the first two benefits cited are gender specific, entitlement must fall on legal recognition as a woman.[43] In the case where Widowed Mother's Allowance is brought to an end due to the issuing of a gender recognition certificate, this benefit may be replaced by a claim for Widowed Parent's Allowance.[44] Where a male-to-female transsexual person is or would be entitled to Widowed Parent's Allowance[45] that person will continue to be eligible for that Allowance after the certificate is issued because the Allowance is gender neutral.[46]

When it comes to retirement pensions there are differences in the **9–49** treatment of men, who reach pensionable age at 65, and women who reach pensionable age at 60. Although these inequalities will begin to disappear from April 2010, the equalisation process will not be complete until 2020. When dealing with Category A pensions—that are derived from the person's own National Insurance Contributions— provisions are made for current or future entitlement to a Category A pension after the full gender recognition certificate is issued on the basis of the transsexual person's acquired gender.[47] So, where a woman who is in receipt of a Category A pension changes gender before the age of 65, entitlement to that pension will cease. However, a claim can be made as a man at the age of 65.[48] Similarly, when a man changes gender and at the time he is under 65 but has attained the age at which a woman reaches pensionable age, that person will be treated as attaining the pensionable age of a woman when the full gender recognition certificate is issued.[49] When dealing with Category

---

[37] This provides for an application to be made to the court in situations where the devolution of property may be adversely affected by the changes brought about by this Act.

[38] See Sch.5.

[39] Under s.37 of the Social Security Contributions and Benefits Act 1992.

[40] Under s.38 of the 1992 Act.

[41] Under ss.40 and 41 of the 1992 Act.

[42] Under s.44 of the 1992 Act.

[43] Sch.5, paras 3 and 4.

[44] Sch.5, para.5.

[45] Under s.39A of the 1992 Act inserted by s.55 of the Welfare Reform and Pension Act 1999.

[46] Sch.5, para.5.

[47] Sch.5, para.7.

[48] Sch.5, para.7(2).

[49] Sch.5, para.7(3).

B pensions, that are based on the contributions of a spouse or former spouse, the general rule is that entitlement will be assessed on the basis of a person's acquired gender.[50]

Constitution of Regular Marriage: Marriage (Scotland) Act 1977 (as amended by the Marriage (Scotland) Act 2002)

9–50   A regular marriage may be either a religious[51] or a civil marriage.[52] In either case each party to the marriage must submit to the registrar of the district in which the marriage is to be solemnised, a notice of intention to marry, accompanied by a birth certificate, and where either party has previously been married, evidence of the dissolution of the previous marriage.[53] There are special provisions where a party to a marriage intended to be solemnised in Scotland is residing in another part of the United Kingdom or is not domiciled in any part of the United Kingdom and also for marriages outside Scotland where a party resides in Scotland.[54] After receipt of the notice, the registrar—if satisfied that there is no legal impediment or if so informed by the Registrar General—issues a marriage schedule which is the authority for the solemnisation of the marriage.[55] The schedule may not, however, be issued before the expiry of 14 days from receipt of the notice unless on the written request of a party to the marriage and with the authority of the Registrar General.[56]

Civil Marriage

9–51   The marriage must be conducted by an authorised registrar[57] and is normally conducted at the registrar's office,[58] although there, Scottish Ministers may make regulations extending the range of places where civil marriages may be solemnised with the approval of local authorities.[59] The marriage schedule must be available to the authorised registrar, both parties must be present together as well as two witnesses who profess to be aged 16 or over.[60] There is no prescribed form

---

[50]   Sch.5, para.8(1). For a detailed analysis of how this works see Sch.5, paras 8(2) through (5).

[51]   1977 Act, ss.9–16.

[52]   *ibid.*, ss.17–20.

[53]   *ibid.*, s.3(1).

[54]   s.3(4), 3(5) and s.7.

[55]   s.6.

[56]   s.6(4).

[57]   This is a district or assistant district registrar appointed in term of s.17 of the 1977 Act.

[58]   In exceptional cases, e.g. where a person is seriously ill or suffering from serious bodily injury and is unable to attend and there is good reason why the marriage cannot be delayed, a registrar may give special dispensation for it to be solemnised elsewhere, e.g. in a hospital. See s.18(4)(a) and (b).

[59]   1977 Act, s.18A added by the Marriage (Scotland) Act 2002. Places are approved by local authorities in accordance with regulations made under s.18A of the 1977 Act. See also the Marriage (Approval of Places) (Scotland) Regulations 2002 (SSI 2002/260).

[60]   s.19(2).

of ceremony laid down by the Act but it generally follows a certain procedure which involves the registrar explaining the nature of marriage in Scots law and asking the parties to declare if they know of any legal impediment to their marriage. The parties are then asked to take each other as husband and wife and to exchange consent to marriage. After they had done so, the registrar declares them to be married and the marriage schedule is then signed by both parties, the witnesses and the registrar. The marriage is then registered.

Religious Marriage

A religious marriage may be solemnised by a minister of the Church **9–52** of Scotland, a minister, clergyman, pastor or priest of a religious body prescribed by the regulations, or other approved celebrant.[61] The marriage schedule must be produced to the celebrant and the parties to the marriage and two witnesses (professing to be aged 16 or over) must be present. Where the celebrant belongs to the Church of Scotland or a prescribed religious body, the marriage must be in accordance with a form recognised as sufficient by the church or body to which the celebrant belongs.[62] In any other case, the statutory requirement is that the form of solemnisation must include a declaration by the parties, in the presence of each other, the celebrant and the witnesses, that they accept each other as husband and wife and a declaration by the celebrant thereafter that they are husband and wife.[63] After the ceremony, the marriage schedule is signed by both parties, the witnesses and the celebrant. It must then be returned to the district registrar for registration within three days of the ceremony.[64]

Unauthorised Celebrant and Validity of Marriage

It is an offence for anyone, who is not within the classes of person **9–53** authorised under the Act to solemnise marriages, to conduct a marriage ceremony in such a way as to lead the parties to believe that he or she is solemnising a valid marriage. It is also an offence for the celebrant of a religious marriage to solemnise it without at the time having the marriage schedule, or for either the celebrant of a religious marriage or an authorised registrar to solemnise a marriage without both parties being present.[65] Provided both parties were present at the marriage ceremony *and* the marriage has been registered, its validity is not to be questioned in any legal proceedings on the ground of failure to comply with a requirement or restriction imposed by the Act.[66] This

---

[61] 1977 Act, s.8(1), s.9 and s.12. See also Marriage (Prescription of Religious Bodies) (Scotland) Regulations 1977 (SI 1977/1670).

[62] s.14(a).

[63] s.14(b) and s.9(3).

[64] s.15(2).

[65] s.24.

[66] 1997 Act, s.23A, as inserted by the Law Reform (Miscellaneous Provisions) (Scotland) Act 1980, s.22(1)(d).

provision does not save a marriage that has never been registered and where no marriage schedule was ever issued.[67] In such a case the marriage is null and void.

Impediments to Marriage

9–54   At any time before the solemnisation of a marriage, any person may submit an objection in writing to the registrar.[68] Where the objection relates to a matter of misdescription or inaccuracy, the registrar may, with the approval of the Registrar General, make any necessary correction. In any other case he or she must, pending consideration of the objection by the Registrar General, suspend the completion or issue of the marriage schedule or, if a marriage schedule has already been issued for a religious marriage, notify the celebrant of the objection and advise him not to solemnise the marriage.[69] If the Registrar General is satisfied that, on consideration of an objection, there is a legal impediment to the marriage as set out in s.5(4) of the 1977 Act[70] he must direct the registrar to take all reasonable steps to ensure that the marriage does not take place. If on the other hand he is satisfied that there is no legal impediment, he must inform the registrar and the marriage schedule may then be completed and issued at that stage so that the marriage may proceed.[71]

Defects and Invalidity: Effect on Marriage

9–55   A marriage will be treated as void, that is as a nullity, where either party is under the age of 16,[72] or falls within the prohibited degrees of relationship.[73] It will also be treated as void where it falls within the statutory legal impediments to marriage under s.5(4) which include in addition to the foregoing, the existence of a prior subsisting marriage, incapacity with regard to understanding or consent, and the fact that both parties are of the same sex. Section 5(4)(f) also contemplates the existence of an impediment under a foreign domicile law of one or both parties. In addition, a marriage may be rendered voidable, that is it remains valid up until the point at which it is successfully challenged, on the ground of impotency.[74] In the past,

---

[67] *Saleh v Saleh*, 1987 S.L.T. 633.

[68] s.5(1).

[69] s.5(2).

[70] See paras 9–11 to 9–27 above.

[71] s.5(3) and s.6(1).

[72] s.1.

[73] s.2.

[74] The SLC recommended the abolition of impotency as a voidable ground of marriage in its *Report on Family Law*, Scot Law Com. No.135 (1992), Recommendations 49 and 50. The Scottish Executive, however, declined their recommendation on the basis that it "provides a facility that would not otherwise be available to a limited number of couples in extreme circumstances": see *Parents and Children: a White Paper on Scottish Family Law* (2000), para.10.10.

the consequences of declaring a marriage void were severe. Each party lost their status as married and, with it, any legal claims to support or property which they might have had arising from the marriage. In addition, the status of any children of the relationship was altered from legitimate to illegitimate, with all the legal consequences that this entailed. The only exception to this rule related to the children of putative marriages, that is, void marriages where one or both parties believed in good faith that the marriage was valid. Over time, the unfortunate consequences attached to nullity have been modified. When it comes to the parties themselves, a court,[75] on granting declarator of nullity, has the same powers to award financial provision in respect of a void or voidable marriage as it has on granting a decree of divorce.[76]

Irrregular Marriage

Under common law only one form of irregular marriage has survived **9–56** until its recent abolition[77]; that is, marriage by cohabitation with habit and repute.[78] This form of marriage arises where a couple have set up home together without going through *any* form of ceremony. It operates on the presumption that *tacit* consent to marriage is constituted by the cohabitation, as man and wife,[79] in Scotland,[80] of a couple free to marry, who are generally reputed to *be* husband and wife. The presumption is rebuttable. There are two major hurdles to be overcome in establishing a marriage of this kind, first, by satisfying the requirement that the cohabitation must be for a considerable period,[81] and secondly, fulfilling the requirements of habit and repute.[82] It has been established that there is no minimum period required for cohabitation.[83] To meet the second requirement however, not only must the parties behave towards one another as husband and wife but they must also be reputed to be such by third parties. According to *Low v Gorman*,[84] "although

---

[75] Until May 4, 2006, only the Court of Session had the power to award a declarator of nullity of marriage (and indeed, declarator of marriage also). This power was extended to the Sheriff court by SSI 2006/207.

[76] Family Law (Scotland) Act 1985, s.17(1).

[77] It has been abolished under s.3 of the Family Law (Scotland) Act 2006 except for certain circumstances: see paras 9–57 to 9–58.

[78] The other two were declaration *de praesenti* and promise *subsequent copula* both of which were abolished by s.5 of the Marriage (Scotland) Act 1939.

[79] Note that it is not cohabitation *per se* that gives rise to the presumption but cohabitation as husband and wife.

[80] See Lord Watson's dicta to this effect in the *Dysart Peerage Case* (1881) L.R. 6 App. Cas. 489 at pp.537–538.

[81] *Campbell v Campbell* (1866) 4 M. 867.

[82] See *Ackerman v Blackburn*, 2002 S.L.T. 37 where the court held that the evidence fell far short of establishing the pursuer's averments of general repute.

[83] See *Kamperman v MacIver*, 1994 S.L.T. 763 where the court held that a period of cohabitation lasting 6 and a half months after an impediment to marriage was removed was not insufficient.

[84] 1970 S.L.T. 356 at 395.

repute need not be universal it must be general, substantially unvarying and consistent and not divided". The opinion of others comes into play and the weight attached to their opinions varies.[85] It is clear that if parties openly admit that they are *not* married then marriage on the basis of cohabitation with habit and repute can never be established. The issue of admissions to certain third parties is, however, less clear cut. In *Mackenzie v Scott*,[86] the court refused to grant a declarator of marriage on the basis that as several friends know that the couple were not in fact married and that they had discussed getting married on several occasions, all they had was a *future* intention to marry and that they did not regard themselves as married. This case may be contrasted with that of *Shaw v Henderson*[87] where the court granted a declarator in circumstances very similar to those of *MacKenzie v Scott*, adopting the view that while relatives knew that the couple had never gone through *any* form of ceremony this did not mean that they did not regard themselves as being husband and wife. This approach was criticised in *Kamperman v McIver*[88] but followed in *Dewar v Dewar*.[89]

9–57 The fact that there was a legal impediment to marriage when the cohabitation began does not preclude the constitution of marriage by continuance of the cohabitation with repute after the parties become free to marry,[90] although circumstances after the removal of the impediment must be sufficient in themselves to establish the inference of tacit consent.[91] Consent to marriage may be proved by cohabitation with habit and repute where spouses have previously been married to one another and divorced.[92] A declarator of marriage must be sought from the court before the legal rights and obligations that attach to marriage will apply to a marriage constituted by consent following relevant cohabitation with habit and repute.[93] The SLC recommended that, given the uncertain status of habit and repute marriage, such marriages

---

[85] See *Petrie v Petrie*, 1911 S.C. 360 where the court placed greater weight on the evidence of the man's professional colleagues and relatives, who considered him unmarried, compared with the views of persons such as the cleaner and the postman. See also *Ackerman v Blackburn*, above, n.82, where the parties were considered married by neighbours, customers of the pursuer's shop and members of the various organisations with which the deceased was involved, but not by close family members of the deceased. In weighing the evidence the views of the latter prevailed. Also *Skeikh v Skeikh*, 2005 Fam. L.R. 7 in which the woman's parents knew she was not married but those encountering the couple in daily life assumed they were. The woman had not wanted to enter marriage via a muslim ceremony as offered by the male. Declarator was granted.

[86] 1980 S.L.T. (Notes) 9.

[87] 1982 S.L.T. 211.

[88] 1993 S.L.T. 732.

[89] 1995 S.L.T. 467.

[90] *Campbell v Campbell* (1867) 5 M. (HL) 115.

[91] *Low v Gorman*, 1970 S.L.T. 356.

[92] *Mullen v Mullen*, 1991 S.L.T. 205.

[93] Where such a declarator is granted the court must, under s.21 of the 1977 Act, state the date on which the marriage was constituted and forward it to the Registrar General for registration. See also n.81 above.

should be abolished.[94] After consultation, the Scottish Executive initially declined to implement this recommendation on the basis that they did not "wish to penalise those who wish to benefit from this form of marriage, however irregular it may be".[95] The Scottish Parliament, however, took the view that this type of marriage was obsolete and abolished it prospectively, except in the case of invalid marriages entered into abroad, where one of parties to that marriage has died.[96] In this situation, where the parties were married "outwith the United Kingdom" and the marriage proves to be invalid under the law of the place where the purported marriage was entered into, a marriage by cohabitation with habit and repute may be established. This is dependent upon *all* the following factors being met, namely:

- both parties belief that they are married to one another up until the death of one of them[97];
- both the deceased and surviving party are domiciled in Scotland at the date of death[98]; and
- that the surviving party only became aware of the invalidity of the purported marriage after the other party's death.[99]

In all other cases, it will no longer be competent to establish marriage by cohabitation with habit and repute for cohabitation entered into *on and after* May 4, 2006 when the Family Law (Scotland) Act 2006 came into effect. This will not, however, have any effect on the validity of marriages of this type entered into before the Act took effect or where the cohabitation with habit and repute: **9–58**

- ended before the commencement of s.3(1)[1]; or
- began before, but ended after commencement[2]; or
- began before, and continues after, commencement.[3]

Declarator of Freedom and Putting to Silence

The 2006 Act also removes the availability of an action for Declarator of freedom and putting to silence at s.42. Such an action was used in days when irregular marriages were common and there was doubt as to whether a couple had privately exchanged consent to marry yet, a Declarator of nullity of marriage was not appropriate if there was not even a semblance of a marriage. The action had become virtually unknown and is now obsolete.   **9–59**

---

[94] See *Report on Family Law* (1992), para.7.9.
[95] See *Parents and Children* (2000), para.10.5.
[96] FLSA 2006, s.3(3) and (4).
[97] s.3(4)(d).
[98] s.3(4)(a) and (b).
[99] s.3(2)(a).
[1] s.3(2)(a).
[2] s.3(2)(b).
[3] s.3(2)(c).

Civil Partnership Act 2004

9–60 Same-sex couples are not permitted to marry but they may form civil partnerships if they fulfil the criteria laid down by the Civil Partnership Act 2004. This has the effect of giving registered civil partners virtually all the same rights as married couples.[4]

Eligibility

9–61 Eligibility is set down in s.86 of the Act which applies to Scotland and which states that two people are *not* eligible to register as civil partners of each other if:

"(a) they are not of the same sex,
 (b) they are related in a forbidden degree,[5]
 (c) either has not attained the age of 16, or
 (d) either is married or already in a civil partnership, or
 (e) either is incapable of—
   (i) understanding the nature of civil partnership, or
   (ii) validly consenting to its formation."

In effect, the same type of restrictions that are placed on marriage apply to a civil partnership. Thus, a man cannot enter into a partnership with another man if he is related to him in a degree specified in column 1 of Sch.10 and a woman cannot enter into a partnership with another woman if she is related to her in a degree specified in column 2 of that schedule.[6] However, (as is also the case with step-relationships established through marriage) provision is made for allowing a man and any man related to him in any degree specified in column 1 of para.2 of Sch.10, and for a woman and any woman related to her in any degree specified in column 2 of that paragraph, to enter into a civil partnership if:

(a) both persons have attained the age of 21, and
(b) the younger has not at any time before attaining the age of 18 lived in the same household as the elder and been treated by the elder as a child of the elder's family.[7]

9–62 The restrictions that were placed on a man entering a civil partnership with:

- the father of his former wife; or
- the father of his former civil partner; or
- the former husband of his daughter; or
- the former civil partner of his son,

---

[4] But see K. Norrie on "What the Civil Partnership Act 2004 does not do", 2005 S.L.T. 35.
[5] These are set out in Sch.10 of the 2004 Act.
[6] 2004 Act, s.86(2).
[7] *ibid.*, s.86(3).

(and vice versa for women) have now been repealed by Sch.3 of the FLSA 2006 consistent with the abolition of the equivalent restrictions placed on marriage with former in-laws.[8]

Where a person wishing to form a civil partnership has acquired a **9–63** new gender under the Gender Recognition Act 2004, this acquired gender is treated as the operative gender for the purposes of determining the forbidden degrees of relationship set out in Sch.10.[9] As with marriage, relationships of the half blood are treated as being of the same order as relationships of the full blood when it comes to the proscribed relationships set out in para.1 of the schedule.[10] What this means is that, in practice, a person could not form a civil partnership with their sibling, whether that sibling was full blood, half blood or adopted.

Registration

Notice of Proposed Partnership

For a civil partnership to take effect in law it must be registered. **9–64** The 2004 Act provides for a system of registration that follows that of marriage.[11] This involves the appointment of authorised registrars by the Registrar General for Scotland who will implement the necessary procedures which imitate those of marriage.[12] Thus, parties to a proposed civil partnership must fulfil the civil preliminaries, including the submission of a notice of proposed civil partnership (together with the prescribed fee) to the appropriate district registrar, who then enters the details in a civil partnership notice book.[13] A notice must be accompanied by:

(a) the birth certificate of the person submitting it,
(b) if that person has previously been married or in civil partnership and—
    (i) the marriage or civil partnership has been dissolved, a copy of the decree of divorce or dissolution, or
    (ii) the other party to the marriage or civil partnership has died, the death certificate of that other party, and
(c) if that person has previously ostensibly been married or in civil partnership but decree of annulment has been obtained, a copy of that decree.[14]

---

[8] See para.9–19 above.
[9] 2004 Act, s.86(5) through (7) which provide that s.86(4) and paras 2 and 3 of Sch.10 are to have effect subject to certain modifications.
[10] s.86(9).
[11] See ss.87 through 100 of the 2004 Act.
[12] s.87.
[13] 2004 Act, s.89. This is to be done according to the Registrar General's prescriptions that include the form and content of the book.
[14] 2004 Act, s.88(2). Provision is also made for those cases where a person is unable to submit the required certificate or decree under s.88(3).

9–65 Accompanying the notice must be a declaration by the person submitting it that s/he believes the intended civil partners are eligible to be in civil partnership with each other.[15] A prescribed period of waiting, namely 14 days,[16] follows during which time the details are publicised[17] by both the district registrar and the Registrar General allowing for any objections to the proposed partnership to be made.[18] Provision is made for early registration to take place "at a date earlier than 14 days after the publicisation of the intended date of signing the civil partnership schedule".[19] This will allow those who are very ill and who are not expected to recover, for example, to enter into an expedited form of partnership. There is also an accelerated procedure under s.96 that provides for the signing of a civil partnership schedule to take place quickly, where the couple were previously married to each other and one of them has changed gender under the provisions of the Gender Recognition Act 2004. Thus the signing of the civil partnership schedule can take place on any of the 30 days immediately following the day that both notices of proposed civil partnerships are given, or if they are given on different days, on the day the second notice is given.[20]

9–66 Where an objection is raised there are two ways in which the district registrar may proceed. In the case of an insubstantial error—such as a misdescription or inaccuracy—the district registrar must notify the intended civil partners, make such enquiries as s/he thinks fit and correct the relevant documents (subject to the approval of the Registrar General).[21] In any other case, s/he must notify the Registrar General at once and, pending consideration of the objection by the Registrar General, suspend the completion or issue of the civil partnership schedule.[22] The Registrar General must either direct the district registrar that there exists a legal impediment to registration or, that there is no such impediment, allowing the parties to go ahead with the registration.[23]

---

[15] s.88(5) and (6).

[16] 2004 Act, s.90 The section provides that the date of signing the civil partnership document "should be a date more than 14 days after publicisation by the district registrar".

[17] Under s.90(2) these include the names of the intended civil partners and the date on which it is intended to register them as civil partners.

[18] 2004 Act, s.92 provides procedures for any person to object in writing to the district registrar against the issue of a civil partnership schedule in order to prevent the registration. As with marriage, such objections must relate to a lawful impediment to the partnership. Under s.92(6) there is a legal impediment to registration where the intended civil partners are not eligible to be in civil partnership with each other (see para.9–61 above).

[19] s.91.

[20] s.96(2).

[21] s.92(4)(a).

[22] s.92(4)(b).

[23] s.92(5).

Civil Partnership Schedule

Where there are no objections to the proposed partnership and the **9–67** district registrar is satisfied that there is no legal impediment to registration s/he issues a civil partnership schedule after the requisite period of notice has expired.[24] This enables the couple to proceed to registration by signing the completed civil partnership schedule before two witnesses aged 16 or over and an authorised registrar.[25] This may be done at a registration office or at any place (other than religious premises)[26] which the intended civil partners and the local registration authority agree.[27] Before signing, the parties must confirm that (to the best of their knowledge) the particulars set out in the civil partnership schedule are correct.[28] As soon as practicable after the civil partnership schedule has been signed, the authorised registrar must enter the particulars into a register known as the "civil partnership register".[29] Thereafter, no alteration is to be made in the civil partnership register except as authorised under the 2004 Act or under any other Act (including an Act of the Scottish Parliament).[30] In addition to providing for the formation of civil partnerships within the United Kingdom, the 2004 Act also provides for the formation of civil partnerships outside the United Kingdom under an Order in Council.[31]

Offences

To underpin its authority the Act creates offences with penalties **9–68** attached to them where its provisions are not complied with in certain circumstances. Where one of the parties enters into a civil partnership knowing that either or both of the parties is already married to or in civil partnership with another, that party will commit an offence.[32] An offence will also be committed where a person knowingly falsifies or forges a civil partnership document,[33] or uses, or gives or sends to any person as genuine any false or forged civil procedure document.[34]

---

[24] s.94.
[25] 2004 Act, s.85. Note that all parties, namely the couple, the witnesses and the authorised registrar must be present.
[26] These are defined under s.93 (3) as premises which "(a) are used solely or mainly for religious purposes, or (b) have been so used and have not subsequently been used solely or mainly for other purposes."
[27] s.93.
[28] s.95(1).
[29] 2004 Act, s.95(2). Under s.98 such registers are subject to certain provisions of the Registration of Births, Deaths and Marriages (Scotland) Act 1965 that provide for the examination of the civil partnership register by district examiners, the searching of indexes kept by registrars or the Registrar General for Scotland and the application to the register of the process of correction.
[30] s.99.
[31] Made under Ch.1, Pt 5 of the Act.
[32] s.100(1).
[33] s.100(2)(a).
[34] s.100(2)(b).

The other offences concern the authorised registrar registering the parties:

- before the civil partnership schedule has been duly completed[35];
- without both parties being present[36];
- as civil partners of each other in a place other than a registration office or place agreed to by the local registration authority.[37]

9–69 Finally, an offence is committed where a person who is not the authorised registrar "conducts himself in such a way as to lead intended civil partners to believe that he is authorised to register them as civil partners of each other."[38] Where an offence is committed, the guilty person will be liable to a fine or imprisonment or both.[39]

Validity

9–70 Once registered in Scotland, a civil partnership can only be set aside as void by either party to the partnership, or any other interested party, on the grounds that the couple were not eligible to enter into such a partnership,[40] or that, even though eligible, "either of them did not validly consent to its formation".[41] For those civil partnerships registered outside Scotland, the 2004 Act sets out special provisions for determining their validity.[42]

In the next chapter we consider the effect of marriage and civil partnership upon the legal rights of individuals entering such a relationship and upon their property.

---

[35] s.100(2)(c).
[36] s.100(2)(e).
[37] s.100(2)(f).
[38] s.100(2)(d).
[39] 2004 Act, s.100(3), The size of the fine and the length of imprisonment will depend upon where there is a conviction on indictment, or on summary conviction.
[40] 2004 Act, s.123(a): see para.9–61 above.
[41] s.123(b).
[42] s.124.

CHAPTER 10

DOMESTIC RELATIONS, PERSONS AND PROPERTY

In Ch.9, we discussed the rules for establishing a valid marriage and **10–01** a valid civil partnership. Logically, the next question that arises is, what legal effect does marriage and civil partnership have on the person and property of spouses and civil partners? Further are such persons treated in a different manner from unmarried heterosexual and same-sex couples?

At one time, a husband acquired, on marriage, complete rights to **10–02** his wife's moveable property, a right known as *the jus mariti*. He also acquired the more limited right to administer her heritable property by virtue of *the jus administrationis*. Even after *the jus mariti* was abolished in 1881,[1] the husband retained the right of administration in respect of the whole of a wife's property, heritable and moveable, until 1920. At that date, however, the Married Women's Property (Scotland) Act 1920 established the basic principle of modern Scots law (now to be found in s.24 of the Family Law (Scotland) Act 1985) that marriage "shall not of itself" affect the respective rights of the parties to the marriage in relation to:

(a) their property, or
(b) their legal capacity.

Thus, spouses are free to acquire, own and dispose of property as though unmarried; enter into contracts as independent persons; sue each other in delict; and may be prosecuted for crimes committed one against the other (such as theft or assault). However, these general propositions are subject to certain qualifications which will be examined in this and succeeding chapters.

MARRIAGE, CIVIL PARTNERSHIP, AND PERSONAL STATUS

Domicile and Residence

At one time, the domicile of both the wife and any children of a **10–03** marriage was dependent on, and followed, that of the husband. The husband also had the right to determine where the matrimonial home

---

[1] Under the Married Women's Property (Scotland) Act 1881, s.1.

should be located and a wife who refused to reside there could be divorced for desertion, unless she could establish that the husband's choice was not genuine or reasonable.[2] Section 1 of the Domicile and Matrimonial Proceedings Act 1973 abolished the wife's domicile of dependence, and established that a married woman could acquire a domicile of choice in the same way as any other person over the age of 16.[3] Further, in 1984, the husband's right to determine the location of the matrimonial home was abolished along with certain other outdated rules affecting spouses.[4]

The domicile of a child is determined by the domicile of his/her parents under the age of 16[5] or, if the parents do not live in the same country as each other, then the domicile "for which the child has for the time being the closest connection".[6] Once a child attains the age of 16 s/he becomes capable of having independent domicile.[7]

Sexual Relations, Fidelity, and Marital rape

10–04   It is clear that spouses have a duty to adhere, i.e. to live together and be sexually faithful with respect to one another. The duty of adherence can no longer be enforced by court action,[8] but where a spouse is unfaithful, grounds exist for divorce.[9] What has been controversial in recent years is the extent to which spouses are obliged to have marital sexual relations. Scots law certainly recognises that sex is an important component of marriage, and that incurable and permanent impotency at the date of marriage (as opposed to wilful non-consummation) gives either party the right to have the marriage declared voidable.[10]

10–05   Does this mean that a husband may use force to compel his wife to accede to sexual relations? Where this occurs between parties who are not spouses, this constitutes the crime of rape. It is only over the last 20 years or so that marital rape has been recognised as a crime by the

---

[2] *Stewart v Stewart*, 1959 S.L.T. (Notes) 70.

[3] Transitional problems persisted for women who had already acquired a domicile of dependence before the 1973 Act came into force: see *I.R.C. v Duchess of Portland* [1982] 1 All E.R. 784.

[4] Law Reform (Husband and Wife) (Scotland) Act 1984, s.4.

[5] Family Law (Scotland) Act 2006 s.22(1) and (2). Prior to the 2006 Act, a legitimate child took domicile of dependence from the father (unless s/he did not reside with him as there was a statutory exception to the general rule under the Domicile and Matrimonial Proceedings Act 1973). Under the common law however, a child whose parents were unmarried took the domicile of his or her mother.

[6] *ibid.*, s.22(3).

[7] Age of Legal Capacity (Scotland)Act 1991, s.7.

[8] Law Reform (Husband and Wife) (Scotland) Act 1984, s.2.

[9] On the basis of adultery under s.1(2)(a) of the Divorce (Scotland) Act 1976.

[10] Impotency is the only ground on which a marriage can be declared voidable in Scots law. The Scottish Law Commission recommended its abolition in *Improving Scottish Family Law* (Scottish Office, 1999). However, as this would effectively remove the only civil law remedy available to those whose religious beliefs forbid divorce, the recommendation was not followed. For a fuller discussion of voidable marriage see Edwards & Griffiths, *Family Law* (1st edn), paras 9.31 *et seq.*

courts, first in Scotland[11] and then in England.[12] The courts were reluctant to accord recognition to marital rape, not only because of difficulties of proof in a situation where the parties already have an intimate relationship, but also because of antique Institutional authority. According to Hume, a husband could not rape his wife.[13] This rested on the belief that when a woman consented to marriage, she thereby irrevocably consented to sexual intercourse with her husband. Over the last 25 years, however, the Scottish courts have unpicked the husband's immunity from prosecution for marital rape, at first only in cases where the parties were actually living apart when the alleged rape took place,[14] and latterly even where spouses continued to cohabit.[15] As the Lord Justice-General put it in *S v HM Advocate*:

> "Nowadays it cannot seriously be maintained that by marriage a wife submits herself irrevocably to sexual intercourse in all circumstances . . . the fiction of implied consent has no useful purpose to serve today in the law of rape in Scotland . . . logically the only question is whether or not as matter of fact the wife consented to the acts complained of".[16]

Name and Citizenship

In Scots law, a woman has always been entitled to retain her own **10–06** surname on marriage. The custom of women adopting their husband's surnames on marriage is said to have crept into Scotland in the first half of the nineteenth century.[17] Prior to that, it was the custom for a married woman to retain her own name.[18] Current practice in formal legal documents is for a married woman to be cited by reference to both her maiden name and her husband's surname. Marriage also now has no automatic effect on British citizenship. A spouse of a British citizen can acquire citizenship only by naturalisation, which is at the discretion of the Secretary of State.[19]

New requirements for naturalisation were introduced by the **10–07** Nationality, Immigration and Asylum Act 2002 ("NIAA 2002")[20] and previous differences between the naturalisation of spouses and non-

---

[11] *S v HM Advocate*, 1989 S.L.T. 469.
[12] *R. v R* [1992] A.C. 599, HL. An attempt to challenge the concept of marital rape by taking the matter to the European Court failed in *SW v UK; CR v UK* [1996] Fam law 275, ECtHR.
[13] Hume, I, 302
[14] *HM Advocate v Duffy*, 1983 S.L.T. 7; *HM Advocate v Paxton*, 1985 S.L.T. 96.
[15] *S v HM Advocate*, 1989 S.L.T. 469.
[16] *ibid.*, at p.473.
[17] See E. Clive, *The Law of Husband and Wife in Scotland* (4th edn, W.Green, Edinburgh, 1997), para.11.019 for further details.
[18] See *Grieve v Pringle* (1797) Mor. 5951.
[19] British Nationality Act 1981 ("BNA 1981"), s.6.
[20] Nationality, Immigration and Asylum Act 2002 ("NIAA 2002"), ss.1–3 and Sch.1; BNA 1981, Sch.1, para.1(2)(c).

spouses, other than the residence requirements,[21] have gone. First, all applicants have to show that they are of full age and capacity and of good character. Secondly, it is necessary for spouses as well as non-spouse applicants to have sufficient knowledge of the English, Welsh or Scottish Gaelic language[22] and sufficient knowledge about life in the United Kingdom, unless it would be unreasonable to expect the applicant to fulfil either requirement because of age, or physical or mental condition.[23] Successful applicants (if of full age) will now have to take an oath and pledge loyalty to the United Kingdom and democracy at a citizenship ceremony.[24] Details of this are set out in a new s.42 and Sch.5 to the British Nationality Act 1981 ("BNA 1981").[25]

Immigration[26]

10–08 Marriage to a United Kingdom citizen does not automatically grant a right to enter and settle in the United Kingdom. A person seeking admission to the United Kingdom as the spouse of a person already settled in the United Kingdom must satisfy the following requirements:

(ii) that the parties to the marriage have met; and
(iii) each of the parties intends to live permanently with the other as his or her spouse and the marriage is subsisting; and
(iv) there will be adequate accommodation for the parties and any dependants without recourse to public funds in accommodation which they own or occupy exclusively; and
(v) the parties will be able to maintain themselves and any dependants adequately without recourse to public funds; and
(vi) the applicant holds a valid United Kingdom entry clearance for entry in this capacity.[27]

10–09 Similar rules apply where a person with limited leave to enter or remain in the United Kingdom seeks an extension on the basis of marriage to a person settled here.[28] In either case, the successful applicant is usually initially allowed to remain in the United Kingdom for

---

[21] Three years for spouses and five years for non-spouses.
[22] BNA 1981, Sch.1, paras 1(1)(c), 3(e) as amended by the NIAA 2002, s.2(1)(a).
[23] BNA 1981, Sch.1, paras 1(1)(ca) and 2(e), 3(e) and 4 as amended.
[24] NIAA 2002, s.3 and Sch.1, substituting BNA 1981, s.42 and Sch.5 and adding new ss.42A and 42B. See also British Nationality (General) Regulations 2003 (SI 2003/548), as amended by SI 2003/3158, SI 2004/1726 and SI 2004/2109.
[25] Macdonald and Webber, *Macdonald's Immigration Law and Practice* (6th edn, Butterworths, London, 2005), paras 2.54–2.56, Ch.2, pp.86–90.
[26] This is governed by the Immigration Act 1971, as amended by the Immigration Rules (1994 HC 395); the Immigration and Asylum Act 1999 ("IAA 1999") and the NIAA 2002. See, further, Macdonald and Webber, above, Ch.11, pp.579–667.
[27] Immigration Act 1971 as amended by the statement of Change in Immigration Rules (1994, HC 395), para.281 as amended by 1997 HC 26, para.1; 2003 HC 538; Cmnd.5597 (2002).
[28] *ibid.*, para.284 as amended by 1997 HC 26 para.2; Cmnd.5949 (2003) and Cmnd.6339 (2004).

up to two years probationary period. After that the Secretary of State may extend the stay if he is satisfied that the requirements listed above are met.[29] The rules are much less stringent where the applicant concerned is an EU citizen or a member of an EU citizen's family.[30]

Section 249 and Sch.23 of the Civil Partnership Act 2004 deal with **10–10** immigration control in relation to civil partnerships. Part 1 of the schedule provides that where two people wish to register as civil partners and one of them is subject to immigration control then the provisions set out in the schedule will apply. A person is subject to immigration control if s/he is not a national of a state which is a contracting party to the Agreement on the European Economic Areas (signed at Oporto on May 2, 1999) and s/he requires leave to enter or remain in the United Kingdom.[31] In such a case s/he must satisfy the qualifying conditions which require the applicant to:

- have an entry clearance granted expressly for the purpose of enabling him to form a civil partnership in the United Kingdom;
- have the written permission of the Secretary of State to form a civil partnership in the United Kingdom; or otherwise to
- fall within a class specified by regulations.

In these circumstances, a notice of proposed civil partnership cannot take effect unless the registration authority is satisfied by the production of specified evidence that the person subject to immigration control fulfils the qualifying condition set out in Pt 1.[32]

Immigration officers and the Secretary of State can refuse leave to **10–11** enter to certain nationalities, if justified by statistical evidence or intelligence.[33] People from "visa national"[34] countries always need to get entry clearance before they can enter the United Kingdom. Some countries' nationals also need transit visas to pass through the United Kingdom.[35] People apply for entry clearance at the United Kingdom embassy or High Commission in their own country.

The Immigration Rules make provision for people who are not **10–12** married but have a permanent relationship.[36] The rules were altered to give effect to the right to family or private life under Art.8 of the ECHR, and now allow for the admission of men and women aged 18 or over to join partners of the same or opposite sex aged 18 or

---

[29] *ibid.*, para.285 as amended by 2003 HC 538.
[30] See Directive 2004/38/EC.
[31] Sch.23, Pt 1, para.1 of the 2004 Act.
[32] Pt 2 of Sch.23, applying to England and Wales, and Pt 3 of the schedule that provides similar procedures to those in Pt 2, which are to apply where the civil partnership is to be formed in Scotland and one of the proposed civil partners is subject to immigration control.
[33] Race Relations (Immigration and Asylum) Authorisation 2001.
[34] HC 395, para.24.
[35] IAA 1999, s.41 and Immigration (Transit Visa) Amendment Order 2000 (SI 2000/1381).
[36] HC 395, paras 295A–O, inserted by Cm.4851 (2000).

over,[37] who are present and settled or being admitted for settlement in the United Kingdom,[38] or who are in the United Kingdom with limited leave for work, business or investment,[39] and with whom they have been living in a relationship akin to marriage for two years.[40] As with spouses, leave to enter to join or accompany an unmarried partner settled in the United Kingdom will normally be for two years in the first instance.[41] Once settlement as a spouse or unmarried partner is achieved, re-admission will be as a returning resident rather than a spouse, and thus subsequent marriage or relationship breakdown does not affect immigration status. However, if settlement has been obtained by means of a false representation made by the immigrant, e.g. as to the subsistence of the relationship, s/he may be subject to administrative removal.[42] Given the concern over "sham" marriages for immigration purposes the government has placed certain restrictions on marriage. For example, there are restrictions on parties switching their short-term "leave to remain" to "leave as the spouse of a British citizen or resident".[43] Other, onerous restrictions are contained in the Asylum and Immigration (Treatment of Claimants) Act 2004.[44] As part of the tightening up process, registrars to whom a notice of marriage/civil partnership has been given are now under a duty to report to the Secretary of State for the Home Department a suspicion on reasonable grounds that the marriage will be a sham marriage/partnership.[45]

Contract and Delict

10–13   As noted earlier, married women and men can sue and be sued, in contract and delict, even though the other party to the action is their spouse.[46] Marriage does not make one spouse automatically liable for the debts, obligations or delicts of the other spouse.

---

[37] HC 395, para.295AA, inserted by 2003 HC 538 and amended by 2004 HC 164.

[38] HC 395, para.295A(i).

[39] HC 395, para.295J.

[40] The policy formulated in October 1997 required four years' cohabitation as a threshold period which made it very difficult for someone who began a relationship as a British citizen while here in a temporary capacity to qualify.

[41] HC 395, paras 295B and 295E.

[42] IAA 1999, s.10(1)(b) inserted by NIAA 2002, s.74.

[43] See HC 395, para.284 as amended, applying to marriage applications from April 1, 2003 that provides there is to be "no switching" if the applicant has not been in the UK beyond six months from the date of last admission, unless admitted as a fiancé.

[44] See, further Macdonald and Webber, above n.25, para.11.67, p.621.

[45] IAA 1999, s.24. See also Reporting of Suspicious Marriages (Scotland) Regulations 2000 (SI 2000/3232). These provisions are additional to the requirements of the Asylum and Immigration (Treatment of Claimants etc.) Act 2004, ss.19–25 which require permission for civil marriage to be obtained from the Home Office. For civil partners see IAA 1999, s.24A inserted by s.261(1), Sch.27, para.162 of the CPA 2004.

[46] While the Married Women's Property Act 1920, s.1, gave married women the same legal capacity to *enter into* contracts as unmarried women, it was not until *Horsburgh*

At one time, a husband was responsible for his wife's antenuptial **10–14** debts, and was also personally liable for household debts contracted by his wife, since by law she had ostensible authority to contract on behalf of her husband in the domestic sphere (*praepositura rebus domesticis*). These rules have now been repealed.[47] But it is still, anomalously, possible for a woman to pledge her husband's credit for necessaries at common law,[48] and he would then be liable for any debt. However, this rule of law has now become obsolete as very few shopkeepers would today hand over goods on a mere private pledge of credit, nor are most members of the public aware the rule exists. The rule extends from a husband's obligation to aliment his wife, however such a duty is also now owed by a wife to a husband.[49] The same obligation applies to those in civil partnerships also.[50] A modern gender-free equivalent therefore is probably for spouse A to allow spouse B to use a credit card which is paid off by spouse A, or alternatively for both spouses to draw cheques on a joint current account. There is, of course, no reason why one spouse cannot expressly or impliedly appoint the other spouse their agent under ordinary principles of contract, and thus allow that spouse to bind them to contracts.

In the field of delict, statutory rules allow the surviving spouse or **10–15** cohabiting partner of a deceased person to claim damages where that person has died due to the negligence of a third party.[51] These rules have been extended to cover civil partners."[52] Such damages include amounts for both financial loss of support and non-financial consequences such as loss of society and grief, distress and anxiety caused.[53] A claim can now be made by a homosexual cohabitant of the deceased, as the definition of relative under Sch.1 of the

---

v Horsburgh, 1949 S.C. 227 that it was established that it was competent for spouses to sue each other in contract. The right to sue one another in delict was established by s.2 of the Law Reform (Husband and Wife) Act 1962.

[47] The ante-nuptial debts rule (by s.6) and the *praepositura* (by s.7) of the Law Reform (Husband and Wife) (Scotland) Act 1984.

[48] As the common law has developed, it has never been, and is not, the case that a *husband* can pledge his *wife's* credit for necessaries.

[49] Married Woman's Property Act, s.4 introduced a limited obligation of aliment on a wife of sufficient means. The current mutual obligation of spouses to each other is governed by the Family Law (Scotland) Act 1985. See s.1(1).

[50] Family Law Scotland Act 1985, s.1(1)(bb) as amended by the Civil Partnership Act 2004, Sch.28, Pt 2, s.11.

[51] Claims may also be made by a parent or child of the deceased: ss.1 and 10 of and Sch.1 to the Damages (Scotland) Act 1976; Administration of Justice Act 1982, ss.9(2) and 14.

[52] CPA 2004, Sch. 28, Pt 4, para.42, that made the necessary amendments to the definition of "relative" in Sch.1 of 1976 Act (interestingly, these amendments were repeated in Sch.2 of the 2006 Act); also Sch.28, Pt 4, para.47 of the 2004 Act makes the necessary changes to the Administration of Justice Act 1982.

[53] See ss.1 and 10 of and Sch.1 to the Damages (Scotland) Act 1976, as amended by the Damages (Scotland) Act 1993 and ss.9(2) and 14 of the Administration of Justice Act 1982.

1976 Act has been amended by s.45(1), Sch.2, para.2 of the FLSA 2006 to include:

> "any person, not being the spouse or civil partner of the deceased, who was, immediately before the deceased's death, living with the deceased as husband and wife or civil partner, or in a relationship which had the characteristics of the relationship between civil partners".[54]

10–16 In the past the courts were generally reluctant to ascribe status to same-sex relationships,[55] but this approach has been challenged by the implementation of the Human Rights Act 1998 and the Court of Appeal's ruling in *Ghaidan v Mendoza*.[56] Subsequent legislation in Scotland takes account of this to provide parity in the treatment of heterosexual and same-sex couples (except with regard to marriage).[57] However, the development of the law in this area has not always been consistent. In *Telfer v Kellock*[58] a woman's claim that she was "family" for the purposes of the 1976 act, after her female partner (with whom she had exchanged vows and rings) had been killed in a road traffic accident, was dismissed. This case was decided five months after the House of Lords ruling in *Ghaidan* that the difference in treatment between same-sex and heterosexual couples was eliminated by the duty under s.3 of the Human Rights Act 1988 to interpret legislation of the United Kingdom parliament in a manner consistent with the provisions of that act.

10–17 Where a person is injured so that he or she finds it necessary to call on a relative for "personal services" such as nursing care or domestic help, a claim may be made against the negligent party to repay these services at a reasonable rate.[59] The definition of relative has been extended to cover civil partners[60] and has been further amended by the 2006 Act to cover same-sex cohabiting partners.[61] Where such a claim is successful, the claimant is under a duty to account to the relative who provided

---

[54] Damages (Scotland) Act 1976, s.10(2), as amended.

[55] See paras 9–37 to 9–44, in particular the UK courts' insistence on interpreting "man" and "woman" in biological terms for the purposes of entry to marriage.

[56] [2002] 4 All E.R. 1162. In this case the court held the statutory meaning of the words "as his or her wife" must be interpreted in the light of Art.8 to mean "as if they were his or her wife" in order to avoid discrimination under Art.14 and thus to enable a same-sex partner to be treated as if he or she were a spouse.

[57] e.g. Adults with Incapacity (Scotland) Act 2000, s.87 and Mortgage Rights (Scotland) Act 2001, s.1(2)(b). For a general overview overview of the way in which same-sex couples were treated in Scots law up to prior to the 2004 and 2006 Acts see B. Dempsey, "Same-Sex Couples in Scots Law—Part 1" (2002) SCOLAG No. 300, 181 and "Same-Sex Couples in Scots Law—Part 2" (2002) SCOLAG No. 301, 201.

[58] 2004 S.L.T. 1290

[59] Administration of Justice Act 1982, ss.7 and 8, as amended.

[60] 1982 Act, s.13(1)(aa), inserted by s.261(2), Sch.28, para.47 of the Civil Partnership Act 2004.

[61] FLSA 2006, s.30.

the services. If the injured person is unable to perform certain personal services *for* a relative, as a result of the negligence of a third party, then that party can also be asked to pay in respect of this loss of services.[62] The "personal services" in question are the kind of domestic duties which would normally be supplied free to a family member, but would be paid for if provided to a stranger, e.g. house cleaning or gardening.

Duty to Give Witness

In civil proceedings, spouses of parties to the action are competent   **10–18** and compellable witnesses: that is, they can both be called and compelled to give evidence.[63] This is, however, subject to the qualification that marital communications between spouses are privileged and therefore cannot be disclosed in court.[64] In criminal proceedings, a spouse is a competent and compellable witness for the *accused*, and is a competent witness for a *co-accused* or the *prosecution*, but is a compellable witness against the accused *only* if that spouse is the victim of the alleged crime or the party injured by it.[65] Thus, if a husband is on trial for murder of a third party, his wife can choose not to give evidence against him.

In a criminal case, the privilege against disclosing any communica-   **10–19** tion made between the spouses during the marriage belongs to the witness and *not* to the accused. Thus, the spouse giving evidence can disclose a marital communication if he or she chooses, and there is nothing to prevent a third party giving evidence of an intercepted or overheard communication between husband and wife. This may be contrasted with the position in a civil action, where the witness spouse cannot disclose interspousal communications even if he or she wishes to do so, although third parties, as in criminal proceedings, *may* reveal the content of such communications if they wish.

The Civil Partnership Act 2004 introduced similar provisions in respect of civil partners. Under s.130 of the 2004 Act, in criminal cases, the civil partner of an accused is a competent but not compellable witness for a co-accused or for a prosecutor and also is not compelled to disclose any communication made between the civil partners while the civil partnership subsists.

Taxation

Only a brief outline can be given here of the key ways in which the   **10–20** taxation system is affected by marriage. Spouses were taxed as one unit for income tax purposes until the late 1980s, with a married

---

[62] Administration of Justice Act 1982, s.9 as amended.
[63] Evidence (Scotland) Act 1853, s.3. At common law the spouse of a party was not, in general, a competent witness.
[64] Evidence (Scotland) Act 1853, s.3 as amended by the Evidence Further Amendment (Scotland) Act 1874, s.1, which removed the limitation on consistorial cases.
[65] Under the Criminal Procedure (Scotland) Act 1995, s.264. See also s.130 of the 2004 Act for civil partners.

woman's income being deemed to be that of her husband.[66] The husband was given the married man's allowance[67] to set off against their joint income, in addition to income relief against any earned income of his spouse.[68] Since the tax year 1990/1991, the married couple has been no longer treated as a tax unit for most tax purposes. Each spouse is responsible for making a return of income and paying the relevant tax.[69] The married couple's allowance was no longer available from the tax year 2000/2001, except for couples in which one of the spouses was aged 65 or more on or before April 5, 2000.[70]

10–21   However, the tax system has not adopted a consistent policy of neutrality as between married couples and those living together outside marriage. For example, transfers between spouses (where on death or by way of lifetime gift) are exempt from inheritance tax[71] as are such transfers between civil partners.[72] However, transfers between a cohabiting couple are not. Similarly, a transfer between spouses or civil partners does not give rise to a chargeable gain for the purposes of capital gains tax[73]; but there is no comparable provision in transfers for cohabiting couples. On the other hand, there are certain situations in which a married couple and, more recently, civil partners may be treated less favourably than an unmarried couple. For example, there is an exemption from capital gains tax on the disposal of a dwelling house which has been the only or main residence[74]; but while a husband and wife or civil partners are only allowed one residence for this purpose,[75] *both* partners in a relationship outside marriage are entitled to relief on a residence. Many of these rules have evolved over time to meet specific problems rather than reflecting any coherent policy towards the taxation of the family unit.

SEPARATION OF PROPERTY: BACKGROUND

10–22 The rule that marriage shall not of itself affect the property rights of spouses is sometimes known as the "separate property" rule.[76]

---

[66] See Income and Corporation Taxes Act 1988 ("ICTA 1988"), s.279.

[67] ICTA 1988, s.257(1).

[68] *ibid.*, s.257(6).

[69] Finance Act 1988, s.32.

[70] ICTA 1988, s.257A.

[71] Under s.18 of the Inheritance Tax Act 1984. There are also limited exemptions from Inheritance Tax in respect of gifts in consideration of marriage under s.22 of the 1984 Act.

[72] Tax and Civil Partnership Regulations 2005 (SI 2005/3229), reg.7(4) which amended s.18 of the Inheritance Tax Act 1984.

[73] Under s.282 of the Income and Corporation Taxes Act 1988, as amended by SI 2005/3229, reg.62 to include civil partners.

[74] Under s.58 of the Taxation of Chargeable Gains Act 1992, as amended by SI 2005/3229, reg.107(2) to cover civil partners.

[75] Under s.222 of the 1992 Act.

[76] Family Law (Scotland) Act 1985, s.24.

Neither spouse acquires a right to own or administer the property of the other on marriage (except by express agreement). This is in line with the emphasis placed in modern family law on marriage as an equal partnership rather than a dependent relationship.[77] However, there are arguments against a strict application of the separate property rule, and in favour of a certain degree of flexibility and pooling of assets. Spouses (and unmarried couples), because of their family obligations, often do not have the same freedom of action as single people. Furthermore, women and men in both marital and cohabiting relationships tend to have different and unequal opportunities to earn and amass property because they take on different roles within the family.[78]

This is particularly so when we consider not just traditional forms **10–23** of wealth such as heritage and capital, but also the so-called "new property",[79] which includes wages from employment, and benefits associated with such labour, or purchased by it, such as pensions, insurance rights and contribution-based social security benefits. The "new property" is of crucial importance in most Scottish households. Recent research estimates that the number of owner-occupied households in Scotland has risen from 57.9 per cent[80] to 63 per cent,[81] and around a third of all households are still rented, with the local authority remaining the single largest type of landlord. In 1981 only 8 per cent of Scots in 1981 had savings of £10,000 or over and only

---

[77] See, e.g. the Family Law (Scotland) Act 1985, ss.9 and 10(1) which deal with the principles to be applied to financial provision on divorce. These provide for a fair sharing of the net value of the property acquired during the marriage, which by s.10(1) means equal shares for spouses except where special circumstances justify a departure from this norm. See further paras 13–07, 13–39 to 13–46 and 13–52 to 13–57.

[78] See J. Flaherty, J. Veit-Wilson and P. Dornan, *Poverty: The facts* (Child Poverty Action Group, 2004), p.170–17; Office for National Statistics, *Social Trends* (No.33) (2003) p.33; Office for National Statistics, *Social Trends* (2004, No.34) p.10; J. Rowlands, *Alive and Kicking: women and men's responses to poverty and globalisation in the UK* (Oxfam, GB, November 2002); The Fawcett Society Briefing Paper on Women and Pensions for Seniors Network downloaded from *www.seniorsnetwork.co.uk// womenpensions/fawcettsociety.htm.*

[79] See Reich, "The New Property" (1963–1964) 73 Yale Law Journal 733.

[80] The Scottish Office: Government Statistical Service, *Statistical Bulletin Housing Series*, HSG/1996/4, 1996. Compare the percentage of owner-occupied dwellings for Great Britain in general at 67%: see OPCS, *Living in Britain, Results from the 1994 General Household Survey* (HMSO, London, 1996), Table 11.2, p.229.

[81] Scottish Executive, *Scottish Household Survey Bulletin* (No.8), November 7, 2005, p.1. Research online downloaded from *www.scotland.govuk/Resource/Doc/46746/0030438.pdf* put the figures at 63% owner-occupied with 29% social renters and 6% renting from a private landlord. Of these 18% of households are in receipt of housing benefit. *Scotland's People: results from the 2003 Scottish Household Survey* (published February 23, 2005), Figure 4–1, p.19 put the figures as 65%, 20% and 6% respectively. Overall, the number of owner-occupied dwellings in Great Britain increased by 44% between 1981 and 2003 while the number of rented dwellings fell by 17% according to *Social Trends—35 years of social change*, News Release (March 22, 2005), p.3. National Statistics downloaded from *www.statistics.gov.uk/socialtrends35.*

15 per cent had savings £5,000 or over.[82] Since then the proportion of households without any type of bank or building society account has fallen, especially since 2000.[83] Nonetheless, the poorest households are still four times as likely to be without an account as those on average incomes.[84] In many Scottish households, therefore, the major assets are rights under life insurance policies and pension schemes. However, when it comes to pensions, women tend to be poorly provided for. According to the Department for Work and Pensions,

> "Married or cohabiting women pensioners have, on average, very low personal incomes compared with married or cohabiting male pensioners. On average, compared with a married or cohabiting woman, a married or cohabiting man will get approximately twice as much in state benefit, far more in private pension, and more in other income. Widowed, divorced and separated women pensioners have more income in their own right than married women pensioners, but less than the equivalent men".[85]

10–24 Statistics demonstrate that women are less likely to acquire these resources than men, for a number of reasons to do with their domestic role within the family, and, in particular, their responsibilities for childcare. The General Household Survey found that about 6.8 million adults aged 16 or over in Great Britain (representing 16 per cent of adults), were informal carers[86] caring for a sick, disabled or elderly person in 2000/2001. Of these carers, 58 per cent were women of whom 73 per cent were married or cohabiting.[87] Over a quarter of these informal carers were working for 20 hours or more a week.[88] Such care responsibilities often prevent women from taking on full-time jobs.[89] In general, where women with dependent children work,

---

[82] See Manners and Rauta, *Family Property in Scotland: An enquiry carried out on behalf of the Scottish Law Commission* (OPCS, HMSO, 1981), Table 2.16, p.9.

[83] *Monitoring poverty and social exclusion in Scotland 2005; findings informing change* (Joseph Rowntree Foundation, December 2005).

[84] *ibid.*, p.6.

[85] Department for Work and Pensions, Report on *Women and pensions: The evidence* (November 2005), p.2.

[86] Their services were provided informally, in addition to care provided by central and local government.

[87] Office for National Statistics, J. Maher and H. Green, *Carers 2000* (The Stationary Office, London, 2002) downloaded from *www.statistics.gov.uk/downloads/theme_health/carers2000.pdf*.

[88] *ibid.*, p.10.

[89] The employment rates for men and women caring for disabled offspring are likely to be lower than those for all people of working age, but far more so in the case of women. Fewer than 50% of all women aged 30–44 caring for disabled children are in work, compared with over 70% of all men aged 30–44 caring for disabled children. See Department for Work and Pensions, "Women, family and households" (Ch.4) in the Report on *Women and pensions: The evidence* (November 2005), p.60.

they do so part time,[90] in order to meet the needs of childcare and domestic responsibilities. Part-time work tends not only to be worse paid than comparable full-time employment, but also gives rise to less in the way of associated benefits, e.g. occupational pension rights. Even where women are employed, and have access to some form of pension scheme, fewer of them are members of such schemes than their male colleagues.[91] This may be due to the fact that women generally earn less than men.[92] Low pay not only affects women but has an impact on those who are dependant on them, such as their children.[93]

A substantial number of women are particularly financially dis- **10–25** advantaged. These are the women who head lone-parent families. In 2002 one in five children in the United Kingdom lived in a lone-parent family.[94] The proportion of children living in lone-parent families in the United Kingdom has increased, it tripled between 1972 and spring 2004 to 24 per cent.[95] Over 90 per cent of lone-parent households in the United Kingdom are headed by women[96] and these households are more likely to be in poverty than other family groups.[97] Almost half of all lone parents in Scotland are in income

---

[90] 42.4% of women worked part time in 2002, with 65.5% doing so when their children were under 4, in contrast to just 9% of men working part time. See Office for National Statistics, *Labour Market Trend* , Vol.110 (No.10) (October 2002). In spring 2002, 52% of women whose youngest dependent child was under 5 were working either part time or full time (36% and 17% respectively). 70% of women whose youngest dependent child was aged 5–10 were working; 26% full time and 44% part time. Office for National Statistics, *Social Trends* (No.33) (2003), p.158.

[91] Overall, 38% of today's working-age women are contributing to a private pension compared with around 46% of working-age men. However women in this position contribute on average less than men. With regard to state pensions in 2005/2006, 30% of women reaching state pension age are entitled to a full basic state pension (24% on their own record). Another 30% have earned less than a full pension, but more than a Category B pension (that is a pension payable by the spouse's qualifying years or earnings). See Department for Work and Pensions, Report on *Women and pensions: The evidence* (November 2005) p.9 and p.6.

[92] According to the Office for National Statistics, *Patterns of Low Pay*, *Labour Market Trends*, Vol.111 (No.4) (April 2003): "women are nearly three times more likely to be in low paid employment than men. Part-time jobs, largely undertaken by women, are about five times more likely to be low paid than full-time jobs; but a full-time job held by a woman is still about twice as likely to be low paid as one held by a man": p.175. In Scotland a third of employees earn less than the £6.50 per hour. Half of all part-time workers earn less than that rate, most of them women. See *Monitoring poverty and social exclusion in Scotland 2005; findings informing change* (Joseph Rowntree Foundation, December 2005).

[93] Fawcett Society, *Fawcett Briefing on Women and Low Pay* (2002), p.2.

[94] See J. Flaherty, J. Veit-Wilson and P. Dornan, *Poverty: The facts* (Child Poverty Action Group, 2004), p.167.

[95] National Statistics *Social Trends 2005*. Downloaded from *www.statistics.gov.uk/cci/nugget.asp?id=1044*.

[96] National Statistics *Focus on Gender* 2004. Downloaded from *www.statistics.gov.uk/downloads/theme_compendia/fog2004/Gender.pdf*.

[97] Office for National Statistics, C. Summerfield and P. Babb (eds), *Social Trends* (No.33) (The Stationery Office, 2003).

poverty, three times the rate for couples with children.[98] Although the number of children living in poverty has been falling,[99] nevertheless, "children in Scotland remain much more likely to be living in income poverty than either working-age adults or pensioners".[1] That such families are amongst the poorest in the United Kingdom is mainly due to the difficulties faced by mothers without partners who try to combine full or even part-time employment with the demands of childcare,[2] the costs of substitute care,[3] and the restrictions imposed by the state system of social security benefits.[4]

10–26   The Department of Work and Pension notes that,

> "the Government has invested over £17 billion in expanding early years and childcare services since 1997. Maternity pay and maternity leave periods increased in 2003. The Sure Start programme of early learning childcare, health and family support assists women and men in their role as parents and in their aspirations to enter and progress in the workforce".[5]

The National Childcare Strategy launched in 1998 aimed to increase the quantity, quality and affordability of childcare, primarily to enable more women to enter paid employment. In addition, the Employment Act 2002 extends parents rights in work and may encourage fathers to become more involved in child rearing as paternity leave became a statutory requirement and new fathers receive two weeks paid leave. The most significant change has been the introduction of flexible working "rights". This allows parents and guardians with children

---

[98] *Monitoring poverty and social exclusion in Scotland 2005; findings informing change* (Joseph Rowntree Foundation, December 2005). Downloaded from *www.jrf.org.uk/ KNOWLEDGE/FINDINGS/socialpolicy/pdf/0585.pdf.*

[99] This is from an average of around 31% of all children in the mid-1990s to around 27% in the years 2001/2002 to 2003/2004, *ibid.*

[1] Above, n.98.

[2] The highest rate of worklessness occurred among lone-parent households with children under 5 years old—64%. Thus, lone-parent households with dependent children are more likely to be workless and economically inactive, than any other type of household. The worklessness rate for lone-parent households was 42% in spring 2004 compared with 5% for couple households with dependent children: see Office for National Statistics, *Workless Households: results of the spring labour force survey* (November 2004), Table 2. While the numbers of women participating in the labour market have risen, in spring 2003, 43% of lone-parent households with dependent children were workless, much higher than the overall household rate of 16%: downloaded from *www.statistics.gov.uk/articles/labour_market_trends/ workless_households.pdf.*

[3] See J. Flaherty, J. Veit-Wilson and P. Dornan, *Poverty: The facts* (Child Poverty Action Group, 2004), p.178. Even with a proportion of costs paid by the childcare element of working tax credit up to a ceiling, parents must still pay 30%, a sizeable amount for low earning parents and possibly enough to make paid work an economically unfeasible option.

[4] See paras 10–64 to 10–77.

[5] Department of Work and Pensions, *Report on Women and pensions: The evidence* (November 2005), p.58.

under six or a disabled child under 18 to request changes in working hours, working times and the place of work. However, an employer is not legally obliged to meet employees' requests. There remain too few childcare places available and it is doubtful if the current measures will create the childcare places needed to meet the Government target for increasing lone-parent employment.[6] A survey of human resource professionals found that 60 per cent said the flexible work regulations would adversely affect their decision to employ women.[7] Further, the £100 a week payment to new fathers under the 2002 Act may not be enough to encourage them to take time out of paid work.

Lone parents as a group are overwhelmingly dependent on state **10–27** benefits.[8] This is because the paid work that is accessible to them, given their other responsibilities, will often pay them no more than state benefit after substitute childcare is paid for, and the cost of losing other "passported benefits" (such as free dental care) is figured in. Thus, the single parent mother has little incentive in the short term to take on paid employment and thus escape the trap of permanent benefit dependency at a subsistence level. This situation is often described as the "poverty trap". While the number of women with children who work *is* on the increase,[9] these tend to be married or cohabiting women, rather than those faced with the difficulties of caring for a child alone.[10] The end result, then, is that women with dependent children earn less than their male equivalents, have less right to work-related benefits, and tend to fail to acquire capital, heritage and pensions in their own right. Rights in property by women are often acquired in *conjunction* with a male partner or as a result of living as a dependant of such a partner. As we shall see, this has serious implications on marital or relationship breakdown.

How far does, and should, Scottish family law take account of **10–28** these economic and social factors? In the next section, we will look at the property rights that apply to domestic relationships *while the*

---

[6] House of Commons Work and Pensions Select Committee, *Childcare for Working Parents: Fifth Report of Session 2002–2003*, Vol.1 (2003), p.6.

[7] Survey conducted by Croner, cited in *Guardian*, April 5, 2003.

[8] Over half of all female lone-parents received 75% or more of their income from benefits or tax credits. See J. Flaherty, J. Veit-Wilson and P. Dornan, *Poverty: The facts* (Child Poverty Action Group, 2004), p.166. It is also the case that women are more likely to be recipients of means-tested benefits, rather than contributory benefits. In 2003, almost two-thirds of claimants reliant on income support were women. See Department for Work and Pensions, *First Release*, Statistical Summary, June 2003.

[9] Female participation in the labour market went from 29% in 1970 to 72% in 2002. See Office for National Statistics, *Labour Market Trends*, Vol.111 (No.6) (June 2003).

[10] While many more women are entering paid work, the employment position for female lone-parents is considerably worse relative to that of mothers in couple families. The employment rate for lone parents in Great Britain was 53% in 2003, in contrast to over 70% for mothers in couple families. See Department for Work and Pensions, *Opportunity for All: Fifth Annual Report 2003* (The Stationary Office, 2003). Even when in work, "lone parents are usually in low-paid jobs with little opportunity for career progression or training": J Casebourne, *A Quality Life for Lone Parents and their Children*, Report of Gingerbread's Annual Conference (April, 2002).

relationship subsists, comparing the position of spouses and civil partners with that of heterosexual cohabiting couples. We shall examine the rules relating to the division of property on termination of a domestic relationship (including "financial provision on divorce") in Chs 11–13.

Exceptions to "Separate Property" Rule

10–29   There are however certain exceptions to the general rule that marriage does not affect the spouses' property rights. These include:

- a spouse's right to aliment[11];
- provisions under the Matrimonial Homes (Family Protection) (Scotland) Act 1981[12];
- spousal presumption of equal shares in household goods[13];
- spousal presumption of equal shares in money and property derived from any housekeeping allowance[14];
- exception to requirement of delivery where insurance policy in favour of spouse and/or children[15];
- right to retain possession of tenancy where spouse who is tenant leaves matrimonial home[16];
- right to succeed to private tenancy on spouse's death as statutory tenant[17];
- right to succeed to public sector secure tenancy on death of spouse[18];

---

[11] 1985 Act, s.1(1)(a). Extended to civil partners by Sch.28, Pt 2, paras 11–13 of the CPA 2004.

[12] Discussed in paras 12–26 *et seq.*

[13] 1985 Act, s.25. This provision has now been extended to cover civil partners and cohabitees both heterosexual and same-sex couples by s.26 of the FLSA 2006. See paras 11–05 *et seq.*

[14] 1985 Act, s.26. This provision has now been extended to cover civil partners and cohabitees by s.27 of the 2006 Act. See paras 12–47 to 12–51.

[15] Married Women's Policies of Assurance (Scotland) Act 1880, s.2. In this case the policy vests in the spouse and his or her representatives as soon as the policy is effected, without delivery. This has now been extended to cover civil partners by s.132 of the Civil Partnership Act 2004.

[16] 1981 Act, s.2(8). This has now been extended to civil partners by s.102(8) of the CPA 2004.

[17] Sch.1, para.2 of the Rent (Scotland) Act 1984. Also protected under para.3 is "a person who was a member of the original tenant's family residing with him". After the House of Lords decision in *Fitzpatrick v Sterling Housing Association* [1999] 4 All E.R. 705, a member of the tenant's family may now be interpreted to include a tenant's same-sex cohabitee. Civil partners now come within the ambit of the 1984 Act through amendment by Sch.28, Pt 4, paras 48–49 of the CPA 2004.

[18] Housing (Scotland) Act 1987, s.52(1). Protection is also extended under s.52(2) to a member of the tenant's family. Cohabitees including same-sex couples are entitled to succeed to a secure tenancy under the 1987 Act and a Scottish Secure Tenancy under the Housing (Scotland) Act 2000, taking together s.108(3), s.22 and Sch 3. Note that the definition of "spouse" under s.108(3) now extends to "another person living together with that person as husband and wife or in a relationship which has

- right to financial provision on divorce where matrimonial property is subject to fair sharing between the spouses regardless of who holds title to it.[19]

ADULTS AND RIGHTS OF SUPPORT

Each spouse owes a duty of support or "aliment" to the other for the **10–30** duration of the marriage. This duty terminates on the dissolution of the marriage. Unmarried partners, apart from civil partners, do not owe each other private law duties of aliment either during or after the termination of the relationship. When a marriage is terminated by divorce or a civil partnership is dissolved, a periodical allowance may be awarded by the court to be paid by one spouse or civil partner to the other for a limited or unlimited time: this should not be confused with an award of aliment which can be made only while the marriage or civil partnership subsists.

During marriage, spouses usually support each other informally and **10–31** do not often seek legal awards. Separated spouses seeking support often prefer to rely on state social security benefits, rather than seek an award from a court which may involve contact with a hostile ex-partner and be difficult to enforce.[20] Aliment, unlike social security benefits, has the advantage that it is awarded at the discretion of the court rather than being set at a fixed amount. However, research evidence indicates that periodical awards made at discretionary levels by courts tend to be on the low side where they are awarded at all.[21] Individuals seeking support for children of the marriage may come to their own voluntary arrangements or will come within the jurisdiction of the Child Support Act 1991.[22] There are very few actions raised for spousal aliment, with those raised most often seeking aliment as an interim award only for the duration of divorce proceedings. Private law rules on spousal aliment therefore are of dwindling importance in comparison to the private law regime governing financial provision on divorce and the public law rules regulating social security and child support.

Nonetheless, current government policies continue to endorse and, **10–32** indeed, aggressively pursue the policy that it is the family, rather than the state, which should be the primary source of maintenance and

---

the characteristics of the relationship between husband and wife except that the persons are of the same sex". Where the parties are cohabitees (heterosexual or same-sex) and a secure tenancy is involved, the property must have been the person's only or principal home throughout the period of six months ending with the tenant's death, a condition which does not apply to spouses.

[19] 1985 Act, s.10. Extended to civil partners by Sch.28, Pt 2, para.16 of the CPA 2004.

[20] *Report of the Committee on One-Parent Families*, Cmnd.5629 (1974), p.115; Dobash and Wasoff, *Financial Aspects of Divorce* (1986), p.31.

[21] See Wasoff *et al, Impact of the Family Law (Scotland) Act 1985 on Solicitors' Practice* (Scottish Central Research Unit, 1990), pp.73–75.

[22] As amended by the Child Support Act 1995 and by the Child Support Pensions and Social Security Act 2000.

provision for family members.[23] While this is not a textbook on social security law, we cannot look usefully at private law rights and duties of support without consideration of the state schemes. There is a complex but crucial inter-relationship between private law aliment and public support, which we will explore below. The relationship between public support and private maintenance of *children* is principally examined in Ch.5.

10–33   Spouses and civil partners, can also claim property rights out of each other's estate on *death* under the rules of both testate and intestate succession. While the FLSA 2006 has for the first time given the courts discretionary powers to make some provision for heterosexual/same-sex cohabiting couples, these are not on a par with the provisions that apply to spouses and civil partners.[24]

Aliment

10–34   The legal obligation on family members to maintain or aliment each other pre-dates the state system of maintenance and support. In the past, the obligation to provide aliment was broadly construed at common law to include the extended, and not just the nuclear, family.[25] So, e.g. grandparents could become liable to aliment grandchildren where the parents were unable to do so,[26] and grandchildren could reciprocally find themselves liable to aliment their grandparents. Within this framework, husbands were liable to aliment their wives, but there was no reciprocal requirement for wives to aliment their husbands until 1920.[27]

Who Owes an Obligation of Aliment?

10–35   The law on aliment is now contained in the Family Law (Scotland) Act 1985.[28] Under this Act, the number of persons liable to pay aliment has been strictly limited. Section 1(1) states that an obligation of aliment is now owed only by:

(a) a husband to his wife[29] *or vice versa* and a partner in a civil partnership to the other partner[30];

---

[23] See the Family Law (Scotland) Act 1985, s.1(1) requiring individuals to maintain their spouse/civil partner and children as well as the Child Support Act 1991 (discussed in full in Ch.5, paras 5–50, 5–61 *et seq.*); and also ss.105 and 78(6) of the Social Security Administration Act 1992.

[24] FLSA 2006, s.28. See also paras 10–90 to 10–97 below.

[25] See Bankton's *Institute of the Laws of Scotland*, i,6,15; Bell's *Principles of the Law of Scotland* (10th edn, 1633).

[26] See, e.g. *Mackenzie's Tutrix v Mackenzie*, 1928 S.L.T. 649.

[27] See Married Women's Property Act 1920, s.4.

[28] References in this section are to the 1985 Act unless otherwise stated.

[29] The terms "husband" and "wife" include parties to a valid polygamous marriage: s.1(5).

[30] Amendment made to the 1985 Act by Sch.28, Pt 2, para.11 of the Civil Partnership Act 2004. References hereafter to spouses should be taken to include civil partners.

(b) a father or mother to his or her child; and
(c) a person to a child who has been accepted as a child of his or her family.[31]

Aliment (and child support) for children is dealt with in Ch.5.[32]

How Much is Owed?

Where aliment is due, it is an obligation to provide a party with **10–36** "such support as is reasonable in the circumstances",[33] having regard to the factors specified in s.4(1), namely:

(a) the needs and resources of the parties;
(b) the earning capacities of the parties; and
(c) generally all the circumstances of the case.

The s.4 factors are also relevant when determining an award of *interim* aliment.[34]

The court is thus given extensive discretion. Unlike social security **10–37** law, where need is defined in terms of set rates of benefit, the "rates" for aliment are flexible, with the needs and resources of the parties being considered in the light of the parties' standard of living during the marriage, their earning capacity, their age and their health. However, it would appear that, in practice, a number of solicitors estimate claims for aliment not on the particular circumstances of the case but rather on the basis of certain "rule of thumb" rates developed over the years.[35]

"Resources" are not just confined to income. They may also include **10–38** capital,[36] (particularly where such capital has regularly been encroached upon for maintenance), support from relatives, third parties or cohabitants or parental contributions.[37] So, e.g. in *Munro v Munro*[38] a wife sued her husband for aliment. The court took into account the fact that the husband's cohabitant was contributing to the joint outlays of that household as these formed part of the resources which were available to the husband. It refused, however, to take account of the cohabitant's *income* and aggregate it with that of the husband, as that would amount to placing the cohabitant under an obligation to aliment the wife, when she was under no such legal obligation.[39]

---

[31] 1985 Act, s.1(1)(d). This does not include a child who has been boarded out for fostering by a local or other public authority or voluntary organisation.
[32] See paras 5–50 *et seq.*
[33] s.1(1) and (2).
[34] *McGeachie v McGeachie*, 1989 S.C.L.R. 99.
[35] See Wasoff *et al, op. cit.*, above, n.21.
[36] *Alexander v Alexander*, 1957 S.L.T. 298.
[37] *ibid.*, at p.303. See also *Syme v Syme* (1833) 11 S. 305.
[38] 1986 S.L.T. 72.
[39] See also *Frith v Frith*, 1990 G.W.D. 5-266.

10–39 "Resources" also include state benefits to which a party is entitled,[40] except those based exclusively on need—such as Income Support and the non-contributory part of the jobseeker's allowance—which will be left out of account. In addition, resources are not limited to present resources but may also include *foreseeable* resources,[41] such as payoffs from insurance or pension plans, rights of inheritance or imminent statutory redundancy payments. Income is normally assessed on the basis of the parties' net income after tax,[42] because aliment is now normally payable out of post-tax income, and is not taxable in the hands of the recipient.[43]

10–40 The court has discretion, when considering "all the circumstances of the case", to take account of any support, financial or otherwise, given by the defender to *any person* whom he or she maintains as a dependant in his or her household, *whether or not* the defender owes an obligation of aliment to that person.[44] Prior to the 1985 Act if a person choose to voluntarily maintain another—not by virtue of a legal obligation of aliment—then such support could not be taken account of by the courts as a drain on the resources of the payer.[45] This often led to the making of an unrealistic assessment.

10–41 *Example:* Husband (H) leaves his wife (W) and sets up a new household with his girlfriend (X) and her children A and B. H has no legal obligation to support X but if he does in fact support her (by paying a portion of his salary towards the household budget for example), his payments can be taken into account when quantifying his resources so as to determine how much aliment he owes W.[46]

10–42 The court is specifically enjoined *not* to take account of the conduct of the parties when quantifying aliment, unless it would be "manifestly inequitable to leave it out of account".[47] This should be

---

[40] See paras 10–22 and 10–23.

[41] 1985 Act, s.27(1). Note that it is within the discretion of the court whether or not to take foreseeable resources into account in the initial action, or whether to leave them to be taken into account at a later date on an application for variation under s.5.

[42] See *Wiseman v Wiseman*, 1989 S.C.L.R. 757; *Harper v Harper*, 1990 G.W.D. 40-2322; *Pryde v Pryde*, 1991 S.L.T. (Sh. Ct.) 26, but *cf. MacInnes v MacInnes*, 1993 S.L.T. 1108 and Lord Marnoch's observation (at p.1109) that the calculation should be on the basis of gross income, where a husband continues to get tax relief in the form of the married person's allowance under s.36 of the Finance Act 1988, despite changes in the tax treatment of his payments.

[43] See further, Barr, *A Vintage Year for Aliment*, 1989 S.L.T. (News) 57.

[44] s.4(3)(a).

[45] See *Henry v Henry*, 1972 S.L.T. (Notes) 26.

[46] Note: Whilst initially H would have no obligation to support the children A and B, if he acts in a manner which indicates he "accepts them as a child of his family" then such a duty will exist: s.1(1)(d) of the 1985 Act. It is interesting to note that in this respect the 1985 Act is far more realistic in its acceptance of the fact that separated spouses tend to acquire new dependants and new responsibilities, than is the Child Support Act 1991, even after considerable amending of its formulae to enable reduced payments in the event of acquired dependants.

[47] s.4(3)(b).

the case only in circumstances where conduct has actually affected the parties' finances, e.g. where a party blatantly disposes of assets or income in order to exhaust their estate, thereby depriving the other party of their right to aliment. Either spouse can claim aliment even if they have given the other grounds for divorce.[48] If one spouse feels aggrieved by the other's matrimonial conduct, then the remedy lies in seeking a divorce which, when granted, terminates the obligation to aliment a spouse (but not children).[49] The statutory attempt to downplay the significance of conduct goes hand in hand with the general move away from a fault-based approach in matrimonial matters.[50]

Court Actions for Aliment

An action for aliment may be raised in the Sheriff Court or the **10–43** Court of Session.[51] It may be raised as an independent action or as an action ancillary to other proceedings such as divorce, dissolution of civil partnership, separation, nullity of marriage or civil partnership, financial provision, or declarator of paternity.[52] Whether an independent action, or ancillary to other proceedings, a court may make an award of interim aliment, pending the final disposal of the action.[53] Those who may apply to the court for aliment are those to whom an obligation of aliment is owed,[54] as well as representatives of children and incapax claimants.[55]

At common law, spouses had to separate before an action of **10–44** aliment could be raised. Section 2(6) of the 1985 Act expressly provides that it is competent to bring an action for aliment, notwithstanding that the pursuer is living in the same household as the defender. Where such an action is brought, however, it may be met with the defence that the defender is fulfilling the obligation of aliment in the household (whether in money or in kind), and intends to continue doing so.[56]

Other defences are also competent. The defender may argue that **10–45** he or she has made an offer to receive the pursuer into his or her

---

[48] *Donnelly v Donnelly*, 1959 S.C. 97.

[49] However, note that even where a decree of divorce has been granted, but a claim for financial provision is still pending, an award of interim aliment remains competent, as in *Neill v Neill*, 1987 S.L.T. (Sh. Ct.) 143.

[50] Compare the similar provision in s.11(7) of the 1985 Act dealing with conduct in respect of financial provision on divorce, discussed in Ch.13; and see also the nonfault grounds for divorce in s.1(2)(d) and (e) of the Divorce (Scotland) Act 1976.

[51] ss.2 and 27(1).

[52] s.2(2)(e).

[53] 1985 Act, s.6(1)(a) and (b). See also n.52 above.

[54] *ibid.*, s.2(4)(a). But note that by ss.27(1) and 17(2), a person may claim *interim* aliment even if they are not owed an obligation of aliment, e.g. a pursuer in an action of nullity of marriage. If she succeeds in her action, the result will be that the defender does not owe her a duty of aliment, but she will nonetheless be entitled to seek and retain interim aliment.

[55] ss.2(4)(b) and (c), and 2(5).

[56] s.2(7).

household and to fulfil the obligation of aliment there, so long as the offer is one which it is reasonable to expect the other spouse to accept.[57] In considering what is "reasonable", the court is expressly allowed to have regard to conduct.[58] For example, where there is a history of domestic violence, adultery or alcoholism, the pursuer may be justified in refusing the offer. However, the mere fact that a husband and wife have agreed to live apart shall not of itself make the offer "unreasonable".[59]

10–46   The court has a number of powers in relation to an action for aliment. It can order either party to provide details of his or her resources.[60] Furthermore, by common law powers, it can grant a commission and diligence to recover documents detailing the parties' resources, such as employment slips. When granting decree, the court usually makes an order for a periodical payment for a definite or indefinite period or until the happening of a specified event, e.g. "two years", or, "until the pursuer re-enters full-time employment".[61] Exceptionally, the court can order the making of alimentary payments of an occasional or special nature, including payments in respect of inlying,[62] funeral and educational expenses.[63] The court can also back-date an award of aliment, either to the date of the bringing of the action or to such later date as the court thinks fit; or, exceptionally, to a date prior to the bringing of the action.[64] The Act expressly states that the court has *no* power to substitute a lump sum for a periodical payment.[65]

Variation and Recall of Court Orders

10–47   Under the 1985 Act the court has power to vary or recall a decree for aliment[66] or interim aliment.[67] Variation normally requires that since the date of the decree there has been a material change of circumstances[68] but this is not necessary in the case of variation of an award of interim aliment.[69] Divorce is not a change of circumstances, but rather an event which causes the obligation of aliment to terminate. A "change of circumstances" must be one which affects the resources of either party, e.g. an increase or decrease in the earnings or means of either party, such as:

---

[57] s.2(8).
[58] 1985 Act, s.2(9), which also refers the court to all other relevant circumstances.
[59] *ibid.*
[60] s.20.
[61] s.3(1)(a).
[62] These are expenses connected with the period of confinement associated with childbirth.
[63] s.3(1)(b).
[64] 1985 Act, s.3(1)(c). The court also has the power to award less than the amount claimed even if the claim is Undisputed: s.3(1)(d).
[65] s.3(2).
[66] s.5.
[67] s.6(4).
[68] s.5(1).
[69] *Bisset v Bisset*, 1993 S.C.L.R. 284.

- where one spouse inherits property[70];
- takes up employment[71]; or
- loses his or her job.[72]

The making of a maintenance assessment under the Child Support Act 1991 is specifically designated as a "material change of circumstances" justifying variation of aliment paid to a spouse as well as to a child.[73]

Recent cases have involved applications to the court to vary a decree **10–48** of aliment in respect of children. In *Ahmed v Ahmed*[74] the mother applied to the Court of Session to increase the amount of aliment payable for the younger child of the marriage. In 1994 the Court of Session awarded aliment of £50 per week for each of the two children. In October 2000 the mother applied for an increase in respect of the younger child. After proof the judge awarded £220 per week and back-dated the increase to the date of the application. The father reclaimed, attacking both the scale of the increase and its backdating. The actual expenditure on the child's recurring needs was found to have been £160 per week. Apportioning four fifths of that to the father meant an award of about £130 per week. The court held, however, that award-ing aliment was not a purely arithmetical exercise, but that the child's needs ought to be related to the standard of living she was entitled to in terms of her parents' earnings and that there should be no dispar-ity between her and the defender's other children in America. Thus the award should not be constrained by what her relatively poorer mother had been able to afford over the past few years without a sufficient contribution from the father.

In this case, costs also involved medical expenses of £10,000. The **10–49** Lord Ordinary had added this sum to the other expenditure and aver-aged it out over the period from the date of the application to the date of decree to arrive at the appropriate amount of aliment. The court held that aliment of £130 per week plus £8,000 (which was the father's share of medical expenses) came to very near the same total as the £220 per week that had been awarded for the period until the child reached 18. It would not, therefore, interfere with the Lord Ordinary's award. It also held that backdating was justified because the father had not been frank about his income and financial circumstances when the application was made, and but for the delay caused by the lengthy proof, an increase would have been awarded soon after the date of application.

In *Sutherland v Sutherland*,[75] the father of two children sought to **10–50** vary an agreement reached in 2001 that provided aliment for his two

---

[70] *Donald v Donald* (1862) 24 D. 499.
[71] *Dowswell v Dowswell*, 1943 S.C. 23.
[72] *Brotherston v Brotherston* (1938) 54 Sh. Ct. Rep. 218.
[73] s.5(1A).
[74] 2004 S.C.L.R. 247.
[75] 2004 Fam. L.B. 70-4.

children and their mother on the grounds that his income had decreased to a material extent since late 2001 while the mother's income had increased as she was now in full-time employment. The sheriff decided that there had been a material change in the father's financial position and that it was appropriate to look at his current income and expenditure. The parties' agents agreed that on the father's current income new statutory rules applied by the Child Support Agency would produce a figure of £475 per month per child. The sheriff regarded this sum as being fair and reasonable and varied the amount of aliment accordingly.

10–51   In this case, as the minute of agreement had been registered in the Books of Council and Session in October 2001, the Child Support Agency would have had to decline jurisdiction to assess child support should the mother have made such an application.[76] Nonetheless, in reaching his decision the sheriff was influenced by the amount that would have been payable by the non-resident parents according to the Child Support Agency's calculations.

10–52   In *Higgins v Higgins*,[77] a couple had two daughters aged 11 and 7. The parents separated in 1998, entered into a minute of agreement in mid 2000 and divorced a few months later. The wife then sought an order for payment of school fees in respect of the younger daughter plus a variation in both children's aliment because childcare costs had risen faster than the retail price indexation allowed for in the agreement. In the agreement, both parents had discharged their rights to financial provision and/or to an order for interim aliment or aliment under the terms of the Family Law (Scotland) Act 1985. They acknowledged that they had been independently legally advised and that the terms of the agreement were fair and reasonable. The father argued that the agreement precluded the mother from claiming an alimentary payment in respect of school fees under s.3(1)(b) of the 1985 Act.

10–53   However, the court held that there had been no express discharge of the right to claim aliment on behalf of a child and, looking at the other terms of the agreement, such a discharge could not be reasonably be inferred from them. All that had been discharged were the financial claims of the couple vis-à-vis one another. It also noted that there had been several material changes in circumstances since the date of the agreement, namely that:

- the father's pay had increased from £160,000 to well over £1 million;
- school fees and associated expenses had risen faster than the inflationary increases granted by the agreement;

---

[76] This is because commissioner's decision CSCS/5/97 reported in 1999 that an extract registered agreement on aliment for a child was equivalent to a maintenance order which removes jurisdiction for the Child Support Agency in *non-benefit* cases.

[77] 2004 Fam. L.B. 67-7.

- the cessation of the wife's allowance at the end of 2003 would mean that her resources and those of the children would fall below their reasonable needs.

It was agreed that the father's ability to pay was not an issue. He considered that he had made a generous agreement and was not prepared to pay all the younger daughter's school fees or "reinstate" his wife's allowance by means of an increase in the children's aliment.

The court held that need was a relative concept but that generally **10–54** speaking it should be assessed against the standard of living which the couple envisaged for the children when the agreement was made. In this case, the agreement had provided in principle for the private schooling of the younger daughter when she became old enough. Thus, the court held that the father should pay school fees to enable the younger daughter to continue at the private school where she had already been for some time. In reaching this decision it took account of the fact that her elder sister and the father's daughter by his remarriage were both being privately educated as well as the fact that the mother's attempts to obtain a better job were constrained by her need to care for the children, especially during school holidays.

The father's argument that the increase in child aliment sought by **10–55** the mother was an attempt to replace her allowance (which was due to come to an end) was met by s.4(4) of the 1985 Act. This section empowers the court in awarding aliment to a child under 16 to include reasonable provision for the expenses of the carer in caring for the child and in this case the evidence showed that the mother's expenditure on herself was modest.

Overall, these cases set out three stages for dealing with aliment: **10–56**

- the first, is to ask whether there has been any material changes in circumstances since the agreement was made[78];
- the second is, if there have been material changes, do they justify any variation in the amount due; and
- if so, by how much should the award be varied?

In assessing need it is also relevant to take account of how a father treats his other children. This is recognised in s.4(3)(a) of the 1985 Act and underpinned by the decision in *Ahmed* that equal treatment of children by parents in old and new families is an important consideration that should be upheld.

Unfortunately the 1985 Act did not extend these powers of varia- **10–57** tion to a court dealing with a variation of aliment payable in terms of an agreement. The FLSA 2006 has corrected this oversight and inserted new powers into s.7[79] of the 1985 Act that are identical to

---

[78] 1985 Act, s.7(2).
[79] subss.(2ZA), (2ZB) and (2ZC) inserted by s.20 of the FLSA 2006.

those for variation of aliment due in terms of a decree discussed above. The FLSA 2006 has also made it clear that when dealing with an action of aliment against a non-Scottish defender the Scottish courts should apply the Scots law on aliment.[80]

Backdating of Court Orders

10–58 At common law, there was no provision for an award of aliment to be backdated to cover time periods before the application was made to the court, because aliment was intended to relieve the present needs of an applicant. Thus a spouse could not, in general, recover arrears of aliment on the basis that the other spouse had failed to provide support in the past[81] unless the aliment was at that time already due under a court decree,[82] separation agreement, or other voluntary obligation.[83]

10–59 However, under the 1985 Act, the court has limited powers to back-date aliment.[84] Aliment can be backdated from the date of the decree to the date of the bringing of the action,[85] or, on special cause shown, to a date prior to the bringing of the action.[86] In addition, the court also has the power to backdate when varying or recalling an award.[87] Where the court exercises this power, it may order any sum paid under the decree to be repaid.[88] But note that where *interim* aliment is concerned, the courts do not have these powers to backdate although, as we have seen, it may vary future payments.[89] Thus, the defender cannot be compelled to pay *interim* aliment in respect of any time period before the award of interim aliment was granted.

Voluntary Agreements

10–60 It is not necessary to go to court to obtain aliment. Parties may reach their own agreements with respect to aliment[90] which the courts will enforce.[91] Parties are also free to make "clean break" agreements excluding future liability for aliment, or barring either party from

---

[80] s.40.
[81] *McMillan v McMillan* (1871) 9 M. 1067.
[82] *Fletcher v Young*, 1936 S.L.T. 572.
[83] *Hood v Hood* (1871) 9 M. 449.
[84] s.3(1)(c).
[85] s.3(1)(c)(i).
[86] s.3(1)(c)(ii).
[87] *Abrahams v Abrahams*, 1989 S.L.T. (Sh.Ct) 11.
[88] s.5(4).
[89] *McColl v McColl*, 1993 S.L.T. 617.
[90] s.7.
[91] An "agreement" under s.7(5) is one that is entered into before or after the commencement of the 1985 Act, and includes a unilateral voluntary obligation. In practice, agreements for aliment are usually in probative writing and registered in the Books of Council and Session for execution to ease any future enforcement. They often combine provisions relating to aliment with other clauses relating to financial provision on divorce, succession and matters relating to children of the marriage. See further, Ch.15.

bringing an action for aliment in the future. However, such agreements can be attacked subsequently in court on the statutory ground that they were not fair and reasonable in all the circumstances at the time they were made.[92] The courts also have power to vary or recall the amount of aliment specified within such agreements where there has been a material change of circumstances since the date of the agreement.[93] The defences which apply when applying for aliment also apply when a party seeks to enforce an *agreement* for aliment.[94]

Termination

An award of aliment terminates at the date indicated by the court **10–61** when making the order. This may be at a definite date, or on the happening of a specified event.[95] The obligation on spouses to aliment each other terminates when the marriage ends, whether by death[96] or divorce. However, an ex-spouse may still be allowed to claim support in the form of a periodical allowance as part of an award of financial provision on divorce.[97]

Enforcement of Aliment

A court order for aliment, or an agreement for aliment executed in **10–62** probative form and registered in the Books of Council and Session, can be enforced under the Debtors (Scotland) Act 1987 by means of a current maintenance arrestment,[98] which requires the employer of the debtor to deduct a sum, determined according to a statutory formula, from the debtor's earnings each pay day, and to pay the sum deducted to the creditor. The deductions continue for as long as the arrestment is in effect, which means that aliment can be recovered at weekly or monthly intervals, as it falls due. But these provisions have certain limitations, namely that: (i) a current maintenance arrestment cannot be used to enforce *arrears* of aliment; and (ii) it can only come into operation four weeks after decree has come into effect, and after the debtor has defaulted on at least one instalment of aliment.[99]

---

[92] 1985 Act, s.7(1). This, of course, refers only to agreements in respect of aliment between spouses. As seen in Ch.5, it is never possible under the Child Support Act 1991 to agree to exclude future liability to support a *child*.

[93] 1985 Act, s.7(2). Again note that under s.7(2A), the making of a child maintenance assessment under the Child Support Act 1991 constitutes a "major change of circumstances".

[94] s.7(3).

[95] s.3(1)(a).

[96] But a widow has an independent claim against her husband's estate for temporary aliment after his death. See *Stair Encyclopaedia*, 1.4.22. The Scottish Law Commission in their *Report on Succession*, Scot. Law Com. No.124 (1990), recommended the abolition of this right (para.9.10.).

[97] See paras 13–72 to 13–76.

[98] Debtors (Scotland) Act 1987, ss.51–56.

[99] Sch.5 to the Child Support Act 1991 has reduced the number of instalments on which the debtor has defaulted from 3 to 1.

Where parties have reached agreements on aliment which have *not* been registered in the Books of Council and Session, a current maintenance arrestment cannot be used. In such cases, where the debtor defaults, a court action must be raised to obtain a decree for aliment, which can then be enforced only by the ordinary means of diligence.[1]

SOCIAL SECURITY AND INCOME-RELATED STATE BENEFITS

10–63 How do private law rules of aliment interact with the public law rules of social security? Where couples cohabit but are either unmarried or not in a civil partnership they are under no obligation to aliment one another. In such cases, where individuals are in need they will have to turn to the state for support under public law.[2] This is also true of married couples and civil partners when they are on low incomes. The people most likely to live in families with low incomes and thus turn to the state for support include:

- lone-parent families;
- the unemployed;
- children, particularly those in workless households;
- pensioners; and
- people from minority ethnic groups, particularly those of Pakistani or Bangladeshi origin.[3]

10–64 Reliance on benefit of some sort is not uncommon; in 2000/2001, 58 per cent of families in Great Britain received some form of social security benefit or tax credit. [4] While getting people into work reduces the chances of poverty "it does not eliminate it",[5] despite the national minimum wage and the introduction of tax credits. However, eligibility for state benefits is dependent upon meeting certain criteria which may prove hard to establish. Each benefit has its own qualifying conditions but benefits are in general divided into those that are

---

[1] Note again that the right to raise an action for aliment in the courts may be barred if aliment for children is also sought under the provisions of the Child Support Act 1991. See, further Ch.5.

[2] Benefits are now administered by the Department for Work and Pensions. The basic legislative framework for benefits is contained in the Social Security Contributions and Benefits Act 1992 ("SSCBA 1992") and the Social Security Administration Act 1992 ("SSAA 1992").

[3] Office for National Statistics, *35 Years of Social Change: Overview, Social Trends,* Vol.35 (2005), p.2.

[4] Office for National Statistics, *Social Trends,* Vol.33 (2003), p.148.

[5] Two fifths of the people in working-age household who are in income poverty have someone in their household in paid work. See *Monitoring Poverty and Social Exclusion in Scotland 2005: Findings Informing Change* (Joseph Rowntree Foundation, December 2005).

contributory and those that are non-contributory.[6] Contributory social security benefits are only payable to individuals who have paid sufficient National Insurance contributions—through deductions from their earnings—which entitle them to make a claim. All other benefits are "non-contributory" as they do not depend on the claimant satisfying a given level of National Insurance contributions.

Under social security law the main income-related benefits, that is, **10–65** those for which eligibility and the amount paid depends on an income *below* a certain level, are the Jobseeker's Allowance,[7] Working Tax Credit,[8] Housing Benefit,[9] Council Tax Benefit[10] and Income Support.[11] Unlike awards of aliment, where the amount of award is set at the discretion of the court, income-related benefits are set at fixed rates intended to reflect the purported minimum amount required for subsistence.

Jobseeker's Allowance

Jobseeker's allowance ("JSA") has two distinct components: a **10–66** time-limited period of support based on past National Insurance contributions for unemployed persons seeking work (replacing unemployment benefit), and an income-based benefit for the unemployed (replacing, in this role, Income Support). To qualify for this benefit a person must not be in full-time work but be capable of work, must be actively seeking it and otherwise satisfy the labour market conditions. The system[12] requires a claimant to attend a Jobseeker's interview, to sign a Jobseeker's agreement and thereafter to attend fortnightly interviews to ensure continued compliance with the labour market requirements, e.g. of availability for work. The two components have separate rules of entitlement.[13] Whereas, in the past, unemployment benefit was paid for a period of up to 12 months, under the 1995 Act the contribution-based element of JSA will be payable for up to a maximum of six months.[14] Income-based JSA (unlike contributory jobseeker's allowance) is a means-tested benefit

---

[6] For detailed discussion of these benefits see *Welfare Benefits and Tax Credits Handbook 2005/2006* (8th edn, Child Poverty Action Group).

[7] Jobseekers Act 1995 ("JSA 1995"), ss.1–3 and 3A.

[8] Tax Credits Act 2002 ("TCA 2002"), s.3(3) and (7), ss.10 and 42.

[9] SSCBA 1992, s.130.

[10] *ibid.*, s.131(1)(a) and (3)–(5).

[11] SSCBA 1992, s.124. Income Support exists as a benefit for those who are not required to satisfy labour market conditions. Those who fall within this group are principally lone parents, those with significant caring responsibilities, the sick and disabled, the bereaved aged over 55 but under 60, pupils, students and people on training courses. For a full list see Income Support (General) Regulations 1987 (SI 1987/1967), reg.4ZA, Sch.1B.

[12] For details, see the Jobseeker's Allowance Regulations 1996 (SI 1996/207).

[13] *ibid.*, ss.2 and 3.

[14] For discussion of the Act see Buck, "Jobseeker's Allowance: Policy Perspectives" (1996) 3 Journal of Social Security Law 149–164; Bonner, "Jobseeker's allowance: an uneasy hybrid" (1996) 3 J.S.S.L. 165.

and provides a weekly cash sum to top up a claimant's income to a minimum level as prescribed by the Secretary of State. Apart from the general requirements of eligibility, a person claiming the income-based JSA must have less than £8,000 in savings, investments and capital and either not be working or working for less than 16 hours a week. Where the claimant has a partner (whether married, civil partner or cohabitant) the partner must either not be working or work less than 24 hours a week. So, where a claimant is a member of a couple, generally both of them must sign all the documentation and meet the qualifying conditions in relation to claims for income-based JSA. Where awarded, income-based JSA also operates as a passport to some other benefits, such as free dental treatment, free prescriptions, and vouchers for spectacles, and maximum Housing Benefit for rent and Council Tax Benefit.

Working Tax Credit[15]

10–67
- Working Tax Credit: paid to those with low incomes.
- Child Tax Credit: paid to people with children, whether they are in, or out of, work.

The new system of Working Tax Credit and Child Tax Credit which replaces working families' tax credit came into force for people who could qualify for income support/income-based jobseeker's allowance from April 2004. Under this system adults are entitled to claim either working tax credit (which may include support for qualifying childcare) or wage replacement benefits (adult-related allowance only). Child Tax Credit is paid for children *in addition* to Child Benefit.[16] A family element in Child Tax Credit replaces the family premium in income support/income-based jobseeker's allowance. The element paid for dependant children as part of some social security benefits continues to be paid, but is generally taken into account as "income" when calculating tax credit entitlement. Child Tax Credit and Child Benefit are therefore the main source of financial support for children.

10–68
The number of households in receipt of in-work tax credits has doubled since 2001, the vast majority of which are families with children.[17] These new payments challenge existing provision based on

---

[15] This has replaced working families' tax credit which was abolished in April 2003, together with child tax credit. See Tax Credits Act 2002, the Working Tax Credit (Entitlement and Maximum Rates) Regulations 2002 (SI 2002/2005); the Tax Credits (Definition and Calculation of Income) Regulations 2002 (SI 2002/2006); the Child Tax Credit Regulations 2002 (SI 2002/2007); the Tax Credits (Income Thresholds and Determination of Rates) Regulations 2002 (SI 2002/2008); the Tax Credits (Claims and Notifications) Regulations 2002 (SI 2002/2014); the Working Tax Credit (Payment by Employers) Regulations 2002 (SI 2002/2172) and the Tax Credits (Payments by the Board) Regulations 2002 (SI 2002/2173).

[16] See paras 10–72 and 10–73 below.

[17] *Monitoring Poverty and Social Exclusion in Scotland 2005; Findings Informing Change* (Joseph Rowntree Foundation, December 2005).

social insurance. They rely on a means-tested system to deliver the most help to families on the lowest incomes and separate benefits for adults and children. These Tax Credits are administered by Her Majesty's Revenue and Customs, formerly the Inland Revenue.

What is Working Tax Credit? ("WTC")

To qualify a person must have an income below a certain level **10–69** and be:

- over 16, have a child and work at least 16 hours a week; or
- over 16, be disabled and work at least 16 hours a week; or
- over 25 and work at least 30 hours a week; or
- 50 or more, work at least 16 hours a week and be receiving certain benefits.[18]

What is Child Tax Credit? ("CTC")

To qualify a person must be at least 16 and be responsible for a **10–70** child, i.e. be the main carer. A child includes a young person under 19 in full-time, non-advanced education.[19]

In separating out support for adults from support for children their **10–71** stated aims were:

- to make work pay for those in low-income households, including those without children, through the WTC;
- to tackle child poverty through the CTC and Child Benefit; and
- to provide a common framework for assessing entitlement to tax credits based more closely on income tax rules, integrating the tax and benefit systems to bridge the divide between work and welfare.

Child Benefit

Child Benefit is a regular payment which is made to anyone bring- **10–72** ing up children regardless of the level or source of income into that household.

To be eligible for Child Benefit a person must be: **10–73**

- bringing up a child who is under 16; or
- bringing up a young person under 19 (under 20 in some cases) who is either studying in full-time non-advanced education or on a government funded training programme; or
- bringing up a young person who is 16–17 years old and who has recently left school and registered for work or training with the Careers or Connexions Service or similar.

---

[18] For more detailed information see Child Poverty Action Group, *Welfare Benefits and Tax Credits Handbook 2005/2006*, pp.1329–1341.

[19] *ibid.*, pp.1309–1328.

The amount of Child Benefit received by a household depends on the number and ages of the children within the family unit. Slightly more is paid for the eldest child than for subsequent children and the amount is increased for older children.

Housing Benefit and Council Tax Benefit

10–74   Housing Benefit (HB)[20] and Council Tax Benefit (CTB)[21] are means-tested benefits which are administered by the local authority for claimants who have a low income to help them meet their rent liability or Council Tax liability for the place where they live. It is available to claimants whether or not they are working full-time and can be claimed in addition to any other benefit. There are, however, some circumstances where HB cannot be claimed regardless of a claimant's income and the fact that he has to pay rent.[22] The rules relating to CTB are often the same as those for HB.

Basic Rules of Entitlement

10–75   To be eligible a claimant must

- be habitually resident in the United Kingdom;
- with his partner, jointly have less than £16,000 in savings, investments and capital;
- have a liability to pay rent as a condition of occupying the property where he resides; and
- be occupying the property that he is claiming benefit for (but there are some exceptions)[23]

Income Support

10–76   Income support ("IS")[24] is a means-tested benefit and provides a weekly cash sum to supplement an individual's income so that it reaches the minimum level as prescribed each year by the Secretary of State. It is available to those who are not in full-time work and who are not required to sign on as available for work as they are of pensionable age or are incapable of work through sickness, disability or pregnancy. Other individuals who are not required to sign on as

---

[20] This comprises Main Council Tax Benefit and alternative maximum Council Tax Benefit (know as second adult rebate). For details see SSCBA 1992, s.130, and Housing Benefit (General) Regulations 1987 (SI 1987/1971) with substitutions made by the Housing Benefit and Council Tax Benefit (State Pension Credit) Regulations 2003 (SI 2003/325).

[21] SSCBA 1992, s.131(1)(A) and (3)–(5), and Council Tax Benefit (General) Regulations 1992 (SI 1992/1814) with substitutions made by the Housing Benefit and Council Tax Benefit (State Pension Credit) Regulations 2003 (SI 2003/325).

[22] Council Tax Benefit (General) Regulations 1992 (SI 1992/1814), reg.7.

[23] Housing Benefit (General) Regulations 1987 (SI 1987/1971), reg.5.

[24] SSCBA 1992, s.124, and Income support (General) Regulations 1987 (SI 1987/1967).

available for work includes people who are bringing up children under the age of 16 on their own and those caring for a disabled person (and in receipt of carer's allowance). For people aged 60 or over IS was replaced from October 2003 by Pension Credit.

To be eligible for IS a claimant must be: **10–77**

- over 16 and under 60; and
- have less than £8,000 in savings investments and capital (£16,000 if in or about to enter permanent residential care/ nursing home care);
- not be in full-time paid work (defined as not less than 16 hours per week paid work)[25]; and
- not be entitled to Jobseeker's Allowance.

While a claimant may undertake some part-time work without removing eligibility, earnings affect the *amount* payable. It is also important to note that a claim is not made simply for an individual but for a family unit, including a spouse, partner and dependent children under 16 living in the home, or under 19 if s/he is still in full-time "relevant" education.[26] This means that only one member of a family can claim income support. The definition of "family" is discussed below.

Aggregation of Resources—What is a Family?

These benefits are all "income-related" in the sense that they are **10–78** assessed on the basis of the resources available to the individual claimant. Under the Social Security Contributions and Benefits Act 1992, these resources include the resources of the claimant's family. The Act provides:

> "Where a person claiming an income-related benefit is a member of a family, the income and capital of any member of that family shall, except in prescribed circumstances, be treated as the income and capital of that person".[27-28]

For these purposes "family" has been broadly defined to include both **10–79** married and unmarried couples, with or without children, as well as single-parent families including a child or young person.[29] The definition has been further amended by the Civil Partnership Act 2004 to incorporate civil partners and same-sex couples living together as if they were civil partners. The 2004 Act provides for the

---

[25] Income Support (General) Regulations 1987 (SI 1987/1967), regs 2, 4 and 6.
[26] *ibid.*, reg.12, the Jobseeker's Allowance Regulations 1996 (SI 1996/207), reg.54 and Child Benefit (General) Regulations 1976 (SI 1976/965), reg.5.
[27-28] s.136(1).
[29] s.137(1).

substitution of "couple" to replace the reference to "married and unmarried couple" and for a new definition of couple under s.137(1) of the1992 Act as:

(a) a man and woman who are married to each other and are members of the same household;
(b) a man and woman who are not married to each other but are living together as husband and wife otherwise than in prescribed circumstances;
(c) two people of the same sex who are civil partners of each other and are members of the same household; or
(d) two people of the same sex who are not civil partners of each other but are living together as if they were civil partners otherwise than in prescribed circumstances.[30]

10–80 Where individuals fall within this definition of family, both entitlement and the amount payable in respect of all benefits are determined by aggregating the claimants capital and income together with that of family members which may well bring him or her above the cut-off point for benefit. The underlying rationale is that the state should not have to support the claimant if sufficient resources are being brought into the household by another member of the family (even if the claimant does not in fact benefit from them). For this reason the "family" is broadly defined under social security legislation to cover married couples, unmarried couples, civil partners and same-sex couples who are living together as if they were civil partners. Such persons are expected to mutually support one another, rather than rely on the state for support, even though unmarried, heterosexual couples and same-sex couples who are not civil partners have no obligations to aliment each other under private law. It is not just the definition of "family" that has been amended by the 2004 Act. Section 254 and Sch.24 of the Civil Partnership Act 2004 apply more generally to amend legislation dealing with social security, child support and tax credits to bring civil partnerships and those living together as though they were civil partners within its ambit.

Recovery from Liable Relatives

10–81 What if a woman living alone, but still married to her husband, applies for an income-related benefit? Although she may qualify for the benefit—and be awarded it, under the private law rules examined above—it is legally the duty of her husband to aliment her. As we have

---

[30] Civil Partnership Act 2004, s.254 and Sch.24, Pt 3, para.46. The Department of Work and Pensions produced a leaflet entitled *Getting it Right?* in 2005 addressed at same-sex couples to advise them that, if on benefit, they would need to inform the DWP. The consequence of so doing of course is that their benefit income could be reduced or, in some instances, stopped.

noted above, it will, however, often be more convenient for a person in this position to claim state benefit rather than to seek and enforce a court award for aliment. Accordingly, the state reserves the right to recover the cost of an award of IS or JSA from those who fall within the category of "liable relatives" under the Social Security Administration Act 1992[31] and the Jobseekers Act 1995.[32] Liability under the 1992 Act previously covered spouses who are liable to maintain each other and parents who are liable to maintain their children.[33] A "child" in this context covers not only a person who is under the age of 16, but one also who is 16 or more but under the age of 19 and in respect of whom either parent, or some person acting in place of either parent, is receiving IS.[34] Under the Civil Partnership Act 2004, however, the definition has been extended to cover civil partners in terms of both the 1992 Act[35] and the Jobseeker's Act 1995.[36] Since the duty to aliment a spouse ends on divorce, an ex-spouse cannot be a "liable relative" under the 1992 Act. The same is the case with a civil partnership that has been formally dissolved. Where "liable relatives" fail to meet their alimentary obligations, then, the Secretary of State is empowered to recover the cost of any award of IS or income-based JSA made in lieu.[37] An application is made to the sheriff who, having regard to all the circumstances, including the defender's resources, may order the defender to pay whatever sum is considered appropriate, on a weekly, monthly or other basis.[38] In the past, the Department of Social Security (now the Department for Work and Pensions) tended to take a broader view of the resources which a liable relative requires for his or her subsistence than the law strictly states, so that in many cases, recovery has not in fact been sought from "liable relatives".[39] The sheriff has a discretion to hold that only a part of what has been paid out as income-related benefit is recoverable from a "liable relative".[40]

However, the likelihood of actions for recovery of benefit from **10–82** "liable relatives" has been considerably reduced by the Child Support Act 1991 as child support payments made by the non-resident parent to the parent with care are paid instead to the Secretary of State to offset any other benefit (such as Income Support) that that individual is in receipt of.[41]

---

[31] s.106.
[32] s.23.
[33] Paraphrased from s.78(6) of the 1992 Act.
[34] s.78(6)(d).
[35] CPA 2004, s.254, Sch.24, Pt 4, para.61(4).
[36] *ibid.*, Sch.24, Pt 7, paras 118–125.
[37] SSCBA 1992, s.106; 1995 Act, s.23.
[38] SSCBA 1992, s.106(2) and SI 1996/207, reg.169(2).
[39] See *Henry v Henry*, 1972 S.L.T. (Notes) 26.
[40] See SSCBA 1992, s.106(2) and SI 1996/207, reg.169(2).
[41] 1991 Act, s.6. See, also, paras 5–62 to 5–63.

SUCCESSION[42]

10–83 Marriage and civil partnership have important consequences for adults in relation to both testate and intestate succession. The provisions of the 1964 Succession (Scotland) Act 1964 dealing with succession have now been extended to cover civil partners.[43]

Intestate Succession

Prior Rights

10–84 Where a person dies without leaving a will, any surviving spouse or civil partner will be entitled to prior and legal rights out of the deceased's estate, according to the law of intestate succession under the Succession (Scotland) Act 1964.[44] Prior rights include rights to the deceased's interest in the dwelling-house which the deceased and surviving spouse/civil partner formerly shared, and the furniture and plenishings,[45] and to monetary provision.[46] As the name implies, these are distributed first out of the deceased's estate before legal rights (although after debts, funeral expenses and taxes). Where the surviving spouse/civil partner was ordinarily resident in a dwelling-house in which the deceased had a "relevant interest" at the date of death,[47] the surviving spouse/civil partner is entitled to the deceased's interest in the house where its value is not in excess of £300,000, or to the sum £300,000 where its value exceeds this limit.[48] The surviving spouse/civil partner is also entitled to furniture and plenishings[49] from the deceased's estate up to a value of £24,000.[50] In addition, the surviving spouse/civil partner is also entitled to monetary provision out of the deceased's estate.[51] The value of the monetary right depends on whether or not the deceased is survived by issue.[52] Where there are issue, the surviving spouse/civil partner is entitled to a sum

---

[42] For fuller details see J. Kerrigan, *Drafting for Succession* (W.Green, Edinburgh, 2004) and D.R. Macdonald, *Succession* (3rd edn, W.Green, Edinburgh, 2001).

[43] Civil Partnership Act 2004, s.261(2), Sch.8, Pt 1.

[44] These rights are extended to civil partners by Sch.28, Pt I, para.1(1) of the 2004 Act.

[45] Succession (Scotland) Act 1964, s.8. For application to civil partners see para.4, Pt 1, Sch.28 of the 2004 Act.

[46] *ibid.*, s.9 as amended by Prior Rights of Surviving Spouse (Scotland) Order 2005 (SSI 2005/252).

[47] A "relevant interest" can be that of an owner or a tenant, other than a tenancy under the Rent and Mortgages Acts, s.8(6). Where there is more than one qualifying house, the surviving spouse has 6 months to elect which is to qualify for prior rights.

[48] 1964 Act, s.8(1).

[49] These are defined in s.8(6)(b) of the 1964 Act.

[50] These can come from a different house from that which the dwelling-house rights were taken.

[51] 1964 Act, s.9; para.1, Pt 1, Sch.28 of the 2004 Act.

[52] "Issue" includes descendants however remote, and makes no distinction between children whose parents were married and those who were born out of wedlock: s.36(1) of the 1964 Act.

of £42,000, and where there are none, to £75,000. The monetary right is borne by the heritable and moveable parts of the estate in proportion to their respective amounts after the dwelling-house and plenishings rights have been taken off.[53] This ensures that the moveable estate, out of which legal rights are claimed, is not unfairly depleted since the children have indefeasible rights in the moveable estate which are exigible only after prior rights have been taken off. In practice, prior rights are fixed at rates such that they exhaust the majority of intestate estates.[54]

Legal Rights

The surviving spouse or civil partner is also entitled to legal rights,[55] which are taken from what is left of the deceased's moveable estate, after prior rights have been deducted. Once again, the sum the surviving spouse receives depends on whether or not there are children or remoter issue of the deceased, since the children are also entitled to legal rights.[56] Where there are no issue, the surviving spouse/civil partner is entitled to half the moveable estate, but otherwise only to one-third. **10–85**

The remaining half or third of the moveable estate (known as the dead's part), plus any remaining heritage, is left for the deceased's heirs to inherit. Under s.2 of the 1964 Act, the heirs of the deceased are listed in order of preferential right. A surviving spouse or civil partner inherits under this head only if there are no children or remoter issue, parents, collaterals or collateral descendants left alive. **10–86**

Testate Succession

Where the deceased leaves a will but fails to provide for the surviving spouse/civil partner or issue, then again legal rights can be claimed by them out of the moveable estate. This right cannot be excluded by the deceased in his or her will. Thus, the surviving spouse/civil partner and issue can only truly be cut out of the will of the deceased if the deceased is willing to convert all the moveable property into heritage (other than a family home). For the surviving spouse/civil partner is entitled to a one-half or one-third share of the moveable estate, depending on whether or not there are surviving children or issue. **10–87**

---

[53] 1964 Act, s.9(3).

[54] SSI 2005/252 amending the 1964 Act. Note, the figures for dwelling-house, plenishings and monetary rights are updated from time to time by statutory instrument.

[55] These used to be referred to under the 1964 Act as the *jus relicti* (where the husband is the surviving spouse) and the *jus relictae* (where the surviving spouse is the wife). These terms have been abolished and replaced with the general term "legal rights" by Sch.28, Pt I, para.6 of the 2004 Act.

[56] In the past these legal rights under the 1964 Act were known as *legitim* but this term, along with *jus relicti* and *jus relictae* has been abolished and replaced with the general term "legal rights" by Sch.28, Pt I, para.6 of the 2004 Act.

10–88   Where the deceased leaves a will in which provision *is* made for the surviving spouse and children, these parties can elect whether to take such provision or whether to renounce it and claim legal rights instead. It is not possible to do both, i.e. to both "approbate" and "reprobate" the will. In some cases, it may be in the interests of the surviving spouse/civil partner to renounce the legacy, even if it is of the whole estate, thereby forcing the whole estate into "artificial intestacy".[57] If the spouse merely took the testamentary gift, and there were also children or remoter issue of the deceased, then those children could claim legal rights which would be taken from the estate leaving only the residue for the surviving spouse. But if the spouse/ civil partner *renounces* the testate gift, then the whole estate falls into intestacy, in which case prior rights take precedence over legal rights. In many cases, these prior rights will exhaust the estate, and so the surviving spouse will obtain the whole estate without having to meet the children's claim for legal rights.

10–89   It should be noted that the divorce or remarriage of a testator does not automatically revoke a will in Scotland. So where a legacy is left to "my wife", for example, it is a question of interpretation as to whether this is merely descriptive or whether the legacy is conditional upon the marriage in question subsisting at the date of the testator's death.[58]

Succession and Cohabitants

10–90   In the past, cohabitants could not claim rights in the estates of their deceased partners unless they had explicitly been left a legacy by that partner. While they are still not entitled to claim prior or legal rights, reforms implemented by s.29 of the Family (Scotland) Act 2006 mean that they can now apply to the court for discretionary provision on intestacy. Under s.25(1) of that Act a cohabitant is defined as either member of a couple consisting of:

    (a) a man and a woman who are (or were) living together as if they were husband and wife;
    (b) two persons of the same sex who are (or were) living together as if the were civil partners.

10–91 In determining whether or not a person is a cohabitant the court is to "have regard to—

    (a) the length of the period during which A and B have been living together (or lived together);
    (b) the nature of their relationship during that period; and
    (c) the nature and extent of any financial arrangements subsisting, or which subsisted during that period."[59]

---

[57] See *Kerr, Petr*, 1968 S.L.T. (Sh. Ct.) 61.
[58] *Couper's Judicial Factor v Valentine*, 1976 S.C. 63; *Burn's Trs*, 1961 S.C. 17.
[59] s.25(2).

In applying to the Court of Session or the Sheriff Court[60] for discre- **10–92** tionary provision, a cohabitant must establish that immediately before the deceased's death the deceased was domiciled in Scotland, was *intestate* and cohabiting with the cohabitant "survivor".[61] Application to the court must be made within six months of the deceased's death.[62] Where the applicant establishes that s/he was a cohabitant the court may make an order or interim order as it thinks fit:

(a) for payment to the survivor out of the deceased's net intestate estate of a capital sum of such amount as may be specified in the order;

(b) for transfer to the survivor of such property (whether heritable or moveable) from that estate as may be so specified.[63]

In reaching its decision the court is directed to consider:

(a) the size and nature of the deceased's net intestate estate;
(b) any benefit received, or to be received by the survivor—
  (i) on, or in consequence of, the deceased's death; and
  (ii) from somewhere other than the deceased's net intestate estate; and
(c) the nature and extent of any other rights against, or claims on, the deceased's net intestate estate; and
(d) any other matter the court considers appropriate.[64]

In the 2006 Act the "net intestate estate" that a surviving cohabitant **10–93** may make a claim for a capital sum out of is defined to mean so much of the intestate estate as remains after provision for the satisfaction of:

(a) inheritance tax;
(b) other liabilites of the estate having priority over legal rights and the prior rights of a surviving spouse or surviving civil partner; and
(c) the legal rights, and the prior rights, or any surviving spouse or surviving civil partner.[65]

Therefore if the deceased died leaving a surviving spouse/civil partner, a surviving cohabitant partner may not receive anything out of the deceased's estate.[66]

---

[60] FLSA 2006, s.25(3). Where the court concerned is the sheriff court it must be in the sheriffdom in which the deceased "was habitually resident at the date of death" or, if this is uncertain, Edinburgh Sheriff Court: s.29(5)(b) and (c).

[61] s.29(1).

[62] s.29(6).

[63] s.29(2)(a).

[64] s.29(3).

[65] s.29(10)

[66] An interesting survey of public opinion regarding succession which included what they believed a cohabitant *should* be able to claim was published by Scottish

10–94   Further, when a court does make an order or interim order it must not exceed "the amount to which the survivor would have been entitled had the survivor been a spouse or civil partner of the deceased".[67] If a capital sum is involved this may be payable by instalments.[68] There is provision for the court, on an application "by any party having an interest", to vary the date or method of payment where a capital sum is concerned.[69]

10–95   If a cohabiting partner dies testate and made testamentary provision for his/her partner then the partner may of course inherit, however this will not defeat the rights of any subsisting spouse or civil partner of the deceased.

10–96   The Scottish Law Commission is currently examining Cohabitants' rights to testate estate when they have been left little or nothing which is intended to be the subject of future legislation.[70]

10–97   The reforms are to be welcomed although they exist on a discretionary footing rather than representing the kind of entitlement that is embodied in the Succession (Scotland) Act 1964. They do go further than the reforms proposed by the Scottish Law Commission in 1990 who, while noting there was some public sentiment in favour of extending succession rights to cohabitants,[71] expressly discounted proposals for extending rights to *same-sex* couples.[72] No doubt the legislative response to including same-sex couples is the result of case law and jurisprudence on human rights emanating from Strasbourg and United Kingdom courts that rejects discriminatory treatment on the basis of sex or gender.[73]

Overview

10–98 It is clear that while public law, most notably in the field of social security legislation, has moved towards a definition of the family which is not dependent upon marital status, private law continues to make important distinctions on this basis, especially in the area of aliment. Only spouses and civil partners (and not unmarried cohabiting heterosexual or same-sex couples), can benefit from the duty imposed by

---

Executive Social Research entitled *Attitudes Towards Succession Law: Findings of a Scottish Omnibus Survey,* July 21, 2005. See also *Report on Family Law,* Scot. Law Com. No.135 (1992), which includes discussion of the range of "permeations" of cohabitation and the inevitable difficulties it poses for legislation: p.16.24

[67] s.29(4).

[68] s.29(7)(b).

[69] s.29(9).

[70] Nichols, D. "The Family Law (Scotland) Act 2006 explained", 2006 Fam. L.B. 79-1.

[71] *Report on Succession,* Scot. Law Com. No.124 (1990); also, *The Effects of Cohabitation in Private Law,* Scot. Law Com. Discussion Paper No.86 (1990).

[72] *The Effects of Cohabitation in Private Law,* Scot. Law Com. Discussion Paper No.86 (1990), p.6.12.

[73] See also 4–75 *et seq.* and 9–41 to 9–44.

s.1 of the Family Law (Scotland) Act 1985. Although we have questioned the extent to which the law of aliment continues to provide a useful form of maintenance for married parties, it is still an option which is open to them, and which is particularly useful as an interim award in divorce proceedings. The period prior to divorce, when a couple are in the process of reorganising their future and finances, but have not yet reached a settlement, is often one of economic vulnerability, particularly for women who most often take primary responsibility for any children of the relationship. For married persons, aliment can provide a useful regime of financial support during this period and is another option to add to that of state support. But for unmarried partners, a claim to support can be established only if a voluntary agreement for support has been entered into by the parties,[74] or by turning to the social security system, and, as we have seen above, this may not be possible where the couple continue to cohabit, even if support from the cohabiting partner is in reality non-existent or inadequate due to the process of relationship breakdown. For such parties, the private and public rules on maintenance combine to create a "catch 22" situation.

Further, whilst existing succession law has been extended to **10–99** accommodate civil partnerships, cohabiting couples—whether of the opposite or same sex—may only claim if their partner was intestate and are only likely to benefit if their partner did not have a prior subsisting marriage or civil partnership.

In the next chapter we will go on to consider the rules relating to marriage, property and the family home.

---

[74] See para.15–20.

CHAPTER 11

THE FAMILY HOME

11–01 For most families, the most important asset they possess is the house in which they live. The family home may be owned privately, or occupied under a public or private sector tenancy.[1] In the case of private ownership, title to heritable property is conferred by a document known as the disposition which must be recorded in the Register of Sasines, or registered in the Land Register of Scotland. It is only on recording or registration of the disposition that ownership of the property passes to the purchaser, who then acquires full rights as proprietor, including the right to occupy and dispose of the property. A mere agreement to purchase property, although (if properly executed) an enforceable contract, does not, of itself, transfer the real right in the property, merely giving the purchaser a personal right against the seller.

11–02 Most house purchases need to be financed by a loan from a building society or bank. Such a loan, colloquially known as a mortgage, is invariably made on condition that the building society or bank becomes a heritable creditor. As such, the lender acquires a real right in security over the property to the value of its interest in the property. This is accomplished by the house purchaser granting a standard security over the house to the lender.[2] This standard security becomes a burden on the property as soon as it is registered or recorded, which gives the lender the right to sell the house if the purchaser fails to make the necessary repayments (including interest). The proceeds of such a sale are held in trust by the lender, and any surplus over from the sale after expenses and the loan have been paid off must be returned to the former debtor.[3]

11–03 Where the house is rented, title to occupy is conferred on the tenant by way of a lease, which lays down the terms and conditions under which the tenancy is held, including the duration of the lease,[4] as well as the period of notice which must be given on either side to

---

[1] Public sector tenancies are regulated principally by the Housing (Scotland) Act 1987 as amended by the Housing (Scotland) Acts of 2001 and 2006. Private sector tenancies are regulated by the Rent (Scotland) Act 1984 and the Housing (Scotland) Act 1988 as amended by the 2001 and 2006 Acts.

[2] Conveyancing and Feudal Reform (Scotland) Act 1970.

[3] *ibid.*, s.27. See, further, G.L. Gretton and K.G.C. Reid, *Conveyancing* (3rd edn, W.Green, Edinburgh, 2004), Ch.19.

[4] Which may not exceed 20 years under Land Tenure Reform (Scotland) Act 1974, s.8.

terminate the tenancy. Statutory provisions have, over the years, provided the tenant with greater security of tenure than existed at common law.[5]

In Ch.10, we discussed the general proposition that marriage has **11–04** no effect on the property rights of the spouses. We noted that the Matrimonial Homes (Family Protection) (Scotland) Act 1981 ("1981 Act") provided an important exception to this rule. In this chapter, we will discuss in detail the key aspects of the 1981 Act[6] as well as the corresponding provisions affording protection to civil partners within the Civil Partnership Act 2004 ("2004 Act").[7] We begin with the 1981 Act as this introduced to Scots law provisions which have only recently been extended to cover registered same-sex partnerships via the 2004 Act.

THE MATRIMONIAL HOMES (FAMILY PROTECTION) (SCOTLAND) ACT 1981

Background to the 1981 Act

Only the person who owns property is entitled to possess it, occupy **11–05** it and alienate it by sale or gift. In respect of heritable property, i.e. land and buildings, the person whose name is on the disposition, i.e. the disponee, is the legal owner (upon registration in the Register of Sasines or the Land Register of Scotland), regardless of who actually financed the sale, e.g. a bank, the other spouse or a relative. Thus, in principle, the person who owns the family home has the power to evict any other occupants, and to interdict them from returning to the premises,[8] provided obligations of aliment are met. A husband or wife may do this if they have sole title.[9]

Clearly, this can cause hardship in the domestic sphere.[10] Parti- **11–06** cular concern arose in the 1970s after empirical research showed that domestic violence[11] was a prevalent and apparently increasing

---

[5] See, further, *Stair Encyclopaedia*, Vol.11, on Public Sector Landlords and their Tenants, pp.625–641; Vol.13, on Landlord and Tenant, pp.49–344.

[6] A full analysis of the conveyancing implications of the 1981 Act is outside the scope of this book. See, further, Gretton and Reid, *op. cit.*, above n.3, at pp.180–195.

[7] Civil Partnership Act 2004, ss.101–116.

[8] In *Maclure v Maclure*, 1911 S.C. 200, a husband who was the sole tenant of the family home was granted an interdict to exclude his drunken wife from the premises, on the condition that he continued to aliment her.

[9] In *Millar v Millar*, 1940 S.C. 56, a wife who let property to her husband gave him notice to quit, just like an ordinary tenant. The court upheld her action regardless of the fact that the property in question was used as the family home and that she had deserted her husband.

[10] See the *Report from the Select Committee on Violence in Marriage* (1974–1975 HC 533) and the *Observations* on that report, Cmnd.6690 (1976).

[11] There are different ways of defining what this entails. See further: Scottish Executive, *The Report of the Scottish Partnership on Domestic Abuse* (2000). Police definitions of domestic violence differ from those used in crime surveys. In Scotland

problem,[12] primarily for women living with violent male partners. It is now widely recognised that "the pattern of abuse is asymmetrical. Overwhelmingly it is men who use violence against women partners, not the obverse."[13] As early as 1976, studies documenting violence and abuse identified a number of key areas for concern,[14] including the family home as a site of abuse.[15]

11–07 Of major concern was the fact that if a violent partner was the sole owner of the home (and most perpetrators of such violence are male) than he had the sole right to occupy and thus to eject all other inhabitants of the house as he pleased, e.g. as a reprisal for calling out police because of assault. If the victim left the house she would have no right to re-enter the family home against his will.

11–08 This had implications for women, namely:

- that they might be rendered homeless, or forced to accept substandard accommodation for themselves and their children; and
- that for this reason many women put up with abuse or violence because they did not have anywhere suitable to go.

11–09 These findings made a great impression on both English and Scottish Law Commissions and led to immediate legislation drafted to deal with the situation. In Scotland this took the form of the Matrimonial Homes (Family Protection) (Scotland) Act 1981. The Act has two main aims:

---

the definition of domestic violence used by the police is "any form of physical, sexual or emotional abuse which takes place within the context of a close relationship". Scottish Executive, *Domestic Violence: Findings From the 2000 Scottish Crime Survey* (2002), p.3.

[12] The police returned details covering 43,678 incidents of domestic abuse in 2004, a 10% increase compared to the 39,643 incidents recorded in 2003. This continues the steady increase in incidents reported since 1999. See: Scottish Executive, *Domestic Abuse Recorded by the Police in Scotland, 1 January–31 December 2004* (Statistical Bulletin, Criminal Justice Series, 2005). Referrals to Scottish Women's Aid have risen steadily over the years. In 1985–1986 there were 10,833 referrals and by 1994–1995 this number had risen to 35,081. See Scottish Women's Aid *Annual Report 1994/1995*, p.3. By 2004 the numbers were up 15% from 72,029 in 2003 to 83,226. See Scottish Women's Aid *Annual Report 2003–2004*.

[13] R. Dobash and R. Dobash, *The politics and policies of responding to violence against women* in *Home Truths About Domestic Violence* (L. Hanmer and K. I. ... ... Routledge, London ... ... incidents with a female victim and male perpetrator represented 88% of all incidents of domestic abuse where this information was recorded. Scottish Executive, *Statistical Bulletin, Criminal Justice Series* (2005), p.3. According to the Scottish Executive, *Domestic Violence: Findings From the 2000 Scottish Crime Survey* (2002), "where the victim's sex was recorded, 93% of incidents of domestic abuse involved a female victim. Where the perpetrator's sex was recorded, 93% were male" at p.5.

[14] *Op. cit.*, above, n.10.

[15] In 2004, the overwhelming majority of incidents of domestic abuse took place in the home—91% of all incidents where the location was recorded. Scottish Executive, *Statistical Bulletin, Criminal Justice Series* (2005). p.3.

- to provide a spouse (and now a civil partner)[16] who has no legal right to live in the home with that right (and to extend this to a limited extent to cohabitees); and
- to provide increased protection for a spouse (and now a civil partner)[17] and children (and to a limited extent a cohabitee)[18] who are at risk from domestic violence or abuse.

Law reform in this area has focused[19] on providing the spouse/civil partner who had no legal title to the house where she[20] resided with the rights: **11–10**

1) to occupy and re-enter the matrimonial home, and
2) to exclude the violent partner, even where he was the sole legal proprietor or tenant.

A principal area for concern which has been subjected to modifications since the passage of the 1981 Act has been how to provide workable *enforcement* mechanisms to protect these rights. **11–11**

The Structure of the 1981 Act

Entitled and Non-Entitled Spouses

The 1981 Act is primarily concerned with providing rights to spouses in respect of the matrimonial/family home. The Act refers throughout to "entitled" and "non-entitled" spouses.[21] These terms are also used to cover "entitled partner" and "non-entitled partner" and their rights in the "family home" under the 2004 Act.[22] The entitled spouse ("ES") or entitled partner ("EP") is the one who has legal title to the matrimonial/family home, as owner or tenant, or who is granted permission to occupy the matrimonial/family home from a third party, e.g. a trustee.[23] The non-entitled spouse ("NES") or non-entitled **11–12**

---

[16] See s.101, Pt 3, Ch.3 of the Civil Partnership Act 2004.

[17] Under ss.102–112 and ss.113–116, Pt 4 of the 2004 Act.

[18] 1981 Act, s.18 dealing with cohabitees, is now amended by s.31 of the Family Law (Scotland) Act 2006 to cover same-sex couples who are not in a civil partnership.

[19] The 1974–1975 Select Committee Report (*op. cit.*, above, n.10) led to the enactment of the Domestic Violence and Matrimonial Proceedings Act 1976 in England, which has now been replaced by Pt IV of the Family Law Act 1996. In Scotland, it took longer for such legislation to be passed in the form of the 1981 Act, which emerged out of the Scot. Law Com. Consultative Memorandum No.41 (1978) on *Occupancy Rights in the Matrimonial Home and Domestic Violence* and the subsequent report on this subject (Scot. Law Com. No.60 (1980)).

[20] In this chapter, the pronoun "he" will be used for the entitled spouse and "she" for the non-entitled spouse as reflecting the commonest situation. The provisions of the 1981 Act are, however, gender neutral.

[21] As defined in ss.1 and 22.

[22] Under ss.101–112 of Pt 3, Ch.3 of the 2004 Act.

[23] 1981 Act, s.1(2). A spouse who is entitled to occupy the matrimonial home along with a third party is also an entitled spouse, but only where the third party has

partner ("NEP") is the spouse or partner who has no legal title to the property, but is given certain rights of occupation under the 1981 or the 2004 Act. The rights of the NES arise automatically under the 1981 Act by virtue of marriage to the entitled spouse as is the case also with registration of a civil partnership under the 2004 Act and such rights do not require any additional form of registration or notification to come into effect. As will be discussed below, without adequate safeguards this could raise problems for third parties who could not tell from examining the title documents of a property that it is a matrimonial or family home and that a NES/P has rights in respect of it.[24]

Matrimonial/Family Home

11–13   The NES/P's rights under the 1981 or 2004 Act apply only in respect of a matrimonial[25] or family[26] home. What counts as a matrimonial home is very broadly defined to include "any house, caravan, houseboat or other structure which has been provided or has been made available by one or both spouses as, or has become, a family residence".[27] This definition may cover more than one residence. So, for example, where a couple buy a house in the town and a cottage in the country, and use them both as family residences, they may both qualify as a "matrimonial" or "family" home within the definition of the Acts. As a house may "become" a matrimonial or family home, the fact that it was purchased before the parties married is irrelevant. A house can be a matrimonial/family home even if neither of the spouses/civil partners has ever lived in it, for the definition is satisfied by a house which is merely "provided" or "made available" as a family residence. On the other hand, not all properties which are purchased during marriage/civil partnership necessarily qualify as a matrimonial/family home. Where, for example, one party buys a property for his or her exclusive use, or for investment purposes, and can argue that it was not acquired as a family residence, the Acts will not apply.[28] Where a house is provided or made available by one spouse/civil partner for the other to reside in *separately* it is not to be regarded as a "matrimonial" or "family" "home".[29] Where the

---

waived his or her right of occupation in favour of the entitled spouse. See *Murphy v Murphy*, 1992 S.C.L.R. 62.

[24] See paras 11–50 to 11–54.

[25] 1981 Act, s.22.

[26] See s.31 of the FLSA 2006 inserting s.18A(3) into the 1981 Act defining "family home" in the same terms as a matrimonial home.

[27] 1981 Act, s.22; see also s.135 of the 2004 Act defining a "family home" for civil partners and at s.18A(3) of the 1981 Act for cohabitees as inserted by s.31 of the FLSA 2006. The definition also includes "any garden or other ground or building attached to, and usually occupied with, or otherwise required for the amenity or convenience of, the house, caravan, houseboat or other structure".

[28] See the attempt to argue against a house being a matrimonial home in *Mazur v Mazur*, 1990 G.W.D. 35-2011.

[29] 1981 Act, s.22 for spouses; 2004 Act, s.135 for civil partners

matrimonial/family home is a tenancy that has been transferred from one spouse/civil partner to the other by agreement or under any enactment it ceases to qualify as a matrimonial/family home.[30]

Application for an order under the 1981/2004 Act may be made to **11–14** either the Sheriff Court or the Outer House of the Court of Session.[31]

Occupancy and Related Rights

Occupancy Rights—Spouses

Under s.1(1) of the 1981 Act, the NES has the right: **11–15**

(a) if in occupation, to continue to occupy the matrimonial home; and
(b) if not in occupation, to enter into and occupy the matrimonial home.

These rights include the right to occupy and re-enter together with any child of the family.[32] The Act was amended to this effect in 1985 to ensure that a non-entitled spouse's occupancy rights could not be defeated by threats to eject any children of the marriage from the matrimonial home. In its initial form, the Act did not confer any occupancy rights on children, who also had no right to occupy the home at common law except by permission of the person with title. It is still the case that children do not have independent rights under the Act, but only indirect rights of occupancy attached to an adult's occupancy rights. Nor is the protection of any child of the marriage a matter of compelling concern in the scheme of the 1981 Act, although the needs of the child are a factor the courts will consider under s.3(3)(c) (discussed in para.11–22).[33] In *Hampsey v Hampsey*[34] the court held that a sheriff had no power to grant an exclusion order simply because the best interests of the child required it. Compare the more recent provisions of the Children (Scotland) Act 1995, ss.76–80, which give the court the right to grant an exclusion order excluding a suspected abuser from the home of a child where this is necessary for the child's protection.[35] Under these provisions, the court *is* enjoined

---

[30] 1981 Act, s.22(2) as inserted by s.7 of the FLSA 2006. The equivalent tenancy provisions for civil partners is at s.135(2) of the 2004 Act (as inserted by Sch.1, para.12 of the FLSA 2006). For cohabitees, similar provision is at s.18A(4) of the 1981 Act as inserted by s.31 of the FLSA 2006.

[31] 1981 Act, s.22 for spouses; 2004 Act, s.135 for civil partners.

[32] Under s.22 this includes "any child or grandchild of either spouse, and any person who has been brought up or treated by either spouse as if he or she were a child of that spouse, whatever the age of such a child, grandchild or person may be". Note that in this context, somewhat unusually, no age limit is placed on the child.

[33] See, e.g. *Assar v Assar*, 1993 G.W.D. 2-102.

[34] 1988 G.W.D. 24-1035.

[35] Discussed in detail in paras 7–49 *et seq.* and 7–69. Note that s.76 exclusion orders last for a maximum of only six months.

to treat the welfare of the child as paramount,[36] and the underlying policy is that it is better, where there is compelling evidence, to prejudice the occupancy rights of an alleged abuser, rather than traumatically remove the child. The 1995 Act does not, however, give children express rights of occupancy in the family home any more than the 1981 Act does.

Occupancy Rights—Civil Partners

11–16 Corresponding rights under s.101 of the 2004 Act apply to civil partners. In this context, a child of the family is defined as,

> "any child or grandchild of either civil partner, and any person who has been brought up or treated by either civil partner as if the person were a child of that partner whatever the age of such a child, grandchild or person".[37] For these purposes "family" is defined as "the civil partners in the civil partnership, together with any child, grandchild or person so treated".[38]

Occupancy Rights—Cohabitees

11–17 In the past the definition of a cohabiting couple was restricted to "a man and a woman who are living with each other as if they were man and wife".[39] However, the section has been extended[40] to include persons living with one another "as if they were civil partners". In determining the issue of whether or not the parties are a cohabiting couple, the court is expressly directed to consider all the circumstances of the case, including the length of the cohabitation and whether there are any children of the relationship.[41]

11–18 Unlike spouses and civil partners, cohabitees *do not* have automatic occupancy rights but must apply to the court to have them declared. Further, occupancy rights may only be granted for a period not exceeding six months requiring further application to obtain another declarator, again for no longer than six months.[42]

11–19 In respect of the definition of "family" home discussed above,[43] similar provision exists and similarly, where a property has been made available by one partner for the other to reside in separately, it falls outwith the definition of family home.[44]

---

[36] 1995 Act, s.16.
[37] Under s.101(7) of the 2004 Act, as amended by Sch.1, para.3(b) of the FLSA 2006.
[38] *ibid.*
[39] 1981 Act, s.18(1). Given this wording a same-sex couple could not come within the definition of a cohabiting couple. The section has now been amended to read "as if they were husband and wife" by s.31 of the FLSA 2006.
[40] By s.31 of the FLSA 2006.
[41] 1981 Act, s.18(2).
[42] *ibid.*, s.18(1).
[43] See para.11–13.
[44] 1981 Act, s.18A(3) for cohabiting couples, inserted by s.31of the FLSA 2006.

Consequential and Subsidiary Rights

Granting occupancy rights to the non-entitled spouse/civil partner **11–20** is not, on its own, enough to guarantee that person's ability to remain in the home. Certain ancillary rights are also necessary. For example, if the right to occupy was not accompanied by a right to the use of furniture and plenishings in the home, then the ES/P might remove such items as belonged solely to him from the matrimonial or family home, thus making occupation very difficult.[45] To prevent this, either spouse or civil partner may apply to the court for an order regulating possession or use of any furniture and plenishings in the matrimonial home.[46] Section 2(1) of the 1981 Act for spouses (at s.102 of the 2004 Act for civil partners), further empowers the NES without the consent of the ES to:

(a) make payments, such as rent, that are due by the entitled spouse[47];
(b) perform any other obligation incumbent on the entitled spouse;
(c) enforce performance of an obligation owed to the entitled spouse by a third party, e.g. a contract to re-paint the house[48];
(d) carry out essential repairs;
(e) carry out non-essential repairs or improvements which the court considers appropriate for the reasonable enjoyment of the occupancy rights[49]; and
(f) take such other steps as an entitled spouse would have been entitled to take to protect his occupancy rights.

It is of little use however, for the NES/P to be given the *right* to pay the mortgage or rent if she has not enough funds with which to pay it because the ES/P is refusing to pay his share. Accordingly, the court

---

[45] This problem, however, is alleviated by s.25 of the Family Law (Scotland) Act 1985, which sets up a presumption that "household goods" are owned in equal shares by spouses. See paras 12–40 to 12–44. This presumption is now extended to civil partners by Sch.28, Pt 1, para.28 of the 2004 Act and to heterosexual cohabiting as well as same-sex couples who are not civil partners by s.22(6) of the FLSA 2006.

[46] 1981 Act, s.3(2) for spouses; 2004 Act, s.103(2) for civil partners. 1981 Act, s.22 for spouses; 2004 Act, s.135 for civil partners: "furniture and plenishings" is defined to include items which are owned, hired or acquired under a hire-purchase or conditional sale agreement by one of the spouses. The court has a discretion as to what order to make having regard to all the circumstances of the case, including the factors set out in the 1981 Act, s.3(3) for spouses; 2004 Act, s.103(3) for civil partners.

[47] Payment includes "rents, rates, secured loan instalments, interest or other outgoings (not being outgoings on repairs or improvements)": 1981 Act, s.2(1)(a) for spouses; 2004 Act, s.102(1)(a) for civil partners.

[48] But only to the extent that the entitled spouse could enforce such performance: 1981 Act, s.2(1)(c) for spouses; 2004 Act, s.102(1)(c) for civil partners.

[49] These must be repairs which the entitled spouse could have legally undertaken and which have been authorised by court order: 1981 Act, s.2(1)(e) for spouses; 2004 Act, s.102(1)(e) for civil partners.

has power to apportion expenditure on rent, mortgage, or essential repairs made by one spouse, between *both* spouses/civil partners,[50] provided application is made within five years from the date on which the payment was made.[51]

Cohabitees

11–21 Sections 2 of the 1981 Act which deals with subsidiary and conse-quential rights and s.3 which concerns the regulation of rights of occupancy of a matrimonial home by court also apply to cohabiting couples by virtue of s.18(3) of that Act.[52] Further, this also now applies to cohabiting same-sex couples by virtue of s.34 of the FLSA 2006.

Regulatory Orders

11–22 Although occupancy rights of the NES/P are granted automati-cally, when it comes to taking any action to enforce or restrict such rights, it may be necessary to ask the court to declare the existence of these rights.[53] The ES/P may also wish to have his common law rights of occupancy declared. The court can also be asked to regulate the exercise of, enforce, or restrict, the occupancy rights of the spouses/civil partners.[54] In each case, it has discretion to make such order as it considers just and reasonable, having regard to all the cir-cumstances of the case including[55]:

(a) the conduct of the spouses/civil partners in relation to each other and otherwise;

(b) the respective needs and financial resources of the spouses/civil partners;

(c) the needs of any child of the family;

(d) the extent (if any) to which—
    (i) the matrimonial (or family) home; and
    (ii) [any relevant] item of furniture and plenishings . . . is used in connection with a trade, profession or vocation of either spouse/civil partner; and

(e) whether the entitled spouse/civil partner offers or has offered to make available to the NES/P any suitable alternative accommo-dation.

These factors are important considerations as they apply not only to regulatory orders but also to exclusion orders, discussed below.

---

[50] 1981 Act, s.2(3) for spouses; 2004 Act, s.102(3) for civil partners.

[51] *ibid.*, s.2(7) for spouses; 2004 Act, s.102(7) for civil partners.

[52] With the exception of s.3(1)(a).

[53] 1981 Act, s.3(1)(a) for spouses; 2004 Act, s.103(1) for civil partners.

[54] *ibid.*, s.3(1) for spouses; 2004 Act, s.103(1) for civil partners.

[55] *ibid.*, s.3(3) for spouses; 2004 Act, s.103(3) for civil partners.

The court has power to grant an interim regulatory order.[56] The **11–23** main restriction on s.3 (1981 Act) and s.103 (2004 Act) is that the court cannot issue an order which would, in effect, amount to excluding an ES/P from the matrimonial/family home.[57] This is because this would be a derogation from the common law rights of the proprietor to occupy his or her own property; rather, this requires a special statutory exclusion order as provided for under s.4 of the 1981 Act and s.104 of the 2004 Act.

Exclusion Orders

The court does, however, have the power to exclude a spouse/civil **11–24** partner whether entitled or non-entitled, from the matrimonial home, under s.4(2) of the 1981 Act and s.104(2) of the 2004 Act. Section 4(2) states:

> "Subject to subsection (3) below, the court *shall* make an exclusion order if it appears to the court that the making of the order is *necessary* for the protection of the applicant or of any child of the family from any conduct *or threatened or reasonably apprehended conduct* of the non-applicant spouse which is *or would be* injurious to the physical *or* mental health of the applicant or child." [Emphasis added.][58]

On first reading, the sections may appear extremely broad in applica- **11–25** tion as:

(i) the court *shall*, not may, grant an order where it feels the test is met;
(ii) the test is met not just by actual conduct, but also by conduct which is threatened or merely apprehended;
(iii) mental, not just physical, injury[59] may be caused by the conduct;
(iv) the injury *itself may* be potential rather than actual.

As Clive[60] has observed, this test could be wide enough to justify excluding a spouse who did nothing worse than smoke tobacco in the family home, were it not for the provisos[61] stating that the court shall *not* make an exclusion order if it would be unjustified or unreasonable having regard to all the circumstances including the factors discussed above (under regulatory orders). In the particular case of a

---

[56] 1981 Act, s.3(4) for spouses; 2004 Act, s.103(4) for civil partners.

[57] *ibid.*, s.3(5) for spouses; 2004 Act, s.103(5) for civil partners.

[58] In s.104(2) of the 2004 act, the words "is to make" are substituted for "shall".

[59] See, e.g. *Anderson v Anderson*, 1993 G.W.D. 35-2258 where the injury complained of was stress-related illness.

[60] E. Clive, *The Law of Husband and Wife in Scotland* (4th edn, W.Green, Edinburgh, 1997), para.15.043.

[61] 1981 Act, s.4(3) for spouses; 2004 Act, s.104(3) for civil partners.

matrimonial home which is, or forms part of, an agricultural holding,[62] or is a tied house, there are further reasons given why a court should not make an exclusion order. Effectively, the court is asked to have regard to the fact that where the family home is a farmhouse and the defender spouse/civil partner is a farm worker, or where that spouse/civil partner is in some other form of employment where residence in the family home is a condition of employment, then his exclusion may not only jeopardise that employment, but possibly also lead to the eviction of the whole family.[63]

Case Law on s.4[64]

11–26   Early judicial interpretation of s.4 was so restrictive that it rendered the section virtually inoperable.[65] The two leading cases of *Bell v Bell*[66] and *Smith v Smith*[67] placed interpretative glosses on the words used in s.4 which made it extremely difficult to obtain an exclusion order. The test of "necessity" was held to be a "high and severe" test[68] which involved an element of "real immediate danger of serious injury or irreparable damage"[69] (although these terms were not to be found in s.4 itself). This emphasis on *physical* violence was reinforced by the finding that unless the applicant was living in the home at the time of the application, an exclusion order was not necessary for protection of the applicant or child, for no immediate danger could be present.[70] In addition, in order to prove the application was necessary, the applicant was required to have already obtained a non-molestation interdict against the other spouse. However, where such an interdict *had been* obtained, but had not been breached, an exclusion order was *also* deemed unnecessary, because there was no indication that the applicant was in imminent danger, or likely to suffer irreparable harm.[71]

11–27   However, subsequent judicial decisions and legislative amendments have reduced the effect of these early decisions almost to nil. It is now clear that an applicant can apply for an exclusion order regardless of whether or not she is living in the matrimonial home.[72] Nor is

---

[62] Defined in Agricultural Holdings (Scotland) Act 1991, s.1.

[63] 1981 Act, s.4(3)(b) for spouses; 2004 Act, s.104(3)(b) for civil partners.

[64] Note: the case law pre-dates the coming into force of the 2004 Act, therefore, references throughout this section are to the 1981 Act and use the term "spouse".

[65] See Robertson and Robson, "Exclusion Orders: The Emerging Criteria", 1983 J.L.S.S. 397.

[66] 1983 S.L.T. 224.

[67] 1983 S.L.T. 275.

[68] *Bell v Bell*, 1983 S.L.T. 224, *per* Lord Robertson at p.230.

[69] *ibid.*, *per* the Lord Justice-Clerk at p.228.

[70] This was the situation in *Bell*, where no order was made since Mrs Bell was, in fact, living temporarily with her son when she applied for the order.

[71] *Smith v Smith*, 1983 S.L.T. 275, *per* Lord Grieve at p.279.

[72] See *Colagiacomo v Colagiacomo*, 1983 S.L.T. 559 and s.13(5) of the Law Reform (Miscellaneous Provisions) (Scotland) Act 1985, which expressly amended s.4 to provide that a spouse may apply for an exclusion order "whether or not that spouse

it any longer a pre-requisite for an exclusion order that the applicant spouse has previously obtained a non-molestation interdict against the other spouse, although it is still a factor to be considered.[73] What amounts to necessity is no longer predicated upon immediate danger, risk of serious injury or irreparable harm. Instead, the court has been directed to consider four questions:

(1) what is the nature and quality of the alleged conduct?;
(2) is the court satisfied that the conduct is likely to be repeated if cohabitation continues?;
(3) has the conduct been or, if repeated, would it be injurious to the physical or mental health of the applicant or to any child of the family?;
(4) if so, is the order sought *necessary* for the future protection of the physical or mental health of the applicant or child?[74]

Since *Bell*,[75] and *Smith*,[76] applications for exclusion orders have **11–28** clearly become more viable, though much still depends on the view the individual first instance judge takes of the facts at hand. Indeed, in a number of cases where application has been made for *interim* exclusion orders,[77] they have been granted on the basis of limited affidavit evidence[78] although it should be noted that interim exclusion orders can be granted only where the non-applicant spouse has been afforded an opportunity of being heard or represented before the court.[79] At one time in danger of interpreting the 1981 Act too restrictively, the courts may now have to guard against too liberal an application of the Act's provisions, and there may be a danger that judges grant orders on the basis of a balance of convenience test (judging

---

is in occupation at the time of the application". Although this is still a factor to be taken into consideration, according to Lord Wheatley in *Colagiacomo*, exclusion orders *have* since been granted (in *Ward v Ward*, 1983 S.L.T. 472 and Brown *v Brown*, 1985 S.L.T. 376), where the applicant spouse has been living outside the home.

[73] See *Brown v Brown*, 1985 S.L.T. 376.

[74] These questions were set out in *McCafferty v McCafferty*, 1986 S.L.T. 650 at 656. They have been approved in subsequent cases. See *Millar v Millar*, 1991 S.C.L.R. 649 where the court held that an exclusion order was still *necessary* to protect the applicant spouse although she had been living apart from her abusive husband for 10 months.

[75] 1983 S.L.T. 224.

[76] 1983 S.L.T. 275.

[77] Under s.4(6). The Act does not specify the test for an interim order but it has been held to be the same as for an ordinary exclusion order: *Bell* (n.68), *Smith* (n.71), *Ward* (n.72) and *Brown* (n.73).

[78] See *Mather v Mather*, 1987 S.L.T. 565 where an interim exclusion order was granted on this basis, although it was then suspended for 3 months to enable the defender to find other accommodation.

[79] See *Armitage v Armitage*, 1993 S.C.L.R. 173 where the court held that, unless there were circumstances in which the need for protection of the applicant was sufficiently urgent to justify a decision being taken immediately, the defender should have been afforded an opportunity to present his case by lodging his own affidavits.

one spouse's interests against the other) rather than on the criteria set out in s.4.[80] The role of the court under the 1981 Act is not to act as arbiter over the spouses' arrangements for sharing the matrimonial home, nor to provide relief to one spouse who no longer wishes to live with the other; but rather to provide protection where one spouse is genuinely causing, or in danger of causing, injury of some kind to the other spouse or any child of the family. The injury complained of should therefore derive directly from the acts of the defender spouse, and not just be stress or unhappiness generally induced by the break-down of the marriage.[81] However, in a few cases, courts have held that stress taken together with the interests of the children can provide sufficient grounds for the granting of an order under s.4.[82]

Cohabitees

11–29 A cohabitee who wishes to exclude a violent partner under s.4 of the Act must first raise an action for full occupancy rights, which, due to the procedure involved, may take several months. Where the application is granted the court can only make an order for a limited period of up to six months, initially, and that may be extended on application for further six month periods.[83]

Additional Orders

11–30 Where the court grants an exclusion order it *must* also make certain other specific orders where these are requested by the applicant, and *may* grant certain others. The court *must* grant[84]:

(a) a warrant for the summary ejection of the non-applicant spouse/civil partner from the home;
(b) an interdict prohibiting the excluded spouse/civil partner from entering the matrimonial home without the express permission of the applicant; and
(c) an interdict prohibiting the non-applicant spouse/civil partner from recovering any furniture or plenishings from the house

---

[80] See *Ward v Ward*, 1983 S.L.T. 472; also *Pryde v Pryde*, 1996 G.W.D. 39-2245. *Cf.*, however, *Barbour v Barbour*, 1990 G.W.D. 3-135 where the court declined to grant an exclusion order because it did not appear that it was necessary to protect anyone.

[81] See *Matheson v Matheson*, 1986 S.L.T. (Sh. Ct.) 2. But see also *Anderson v Anderson*, 1993 WL 966116; *Assar v Assar*, 1994 WL 1716350; and *Roberton v Roberton*, 1999 S.L.T. 38 (1st Div) where the court upheld the sheriff's granting of an interim exclusion order on the basis that the defender's conduct was part of a continuing process with which the pursuer's deteriorating health was consistent and that on the material before him the sheriff was entitled to conclude that the pursuer's health problems were not attributable simply to the distress of the breakup but to the defender's conduct which might be expected to damage her health.

[82] See *Anderson v Anderson*, 1993 WL 966116 and *Assar v Assar*, 1994 WL 1716350.

[83] 1981 Act, s.18(1) which as amended by s.31 of the FLSA 2006 applies to same-sex as well as opposite-sex partners.

[84] 1981 Act, s.4(4) for spouses; 2004 Act, s.104(4) for civil partners.

except with the consent of the other spouse or by further order of court.

In the case of (a) and (c), however, the defender spouse/civil partner can plead that the order is unnecessary.

The court *may*, in addition, grant certain other orders, including, **11–31** importantly, an interdict prohibiting the other spouse/civil partner "from entering or remaining in a specified area in the vicinity of the matrimonial home",[85] ("family home" in the 2004 Act). Such an interdict may be particularly useful, as the protection that can be afforded by s.4(4) of the 1981 Act/s.104(4) of the 2004 Act alone is limited. Orders made under these sections cannot prevent a spouse/civil partner entering a house bought or rented after separation which is *not* a matrimonial/family home, nor a refuge where a spouse/civil partner is staying temporarily, nor the place of work of a spouse/civil partner, nor the school which the parties' children attend. These are all areas, as experience demonstrates, where couples are likely to come into contact and where one party may be vulnerable and put at risk. Where the NES/P wishes to keep the ES/P away, not only within the home but also, for example, when picking up the children from school or when getting the car out of a nearby car park, then the protection an interdict under s.4(5) of the 1981 Act/s.104(4) of the 2004 Act offers some help but may still be inadequate.

Thus, the Scottish Law Commission recommended that the **11–32** definition of matrimonial interdicts be extended to cover areas outwith the matrimonial home, such as schools and work places,[86] and this has been implemented by the FLSA 2006. This amends s.14(2)(b) of the 1981 Act and s.113(2)(b) of the 2004 Act[87] so that a spouse/civil partner is prohibited from entering or remaining in:

(i) the matrimonial (or family) home;
(ii) any other residence occupied by the applicant spouse (or civil partner);
(iii) any place of work of the applicant spouse (or civil partner);
(iv) any school attended by a child in the permanent or temporary care of the applicant spouse (or civil partner).

These additional orders are important because they help to secure the position of the applicant spouse/civil partner. In particular, as we will see below, an interdict can be enforced by the police if a power of arrest is attached by the court.[88]

---

[85] 1981 Act, s.4(5)(a) for spouses; 2004 Act, s.104(5)(a) for civil partners.
[86] Recommendation 57(c), *Report on Family Law*, Scot. Law Com. No.135 (1992).
[87] FLSA 2006, s.10 amends s.14(2)(b) of the 1981 Act; Sch.1, s.8 of the FLSA 2006 amends s.113 of the 2004 Act.
[88] See paras 11–38 to 11–42.

Cohabitees

11–33   The FLSA 2006 introduced "domestic interdicts" into the 1981 Act by the insertion of ss.18A and 18B.[89] These domestic interdicts offer protection to both same-sex and opposite-sex cohabitees.

Enforcement of Interdicts

Matrimonial Interdicts

11–34   An interdict is an order granted by a court prohibiting certain conduct of one person towards the other. For the purposes of the 1981 Act, a *matrimonial* interdict is defined under s.14(2) as any interdict or interim interdict which:

(a) restrains or prohibits any conduct of one spouse towards the other spouse or child of the family, or
(b) prohibits a spouse's movements as outlined above.[90]

11–35   Section 14(1) makes it clear that a matrimonial interdict may be granted where the spouses are still cohabiting. A s.14(2)(a) interdict must specify in detail the conduct which is prohibited, and this should be no wider than is necessary to prevent the illegal act, i.e. the molestation of the other spouse or child of the family.[91] A s.14(2)(b) interdict, like a regulatory order under s.3, *cannot* serve to exclude the entitled spouse from his own home, since the function of an interdict is merely to enforce existing legal rights, not to declare new rights or restrict existing ones.[92] The 1981 Act has been amended by s.10 of the FLSA 2006 to allow that a matrimonial interdict may be granted which excludes an ES from his property when the matrimonial interdict is *ancillary* to an exclusion order *or*, by virtue of s.1(3), the court refuses leave to exercise occupancy rights. This amendment was included to ensure that a matrimonial interdict not be used as an easy alternative to an exclusion order.

11–36   A s.14(2)(b) interdict is, in practice, usually ancillary to an exclusion order as—due to the nature of domestic relationships—it is a difficult remedy in practical terms if the parties are still residing in the same house.[93] Furthermore, a NES who wishes to exclude the other spouse *has* to seek the statutory remedy under s.4. The difference between seeking an interdict and an exclusion order is that, as we have

---

[89] Inserted by s.31 of the FLSA 2006.
[90] See paras 11–31 and 11–32.
[91] See *Murdoch v Murdoch*, 1973 S.L.T. (Notes) 13, where an interim interdict preventing a husband from telephoning his wife or calling at her house was rejected on the basis that its scope was too wide.
[92] *Tattersall v Tattersall*, 1983 S.L.T. 506. This is now expressly embodied in the new s.14(2)(b)–(5) of the 1981 Act inserted by s.10 of the FLSA 2006.
[93] K. Norrie, E. Sutherland, A. Cleland, *The Laws of Scotland, Stair Memorial Encyclopaedia*, Reissue, Edin., Law Society of Scotland (2004), pp.495–496.

seen, an exclusion order can be granted only where the court is satisfied that it is *necessary*; whereas an interdict may be granted, like any ordinary civil order, on the balance of probabilities.

Interdicts for Civil Partners

Section 113 of the 2004 Act governs interdicts obtainable by civil **11–37** Partners. This mirrors s.14 of the 1981 Act as amended by the FLSA 2006 Act.[94]

The Importance of Powers of Arrest Under the 1981 Act

At common law, a interdict (including a matrimonial interdict), like **11–38** other civil orders, could be enforced only by going back to the civil court and seeking to have the party who had failed to obey the interdict penalised for breach of interdict.[95] Such a return to the courts would inevitably involve expense and, even worse in the context of domestic violence, delay. Without further provision, an exclusion order under s.4 of the 1981 Act and s.104 of the 2004 Act would also be enforceable by civil means only.

For most NESs faced with a violent spouse attempting to re-enter **11–39** the family home in breach of an interdict or exclusion order, clearly the most useful remedy would be if the police could be asked to enforce the interdict. But as a general rule the function of the police is to enforce the *criminal* law, and although conduct in breach of a matrimonial interdict might also be criminal, e.g. an assault, the police have tended in the past to be reluctant to become involved in domestic disputes of this kind.[96]

The 1981 Act, heeding these problems, provides a novel enforce- **11–40** ment mechanism now mirrored in the 2004 Act, whereby the civil exclusion order, or matrimonial interdict, can nonetheless be enforced by the police. As we saw at para.11–30 above, where an exclusion order is granted by the court under s.4,[97] an ancillary matrimonial interdict *must be* made as well by virtue of s.4(4).[98] Other interdicts may also be granted under s.4(5).[99] These interdicts

---

[94] FLSA 2006, s.33 and Sch.1, para.8.

[95] For practice and procedure in the Sheriff Court see further, Macphail, *Sheriff Court Practice* (Sheriff Tom Welsh Q.C. (ed.), 3rd edn, W.Green, Edinburgh, 2006). For the Court of Session rules, see Court of Session Act 1988, s.47(1).

[96] See Morley and Mullender, *Preventing Domestic Violence to Women* (Police Group Crime Prevention Series, Paper No.48, HMSO, 1994). See also Grace, *Policing Domestic Violence in the 1990s* (Home Office Research Study, No.139, London, HMSO, 1995). Theoretically, another remedy for potential victims of domestic violence lies in the common law remedy of lawburrows, under which a potential lawbreaker is asked to give security in respect of future behaviour. In practice it is of little use in preventing domestic violence from materialising: see *Liddle v Morton*, 1996 G.W.D. 22-1292.

[97] 2004 Act, s.104.

[98] *ibid.*, s.104(4).

[99] *ibid.*, s.104(5).

qualify as "matrimonial interdicts" under s.14(2) of the Act. By s.15(1)(a), the court is *required* to attach a power of arrest to any matrimonial interdict which is made ancillary to an exclusion order.[1] This provision is mandatory in order to avoid the prior English experience, which was that the courts were reluctant to attach a power of arrest when given unfettered discretion.[2] The courts also have discretion to attach a power of arrest to a matrimonial interdict which is *not* ancillary to an exclusion order. In that kind of case, the non-applicant spouse must have had the opportunity of being heard or represented before the court, before the power of arrest can be granted.[3]

11–41 The power of arrest gives the exclusion order "teeth". It enables the police to arrest the non-applicant spouse without warrant, where they have "reasonable cause for suspecting that spouse of being in breach of the interdict".[4] It is not necessary for a breach of the ordinary criminal law to have occurred, or be suspected, before the power of arrest can be exercised by a constable, merely actual or suspected breach of the interdict.[5] This represented a major step forward in providing protection for those at threat from domestic violence. However, the efficacy of exclusion orders with powers of arrest was limited by the fact that under the 1981 Act they terminate when the marriage comes to an end.[6] Although powers to regulate the occupation of the matrimonial home on divorce do exist, they are very rarely used.[7] This is a serious defect for the applicant spouse who may suddenly be left unprotected on divorce. The difficulty lies in the fact that, while the law may regard the parties' relationship as at an end, this does not necessarily reflect reality, particularly where a violent partner is concerned. Experience shows that a violent partner often continues to harass a former spouse or cohabitee, regardless of the fact that a divorce has taken place or that the parties are no longer cohabiting.[8] Recognising the problems that this caused, the Scottish

---

[1] 2004 Act, s.114. Power of arrest may be attached to an interdict which is ancillary to an *interim* exclusion order.

[2] See *Report on Occupancy Rights in the Matrimonial Home and Domestic Violence*, Scot. Law Com. No.60 (1980), para.4.35 and *Lewis v Lewis* [1978] 1 All E.R. 729.

[3] 1981 Act, s.15(1)(b) for spouses; 2004 Act, s.114(1)(b) for civil partners.

[4] 1981 Act, s.15(3) for spouses; 2004 Act, s.114(4) for civil partners.

[5] See s.15(3) and Lord Advocate's guidelines to chief constables on the Matrimonial Homes (Family Protection) (Scotland) Act 1981 (outlined in 1986 SCOLAG 170).

[6] 1981 Act, s.5(1)(a) for spouses; 2004 Act, s.105(2)(a) for civil partners.

[7] Family Law (Scotland) Act 1985, s.14(2)(d). Incidental orders (of all kinds) were made in only 2% of all ordinary divorce actions for 1989 and 1% in 1991. See Morris, Gibson and Platts, *Untying the Knot: Characteristics of Divorce in Scotland* (Scottish Central Research Unit, Edinburgh, 1993), p.34.

[8] In Scottish Executive Social Research, *An Evaluation of the Protection from Abuse (Scotland) Act 2001* (2003), the authors K. Cavanagh, C. Connelly and J. Scoular reported that: "Much literature indicates that separating from an intimate partner is a dangerous and potentially lethal time for women. This was significantly reinforced in our finds. Men's threats to maim, disfigure and kill an intimate partner who

Law Commission recommended that the law be reformed to provide that a power of arrest would last for a fixed term of three years and remain effective even where the parties; marriage had come to an end.[9]

This recommendation has been enacted in the Protection from **11–42** Abuse (Scotland) Act 2001[10] that also provides for powers of arrest to be attached to interdicts granted under it.[11] For reasons outlined below,[12] there were discrepancies in the procedures dealing with powers of arrest under the 1981 and 2001 Acts. To maintain consistency in dealing with such powers, an amendment has been made to the 2001 Act instructing the court to attach a power of arrest to a matrimonial interdict which is ancillary to an exclusion or interim order made under the 1981 Act,[13] or to any relevant interdict as defined by s.113(2) of the 2004 Act, which is ancillary to an exclusion or interim order made under the 2004 Act.[14] In light of these amendments, ss.15–17 of the 1981 Act, dealing with attachment of powers of arrest to matrimonial interdicts, police powers after arrest and procedure after arrest have now been repealed.[15] This means that it is the 2001 Act that now has *exclusive* jurisdiction over powers of arrest attached to interdicts dealing with domestic violence or abuse.[16]

Cohabitees

Protection in the form of "domestic interdicts" has been extended **11–43** to cohabitees by s.31 of the FLSA 2006 which introduces ss.18A and 18B into the 1981 Act. Further, as s.32 of the FLSA 2006 amends the Protection from Abuse (Scotland) Act 2001 so that the power of arrest is attached "in the case of any other interdict", it may be attached to these domestic interdicts subject to conditions.[17]

---

had left them were widely and vividly reported in the court records, as was the actual execution of many of these threats. The need for effective legal protection for women at this time is absolutely critical": p.85.

[9] Recommendation 60 of the *Report on Family Law*, Scot. Law Com. No.135 (1992).
[10] Protection from Abuse (Scotland) Act 2001, s.1(3).
[11] See paras 11–66 to 11–69 below.
[12] See paras 11–65 to 11–67.
[13] Protection from Abuse (Scotland) Act 2001, s.1A(a), inserted by s.32 of the FLSA 2006.
[14] *ibid.*, s.1A(b). Domestic interdicts dealing with cohabitees under s.18A of the 1981 Act are covered by the amendment made to s.2(1) of the 2001 Act that inserts the words "in the case of any other interdict" into that section that deals with the duration, extension and recall of powers of arrest.
[15] FLSA 2006, s.45(2) and Sch.3, repealing ss.15–17, of the 1981 Act provisions and s.45(2) and Sch.3 of the FLSA 2006 repealing ss.114–116 of the 2004 Act dealing with powers of arrest for civil partners.
[16] See further, discussion at paras 11–67 and 11–68 below.
[17] Protection from Abuse (Scotland) Act 2001, s.1(2).

THIRD PARTY DEALINGS AND THE MATRIMONIAL/FAMILY HOME

11–44 Sections 1 and 4 of the 1981 Act and ss.101 and 104 of the 2004 Act, as we have seen, combine to give the NES/P the right to occupy and re-enter the matrimonial home and, if necessary, even to exclude the ES/P. But, crucially, the NES/P does *not* acquire any rights of ownership in the home under the 1981 or 2004 Acts. The ES/P is still entitled to sell the whole of the property. Since, under s.1(1) of the 1981 Act,[18] the NES's occupancy rights depend on there being an *entitled* spouse in respect of the particular home in question, without further provision, these occupancy rights would fall at the moment of sale. Thus the NES/Ps rights could be easily defeated by selling the property, either to a bona fide third party or perhaps just to a "straw man", such as a relative or friend, who could then re-convey the house to the originally entitled spouse.

11–45 A similar problem arises where the spouses/partners are co-owners. At common law, each is entitled to sell his or her *pro indiviso* share to another party. Spouse A therefore could sell his half of the house to stranger X who as co-proprietor would then be entitled to occupy the former matrimonial home along with spouse B. Effectively this would be likely to render spouse B's common law occupancy rights unworkable.

11–46 In order to prevent the first problem, the 1981 Act provides at s.6(1)(a) that the NES is not to be prejudiced by reason only of any dealing of the ES relating to the matrimonial home.[19] "Dealing" is very broadly defined to include the sale or lease of the matrimonial home, or grant of a heritable security over it or the creation of a trust over it.[20] Although the ES/P retains his legal right to sell the home, under s.6(1A)[21] the NES's occupancy rights are protected from the entitled spouse's dealing except in the circumstances outlined in paras 11–53 and 11–54 below. Not only that, but the purchaser is not entitled to claim rent from the non-entitled spouse in respect of her continued occupancy. These provisions protect the NES from eviction by a third party. The protection against dealings given to NES in s.6 is extended in similar terms to protect *co-owning* spouses under s.9(1) of the 1981 Act and to *co-owning* civil partners under s.109 of the 2004 Act.

11–47 *Example*: A and B are married to each other and own the matrimonial home in common. A sells his *pro indiviso* half share to a third party, X. X now co-owns with B but cannot occupy because B has the

---

[18] 2004 Act, s.101(1) for civil partners.
[19] *ibid*., s.106 for civil partners.
[20] 1981 Act, s.6(2); 2004 Act, s.106(2).
[21] Substituted by s.6(2) of the FLSA 2006 in place of s.6(1)(b) of the 1981 Act. Sch.1, para.5 of the FLSA 2006 substitutes s.106(1A) in place of s.106(1)(b) of the 2004 Act.

protection of s.9(1)(a) and (b). Obviously this will usually discourage X from purchasing.[22]

Consents, Renunciations and Affidavits

Although the function of the provisions of the 1981 Act (which **11–48** have been mirrored in the 2004 Act) is to protect the interests of NESs, it also has to balance them against the interests of third parties, and provide for the ordinary situation where a married couple both wish to sell the family home to a third party. No third party will purchase a matrimonial home which is burdened with the occupancy rights of a NES. The Act's solution is to provide that where the NES consents to the "dealing" in writing, and in prescribed form, the protection afforded against adverse dealings will not apply.[23] The court can dispense with the consent of the NES/P in certain circumstances,[24] especially where consent is unreasonably withheld[25]; where the spouse/civil partner cannot consent because of physical or mental disability; or the spouse/civil partner cannot be found.[26] However, an order dispensing with consent can only be made if the heritable security is granted for a loan of no more than such amount as the court specifies in the order, and the security is executed before the date prescribed in the order.[27] Where the court refuses an application for an order, it has power to require a NES/P "to make such payments to the owner of the home in respect of that spouse's occupation of it as may be specified in the order" and "to comply with such other conditions relating to that spouse's occupation of the matrimonial home as may be so specified".[28]

---

[22] But if he does, X still has the indefeasible common law right as co-owner with B to raise an action of division and sale of the house. Note that the protection given in respect of such actions under s.19 applies only where the co-owners are spouses.

[23] 1981 Act, s.6(3)(a) for spouses; 2004 Act, s.106(3)(a) for civil partners. The prescribed form is set down by the Matrimonial Homes (Form of Consent) (Scotland) Regulations 1982 (SI 1982/971). The writing requires to be carried out in the presence of a notary public.

[24] These now include a proposed sale where negotiations with a third party have not begun, or where they have begun but a price has not been agreed under s.7 of the FLSA 2006 which amends s.7 of the 1981 Act. Under these circumstances an order dispensing with consent may only be made if the price agreed for the sale is no less than such amount as the court specifies in the order and the contract for the sale is concluded before the expiry of such period as may be so specified under s.7(1B) inserted by s.7 of FLSA 2006. In the case of civil partners see s.107 of the 2004 Act as amended by s.33, Sch.1, para.6 of the FLSA 2006.

[25] e.g. *O'Neill v O'Neill*, 1987 S.L.T. (Sh. Ct.) 26.

[26] 1981 Act, s.6(3)(b). Similar provisions apply to the dispensation with a civil partner's consent to dealing under s.107 of the 2004 Act.

[27] 1981 Act, s.7(1D) inserted by s.7 of the FLSA 2006. For civil partners see s.107(1D) of the 2004 Act inserted by Sch.1, para.6 of the FLSA 2006.

[28] 1981 Act, s.7(3A) inserted by *ibid*. For civil partners see s.107(3A) inserted by *ibid*.

11–49   It is also competent for the NES/NEP to renounce his or her rights in the matrimonial/family home.[29] To guard against undue pressure on the non-entitled spouse, such renunciation must be done in writing before a notary public.

11–50   From a conveyancing perspective, the important question is how is the prospective purchaser of a house to know if he or she is buying a matrimonial home in respect of which a NES has occupancy rights? Given that occupancy rights under the 1981 Act are not registered, there is no way in which a potential purchaser can check to find out if a NES exists.[30] This places the purchaser in a difficult position. The solution, as provided by s.6(3)(e), is that where there has been "a transfer for value",[31] a third party who acquires an interest in heritable property will not be prejudiced by the occupancy rights of any spouse of the seller, if:

"(a) the third party acted in good faith, and
(b) the transferor[32] produces to the third party *either*
    (i) a written declaration signed by the transferor, or a person acting on behalf of the transferor under a power of attorney or as a guardian (within the meaning of the Adults with Incapacity (Scotland) Act 2000 (asp 4), that the subject of the transfer are not, or were not at the time of the dealing, a matrimonial home in relation to which a spouse of the transferor has or had occupancy rights; or
    (ii) a renunciation of occupancy rights or consent to the dealing which bears to have been properly made or given by the non-entitled spouse or person acting on behalf of the non-entitled spouse or a person acting on behalf of the non-entitled spouse under a power of attorney or as a guardian (within the meaning of the Adults with Incapacity (Scotland) Act 2000 (asp 4)".[33]

---

[29] 1981 Act, s.6(3)(a)(ii) for spouses. The Act allows rights to be renounced in respect of: (a) a particular matrimonial home; or (b) a particular property which it is intended by the spouses will become a matrimonial home. For civil partners see s.106(3) of the 2004 Act.

[30] The NEP's rights are treated as an overriding interest over the property, and as such are not noted in the title sheet. See s.6(4) which amends the Land Registration (Scotland) Act 1979. Checking the Register of Marriages is not conclusive either, as the parties may have married abroad or be married by cohabitation with habit and repute.

[31] These word replace the word "sale" that existed under the original s.6(3)(e) by s.6(3) of the FLSA 2006. For civil partners the same substitution has been made by the insertion of subs.(1A)(b)(i) after s.106(1) of the 2004 Act by s.33, Sch.1, para.5 of the FLSA 2006.

[32] This has been substituted for the word "seller" that existed under the original s.6(3)(e) by s.6(3) of FLSA 2006. For civil partners see insertion of subs.(1A)(b)(ii) after s.106(1), *ibid*.

[33] 1981 Act, s.6(3)(e) as amended by s.6(3) of the FLSA 2006. For civil partners see subs.(1A)(b)(ii)(i) and (ii), *ibid*.

In practice, therefore, during exchange of missives for sale of a house, the seller is routinely required as a condition of the sale to produce either a consent to the dealing or renunciation of occupancy rights which appears to have been given by the NES/P, or an affidavit declaring *either* that the subjects of the transfer for value are not a matrimonial/family home *or* that there is no spouse/partner with occupancy rights in respect of that home.

Where the correct documentation, detailed above, is supplied and the third party has acted in good faith, then s/he can enter the contract free of any occupancy rights of a NES. The Act does not specify what amounts to good faith. It is clear that where the purchaser has actual knowledge of the existence of a NES, e.g. because they are a relative of the family, then he or she will not be in good faith. What is not clear is whether the third party is under any duty to make inquiries about the marital/civil partnership position of the seller. As Clive points out, the result of a requirement to make reasonable inquiries could be an unacceptable and embarrassing invasion of privacy.[34] **11–51**

What if a seller fraudulently declares in the matrimonial affidavit that there is no NES, or forges a consent or renunciation? It is clearly the intent of the section that the purchaser can still enter and occupy the subjects and that the non-entitled spouse's occupancy rights fall. The only remedy open to the NES will then be to apply to the court for "just and reasonable" compensation from the entitled spouse.[35] **11–52**

Double Dealing

Consider the scenario where A and B are married and A, the sole owner of the family home, sells it to C who then in his turn sells it to D. It is clear that the sale to C could not have prejudiced B's right of occupancy as NES (unless a matrimonial affidavit, consent or renunciation was fraudulently given by A). But in this scenario, does D have the right to occupy? Do B's occupancy rights still operate to prevent him? In Clive's view, the NES's occupancy rights are no longer enforceable in this situation, but the wording of s.6(1) was ambiguous enough to make this contestable.[36] To clarify the position s.6 has now been amended to provide that the NES's occupancy rights will not be exercisable, following a dealing by the entitled spouse where: **11–53**

(a) a person acquires the home, or an interest in it, in good faith and for value from a person other than the person who is or, as the case may be, was the entitled spouse; or

---

[34] *Op.cit.*, n.60, para.15.076.

[35] 1981 Act, s.3(7) for spouses; 2004 Act, s.103(8) for civil partners.

[36] *Op.cit.*, no. 60. paras 15.081, 15.083. This is also the argument put forward by the Scottish Law Commission in its *Report on Family Law*, Scot. Law Com. No. 135(1992), para.11.10. But see a contrary view in Nichols and Meston, *The Matrimonial Homes (Family Protection) (Scotland) Act 1981* (2nd edn, 1986), para.6.05.

(b) a person derives title to the home from a person who acquired title as mentioned in paragraph (a).[37]

Pre-Marital and Pre-Act Dealings or Obligations

11–54　Where a dealing or obligation entered into by the entitled spouse with respect to property takes place before his or her marriage to the non-entitled spouse, it remains unaffected by s.6 of the 1981 Act.[38] The same is true of those dealings or obligations entered into by such a spouse before the 1981 Act came into effect.[39]

Co-owners/Co-tenants of the Matrimonial Home

11–55　Until now, we have been dealing mainly with the remedies granted by the 1981 Act (and mirrored by those of the 2004 Act) where one spouse (the ES) is sole owner and the other (the NES) is not. However, it is increasingly common for both spouses to share legal title to the matrimonial home, whether as co-owners or co-tenants. Neither party in this situation may eject the other from the matrimonial home.[40] But the Act makes it clear that a regulatory order under s.3, and an exclusion order under s.4, can be obtained where both spouses are entitled to occupy the matrimonial home.[41]

11–56　As noted above, at common law, where parties own property in common, each party is free to sell his or her *pro indiviso* share of the property without the other's agreement. The protection given by s.9(1) in this situation was discussed in paras 11–45 and 11–47 above. Another right given to co-owners, however, is the right to raise an action of division and sale. Until the 1981 Act, the court had no discretion to refuse an application of this kind, even if it left the non-applicant spouse without a home. Effectively, therefore, raising an action of division and sale was a foolproof way to defeat the occupancy rights of the co-owning spouse.

11–57　To deal with this, s.19 of the Act provides that when an action is brought for division and sale, the court has a discretion to refuse or postpone the granting of decree, or to grant decree subject to conditions, having regard to all the circumstances of the case including the factors listed in s.3(3).[42] Similar provisions apply to civil partners under s.110 of the 2004 Act. Whether the applicant spouse/civil

---

[37] 1981 Act, s.6(1A) as inserted by s.6(2) of the FLSA 2006. For civil partners, see s.106(1A) inserted to the 2004 Act by s.33. Sch.1, para.5 of the FLAS 2006.

[38] 1981 Act, s.6(3)(c) for spouses; 2004 Act, s.106(3)(c) for civil partners.

[39] 1981 Act, s.6(3)(d) for spouses; 2004 Act, s.106(3)(d) for civil partners, in which the wording is "before commencement of this section".

[40] 1981 Act, s.4(7) and the 2004 Act, s.104(8) make it clear that common-law powers to eject, if they were ever competent between co-owning spouses/partners, no longer apply.

[41] 1981 Act, s.4(1) for spouses and the 2004 Act, s.104(1) for civil partners.

[42] s.19(a).

partner has made an offer of suitable alternative accommodation to the other spouse/civil partner is also relevant.[43] Children are regarded as a very important consideration under s.19, although as is always the case with the 1981 Act, their needs are not paramount. In *Crow v Crow*[44] the court held it competent to postpone granting decree for division and sale beyond a date when the marriage would be terminated by divorce where the needs of the children required this.[45]

While there is some doubt as to where the onus of proof lies in s.19 applications,[46] the court is, in practice, unlikely to allow a sale to go ahead where this would adversely affect the children's interests and those of the parent with whom they live. It is important to note that s.19 of the 1981 Act and s.110 of the 2004 Act apply only to co-owners who are spouses or civil partners. In all other cases where a house is jointly owned, e.g. by cohabitees, or *ex*-spouses or *ex*-civil partners, the court *must* grant decree where it is applied for, as a matter of common law. **11–58**

TENANCIES

In many cases, the matrimonial/family home is held under a sole or shared tenancy agreement rather than owned by the spouses or partners. Particular problems may arise for NES/P living in homes of this kind. In some tenancies, security of tenure can be guaranteed only where the legal tenant is in continuous occupation. This requirement will be met under the 1981 Act even if the sole legal tenant has abandoned the tenancy if the tenant's spouse is in occupation.[47] Where the ES/P fails to meet his or her obligations, or has left or been excluded from the matrimonial/family home, the NES/P may wish to have the tenancy transferred into her name. **11–59**

Transfer

This may be accomplished in one of two ways. Under the Housing (Scotland) Act 1987, social landlords (such as local authorities) may apply to the court for recovery of possession on the basis that he or she wishes to transfer the tenancy to the tenant's spouse, former **11–60**

---

[43] 1981 Act, s.19(b). The offer must be of specific alternative accommodation. So, e.g. a general offer to help a co-owning spouse find somewhere to live, as in *Hall v Hall*, 1987 S.L.T. (Sh. Ct.) 15, is not sufficient. For civil partners see s.110(b) of the 2004 Act.

[44] 1986 S.L.T. 270.

[45] See also *Milne v Milne*, 1994 S.L.T. (Sh. Ct.) 57.

[46] Compare *Hall v Hall*, 1987 S.L.T. (Sh. Ct.) 15 and *Milne v Milne*, 1994 S.L.T. (Sh. Ct.) 57, where it was held that the onus lay on the spouse seeking decree to establish that the sale was reasonable, with *Berry v Berry*, 1988 S.C.L.R. 296 where it was held that the onus lay on the defender to show why it was unreasonable for the sale to go ahead.

[47] 1981 Act, s.2(8) for spouses; 2004 Act, s.102(8) for civil partners.

spouse, civil partner, former civil partner or cohabitee.[48] This is competent where one of these parties has applied for the transfer, and one of the parties to the relationship no longer wishes to live with the other in the house. Alternatively, the NES may apply to the court for a transfer under s.13 of the 1981 Act, provided that he or she is prepared to pay the other spouse such compensation as the court deems just and reasonable in the circumstances.[49] Where an application is made under s.13, the court is directed to have regard to all the circumstances of the case[50] including the suitability of the applicant to become a tenant and the applicant's capacity to perform the obligations under the lease.[51] In assessing the situation, the court may take account of the parties' conduct[52] as well as the children's interests.[53] Where both spouses are common tenants, the court may vest the tenancy solely in the applicant's name, provided that the applicant pays just and reasonable compensation to the other spouse.[54]

11–61   In such cases, a copy of the application for transfer must be served on the landlord, who must be given an opportunity of being heard or represented before the court makes a transfer order.[55] The court may not transfer a tenancy in certain cases where it represents an incident of employment, or is an agricultural holding or croft, or let on a long lease.[56] Where, however, the transfer is competent and the court makes an order, the tenancy vests immediately in the transferee and the transferee becomes subject to all the liabilities under the lease, except for arrears of rent, which remain the liability of the transferor.[57]

---

[48] See s.48 of, and Sch.3, para.16 to, the 1987 Act. Sch.28, para.54 amends s.83 of the Housing (Scotland) Act 1987.

[49] 1981 Act, s.13(1) for spouses; 2004 Act, s.112(1) for civil partners.

[50] Including the factors set out in s.3(3) of the 1981 Act. See s.103(3) of the 2004 Act for civil partners.

[51] 1981 Act, s.13(3) for spouses; 2004 Act, s.112(3) for civil partners.

[52] See *McGowan v McGowan*, 1986 S.L.T. 112 where the court granted a transfer partly because the husband's extremely unreasonable conduct had been solely responsible for the breakdown of the marriage and partly because the wife had been having to stay with her daughter and her family in a house which was too small for them. See also the case of *McMillan v McMillan*, 2004 Fam. L.B. 70-5 where the court also took the view that given that the incomes of husband and wife were roughly similar, it was reasonable for the tenancy to be transferred as the husband's behaviour had been the principal reason for the breakdown of the marriage.

[53] In *Guyan v Guyan* (Note), 2001 Fam. L.R. 99, the wife sought a transfer of her husband's share of a joint tenancy into her name. He did likewise. In reaching its decision the court held that in balancing the interests of adults and children, the children had to come first and made an order transferring the tenancy to the wife on the grounds that the children would have more security, live in better accommodation and surroundings (than their current temporary accommodation) and be able to continue at their existing school.

[54] 1981 Act, s.13(9) for spouses; 2004 Act, s.112(10) for civil partners.

[55] 1981 Act, s.13(4) for spouses; 2004 Act, s.112(4) for civil partners.

[56] 1981 Act, s.13(7) for spouses; 2004 Act, s.112(8) for civil partners.

[57] 1981 Act, s.13(5) for spouses; 2004 Act, s.112(5) for civil partners.

The court's power to transfer a tenancy under s.13 can be exercised **11–62** on decree of divorce[58] or nullity of marriage.[59] In either case, the court may make an order transferring the tenancy when it grants decree, or within a specified period thereafter.[60]

Cohabitees

When it comes to a transfer of tenancy the court can only make **11–63** such an order in favour of the NEP if that party has been granted occupancy rights by the court, or to either partner, if both are entitled to jointly occupy the home, e.g. as joint tenants.[61]

Termination of Rights Under the 1981 and 2004 Acts

Rights for spouses and civil partners will cease to exist where: **11–64**

- the marriage/partnership comes to an end by death or divorce/dissolution of partnership (except where a transfer of tenancy is concerned[62] or where powers of arrest have been attached to a matrimonial or domestic interdict in which case such powers of arrest expire three years after they have been granted (regardless of whether or not a marriage is still in existence)[63];
- where the ES/P ceases to be entitled[64];
- where the NES/P consents to the dealing or renounces his or her occupancy rights[65];
- The NES/P's rights under s.6 of the1981 Act or s.106 of the 2004 Act do not operate where the ES/P has permanently ceased to be entitled to occupy the home in question and for a continuous period of two[66] years thereafter, during which time the NES/P has not occupied the home[67];

---

[58] 1981 Act, s.13(2)(a) 1981 Act. Also dissolution of civil partnership at s.112(2)(a) of the 2004 Act.

[59] 1981 Act, s.13(2)(b) 1981 Act. Also nullity of civil partnership at s.112(2)(b) of the 2004 Act.

[60] 1981 Act, s.13(2) for spouses; 2004 Act, s.112(2) for civil partners.

[61] 1981 Act, ss.13 and 18(4).

[62] *ibid.*, ss.1(1) and 5(1)(b); 2004 Act, s.105(2)(a). Also see *Clarke v Hatten*, 1987 S.C.L.R. 527.

[63] Protection from Abuse (Scotland) Act 2001, s.1(3).

[64] As the NES's rights under the 1981 Act are derived from the ES's rights, it follows that where the ES ceases to have such rights those of the NES must fall (except in relation to dealings under s.6). The same applies to civil partners (except in relation to s.106 of the 2004 Act).

[65] 1981 Act, s.6(3)(a)(i) and (ii) and s.6(3)(e); 2004 Act, s.106(3)(a)(i) and (ii).

[66] Originally this was five years but it has been changed to two by s.5 of the FLSA 2006. For civil partners see insertion of subs.(6A) after s.101(6) by s.33, Sch.1, para.3 of FLSA 2006.

[67] 1981 Act, s.6(3)(f). *Stevenson v Roy*, 2002 S.L.T. 445.

- the six-month period of occupancy rights granted to a cohabitee by a court has elapsed (and a re-application to the court has not been made).[68]

Limitations of the 1981 Act

11–65   Our discussion of the 1981 Act highlights the difficulties that arise in framing legislation aimed at combating domestic violence on the paradigm of marriage. While the 1981 Act has been amended to allow interdicts with powers of arrest to continue after divorce and for domestic interdicts with powers of arrest to apply to cohabiting heterosexual and same sex-couples, and while provisions similar to those contained in the 1981 Act have been enacted to apply to same-sex couples who are registered as civil partners under the 2004 Act, there are still situations in which family members find themselves without adequate protection from domestic violence. So, for example, a sister cannot seek a matrimonial or domestic interdict against her brother, a child cannot seek such an interdict against his or her parents, nor can parents seek such an interdict against their children. Although such persons can apply for a common law interdict, this is of limited value as it does not have powers of arrest attached to it. As we noted earlier, one of the advantages of having a "matrimonial", "domestic" or "relevant" interdict with powers of arrest attached to it is that it enables the police to arrest the non-applicant spouse or partner without warrant, where they have reasonable cause for suspecting that person of being in breach of the interdict.[69] This means that the police do not need to wait for a breach of the ordinary criminal law to have occurred, or be suspected, before the power of arrest can be exercised by a constable, as it will be sufficient for a constable to take immediate action removing the violent or abusive person from the scene where he or she forms the view that an actual or suspected breach of interdict has occurred.[70] Concern about the flaws inherent in the 1981 Act (especially prior to its amendment under the FLSA 2006) and the inadequate protection afforded to individuals at risk of abuse from other family members or individuals led to the passing of the Protection From Abuse (Scotland) Act 2001.

PROTECTION FROM ABUSE (SCOTLAND) ACT 2001

11–66 This Act[71] extends the range of interdicts to which powers of arrest may be attached. These include any interdicts (or interim interdicts) obtained before or after the passing of the Act for the purposes of

---

[68] s.18(1).

[69] The power of arrest is now solely governed by s.4 of the Protection From Abuse (Scotland) Act 2001 as the FLSA 2006 has repealed s.15(3) of the 1981 Act and s.114(4) of the 2004 Act.

[70] Protection From Abuse (Scotland) Act 2001, s.4.

[71] Which came into force on February 6, 2002.

protecting against "abuse". Under its provisions, applicants no longer need to demonstrate any particular personal relationship to an alleged abuser. Nor are occupancy rights of any relevance. There is therefore no need for any person applying for a power of arrest to share, or to have shared, a home with the abuser. Instead the court simply has to find that granting the power of arrest is necessary to protect the applicant from the risk of abuse through a breach of interdict. Those currently excluded from using the 1981 Act, noted above, may use the 2001 Act to have powers of arrest attached to an interdict that has been obtained, or is being sought, to provide protection from abuse. Such an order may be obtained from either the Court of Session or the Sheriff Court.[72] Abuse under the Act is widely defined to cover psychological as well as physical abuse as well as:

> "violence, harassment, threatening conduct, and any other conduct giving rise or likely to give rise, to physical or mental injury, fear, alarm or distress".[73]

It includes conduct, which need not be active, and which covers a relatively wide category of behaviour including presence in a specified place or area.[74]

The FLSA 2006 has repealed ss.15(3) of the 1981 Act and s.114(4) of the 2004 act, the sections dealing with power of arrest without warrant. There was a risk under the previous regime of two powers of arrest being attached to interdicts prohibiting the same person from doing the same thing, although provision was made in both acts to try to ensure that two powers of arrest could not be attached to interdicts prohibiting the same person doing the same thing.[75] **11–67**

Before granting powers of arrest the court must be satisfied that: **11–68**

"(a) the interdicted person has been given an opportunity to be heard by, or represented before, the court;
(b) attaching the power of arrest is necessary to protect the applicant from a risk of abuse in breach of the interdict".[76]

The court must be satisfied that the attachment of the power of arrest is necessary to protect the applicant from a risk of abuse in the interdict. The fact that a woman has an interdict and that the interdicted person is abusive or potentially abusive is not sufficient proof to the court of risk of abuse. The court must be satisfied that

---

[72] 2001 Act, s.7.
[73] *ibid.*
[74] *ibid.*
[75] Protection From Abuse (Scotland) Act 2001, s.1(2)(b) and s.15(1A) of the 1981 Act inserted by s.6 of the 2001 Act.
[76] s.1(2).

attaching the power of arrest is necessary to protect the applicant from a risk of abuse in breach of the interdict.[77] So, for example, fear of another's presence in a specified place will not in itself justify the granting of powers of arrest unless there is an interdict prohibiting that person's presence. If a power of arrest is attached to an interdict under the terms of the legislation, police have discretionary powers to arrest and detain the person in breach of the interdict.[78] There is a two-step test before the police can use this power. They must:

(a) have reasonable cause to suspect that a breach of the interdict has occurred[79]; and
(b) also be satisfied that if not arrested, the person in breach will continue to cause abuse, or further abuse, which will be in breach of the interdict.[80]

In other words the police have to carry out a risk assessment on the spot. It is not enough for the police to suspect that the interdict has been breached. They must also be satisfied that there is a potentially abusive situation that the victim needs to be protected from and that this abuse would be in breach of the interdict. It is also not enough to satisfy this test for the police to suspect that the interdicted person would be likely to be abusive if not arrested where the likely abusive behaviour is not prohibited by the interdict. This is now the test that applies to *all* interdicts that have powers of arrest attached to them given the repeal of ss.15–17 of the 1981 Act and ss.114–116 of the 2004 Act by the FLSA 2006.[81]

11–69 Where a power of arrest is attached to an interdict under the 2001 Act, the court must specify the length of its duration up to a maximum period of three years from the date of attachment.[82] After this date it will cease to have effect, although an application may be made to the court for an extension of up to three years.[83] There is no limit to the number of times an extension may be granted. On arrest, a person must be detained in police custody until s/he is either charged with an offence or brought before a court.[84] In a study evaluating the 2001 Act, the authors noted that it appeared "to be

---

[77] s.1(2).
[78] Protection From Abuse (Scotland) Act 2001, s.4(1). However, this discretionary power may be compared with the discretionary power that was (prior to the FLSA 2006) exercised under the 1981 Act where the Lord Advocate's guidelines issued in 1986 provided that "the offending spouse will be arrested in all but the most trivial cases".
[79] s.4(1)(a).
[80] s.4(1)(b).
[81] See s.45(2), Sch.3.
[82] s.1(3).
[83] s.2(4).
[84] s.4(2).

successful in increasing access to powers of arrest".[85] However, the study also noted that these gains were limited,

> "due to the continued reliance on police discretion and the requirement that the breach of the interdict must amount to a crime before prosecution can be considered".[86]

It also observed that:

> "Civil law interdicts place an unfair burden on victims of abuse to pursue actions due to strict criteria for legal aid and the cost of privately funding civil court actions".[87]

Protection From Harassment Act 1997

Another way of regulating abusive or violent conduct is to utilise the **11–70** provisions of the Protection From Harassment Act 1997. The Act imposes an obligation on persons not to,

> "pursue a course of conduct which amounts to harassment of another which is either intended to amount to harassment of that other or which he knows or ought to know amount to harassment of another. For these purposes such conduct occurs in circumstances where it would appear to a reasonable person that it would amount to harassment of that other".[88]

Where such conduct occurs, a civil delict is created in Scotland against which an order restraining harassment may be sought. In this context, "conduct" is broadly defined to include speech[89] and that harassment includes "causing the person alarm or distress".[90] Where an application is made to the court it may award damages[91] as well as granting an interdict or interim interdict.[92] As such an interdict is designed to protect the applicant from abuse, it may have a power of arrest attached to it in terms of the Protection From Abuse (Scotland) Act 2001. Damages may include damages for any anxiety caused by the harassment or any financial loss arising from it.[93] The court may also, if appropriate, issue a non-harassment order

---

[85] K. Cavangh, C. Connelly and J. Scoular, *An Evaluation of the Protection From Abuse (Scotland) Act, 2001* (Scottish Executive Social Research, 2003), p.86.
[86] *ibid.*, p.87.
[87] *ibid.*
[88] ss.1(1) and (2).
[89] s.8(3).
[90] s.8(3).
[91] s.8(5)(a).
[92] s.8(5)(b)(i).
[93] s.8(6).

("NHO").[94] An NHO is more difficult to obtain than an interdict, as the applicant has to prove a "course" of harassing conduct on more than two separate occasions before the court will make an order.[95] A defence to an action exists where the conduct was:

- authorised by, under or by virtue of any enactment or rule of law;
- was pursued for the purpose of preventing or detecting crime; or
- was, in the particular circumstances, reasonable.[96]

11–71 Case law has demonstrated that the courts have encountered difficulties, and have adopted differing interpretations of the Act when it comes to the granting of NHOs. In *Heenan v Dillon*[97] the sheriff questioned the proposition set out in *Furber v Furber*,[98] that a court could grant an NHO at any time during the proceedings without the defender having an opportunity of being heard.[99] In *Alexandra v Murphy*,[1] the Sheriff Principal upheld this view on the grounds that, given the order could render the defender liable to imprisonment, such an action would amount to a fundamental breach of natural justice. He also formed the view (which was obiter) that:

- it is incompetent to make an interim NHO[2];
- a determinative NHO can be pronounced once only and that having been pronounced , it cannot be continued, varied or reviewed by application under s.8 of the 1997 Act or by appeal;
- in a defended cause a determinative order should not generally be granted without proof.[3]

---

[94] s.8(5)(b)(ii).

[95] This understanding was established following the case of *Glennan v McKinnon*, 1998 SCCR 285. In this case the court held that it was not permissible to take previous convictions into account so that for an NHO to be available there had to have been averments of conduct *on at least two occasions* in relation to the current offence. However see *Riley v HM Advocate*, 1999 S.C.C.R. 644 which somewhat mitigates the effects of the previous case although it still upholds the position that "a course of conduct" must be demonstrated before an NHO can be contemplated. In the Scottish Executive Consultation Paper, *Stalking and Harassment* (2000), reform was canvassed on whether such conduct should "cover not only the present charge but also a previous incident where that had formed part of a previous conviction" at p.3.

[96] s.8(4).

[97] 1999 S.L.T (Sh Ct) 32.

[98] 1999 S.L.T. (Sh Ct) 26.

[99] The sheriff in *Heenan* did observe that it was not clear from the judgment whether the "interim" NHO made by the sheriff in that case was made without the defender having had an opportunity of being heard. The sheriff observed that while the order was made ex parte, "that does not mean that the defender did not have notice of the motion" (at 32L).

[1] 2000 S.L.T. (Sh Ct) 44.

[2] Note: for the avoidance of confusion, it is the non-harassment order that in the Sheriff Principal's opinion could not be interim. This is not to be confused with an interim interdict which may be granted under the Act at s.8(5)(b)(ii).

[3] *Op. cit.* above, n.1 at 48G.

While the court is empowered to grant an interdict or a NHO, this is **11–72** subject to the proviso that,

> "a person may not be subjected to the same prohibition in an interdict or interim interdict and a non-harassment order at the same time".[4]

In *McCann v McGurran*,[5] the court held that the clear implication is that in exercising its power it cannot "grant both remedies but must, if circumstances require it, choose between the two".[6] It goes on to note:

> "This is perfectly consistent with the situation where in the same action, in applying remedies, the different remedies may be thought appropriate at different times (or perhaps even in respect of different conduct). Thus, since the non-harassment order is not an interim provision, there can be occasions where the court thinks it appropriate to pronounce at the early stage of the action an interdict but then, if the harassment is proved at a later stage of the case, wants to confer on the pursuer the more powerful protection of a non-harassment order".[7]

In stating this the court held that the restriction on the power to pronounce a NHO was "aimed alone at interdict orders pronounced within the framework of the action of harassment" and went on to observe that:

> "while the fact that the pursuer had the protection of a permanent interdict [granted in an earlier divorce action] was a significant factor to be considered in determining whether or not to grant a non-harassment order, the application was technically competent".[8]

However, in this case, the court held that there were no circumstances **11–73** which justified the granting of a NHO *at this stage* as the defender had given notice of intention to defend and the issues relevant to the merits could not be identified until they had been focused by the defences and the defender had had the opportunity to be heard.

Where an NHO is made and breached, the party breaching it is guilty of an offence and may be liable to imprisonment,[9] or to a fine,[10–11] or

---

[4] s.8(5)(b)(ii).
[5] 2002 Fam. L.R. 74.
[6] *ibid.*, at 13-11, p.76.
[7] *ibid.*
[8] *ibid.*, at 13-02, p.74.
[9] This may be up to five years where conviction is on indictment or up to six months on summary conviction under s.9(1)(a) and (b).
[10–11] *ibid.*

both (see above). Note that breach of the order is still a criminal offence even if the order is granted in a civil court which means that it automatically attracts greater sanction than the civil protection orders outlined above. However, in the past, breach of an NHO did not in itself constitute an offence for which the police could arrest without a warrant. Amendments to the 1997 Act and the Criminal Procedure (Scotland) Act 1995[12] now give the police statutory powers to arrest those in breach of the order without such a warrant.[13]

11–74 Finally, it should be noted that for many women faced with violence in the home, establishing or claiming rights of occupancy in the matrimonial home is, in itself, a risky exercise. For these parties, the problem is often whether they would rather face domestic violence or homelessness. Under the Housing (Scotland) Act 1987, local authorities have specific duties to provide accommodation for those who qualify as "homeless". But this obligation falls if the person concerned is deemed to be intentionally homeless. There are a number of circumstances in which this may occur,[14] but one of particular interest here is that in *McAlinden v Bearsden and Milngavie District Council*[15] where a woman was held to have rendered herself intentionally homeless, because she had not applied for occupancy rights as a cohabitee under the 1981 Act.

11–75 However, homelessness and domestic violence interact. Many individuals intentionally leave otherwise suitable accommodation because of the threat or presence of violence to themselves or their children. This has now been recognised by the 1987 Act, which expressly provides that a person is not intentionally homeless simply because he or she leaves accommodation which it was unreasonable to expect him or her to occupy, e.g. because of the fear of domestic violence.[16] This means that even a person who has legal rights to accommodation, e.g. a co-owning spouse, may, nonetheless, qualify as a homeless person under the Act. The definition of a homeless person in terms of the 1987 Act[17] is normally a person who has no accommodation in Scotland or England or Wales, but it also includes a person who has accommodation, but:

(a) cannot secure entry to it, or

(b) it is probable that occupation of it will lead to violence from some other person residing in it or to threats of abuse (within the meaning of the Protection from Abuse (Scotland) Act 2001

---

[12] Made by s.49 of the Criminal Justice (Scotland) Act 2003.

[13] Protection From Harassment Act 1997, s.9 and s.234A of the Criminal Procedure (Scotland) Act 1995.

[14] Housing (Scotland) Act 1987, s.26.

[15] 1986 S.L.T. 191.

[16] Above, s.26(1).

[17] As amended by the Law Reform (Miscellaneous Provisions) (Scotland) Act 1990 and by the Homelessness etc. (Scotland) Act 2003 (asp 10).

(asp 14) from some other person residing in it and likely to carry
out the threats, or
(bb) it is probable that occupation of it will lead to
    (i) abuse; or
    (ii) threats of violence which are likely to be carried out, from
        some other person who previously resided with that person,
        whether in that accommodation or elsewhere.[18]

These provisions attempt to provide individuals fleeing domestic vio- **11–76**
lence and seeking a home, with at least the choice of asserting occupancy rights under the 1981 Act, or seeking accommodation from the
local authority. However, although victims of domestic violence are
given priority on the housing list, public housing is still difficult to
obtain[19] and, even where provided, may not come up to the same
standard as previous accommodation. For those women who have
left husbands who own or co-own the family home, a third option is
to initiate divorce proceedings, and to attempt to stake a claim to all
or part of the family home as part of a claim for financial provision
on divorce. We examine this further in Ch.13 along with the rights
that apply to civil partners. In Ch.12, however, we will look at other
strategies for disputing *ownership*, as opposed to *occupation*, of the
family home, while the marriage or civil partnership subsists, as well
as looking at ownership of other types of matrimonial or family
property.

---

[18] Housing (Scotland) Act 1987, s.24(3) as amended by the Law Reform
(Miscellaneous Provisions) (Scotland) Act 1990 and by the Homelessness etc.
(Scotland) Act 2003 (asp 10). Para.(bb) was added by the Law Reform
(Miscellaneous Provisions) (Scotland) Act 1990.
[19] This may be due to a shortage of housing stock or a local authority's reluctance to
accept jurisdiction. See *Mcmillan v Kyle and Carrick District Council*, 1995 S.C.L.R.
365 where a local authority alleged it had no jurisdiction over the homeless applicant, and therefore no duty to provide housing, because the applicant did not have
sufficient family or local connections with the area.

CHAPTER 12

OWNERSHIP OF FAMILY PROPERTY

Ownership and the Family Home

12–01 In the last chapter, we looked at the rights of occupancy given to spouses, civil partners and, in some circumstances, cohabiting unmarried partners under the Matrimonial Homes (Family Protection) (Scotland) Act 1981. As we stressed at that point, these rights are not rights of *ownership* in respect of the family home. Ownership of property is determined by who acquires the object in question. Where this is not clear, the matter has to be proved by evidence. When heritage, i.e. houses or land, is purchased, particular steps must be gone through before the purchaser can acquire a valid title. These include signing a formal written disposition of the heritage in question and registering it or recording the disposition in the appropriate land register.[1] When moveable property is acquired, no such steps are usually required, and there is often no formal written document which proves who is the owner of the property in question. As we shall see, this can cause problems, particularly in relation to money in bank accounts.

12–02 With couples, property is often owned by both together, as common property. But not always. The house may be owned by only one party to the marriage. The car may be owned by the other. Sometimes this is through deliberate choice, but sometimes it is a matter of accident. The consequences can be unfair. A party may have contributed directly or indirectly to the purchase of a particular asset, yet matters may have been arranged so that the asset is the sole property of the other party. For example, the family home may be owned solely by the husband notwithstanding that the wife:

- may have contributed *financially* to the purchase price or mortgage paid on the house, by, e.g. paying half or some proportion of the mortgage instalments, or by paying for household day-to-day expenses so that the husband's income can be reserved for paying the mortgage; or

---

[1] Either the Register of Sasines or the Land Register, depending on the date of sale and the location of the subjects of sale. The person whose name is on the title may of course owe a *personal* obligation to convey the heritage to another person, e.g. where title is taken by trustees.

- may have contributed *in kind* to the global resources of the household, thereby creating or releasing other resources, which can then pay towards the purchase price or the mortgage. For example, she may have provided unpaid domestic services, e.g. cooking, cleaning, childcare, which freed the husband to take on paid work; or
- may have *enhanced* the value of the house by financial contributions towards its upkeep; or perhaps by physically repairing or redecorating it.

As we commented in Ch.10, many women acquire less in the way of **12–03** financial assets in their own name than men, due to their need to balance paid employment with family commitments, such as childcare. In the nature of domestic relationships, while the relationship subsists, resources tend to be pooled on a de facto basis and so this may not raise difficulties. However, when parties separate, or become hostile to each other, it becomes of vital importance who has the strict legal right to the formerly shared assets of the domestic relationship. No right exists to a share in the family home merely by virtue of shared occupancy or financial dependency; the crucial matter is whose name is on the title.[2]

The problem is alleviated to some extent by the growing tendency **12–04** for couples, both married and unmarried, to take title to property bought as a family home in common,[3] but this is not always the case. Title to the family home may have been acquired by one spouse when he or she was single and not altered on marriage; or one spouse may have acquired sole title to the matrimonial home after the dissolution of a former marriage and then re-married; or the property may have been put in the name of one spouse only for business, tax or bankruptcy purposes. In all these cases, the spouse or cohabitee without title has no right to a share in the house concerned. For married and civil partners, these consequences are blunted by the possibility of a claim to financial provision in any divorce or dissolution of partnership proceedings, so long as the home falls into the definition under the Family Law (Scotland) Act 1985 of "matrimonial or partnership property".[4] As we will discuss in Ch.13, at the time of divorce or dissolution of a civil partnership, existing legal rights in the matrimonial or partnership property can be discarded at the discretion of the court and that property,

---

[2] See the important case of *White v White* [2001] 1 A.C. 596 which affirms there is no presumption of equal division of the total of what the two individuals own if it falls outwith matrimonial property.

[3] Over the years, the rise in owner-occupation of the family home has continued so that the number of owner-occupied dwellings in the UK increased by 88% from 9.6 million in 1971 to 18.1 Million in 2003. Office for National Statistics, *35 Years of Social Change: Overview, Social Trends*, Vol.35 (2005), p.5.

[4] Family Law (Scotland) Act 1985, ss.8–10 as amended by s.261(2), Sch.28, Pt 2, paras 14–16 of the Civil Partnership Act 2004. See further, Ch.13.

including the home, can be reallocated between the spouses or civil partners. Furthermore, it is competent at this stage to make a claim based on non-financial contributions to the joint resources of the matrimonial or partnership household.[5]

12–05   Heterosexual cohabiting partners and same-sex cohabiting partners (who are not civil partners), however, do not have the opportunity of seeking reallocation of family assets on breakdown in the same way that married couples on divorce do and are thus in a particularly vulnerable position. Importantly, the Family Law (Scotland) Act 2006[6] now provides that such couples can apply to the court for discretionary provision but this is not on a par with the financial provision that spouses and civil partners can claim on divorce or dissolution of partnership.[7] Cohabitees may also look for remedy in the general law of unjustified enrichment. Attempts have been made in other jurisdictions, such as England and the United States, to provide remedies to cohabitees seeking rights to a share in the family home in terms of certain principles under the law of property and constructive trusts. So far this approach has not succeeded in the Scottish courts, for reasons discussed below.

Claims Under the Law of Unjustified Enrichment

12–06   Where a spouse or cohabitee has made financial contributions towards a property he or she does not own, e.g. by paying towards the deposit on the purchase price of the family home, or by making contributions towards the mortgage payments, or by paying for improvements to the house like a conservatory, then in theory, one option is to seek a remedy in unjustified enrichment, in practice usually under the law of recompense. Thus,

> "a person may be said to be unjustly enriched at another's expense when he has obtained a benefit from the other's actings or expenditure without there being a legal ground which would justify him in retaining that benefit".[8]

12–07   The requisites for claims of recompense are not wholly settled but it seems necessary to establish that[9]:

(a) the claimant spouse had no intention of donation;
(b) the claimant suffered loss, while the other spouse or cohabitee was enriched as a result;

---

[5] Family Law (Scotland) Act 1985, s.9(1)(b). See paras 13–15, 13–40 to 13–41.

[6] s.28.

[7] Under the provisions of the Family Law (Scotland) Act 1985. See further discussion in Ch.13.

[8] *Dollar Land (Cumbernauld) Ltd v CIN Properties Ltd*, 1996 S.C. 331 at 348–349.

[9] See, inter alia, *Edinburgh Tramways Co. v Courtney*, 1909 S.C. 99; *Newton v Newton*, 1925 S.C. 715.

(c) the claimant did not act so as to benefit herself, i.e. did not act *in suo;* and

(d) no other remedy is available, e.g. under a contractual agreement, or in delict.

If the claim is proven, the party who benefits must compensate the other party to the extent of enrichment, so long as this is equitable in the circumstances.

In practice, it is very difficult to succeed in an action for unjustified **12–08** enrichment in the domestic sphere.[10] The case law on the subject is in need of clarification, but what tends conclusively to extinguish any claim is the need to prove that the claimant did not in some way act to his or her own benefit.[11]

Example: A and B live together as cohabitees. They live in a house **12–09** solely owned by B. A expends labour upon painting the outside of the house, without pay from B. B then breaks up with A and asks her to leave the house.

In theory, a claim can be made by A in respect of her labour, to the extent of B's gain. But she is likely to fail because, in the circumstances, B can probably prove that the labour was donated[12] or he may prove that A was knowingly acting to her own advantage, in improving her living conditions, since she knew the house was not her own. A different result might be reached if it was proven that A erroneously thought that the house was owned by her in common with B. In that case, arguably she would have objectively not been acting to her own advantage by merely improving her living conditions, but rather acted in the mistaken belief she was improving her own property.[13] According to Clive,[14] a claim for recompense is likely to be successful only if the claimant can establish an element of error. If this is true, an error of law should now be as effective in founding a claim as an error as to fact.[15]

---

[10] See J. Thomson, "*Unjustified Enrichment and Family Law*", 2003 S.L.G. 119.

[11] *Edinburgh Tramways Co. v Courtney*, above. But see *Shilliday v Smith*, 1998 S.C. 725 where pursuer sought to recover payments made, in contemplation of marriage, for repairs and for material used in repairs and for work done to and on the defender's home, from the defender. Exceptionally, the court in this case rejected the argument that the pursuer benefited *in suo* (because she lived in the house for part of the period) on the basis that the critical factor in her ground of action was that she only acted as she did in contemplation of the parties' marriage which did not take place.

[12] Although the presumption against donation does still stand between spouses and cohabitees—see *Newton* (above, n.9).

[13] This was the result in *Newton*, above n.9.

[14] Clive, *The Law of Husband and Wife in Scotland* (4th edn, W.Green, Edinburgh, 1997), para.14.085.

[15] But see *Morgan Guaranty v Lothian Regional Council*, 1995 S.L.T. 299 where the court held that an appropriate remedy for recovery of money paid or property transferred under an obligation that was void but was erroneously thought to be valid, was an action of repetition under the *condictio indebiti* and not a claim based

Claims Under the Law of Trusts

12–10   Under English common law, it is accepted that one party may have the "beneficial interest" in a piece of property while another party has the formal legal interest. In a number of English cases, claims have been made on behalf of both spouses and cohabitees, that although formal legal title to a property lies with the other spouse or cohabitee, the claimant has a beneficial or equitable interest in the property which the courts should recognise. These claims have been made on the basis of the law of trusts, in particular in terms of implied,[16] resulting in constructive[17] trusts. Claims are often of the following form. Although partner A owns the former family home in his sole name, actually that home was purchased with assets generated by both himself and partner B. A, therefore, should be regarded in law not as unfettered proprietor, but as holding the property as a trustee on behalf of himself and partner B. On this basis, partner B asserts that a trust favouring herself as a beneficiary has been constructed or implied by the law, even although A never *expressly* constituted a trust favouring B. What substitutes for express constitution of trust, and therefore crucially founds the claim, is a finding of an express or implied agreement or "imputed common intention" between the parties A and B, that the ownership of the house was to be shared.

12–11   Although such claims have succeeded in England,[18] this is an area of law of labyrinthine complexity,[19] especially from the viewpoint of Scots lawyers where the system of trust law and title to land is very different. In the absence of any kind of express agreement, when have the courts imputed an intention to the parties to share the equitable ownership? The indeterminate answer is that they will do so when it is "reasonable" to do so.[20] These English cases have tended to accept that financial contribution on the part of the claimant will reasonably prove such a

---

on recompense. In such a case a payment might be recovered under the *conditio indebiti* irrespective of whether the mistake under which it was paid was one of fact or of law.

[16] *Pettit v Pettit* [1970] A.C. 777; *Gissing v Gissing* [1971] A.C. 886; *Burns v Burns* [1984] Ch. 317; *Thomas v Fuller-Brown* [1988] 1 F.L.R. 237; *Lloyds Bank v Rosset* [1991] 1 A.C. 107.

[17] *Cooke v Head* [1972] 2 All E.R. 38; *Eves v Eves* [1975] 3 All E.R. 768; *Grant v Edwards* [1986] Ch. 638.

[18] Where a claimant has established an interest in the property but the parties cannot reach agreement on sale and division of the proceeds the issue will be determined under the Trusts of Land and Appointment of Trustees Act 1996.

[19] See Wragg, "Constructive Trusts and the Unmarried Couple" (1996) 26 Family Law 298; and Glover and Todd, "The Myth of Common Intention" (1996) 16 (3) Legal Studies 325; Hogget and Pearl, *The Family, Law and Society* (5th edn, 2002), pp.164–184; S. Cretney, J. Masson and R. Bailey-Harris, *Principles of Family Law* (7th edn, 2002), pp.101–143; see I. Moore, "Proprietary Estoppel, Constructive Trusts and Section 2 of the Law of Property (Miscellaneous) Provisions Act 1989", 2002 63 M.L.R. 912; R. Probert, *Cretney's Family Law* (5th edn, 2003), pp.77–105.

[20] See Lords Reid and Diplock in *Pettitt v Pettitt* [1970] A.C. 777.

common intention[21] but have been less inclined to accept the same about household contributions of a non-financial kind.[22] However, where the claimant can establish the existence of an express, even if informal, promise by the other party that the claimant would have a share in the property, the claim may have a chance of success even where the contribution made by the claimant is of a non-financial type.[23]

In Scotland, the law of trusts is very different from the equivalent **12–12** English law, and it is unclear whether equivalent claims can be made. Historically, restrictions in the Scots law of evidence have inhibited the development of claims under trust. Under the Blank Bonds and Trusts Act 1696, proof of trust where the alleged trustee held a written title that is valid on the face of it was restricted to the writ or oath of the alleged trustee. This meant that where one party had a written title to property which on the face of it named him or her as sole and unfettered proprietor, no one else could prove that, in fact, that property was held in trust for other parties, unless the challenger could produce a writ from the title-holder to that effect, or get the title-holder to admit to this on oath. (The latter would obviously be particularly unlikely.)

So in *Newton v Newton*,[24] a man who bought a house and put it in **12–13** his fiancée's name, intending that she should hold the property in trust for him, was unable, when they later fell out, to challenge her title to the property, because he was unable to prove that she held as trustee by her own writ or oath. There is a strong argument that the 1696 Act in fact never applied to the proof of a trust constructed by law, as opposed to a trust voluntarily constituted by a truster.[25] However, this argument need not be pursued since the Requirements of Writing (Scotland) Act 1995 has now repealed the 1696 Act.[26] Norrie[27] has

---

[21] Such as the payment of a deposit on a home, or any other direct financial contribution to its purchase (*Pettit v Pettit* [1970] A.C. 777), or any payment of mortgage instalments (*Gissing v Gissing* [1971] A.C. 886).

[22] Such as redecorating or renovating the family home (*Thomas v Fuller-Brown* [1988] 1 F.L.R. 237); supervising building works (*Windeler v Whitehall* [1990] 2 F.L.R. 505); caring for children and running the household (*Burns v Burns* [1984] Ch. 317); contributing to the housekeeping (*Burns*, above); assisting with business entertaining (*Windeler*, above); or buying consumer goods, clothes or furnishings for the family (*Burns*, above). But see also *Midland Bank v Cooke and Another* [1995] 2 F.L.R. 915.

[23] See *Cooke v Head* [1972] 2 All E.R. 38, where a female partner was awarded one-third of the net proceeds of sale of the house on the basis of her contribution in labour to the construction of the property. See also *Eves v Eves* [1975] 3 All E.R. 768; *Hammond v Mitchell* [1991] 1 W.L.R. 1127.

[24] 1923 S.C. 15.

[25] See Norrie, "Proprietary Rights of Cohabitants", 1995 J.R. 209 at p.216: "If the Scottish courts refuse to recognise that the constructive trust can be used to confer property benefits on cohabitants it will not be because they are prevented from doing so by the Blank Bonds and Trusts Act". *Cf.* Thomson, *Family Law in Scotland* (3rd edn, 1996), p.70.

[26] Requirements of Writing (Scotland) Act 1995, s.14(2) and Sch.5.

[27] *Op. cit.*, Norrie above, n.25.

suggested that there is possible scope for opening up the remit of constructive trusts to include claims made by cohabitees. It is unlikely,
however, that the Scottish courts will be receptive to such claims for a
number of reasons.

12–14   First, Scots law has historically taken a very restrictive approach to
the occasions where it is willing to impose a trust by law upon unsus-
pecting parties. By contrast, in the United States especially, constructive trust has been used extensively and flexibly as an equitable
doctrine which allows reallocation of rights to property in a whole
variety of scenarios where one person has become unfairly enriched
at the expense of another party. In Scots law, this flexible equitable
role is traditionally taken by the law of unjustified enrichment, rather
than the law of trusts. As a result, in Scotland, constructive trusts
have usually been limited to situations where:

  (i) A holds property belonging to B; and
  (ii) A owes fiduciary obligations towards B; and
  (iii) A abuses this fiduciary relationship so as to enrich himself.

12–15 The paradigm scenario is that found in *Jopp v Johnston's Trustee*,[28]
where a lawyer A, acting for client B, held funds of B's for investment
purposes. He took the profits derived from these investments and
placed them in a bank account in his own name. The court held on
his death that the money in that account was actually held by him in
constructive trust for client B. This had the benefit of protecting the
funds from A's creditors.

12–16   While it is well established that husband and wife owe each other a
fiduciary relationship, and the same is at least possibly true of cohabiting partners, most domestic situations will not involve the element
of deception which underlies the equitable construction of a trust in
cases like *Jopp v Johnston's Trustee*.

12–17   Secondly, there are strong policy reasons for opposing the extension of the doctrine of constructive trust in Scots law. For example,
such claims undermine the general basis of the land tenure system,
namely that it can be relied on that the person whose name is on the
title is the owner of the property and can transfer a valid title. This is
not a conclusive criticism, as a third party purchaser for value will
always acquire a good title to the property transferred, even where the
seller turns out to be a trustee selling in breach of trust.[29] However,
there are also difficult implications for the law of bankruptcy,[30] as

---

[28] (1904) 6 F. 1028.
[29] Trusts (Scotland) Act 1961, s.2. See *Brodie v Secretary of State for Scotland*, 2002
G.W.D. 20-698.
[30] See *Gibson v Hunter Home Designs*, 1976 S.C. 23. See also *Sharp v Thomson*, 1997
S.L.T. 636, where the House of Lords overruled the decision of the Inner House (1995
S.L.T. 836) by holding that where a company accepted the purchase price and delivered the disposition, it ceased to have any beneficial interest in the heritable property
in question. This meant that the property was beyond the remit of a floating charge

property which is held in trust for another person is protected in the bankruptcy of the trustee from the claims of his personal creditors.[31]

Example: A is the owner of house X. A goes bankrupt and his credi- **12–18** tors seek to attach his assets including house X. A's former unmarried partner B, at A's instigation, goes to court and claims that as she paid half the mortgage on the house for many years and received no other consideration, the court should declare that although A's name is on the title he held it in constructive trust for A and B; and she may then seek an action of accounting to recover half the value of the house. A's creditors may well feel aggrieved. Effectively, B has been given a higher ranking than they in order of claim to A's assets, without benefit of being a secured creditor.[32]

Thirdly, as was perhaps apparent above, the English common law rules **12–19** on constructive trust and family homes are themselves not a model for adoption, being flawed, confusing and to some extent unsuccessful in what they seek to achieve.[33] A far more appealing option is to provide some kind of statutory discretion to the court to reallocate ownership of a family home shared by a cohabiting couple, along the lines of the right to financial provision on divorce which can be claimed by spouses. The Scottish Law Commission recommended that a limited right to apply for such an award under the Family Law (Scotland) Act 1985 should be extended to cohabitants[34] on the basis only of s.9(1)(b) of the 1985 Act which allows for "fair account" to be taken of,

> "any economic advantage derived by either person from contri-butions by the other, and of any economic disadvantage suffered by either person in the interests of the other person or of the family".[35]

---

granted by the company over its property, which crystallised the day after the dispo-sition was delivered (yet before registration). However, *Sharp v Thompson* has been limited to floating charges by the case of *Burnett's Trustees v Grainger*, 2004 S.C. (HL) 19, where the House of Lords declined to apply *Sharp v Thompson* to ordinary per-sonal insolvency.

[31] *Heritable Reversionary Co. v Millar* (1891) 19 R. (H.L.) 43; Bankruptcy (Scotland) Act 1985, s.34.

[32] A creditor with a heritable security would, of course, still take in preference to B. (In England, by contrast, in *Midland Bank v Cooke* [1995] 2 F.L.R. 915, the rights of the claimant wife were preferred to those of the secured lender.)

[33] e.g. in their failure to recognise uniformly the value of non-financial contributions towards the shared household. Gretton has commented that "few English lawyers would regard their system in this regard as being a suitable article for export" and, later, "The idea that into this labyrinth [the Scottish legal system] should walk and lose ourselves fills me with horror", *Constructive Trusts* (1997) 1(3) E.L. Rev 281.

[34] *Report on Family Law*, Scot. Law Com. No.135 (1992), para.16.32; following on from discussion on *The Effects of Cohabitation in Private Law*, Scot. Law Com. Discussion Paper No.86 (1990), paras 5.1–5.21.

[35] Their alternative proposal for reform was the introduction of a system of commu-nity of property during marriage which could possibly be extended to cohabiting partners. This was rejected in favour of the system of financial provision on divorce now embodied in the 1985 Act.

This is what has now been implemented by s.28 of the FLSA 2006. Thus the court *may* make a discretionary award of capital where cohabitation of heterosexual and same-sex couples comes to an end (other than through death)[36] and a claim is made "not later that one year after the day on which the cohabitants cease to cohabit".[37] Such an award may also represent a figure set by the court in respect of "any economic burden of caring, after the end of the cohabitation, for a child of whom the cohabitants are the parents".[38] It is to be based on whether, and to what extent, the defender has derived economic advantage from contributions made by the applicant and the extent to which the applicant has suffered economic disadvantage in the interests of the defender or "any relevant child".[39] For these purposes a child is defined as someone under 16[40] and the reference to "contributions" is expressly defined to cover "indirect and non-financial contributions"[41] so that this provision avoids the kind of difficulties experienced in England over financial and non-financial contributions.

12–20   Our view then is that the new statutory remedy is to be preferred to a judicial extension of the role of the constructive trust, although it may be argued it does not go far enough. Experience of the 1985 Act in operation has shown that the courts are extremely reluctant to make awards on the basis of economic advantage and disadvantage and this provision has been very much under-utilised to date.[42–43] It is hard to believe that the courts would not be even less willing to make awards in favour of unmarried parties.[44]

DEBTS AND BANKRUPTCY

12–21 Unfortunately, family assets may be put at risk where one member of a couple, or both of them, gets into debt. In these circumstances the law seeks to balance the interests of creditors with those of families to ensure that both are fairly treated. In the past, marriage had effects on the liability of one spouse for the debts incurred by the

---

[36] Where a man and a woman, where the court would have jurisdiction if they were married to one another under s.29(9)(a) ,or where a same-sex couple where the court would have jurisdiction to hear an action for dissolution of the civil partnership if they were civil partners of each other under s.29(9)(b).

[37] FLSA 2006, s.28(8).

[38] s.28(2)(b).

[39] s.28(3)(a)–(b).

[40] s.28 (9).

[41] *ibid.*

[42–43] See paras 13–58 to 13–65.

[44] The Scottish Law Commission already specifically rejected a proposal that cohabitees, like spouses, should have a right to claim a fair share of the net value of the assets of both parties to the relationship on its breakdown: Scot. Law Com. No.135 (1992), para.16.15.

other,[45] but other than for certain statutory debts,[46] this is no longer the case. This means that debts incurred by one domestic partner today impose no liability on the other, regardless of whether the parties are married, unmarried or in a civil partnership. This means that the bankruptcy of one spouse or domestic partner does not entitle the trustee to lay claim to any property owned by the spouse or partner of the debtor. It also means that a spouse or partner of the debtor who seeks to rank as a creditor in the debtor's sequestration does so as an ordinary creditor as his or her relationship with the debtor is not privileged in any way. However, a domestic relationship does have implications for the way in which property may be held, e.g. transfer of property from one partner to another to pre-empt creditor's rights. Where there is a sham transfer of assets from a debtor to a debtor's partner, a creditor may challenge the transfer.[47] Or, the creditor may argue that in such cases the transfer is defective or not complete, thus the debtor would not have been divested of his or her property which would still be subject to a creditor's claims.

In the case of a debtor's sequestration a creditor may make other **12–22** claims over property that the debtor has transferred to his or her domestic partner. Until 1985, it used to be the case that inter-spousal gifts made within a year and a day of bankruptcy could be revoked by the trustee in sequestration.[48]

However, it is now the case that under the provisions of the **12–23** Bankruptcy (Scotland) Act 1985, any transfer made by a debtor to his or her spouse or civil partner[49] within a stated period of his or her sequestration can be *challenged* by the trustee in sequestration. Where this occurs, the onus then shifts to the debtor to show either solvency at the date of the transfer, or that the transfer had been made for adequate consideration.[50] The stated period varies according to whether the transferee qualifies as an "associate" in which case the period is

---

[45] Thus a husband was liable for his wife's ante-nuptial debts until this was abolished by the Law Reform (Husband and Wife) (Scotland) Act 1984, s.6(1) and (2) and he was bound by his wife's capacity to act as his agent in domestic affairs (under the *praepositura domesticiis rebus*) until this was abolished under s.7 of the 1984 Act.

[46] See the Local Government Finance Act 1992, s.77 which imposes joint and several liability on spouse and cohabitants for council tax, and the Social Security Administration Act 1992, s.78 that does the same for repayment of social fund loans.

[47] *Anderson v Andersons's Trustees* (1892) 19 R. 684. In this case there was no indication that the approach taken by the court depended on marriage and dicta in the House of Lords in *Barclays Bank v O'Brien* [1994] 1 A.C. 180 at 198D suggest that the law is not limited to taking account of spouses only but should recognize "unmarried cohabitation, whether heterosexual or homosexual (at 198D).

[48] Married Women's Property (Scotland) Act 1920, s.5, repealed by the Family Law (Scotland) Act 1985, s.28(2), Sch.2.

[49] Provisions of the 1985 Act have been extended to civil partners by the Civil Partnership Act 2004, Sch.28, Pt 3, paras 31–41.

[50] 1985 Act, s.34.

five years, whereas in all other cases it is limited to two years.[51] The definition of an associate is very wide, including not only the debtor's spouse or civil partner,[52] but also any relatives of the spouse or civil partner.[53] If the debtor can establish that he or she was absolutely solvent (at the time of the transfer)[54] or that the consideration was adequate,[55] or, where the transaction was a gift[56] that it was reasonable having regard to all the circumstances, then the transaction will stand. Otherwise, the court may reduce the transaction or grant such other redress as is appropriate.

12–24   Remedy at common law still exists and a creditor may challenge a transfer made by the debtor (regardless of the debtor's relationship with the person to whom it is transferred) if:

- it was made at a time when the debtor was insolvent; or
- making the transfer rendered the debtor insolvent and the debtor remains insolvent at the date of the challenge,

and in *both* cases there was no onerous consideration for the transfer.[57] However, as it is difficult for creditors to establish that the debtor was insolvent at the time of the transfer, the statutory remedy under the 1985 Act is more usually relied upon.

12–25   Where premiums are paid by spouses or civil partners in respect of a policy under the Married Women's Policies of Assurance (Scotland) Act 1880,[58] a creditor may seek to recover their repayment but only if it can be established that they were paid with intent to defraud the creditor, or if the person effecting the policy is made bankrupt within two years from effecting the policy.[59]

PROTECTION OF HERITABLE CREDITORS

The Matrimonial Homes (Family Protection) (Scotland) Act 1981

12–26   As we have seen in Ch.11, a spouse or civil partner is protected from the consequences that may ensue from the other spouse's or partner's dealing in respect of the matrimonial or family home, subject to the protections enacted for a transferor who has acted in

---

[51] 1985 Act, s.34(3).

[52] *ibid.*, s.74. Note that spouse includes a former spouse as well as those "reputed" to be husband and wife, although it does not extend to cohabitees as such.

[53] *ibid.* "Relative" is defined as ancestor, descendant, adopted child, stepchild, sibling, uncle, aunt, nephew or niece (whether of the full blood or the half blood).

[54] *ibid.*, s.34(4)(a).

[55] *ibid.*, s.34(4)(b).

[56] *ibid.*, s.34(4)(c), e.g. for a birthday, Christmas or other conventional gift.

[57] *Boyle's Trustee v Boyle*, 1988 S.L.T. 581.

[58] This Act's provisions are extended to cover civil partners by s.132 of the Civil Partnership act 2004.

[59] Married Women's Policies of Assurance (Scotland) Act 1880, s.2.

good faith and given value.[60] As many families rely on mortgages to purchase their homes this results in them granting a standard security over the house to the lender. Such lenders have the status of heritable creditors whose loans are secured. Where the purchaser fails to make the necessary repayments they are entitled to sell the property and reimburse themselves from the proceeds of sale. The Matrimonial Homes (Family Protection) (Scotland) Act 1981 protects the rights of such creditors under s.8[61] by providing that their rights are not to be prejudiced "by reason only of the occupancy rights of the non-entitled spouse".[62] However, it does make provision for the NES to make loan payments due by the entitled spouse.[63] This is important because it enables the NES to take over the repayments from the ES and thus be less vulnerable to ejection by lenders such as banks or building societies.

There are, however, restrictions on the right of a lender to benefit **12–27** from a s.8 court order being:

Prior to December 30, 1985 the lender must have acted in good faith and, before granting the loan, must have had produced to it by the entitled spouse either:

- an affidavit sworn or affirmed by the entitled spouse declaring that there is no non-entitled spouse; or
- a renunciation of occupancy rights or consent to the taking of the loan which bears to have been properly made or given by the non-entitled spouse.[64]

In the case of loans granted from December 30, 1985 the lender will forfeit protection unless the lender acted in good faith and, at or before the granting of the security, there was produced to the lender by the granter:

- an affidavit sworn or affirmed by the granter declaring that the subjects are not a matrimonial home in relations to which a spouse of the granter has occupancy rights; or

---

[60] Matrimonial Homes (Family Protection) (Scotland) Act 1981, s.6 as amended by s.6 of the FLSA 2006, and s.106 of the Civil Partnership Act 2004 as amended by s.33, Sch.1, para.5 of the FLSA 2006.

[61] As amended by the Law Reform (Miscellaneous Provisions) (Scotland) Act 1990, s.74(1) and (2), Sch.8, para.31(2) and Sch.9.

[62] Matrimonial Homes (Family Protection) (Scotland) Act 1981, s.8(1). See s.108 of 2004 Act that enacts the same protection for heritable creditors in the case of a civil partnership.

[63] Matrimonial Homes (Family Protection) (Scotland) Act 1981, s.8(1). In the case of civil partners see s.108(1) of the 2004 Act.

[64] Matrimonial Homes (Family Protection) (Scotland) Act 1981, s.8(2) as amended by the Law Reform (Miscellaneous Provisions) (Scotland) Act 1985, s.13(8). The same provisions apply to civil partners by virtue of s.108(2) of the 2004 Act.

- a renunciation of occupancy rights or consent to the granting of the security which bears to have been properly made or given by the non-entitled spouse.[65]

The Family Home and Cautionary Obligations

12–28 Where a creditor has a standard security over property and the debtor defaults on repayment of the loan the creditor may take possession of the property and sell it to acquire repayment of the loan. For many families their home is their most valuable asset. A number of cases have arisen in the last decade involving the situation where one member of a couple, who wishes to raise money by pledging the family home as security for the loan, persuades the other to consent to a standard security over their interest in the home where title to the property is held in common. This means that if the debtor defaults, the creditor may call up the standard security and sell the house. Raising money in this way has implications for families, given the substantial growth in home ownership in recent decades and the great increase in the number of homes "jointly" owned, for if the debtor defaults, such families may find themselves homeless.[66] A number of wives who found themselves in this position sought to challenge the creditor's right to call up the standard security on their share of the property on the basis that their consent to it had been obtained through their husbands' undue influence or misrepresentation.[67] The problem they had to overcome was the fact that the standard security represented a contract between the creditor and the wife to which the husband was not a party.

12–29 In *Barclay's Bank v O'Brien*[68] a husband and wife agreed to execute a second mortgage of their matrimonial home as security for overdraft facilities extended by the bank to a company in which the husband had an interest. The wife had no such interest. The branch manager of the bank sent the documents to another branch for execution with instructions to ensure that both defendants were fully aware of the nature of the documents, and that, if in doubt, they should consult their solicitors before signing. Alas, the instructions were not carried out and the wife signed the deed without reading it. She relied on her husband's false representation that it was limited to £60,000 and would last only three weeks. When the

---

[65] Matrimonial Homes (Family Protection) (Scotland) Act 1981, s.8(2A). The same provisions apply to civil partners by virtue of s.108(3) of the 2004 Act.

[66] While the local authority has the duty to provide accommodation for those who are homeless (see the Housing (Scotland) Act 1987 (as amended by the Housing (Scotland) Act 2001) and the Homelessness etc. (Scotland) Act 2003), qualifying for priority on the waiting list for housing and acquiring accommodation of the equivalent standard to that which a family has given up creates problems for the family.

[67] The key cases here include *Barclay's Bank v O'Brien* [1994] 1 A.C. 180; *Smith v Bank of Scotland*, 1997 S.C. (HL) 111; *Royal Bank of Scotland v Etridge (No.2)* [2001] 4 All E.R. 449.

[68] [1994] 1 A.C. 180.

company's overdraft exceeded £154,000, the bank sought to enforce the mortgage and obtained an order for possession.

The wife appealed but the judge dismissed her case on the ground **12–30** that since there was no evidence that in deceiving his wife the husband was acting on behalf of the bank, they could not be held responsible for his misrepresentation. The case went all the way to the House of Lords who held that where a wife had been induced to stand as surety for her husband's debt by his undue influence, misrepresentation or some other legal wrong, she had an equity against him to set aside that transaction which would be enforceable against a third party who had actual or constructive notice of the circumstances giving rise to her equity. This would apply where a wife offers to stand surety in a trans- action which is *not to her financial advantage* and which carried a *sub- stantial risk* of her husband committing a legal or equitable wrong. In these circumstances the creditor was put on inquiry and would have constructive notice of the wife's rights unless he took *reasonable steps* to ensure that her agreement had been property obtained.[69]

What amounted to reasonable steps in *Barclay's Bank* was later **12–31** cut back by the House of Lords in the subsequent case of the *Royal Bank of Scotland v Etridge (No.2)*[70] to the requirement that the creditor need do no more than to take reasonable steps to satisfy itself that the practical implications of the proposed transaction have been brought home to the wife in a meaningful way so that she enters into the transaction with her eyes open so far as its basic ele- ments are concerned. To meet this requirement the bank need do no more than inform the wife that for its own protection it will require written confirmation from a solicitor acting for her to the effect that the solicitor has fully explained to her the nature of the documents and the practical implications that they will have for her.[71] In *Etridge*, the House of Lords made it clear that any deficiencies in the advice given are a matter between the wife and the solicitor so that the bank is entitled to proceed in the belief that a solicitor in advis- ing the wife has done so properly.[72] Not only that, but the solicitor advising the wife may *also* act for her husband or the bank provided s/he is satisfied that s/he is acting in the wife's best interests and that acting on her behalf will not give rise to a conflict of interest.[73] The

---

[69] [1994] 1 A.C. 180.

[70] [2001] 4 All E.R. 449.

[71] In *Barclay's Bank v O'Brien* the bank was required to discharge its obligation by means of a personal meeting with the wife (in the absence of her husband) where she would be informed of the extent of her liability as a surety, warned of the risk she would be running, i.e. that the home may be possessed by the bank, and urged to take independent legal advice.

[72] The responsibilities of a solicitor acting for a wife in this situation were set out in detail.

[73] In 2003 The Law Society of Scotland's Conveyancing Committee stated that the same solicitor must not advise both debtor and guarantor. It also published a stan- dard letter for use by solicitors advising guarantors. See "Inter-Spouse Guarantees: An Update", 2003 J.L.S.S. 34.

House of Lords also upheld the view that the creditor would not only be put on inquiry in cases involving spouses[74] but in any case where the relationship between the surety/cautioner and the debtor is non-commercial.[75]

12–32   In Scotland, the key case is the House of Lords ruling *Smith v Bank of Scotland*,[76] which was heavily influenced by *Barclay's Bank v O'Brien*.[77] In this case, the concept of good faith was used to extend a creditor's duty not to mislead and to provide disclosure in certain circumstances. Thus the concept was used to extend the creditor's duty to act not only where misapprehensions *were known to be present* but also where misapprehensions *might be present as a possible wrongful act* by the debtor.[78] The nature of the debtor's actions must have compromised the consent of the cautioner to the extent that, had the contract been between the debtor and the cautioner, the obligation would have been rendered voidable. The cautioner must show that had it not been for the undue influence or misrepresentation s/he would not have entered into the transaction. The onus of proof remains on the cautioner to show that s/he placed trust and confidence in the debtor (because of their personal relationship) as well as, that the transaction s/he entered into was plainly to his or her disadvantage and that this was not explicable without the presence of some wrong being perpetrated by the debtor.

12–33   Where this burden is met and the transaction is held to be "inexplicable" the burden of proof then shifts to the creditor. Although the case of *Smith* involved a wife acting as cautioner for her husband's debt, the banks have made it their practice to advice and disclose whenever:

> "the person providing security is an individual rather than a business or a company, including the situation where a director is to provide security for a company".[79]

---

[74] In *Barclay's Bank v O'Brien* [1994] 1 A.C. 180 Lord Browne-Wilkinson did not restrict the court's ruling to married couples but noted that "in my judgment the same principles are applicable to all other cases where there is an emotional relationship between cohabitees . . . Now that unmarried cohabitation, whether heterosexual or homosexual, is widespread in our society, the law should recognise this. Legal wives are not the only group which are exposed to the emotional pressure of cohabitation (at 198D)".

[75] For discussion of these cases see D. Morris, "Wives are Told Don't Blame the Bank Sue your Solicitor!", 1999 Feminist Legal Studies, Vol.7, pp.193–202; G. Gretton, "Sexually Transmitted Debt", 1997 S.L.T. (News) 195; R. Auchmuty, "Men Behaving Badly: An Analysis of English Undue Influence Case", 2002 Social and Legal Studies, Vol.11, pp.257–282; R. Russell, "Royal Bank of Scotland v Etridge No.2: The End of a Sorry Tale", 2002 S.L.T. (News) 55; "Inter Spouse Guarantees: An Update", 2003 J.L.S.S., Vol.48, pp.34–38.

[76] 1997 S.C. (HL) 111.

[77] [1994] 1 A.C. 180.

[78] For a detailed discussion of the Scottish position see S. Eden, "Cautionary Tales: The Continued Development of Smith v Bank of Scotland", 2003 7 (1) E. L. Rev 107.

[79] *ibid.*, p.113.

In Scotland, it would appear sufficient for a creditor to warn the potential cautioner of the consequences of entering into the proposed cautionary obligation and to advise him or her to take independent advice.[80] Thus as long as a lender has reasonable ground to believe that the cautioner is receiving legal advice, no further steps need be taken to ascertain whether or not the cautioner understands what s/he is undertaking (regardless of whether his or her solicitor is also acting for the bank or the debtor).[81] Not only that, but it would appear to be sufficient in Scotland for the warning and advice to be contained within the guarantee, that is as part of the security document. In the *Royal Bank of Scotland v Wilson*[82] the court held that wives acting as cautioners were expected to look after their own interests and make their own inquiries and that there was nothing in *Royal Bank of Scotland v Etridge*[83] to suggest that the specific duties on creditors prescribed therein were part of the law of Scotland. While the law in Scotland obliged the creditor in the interests of good faith not to mislead the debtor, the only misrepresentation averred was one of silence and there was no duty of disclosure on the creditor in such circumstances. Unless expressly asked to, the creditor was not obliged to make any disclosure to the prospective cautioner as to the extent of the borrower's indebtedness. Thus the creditor's obligations in Scotland appear to be less onerous than those of their English counterparts.

Protection of Spouses/Civil Partners

Up until the introduction of the Mortgage Rights (Scotland) Act **12–34** 2001, there was no protection for domestic partners of persons who took out a standard security over the family home where a creditor called up the standard security and put the property up for sale to repay the outstanding amount due on the loan. In other words, the family home was treated no differently from any other form of heritable property. Concern over families being rendered homeless in such a situation led to the 2001 Act which enables a person to apply to the court for a suspension of the creditor's rights on default, where the security subjects form a person's sole or main residence (regardless of whether he or she owns the property). Such an order can be applied for by:

- the debtor or the proprietor of the property;
- his or her NES;
- a person living with the proprietor as husband and wife or in a same-sex relationship with all the characteristics of a relationship of husband and wife;

---

[80] See Lord Clyde in *Smith v Bank of Scotland*, 1997 S.C. (HL) 111 at 122.

[81] See Lord Sutherland in *Clydesdale Bank plc v Black*, 2002 S.L.T. 764 at 776H.

[82] 2003 S.L.T. 910.

[83] [2001] 4 All E.R. 449. Note that in this case neither of the wives averred that their husbands had made any positive misrepresentation to them and the bank was off the opinion the wives had had benefit of independent legal advice.

- any person who no longer lives in the security subjects but had lived there for at lease six months ending with the date on which the security subjects ceased to be the sole or main residence of the debtor or the proprietor *and* the security subjects are the sole or main residence of a child under 16 who is a child of that person and of the debtor or proprietor.[84]

In this situation the court may make such an order as it thinks fit, including suspending the creditor's rights for a period, but only if it considers it reasonable in all the circumstances, having regard to:

- the nature and reasons for the default;
- the applicant's ability to fulfil within a reasonable period the obligations under the standard security in respect of which the debtor is in default;
- any action taken by the creditor to assist the debtor to fulfil those obligations; and
- the ability of the applicant and any other person residing at the security subjects to secure reasonable alternative accommodation.[85]

12–35 Where a spouse or civil partner is sequestrated and s/he is an "entitled" spouse/partner,[86] and the non-debtor is the "non-entitled" spouse/partner, the latter is entitled to receive intimation of the sequestration from the trustee and be advised of the right to apply under the Bankruptcy (Scotland) Act 1985[87] for recall or for such order as the court thinks fit to protect the occupancy rights of the NES/P. This is only possible where the court is satisfied that the purpose of the petition for sequestration was wholly or mainly to defeat the occupancy rights of the NES/P.

12–36 It is not only the matrimonial or family home that is at risk where a person gets into debt; its contents may also be subject to seizure. Some protection relating to the possession and use of its contents was provided by the Debtors (Scotland) Act 1987 which listed items that were to be exempt from seizure through poinding.[88] However these exemptions have been repealed as the Debt Arrangement and Attachment (Scotland) Act 2002 now makes it incompetent to

---

[84] See s.1(2) of the 2001 Act. Under s.1(3) the definition of "child" includes a stepchild and any person brought up or treated by the applicant and debtor or proprietor as their child. The definition would appear to cover a child of both members of a same-sex couple.

[85] *ibid.*, s.2(2).

[86] Under ss.1 and 22 of the Matrimonial Homes (Family Protection) (Scotland) Act 1981 for spouses; s.101 of the Civil Partnership Act 2004 for civil partners.

[87] 1985 Act, s.16. See s.261(2), Sch.28, Pt 3, para.37 of the Civil Partnership Act 2004 which amends s.41 of the Bankruptcy (Scotland) Act 1985 so that the same protection is afforded civil partners.

[88] Debtors (Scotland) Act 1987, s.16 and Sch.5, para.5 including things such as beds, bedding, household linen, chairs, settees, tables, etc.; this was amended by SI 2000/189 to include computers, microwaves, telephones and televisions.

enforce payment of *any* debt by poinding or warrant sale.[89] The 2002 Act also limits that which may vest in a trustee in sequestration under the Bankruptcy (Scotland) Act 1985, to that falling outwith the limitations imposed by the 2002 Act.[90]

OTHER TYPES OF FAMILY PROPERTY

Although the family home, where owner-occupied, usually represents **12–37** the major heritable asset of the marriage, issues also arise during the marriage as to ownership of moveable goods and cash assets, e.g. furniture, the car, and money in bank accounts. Particular problems arise, again, because of the close personal relationship between spouses, and the norm of domestic sharing of assets regardless of who has actual title to those assets.

As a general rule, where A hands over property or money to B, **12–38** there is a presumption *against* donation by A to B. (A may, for example, merely be depositing the item with B for safekeeping). As with all presumptions, it may be rebutted. While the nature of the relationship between husband and wife is such that one might expect them to exchange gifts, case law suggests that the courts are wary to hold that the presumption is rebuttable simply because the donor and donee are married to each other.[91] The courts are, however, aware that intention to donate is more likely between spouses than between strangers.[92] Gifts made between spouses are as irrevocable as gifts to other people.[93] However, gifts between spouses to defraud creditors in the bankruptcy of the donor spouse may be struck down as gratuitous alienations under s.34 of the Bankruptcy (Scotland) Act 1985 which now applies also to civil partners.[94]

---

[89] s.58(2).

[90] 1985 Act, s.33 as amended by Sch.3, para.15 of the 2002 Act. Protection is extended to civil partners by Sch.28, Pt 3 of the 2004 Act which amends the 1985 Act. See also s.127 of the 2004 Act.

[91] See, e.g. *Jamieson v McLeod* (1880) 7 R. 1131; *Newton v Newton*, 1923 S.C. 15; *A. v B.* (1925) 41 Sh. Ct. Rep. 23.

[92] Thomson, *Family Law in Scotland* (4th edn, Butterworths, Edinburgh, 2002), p.69, asserts the presumption is "not difficult" to rebut between spouses. Clive, *op. cit.*, at para.14.029 comments that while "the natural affection and obligation to provide support which subsists between parent and child can cancel out a presumption against donation . . . these considerations have, for some reason, not been given much weight in husband and wife cases" although he acknowledges that "there is no reason to doubt that they at least reduce the strength of the presumption".

[93] The old common law rule that gifts between spouses were revocable during the donor's lifetime was abolished by s.5 of the Married Women's Property (Scotland) Act 1920. But death-bed gifts by a spouse may still be revocable where the donor unexpectedly recovers, under the general rules of *donatio mortis causa*.

[94] Extended to civil partners by s.132 of the 2004 Act. Gifts made by a spouse/civil partner to 3rd parties up to 5 years before a divorce/dissolution of partnership that are intended to reduce a person's resources in order to avoid an order for financial provision are also struck down by s.18 of the Family Law (Scotland) Act 1985,

12–39   Scots law does recognise that there are certain occasions when it is equitable to modify the operation of the separate property rule in relation to the moveable property of spouses and civil partners; but only in limited circumstances involving household goods, savings from housekeeping allowances, and life insurance policies.

Household Goods

12–40   As a rule of evidence, spouses/civil partners are presumed to own household goods in equal shares.[95] Ownership of these goods, like all moveable property, depends upon who actually purchases them. *Proof* of this ownership is a matter of evidence and, as stated earlier, there is usually no conclusive written document proving who owns moveable property. For example, a vehicle registration document for the family car in the name of the husband does not prove the husband *owns* that car, merely that he is the registered keeper. The car may in fact have been purchased by the wife, in which case she is the owner. The registration document, however, will be *evidence* to help prove who is the owner if this is disputed.

12–41   For many household goods, who actually purchases certain goods is often wholly accidental. The husband may purchase the fridge with his cheque book, while the wife buys the microwave oven on credit. Both purchases are intended to be used and owned jointly in the family home, and who bought which is of no concern. Since assets are frequently commingled in marriage, it was often difficult in the past to prove conclusively who had bought what when ownership of matrimonial assets later fell into dispute.

12–42   Section 25(1) of the Family Law (Scotland) Act 1985 now meets this problem by providing that,

> "if any question arises (whether during or after a marriage) [or civil partnership]) as to the respective rights of ownership of the parties to a marriage [or the partners in a civil partnership] in any household goods obtained in prospect of or during the marriage [or the civil partnership] other than by gift or succession from a third party, it shall be presumed, unless the contrary is proved, that each has a right to an equal share in the goods in question".

The presumption which arises under s.25 is merely a rule of evidence, and may be rebutted on the balance of probabilities. Indeed, it is no different from the rule of evidence which existed at common law. What does alter the common law significantly is s.25(2), which provides that the presumption of equal shares shall *not* be rebutted

---

as amended by s.261(2), Sch.28, Pt 2, para.24 of the 2004 Act (to apply to civil partners).

[95] Family Law (Scotland) Act 1985, s.25(2) as amended by s.261(2), Sch. 2, para.28 of the 2004 Act.

merely by the fact that if while the parties were married or in a civil partnership *and* living together, the goods in question were purchased from a third party by either party alone or by both in unequal shares. This means that actual proof of payment (or of payment in unequal shares) cannot, in itself, overcome the presumption.[96] Effectively, this means that the best evidence to prove who owns a household item, namely proof of purchase, is not admissible as evidence. The policy behind this rather bizarre result is clear: but it might have been better achieved by a simple rule that household goods are owned in common.

Household goods are very broadly defined to cover:　　　　**12–43**

> "any goods (including decorative or ornamental goods) kept or used at any time during the marriage [or civil partnership in any family] home[97] for the joint domestic purposes of the parties to the marriage [or the partners], other than—

(a) money or securities;
(b) any motor car, caravan or other road vehicle;
(c) any domestic animal".[98]

This definition of household goods covers a suitably wide range of property although the exclusion of the family car, often a major asset, can be queried. Where goods are not kept or used "for joint domestic purposes" they will not qualify as household goods and s.25(1) will not apply. This means that where one spouse/civil partner has specifically purchased goods for his or her own purposes, e.g. in connection with a hobby which the other spouse does not share, then that spouse will retain sole ownership of the goods in question. So a husband who buys model trains, or a wife who collects Japanese prints, can attempt to prove that these were not acquired for "joint domestic purposes" and the presumption of ownership in equal shares will not arise.

Gifts from third parties do not fall within the presumption of equal **12–44** sharing of household goods under s.25(1) of the 1985 Act. Nor do gifts made to the couple before they marry or enter a civil partnership. Where wedding or engagement presents are concerned, ownership depends, under common law, on the intention of the donor. Was the gift meant to be owned in common by the couple, or by one party only? As Thomson has pointed out,[99] although a gift may be intended

---

[96] Although note that if the parties are married *but not living together*, then the provisions of s.25(2) will not apply and so evidence of payment alone *may* be sufficient to rebut the presumption.

[97] This has the same meaning as "matrimonial home" in s.22 of the Matrimonial Homes (Family Protection) (Scotland) Act 1981. See Ch.11.

[98] 1985 Act, s.25(3).

[99] J. Thompson, *Family Law in Scotland* (4th edn, Butterworths, Edinburgh, 2002), pp.68–69.

for the parties' joint *use*, it does not necessarily follow that the donor intended that the gift should be *owned* jointly by them, even though that may be the intention in many cases. A gift of antique jewellery, passed down in the husband's family for generations for example, may be made to the couple for the *use* of the wife, but with the intention of sole *ownership* going to the husband, so that the items can be retained on that side of the family.[1] Where the donor is still alive to speak to his or her intention, or there is express proof of the donor's intention, there may be no problems in proof of ownership. In other cases, it may be possible to infer the correct intention from the circumstances surrounding the gift, such as who it came from, e.g. a friend of the groom, or of the bride (or their respective families).[2] Clive has suggested that a presumption of joint ownership of wedding presents would be appropriate.[3]

Cohabitees

12–45 For cohabitees the definition of "household goods" is the same as contained in the 1985 Act.[4]

12–46 Under s.26 of the FLSA 2006, cohabitants benefit from an assumption of equal ownership of goods acquired during the period of cohabitation. However, in their case, the presumption is rebuttable and there is no equivalent exclusion of certain objections to the assumption as is provided by s.25(2) of the 1981 Act for spouses and civil partners.

Money and Bank Accounts

12–47 As the definition of "household goods"[5] expressly excludes money and securities from its remit, the ordinary rules of ownership of moveables apply to these assets. Confusion about these rules sometimes arises where money is held in a bank or building society account opened in the joint names of spouses or other parties. In such cases, the names on the account are not conclusive of ownership of the funds held in the account; instead, they merely indicate to the bank or building society concerned that each of the named account-holders may draw freely on the account. Crucially, there is no presumption of joint ownership of the funds raised by the fact that they are in joint names. Instead, ownership must be proved by reference to the actual contributions made by the account-holders, and whether or not there is any evidence of donation.

---

[1] Note that such items may be regarded as "heirlooms" and therefore be unaffected by the wife's prior right to furniture and plenishings if the husband dies first and does not leave a will: Succession (Scotland) Act 1964, s.8(6)(c).

[2] See *McDonald v McDonald*, 1953 S.L.T. (Sh. Ct.) 36.

[3] *Op. cit.*, above, n.14, at para.14.041.

[4] FLSA 2006, s.26(4).

[5] 1985 Act, s.25 for spouses and civil partners; FLSA 2006, s.26 for cohabitees.

Example: H and W set up a joint bank account with the Royal Bank **12–48** of Scotland. Only W earns, and she pays a certain amount of her salary into the account per month. Both parties draw on the funds to pay household bills and buy domestic necessaries. In the absence of evidence to rebut the presumption against donation, it will be assumed that the funds in the account still belong solely to the wife and that the account was opened merely to allow the husband to draw conveniently on the funds of the wife.[6]

Where there is evidence that *both* parties have contributed to the funds in a joint account, but the precise amounts remain vague, it is submitted that donation of whatever amount is necessary to give each a half share should be inferred, unless there is specific evidence to the contrary.[7]

Joint accounts set up by spouses frequently incorporate a sur- **12–49** vivorship clause which allows the surviving spouse to withdraw all the funds on the death of the other. Such a clause does not of itself imply that the deceased spouse intended to leave such proportion of the funds as belonged to him or her to the surviving spouse on death. It merely allows the surviving spouse to ingather the funds, which will then be due to the deceased's heirs. However, it is sometimes possible in these circumstances to prove *donatio mortis causa*.[8]

Savings from Household Allowance

At common law, where a wife managed to save money from a **12–50** housekeeping allowance paid to her by her husband, the savings were considered to belong to her husband.[9] This was because the source from which the funds derived was property owned by her husband. The wife merely held and spent the funds as her husband's agent, and owed him the duty to return any un-spent surplus. Injustice arose, however, where the wife saved money out of the allowance by, e.g. spending her own earnings on household provisions. The money saved was still her husband's. The only way in which a wife could claim a share of the money saved was if she could establish, as in *Pyatt v Pyatt*,[10] that the savings had increased due to her management skills. In *Pyatt*, the wife saved money out of her allowance and used it to put a winning stake on the football pools. The question was whether the pay-out from the win on the pools should go wholly to the husband since the stake had been bought using his money. The

---

[6] See *Cuthill v Burns* (1864) 24 D. 849.
[7] Proposals for the introduction of a presumption of equal ownership of money held in joint accounts by spouses were dropped, reportedly because of the opposition of the Committee of Scottish Clearing Banks. See *Report on Matrimonial Property*, Scot. Law Com. No.86 (1984), para.4.9.
[8] *Forrest-Hamilton's Trs*, 1970 S.L.T. 338.
[9] *Preston v Preston*, 1950 S.C. 253.
[10] 1966 S.L.T. (Notes) 73.

court held that the winnings had derived not only from the stake money which had come out of the housekeeping money provided by the husband, but also from the wife's luck and skill. Accordingly, both were entitled to an equal share of the winnings.

12–51   Section 26 of the Family Law (Scotland) Act 1985[11] now provides that:

> "If any question arises (whether during or after a marriage) [or civil partnership]) as to the right of either party to a marriage [or as the case may be of a partner in a civil partnership] to money derived from any allowance made by either party [or partner] for their joint household expenses or for similar purposes, or to any property acquired out of such money, the money or property shall, in the absence of any agreement between them to the contrary, be treated as belonging to each party [or partner] in equal shares".[12]

The section appears wide enough to cover savings made before, as well as after, the section came into force.

Cohabitees

12–52   Almost identical provision as that found in s.25 of the Family Law (Scotland) Act 1985 (presumption of equal shares in household goods) is now to be found at s.26 of the FLSA 2006 pertaining to cohabitees. Further, the presumption of equal shares in money and property derived from a housekeeping allowance at s.26 of the 1985 Act is also to be found in the 2006 Act at s.27.[13] Importantly, however, there is an express exclusion of the residence in which the couple live (or lived) together from the presumption of equal shares.[14]

Married Women's Policies of Assurance (Scotland) Act 1880

12–53   Where one person takes out insurance on his or her life for the benefit of another, normally the policy must be delivered, or intimation of the policy made, to that third party before he or she can acquire rights under the policy. This is because the contract of insurance is constituted between the insurance company and the insured, under which the third party is given a right known as *a jus quaesitum tertio*.[15] Without delivery or intimation, the third party right under the policy cannot be enforced against the insurance company. Where,

---

[11] As amended by Sch.28, Pt 2, para.29 of the 2004 Act.

[12] This section (prior to its redrafting by the 2004 Act to include civil partners) replaced the similar provision in s.1 of the Married Women's Property Act 1920, which only covered savings made by a *wife* from a housekeeping allowance made to her by her *husband*. The provisions of s.26 of the 1985 Act clearly apply equally to husband and wife.

[13] Implementing *Report on Family Law*. Scot. Law Com. No.135 (1992), para.16.12.

[14] FLSA 2006, s.27(3).

[15] *Carmichael v Carmichael's Exrx*, 1920 S.C. (H.L.) 195.

say, a husband takes out insurance on his life for the benefit of his wife, it is artificial to demand delivery or intimation because of the nature of the relationship. Section 2 of the Married Women's Policies of Assurance (Scotland) Act 1880[16] therefore makes an exception to the ordinary rule in the case of a husband or wife taking out a life policy in favour of the other spouse or children of the marriage. The effect of the statute is that the policy proceeds are deemed to be held in trust by the insured for the third party beneficiaries whose rights are therefore enforceable against the insured (or his estate) even if there was no delivery or intimation. This provision has now been extended to civil partners by s.132 of the 2004 Act. Although the Scottish Law Commission recommended that it should also be extended to cohabitees[17] this has not been implemented by the FLSA 2006.

In the following chapter we consider in detail the division of property upon divorce or dissolution of a civil partnership which includes the need to ensure adequate provision is made for parties dividing up their assets to cover two households in place of the previous one.

---

[16] As amended by the Married Women's Policies of Assurance Act (Scotland) (Amendment) 1980.
[17] *Report on Family Law*. Scot. Law Com. No.135 (1992), para.16.45.

CHAPTER 13

FINANCIAL PROVISION ON DIVORCE AND DISSOLUTION OF CIVIL PARTNERSHIP

13–01 When spouses or partners decide to terminate their relationship, this affects them not only emotionally but also financially. The resources which previously financed one home now have to sustain two separate households and assets shared during the course of the relationship must be divided between the couple. Where the parties are married, on their divorce, the court is empowered to redistribute the assets of the marriage regardless of who had legal title to those assets during the marriage, by making orders for financial provision on divorce under the Family Law (Scotland) Act 1985,[1] in particular ss.8–16. These provisions have now been extended to civil partnerships, where the partnership is being dissolved, through amendments made to the 1985 Act by Sch.28, Pt 2 of the Civil Partnership Act 2004, ss.11–30. Under the 1985 Act spouses/civil partners must establish grounds for divorce/dissolution before they can apply for an award of financial provision.[2] However, the grounds for divorce are rarely contested these days, and divorce by mutual consent after two years' non-cohabitation has become the most popular option.[3] This period has, of course, been controversially reduced to one year for both spouses and civil partners by the Family Law (Scotland) Act

---

[1] References in this chapter are to the 1985 Act, unless otherwise indicated.

[2] Divorce (Scotland) Act 1976, s.1 for spouses; Civil Partnership Act 2004, s.117 for civil partners. The grounds for dissolution, set out in Pt 3, Ch.5 of the 2004 Act, s.117 (as amended by Sch.1 of the FLSA 2006) are the same as they are for marriage with the exception of "adultery" which is omitted from the 2004 Act. See discussion in Ch.14.

[3] See Ch.14. Non-fault-based grounds for divorce have recently overtaken fault-based grounds in Scottish divorce cases. For the years 1989–1991 the most common ground for divorce was that of behaviour, cited in 44%, 46% and 44% of cases respectively, followed by non-cohabitation in 29%, 28% and 30% of cases, and adultery in 17%, 15% and 15% of cases. See Morris, Gibson, and Platts, *Untying the Knot: Characteristics of Divorce in Scotland* (Scottish Office Central Research Unit, Edinburgh, 1993). But more recently, *Civil Judicial Statistics for 2002, Scotland* (HMSO) (which are the most up-to-date figures at the time of going to press) show that out of 136 divorces in the Court of Session and 10,690 divorces in the Sheriff Court, 56% of divorces in both courts were based on two Years' non-cohabitation, compared with 15 % on grounds of behaviour and 6% of cases in the Court of Session and 4% of cases in the Sheriff Court were based on adultery.

2006.[4] It is the financial aspects of divorce together with childcare arrangements which are overwhelmingly the most crucial and disputed matters in modern divorce, both in and out of court. For this reason, we will turn our attention first to the principles governing financial provision, before examining the grounds for divorce and dissolution in the next chapter. Court orders relating to arrangements for children after divorce were considered in Ch.4. Issues of childcare and finance are, of course, not always separable. In many divorces where there are children, residence and contact will be key bargaining issues when negotiating a division of property and we may expect the same to be true of dissolution of civil partnerships,[5] as is the subsequent question of whether the spouse/civil partner with care of the children may retain the family home while they are growing up.

The rules regulating distribution of resources after divorce can be **13–02** tailored to implement one or more not always compatible objectives and different jurisdictions favour some objectives over others. For example, they could be intended to penalise the party responsible for marital breakdown or to ensure continued support of the economically weaker spouse by the other or, to provide *transitional* support while former spouses re-establish financial independence. Further, they may seek to equitably adjust any economic disadvantage one spouse may have suffered in the interests of the family.[6] In Scotland, the law on financial provision on divorce prior to the 1985 Act, found in s.5 of the Divorce (Scotland) Act 1976,[7] suffered from the lack of any clear statement of its objectives. The court was given almost no guidelines to aid it in the exercise of its discretion to make an award. By contrast, under the 1985 Act, the court is assisted by a set of principles laid out "in considerable and almost clinical detail"[8] in s.9, which to some extent incorporates all the objectives mentioned above bar the first.

The two grounds for divorce/dissolution are irretrievable break- **13–03** down of marriage/civil partnership or the granting of an interim gender recognition certificate to either party to the marriage/civil partnership.[9] The principal philosophy underlying the 1985 Act— now mirrored in the 2004 Act for civil partners—is that divorce should be as far as possible a "clean break" between the parties, that

---

[4] FLSA 2006, s.11(a) amending s.1(2) of the 1976 Act for spouses; s.33, Sch.1, para.9 of the FLSA 2006 amending s.117(3) of the 2004 Act for civil partners.

[5] The first couple seeking an action for dissolution was reported in the *Telegraph* on May 19, 2006. The will, of course have to fulfil the time requirement on non-cohabitation first. The lesbian couple entered civil partnership in February 2006 but 2 months later decided to terminate their relationship.

[6] See *Report on Aliment and Financial Provision*, Scot. Law Com. No.67 (1981).

[7] See further, *Aliment and Financial Provision*, Scot. Law Com. Memo No.22 (1976), Vols 1 and 2, and *ibid.*, paras 3.41–3.46.

[8] *Per* Lord President Hope in *Little v Little*, 1990 S.L.T. 785 at 786L–787A.

[9] Divorce (Scotland) Act 1976, s.1(1)(a)–(b) for spouses; 2004 Act, Pt 3, Ch.5, s.117(2)(a)–(b) for civil partners. Note that prior to the passage of the Gender Recognition Act 2004, irretrievable breakdown was the sole basis for divorce.

is, the former spouses should be free to lead separate lives after divorce, unrestricted by continuing financial obligations to each other. Marriage is seen as a partnership "wound up" by divorce and, ideally, the assets of that partnership should be distributed once and for all on its termination to the former partners in the form of capital, or by transfer of property. Accordingly, the 1985 Act restricts the making of a periodical allowance award, requiring one spouse to continue to maintain the other after divorce, to occasions where a capital or property transfer award is insufficient to meet the objectives of the Act.[10] Furthermore, the court is given a wider range of powers than was provided under the 1976 Act to make it easier for it to award an equitable clean break settlement. In particular, the court can make an award of capital by instalments,[11] and make a property transfer order.[12]

13–04   It is important to note that ex-spouses cannot expect a clean break from any *children* of the marriage. While divorce may end the legal relationship between spouses, that existing between parent and child persists, and the divorce court, where it has jurisdiction still to do so since the advent of the Child Support Act 1991,[13] will make such award of aliment for children of the marriage as is justified in the circumstances, before turning to any question of financial provision.[14]

<h2 style="text-align:center">THE LEGAL FRAMEWORK</h2>

13–05 Where an application is made for financial provision on divorce/dissolution, under s.8(2), the court[15] is directed to make such orders as are:

(a) justified by the principles set out in s.9; and
(b) reasonable, having regard to the resources of the parties.

Both considerations must be taken into account before an order can be made. Thus, lack of resources on the part of one party at the date of divorce may sometimes lead the court to award a lower sum than would be suggested by the norm of equal sharing of matrimonial property set out in s.10(1) (see paras 13–07 *et seq.*). For example, in *Crockett v Crockett*,[16] a slump in the value of the husband's business

---

[10] s.13(2)(a) and (b).
[11] s.12(3).
[12] s.12(1).
[13] As amended by the Child Support Act 1995 and the Child Support, Pensions and Social Security Act 2000.
[14] See Ch.5 for discussion of child support and child aliment.
[15] Under s.27, this may be the Court of Session or the Sheriff Court.
[16] 1992 S.C.L.R. 591. But *cf. Shand v Shand*, 1994 S.L.T. 387, where the husband's lack of assets at the date of divorce was due to his having caused his own bankruptcy.

between the relevant date[17] and the date of divorce led the court to make a much lower award to the wife than it would have made purely on the basis of the s.9 principles. However, *resources* are not limited to those assets which qualify as "matrimonial" or "partnership" property[18] but comprise all assets available to the parties,[19] including "foreseeable" resources.[20] These might include assets such as insurance policies which are due to mature after the divorce/dissolution, lump sum payments and "golden handshakes" due on retirement or termination of employment.

THE S.9 PRINCIPLES

Section 9 of the 1985 Act sets out the five principles which govern **13–06** financial provision. The basic premise in s.9(1)(a) is that all matrimonial/partnership property should be shared fairly between the parties. Fair sharing, as we shall see, is defined to mean equal sharing unless there are special circumstances to depart from this norm. In addition, account is also to be taken under ss.9(1)(b)–(e) of economic advantages or disadvantages which have been sustained by either person; the economic burden of childcare; substantial dependence; and severe financial hardship. Where one party would not be adequately compensated in any of these circumstances by an equal share of the property under s.9(1)(a), then the court may, in theory, award more than a half share to that person. However, this is rarely done in practice.[21] The s.9 principles are intended to be flexible enough to produce a fair result in a variety of different types of marriage/civil partnership, including those of long and short duration, as well as those which have children or are childless. Even after a division of property has been worked out in principle, under s.8(2) the court has substantial discretion as to what orders to make to implement that division. That is, depending on the available resources at the date of divorce/dissolution, it may make an order for immediate payment of a capital sum or for payment deferred to a certain date or for payment of the capital sum by instalments, possibly out of the salary of the payer.

The wife was awarded the maximum possible sum out of the assets remaining at the date of divorce.

[17] FLSA 2006, s.16 now requires matrimonial/partnership property be valued at either a date the parties agree upon or the date of the order or a date as close to the date of making the order as the court may determine. See discussion at paras 13–11 and 13–21 to 13–23 below.

[18] See para.10–39 below.

[19] See, e.g. *Buczynska v Buczynski*, 1989 S.L.T. 558 where a flat purchased for one spouse by a third party as a gift was taken into account as a "resource" when determining financial provision.

[20] s.27(1).

[21] See, also, 13–57 below.

First Principle: s.9(1)(a)—Fair Sharing of Value of Matrimonial/Partnership Property

13–07   The first principle contained in s.9(1)(a) is that:

> "the net value of the matrimonial property should be shared fairly between the parties to the marriage [or as the case may be the net value of the partnership property should be so shared between the partners in the civil partnership]".

Under s.10(1), fair sharing is defined as equal sharing except where "special circumstances" justify an alternative division.

Matrimonial/Partnership Property

13–08   The first question, then, is what qualifies as "matrimonial" or "partnership" property? Section 10(4) of the 1985 Act defines "matrimonial" property as,

> "all the property belonging to the parties or either of them at the relevant date which was acquired by them or him (otherwise than by gift or succession from a third party)—
> (a) before the marriage for use by them as a family home or as furniture or plenishings for such a home; or
> (b) during the marriage but before the relevant date".

Section 10(4A) of the Act defines "partnership" property in conformity with this definition.

13–09   It is crucial to note that matrimonial/partnership property includes all property acquired during the relevant period by *either* or *both* spouses/civil partners (subject to the stated exceptions), regardless of whether one or both parties had legal title to the property in question during the subsistence of the marriage. So, if a husband purchases the family home during the marriage in his sole name, then it falls into the matrimonial property pot, and subject to any "special circumstances" will prima facie be divided equally between the spouses on divorce. The same applies to money held in a bank account solely belonging to the wife, or to furniture owned in common by both.

13–10   One of two dates may qualify as the "relevant date" for the purpose of assessing what is matrimonial/partnership property being, either the date on which the parties ceased to cohabit[22] or the date of service of the summons in the divorce/dissolution action,[23] whichever one is the earlier.[24] Parties to a marriage cease to cohabit only when they

---

[22] s.10(3)(a).
[23] s.10(3)(b).
[24] 1985 Act, s.10(3). For effect of resumption of cohabitation with regard to fixing the relevant date see *Brown v Brown*, 2003 Fam. L.B. 64-2.

cease in fact to live together as man and wife.[25] As discussed in Ch.10, this is a question of fact which may or may not involve cessation of sexual relations. The fact that parties live together in the same house does not necessarily mean that they are still "cohabiting" for the purposes of the Act.[26] Where the parties initially cease to cohabit, but have since made an attempt at reconciliation, there are special provisions setting out how the relevant date is to be calculated under s.10(7) so as not to discourage reconciliation.

Until the passage of the Family Law (Scotland) Act 2006, this **13–11** "relevant date" was also used as a cut-off point for the *valuation* of matrimonial property. It was intended to be a logical and convenient device-preventing the various matrimonial assets having to be repeatedly revalued during negotiations right up to the final date of divorce. However, increases and decreases in the value of assets between the relevant date and the final date of divorce have led to some unfortunate outcomes as shall be discussed at paras 13–21 to 13–24. For this reason, it is now the case that when property is *transferred* between spouses/civil partners as part of a divorce/dissolution settlement, the relevant date for *valuation* is now either a date the parties agree or a date as close to the date of transfer as the court considers appropriate.[27]

Case law[28] has established that damages for personal injury or **13–12** criminal injuries compensation payments form part of the matrimonial property, even if they have not been paid over before the relevant date, so long as the act *giving rise* to the claim occurred before the relevant date. Thus, in *Skarpaas v Skarpaas*[29] the husband received damages for personal injury after the relevant date, but in respect of an accident which had befallen him during the marriage and before the relevant date. The damages were held to be matrimonial property, as they were in the case of *Louden v Louden*[30] where they were paid after the relevant date in respect of a claim for wrongful dismissal which arose during the marriage. However, the time and nature of such a payment may constitute "special circumstances" to depart from the norm of equal sharing.[31] It is also important to note that deductions for certain aspects of the damages may be made, e.g. in

---

[25] 1985 Act, s.27(2). Neither the Civil Partnerhsip Act 2004 nor the FLSA 2006 amended the wording of this section.

[26] See *Buczynska v Buczynski*, 1989 S.L.T. 558 where the court held that cohabitation ceased while the parties were still living in the same premises, but had ceased to share the same bedroom, the wife had ceased to cook for her husband and the husband's solicitor had notified the wife of the husband's intention to raise a divorce action.

[27] 1985 Act, s.10(2A) and (2B) as amended by s.16 of the FLSA 2006.

[28] Note: all case law discussed concerns the division of "matrimonial" property between "spouses" as the registration of civil partnership has only been possible since December 5, 2005.

[29] 1993 S.L.T. 343.

[30] 1994 S.L.T. (OH) 381.

[31] See *Skarpaas v Skarpaas*, 1991 S.L.T. (Sh. Ct.) 15 at p.19.

Skarpaas the sheriff deducted that portion of the award that was referable to solatium and loss of future earnings.[32] If the accident giving rise to the claim for damages falls outwith the relevant period, i.e. before the marriage or after the relevant date, then the damages awarded will not be considered matrimonial property even if they are paid over before the relevant date.[33] Redundancy payments may qualify as matrimonial property if they have been paid to one spouse before the relevant date, even though they are payments made in compensation for loss of future earnings.[34] A refund of income tax may also qualify as matrimonial property, even where it is paid after the relevant date, if the right to repayment refers to a financial period before the relevant date.[35]

Some items are specifically excluded from the definition of matrimonial property.

Excluded Property

Property Acquired Before Marriage

13–13   As we have seen, under ss.10(4) and 10(4A) matrimonial/partnership property must be acquired by either or both spouses/civil partners either:

- before the marriage/registration of partnership for use by them as a family home or as furniture or plenishings; or
- during the marriage/partnership but before the relevant date.

Property acquired before marriage/civil registration will thus not form part of the matrimonial property unless it was acquired by the prospective spouses/civil partners "for use by them as a family home". Case law has established it is not a requirement of this provision that either party need have contemplated marriage when purchasing such a home.[36] If, for example, a man purchases a house for himself and his girlfriend to live in together as a "family", with no intent of marriage at that date, but then subsequently the parties do marry, then there is no reason why the house should not fall into matrimonial property under s.10(4). In *Buczynska v Buczynski*,[37] the husband bought a house at a time when he was still married to his first wife but having a sexual relationship with the pursuer. He and the

---

[32] See also *Carroll v Carroll*, 2000 Fam. L.B. 58-6 where the sum representing future earnings was excluded from the award.

[33] See *Petrie v Petrie*, 1988 S.C.L.R. 390 where damages awarded after the relevant date for injuries sustained before the marriage were held not to constitute matrimonial property because the property right in that case, the right to damages, had accrued before the date of the marriage.

[34] See *Smith v Smith*, 1989 S.L.T. 668; *Tyrrell v Tyrell*, 1990 S.C.L.R. 244.

[35] *MacRitchie v MacRitchie*, 1994 S.L.T. (Sh. Ct.) 72.

[36] See *Mitchell v Mitchell*, 1995 S.L.T. 426 at 428.

[37] 1989 S.L.T. 558.

pursuer cohabited there from the date of purchase of the home, and continued to do so after their marriage in 1969, and until the relevant date in 1987. The court held that the house was matrimonial property since it had been bought "for use as a family home", apparently having no difficulty in finding that a cohabiting couple could be a "family" even where one party was still married to another person. However, in these circumstances, it must still be proved that there was an intention to purchase the house for use as a family home: not, for example, as a single person's residence, as an investment, or as a home for another person, e.g. an ex-spouse. In *Maclellan v Maclellan*,[38] the husband bought a croft before marriage for his sole use. Later the wife moved into the croft and it became the family home. The court held that although the couple had lived together there for 26 years, it was not matrimonial property, as it was not bought "for use . . . as a family home".

Maclellan illustrates a real source of hardship in the way the legis- **13–14** lation is phrased. The wife had no claim on the family home, which was the sole substantial asset of the marriage, despite having lived in it and helped maintain it for 26 years. If the husband had chosen to sell that croft and purchase another home, either during or in contemplation of the marriage, then the new home would have comprised matrimonial property.[39] A similar problem arises where a husband purchases a house to live in with wife 1, divorces her but goes on living in that home, and then marries wife 2 who moves in. However long he and wife 2 live in that home, it will not be regarded as matrimonial property in respect of the second marriage. In *Buczynska*, Lord Morton suggested[40] that by analogy with the Matrimonial Homes (Family Protection) (Scotland) Act 1981, s.22, a home which "becomes" a family home should be regarded as falling into matrimonial property, whatever the intention at the time of purchase. Helpful as this approach might be, it cannot be said to be justified by the wording of the 1985 Act.[41]

Some courts have attempted to mitigate the hardship caused by **13–15** cases like these, by including in the matrimonial property any increase in the value of the home over the period of the marriage up to the relevant date, where this increase is due in part to the contributions (financial or otherwise) of the disfavoured spouse. In *Budge v Budge*,[42] the wife's efforts during the marriage enhanced the value of a croft which had been bought by the husband with the proceeds of a house

---

[38] 1988 S.C.L.R. 399.
[39] See, e.g. *Jacques v Jacques*, 1995 S.L.T. 963, affirmed by House of Lords at 1997 S.L.T. 459.
[40] At p.560. S.22 of the 1981 Act defines a "matrimonial home" as including a house which "has become" a family residence.
[41] For criticism of this approach, see Clive, *The Law of Husband and Wife in Scotland* (4th edn, W.Green, Edinburgh, 1997), para.24.025, n.74; Meston, "Matrimonial Property and the Family Home", 1993 S.L.T. (News) 62.
[42] 1994 G.W.D. 38-2234.

inherited solely by him. The court awarded her a capital sum which represented half the increase in value of the property from the date of the marriage to the relevant date.[43]

13–16 It is not necessary for a house acquired in contemplation of marriage to be used continuously by the parties as a family home from the date of acquisition. In *Mitchell v Mitchell*[44] the parties married, bought a family home, divorced, remarried and then divorced again. The husband retained the house used as a family home after the first divorce, and the question arose whether it was "matrimonial property" in respect of the second marriage. The husband argued that the house was purchased in contemplation of the first marriage, not the second, and therefore should not be regarded as "matrimonial property". The court held that the parties had, as a matter of intention, acquired the house "for use by them as a family home", and nothing in the section stipulated that the property should have been acquired for use in relation to a particular marriage.

Property Acquired by Gift or Succession from a Third Party

13–17 Property acquired by either party before or during the marriage, by way of gift or succession from a third party, is excluded from matrimonial property, under s.10(4) of the 1985 Act. This is true even if the property is a gift from a third party to *both* parties to the marriage.[45] (Gifts from one spouse to the other are not excluded from matrimonial property by this provision.) However, if property excluded under this head changes its form or substance during the marriage, then it may be regarded as having been converted into matrimonial property.

13–18 In *Latter v Latter*,[46] questions arose as to whether: (i) the family home; and (ii) shares belonging to the husband fell into matrimonial property. The family home had been purchased with a sum of money donated by the wife's family and handed over to her solicitors to buy the property, title to which was then taken in the wife's name alone. On divorce, the court held that the home was not matrimonial property as it had been acquired as a gift, choosing to disregard the fact that the gift had been of the sum of money used to purchase the home, and not the home itself. In Lord Marnoch's view,

> "to draw a distinction as between a gift of the purchase price and a gift of the heritable property itself, simply because of the conveyancing techniques employed, would be over precise".[47]

---

[43] See also *Ranaldi v Ranaldi*, 1994 S.L.T. (Sh. Ct.) 25 where the court awarded the second wife half of the increase in value of the home, on the basis that she had contributed to the successful running of it as a guest house throughout the marriage.

[44] 1995 S.L.T. 426.

[45] *Smith v Smith*, 1992 G.W.D. 23-1324.

[46] 1990 S.L.T. 805.

[47] *ibid.* at 808.

On the other hand, the court held that the husband's shares *did* amount to matrimonial property. These shares had been acquired by the husband prior to marriage, and so were prima facie excluded. However, during the course of the marriage, these shares, which were originally held in a number of family companies, were reconstructed into a single holding of shares in one parent company and this change of form was sufficient to transmute them into matrimonial property. The court noted that even if the shares had been excluded from matrimonial property, the increase in value of the shares over the period of the marriage could have been included.

Contrast *Whittome v Whittome (No.1)*[48] where Mr Whittome **13–19** acquired shares, by gift and as a beneficiary under trusts, which formed part of a private family company. Although the nature of the shareholding changed considerably over time, e.g. the private company in which shares were held was publicly floated, it was held that none of these developments led to the creation of new property which would fall to matrimonial property. The facts were distinguished from *Latter* in that Mr Whittome's shares were held in one company which existed throughout the whole period of the marriage.[49] Furthermore, the court rejected the *Latter* approach in holding that the whole value of the gift at the relevant date, not just the original value at the date of donation, should be excluded from matrimonial property. The general rule seems to be that if the reorganisation of a company results in new shares being acquired in place of the old, the new shares will be matrimonial property; but, if the shareholding remains as it was before, albeit in a different structural form, the property will not qualify as matrimonial property.

These cases must not be confused with the common scenario where **13–20** property acquired by gift or succession is sold during the course of the marriage, and the proceeds used to purchase some other form of property. For example, a gift of shares may be sold to purchase a house, furniture or other shares. In these cases, what is purchased with the money so derived will fall into matrimonial property.[50] However, the fact that the funds used to acquire this property came from a gift to one spouse/civil partner, may be taken into account as "special circumstances" under s.10(6)(b).[51]

Valuation

Valuation is important because it is the *net value* of the matrimo- **13–21** nial property that is to be divided fairly between the spouses for the purposes of s.9(1)(a). Prior to s.16 of the FLSA 2006, matrimonial

---

[48] 1994 S.L.T. 115.

[49] *ibid.* at 125.

[50] See *Jacques v Jacques*, 1995 S.L.T. 963. See also *Fulton v Fulton*, 1998 S.L.T. (OH) 1262 where the court held that shares purchased with money that was a gift were matrimonial property.

[51] See also 13–41.

property was also *valued* as at the "relevant date".[52] Problems arose therefore when items went up or down in value after the relevant date. For example, with the fluctuation of homes prices, there is often a considerable difference between the value of a house at the relevant date and the date of divorce, particularly where divorce is sought after years of non-cohabitation.

13–22   In *Wallis v Wallis*,[53] the spouses owned the family home in common. The property was worth a gross amount of £44,000 at the relevant date but £68,000 at the date of divorce, an increase in value of £24,000. The husband sought an order transferring the wife's half of the house to himself. At first instance, the sheriff agreed to make such an order and, by compensation, awarded a half share in the value of the house as at the date of divorce to the wife. The husband appealed. Both the Inner House and the House of Lords subsequently held that the value of an item of matrimonial property had clearly to be established as at the *relevant date*, and that accordingly the wife could only be compensated by an award of half the value of the house at that date, unless there were special circumstances to do otherwise. An increase in value in a house after the relevant date could not be treated as matrimonial property.[54] Effectively this meant that the husband received the wife's half of the house, worth £34,000 gross, for an outlay of £22,000, a result clearly unreasonable to the wife and recognised as such by the House of Lords.[55] Although the increase in value in the house after the relevant date had enhanced the husband's *resources*, it had not increased the value of the *matrimonial property;* and, as already noted, only a decline, not an increase, in resources can justify a departure from the norm of equal sharing of the matrimonial property under s.8(2)(b). Furthermore, a change in value of an asset after the relevant date was not sufficiently uncommon to amount to "special circumstances" which could be taken into account in terms of s.10(1).[56] However, although an increase in value in the matrimonial home after the relevant date post-*Wallis* could not qualify as matrimonial property, it was still a "resource" that could be taken into account and accessed, if it could be justified by one of the other s.9 principles (that are not limited in their application to matrimonial property).[57] The decision in *Wallis* has now been rendered obsolete by s.16 of the FLSA 2006.

---

[52] s.10(2).

[53] 1992 S.L.T. 676 (1st Div.); affirmed by the House of Lords at 1993 S.L.T. 1348.

[54] See also *Lewis v Lewis*, 1993 S.C.L.R. 32.

[55] See also academic criticism by Clive, 1992 S.L.T. (News) 241; Thomson, 1992 S.L.T. (News) 245; Bissett-Johnson, 1994 S.L.T. (News) 248.

[56] For a more detailed discussion of the Inner House decision see E. M. Clive, "Financial Provision on Divorce: 'A Question of Technique'", 1992 S.L.T. (News) 241; see also J. M. Thomson, "Financial Provision on Divorce: Not Technique but Statutory Interpretation", 1992 S.L.T. (News) 245 and E. M. Clive, "Dr Clive Replies", 1992 S.L.T. (News) 247.

[57] See *Cunniff v Cunniff*, 1999 S.L.T. 992 (Ex Div) where the court held that there was no reason why the increase in value of the defender's pension, which the Lord

Section 16 Family Law (Scotland) Act 2006

The Scottish Executive, aware of the problems linking valuation of **13–23** matrimonial property to the relevant date,[58] implemented reform in s.16 of the FLSA 2006. For the purposes of the valuation of family property the FLSA 2006 replaces the term "relevant date" with "appropriate valuations date", defining that to mean:

(a) where the parties to the marriage or, as the case may be, the partners agree on a date, that date;
(b) where there is no such agreement, the date of the making of the order under s.8(1)(aa).[59] An earlier draft of this section gave rise to criticism, especially regarding the valuation of pension rights and is discussed at para.13–33 below.[60]

In exceptional cases, where the court decides that the date of making the order should not apply, "the appropriate valuation date shall be such other date as the court may determine",[61] however that date should be as near as possible to the making of the order.[62]

Prior to s.16 of the FLSA 2006, in order to avoid the inequity **13–24** arising from *Wallis*, parties owning the house in common were free either to agree that one should sell his or her half interest to the other or, in the absence of agreement, to seek an order for division and sale.[63] In both cases, the value of the house at the date of sale is divided and so both parties receive their due. The disadvantage in the latter case, however, is that the party wishing to realise the value of his or her share in the house must raise a separate action to do so after concluding divorce proceedings. Another alternative, therefore, is to seek an incidental order for sale and equal division of the proceeds on divorce, rather than a property

---

Ordinary had concluded was achieved by the defender at the expense of other resources, should not be considered as a "resource" to be included in the assessment. See also *Vance v Vance*, 1997 S.L.T. (Sh Ct) 71 where the court held that the increase in value can be accessed in a claim under the other s.9 principles, none of which is limited to matrimonial property.

[58] In its Consultation Paper, *Family Matters: Improving Scottish Family Law* (Scottish Office, Edinburgh, March 1999) the Scottish Office raised the issue of whether the effect of *Wallis* should be Reversed, while the White Paper on *Parents and Children: A White Paper on Scottish Family Law* (2000) postponed any changes in this area until a comprehensive review of matrimonial property had been undertaken.

[59] See s.16 of the FLSA 2006 inserting subss.(2A), (3A) and (2B) after s.10(2) of the 1985 Act.

[60] J. Buchanan, "Pension Rights: Valuation and Sharing Issue", 2005 Fam. L.B. 75-4; A. Gibb, 2005 Fam. L.B. 76 (July Editorial); J. Buchanan, "Pension Rights: A Response to the July Editorial", 2005 Fam. L.B. 77-2.

[61] 1985 Act, s.10(2B) as inserted by s.10 of the FLSA 2006. In this case, where the court selects a date, it should be as near as possible to the date of making the order.

[62] For a discussion of s.16 see David Nichols' "Comment" in 2006 Fam. L.B. 80-2.

[63] See *MacKenzie v MacKenzie*, 1991 S.L.T. 461 and *Crockett v Crockett*, 1992 S.C.L.R. 591.

transfer order.[64] In *Jacques*,[65] in order to avoid the problems presented by *Wallis*, at first instance the sheriff expressly refrained from making any order at all with respect to the matrimonial property. On appeal, the Inner House found that the sheriff should have granted an order for sale and equal division of the property under the 1985 Act, rather than forcing the parties to resort to separate proceedings for division and sale of the property which would involve them in further expense and delay.[66] This was what had been done in *Quinn v Quinn*[67] where the sheriff declined to make a property transfer order and opted, instead, for granting an order for the sale of the parties' matrimonial home.[68] Although a transfer is justified by the fair sharing of matrimonial property principle, it is often not reasonable in the light of the spouse's resources. However, it may be a preferable option where it is considered necessary for maintaining a family home for children of the marriage, especially if they are young[69] and may be offset, for example, by a transferee spouse not making a claim on the pension of the transferor spouse.

13–25 Some types of matrimonial property are particularly difficult to value. Notable amongst these are family or small businesses, and rights in occupational pension schemes. The value of a public limited company can be determined by Stock Exchange prices. But the value of other types of businesses may be dependent on a number of factors, such as whether there is a prospective purchaser,[70] whether the business is sold on a voluntary or forced basis,

---

[64] Under s.14(2)(a) and (k). See *Jacques v Jacques*, 1995 S.L.T. 963; *MacKenzie v MacKenzie*, 1991 S.L.T. 461; *Reynolds v Reynolds*, 1991 S.C.L.R. 175; *Symon v Symon*, 1991 S.C.L.R. 414; *Crockett v Crockett*, 1992 S.C.L.R. 591; *Lewis v Lewis*, 1993 S.C.L.R. 32. The case of *Lewis* established that this did not run counter to *Wallis* since that only governs where a property transfer order is made.

[65] 1995 S.L.T. 963

[66] *ibid.* at 966.

[67] 2003 S.L.T. (Sh Ct) 5.

[68] See *Webster v Webster*, 2003 Fam. L.B. 62-6 and 62-7 where the sheriff endorsed the sheriff's observations in *Quinn* that the court should consider whether special circumstances exist (see para.13–40 below) to justify the transfer of one party's share to the other—with the consequent inequality of division—as opposed to allowing the parties to sell the property and divide the proceeds. In this case there were no special circumstances justifying an unequal division of the matrimonial property which had increased substantially in value since the relevant date. So, the sheriff opted for an sale of the property, with the husband paying the wife a lump sum out of his share of the proceeds. He viewed this as representing an easier and fairer way of equalizing matrimonial property. See also *McCaskill v McCaskill*, 2004 Fam. L.B. 72-3. See also *Weir v Weir*, 2005 Fam. L.B. 76-5 where because post-*Wallis* the transfer of the wife's half share of the family home to the husband would have produced a result not fair to her the court felt obliged to order division and sale rather than property transfer.

[69] See paras 13–43 and 13–44 below discussing deviation from equal sharing under "special circumstances" relating to the nature and use of the property under s.10 (6)(d) of the 1985 Act.

[70] See, e.g. *Savage v Savage*, 1993 G.W.D. 28-1779, where the value of the business was reduced to reflect the difficulty of selling it for full value.

whether the business is geared for short or long term profits, or for maximum income or maximum capital growth, and how far the value of the business lies in the persons currently running it, and the goodwill they personally command.[71]

Pensions—Valuation of[72]

Pensions have, in the past, created special problems with regard to valuation. As noted in earlier chapters, pension rights are an important asset in modern marriages. Indeed, where matrimonial property is in existence, an occupational pension will often be the largest asset in the marriage overall. The 1985 Act expressly provides in s.10(5)[73] that rights to, or interests in, pension schemes[74] or life policies, and similar arrangements[75] fall within the definition of matrimonial or partnership property. This recognition that pension rights are part of the shared assets of a marriage/civil partnership has been of particular importance to married women, who tend to acquire less in the way of pension rights in their own name than men.[76] Women with children often fail to make contributions sufficient to acquire their own full occupational pension because of withdrawal from the job market in favour of domestic responsibilities, and even women who have been in steady employment tend to have earned lower salaries and had more interrupted working careers, and consequently acquire less in the way of pension rights.[77] Women are, therefore, as a group,

13–26

---

[71] See *McConnell v McConnell*, 1993 Fam. L.B. 6-7, where evidence was led to the effect that the company was a "people" company.

[72] See also 13–35 to 13–38 and paras 13–47 to 13–51 for a more detailed discussion.

[73] As amended by the Pensions Act 1995, s.167(2).

[74] The definition of "pension scheme" under s.10(10) is not limited to tax-approved schemes, to funded schemes, or to schemes which provide pension benefits as opposed to lump sum benefits. It includes Hancock annuities, provision for parties' pensions payable by the continuing partners in terms of a partnership agreement, and the state pension including the State Earnings Related Pension Scheme (SERPS).

[75] Similar arrangements have been held to include private pension plans for employed or self-employed people, but not gratuities paid by employers after separation (*Gibson v Gibson*, 1990 G.W.D. 4-213) or redundancy payments (*Smith v Smith*, 1989 S.C.L.R. 308).

[76] See Field and Prior, *Women and Pensions* (DSS Research Report No.49, 1996) and *Pensions and Divorce* (DSS Research Report No.50, 1996). According to the Department of Work and Pensions, *Report on Women and Pensions: The Evidence* (November, 2005) there are 2.2 million women in total not accruing a basic state pension. Of these about 1.3 million are married and National Insurance Inheritance Rules may apply. Around 600,000 of the 2.2 million women are earning under the lower earnings limit. The Family Resources Survey estimates are that around 390,000 carers are not accruing basic state pension entitlement, around 120,000 of them caring for 20 hours or more a week (at p.80). The figures show that only "30% of women reaching State Pension Age are entitled to a full basic State Pension (24% on their own accord) (at p.81). As a result two thirds of people in receipt of Pension Credit are women (at p.82)."

[77] This is because women are more likely than men to take on caring responsibilities and therefore time out of the labour market which affects their entitlement to the

vitally dependent on the pension rights of their husbands, including any associated benefits to wives and widows, to protect them from old-age poverty.[78] Once a couple are divorced, any rights accruing in terms of the pension scheme to the husband's "spouse or widow" will generally go to the second wife (if any) and not to an ex-wife. By including pension rights in the definition of matrimonial property, therefore, the Act recognises that women have a right to (prima facie) an equal share in the pensions earned by their husbands for the period during which they were married, and that this right cannot be extinguished by the simple expedient of divorce.

13–27 The rules relating to valuation of pensions have recently been clarified by the Divorce etc. (Pensions) (Scotland) Regulations 1996.[79] The proportion of the pension rights which fall into matrimonial property at the relevant date is calculated according to a formula set out in reg.3 of the 1996 Regulations. This involves an apportionment of the total value of the pension rights over the time of the marriage, according to the formula "A × B/C" where:

A is the value of the pension rights at the "relevant date";
B is the period during the marriage when the party is a member of the pension scheme; and
C is the total period of membership of the scheme before the relevant date.

13–28 *Example:* H started contributing to a pension plan in 1985. He married W in 2000 and separated from her in 2005, the relevant date. His pension was valued at the relevant date at £40,000. The proportion of the pension which represents matrimonial property is as follows:

$$\frac{\text{value at relevant date (A)} \times \text{years' marriage (B)}}{\text{total years in pension scheme before the relevant date (C)}} = \frac{£40,000 \times 50}{20}$$

---

state pension. They are also more likely to be in low-paid work and to work part time which affects their access to occupational pension schemes and their ability to pay into any pension scheme. They have also suffered because the welfare system has been geared to a pattern of lifetime earnings, to full-time employment with no or only brief periods out of employment. The problem is that the welfare system assumed that women would be able to rely on husband's pensions to support them in their old age. See The Fawcett Society Briefing Paper on *Women & Pensions* for Seniors Network: *www.seniorsnetwork.co.uk/womenspensions/fawcettsociety.htm.*

[78] Attempts have been made to alleviate this poverty through the introduction of Pension Credit in 2003. This is an income-related entitlement for people aged 60 or over living in Great Britain that provides them with a contribution to a guaranteed minimum level of income of at least £114.05 a week for a single pensioner and £174.05 a week for couples (2006/2007). The level of minimum income may be higher for people with caring responsibilities, severe disability and certain housing costs.

[79] SI 1996/1901. See Bissett-Johnson, "Recent Changes in Valuation and Division of Pensions on Divorce", 1996 S.L.T. (News) 295.

The value of the pension rights falling into matrimonial property therefore comes to £10,000.

The 1996 Regulations also determine what method should be used to value occupational pension scheme rights. In the past, two methods have been adopted:

(i) *Continuing service method* This assumes that the member of the **13–29** pension scheme will continue in service until retirement. The value of the pension is calculated using an estimated value for final salary at the date of retirement.

(ii) *Leaving service method* This assumes that the member leaves **13–30** service at the relevant date. The final salary at that date is used to calculate the value of the pension at that date. This value is also known as the "transfer value" of the pension, because it is the value the member would be entitled to transfer into another pension scheme, if he left his current employment at the relevant date.

The most important difference between the two approaches is that **13–31** the continuing service valuation tends to give a higher value for the pension, since salaries at the date of retirement obviously tend to be higher than at date of separation. Although the majority of Scottish lawyers and judges preferred to use continuing service valuation prior to 1996, the transfer value of a pension has the advantage of being more readily and cheaply available, because under the legislation requiring that pensions be transferable between employers, all pensions administrators are required to supply this information. Transfer value is also much easier to calculate than continuing service value, because it is based on a known final salary at the relevant date, and thus involves far less projection as to uncertain future events.

However, it is now well established that the valuation of pension **13–32** and other rights is done according to the cash equivalent transfer value ("CETV"), that is, the cash equivalent to which the pension holder would be entitled at the relevant date.[80] The fact that this may give rise to unfairness in particular instances, because one method of valuation may be appropriate in connection with one pension scheme but not another,[81] does not justify deviation on the grounds of

---

[80] There was some doubt as to whether the court was obliged in terms of the earlier regulations to use the "cash equivalent" figure in valuing benefits at the relevant date for divorce proceedings raised between August 19, 1996 and December 1, 2000. The Divorce etc. (Pensions) (Scotland) Regulations 2000 (S SI 2000/112) now make it clear that for all divorce actions commencing after December 1, 2000, it is the cash equivalent value that should be applied.

[81] S. Eden, "Pensions and Divorce (Pt II)", 1996 Fam L.B. 23-3; S. Smith, "Valuation of Pension Rights on Divorce", 1999 Fam L.B. 38-3; I. Talman, "Pensions on Divorce", 1999 Fam. L.B. 41-3 and H. Smith, "Valuation of Pension Rights Revisited", 1999 Fam. L.B. 42-3.

"special circumstances".[82] While CETV gives an acceptable value in the majority of cases, there are those cases where it may understate or overstate the true value of the pension rights that are likely to be payable. This is because CETV is based on the rights to which a member would be entitled to if he or she *leaves* the scheme. When dealing with a final salary pension scheme, for example, the rights offered to leavers of the scheme are materially different, in respect of the same period of service, to those that will be payable to someone who remains in the scheme.[83] As the law currently stands this discrepancy cannot be taken into account. To deal with this it is been proposed that the court should be given the discretion to substitute a fair value through regulations that state,

> "where it is demonstrated that the pension rights, on which a value provided under the regulations has been calculated, are materially different from those which are likely to be payable, the court will have discretion to substitute an alternative value provided by a prescribed person".[84]

13–33 Another area that poses problems that s.16 does not deal with is where there are changes in value after the relevant date. This most commonly arises where pension sharing is involved because this cannot occur until after the divorce. In this situation, the scheme will use the CETV at the date of implementation, rather than the relevant date value to implement the share and this according to Buchanan can lead to,

> "unexpected and undesirable outcomes. If changes in value after the relevant date were due solely to economic factors then it would normally be reasonable that they should be dealt with in the same way as other matrimonial assets. However, what may not be generally appreciated is that significant changes can occur in both values *and* the nature of the pension rights after the relevant date, that are often due to other than economic factors".[85]

After outlining the situations in which this may occur he proposes that, if the relevant date value is fair, courts should be given more discretion to share the pension rights unequally.

---

[82] *Stewart v Stewart*, 2001 S.L.T. (Sh Ct) 114; *Logan v Logan*, 2002 Fam. L.B. 55-4; *Webster v Webster*, 2003 Fam. L.B. 62-6.

[83] See *Logan v Logan*, 2002 Fam. L.B. 55-4.

[84] This solution has been put forward by J. Buchanan, "Pension Rights: Valuation and Sharing Issues", 2005 Fam. L.B. 75-4, who was commenting on an earlier draft of s.17 of the FLSA 2006, which was s.14 under the Bill. He proposed adding a further subsection on these lines to ss.10(8) and 10(8A) of the 1985 Act. However, this has not effected the actual wording of what is now s.17.

[85] J. Buchanan, "Pension Rights: Valuation and Sharing Issues", 2005 Fam. L.B. 75-4 at 75-5.

As things stand, practitioners are advised to "check around the **13–34** time of divorce that the proposed arrangement still produces results in line with their expectations"[86] as it is possible that,

> "a sharp drop in the CETV, in the interval between agreeing the sum to be transferred and implementation, can leave the transferor spouse with no pension fund".[87]

Pension Options—Earmarking, Lump Sum Orders and Pension Sharing Orders

Under s.12A,[88] the courts have power to "earmark" a proportion or **13–35** fixed lump sum amount of the pension for the benefit of the non-members spouse/civil partner, payable at the date when the pension matures. Such a "pension lump sum order"[89] can be ordered by the courts when making an order for a capital sum but is ordered against the trustees or managers of the pension scheme of the payee spouse/civil partner, rather than against the spouse/civil partner him or herself. The court's power to make such an order only arises if it is making a capital sum order, not an order for a periodical allowance. Where made, it does not accelerate payment, so that both the member and non-member will receive payment only when the pension right becomes due, normally on the retirement or earlier death of the member spouse/civil partner. However, it is now possible for the spouses/civil partners to share a pension when it matures.[90] This is done by the parties reaching agreement (a qualifying agreement)[91] or by obtaining a pension sharing order under s.8(1)(baa) of the 1985 Act.[92] Where there is to be pension sharing the court cannot make a pension lump sum order under s.12A of the 1985 Act.[93] The advantage of these options is that they do not require any immediate payment out of available resources. The idea is that on divorce/dissolution the transferor's shareable rights in his or her pension arrangement are subject to a debit of the appropriate amount and the transferee spouse/civil partner becomes entitled to a credit of that amount which is enforceable against the person responsible for running the pension scheme.[94] The

---

[86] J. Pollock, "Pensions", 2006 Fam. L.B. 80, p.4.

[87] *ibid.*

[88] Added by s.167(3) of the Pensions Act 1995.

[89] Welfare Reform and Pensions Act 1999 ("WRPA 1999"), s.28(1)(f); Pensions on Divorce etc. (Pension Sharing) (Scotland) Regulations 2000 (SI 2000/1051), regs 3 and 5.

[90] This does not apply to state pensions. For discussion of changes in non-state pension rules see A. Bissett-Johnsons, "Changes in Pension Division on Divorce", 2000 S.L.T. (News) 297.

[91] WRPA 1999, s.28(1)(f); Pensions on Divorce etc, (Pension Sharing) (Scotland) Regulations 2000 (SI 2000/1051), regs 3 and 5.

[92] The order is defined in the 1985 Act, s.27 (as amended by WRPA 1999, s.20).

[93] 1985 Act, s.8(4), (5) and (6), added by WRPA 1999, ss.28(6) and 84 and Sch.12, para.6.

[94] WRPA 1999, s.29.

pension credit can then be used to purchase rights in the pension arrangement in the transferee's own name. The pension will become payable when the transferee retires. Before a qualifying agreement is signed, the transferor must have intimated his intention to share his or her pension rights with the transferee to the managers of his or her pension fund. Such agreements must be registered in the Books of Council and Session and cannot be made after the parties have divorced. Alternatively, the court can make a pension sharing order[95] which will specify the percentage value or the amount to be deducted from the transferor's pension rights.[96] On divorce/dissolution, the spouses/civil partners send the decree[97]and the qualifying agreement or pension order to the pension scheme managers so that pension sharing can be effected.

13–36   A final valuation problem is what associated benefits should be included when calculating the total value of the pension. Typically, occupational pensions give rise to a bundle of benefits on top of the basic member's pension, including a spouse's pension and lump sum (if the pensioner survives to retirement) or death in service benefit and widow/widower's pension if he or she does not.

13–37   Until recently, there was considerable doubt as to which of these extra benefits should be included when valuing an occupational pension for divorce purposes.[98] Amendments made to s.10(5) by the Pensions Act 1995[99] now make it clear that any benefit given by a pension to the surviving spouse or civil partner, including any death in service benefit, is to be included in the value of that pension for divorce/dissolution purposes.

Pension Protection Fund

13–38   Given the problems with employers going bankrupt and the effect this has on employees' pension rights, the government has introduced the Pension Protection Fund under the Pensions Act 2004. This is a government fund to which pension schemes contribute by way of a levy. Its purpose is to pay out compensation to members whose pension schemes have collapsed. Where such a payout is made, s.17 of the FLSA 2006 governs how such compensation is to be dealt with in relation to financial provision as it may well form part of the matrimonial or civil partnership property. The 1985 Act is amended by adding a new subs.(5A) to s.10 of that Act[1] which makes it clear that

---

[95] *Galloway v Galloway*, 2003 Fam. L.B. 61-5 is the first reported instance of a pension sharing order being made in Scotland. The case also established that in terms of s.17(2B) of the Legal Aid (Scotland) Act 1986 the full value of a pension sharing order is liable for clawback.

[96] 1985 Act, s.27 (as amended by the WRPA 1999, s.20(3)).

[97] Within two months of the extract decree.

[98] See previously, *Brooks v Brooks*, 1993 S.L.T. 184; *Crosbie v Crosbie*, 1996 S.L.T. (Sh. Ct.) 86 and *Gribb v Gribb*, 1996 S.L.T. 719.

[99] s.167(2).

[1] By s.17 of the FLSA 2006.

the compensation may form part of the matrimonial (or civil partnership) property. As with ordinary pensions, compensation received also has to be apportioned so that only that part attributable to the marriage or civil partnership is available for distribution between the parties.[2] Unlike other rights under a pension scheme, however, which can be shared by a pension sharing order[3] or be made subject to an order earmarking a lump sum,[4] the court cannot make any such orders against the compensation payable from the pension protection fund.[5]

Valuation is of course only the start of the difficulties associated with pensions. Dividing an asset such as a pension, which has a nominal value at the relevant date, but in fact may not be realisable as a liquid asset until many years after the divorce, presents severe practical problems. We discuss possible solutions to this problem at paras 13–47 to 13–51 below.

Net Value of Matrimonial/Partnership Property

It is the "net" value of the matrimonial/partnership property which **13–39** is to be shared between the parties under s.9(1)(a). This is calculated by taking the gross value of the matrimonial/partnership property at the relevant date, and deducting any outstanding debts. The debts must have been incurred by either party before or during the marriage/partnership, in connection with matrimonial property, and be outstanding at the relevant date.[6] For example, a mortgage taken out on the security of the family home will be deducted to produce the net value of the home; while loans incurred to purchase moveables should similarly be deducted.[7] However, capital gains tax which is notionally payable on such property is not deductible.[8]

---

[2] This is to be done in accordance with regulations made by the Scottish Ministers under s.10(8B).

[3] Under s.12A(2).

[4] Under s.12A(3).

[5] See s.8(4A) inserted by s.17(2) of the FLSA 2006.

[6] 1985 Act, s.10(2). In *Mackin v Mackin*, 1991 S.L.T. (Sh. Ct.) 22, a house was purchased from the husband's employers with a penalty attached to resale within 5 years. When this penalty was imposed because the spouses separated within 5 years, the value of the property was treated as being the market value less the imposed penalty. In *Buchan v Buchan*, 1992 S.C.L.R. 766, arrears of tax and penalties relating to the period before separation were held to be deductible debts although not calculated until after separation. But *cf. McCormick v McCormick*, 1994 G.W.D. 35-2078 where estimated tax on H's business profits was not deductible; and *Latter v Latter*, 1990 S.L.T. 805, where notional capital gains tax was not deductible from the value of shares held by one spouse.

[7] See *Jesner v Jesner*, 1992 S.L.T. 999.

[8] The Lord Ordinary in *Sweeney v Sweeney*, 2003 S.L.T. 892 held that in determining the net value of the matrimonial property it was permissible to deduct the capital gains tax notionally payable by the husband. However, the Inner House in *Sweeney v Sweeney*, 2004 S.C.L.R. 256 found that the Lord Ordinary had erred in upholding such a deduction for: "it is, rightly, conceded on behalf of the husband that any hypothetical liability of his to capital gains tax arising on the assumption that he had disposed of matrimonial property on that date does not fall to be deducted as

Special Circumstances

13–40   After the net value of matrimonial/partnership property has been calculated, in principle under s.10(1) the property is to be shared equally between the parties unless there are "special circumstances" to justify a different division. Without prejudice to the generality of s.10(1),[9] s.10(6) lists certain circumstances which particularly justify such a departure, and which are examined below. It should be noted that although these circumstances may justify departure from equal sharing, they cannot *require* it: where the circumstances cited are of negligible significance, or opposing special circumstances counterbalance each other, then equal division may be allowed to stand.[10] In each case, what matters is what constitutes *fair* sharing under s.10(1).

(i) "the source of the funds or assets used to acquire any of the matrimonial property [or partnership property] where those funds or assets were not derived from the income or efforts of the [persons] during the marriage [or partnership]"[11]

13–41   As we have seen above, where property owned by a spouse/civil partner is acquired by gift or succession from a third party, then it is prima facie not matrimonial/partnership property. However, where such property is sold and the proceeds are then used to acquire new assets which do constitute matrimonial/partnership property, then unequal sharing of these assets may be justified.[12] Similarly, where property owned solely by one party before the marriage/civil partnership, e.g. a bachelor flat, is sold during the marriage/partnership

---

being an outstanding debt. No 'netting' provision in respect of matrimonial property other than for outstanding debts is expressly made in the statute [1985 Act]", at 264D.

[9] One "special circumstance" not listed in s.10(6) is where one party has had the sole use of the family home since the date of separation. The usual practice in these circumstances is, however, to seek an incidental order for interest: see paras 13–88 and 13–89 below.

[10] *Jacques v Jacques*, 1997 S.L.T. 459, *per* Lord Clyde.

[11] s.10(6)(b).

[12] See *Davidson v Davidson*, 1994 S.L.T. (OH) 506 where the court awarded the wife more than a half share of the value of the matrimonial home, which represented the parties' only matrimonial property, on the grounds that it had been purchased entirely by the wife with money derived from her inherited shareholdings. See also *R v R*, 2000 Fam. L.R. 43 where the court held that the fact that to a large extent the net value of the matrimonial property derived from assets donated to or inherited by the defender did constitute a special circumstance which justified departure from the presumption of an equal division of these assets. However, in this case the court also acknowledged that, although special circumstances existed, due weight had to be given to the other s.9 principles, especially s.9(1)(b), as the wife had suffered a financial disadvantage in being unable to pursue her career because of her commitment to caring for their children and the family home (although it did not quantify this). This case has been criticised on the grounds that whatever special circumstances exist they *cannot* be circumstances which constitute successful claims under other s.9 principles because the other principles are not factors to be used in determining a fair division of assets under s.9(1)(a). They represent claims that exist *in addition to* those associated with a fair division.

to purchase items which are matrimonial/partnership property, then the same argument may be raised. In *Cordiner v Cordiner*,[13] for example, the court held that where the husband's assets had amounted to £107,000 prior to marriage and the wife had had no capital assets, this justified a departure from equal sharing of matrimonial property under ss.10(1) and 10(6)(b) and deducted the value of the husband's pre-marital assets from the net value of the matrimonial property at the relevant date, distributing what remained in equal shares. In *Kerrigan v Kerrigan*,[14] the husband's mother provided the whole of the deposit put down on the matrimonial home, and the husband paid the whole mortgage during the marriage, which lasted only two months. Although title to the house was taken in joint names, the court awarded the whole of the house to the husband. A similar decision was reached in *Mukhtar v Mukhtar*[15] where sheriff Horsburgh ordered the husband to transfer his half share of the family home over to his wife, effectively giving her the whole of the matrimonial property. In this case, the wife's father had provided a £50,000 deposit toward the house and guaranteed a secured loan for the balance of £146,000, He also made all but two of the monthly payments on the property. The marriage, with no children, was very short lived lasting less than two months. In these circumstances the sheriff rejected the husband's claim that the house was a joint gift by the wife's father, and hence not matrimonial property under s.10(4). If this had been the case then under ordinary property law the division of its value would have had to be in equal share. The sheriff, however, held that the father had never intended the make a joint gift and that all his expenditure had been undertaken to benefit his daughter. The title had only been put in joint names because both the husband and the wife's income had to be taken into account to support the loan that was taken out. In reaching his decision, the sheriff declined to follow the dictum of Lord MaFadyen in *Cunningham v Cunningham*[16] to the effect that the source of funds used to purchase the matrimonial home is less important than would be the case with other kinds of matrimonial property. He observed that the remark in *Cunningham* had been made in the context of a long-standing marriage where both parties had used their separate and substantial inheritances to purchase matrimonial property. How intention is interpreted in these circumstances is important. In *Le Riche v Le Riche*,[17] where the couple were married for two years, Sheriff Lothian declined to depart from the norm of equal sharing where the funds for the family home had come almost entirely from the wife's family. He took the view that if the couple had intended to reflect the substantial contribution by the

---

[13] 2003 Fam. L.R. 39.
[14] 1988 S.C.L.R. 603.
[15] 2002 Fam. L.B. 60-7.
[16] 2001 Fam. L.R. 12.
[17] 2001 Fam. L.B. 51-8,

wife's family, the title to the property should have been taken in unequal shares.

13-42 How courts of first instance view all the circumstances of the case is important. In *Phillip v Phillip*,[18] a quarter of the original price of the family home came from the sale by the husband of his house owned prior to the marriage, some 20 years before. Despite the lapse of time, the court held that a quarter of the value of the home at the relevant date was to be deducted from the assets and given to the husband, before dividing the remainder equally between the spouses.[19] However, in *Jacques v Jacques*,[20] the Inner House and, subsequently, the House of Lords held that although the matrimonial home had been purchased during the marriage with the proceeds of a house owned solely by the husband prior to the marriage, this was, in the circumstances, of little importance and did not justify unequal division. The particular facts of the case justifying this decision were that the spouses had occupied the house owned by the husband together before their marriage, and had agreed to take title to the new home in both names.[21] As the Lord President observed in *Little v Little*[22]:

> "The concept of sharing the net value of the matrimonial property fairly, the flexibility which is given by the expression 'special circumstances' in section 10(6) and the repeated references in section 11 to all the other circumstances of the case serve to emphasise that, despite the detail, the matter is essentially one of discretion, aimed at achieving a fair and practicable result in accordance with common sense. It remains as important as it always has been that the details should be left in the hands of the court of first instance and not opened up for reconsideration on appeal".

(ii) "the nature of the matrimonial property [or partnership property], the use made of it (including use for business purposes or as a [family] home) and the extent to which it is reasonable to expect it to be realised or divided or used as security"[23]

13-43 *Nature of property* In *Skarpaas v Skarpaas*,[24] the court held that damages paid to a husband, to compensate him for personal injury

---

[18] 1988 S.C.L.R. 427.

[19] See also *Budge v Budge*, 1990 S.C.L.R. 144, where the matrimonial home was purchased with £7,000 derived by the husband from the sale of a home inherited solely by him: the court held that only the increase in value of the house since the marriage should be equally shared with the wife.

[20] 1995 S.L.T. 963; affirmed by the House of Lords, 1997 S.L.T. 459.

[21] The agreement to take the house in joint names was arguably another "special circumstance" under s.10(6)(a) which counter-balanced the issue of the source of the purchase price of the house.

[22] 1990 S.L.T. 785 at 787B-C.

[23] s.10(6)(d).

[24] 1993 S.L.T. 343.

inflicted on him before the relevant date (but during the subsistence of the marriage) were matrimonial property. However, the part of this award representing solatium and compensation for loss of future earnings was held to be so "essentially personal to the defender" that there were special circumstances to award the husband more than half of the sum in question.[25] In *McGuire v McGuire's Curator Bonis*,[26] however, only a small part of the solatium element of an award of criminal injuries compensation was unevenly divided on this basis, the rest of the award being split 50:50. Similar reasoning may apply to redundancy payments aimed at compensating one spouse personally for his or her loss of future earnings.

Use of property The use of the matrimonial home, particularly as a **13–44** home for young children, may be invoked to justify unequal division of that home.[27] In *Peacock v Peacock*,[28] it was argued that if the value of the matrimonial home was to be divided equally between the spouses, then neither spouse would have sufficient funds to purchase a new home which could house the two children of the marriage. In these special circumstances, the sheriff ordered the husband to transfer his half share in the matrimonial home to the wife, who had legal custody of the children, although all she could transfer to him in return was an insurance policy worth £643. The decision was upheld by both the sheriff principal and the Inner House.[29] But in *Adams v Adams (No.1)*[30] the Lord Ordinary refused to accept an argument that the two children of the marriage, aged 14 and 12, would experience an unacceptable disruption to their lives if they were forced to leave the family home.[31]

An alternative approach may be to accept that the matri- **13–45** monial/family home should be divided in equal shares, but to ask the court to make an incidental order that sale be delayed and that the spouse/civil partner with care of the children should continue to reside there as a sole occupier until the last child reaches, say, the age

---

[25] See also *Petrie v Petrie*, 1988 S.C.L.R. 390.

[26] 1991 S.L.T. (Sh. Ct.) 76.

[27] See *Cooper v Cooper*, 1989 S.C.L.R. (Sh Ct) 347 where the sheriff held that the fact the house was required as a home for the pursuer and the three children of the marriage (one of whom was under 16 and another who was still in full-time education and had special needs) that if sold would render them homeless was a circumstance that made it unreasonable to expect the house to be realised and that s.19(6)(d) applied. See also *Murphy v Murphy*, 1996 S.L.T. (Sh CT) 91 where the court held that given the wife would have care of the parties' child after divorce, that the house was necessary for the child's welfare, that the husband had alternative accommodation and that the wife would receive no payment from the pension rights or otherwise, special circumstances existed justifying an unequal division of matrimonial property in the wife's favour to the extent of transferring the husband's interest in the matrimonial home.

[28] 1994 S.L.T. 40.

[29] See also *Murphy v Murphy*, 1996 S.L.T. (Sh. Ct.) 90.

[30] 1997 S.L.T. 144.

[31] *ibid.* at 148.

of 16.[32] Orders of this kind were once frequently used in the English courts. They have, however, fallen from favour because, on the one hand, they create short-term hardship for the non-resident spouse, whose capital is locked up without compensation and, on the other hand, may produce sudden homelessness for the spouse with care of the children at a future date, when there is no guarantee that he or she will have more in the way of assets to acquire a new home.

13–46   Another case where matrimonial property may be unevenly divided because of its use is where the family home is used by one spouse to run a business, e.g. a farm, a "bed and breakfast" or a dental practice. In *Geddes v Geddes*[33] the husband purchased a farm with his own money for use as a family home. This was the couple's only significant asset. The sheriff awarded the wife not one-half of the net value, which would have required the sale of the farm, but only one-fifth, to be paid by six instalments from the date of divorce. This was because, as the court remarked in *Mayor v Mayor*,[34] "one should hesitate long and hard before ordaining the disposal of an income producing asset such as the family business". As in *Geddes*, the power of the court to order the payment of a capital sum by instalments out of the income of the payer may be usefully applied to resolve the conflict between giving one spouse a reasonable award, and not destroying the livelihood of the other spouse, where the marriage is poor in capital assets.

13–47   *Realisability of property*   Most cases relating to this issue have dealt with the division of rights under pension schemes. As we noted above, dividing pensions rights at the date of divorce presents difficulties, because although the rights in question can be valued as matrimonial property using the rules outlined at paras 13–27 and 13–28 above, in most divorces the pension will not yet have reached maturity, and it may be many years before any funds are due to be paid out. The courts are therefore faced with the difficulty of equitably sharing the value of an asset which does not yet exist in liquid form.

13–48   *Example:* H and W divorce in 2006. H is a member of an occupational pension scheme, with benefits payable on either retirement or death in service. His date of retirement is 2023. His rights in the scheme, as at the relevant date and referable to the period of the marriage, are valued at £80,000. Applying the norm of equal sharing, W should receive £40,000. But H may have no other realisable resources at the date of divorce, in which case he can only make such a payment, if at all, by borrowing money. H cannot sell or assign his rights in the pension fund to a third party to procure immediate cash because, for tax reasons, pension schemes invariably do not allow their members

---

[32] Under s.14(2)(d)(i) and (ii).
[33] 1993 S.L.T. 494.
[34] 1995 S.L.T. 1097 at 1101.

to do this, even where the third party is a spouse or ex-spouse. If W receives the £40,000 at the date of divorce, she is effectively receiving accelerated rights in H's pension while H must wait, as usual, until the pension matures. However, W may suffer in the long term, as she may well spend the lump sum received at the date of divorce, e.g. on new housing for herself and the children, and then have no pension (unless she has made sufficient contributions into her own independent pension) to sustain her in old age.

A number of options exist to circumvent this problem. The parties **13–49** may agree, among themselves, to trade off the value of the pension rights against some other asset of matrimonial property, notably the member spouse's interest in the matrimonial home where it is owned in common. Research suggests that such trade-offs are commonly agreed in preference to splitting the value of pension rights.[35] Where both spouses have a pension, their respective rights may cancel each other out. Where agreement is not reached, however, it is possible to argue that "special circumstances" exist to depart from equal sharing of the value of the pension rights because of the unrealisable nature of the asset.[36] In a number of cases, judges have on this basis awarded less than 50 per cent of the value of the pension rights to the non-member spouse, and sometimes as little as a third.[37]

It is submitted, however, that such discounting is both inequitable **13–50** and unnecessary. There are other ways to get around the lack of liquid assets accessible by the member spouse at the date of divorce. The courts can order payment of a capital sum by instalments out of the income of the member spouse[38] or defer payment of part or all of the capital sum until a fixed date in the future, such as death or retirement.[39] Most usefully, the courts have the power under s.12A[40] to "earmark" a proportion or fixed lump sum amount of the pension for the benefit of the non-member spouse, payable at the date when the pension matures. This avoids altogether the difficulty of the lack of liquid resources at the date of divorce. Such a "pension lump sum order" can be ordered by the courts when making an order for a capital

---

[35] Wasoff, McGuckin and Edwards, *Mutual Consent: Written Agreements in Family Law* (Scottish Office Central Research Unit 1997), Ch.4.

[36] This approach was expressly approved by the Inner House in *Little v Little*, 1990 S.L.T. 785.

[37] See *Fleming v Fleming*, 1993 G.W.D. 9-621; *Stephen v Stephen*, 1995 S.C.L.R. 175 where only a third of the transfer value of the pension was awarded to the pensioner's wife (amounting to £38,240) and, of that sum, payment of £15,000 was deferred until the death or retirement of the husband (who was aged 52 and expected to retire at 65).

[38] 1985 Act, s.12(3). *Johnstone v Johnstone*, 1990 S.L.T. (Sh. Ct.) 79.

[39] 1985 Act, s.12(1)(b). *Stephen v Stephen*, 1995 S.C.L.R. 175 *Bannon v Bannon*, 1993 S.L.T. 999, where the court deferred payment until date of retirement but with an increased award to allow for the saccumulation of interest during this period; *Shand v Shand*, 1994 S.L.T. 387.

[40] As inserted by s.167(3) of the Pensions Act 1995.

sum but is ordered against the trustees or managers of the pension scheme of the payee spouse, rather than against the spouse him- or herself. This allows for easier enforcement of the order. It is important to note that: (i) the court's power to make such an order arises only if it is making a capital sum order, not an order for a periodical allowance; and (ii) that where such an order is made, it *does not accelerate* the right to payment. Both the member and non-member spouses will receive payment only when the pension rights become due: normally, on the retirement or earlier death of the member spouse.

13–51   "Earmarking" was a major improvement to the scheme of the 1985 Act and should help considerably to alleviate old-age poverty for women, particularly those who have been traditional homemakers. A problem which remains with earmarking, however, is that the rights of the non-member spouse are dependent on the pension fund of the member spouse. What happens, for example, if the pension scheme is fraudulently denuded of assets before the date of maturity, as in the *Maxwell* case? Or if, at the date of maturity, no pension materialises because it has been lost due to the misconduct of the member spouse, as is sometimes the case with military pension schemes? This problem can be avoided by craving the court to make a pension lump sum order against the pension fund trustees, but also, as an alternative and subsidiary remedy only, to make a capital sum order directly against the member spouse. Another problem is that earmarked benefits will usually be payable on the date of retirement or death in service of the *member spouse*. This may be an unhelpful date of payment for the non-member spouse who may reach retirement earlier or later. A better option still, therefore, is that of "pension splitting" discussed at para.13–35 above, where parties make a qualifying agreement[41] or the court makes a pension sharing order under s.8(1)(baa) of the 1985.[42] This permits the court to split the current value of the pension rights in question at the time of divorce/dissolution, and to transfer the non-member's share of these pension rights into independent rights in the same scheme, or into any other occupational scheme or money purchase scheme of their choice. The effect is to give the non-member spouse/civil partner an independent pension which can then be enhanced, if desired, by the payment of further contributions after the date of divorce.

(iii) "any destruction, dissipation or alienation of property by either [person]"[43]

13–52   The rationale of this head is that a spouse/civil partner who has wilfully reduced the total value of the matrimonial property which

---

[41] WRPA 1999, s.28(1)(f), s.28 (1)(f), Pensions on Divorce etc. (Pension Sharing) (Scotland) Regulations 2000 (SI 2000/10510), regs 3 and 5.

[42] The order is defined in the 1985 Act, s.27 (as amended by WRPA 1999, s.20).

[43] s.10(6)(c).

would otherwise have been available for distribution should not be entitled to a full half-share of the property. In *Short v Short*[44] a wife dissipated assets by fraudulently borrowing £20,000 on the security of the matrimonial home without the knowledge of her husband. Her half-share of the matrimonial property was reduced by subtracting nominally the debt she had run up from the total value of the matrimonial assets, before equal division of what remained.[45] Dissipation requires some positive action by a spouse. Thus, in *Park v Park*[46] the husband's failure to meet mortgage payments led to the forced sale of the matrimonial home at a loss. The court did not reduce his share of the matrimonial property, holding that "a passive failure to take definite steps to prevent destruction, dissipation or alienation is not sufficient".[47] The spouses were joint owners in *Park* and the wife could have made the payments herself or at least taken steps to deal with the situation.

Where dissipation occurs its effects cannot always be rectified, **13–53** especially where there are few matrimonial assets. In *Fraser v Fraser*[48] the only matrimonial property was the husband's interest in a pension scheme valued at £105,000 at the relevant date. On equal division of the matrimonial property the wife should have been entitled to £52,500. However, the husband retired early, received a lump sum and dissipated it on a failed business. At the date of divorce no resources existed sufficient to justify the making of a capital award in favour of the wife.[49]

(iv) "the terms of any agreement between the [persons] on the ownership or division of any matrimonial property [or partnership property]"[50]

Where parties have entered into an agreement as to the division of **13–54** their matrimonial/partnership property, the court will enforce it unless any term in it is successfully challenged on the ground that it was not fair and reasonable at the time that it was entered into.[51] The way in which couples have agreed to take title to property, e.g. buying the family home in both names, is not generally regarded as an

---

[44] 1994 G.W.D. 21-1300.
[45] See also *Goldie v Goldie*, 1992 G.W.D. 21-1225.
[46] *Park v Park*, 1988 S.C.L.R. 584.
[47] *ibid.* at 587. This approach was followed in *Russell v Russell*, 1996 G.W.D. 15-895 where the court held that s.10(6)(c) required something more than the course of bad luck which had affected the wife's business decisions including losing her job and investing capital in unsuccessful business ventures.
[48] 1994 Fam. L.B. 10-3.
[49] The court *could* have awarded a capital sum payable by instalments out of the annual periodical element of the pension, which still existed. It did not do so, however, because the husband needed this income to support his 13-year-old son who lived with him.
[50] s.10(6)(a).
[51] See s.16(1)(b). This is discussed further at paras 15–08 *et seq.* and 15–20.

"agreement", since it does not relate explicitly to division of matrimonial property.[52]

(v) "the actual or prospective[53] liability for any expenses of valuation or transfer of property in connection with the divorce [or the dissolution of the civil partnership]"[54]

13–55   This provision ensures that any one spouse/civil partner who is ordered to transfer all or part of an item of property to the other is not unfairly burdened with the expenses of the transfer. The expenses of valuation or transfer undertaken by one spouse/civil partner can be taken into account to reduce the other spouse's share of the matrimonial property. However in *Sweeney v Sweeney*,[55] the court took the view that capital gains tax payable on a transfer of property is not an expense for this purpose.

Conduct

13–56   In reaching a decision as to whether or not special circumstances apply to divert from equal sharing in any particular case, the court is expressly directed to ignore the issue of conduct on the part of either spouse/civil partner unless it has adversely affected relevant financial resources or it would be manifestly inequitable to leave the conduct out of account.[56] This is most likely to arise under the head of dissipation of assets, e.g. where a spouse has gambled away the assets of the marriage. The amoral behaviour is not relevant as "special circumstances" *per se*, but the financial consequences of that behaviour are. This provision on conduct, is not just limited to a consideration of special circumstances, but pertains generally to the application of s.9 principles.

Special Circumstances Overall

13–57   The foregoing give rise to situations in which special circumstances may come into play, but the mere fact that they are found to exist does not render it mandatory for the court to depart from the norm of equal sharing, for the court must not only be satisfied that such circumstances justify a departure but also that such a departure is fair and reasonable having regard to the parties' resources. In considering the facts of a case there may well be an overlap between circumstances that may support the application of other s.9 principles (apart from

---

[52] But see obiter comments of Lord Clyde in *Jacques v Jacques*, 1997 S.L.T. 459, who felt s.10(6)(a) might not be so limited.

[53] See *Farrell v Farrell*, 1990 S.C.L.R. 717, where the court took account of the future costs of division and sale of the matrimonial home at a date after divorce; but *cf. Adams v Adams (No.1)*, 1997 S.L.T. 144.

[54] s.10(6)(e).

[55] 2003 S.L.T. 892 (OH) at 901C–D.

[56] s.11(7)(a)–(b).

s.9(1)(a)) and that may also fall within the remit of the special circumstances referred to in s.10(1) of the 1985 Act. Where this is the case, as a commentator on the case of *Dehvasati v Dehvasati*[57] has observed, courts must be careful not to focus unduly on such circumstances, as "the tendency to treat everything as special circumstances devalues these other principles".[58]

Second Principle: s.9(1)(b)—Economic Advantage and Disadvantage and Contributions

In some cases, the norm of equal sharing of matrimonial/partner- **13–58** ship property is inappropriate for reasons which do not fall within the special circumstances in s.10(1) and (6). Section 9(1)(b) is designed primarily to deal with the not uncommon situation where one party (the "homemaker") has given up or reduced his or her career prospects to care for the other and, possibly, the children of the family, while the other party (the "wage-earner") has continued to work and benefited from this arrangement in terms of earnings and career advancement.[59] The homemaker will often find it difficult to maintain his or her standard of living after divorce/dissolution without the support of the wage-earner. Prior to the 1985 Act, such a spouse could have expected to be supported for at least some while after divorce by periodical payments ordered against the wage-earner spouse. The scheme of the 1985 Act, however, prefers to foster clean breaks and capital settlements, rather than continuing dependent relationships. But a capital settlement based on equal sharing of the matrimonial/partnership property may not be sufficient to compensate for the long-term economic disadvantage the homemaker may have suffered in terms of blighted career prospects, earnings level, and the associated benefits such as occupational pension rights. For this reason, the 1985 Act provides that, in addition to the principle of fair sharing under s.9(1)(a), the court must also consider whether,

> "fair account should be taken of any economic advantage derived by either [person] from contributions by the other, and of any economic disadvantage suffered by either [person] in the interests of the other [person] or of the family" (s.9(1)(b)).[60]

---

[57] 2003 Fam. L.B. 63-3.

[58] *ibid.* at 63-4. In this case what amounted to "special circumstances" could just as easily have been dealt with under principles 9(1)(b) and (c).

[59] For a particularly clear and comprehensive analysis of the disadvantages experienced by the "homemaker" post divorce and the comparative advantages of the "wage earner" post divorce, see the opinions of the House of Lords in the recent joint English cases of *Miller v Miller* and *McFarlane v McFarlane*, 2006 UKHL 24, in particular the opinion of Lord Nicholls of Birkenhead, especially paras 90–99.

[60] See *Buchan v Buchan*, 2001 Fam. L.R. 48 where the court held that it was pertinent to take into account the pursuer's various roles throughout the marriage as joint breadwinner, housekeeper, mother and teacher which justified an award under this heading. The court also took other factors into account, such as the contribution of

13–59 "Economic advantage" extends to include any advantage gained before or during the marriage or civil partnership and includes gains in capital, income and earning capacity, while "economic disadvantage" is defined as the converse.[61] "Contributions" are defined to include any contributions made before or during the marriage or civil partnership[62] and expressly cover indirect and non-financial contribution, in particular, any such contributions made by looking after the family home or caring for the family.[63]

13–60 The great advantage of this principle is that it can be used to make an award where there is little or no matrimonial/partnership property.[64] However, in practice, the courts have tended to be reluctant to

---

a capital sum made by the pursuer's parents towards the family home (which was repossessed through the defender's failure to maintain mortgage payments) as well as the defender's conduct which had an adverse affect on the parties' financial resources. As a result of all these considerations the court elected to depart from the norm of equal sharing and to make property transfer orders that would have the effect of giving the pursuer sole title to the matrimonial home and to an endowment policy. See also *Symanski v Symanski (No.2)*, 2005 Fam. L.R. 2 where the Sheriff Principal upheld a finding by the sheriff that no share of the matrimonial property should be paid to the defender/husband because, inter alia, he had gained economic advantage from the pursuer before the marriage from the injections of capital into his businesses (which subsequently failed). The defender had attempted to argue that when he was discharged from bankruptcy this had the effect of discharging him of all debts and obligations from the date of discharge, including any economic advantage derived from the pursuer. He argued that the pursuer, in seeking an unequal share of the matrimonial property as a spouse, was seeking to derive a financial benefit which would not be available to the defender's creditors. His argument was unsuccessful because the court held that the matrimonial property was entirely derived from property owned by the pursuer and so, far from seeking to obtain any advantage over other creditors, the pursuer was simply seeking to prevent the defender from obtaining a share of that property on account of the imbalance between contributions made by the pursuer and the total absence of any contributions by the defender.

[61] 1985 Act, s.9(2). See *Wilson v Wilson*, 1999 S.L.T. 249 (OH) where the court held that where a wife did not receive the expected gains in lifestyle during marriage because her husband ploughed his earning back into his farming business this amounted to a "contribution" by the wife. See also *Quinn v Quinn*, 2003 S.L.T. (Sh Ct) 5 where the court observed that maintaining the family home after separation, which on divorce will be shared equally, might qualify as a disadvantage if it can be quantified appropriately.

[62] s.9(2).

[63] *ibid.* See *Cahill v Cahill*, 1998 S.L.T. (Sh Ct) 96 where the court took into account renovations that that the pursuer husband had made during the marriage to a cottage owned by the defender that was not matrimonial property. The court held that the economic advantage that the defender derived from the improved cottage was one that came about through the pursuer's efforts during the marriage, the advantage being gained when the improvements were carried out although the benefit might not be realised until a subsequent date.

[64] In *Dougan v Dougan*, 1998 S.L.T. (Sh Ct) 27 there was no matrimonial property to be shared out but the court did make an award to the pursuer under s.9(1)(b) because "it is quite clear that the pursuer suffered an economic disadvantage in giving up a well paid position in the interests of the family and, even though the marriage was a short one, the disadvantage to the pursuer was substantial" at 30. See also *Johnston v Johnston*, 2004 Fam. L.B. 70-6 where a wife tried unsuccessfully

make awards under s.9(1)(b). This is because they are instructed when applying s.9(1)(b) to take into account the extent to which:

"(a) the economic advantages or disadvantages sustained by either [person] have been balanced by the economic advantages or disadvantages sustained by the other [person], and

(b) any resulting imbalance has been or will be corrected by a sharing of the value of the matrimonial property [or the partnership property] or otherwise".[65]

The kind of problems that arise in establishing a claim under the section are demonstrated in *Coyle v Coyle*.[66] In this case the wife pursuer had given up a successful career at her husband's request to undertake domestic tasks and childcare after the marriage. Had she continued working she would have earned substantial sums during the marriage and have built up a substantial pension. She argued that these losses should be compensated. However, the court held that the section did not provide for automatic compensation and that the pursuer had not established an identifiable economic advantage her spouse had enjoyed which derived from an identifiable contribution of hers and which was fair to take account of. While it was true that the husband would have had to pay for domestic and childcare services if she had continued to work it was also the case that she would have been earning a good salary and thus increasing the family's wealth. There was not any obvious connection between the increase in the value of his business and her non-financial domestic contributions. **13–61**

In dealing with this ground the court had to balance the economic disadvantages suffered by each party and then see whether any resulting imbalance had been corrected by a fair sharing of the matrimonial property or otherwise. It had to take account of the interplay between the two principles and reach an overall view of the fairness and reasonableness of the financial provision to be awarded. In this case an additional award was not justified as there was sufficient matrimonial property to compensate her adequately by a share of it. Indeed the wife benefited from a property transfer order in relation to the former family home which had increased substantially in value from the relevant date to the date of proof. This was held to correct any economic disadvantage which she suffered in the interests of her husband and family. While this appears to be fair in the circumstances of this case, the failure to make an award on the basis of the wife's non-financial contributions to the home and family because of the failure to establish a nexus between her domestic activities and the **13–62**

---

to get an award under this heading in order to get at the much more valuable non-matrimonial property that represented her husband's interest in a farming partnership.

[65] s.11(2).

[66] 2004 Fam. L.B. 67-6 and 67-7.

increase in the value of her husband's business may cause hardship in other cases where there is insufficient matrimonial property to be divided among the parties.

13–63   It is often successfully argued that either the advantages and disadvantages suffered or gained by the spouses have balanced themselves out,[67] or that any imbalance has been sufficiently accommodated through the equal sharing of matrimonial property under s.9(1)(a). So, for example, in *Welsh v Welsh*,[68] the husband was employed throughout the whole 18 years of the marriage and had acquired a full pension and other benefits. The wife argued that their standard of living had only been achieved because she had given up a good job to look after the family and home, and as a result she had been economically disadvantaged. The court found, however, that as the husband had supported her throughout the marriage and as she was now sharing in the value of the home purchased solely with his earnings, their contributions balanced each other out, and so no s.9(1)(b) award was appropriate.[69]

13–64   The prevailing judicial view seems to be that in most cases, domestic family arrangements work to the mutual benefit of both spouses, and that the spouse who earns the most does not necessarily gain an unfair advantage over the spouse who opts not to work, or to work part-time. Where awards have been made under s.9(1)(b), they have tended to provide compensation for actual financial contributions made during the marriage by one spouse to the other,[70] or where the labour of one spouse has enhanced the value of an asset which does not form part of the matrimonial property, e.g. a house acquired before marriage by one spouse and subsequently used as the family home or business.[71] However, giving up professional employment to look to the family's needs over a number of years *has* been taken account of by some courts, especially where this has resulted in reduced employment prospects for that spouse.[72]

---

[67] *Adams v Adams (No.1)*, 1997 S.L.T. 144.

[68] 1994 S.L.T. 828.

[69] See also *Petrie v Petrie*, 1988 S.C.L.R. 104.

[70] See *Buchan v Buchan*, 1993 G.W.D. 23-1515, where the court took into account the fact that the wife continued to make the same financial contribution to the parties' joint bank account despite the fact that she had taken a substantial cut in salary on marriage. See also *Macdonald v Macdonald*, 1994 G.W.D. 7-104 and *Farrell v Farrell*, 1990 S.C.L.R. 717.

[71] See *Ranaldi v Ranaldi*, 1994 S.L.T. (Sh. Ct.) 25 where the court awarded the wife half the increase in value of the family home (which was not matrimonial property) over the period of the marriage, to reflect the labour she had put into running it as a boarding house.

[72] See *Louden v Louden*, 1994 S.L.T. 381, where 55% of the property was awarded to the wife because she had given up a job as a secretary and looked after a child, while the husband pursued a successful business career during their 17-year marriage. In *Clokie v Clokie*, 1994 G.W.D. 3-149, the property was unequally divided in favour of the wife because she had prejudiced her academic career to further that of her husband. See also *McCormick v McCormick*, 1994 G.W.D. 35-2078.

The court's restrictive approach to s.9(1)(b) is well illustrated in **13–65** *De Winton v De Winton*.[73] In this case, although the marriage was a wealthy one, there was no matrimonial property at all to divide under s.9(1)(a), as all the property had been acquired by the spouses prior to the marriage. The husband owned property amounting to some £1 million, while the wife had a shareholding in a family company worth £160,000. During the marriage, the wife used her money to pay for the children's education at private schools and to raise the standard of living in the household. On divorce, the wife's only possible claim was under s.9(1)(b) as there was no matrimonial property and the children were over the age of 16. The court accepted that she had suffered economic disadvantage, but found that no economic *advantage* had been conferred on the husband, as he would not have chosen by himself to pay for the children to attend private schools, and her other expenditures were on unnecessary luxuries. An award of £30,000 was, however, made, to compensate the wife for financial contributions she had put into the husband's business.

Third Principle: s.9(1)(c)—Fair Sharing of Economic Burden of Childcare

Section 9(1)(c) requires that: **13–66**

"any economic burden of caring,
[(i)] after divorce, for a child of the marriage under the age of 16 years should be shared fairly between the [persons]".
[(ii) after dissolution of the civil partnership, for a child under that age who has been accepted by both partners as a child of the family,]

Section 9(1)(c) is not designed directly to provide for the maintenance of the child, as this is the function of the rules relating to aliment and child support,[74] but rather to make allowance for the fact that even where aliment or child support is paid, there may be economic costs involved in caring for a child which ought to be taken into account when adjusting the spouses' financial position on divorce. As some 40 per cent of divorcing couples have children under 16[75] this is an important consideration. When assessing the level of award under s.9(1)(c), the court is directed to consider a range of factors under

---

[73] 1996 Fam. L.B. 23-6.
[74] See Ch.5.
[75] See *Annual Report of the Registrar General for Scotland, 1995*. Also National Statistics Online, *Dependent Children by Family Type UK, 2004*—1 in 4 children now reside in lone parent families (22% headed by a lone mother; 2% by a lone father) In 2003, 153,500 children under 16 were affected by their parents divorcing in England and Wales, just over 1 in 5 were under 5 years old. Downloaded from *www.statistics.gov.uk/CCI/nugget.asp?ID=1163*.

s.11(3) which include the age and health of the child,[76] the educational, financial and other circumstances of the child,[77] and the needs and resources of the persons.[78] The court may also take into account any support provided by the defendant to dependants, whether or not he or she is legally obliged to provide such support.[79]

13–67   An award under s.9(1)(c), unlike s.9(1)(a) and (b), may be made in the form of a periodical allowance order as well as an order for a capital sum or transfer of property.[80] The courts have often appeared less reluctant to make substantial capital awards under s.9(1)(c) than s.9(1)(b). In *Morrison v Morrison*,[81] for example, the wife was awarded two-thirds of the value of the home and contents so that she could look after the children aged 13 and 10. In *Macdonald v Macdonald*,[82] a wife who assumed the financial burden of bringing up five children, paying for the mortgage and hiring domestic help, was awarded more than half of the capital of the marriage. In some cases the burden of childcare may constitute "special circumstances" to divert from equal sharing under s.9(1)(a), as well as justify an award under s.9(1)(c).[83]

13–68   Since the introduction of the Child Support Act 1991, s.9(1)(c) has become less important. However, in *Maclachlan v Maclachlan*[84] Lord Macfayden expressed the view that although the enactment of the Child Support Act 1991 had greatly reduced the scope for reliance on s.9(1)(c), it had not wholly superseded it, for,

> "The fact that one parent has to purchase a house large enough, not only to accommodate herself, but also to provide suitable accommodation for the children, seems to me to be an aspect of the economic burden of caring for the children after divorce. If an award of a capital sum would enable that burden to be more fairly shared, I see no reason why reliance cannot be placed on section 9(1)(c) as justifying such a capital sum".[85]

---

[76] s.11(3)(d).
[77] s.11(3)(e).
[78] s.11(3)(g).
[79] s.11(6).
[80] s.13(2).
[81] 1989 S.C.L.R. 574.
[82] 1994 G.W.D. 7-104.
[83] See, e.g. *Peacock v Peacock*, 1994 S.L.T. 40.
[84] 1998 S.L.T. 693 (OH).
[85] *ibid.* at 698K. However, such an award was not justified in this case as the wife would have more than sufficient resources to purchase a suitable house for the children and herself out of the proceeds of sale from the matrimonial home. Nor was he prepared to award a capital sum to the wife to enable her to make provision for future school fees. He took the view that: "While I do not go so far as to exclude the possibility of its ever being appropriate to make a capital award to enable such future expenditure to be provided for, I am of opinion that the court should be slow to make capital provision for a revenue expense" (at 698F).

Further, where a maintenance assessment has not been made,[86] or in **13–69** certain other circumstances, a claim under s.9(1)(c) may still be viable.

In *Russell v Russell*,[87] for example, the husband received substantially more than a half share of the pension rights which were the entirety of the matrimonial property, on the basis that in order to bring up the three children of the marriage, he had had to take early retirement, which meant reduction of these rights. Under these circumstances a s.9(1)(c) award was justified. Courts are, however, reluctant to give the parent who is caring for children an increased share of the value of the matrimonial home, through ordering the other parent to make a property transfer order, where there are insufficient funds or resources to maintain the property. In *Shipton v Shipton*,[88] for example, the court declined to order the husband to transfer his half share in the family home over to the wife who wanted to continue living there with the children because the wife could not afford to keep up the mortgage payments. For this reason the sheriff ordered the home to be sold.[89]

REMAINING S.9 PRINCIPLES

Sections 9(1)(d) and (e) allow for an award to be made on divorce/dis- **13–70** solution by the court where the principles in s.9(1)(a)–(c) are insufficient to provide adequately for one spouse/civil partner after the divorce/dissolution, i.e. where one spouse has been financially dependent on the other to a substantial degree[90] or is likely to experience serious financial hardship on divorce.[91] When introduced, it was envisaged these sections would be invoked only in fairly narrow circumstances, namely where one spouse, usually the wife, had removed herself for some time from the labour market in order to look after the family and home and had become financially dependent on the husband and could not now be expected to re-enter employment. Even in such a case, an adequate "clean break" settlement can often be constructed under s.9(1)(a)–(c). In some marriages, however, perhaps because there is little or nothing in the way of capital assets to share under s.9(1)(a), or because the wife has taken her half share of the matrimonial property in the form of the family home, leaving her with no resources for day-to-day expenses, a s.9(1)(d) or (e) award may be appropriate.

It is open to the courts to apply s.9(1)(d) or (e) or both, where it con- **13–71** siders that appropriate.[92] In dealing with claims under both s.9(1)(d)

---

[86] See *Proctor v Proctor*, 1994 G.W.D. 30-1814.
[87] 1996 Fam. L.B. 21-5.
[88] 1992 S.C.L.R. (Sh Ct) 23.
[89] The same result occurred in *Symon v Symon*, 1991 S.C.L.R. (Sh Ct) 414 and in *Adams v Adams (No.1)*, 1997 S.L.T. 144 (OH) for the same reason.
[90] s.9(1)(d).
[91] s.9(1)(e).
[92] *Stott v Stott*, 1987 G.W.D. 17-645.

and (e), the court must consider a number of factors including the age, health, and earning capacity of the claimant, as well as the needs and resources of both parties[93] together with all other circumstances of the case.[94] In addition, the court has a discretion to take account of any support given by the defender spouse to dependants within the household.[95] Conduct is relevant to s.9(1)(d) and (e) not only where it has affected the financial resources of the marriage, but also where it would be manifestly inequitable to leave it out of account.[96]

Fourth Principle: s.9(1)(d)—Adjustment from Financial Dependence

13–72   Section 9(1)(d) provides that a person who has been financially dependent to a substantial degree on the financial support of the other person should be awarded such financial provision as is reasonable to allow him or her to adjust to the loss of that support on divorce/dissolution, over a period of not more than three years from the date of divorce/dissolution.[97] What the Act clearly envisages is that for many homemakers the three-year period will provide a transitional stage during which they can retrain or re-enter the labour market with a view to reacquiring financial independence.[98] Section 11(4) lists various factors the court should consider when making an award under s.9(1)(d), including notably "the duration and extent of the dependence of [the claimant] prior to divorce". In *Sweeney v Sweeney*,[99] the sheriff made an order for periodical allowance to be payable monthly for one year from the date of decree of divorce. This was justified by the fact that the pursuer had not worked independently since the birth of her first child in 1982 (twenty years earlier), during which time she had been wholly dependent upon the defender, who had been making monthly payments to her backdated to the date of separation. The sheriff accepted her contention that she would try to retrain, but that while she would like to do office work again, it might be hard for her to get a job given the length of time since she had last worked and her age.

---

[93] 1985 Act, s.11(4)(a) and (d) and (5)(a) and (d). "Needs and resources" are defined to include foreseeable needs and resources under s.27(1).

[94] s.11(4)(e) and (5)(e).

[95] s.11(6).

[96] s.11(7)(b).

[97] But see *Sullivan v Sullivan* (OH), 2003 Fam. L.R. 53 where the court held that an award of a periodical allowance until remarriage or death was competent (although it might extend beyond a three-year period) given that the capital sum awarded to the defender was modest and that she also had the burden of looking after the two children of the marriage. Lord Emslie held: "In such circumstances, it was in my view open to the sheriff to conclude that there was a continuing dependency here which could not adequately be satisfied by means of a capital award alone, and that in order to avoid hardship a continuing periodical allowance at the specified date would be justified", at 59.

[98] 1985 Act, s.11(4) specifically requires the court when making a s.9(1)(d) award to have regard to the claimant spouse's earning capacity, and any intention they have to undertake a course of education or training.

[99] 1993 S.L.T. (Sh Ct) 892.

As a result she would need time to adjust to the loss of support and while acknowledging that she would in due course,

> "be able to have the benefit of income produced by any capital paid, it will, on the face of it, take some time for her to obtain the full benefit of that, and I see no reason why she should be expected to use part of the capital to meet her income needs".[1]

However, where a spouse has managed to survive in the period **13–73** between separation and divorce without any alimentary support from his or her partner, even if only by reducing his or her standard of living, this is often viewed by the courts as showing lack of dependence and hence prejudice any award under this head, especially if the period between separation and divorce has been lengthy.[2]

Where a s.9(1)(d) award is made, it usually takes the form of a peri- **13–74** odical allowance order[3] although a capital sum or property transfer order is also competent.

The time limit of three years for a periodical allowance payable **13–75** under s.9(1)(d) has been recently criticised in the House of Lords as part of the opinions in the joint case of *Miller v Miller* and *McFarlane v McFarlane*.[4] In both cases there was insufficient capital to enable a clean break. The McFarlanes sought a "joint lives" order,[5] the dispute being the actual amount that should be paid in respect of each of the children of the marriage and for Mrs McFarlane. By the time the case reached the House of Lords, Mrs McFarlane was also trying to have the original period of payment reinstated after the Court of Appeal had limited this to five years only. In his judgement, Lord Hope of Craighead took the opportunity to discuss principle 9(1)(d) of the Family Law (Scotland) Act 1985 and to criticise the limitation of three years it places on a periodical allowance payable to enable a person to adjust to life post-divorce. He states:

> "The length of the period for which a periodical allow- ance should be awarded should no longer be confined to an absolute maximum of three years. The court should have a discretion to provide for a longer period . . . in exceptional circumstances".[6]

---

[1] *ibid.* at 2003K.
[2] See *Dever v Dever*, 1988 S.C.L.R. 352; also *Millar v Millar*, 1990 S.C.L.R. 666, where the Sheriff Principal commented that one must consider the level of support prior to the date of divorce and ask whether an award of financial provision is desirable to enable the claimant to adjust to that loss.
[3] s.13(2)(a).
[4] 2006 UKHL 24. Note: these are cases decided under English law.
[5] Being an order available in the law of England and Wales for periodical payment which cannot extend beyond the joint lives of the parties and automatically comes to an end if the party receiving the periodical payment remarries or upon the death of one party.
[6] Above, n.4, para.121.

The Scottish Executive are reported to have said in response that they are considering carefully the cases down south and any implications for Scotland.[7]

13–76 However, there are a number of other means by which payments from income may be made when capital is insufficient to meet the s.9 principles. For example, a capital sum can be made payable by instalments out of income[8] or a periodical allowance granted under of s.9(1)(c) and (e) may be made for a definite or indefinite period or until the happening of a specified event.[9] It is also not unknown for a court to award a three-year periodical allowance followed by an immediately subsequent order under s.9(1)(e) of the Act.[10] For further discussion of these orders see paras 13–81 to 13–89 below.

Fifth Principle: s.9(1)(e)—Serious Financial Hardship

13–77 Section 9(1)(e) provides that a person who, at the time of the divorce/dissolution seems likely to suffer serious financial hardship as a result of the divorce/dissolution should be awarded such financial provision as is reasonable to relieve this hardship over a reasonable period.[11] There are two crucial points to note here. First, whereas an award under s.9(1)(d) is limited in duration to three years, a s.9(1)(e) award can be of unlimited duration.[12] Secondly, the "serious financial hardship" that is to be relieved is restricted to that occurring at the time of, and *as a result of*, the divorce. A direct causal link between the divorce and the hardship is thus required. In *Barclay v Barclay*,[13] the wife was permanently disabled by multiple sclerosis. The court, however, declined to make an award under s.9(1)(e) because although the wife was indeed suffering serious financial hardship, this was caused not by the separation and pending divorce, but by a deterioration in her medical condition. However, a periodical allowance for three years was awarded under s.9(1)(d) to allow for adjustment from dependence.

13–78 Interestingly, although s.9(1)(e) requires that the hardship stem from the divorce itself and not any other factor such as illness, it does

---

[7] 2006 Edinburgh Law News 556. Downloaded from *www.law.ed.ac.uk/sln/index.aspx?page=563*.

[8] s.12(2) and s.12(3).

[9] s.13(3).

[10] We are grateful to David Nichols for his insightful comments on court practice in this respect.

[11] See *Galloway v Galloway*, 2003 Fam. L.R. where court awarded a periodical allowance of £1,000 a month on this ground to be payable until the pursuer, aged 55, reaches the age of 60 (when she could access deferred pension rights) or her death or remarriage, whichever of the foregoing dates comes first.

[12] See *Mackenzie v Mackenzie*, 1991 S.L.T. 46 and *Johnstone v Johnstone*, 1990 S.L.T. (Sh. Ct.) 79, where in each case periodical allowance awards were made to wives until their remarriage or death; *Bell v Bell*, 1988 S.C.L.R. 457 where an award was made payable until the wife reached 60 or remarriage or death, whichever was earlier.

[13] 1991 S.C.L.R. 205.

not apparently require, as s.9(1)(d) does, that the claimant spouse be financially dependent on the other spouse. In *Haugan v Haugan*[14] a 51-year-old woman was left by her high-earning husband after 27 years of marriage. There was no matrimonial property nor capital assets and she applied for a periodical allowance for an indefinite period under s.9(1)(e) on the basis that she had negligible employment prospects due to physical and mental illness as well as the lack of any qualifications. Her husband argued that any hardship suffered by her was not "as a result of the divorce" as, since their separation a year or so earlier, he had not paid her any aliment. During this time she had lived off income support and was thus strictly financially dependent at the date of divorce on the state, rather than her husband, which would normally exclude a s.9(1)(d) claim. The court found that the loss of the right to aliment on divorce would itself be a hardship brought about by the divorce, and that accordingly a s.9(1)(e) award, of unlimited duration, was appropriate. This view was upheld by an extra division of the Inner House[15] who made it clear that,

> "While the pattern of actual support afforded prior to the divorce, including any period of separation, is among the factors to be taken into account when assessing whether the loss of the right to aliment is likely to give rise to that hardship, the presence or absence of such actual support cannot be determinative of that matter. The fact that prior to divorce a spouse has failed to fulfil his or her obligation of support to the other cannot, even when active steps have not been taken to enforce it, exclude the making of financial provision in accordance with the principle set out in section 9(1)(e); nor can the fact that at the date of the divorce the claiming party is already suffering such hardship".[16]

However, the court accepted that since the first case there had been a material change in the defender's financial circumstances and that a reduction to £500 a month was reasonable having regard to the parties' resources.

At the end of the day *Haugan* has the rather odd result that it may **13–79** in some cases be easier to establish a right to unlimited support under s.9(1)(e) than three-year support under s.9(1)(d), a result surely not intended by the drafters of the Act. But, as Thomson has suggested,[17] a better approach might have been to order a capital award under s.9(1)(b), payable if necessary by instalments out of the husband's income.[18]

---

[14] 1996 S.L.T. 321.

[15] 2002 S.L.T. (Ex Div) 1349.

[16] *ibid.* at 1352H-I.

[17] Thomson, *Family Law in Scotland* (3rd edn, 1996), p.146.

[18] But see A. Bissett-Johnson's concerns about the limitations of a capital sum in "Financial Provision on Divorce in Scots law—Does it Need Reform?", 2000 J.R. 265 discussed at para.13–97 below.

13–80   In assessing what amounts to "serious" financial hardship, the applicant's access to sources of support other than the spouse, which includes state benefits, must be considered.[19] As *Haugan* demonstrates, the fact that a spouse may be entitled to state benefits does not automatically mean he or she is not suffering serious financial hardship (indeed it is often the fact of serious financial hardship which makes a person eligible for state benefits). The courts have tended to consider the degree to which the standard of living of a particular spouse will drop on divorce,[20] and the extent to which this has already been cushioned by an award for financial provision based on s.9(1)(a)–(d) of the Act.[21] Where the drop in standard of living as a result of divorce is minimal, because the spouses were already living at a low income level prior to separation, an award has usually not been granted.[22] It must be remembered that s.9(1)(e) is concerned not with alleviating serious financial hardship in general, but only that arising as a result of the divorce/dissolution. Hence it is has been sometimes said anecdotally that s.9(1)(e) is mainly of use to middle-class wives, who are accustomed to a standard of living which may plummet as a direct result of divorce.

COURT ORDERS

13–81   In order to implement the objectives of the 1985 Act, the courts are given power to make a wide range of orders. These can be divided into:

   (a) orders making financial provision for the parties, including an order for payment of a capital sum,[23] for transfer of property,[24] and for payment of a periodical allowance[25];
   (b) incidental orders under s.14(2);
   (c) anti-avoidance orders under s.18; and
   (d) enforcement orders under ss.19 and 20.

Financial Orders

13–82   As a periodical allowance takes the form of a regular payment made by one spouse to another, it undermines the principle of a clean break. For this reason, the courts are directed as far as possible to deal

---

[19] See s.11(5)(a) and (d).
[20] s.11(5)(c).
[21] But see *MacKenzie v MacKenzie*, 1991 S.L.T. 461 where an award under s.9(1)(e) was made to a wife although she was also receiving a substantial capital sum under the other principles.
[22] See *Barclay v Barclay*, 1991 S.C.L.R. 205 where s.9(1)(e) was not applied because the reduction in the wife's weekly income post divorce amounted to only around 5%.
[23] s.8(1)(a).
[24] 1985 Act, s.8(1)(aa), as inserted by the Law Reform (Miscellaneous Provisions) (Scotland) Act 1990, Sch.8, para.34.
[25] s.8(1)(b).

with financial provision by means of orders for payment of a capital sum or transfer of property. The courts may make an order for a periodical allowance only where it can be justified by s.9(1)(c), (d), or (e), and only where a capital sum or property transfer order would be inappropriate or insufficient to meet the demands of the s.9 principles, given the resources available to the parties.[26] In many marriages it is difficult to order a capital "clean break" settlement because there are few or no liquid capital assets available at the date of divorce. However, a spouse or civil partner who has no current access to capital may nonetheless have an expectation of acquiring some at a future date, e.g. under an insurance policy, pension scheme, or other investment. Alternatively, the paying spouse/civil partner may have a high enough salary to be able to pay off a capital sum by instalments out of income. The courts are therefore given the power to defer the date of payment of the capital sum,[27] and to order payment of capital by instalments.[28] The kind of flexibility that the courts have can be illustrated by *Crosbie v Crosbie*,[29] where the sheriff made an order for payment of a capital sum to be made in three stages. The first payment was to be made on decree of divorce; the second within seven days of settlement of sale of the matrimonial home; and the third was to be made out of fixed monthly instalments payable after the divorce.

It is important to note that an order for payment of capital by instalments is quite different from an order for payment of a periodical allowance, because although both may be paid out of recurrent income, the amount payable under a capital sum order cannot be varied once made. The courts are, however, empowered to vary the date or method of payment on a material change of circumstances,[30] e.g. if an expected pay-out from an investment fails to materialise or if a job is lost or pay-cut imposed.

The flexibility of capital sum orders has been enhanced further by **13–83** the insertion of s.12A into the 1985 Act, which empowers the court to make an order for payment of a lump sum out of a pension fund at the date of maturity of the pension (a "pension lump sum order")[31] against the trustees or managers of a pension scheme. The effect of such an order was discussed above at para.13–35.

Given the importance of clean break settlements in the scheme of **13–84** the 1985 Act, the number of capital sum orders made by the courts is at first glance surprisingly low. In 1991, such orders were only made in five per cent of ordinary divorce actions with an average amount payable of £4,000–£6,000.[32] One of the reasons for the

---

[26] s.13(2).
[27] s.12(2).
[28] s.12(3).
[29] 1995 Fam. L.B. 14-6.
[30] s.12(4).
[31] Under s.8(1)(ba) as inserted by s.167(1) of the Pensions Act 1995.
[32] See Morris, Gibson and Platts, *op. cit.* above, n.3, at p.33.

relatively low incidence of court orders for capital sums is because in many marriages with substantial amounts of capital, such payments are agreed under the terms of a separation agreement rather than sought by means of a court order.[33] However, it remains to be shown whether application to the court for capital sum orders have increased with the introduction of pension lump sum orders under s.12A.

13–85   Another option open to the courts, and in keeping with the philosophy of a clean break, is to make a property transfer order. The transfer may be stipulated to take place at the date of divorce or at a future specified date.[34]

13–86   As noted above, in theory, periodical allowance orders should only exceptionally be made under the s.9 principles.[35] However, in practice they still feature in divorce although there is some evidence that their numbers are declining.[36] Awards are most likely to be made in cases where the marriage has lasted for 30 years or more, and least likely to be ordered where the marriage lasted 10 years or less.[37] A periodical allowance order can be granted for a definite or indefinite period or until the happening of a specified event, e.g. the youngest child reaching the age of 16.[38] A periodical award under s.9(1)(d) is of course limited to a maximum duration of three years.[39] A periodical allowance award falls on the death of or remarriage/entering into a

---

[33] Capital sum payments from one spouse to the other are agreed in some 30% of minutes and joint minutes of agreement: see Wasoff, McGuckin and Edwards, *op. cit.*, above, n.35, at p.20.

[34] 1985 Act, s.12(2). For discussion of the difficulties that this may create see Cousine, "Property Transfer Orders: Some Conveyancing Imponderables" (1990) 35 J.L.S.S. 52 and "Reply" by E. Clive, (1990) 35 J.L.S.S. at p.118.

[35] For an argument in favour of extending their use see A. Bissett-Johnson, "Lifestyle Support or Provisions for the Middle Aged Wife", 1999 S.L.T. 37.

[36] See Morris, Gibson and Platts, *op. cit.* above, n.3, p.32. Periodical awards were made in 20% of ordinary divorce actions in 1989, 16% in 1990 and 15% in 1991. Note, there is a lack of available statistical information on the awards granted in divorce actions. Other statistics pertaining to divorce and civil proceeding in general however may be downloaded from the Scottish Executive website: *www.scotland.gov.uk/Publications/2004/02/18897/33079*.

[37] See Morris, Gibson and Platts, *op. cit.* above, n.3, p.32, Table 26. Interesting recent discussion of the relevance of the length of the marriage in respect of the amount of award, can be found in the opinions of House of Lords in the case of *Miller v Miller* [2006] UKHL 24 in which a wife was awarded £5 million pounds when her marriage failed in under three years. This was, however, only one-sixth of her husbands estimated worth and it was said she had had "reasonable expectation" of a lengthier marriage. She had petitioned for divorce on the grounds of his adultery. The House of Lords also discussed the relevance of conduct in the making of an award.

[38] s.13(3).

[39] An award under s.9(1)(d) need *not* of course be made for the full possible period of three years. See *Muir v Muir*, 1989 S.L.T. (Sh. Ct.) 20 where a wife was awarded a periodical allowance for one year under s.9(1)(d); *Sheret v Sheret*, 1990 S.C.L.R. 799 (periodical allowance awarded for 13 weeks). But see *Sullivan v Sullivan*, above, para.13–72, n.97, where a sheriff's award until remarriage or death was upheld even although it might extend beyond the three year period.

civil partnership of the payee.[40] Like an order for transfer of property or payment of a capital sum, a periodical allowance can be postponed until the defender is in a position to pay it.[41]

Either party or his executor may apply to the court for variation or **13–87** recall of a periodical award if they can show that a material change of circumstances has occurred.[42] The court has power to backdate, vary or recall any award to the date of the application, or on cause shown, to an earlier date.[43] In addition, it has the power to convert a periodical allowance order into a capital sum or property transfer order.[44]

Incidental Orders

The court has the power to make one or more incidental orders to **13–88** assist it in implementing its decision under the s.9 principles.[45] Section 14(2) gives the court power, inter alia, to order the sale or valuation of property,[46] to regulate the occupation of the matrimonial home after divorce/dissolution, to declare the property rights of the spouse/ partners, to allocate liability for household outgoings after the divorce/dissolution, and to order that security be given in respect of any financial provision ordered.[47] In general, the court can make any ancillary order which it feels necessary in order to give effect to the s.9 principles.[48] Any incidental order made must be justified under the s.9 principles and be reasonable having regard to the resources of the parties.[49]

An incidental order for interest[50] is frequently sought where there **13–89** is a lapse in time between the date at which payment of a capital sum or transfer of property is ordered—usually the date of divorce— and the date at which the capital is actually paid or the property transferred. There was for a time some disagreement as to whether interest

---

[40] 1985 Act, s.13(7)(b). Where the *payer* rather than *payee* dies, the order continues to operate against the Deceased's estate: s.13(7)(a).

[41] *Shipton v Shipton*, 1992 S.C.L.R. (Sh Ct) 23.

[42] s.13(4).

[43] s.13(4)(a) and (b).

[44] 1985 Act, s.13(4)(c). This is useful where the payer dies since the liability for payment on his estate can be converted into a lump sum.

[45] A spouse cannot apply for an incidental order under s.14(2) in isolation but only in connection with an order for financial provision: *MacClue v MacClue*, 1994 S.C.L.R. 933. See Also *Reynolds v Reynolds*, 1991 S.C.L.R. (Sh Ct) 175.

[46] See *Thomson v Thomson*, 2003 Fam. L.R. (Sh Ct) 22 where the sale was ordered but postponed.

[47] In *Murley v Murley*, 1995 S.C.L.R. 1138, the court used this power to guarantee payment to the husband of a certain percentage of the value of the family home at a date after the divorce. The husband was ordered to transfer his share in the house to his wife, on condition that she took out a standard security over the property to the value of a certain sum which would be payable to the husband on either the wife's sale of the home, or the youngest child's 18th birthday, whichever was earlier.

[48] s.14(2)(k).

[49] See *Geddes v Geddes*, 1993 S.L.T. 494 at 499.

[50] s.14(2)(j).

on a capital sum could be awarded in respect of a period prior to the date of divorce. The Inner House made it clear in *Geddes v Geddes*[51] that such an award is competent[52] and would be justified, inter alia, where one spouse had had sole occupation of a family home owned in common since the date of separation, and the other party had therefore suffered loss of use for that period.[53]

13–90 Sheriffs now have power to dispense with the grantor's execution of a deed dealing with moveable property in favour of execution by the sheriff clerk.[54]

Anti-Avoidance Orders

13–91 It is possible a spouse/civil partner may seek to reduce his or her potential liability to make financial payments to the other spouse/civil partner on divorce, by giving away property or selling assets at a below market value, with the intention of reducing the total value of the matrimonial property or reducing his or her apparent resources at the date of divorce/dissolution. In order to prevent such fraudulent behaviour, the court may, under s.18, set aside or vary the terms of any transaction or transfer of property which had the effect of defeating a claim for financial provision.[55] The court may in addition make such an order in relation to the property as it thinks fit.[56] Application under s.18 may be made up to a year after the date of the divorce.[57] However, transactions or transfers can only be reduced or varied if they have occurred within the previous five years.[58] The court also has power to act proactively to prevent such fraudulent transactions, by issuing interdict against either spouse/civil partner.[59] The rights of third parties who acquire property in good faith and for value from a spouse/civil partner or a party further down the chain are protected.[60]

13–92 *Example:* H gives away a flat worth £100,000 to his girlfriend G in 1995. In 1997 he seeks a divorce. The flat was acquired in H's sole name but during the marriage and so would have fallen intomatrimonial

---

[51] 1993 S.L.T. 494.

[52] Overruling *Carpenter v Carpenter*, 1990 S.L.T. (Sh. Ct.) 68 and *Skarpaas v Skarpaas*, 1991 S.L.T. (Sh. Ct.) 15.

[53] See also *Welsh v Welsh*, 1994 S.L.T. 828.

[54] See subpara.(ja) inserted into s.14(2) by s.18 of the FLSA 2006. Sheriffs previously could do so in relation to heritable property where the grantor of deeds could not be found, refused or was unable, or failed to execute the deed. However, in an increasing number of matrimonial cases, courts are being asked to make orders for the transfer of moveable property such as insurance policies.

[55] s.18(1).

[56] 1985 Act, s.18(2). In *Tahir v Tahir (No.2)*, 1995 S.L.T. 451 the court set aside decree pronounced against the former husband for payment of a loan which was found to be fictitious.

[57] s.18(1).

[58] s.18(1)(i).

[59] 1985 Act, s.18(1)(ii). See *Hernandez-Cimorra v Hernandez-Cimorra*, 1992 S.C.L.R. 611.

[60] See s.18(3).

property if he had still owned it at the date of divorce. The gift to G can clearly be reduced as she did not take for value.[61] But what if G had sold the flat in 1996 to third party X, who took for full market value and without knowledge of H, or the divorce? X appears at first glance to take for value and in good faith, in which case the sale will not be reducable. Nor, it seems, can the proceeds of the sale to X be regarded as "resources" available to H under s.8(2), as they belong to G. It can be argued however that if X knew when purchasing that G had acquired the flat for free—as he is likely to do from examining the title—then he might be barred from pleading good faith.[62]

Enforcement Orders

The court has the power, on cause shown, to grant warrant for inhibition or arrestment on the dependence of the action in which a claim is made.[63] The court may also order that either spouse/civil partner reveals details of their financial resources.[64]   **13–93**

Finally, it should also be noted that until decree of divorce/dissolution is granted, the court has power to award interim aliment to either spouse/civil partner.[65]   **13–94**

ASSESSMENT

The five principles contained in s.9 of the 1985 Act attempt to strike a balance between providing a framework which limits and regulates the discretion of the court when awarding financial provision on divorce, and now on dissolution of civil partnership, and allowing the court room for manoeuvre to produce an equitable solution on the very different facts of each case. The principles can only ever be guidelines in a process whose aim is to reach an outcome that is both justified by the law and fair to the parties. Each case will be solvable by a number of different disposals, each of which can be justified under the law. In certain cases, such as, notably, *Little v Little*,[66] the courts have quite clearly not restricted themselves to a textbook application of the s.9 principles but have taken a more flexible approach in the interests of efficiency and equity. On the other hand, as we saw in   **13–95**

---

[61] s.18(3)(a).

[62] *Hay v Jamieson* (1672) Mor. 1009; Erskine IV, I, 36; Bell, *Comm.*, iii, 183. Where this argument fails, however, the gift can be regarded as dissipation, and thus as special circumstances to justify W being given more than 50% of the matrimonial property under s.10(6)(c). But this will be of little consolation if there is no matrimonial property by the date of divorce to divide.

[63] s.19.

[64] s.20.

[65] s.6.

[66] 1990 S.L.T. 785. A similar broad practical approach was applied in the case of *McVinnie v McVinnie (No.2)*, 1996 G.W.D. 24-1383 and upheld by the Sheriff Principal.

the discussion of the pre-FLSA 2006 case of *Wallis*, the courts cannot ignore the clear words of the statute simply to produce what seems a fairer result. In *Little* itself, the Lord Ordinary declined to aggregate the total net value of the spouses' assets and share it equally between them, or in some other division justified by special circumstances, as is the normal procedure under s.9(1)(a). Instead, he held that certain items of matrimonial property already de facto divided up by the spouses, such as their cars, were to be left out of calculation, and then went on to split the remaining assets, including the matrimonial home, in equal shares according to their valuation at the date of divorce. In effect, this did not produce an equal split of the total value of the matrimonial property as at the relevant date. The Inner House, found this approach a practical one, which, in the special circumstances of the case, gave rise to fair sharing of the property as required in s.10(1). Thomson has criticised the decision in *Little* as erroneous in terms of the s.9 scheme[67]; but it can also be endorsed as reflecting an underlying current of equity and pragmatism often found in first instance decisions on financial provision.

13–96 The fact that the decision in *Little* was upheld by the Inner House highlights the extent to which appeal courts are reluctant to reverse the decisions of the court that first hears the case and has the benefit of hearing all the evidence first hand. This is particularly true in relation to decisions on financial provision, where despite the detail of the legislation, the decision taken is fundamentally an exercise of discretion. An appeal court will thus only reverse the decision reached by a lower court if the court misdirected itself in law, failed to take into account a relevant or material factor or reached a result which was manifestly inequitable or plainly wrong.[68] To reiterate Lord Hope's comment in *Little*:

> "the matter is essentially one of discretion, aimed at achieving a fair and practicable result in accordance with common sense. It remains as important as it always has been that the details should be left in the hands of the court of first instance and not opened up for reconsideration on appeal".[69]

13–97 It is important to realise that the s.9 principles, and the powers of the court, however skilfully manipulated, are not in themselves capable of preventing poverty on the breakdown of every relationship. In many marriages, there simply is no property to divide on

[67] J. Thomson, "Financial Provision on Divorce—Undermining the 1985 Act", 1990 S.L.T. (News) 313.

[68] *Per* Lord President Hope in *Little* at p.786K-L, citing Lord Guthrie's dictum in *Gray v Gray*, 1968 S.L.T. 254 at 258. But see J. Thomson, "Essentially Discretionary? Financial Provision on Divorce", 2000 Scottish Law Gazette 169 critiquing this approach on the grounds that it ignores the clear and rational structure of the Act by over privileging judicial discretion.

[69] At 787D; affirmed by the House of Lords in *Jacques v Jacques*, 1997 S.L.T. 459.

divorce,[70] although the 1985 Act does help by providing the possibility of the payment of a capital sum by instalments out of income or future resources, and by contemplating the splitting of pension rights. However, Bissett-Johnson has drawn attention to what he perceives to be weaknesses under the Act,[71] especially where dealing with support for older, home-based wives following divorce. He not only argued in favour of giving courts discretion to take into account the increase in value of non-matrimonial assets during a marriage, as well as any increases in the value of matrimonial property after the relevant date—proposals taken on board by the Executive in the FLSA 2006—but also questioned whether a "clean break" on divorce, established through a capital award, is always desirable. He makes the case for extending the courts discretion to award a periodical allowance on the grounds that capital sums may in some cases be disadvantageous. Further to this, as we have discussed,[72] the House of Lords in the recent joint case of *Miller v Miller* and *McFarlane v McFarlane*[73] have also discussed the undesirability of limiting the time period over which any periodical allowance can be made. In the current climate, lump sum payments are not inflation proof and low return on interest rates may force the recipient to encroach on capital in order to meet living costs. Furthermore, in such circumstances it is questionable whether the lump sum will adequately provide a wife with a sum equal to the loss of salary and career prospects that she may have suffered during marriage. In addition the payment of a capital lump sum will (unlike transfer of the matrimonial/family home) usually result in excluding eligibility to apply for state support and passported benefits such as free dental care, by taking the transferees savings over the statutory limit for state support. Those most at risk here are older women who may find it hard to increase their income through employment given the "age prejudice" they may encounter. Despite European legislation[74] outlawing such discrimination, this is hard to police in practice. The difficulties such women experience may be compounded by

---

[70] Financial awards other than aliment for children were only made in some 14% of ordinary divorces in Morris, Gibson and Platts, *op. cit.* above, n.3 at p.28. In many of the other 86% of cases, of course, property will exist but have been divided by agreement rather than court order. See also paras 15–01 and 15–06.

[71] A. Bissett-Johnson, "Lifestyle Support or Provision for the Middle Aged Wife", 1999 S.L.T. 37, A. Bissett-Johnson, and C. Barton, "Financial Provision on Divorce in Scots Law—Does it Need Reform?", 2000 J.R. 265.

[72] Para.13–75.

[73] [2006] UKHL 24.

[74] See Framework Equality Directive, Council Directive 2000/78 establishing a general framework for equal treatment in employment and occupation (Official Journal L 303/16.2 December 2000). For discussion, see C. O'Cinneide, *Age discrimination and European Law*, Employment & Social Affairs: Fundamental rights and anti-discrimination, European Commission Directorate-General for Employment, Social Affairs and Equal Opportunities Unit D.3, (April 2005). Legislation on age in the UK is scheduled to be implemented in October 2006 and it will cover employment

the fact that there is some evidence from English solicitors that the lump sum payments sought may not have been adequately calculated where they are intended to cover both lost income and relocation and housing expenses or where they are used to "top up" a pension or provide a retirement income.[75] In addition, if such capital is payable by instalments, there is a risk that the balance of the sum may be lost if the husband becomes bankrupt.[76] The advantage of awarding a periodical allowance is that, unlike a capital sum, it can be varied up or down to take account of a material change in the parties' circumstances, and where bankruptcy occurs, periodic payments from income to meet the needs of a bankrupt's former spouse and family are protected as they are excluded from vesting in the trustee in bankruptcy.[77]

Cohabitants

13–98   It is important to note that, as we have commented in earlier chapters, *unmarried* partners have no right to seek an award *equivalent* to that of financial provision on divorce/dissolution upon the breakdown of their relationship. However, couples separating after the May 4, 2006 are able under s.28 of the FLSA 2006 to apply for a financial award within a year of the date of ceasing to cohabit (other than by reason of the death of one of them).[78] Section 28 is modelled on the economic advantages and disadvantages principle in s.9(1)(b) of the 1985 Act yet with no requirement for an award to be reasonable with regard to the resources of the parties. The Law Commission in England has undertaken a consultation to ascertain whether people south of the border consider whether family law, as it pertains to cohabitants, requires reform.[79] It has been said that the modest reforms introduced in Scotland by the FLSA 2006 give "cavernous" discretion to the courts[80] who are likely to attach a lot of weight to the period of cohabitation.[81]Importantly, there remains no entitlement to aliment or to a periodical allowance but award is limited to

---

and vocational training for people of all ages. It will be the final strand of equality legislation to be implemented and it will be enforced alongside existing legislation on race, sex, disability, sexual orientation, religion or belief.

[75] S. Arthur, and J. Lewis, *Pensions and Divorce: Exploring Financial Settlements* (HMSO Research Report 118, Social Security, 2000), p.31.

[76] W. McBryde, "Financial Provision on Divorce and Sequestration", 1996 S.L.T. (News) 389.

[77] Bankruptcy (Scotland) Act 1985, s.32 as amended by s.261(2), Sch.28, Pt 3, para.34 of the 2004 Act extending cover to civil partners.

[78] 1985 Act, s.28(1). Note that the definition of cohabitant under s.25 of the Act includes same-sex cohabitant couples.

[79] The Law Commission, *Cohabitation: the Financial Consequences of Relationship Breakdown*, Consultation Paper, No.179 (May 4, 2006): *www.lawcom.gov.uk/docs/cp179.pdf*.

[80] So described by Morag Wise, Q.C. in 2006 Fam. L.B. 80-3.

[81] *ibid.*

payment of a capital sum, either on a specified date or in instalments[82] and an interim order is permissible [83]

Prior to the passage of the FLSA 2006, cohabiting couples could **13–99** only regulate the division of their assets on breakdown of relationship by entering a separation or cohabitation contract, an option that remains open to them. Married couples and now civil partners may also sometimes have good reason to wish to exclude the jurisdiction of the courts and make their own enforceable agreements about division of property should their relationship end in divorce/dissolution.[84] The benefits for them are the avoidance of uncertainty as to how a court will exercise its discretion under the Act, the fact that the couple are empowered to regulate their own affairs rather than submitting to the approach taken by the court, and the possibility of conducting often acrimonious disputes in privacy rather than in open court.[85] Agreements have become of increasing importance since the introduction of the 1985 Act, and will be discussed in detail in Ch.15.

---

[82] s.28(7)(a)–(b).
[83] s.28(1)(c).
[84] See s.16. Grounds for setting aside such agreements under common law and by virtue of s.16(1) are discussed in Ch.15.
[85] Solicitors are conscious of, and promote these benefits: see Wasoff, Dobash and Harcus, *The Impact of the Family Law (Scotland) Act 1985 on Solicitor's Divorce Practice* (Scottish Central Research Unit, Edinburgh, 1990), pp.77–79.

CHAPTER 14

DIVORCE AND DISSOLUTION: GROUNDS AND PROCESS

DIVORCE

14–01 The Divorce (Scotland) Act 1976 ("1976 Act"), s.1(1), provides that the only two grounds for divorce are that the marriage has broken down irretrievably or that an interim gender recognition certificate has been issued to either party after the date of marriage.[1] Irretrievable breakdown can be established only on the basis of one of the five fact situations set out in s.1(2). As Lord Prosser observed in *Findlay v Findlay*:

> "The question for the court is thus not a general one, as to whether the marriage has broken down irretrievably in any ordinary sense of those words, but is a particular question as to whether the subsequent provisions of the Act have been satisfied".[2]

OVERVIEW

14–02 Prior to reforms instituted by the Family law (Scotland) Act 2006, irretrievable breakdown of the marriage could be established on the following grounds:

- adultery (s.1(2)(a));
- intolerable behaviour (s.1(2)(b));
- desertion (s.1(2)(c));
- two years non-cohabitation with consent (s.1(2)(d));
- five years non-cohabitation without the need for consent (s.1(2)(e)).

Since the May 4, 2006,[3] the grounds for establishing irretrievable breakdown are:

---

[1] Under the Gender Recognition Act 2004 Sch.2, Pt 2, para.6 which amended s.1(1) of the 1976 Act.

[2] 1991 S.L.T. 457 at 458.

[3] The Family Law (Scotland) Act 2006 (Commencement, Transitional Provisions and Savings) Order 2006 (SSI 2006/212).

- adultery;
- intolerable behaviour;
- non-cohabitation for one year with the other party's consent to divorce; or
- non-cohabitation for two years without the need for consent.

Actions for divorce raised prior to the May 4, 2006 Act are dealt with under the old law contained in the unamended 1976 Act.

Civil Partnership[4]

The provisions governing the dissolution of a civil partnership are to **14–03** be found at Pt 3, Ch.5, ss.117–122 of the Civil Partnership Act 2004.[5] As is the case for divorce, there are two grounds on which an action for dissolution may be founded, being irretrievable breakdown of the civil partnership or the granting of an interim gender recognition certificate to either party after the registration of the civil partnership.[6] The grounds for establishing irretrievable breakdown are the same of those for married couples with the omission of adultery as a ground.[7] Consistent with the changes to the 1976 Act, desertion was removed as a grounds for dissolution by the FLSA 2006.[8]

The Grounds for Divorce—Discussion

Divorce can only be obtained on the basis of "irretrievable break- **14–04** down" if it is established on one of the grounds set out in s.1(2) of the 1976 Act. These may be summarised as adultery, behaviour, one years' non-cohabitation by the spouses where both consent to the divorce, and two years' non-cohabitation by the spouses where there is no mutual consent. When the Gender Recognition Act 2004 came into force on the April 4, 2005, the second basis on which divorce may be granted was added to Scots law, namely, that an interim gender recognition certificate has been issued to either spouse.[9] Divorce for adultery was recognised at common law from the

---

[4] For a discussion on the formation of a civil partnership see Ch.9, paras 9–60 *et seq.*
[5] As amended by s.33, Sch.1 of the FLSA 2006.
[6] 2004 Act, s.117(2)(a)–(b).
[7] This is because, due to the heterosexual definition of adultery, there was broad consensus at the time of consultation that sexual infidelity need not be a separate ground, for it could be incorporated within unreasonable behaviour. See Scottish Executive, *The Consultation on Civil Partnership Registration: Analysis of the Responses* (February 5, 2004), para.7.27.
[8] FLSA 2006, s.45(2), Sch.3.
[9] Divorce (Scotland) Act 1976, s.1 as amended by the Gender Recognition Act 2004, Sch.2, Pt 2, para.6.

Reformation onwards[10] while desertion was introduced as a ground by statute in 1573. These were the only grounds of divorce until 1938, when the Divorce (Scotland) Act 1938 introduced the grounds of cruelty, incurable insanity, sodomy and bestiality. It was not until 1976 that it became possible to obtain a divorce without proof of matrimonial fault on the part of one of the spouses. The current mixture of fault- and non-fault-based criteria is thus the product of continuing reform over the years. As a result, Scots law has moved from a position where marriage could be ended only by proof of matrimonial offence on the part of one spouse, to the current regime where more divorces are obtained by mutual consent after a period of non-cohabitation than on any other basis.[11] How successful this process of reform has been in establishing a satisfactory level of access to divorce is still controversial. On the one hand, there has been much support for further liberalisation of the divorce laws,[12] but, on the other, concern for the high and increasing rate of breakdown of marriage and its effect on the family.[13] Before turning to the issue of reform, we shall consider the grounds prior to the FLSA 2006.

Adultery

14–05   Under s.1(2)(a), it is a ground of divorce that "since the date of the marriage the defender has committed adultery".

14–06   Adultery has been defined as "voluntary sexual intercourse between a married person and a person of the opposite sex, not being the marriage partner".[14] Accordingly, pre-marital sex with someone other than the future spouse cannot be adultery. A single act of adultery will suffice to give rise to grounds for divorce. If the sex is not voluntary, e.g. if rape is involved, then there is no adultery.[15] If consent cannot be given due to mental incapacity, e.g. dementia, then again there is no adultery even if the sexual act physically took

---

[10] See Fraser, *Husband and Wife*, Vol.II (2nd edn, 1878), pp.1139–1140.

[11] See "The Future for Scottish Divorce Law, A 'No Fault' or Mixed system for Scotland" in S. Harvie-Clark, *Family Law (Scotland) Bill: Grounds for Divorce (Updated)* (SPICe briefing, April 21, 2005, The Scottish Parliament) pp.12–13. See also n.2 to Ch.13.

[12] See *The Ground for Divorce: Should the law be changed?*, Scot. Law Com. Discussion Paper No.76 (1988); *Report on Reform of the Ground for Divorce*, Scot. Law Com. No.116 (1989), paras 2.1–2.11.

[13] Recent years have seen a decline from the number of divorces taking place in the 1980s and 1990s, in 1995 almost 40% of marriages in Scotland ended in divorce (RGS, *Annual Report 1995*). In 2003 there were 10,928 divorces in Scotland representing just over one-third of the 30,757 marriages taking place in the same year (RGS, *Annual Report 2003*). In 2004 there were 11,277 divorces representing just under one-third of the 32,154 marriages that took place, (RGS, *Annual Report 2004*) downloaded from *www.gro-scotland.gov.uk/statistics/library/ annep.reg-annual review-2004/inde*, Ch.1, p.9.

[14] Clive, *The Law of Husband and Wife in Scotland* (4th edn, 1997), para.21.004.

[15] *Stewart v Stewart* (1914) 2 S.L.T. 310.

place.[16] So long as sexual intercourse is voluntary, then the state of mind in which it was undertaken (such as belief that one's spouse is dead) is irrelevant.[17] For the purposes of establishing adultery, sexual intercourse must involve some degree of physical penetration of the vagina by the penis. Penetration elsewhere, or by other means, does not amount to adultery. Nor do acts that fall short of such penetration, such as oral sex. Accordingly, if a wife is artificially inseminated with the sperm of someone other than her husband, this does not found adultery, even if the insemination was done without the husband's knowledge or consent.[18] These types of activity, less than full intercourse, can, however, found an action for divorce on the basis of unreasonable behaviour under s.1(2)(b) (see para.14–08 below).

Adultery is not commonly used as a ground of divorce today. In 1995 only eight per cent of divorces were obtained on that ground[19] and in 2002 this number had dropped to six per cent of divorce in the Court of Session and four per cent in the Sheriff Court.[20] For this reason, we will not discuss in full two, somewhat archaic and now very rarely pled, defences to adultery. These are *condonation*,[21] that is, the claim that the pursuer forgave the defender for his or her adultery in the full knowledge it had occurred, and *lenocinium* (or "whore-mongering"),[22] the claim that the pursuer actively encouraged or induced the defender to commit adultery.[23] Collusion—where parties to a marriage agree to permit a false case most usually in order to achieve a quicker divorce—discussed below at para.14–28, was also a defence to adultery and indeed to other grounds until s.14 of the FLSA 2006 removed this as a bar to divorce.[24] **14–07**

Behaviour

Under s.1(2)(b) a marriage has irretrievably broken down if, **14–08**

"since the date of the marriage the defender has at any time behaved (whether or not as a result of mental abnormality and

---

[16] Difficulty may arise where incapacity to consent is due to the voluntary consumption of drink or drugs ingested: see Clive, *op. cit.* above, n.14, at para.21.005.

[17] *Hunter v Hunter* (1900) 2 F. 771.

[18] The physical requirements for adulterous sexual intercourse were discussed in *MacLennan v MacLennan*, 1958 S.C. 105 where the issue was indeed that of non-consensual artificial insemination by donor (AID).

[19] See RGS, *Annual Report 1995*, Table 8.1.

[20] Scottish Executive, *Civil Judicial Statistics for 2002* (HMSO, Scotland, 2004).

[21] 1976 Act, s.1(3). Condonation requires something more than *verbal* forgiveness, e.g. resumption of cohabitation after the adultery (subject to a three-month grace period for attempted reconciliation—see s.2(2). See further, Clive, *op. cit.* above, n.14 at paras 22.011–22.021.

[22] Which translates into modern usage as "no pimping".

[23] 1976 Act, s.1(3). See, further, Clive, *op. cit.* above, n.14 at paras 22.002–22.010.

[24] However, it remains the case at common law that the court should not grant a decree of divorce if satisfied that the pursuer has put forward a false case or the defender has withheld a good defence.

whether such behaviour has been active or passive) in such a way that the pursuer cannot reasonably be expected to cohabit with the defender".

Identical provision is to be found at s.117(3)(a) of the 2004 Act with the substitution of the word "registration" for "marriage".

14–09 While behaviour was the commonest ground for divorce at the beginning of the 1980s,[25] in recent years it has been overtaken in popularity by the two years' non-cohabitation and consent ground. In 2002, one-half of the divorces in both the Court of Session and the Sheriff Court were based on this ground, that is, 56 per cent[26] compared with 15 per cent on behaviour.[27]

14–10 It is only behaviour which has occurred "since the date of the marriage" which is relevant. Thus, if a woman fraudulently induces a man to marry her on the grounds that he is the father of her expected child then this behaviour will not found a divorce, as it occurred prior to the marriage.[28] However, where behaviour commenced prior to marriage continues after marriage, then provided it meets all the other requirements of the section, it may justify a divorce. While the word "behaviour" suggests a course of conduct which takes place over time, the wording "at any time" makes it clear that one single act or occurrence will qualify.[29]

14–11 The behaviour must be "such that the pursuer cannot reasonably be expected to cohabit with the defender". Under s.13(2), parties to a marriage cohabit only where they are "in fact living together as man and wife". While at one time the only behaviour that could be taken into account was that which amounted to cruelty,[30] the current Act makes it clear that conduct need not be culpable, unjustifiable, or even directed towards the pursuer, to found a divorce. The statute expressly states that the behaviour may be "active" or "passive" and may arise as the result of a "mental abnormality". Thus, insanity is not a defence to divorce under this head[31] and behaviour related to illness may justify a divorce. It is no defence that the defender spouse is not to blame for his or her behaviour, and does not intend in any way to

---

[25] Behaviour was the commonest ground of divorce in 1981. By 1984 the combined total of divorces obtained on two or five years' non-cohabitation had overtaken the number obtained on behaviour grounds. By 1986 the total number of divorces obtained on the basis of two years' non-cohabitation alone had overtaken those on the behaviour ground.

[26] *Op. cit.* above n.20.

[27] *ibid.*

[28] But *cf. Hastings v Hastings*, 1941 S.L.T. 323 where a wife's fraudulent inducement of marriage by pretending that her husband was the father of her expected child, was held to give husband reasonable cause for desertion (under the Divorce (Scotland) Act 1938).

[29] See dicta in *Gray v Gray*, 1991 G.W.D. 8-477.

[30] Under the Divorce (Scotland) Act 1938.

[31] This was also the case under the Divorce (Scotland) Act 1964, s.5(2)(b), and see the English case of *Williams v Williams* [1964] A.C. 698.

harm or upset the other spouse.[32] For example, in *Fullarton v Fullarton*,[33] a husband was divorced on the basis that as a result of a schizophrenic condition, he had lost all interest in his wife and children and slept abnormally long hours. There must, however, be something more than a mere state of affairs that exists, i.e. there must be some degree of action or conduct by one party which affects the other.[34] It is unsettled whether some minimal mental element is required in order to distinguish behaviour from a mere state of being.[35]

When considering whether it is reasonable to expect the pursuer to **14–12** cohabit with the defender, the court will consider the personality and experiences of the actual pursuer in question, not some hypothetical reasonable, objective pursuer.[36] In other words, a subjective, not objective, approach is taken in this regard. On the other hand, the court is then asked objectively to assess whether it is reasonable for the pursuer to cohabit with the defender. It is important to stress that the court is not asked to discuss whether the defender's behaviour *itself is* unreasonable, but only whether or not the pursuer can reasonably be expected to cohabit with the defender. What is crucial is that there is a causal link between the defender's behaviour and the pursuer's desire to no longer cohabit with the defender. In *Knox v Knox*,[37] a husband raised an action of divorce on the basis that his wife nagged and shouted at him and had written abusive letters to him while he was living with another woman. The court found that the letters had no effect upon the pursuer, and that the real reason for his leaving home was not his wife's alleged nagging, but his desire to pursue a relationship with another woman. The action for divorce was therefore dismissed since the husband had failed to show that his unwillingness to continue cohabiting with his wife was actually caused by her behaviour.[38]

---

[32] See *O'Neill v O'Neill* [1975] 3 All E.R. 289 (where husband was an excessive do-it-yourself enthusiast and made his family's life a misery although his behaviour was not intended to upset them in any way); *Gollins v Gollins* [1964] A.C. 644 (where an idle, lazy husband got into debt while the wife struggled to maintain the family); *Thurlow v Thurlow* [1975] 2 All E.R. 979 (where a wife, because of a neurological disorder, took to bed and ceased to do any housework); and *Friday v Friday* [1970] 3 All E.R. 554 (where a wife existed in a state of blank passivity as a result of a schizophrenic condition).

[33] 1976 S.L.T. 8.

[34] See *Katz v Katz* [1972] 1 W.L.R. 955, *per* Sir George Baker at 960.

[35] There seems to be no such requirement in England: see *Thurlow v Thurlow, op. cit.* above, n.32. *Cf.* Clive, *op. cit.* above, n.14, at para.21.013.

[36] *Meikle v Meikle*, 1987 G.W.D. 26-1005.

[37] 1993 S.C.L.R. 381.

[38] See also *Smith v Smith*, 1976 S.L.T. (Notes) 26, where a wife raised an action for divorce for cruelty on the basis that her husband had been convicted of murder and she was undergoing treatment for her nerves. The court found she had failed to establish any causal connection between her husband's crime and her unwillingness to cohabit with him.

14–13   When parties separate prior to divorce, the pursuer's acts *after* separation are relevant when assessing whether or not it is reasonable to expect him or her to cohabit with the defender. This is because facts sufficient to form a ground of divorce must be established as at the date of proof, not the date of separation. In *Findlay v Findlay*[39] the wife formed an association with another man after she and her husband had separated. She raised an action divorce based on her husband's behaviour. The issue was whether she was unwilling to cohabit with her husband because of her husband's behaviour, or because she had entered a relationship with another man. Lord Prosser held that:

> "On its own, I should doubt whether a party could contend that an association formed since separation by that party could make it unreasonable to expect that party to cohabit with the other party to the marriage".

But he went on to state that he had, however,

> "come to the view that where, as here, a pursuer originally separated from a defender for reasons which flowed from the conduct of the defender, and where after such a separation the parties' lives change over a period of time, and a new association is formed, then it is only realistic to see that association as arising in a sense from the earlier conduct and separation, and as being a relevant factor in considering whether, at the date of proof, the pursuer can reasonably be expected to cohabit with the defender".[40]

Thus, Lord Prosser was satisfied that, taking account of the whole history of events leading up to and since separation, the pursuer could not reasonably be expected to cohabit with the defender, and that this flowed directly from the original conduct of the defender.

14–14   The range of behaviour which may found a divorce under s.1(2)(b) is very broad. It includes non-physical assaults on the pursuer's person or feelings as well as physical violence.[41] It also covers various types of sexual conduct, including sodomy and bestiality (which were formerly grounds of divorce in their own right),[42] along with habitual drunkenness or drug use, and neglect, indifference, taciturnity, and passive or obsessive behaviour. It can include behaviour towards third

---

[39] *Findlay v Findlay*, 1991 S.L.T. 457 at 461.
[40] *ibid.*
[41] See *Macleod v Macleod*, 1990 G.W.D. 14-767 (where a jealous husband constantly accused his wife of being unfaithful, although such claims were unfounded).
[42] Under the Divorce (Scotland) Act 1938.

parties within or outwith the family,[43] the latter even where there is no sexual relationship involved.[44]

In *AB v CB*[45] a husband, while temporarily insane, murdered his **14–15** child. His wife, the child's mother, refused to live with him after he was released from hospital. He raised a divorce action on the grounds of her desertion, but the court held that she had reasonable grounds for non-adherence and dismissed the action. A single act of this type would certainly give rise to grounds for divorce under s.1(2)(b) of the 1976 Act. In *Hastie v Hastie*,[46] the wife made false allegations that her husband was unfaithful and had committed incest with his niece. The court held that, although the wife's conduct was unlikely to recur, nonetheless her allegations had been destructive of the mutual confidence essential to the continuance of a marriage, and so the husband was granted a divorce.

One Year's Non-Cohabitation Plus Consent

Under s.1(2)(d), a marriage has irretrievably broken down if, **14–16**

> "there has been no cohabitation between the parties at any time during a continuous period of one year after the date of the marriage and immediately preceding the bringing of the action and the defender consents to the granting of decree of divorce".[47]

Identical provision exists for civil partners at s.117(3)(c) with the obvious substitution of the words "registration" for "marriage" and "dissolution" for "divorce".[48]

Before amendment by the FLSA 2006, the predecessor of this pro- **14–17** vision—two years' non-cohabitation plus consent—was the most common ground for divorce, with 48 per cent of divorces obtained in this way in 1995[49] and 56 per cent of divorces in 2002.[50] There must be a continuous period of non-cohabitation, together with the consent to divorce of the spouse who has not raised the action. Non-cohabitation is a question of fact, regardless of the actual intentions of the parties and therefore cohabitation depends simply on whether the parties are "in fact living together as man and wife".[51] The period

---

[43] See *White v White*, 1966 S.L.T. 288 (where a husband's criminal conviction for an act of gross indecency with another man in a public toilet held grounds for divorce for behaviour).

[44] See *Stewart v Stewart*, 1987 S.L.T. (Sh. Ct.) 48 (where a husband's non-sexual association with another woman after work and late at night was considered sufficient to give his wife grounds for divorce).

[45] 1959 S.C. 27.

[46] 1985 S.L.T. 146.

[47] As amended by s.1 of the FLSA 2006.

[48] As amended by s.33, Sch.1, para.9 of the FLSA 2006.

[49] *Op. cit.* above, n.20.

[50] *ibid.*

[51] s.13(2).

of non-cohabitation must be "continuous", and rules exist on exemption of periods of cohabitation to encourage reconciliation.[52] That is, if parties separate but then resume cohabitation for a period before separating once again, when considering whether the period of non-cohabitation has been "continuous", no account is taken of periods of resumed cohabitation as long as such periods do not exceed six months in *total*.

14–18 *Example 1:* Sue leaves Joe on March 31, 2006. Joe implores her to come back and the couple attempt a reconciliation when Sue resumes cohabitation with Joe on August 1, 2006. Their attempt is unsuccessful and they agree Sue should leave for good on December 1, 2006. The four-month period of cohabitation from August 1 until the beginning of December will not interrupt the running of the one-year period but it will not count towards it either. This means that either party can raise an action for divorce on the basis of one year's non-cohabitation but not until July 31, 2007. If they had not had a period of attempted reconciliation such an action could be raised on March 31, 2007.

14–19 *Example 2:* Sue leaves Joe on March 1, 2006. They resume cohabitation on August 1, 2006 until March 15, 2007. As the resumption of cohabitation has extended beyond the six-month period provided for in s.2(4), it has interrupted the running of the one-year period. This means that if either party wished to raise an action for divorce the one-year period can only start to run from March 15, 2007.

Similarly, for civil partners, identical provision is made for calculating a period of non-cohabitation at s.119(3) of the 2004 Act.

14–20 A defender must positively consent to the divorce/dissolution, and has the power to withdraw consent at any time during the one-year period right up until the granting of the decree.[53] Withdrawal of consent is competent even where it represents a tactical manoeuvre on the part of the defender to improve his or her bargaining position.[54]

14–21 For civil partners, it was included in the 2004 Act that provision was to be made for an Act of Sederunt to be passed to ensure that in an action for dissolution raised on the basis of one year's non-cohabitation with consent that:

- the defender be given such information as enables that civil partner to understand—
    - (i) the consequences of consenting to the granting of decree; and
    - (ii) the steps which must be taken to indicate such consent; and
    - (iii) as to the manner in which the defender in such an action is to indicate such consent and withdrawal of such consent;

---

[52] s.2(4).

[53] *Taylor v Taylor*, 1988 S.C.L.R. 60 (Sh. Ct.). This has been enabled by statute for civil partners at s.117(3)(4).

[54] *Boyle v Boyle*, 1977 S.L.T. (Notes) 69.

- and where the defender has indicated and not withdrawn such consent in the prescribed manner, that indication will be sufficient evidence of consent.[55]

Two Years' Non-Cohabitation without the Need for Consent

Finally, under s.1(2)(e), a marriage has irretrievably broken down if, **14–22**

> "there has been no cohabitation between the parties at any time during a continuous period of two years after the date of the marriage and immediately preceding the bringing of the action".[56]

Identical provision exists for civil partners at s.117(3)(d) with reference to the "date of registration" rather than to a "marriage".[57]

The same rules discussed under "one year's non-cohabitation with **14–23** consent" apply in relation to what is non-cohabitation[58] and what amounts to a continuous period.[59] Prior to the amendment by the FLSA 2006, its predecessor—five years' non-cohabitation without the need for consent—was the third most popular ground with 18 per cent of divorces obtained in this way in 1995.[60]

This is the only ground which allows a disgruntled spouse/civil **14–24** partner to unilaterally terminate his or her marriage/partnership without the other party having committed any fault. Prior to amendment by the FLSA 2006, the court had discretion under s.1(5) of the 1976 Act and s.117(6) of the 2004 Act to refuse an action for divorce/dissolution on this grounds, "if in the opinion of the court the grant of decree would result in grave financial hardship to the defender".[61]

"Hardship" included the loss of the chance of acquiring any **14–25** benefit, e.g. a wife's or widow's benefit under the occupational pension scheme of a husband, or a life policy. This discretionary power might be used or not by the court even if grave financial hardship was established.[62] Courts determined only *financial* hardship as a consequence of a divorce was relevant.[63] Emotional hardship

---

[55] Such notices of consent to dissolution of civil partnership or separation of civil partnership may be found at Ch.33A.18 of the Act of Sedurunt (Sheriff Court Ordinary Cause Rules) 1993 No. 1956 (s.223), Sch.1, Ch.33A (Civil Partnership Cases).

[56] As amended by s.11 of the FLSA 2006.

[57] As amended by s.33, Sch.1, para.9 of the FLSA 2006.

[58] 1976 Act, s.13(2).

[59] *ibid.*, s.2(4).

[60] See RGS, *Annual Report 1995*, Table 8.1.

[61] FLSA 2006, s.13 repeals s.1(5) of the 1976 Act.

[62] See *Norris v Norris*, 1992 S.L.T. (Sh. Ct.) 51.

[63] If the defender is already living at an impoverished level before the divorce, the defence will not be competent. In *Boyd v Boyd*, 1978 S.L.T. (Notes) 55, the wife had already suffered grave financial hardship during the subsistence of the marriage because her husband was able to pay her only £4.50 per week in aliment. Hence the court found that she would not be significantly worse off as a result of the divorce, and so the defence failed.

arising from, e.g. loss of companionship or belief that divorce is not proper, was held to be of no significance.

14–26   This hardship defence was successful mainly where future benefits would be lost as a result of a decree of divorce. Spouses, particularly older wives in professional marriages who have never worked, or failed to work long enough to build up independent pensions, could claim with reason that divorce would defeat their rights in their husbands' pensions and that this will directly cause them grave financial hardship in the future. In *Nolan v Nolan*[64] the court agreed to refuse decree of divorce because the defender, if divorced, would have lost: (i) a chance of receiving two-fifths of the income element of her husband's index-linked pension; (ii) her indefeasible legal rights in succession in respect of the lump sum element of the pension if it still formed part of his estate on his death and she survived him; and (iii) dependent again on survivorship, her entitlement to the State widow's pension. Although the husband offered to take out an insurance policy for her benefit, the judge was not satisfied that this would adequately compensate her for the potential loss.

14–27   However, as discussed in Ch.13, since the enactment of the Family Law (Scotland) Act 1985, s.10(5), this is no longer a compelling issue as the matrimonial property divisible on divorce is expressly defined to *include* the value of any pension rights of either spouse referable to the period of the marriage.[65] Furthermore, since the Pension Regulations 1996 have been enacted they have eliminated the previous doubt as to whether any widow's or widower's benefit portion of the pension forms part of the value. Even if there are no liquid assets with which to pay off pension rights at the date of divorce, a pension lump sum order can now be made under s.12A, earmarking a portion of the benefits to be paid at the date the pension matures. Thus we arrived at a point where there seemed no case to justify—purely for financial reasons—keeping alive a marriage which had irretrievably broken down. To do so goes against the general spirit of the 1976 Act.[66] Hence, this discretionary power had been abolished by the FLSA 2006.[67]

Collusion

14–28   This defence was abolished by s.14 of the FLSA 2006 as there was broad agreement that the legislative provision no longer served a useful purpose. Previously, where the spouses agreed to put forward a false case to obtain a divorce, or to hold back a good defence, if discovered, divorce was refused on the ground of collusion.[68] If

---

[64] 1979 S.L.T. 293.

[65] See paras 13–26 *et seq.*

[66] This is the view of the Scottish Law Commission; see *Report on Family Law*, Scot. Law Com. No.135 (1992), para.13.12.

[67] FLSA 2006, s.13 repealing s.1(5) of the 1976 Act, and FLSA 2006, Sch.3 repealing s.117(6) of the 2004 Act.

[68] *Walker v Walker*, 1911 S.C. 163 at 169.

collusion emerged *after* decree had been granted, then it could be reduced. Nevertheless, it is still the case at common law that a court should not grant a decree of divorce if satisfied that the pursuer has put forward a false case or the defender has withheld a good defence. Co-operation by spouses in seeking a divorce or reaching agreement on its terms, e.g. relating to finance, did not amount collusion unless there was also deceit.[69]

REFORMING THE GROUNDS FOR DIVORCE

Given that divorce is supposed to be based on the concept of irre- **14–29** trievable breakdown of marriage, current law remains an uneasy partnership between fault and non-fault-based grounds. It is evident that despite the introduction of no-fault divorce, many divorce actions are still obtained on the basis of behaviour or adultery, primarily because the parties do not wish to wait what was until recently *two* years for a divorce.[70] This subverted one of the main aims of the 1976 Act, which was to avoid "an unnecessary emphasis on blame and recrimination and an unnecessary increase in bitterness and hostility".[71] In 1988, the Scottish Law Commission consulted on the idea of making divorce available after a period of notice, or after a short period of non-cohabitation lasting from three months to a year.[72] This proposal proved too radical however and in its subsequent report, it merely recommended the dropping of the ground of desertion and shortening the periods of non-cohabitation to one year with consent, and two years without.

Reforms Made by the Family Law (Scotland) Act 2006—Overview

While other countries, such as Australia, New Zealand, Sweden and **14–30** Finland have opted for "no fault" systems of divorce,[73] the reforms implemented by the FLSA 2006 continue to promote a mixed system of divorce, that is, a combination of fault and non-fault grounds along the lines of the Scottish Law Commission's recommendations.[74]

---

[69] *McKenzie v MacKenzie*, 1935 S.L.T. 198.
[70] See *Report on Reform of the Ground for Divorce*, Scot. Law Com. No.116 (1989), para.2.2.
[71] *ibid.*, para.2.3.
[72] See *The Ground for Divorce: Should the Law be Changed?*, Scot. Law Com. Discussion Paper No.76 (1988).
[73] England also attempted to institute no-fault divorce by providing that irretrievable breakdown would only be inferred after the expiry of a one-year period for consideration of the practical consequences of divorce, and reflection on whether the marital relationship was irreparable under Pt II of the Family Law Act 1996. However, in 2001 the UK government repealed this part of the Act with the result that England and Wales continues to retain its mixed system of divorce on irretrievable breakdown of marriage.
[74] See *Report on Reform of the Ground for Divorce*, Scot. Law Com. No.116 (1989).

While the grounds of adultery and intolerable behaviour have been retained, desertion as a ground has now been abolished under s.12.[75] The periods of non-cohabitation attached to the non-fault grounds under s.11 of the FLSA 2006 have been reduced to one year, where both parties consent to divorce, and to two years where there is no consent. The defence of collusion has been removed as a bar to divorce[76] and the court is no longer empowered to refuse to grant a divorce following non-cohabitation under s.1(5) of the 1976 Act if it considers that to do so would result in grave financial hardship to the party who does not consent to the divorce.[77] However, a further amendment made by the FLSA 2006 is the insertion of a new s.3A into the 1976 Act providing the court with the discretion to postpone decree of divorce where a religious impediment to remarry exists. In such a case the court has to be satisfied that the party seeking divorce has removed or has contributed to the removal of the impediment preventing the other party from remarrying once divorced. A power is given to Scottish Ministers to make regulations to prescribe the religious faiths which can rely on this provision.[78] A similar provision has not been extended to civil partners as a civil partnership cannot be established through a religious ceremony.

JUDICIAL SEPARATION—SPOUSES AND CIVIL PARTNERS

14–31 For those who wish to separate but are both opposed to divorce or dissolution, the option of judicial separation remains.[79] Judicial separation is rarely resorted to today,[80] given the decline in the social stigma of divorce and the possibility of obtaining a divorce without proof of matrimonial fault. The grounds for obtaining a decree of judicial separation are now identical to those for obtaining divorce or dissolution and subject to the same defences and bars. A spouse who has obtained a judicial separation thus always has grounds subsequently to raise an action of divorce if he or she wishes[81] as will a civil partner to obtain dissolution having previously obtained judicial separation.[82]

14–32 If in an action for judicial separation between *spouses* it appears to the court there is a reasonable prospect of a reconciliation between

---

[75] This provision is no longer necessary because of the reduction in periods of non-cohabitation introduced by s.11 of the FLSA 2006. Desertion as a grounds for dissolution of a civil partnership was removed by s.45(2), Sch.3 of the FLSA 2006.

[76] Under s.14 of the FLSA 2006.

[77] This is abolished by s.13 of the FLSA 2006.

[78] 1976 Act, s.13(3A)(9) inserted by s.15 of the FLSA 2006.

[79] 1976 Act, s.4 for spouses; 2004 Act. s.120 for civil partners

[80] For a discussion of the importance of judicial separation in the past, see Clive, *op. cit.* above, n.14, at para.19.043.

[81] 1976 Act, s.3(1); Law Reform (Miscellaneous Provisions) (Scotland) Act 1968, s.11.

[82] 2004 Act, s.121.

the parties, it shall continue the action for such a period as it thinks proper to enable attempts to be made to effect such a reconciliation.[83] No similar provision has been included in the 2004 Act for civil partners in an action for separation in Scotland, however[84] such provision does exist in an action for *dissolution*[85] and a court cannot grant dissolution without hearing evidence from the pursuer even where a decree for separation has previously been granted.[86]

In an action for judicial separation between spouses where the **14–33** defender is suffering from mental illness, the court is directed to appoint a curator *ad litem* to the defender.[87] Similar provision exists for the appointment of a curator *ad litem* for defenders to an action for judicial separation for civil partners.[88]

A decree of judicial separation provides judicial sanction for **14–34** spouses or civil partners to separate and live apart without terminating the marriage/civil partnership. Apart from this, the ordinary obligations and restrictions of marriage/civil partnership continue to apply. Thus, neither can remarry and the obligation of aliment subsists. The 1976 Act makes reference to actions for "separation and aliment",[89] whilst the 2004 Act refers to actions for "separation" only.[90] However, the 2004 Act amends the Family Law (Scotland) Act 1985 to make actions for aliment competent in an action for separation.[91]

Prior to the FLSA 2006, the most significant consequence of judi- **14–35** cial separation was that the husband lost the legal rights he would normally have had in his wife's property acquired *after the* date of separation, if she died before him without making a will.[92] There was no reciprocal provision in relation to a *wife's* claim on her husband's estate. There seems little point in retaining the remedy of judicial separation today, as it simply provides a legal remedy for one party who wishes to live apart from the other, and there are other more effective ways to protect that right, such as those found in the Matrimonial Homes (Family Protection) (Scotland) Act 1981. The Scottish Law Commission views it as an anachronism and has recommended its abolition, but this recommendation has not yet been implemented.[93]

---

[83] 1976 Act, s.2.
[84] Note: such provision however, does exist at s.118 in an action for *dissolution* and, at s.121(2), a court cannot grant dissolution without hearing evidence from the pursuer even where a decree for separation has previously been granted.
[85] 2004 Act, s.118.
[86] 2004 Act, s.121(2).
[87] 1976 Act, s.11 as enacted by OCR 33.16, SI 1993/1956 (S.223).
[88] OCR 33A.16, SSI 2005/638.
[89] s.4(1).
[90] s.120.
[91] 2004 ct, s.261(2), Sch.28, Pt 2, para.11 inserting s.2(2)(aa) into the 1985 Act.
[92] Conjugal Rights (Scotland) Amendment Act 1861, s.6. The whole Act has been repealed by the FLSA 2006.
[93] *Report on Family Law*, Scot. Law Com. No.135, (1992), para.12–19.

JURISDICTION AND PROCEDURAL ASPECTS OF DIVORCE/DISSOLUTION

Jurisdiction—Spouses

14–36   Until 1983, all actions dealing with personal status, including divorce, could be raised only in the Court of Session. However, the Sheriff Court now has concurrent jurisdiction[94] and most divorces are raised in that forum. The Court of Session has jurisdiction to hear a divorce where either party to the marriage:

(a) is domiciled in Scotland on the date of commencement of the action; or
(b) was habitually resident in Scotland through the period of one year ending with that date.[95]

Jurisdiction exists in the Sheriff Court where either (a) or (b) above is satisfied *and* either party to the marriage:

(i) was resident in the sheriffdom for a period of 40 days ending with that date; or
(ii) was resident in the sheriffdom for a period of not less than 40 days ending not more than 40 days before the said date, and has no known residence in Scotland that date.[96]

14–37 Unlike the position in England, where spouses must be married for one year before either one of them can raise an action for divorce,[97] there is no minimum time bar in Scots law.

Jurisdiction—Civil Partners[98]

14–38   The courts[99] in Scotland have jurisdiction in relation to proceedings for the dissolution or annulment of a civil partnership or for the separation of civil partners where:

(a) both civil partners are habitually resident in Scotland;
(b) both civil partners were last habitually resident in Scotland and one of the civil partners continues to reside there;
(c) the defender is habitually resident in Scotland;
(d) the pursuer is habitually resident in Scotland and has resided there for at least one year immediately preceding the date on which the action is begun; or

---

[94] Divorce Jurisdiction, Court Fees and Legal Aid (Scotland) Act 1983, s.1.
[95] Domicile and Matrimonial Proceedings Act 1973, s.7.
[96] *ibid.*, s.8(3) as amended by the Divorce Jurisdiction, Court Fees and Legal Aid (Scotland) Act 1983, Sch.1, para.18.
[97] Family Law Act 1996, s.4.
[98] The Civil Partnership (Jurisdiction and Recognition of Judgments) (Scotland) Regulations 2005 (SSI 2005/629).
[99] Both the Court of Session and the Sheriff Court under s.135 of the 2004 Act.

(e) the pursuer is domiciled and habitually resident in Scotland and has resided there for at least six months immediately preceding the date on which the action is begun.

Brussells II

Since March 1, 2001, the Convention on Jurisdiction and the **14–39** Recognition and Enforcement of Judgments in matrimonial matters dealing with Member States has been effective.[1] The Convention's aim is the reciprocal recognition and enforcement of decrees relating to divorce, separation and nullity throughout the EU.[2] As a result appropriate amendments have been made to Scottish legislation to bring it into line with the Convention[3] although jurisdiction still remains primarily dependent on the parties' habitual residence or domicile and if either or both party is habitually resident in Scotland then the Scottish courts will have jurisdiction. However, this may encourage forum shopping, with parties rushing to raise an action in the court that they perceive of as being most favourable to them, as a court first seised of the issue, as defined in Art.16, has jurisdiction over courts later seised in the matter.[4] Concern over this issue has led to the EU Green Paper on Applicable law and Jurisdiction in Divorce (Rome III) questioning whether the Convention can be made to work in such a way to avoid parties rushing to court to secure the most favourable jurisdiction for themselves, either by allowing parties to agree a forum in advance, or empowering the court with jurisdiction to transfer the case to a more convenient court in another Member State.[5]

The current convention applies to "the attribution, exercise, dele- **14–40** gation, restriction or termination of parental responsibility".[6] In particular, it will apply to the following:

- rights of custody and access (residence and contact);
- guardianship;

---

[1] See Council Regulation (EC) No.1347/2000 known as "Brussels II" now repealed and replaced by Council Regulation (EC) No.2201/2003 known as "Brussels II *bis*" that came into effect on March 1, 2005. Note that much of the earlier regulation has been retained and incorporated into its replacement, although the scope of Brussels II *bis* in addressing issues relating to children is broader than that of the original and is independent of the previous link to parental matrimonial proceedings. For further details see Morris, *The Conflict of Laws* (6th edn).

[2] According to *Singh v Singh*, 2005 S.L.T. 749 the Council Regulation was not restricted to cases where both parties could found jurisdiction under Art.2(1) and applied in a case, such as the present, where the respondent was not habitually resident or domiciled in, or a national of, a Member State.

[3] See EC (Matrimonial Jurisdiction and Judgments) (Scotland) Regulations 2001 (SSI 2001/36) repealed and replaced by EC (Matrimonial and Parental Responsibility Jurisdiction and Judgments) (Scotland) Regulations 2005 (SSI 2005/42). Also, The Civil Partnership (Jurisdiction and Recognition of Judgments) (Scotland) Regulations 2005 (SSI 2005/629).

[4] See A. Bissett-Johnson's "Comment" in 2005 Greens Fam. L.B. 73-1.

[5] See Editorial in Greens Fam. L.B. 77-1.

[6] Brussels II *bis*, Art.1(1)(b).

- the designation and functions of a person having charge of the child's person or property;
- the placement of a child in a foster family or institutional care; and
- protective measures relating to the child's property.[7]

It does not, however, apply to:

- establishing a parent/child relationship;
- adoption;
- the child's name;
- emancipation;
- maintenance obligations;
- trusts or succession;
- measures taken in respect of a criminal offence committed by a child.

14–41 Under the Convention, the child is given the right to be heard on matters relating to his or her custody "unless this appears inappropriate having regard to his or her age or degree of maturity".[8]

Cross-Border Divorce and Dissolution

14–42   In respect of cross-border divorces within the United Kingdom, jurisdiction in these cases is dependent upon one of the spouses or civil partners having been domiciled within a particular United Kingdom legal jurisdiction or having been resident there for at least a year immediately preceding the raising of the action. Where spouses/civil partners are domiciled or resident in different United Kingdom legal jurisdictions then each has a choice as to where to raise the divorce action.

14–43   In actions for divorce where there is competition between actions raised in different United Kingdom legal jurisdictions it is governed by the Domicile and Matrimonial Proceedings Act 1973, Sch.3 which provides for the mandatory sisting by Scottish courts of actions raised here where the criteria set out in para.8 are met. These are:

- the competing proceedings relate to the same marriage;
- the couple resided together after the marriage;
- the couple were resident together in the other jurisdiction when the Scottish action was raised or they last resided together there; and
- either spouse was habitually resident in that other jurisdiction for at least a year immediately preceding their last residence together.

---

[7] Brussels II *bis*, Art.1(2).
[8] Above, Art.11(2).

There are also provisions set down in para.9 for a discretionary sist **14–44** where this would serve the balance of fairness and convenience, including the convenience of witnesses and time-scales and expenses in the competing jurisdictions.[9]

Cross-Border Recognition of Decree

Marriage

Provision is made for recognition throughout the United Kingdom **14–45** of a decree of divorce, annulment or legal separation granted by any court of civil jurisdiction in the British Islands[10] by the Family Law Act 1986.[11] There are only two grounds for refusal of recognition. These are:

- that it was granted or obtained at a time when it was irreconcilable with a decision determining the question of the subsistence or validity of the marriage previously given by a court of civil jurisdiction in Scotland or by a court elsewhere and recognised or entitled to recognition in Scotland[12];
- that the divorce or legal separation was granted or obtained at a time when, according to Scots law, there was no subsisting marriage between the parties.[13]

However, even where these circumstances arise, the court is not obliged to refuse recognition but may go ahead and uphold the divorce, annulment or legal separation.

Civil Partnership

In respect of civil partnerships, s.233 of the 2004 Act provides that **14–46** the validity of a dissolution or annulment of a civil partnership or a legal separation of civil partners which has been obtained from a court of civil jurisdiction in one part of the United Kingdom is to be recognised throughout the United Kingdom unless irreconcilable with a decision determining the question of the subsistence or validity of the civil partnership.

Recognition of Overseas Decrees

Provision is also made for the recognition of overseas divorces, **14–47** annulments and legal separation from countries outside the British

---

[9] For further discussion see L. Mair, "Cross-Border Divorces within the UK", 2004 Fam L.B. 70-3.

[10] These cover England and Wales, Scotland, Northern Ireland, the Channel Islands and the Isle of Man.

[11] s.44(2).

[12] s.51(1).

[13] This includes the rules of Scottish private international law, see s.51(2).

Islands.[14] Jurisdiction in the Court of Session and the Sheriff Court has been devised for those actions where a pursuer is seeking recognition in Scotland of a decree of divorce, nullity or separation granted in a country outwith the EU.[15]

Proof

14–48   Before a decree of divorce/dissolution can be granted, the ground of the action must be proven on the balance of probabilities.[16] The burden of proof rests with the pursuer who must prove the ground in all cases, regardless of whether the action is defended or undefended.[17] While corroboration is no longer necessary,[18] there must be evidence from someone other than the spouses/civil partners to support the conclusion for divorce.[19] Such evidence need not, however, take the form of parole evidence, i.e. evidence given by witnesses in court, but may be tendered by way of affidavit, i.e. a statement in writing sworn and affirmed in the presence of a notary public or other competent authority). In undefended actions—which are overwhelmingly the majority of divorces in Scotland—the rules of court provide that evidence is to take the form of affidavit evidence unless the court directs otherwise.[20]

Simplified Divorce/Civil Partnership

14–49   In addition, a simplified, speedy and cheap form of do-it-yourself divorce was introduced in 1982. This is available only where certain conditions are met.[21] These are that:

"(i)   the action is undefended;
(ii)   the action is brought on the basis of—
      a)   one or two years' non-cohabitation;
      b)   or a interim gender recognition certificate has been issued to one of the parties;
(iii)   the pursuer is able to state that there are no other proceedings pending in any court which could have the effect of bringing the marriage to an end;

---

[14]   For further discussion see *Scottish Family Law Service* (Issue 20, LexisNexis/ Butterworths, 2005), paras 1101–1140.
[15]   Domicile and Matrimonial Proceedings Act 1973 as amended by s.37 of the FLSA 2006.
[16]   1976 Act, s.1(6) for spouses; 2004 Act, s.117(8) for civil partners.
[17]   Civil Evidence (Scotland) Act 1988, s.8(1) as amended.
[18]   *ibid.*, s.1(1) abolished the need for corroboration in all civil proceedings.
[19]   *ibid.*, s.8(3) as amended by s.261(2), Sch.28, Pt 4, para.55 of the 2004 Act to include civil Partners.
[20]   See RCS 49.28(2), as amended by the Act of Sederunt (Rules of the Court of Session Amendment No.5) (Family Actions and Miscellaneous) 1996 (SI 1996/2587), para.2(20), and the Act of Sederunt (Rules of the Court of Session Amendment No.9) (Civil Partnership Act 2004 etc.) 2005 (SSI 2005/632), para.14; and OCR 33.28(2) for spouses and OCR 33A.28 for civil partners.
[21]   RCS 49.72 (derived from SI 1982/1679) and OCR 33.73.

(iv) there are no children of the marriage under the age of 16 years;
(v) neither partner is applying for an order for financial provision on divorce;
(vi) neither party suffers from mental disorder; and
(vi) there is no religious impediment to the remarriage of either party in terms of section 3A of the Act of 1976."[22]

Similar procedure is available for civil partners as contained within the Act of Sederunt (Ordinary Cause Rules) Amendment (Civil Partnership Act 2004) 2005.[23]

Legal representation is not required in this form of action. The **14–50** action can be initiated using a standard application obtainable from the sheriff Clerk, the Court of Session or the local Citizens Advice Bureau. To simplify matters further, the general requirement for evidence from someone other than the spouses/civil partners is dispensed with.[24] On introduction, the aim of rendering the divorce process more accessible to ordinary people was laudable. However, given that many divorces in Scotland involve spouses who have children under 16,[25] or who wish to apply to the court for financial provision,[26] or both, the value of this procedure is limited. Nonetheless, in 1994–1995 the procedure was used in one-third of divorces.[27]

ORDINARY DIVORCES

Divorces/dissolutions which do not qualify for the simplified proce- **14–51** dure (being the majority of divorces) are known as "ordinary" and proceed through the formal court system. Some particular points relating to procedure should be noted.[28]

---

[22] RCS 49.72 as amended by the Act of Sederunt (Rules of the Court of Session Amendment No.3) (Family Law (Scotland) Act 2006) 2006 (SSI 2006/206), para.15.
[23] SSI 2005/638.
[24] Civil Evidence (Scotland) Act 1988, s.8(4) and (5) empower the Lord Advocate to dispense with the requirements of s.8(3) in specified classes of action by statutory instrument.
[25] In 1995, over one-third of divorces ended by final judgment involved children under 16, see Scottish Courts Administration, *Civil Judicial Statistics 1995*, pp.26–28. Current Civil Judicial Statistics no longer record this information. However, in England and Wales in 2003, 153,500 children under 16 were affected by their parents divorcing in England and Wales, just over one in five were under five years old. Downloaded from *www.statistics.gov.uk/CCI/nugget.asp?ID=1163.*
[26] There was an award for aliment for children or financial provision in 35% of ordinary divorces in 1991: Morris, Gibson and Platts, *Untying the Knot: Characteristics of Divorce in Scotland* (Scottish Central Research Unit, Edinburgh, 1993), p.27. However, around 80% of these awards were for aliment, which has largely been removed from the jurisdiction of the court under the Child Support Act 1991.
[27] See *Civil Judicial Statistics 1994*, p.30 and *Civil Judicial Statistics 1995*, p.28. Current Civil Judicial Statistics no longer record this information.
[28] For general discussion of procedure see S.A. Bennett, *Divorce in the Sheriff Court* (7th edn, Barnstoneworth, Edinburgh, 2005).

Options Hearings in the Sheriff Court

14–52   Where a divorce is defended in the Sheriff Court, rules of court[29] now provide for an additional step in the legal process, known as an options hearing, to take place. This hearing is intended to give the parties a chance to meet together before the sheriff in order to ascertain if agreement can be reached without proceeding to a full proof, or if this is not possible, to focus the precise disagreement between the parties. The aim is to save judicial time as well as legal aid,[30] and also to reduce delays in concluding the action. To this end, both parties are required to attend the hearing in person[31] and the sheriff is directed to adopt an interventionist role.[32] On the basis of information gathered, the sheriff may order a proof[33] or proof before answer,[34] or remit the action to additional procedure.[35] S/he may also appoint the cause to debate if satisfied that there is a preliminary matter of law which if established following debate would lead to decree in favour of either party, or to limitation of proof to any subsequent degree.[36] In addition, a sheriff has power, on cause shown, to continue the options hearing for up to 28 days.[37] However, this power may be used only once.[38] While the aims of the options hearing are to be applauded, questions have been raised as to how effective this new procedure is in practice.[39] As the rules currently stand it is not actually necessary for a defender in a family action to appear at an options hearing in person as representation by a solicitor will suffice to avoid being held in default by the court,[40] except possibly where a sheriff has expressly ordered the defender to appear in person and he or she has failed to obey that order.[41] Such a situation undermines the purpose of the hearing, which is to give the parties every opportunity to resolve their differences at an early stage in the proceedings before proceeding to a proof. It is clear that if options hearings are to represent more than a mere formality then both parties must make a personal

---

[29] OCR 9.12; OCR 33.36 for spouses and OCR 33A.36 for civil partners.

[30] But see A. Gibb, "Time Heals–But not on Legal Aid", 2005 Fam. L.B. 75-1 where the author is critical of the present block fee regime for civil legal aid setting out the problems that practitioners face in recovering fees for attending options hearings and the impact that this is having on the court system.

[31] OCR 33.36 for spouses; OCR 33A.36 for civil partners.

[32] OCR 9.12.

[33] OCR 9.12(3)(a).

[34] OCR 9.12(3)(b).

[35] OCR 9.12(4).

[36] OCR 9.12(3)(c) added by the Act of Sederunt (Ordinary Cause, Summary Application and Small Claim Rules) Amendment (Miscellaneous) 2004 (SSI 2004/197) (effective May 21, 2004), para.2(6).

[37] OCR 9.12(5).

[38] *ibid.*

[39] See Gibb, 1994 Fam. L.B. 7-2 and McTaggart, 1995 Fam. L.B. 13-10.

[40] OCR 33.37 and 9.12(7).

[41] *Grimes v Grimes*, 1995 S.C.L.R. 268.

appearance in court and the rules should make it clear that representation by a solicitor will not suffice in these circumstances.

Children—Child Welfare Hearing

Many divorces involve children under 16 and it is not uncommon **14–53** for parents to seek a s.11 residence, contact or parental responsibilities order at the same time as the principal decree of divorce. The court may exceptionally refuse to grant a decree of divorce/dissolution if it is not satisfied that appropriate arrangements have been made for the children dependant on the spouses/civil partners.[42] In such cases, the best option for the court may be to refer the child to the reporter who will then convene a children's hearing. In such a case, a proof will have to be held to decide if a ground of referral to the hearing exists.[43] Where divorce/dissolution proceedings involve a child under 16, the court has a duty to give that child an opportunity to express his or her views, which must then be given due regard, depending on the age and maturity of the child.[44] The action must be intimated to that child so that he or she knows that the action is underway and has a chance to participate. Where the child is considered too young to be able to give a view, or distress might be caused to the child, the court can dispense with intimation.[45]

It is strongly desirable for the welfare of the child that disputes **14–54** involving children should be resolved as speedily as possible. This is particularly true in disputes over residence for, where the longer the child remains settled with one parent on an interim basis pending resolution of the dispute, the harder it is for the court to contemplate making a change.[46] For this reason, a new "fast-track" procedure, known as the child welfare hearing, was created to deal with any defended actions in the Sheriff Court[47] which involve a s.11 order under the Children (Scotland) Act 1995, or any other actions where a sheriff considers that such a hearing should be fixed.[48] The aim of the child welfare hearing is to identify and process any disputes concerning children as expeditiously as possible. Three weeks must usually elapse after the notice of intention to defend is lodged before the hearing can be held.[49] All parties (including a child who has indicated his or her wish to attend) are required to attend the hearing personally, except on

---

[42] Children (Scotland) Act 1995, s.12(2)(c) as amended by s.261(2), Sch.28, Pt 4, para.60 of the 2004 Act.

[43] 1995 Act, s.54 as amended by s.261(2), Sch.28, Pt 4, para.61 of the 2004 Act. See further, paras 8–15 *et seq.*

[44] 1995 Act, s.11(7). A child is presumed competent to express a reasonable view at the age of 12 (s.11(10)).

[45] OCR 33.7(7), as amended, for spouses; OCR 33A.7(7) for civil partners.

[46] See para.4–66.

[47] OCR 33.22A, as amended, for spouses; OCR 33A.23 for civil partners.

[48] OCR 33.22A(1)(c) for spouses (these might include for, e.g. paternity proceedings); OCR 33A.23(1)(c) for civil partners.

[49] OCR 33.22A(1), as amended, for spouses; OCR 33A.23(1) for civil partners.

cause shown.[50] Parties are also under a duty to provide the sheriff with as much information as possible so that he or she can take whatever steps are necessary to deal with the matter.[51] In conducting the hearing, the sheriff is expected to adopt the same kind of interventionist role that is promoted in the options hearing, in the hope that disputes involving children can be processed as efficiently as possible.[52]

Power to Refer Parties to Mediation

14–55 The court also has power to suspend the divorce/dissolution proceedings and to refer the parties to mediation.[53] The purpose here is not to encourage parties to reconcile,[54] but to bring them together with the help of a third party mediator so that they can try to reach agreement about the terms of their divorce, especially with regard to children and, more recently, property. Mediation helps the parties to reach agreement by operating outwith the formal adversarial process of the courts and legal advisers.[55] Both the Court of Session[56] and the Sheriff Court[57] have power to refer parties in any dispute involving parental responsibilities or rights to a family mediation service.

REGISTRATION

14–56 When decree of divorce or dissolution is granted, the clerk of court is required to notify the content of the decree to the Registrar General who must make an entry in the relevant register, being the Register of Divorces[58] or the Register of Dissolution of Civil Partnership.[59]

In the final chapter, we consider how parties in Scotland can themselves regulate the terms of dissolution of their marriage/civil partnership or other relationship by agreement—with or without the help of a mediator—and to what extent the courts can, or should, act to protect the weaker party in the relationship, as well as the public interest in the stability of family life.

---

[50] OCR 33.22A(5), as amended, for spouses; OCR 33A.23(5) for civil partners.

[51] OCR 33.22A(6), as amended, for spouses; OCR 33A.23(6) for civil partners.

[52] See A. Gibb, above, n.30 where he talks about the difficulties that practitioners face regarding the payment of legal aid fees in respect of a child welfare hearing and where he observes that where family litigation is concerned, "The situation is at crisis point" (at 75-2).

[53] Note: s.261(2), Sch.28, para.58 of the 2004 Act amends s.1(2) of Civil Evidence (Family Mediation) (Scotland) Act 1995 pertaining to the inadmissibility in civil procedure of information as to what occurred during family mediation.

[54] Mediation was originally referred to as conciliation, but this term was changed to avoid confusion with reconciliation.

[55] See further, Ch.15.

[56] RCS 49.23 as amended.

[57] OCR 33.22, as amended, for spouses; OCR 33A.22 for civil partners.

[58] Registration of Births, Deaths and Marriages (Scotland) Act 1965, s.48.

[59] 2004 Act, s.122.

CHAPTER 15

PRIVATE ORDERING: MINUTES OF AGREEMENT AND JOINT MINUTES OF AGREEMENT

Despite the emphasis which has been placed on conflict in divorce in **15–01** earlier chapters, by no means all divorces are defended in court and resolved by full adversarial proceedings. While couples do get into dispute with one another which may require adjudication in court this is by no means always the case. In fact the cases that make it to court tend to be in the minority of cases rather than the majority. Despite the image of the legal profession as an adversarial profession rather than an enabling one, many couples opt to reach their own agreements on matters such as childcare, aliment and the distribution of their property at the end of their relationships. Although all divorces (and now dissolutions of civil partnerships) must go to court, very few in practice are defended or involve litigation.[1] Research on what people do and think about going to law in both Scotland[2] and England and Wales[3] also reveals that very limited use is made of formal legal proceedings to resolve justiciable problems. Reaching consensus has been the goal of much contemporary family law in Scotland (see the Children (Scotland) Act 1995) and England and Wales (see the Family Law Act 1996). It is not therefore surprising to find that many couples reach their own agreements on matters like childcare, aliment and the distribution of their property.[4] One Scottish study estimates that these agreements, referred to as minutes of agreement ("MoA") and joint minutes of agreement ("JMoA") account for around one-third of the total number of divorces in any year.[5] Among the claimed benefits of reaching agreements are that they:

---

[1] See Morris, Gibson and Platts, *Untying the Knot: Characteristics of Divorce in Scotland* (Scottish Central Research Unit, Edinburgh, 1993), p.15.

[2] H. Genn and A. Paterson, *Paths to Justice Scotland* (Hart Publishing, Oxford, 2001).

[3] H. Genn, *Paths to Justice* (Hart Publishing, Oxford, 1999).

[4] See A.M. Cubie, "Comment: Agreements and Divorcing Clients", 2003 Fam. L.B. 62-2.

[5] Wasoff, McGuckin and Edwards, *Mutual Consent: Written Agreements in Family Law* (Scottish Central Research Unit, Edinburgh, 1997). It is surprising to note that in reaching these agreements, mediation as an alternative form of dispute processing is so little in evidence. This was especially true for Scotland, *op cit.* above, n.2., pp.211–213, where out of all 472 respondents to the main questionnaire only seven stated that they had had any involvement with a mediation or conciliation organisation.

- save time and money; and
- may reduce the kind of hostility that full open court proceedings generate.[6]

15–02 It is worth noting, however, that parties who make agreements,

> "reported that high emotion, conflict, antagonism and compromise were the norm in reaching such agreements. The term 'agreement' is, in itself, misleading, since almost all of those interviewed said that they had not willingly agreed but had felt pressured into signing because they thought that the alternatives were worse. They did not feel in control of the process or the outcome. No one felt empowered".[7]

In fact, Wasoff suggests that the term "settlement" would be a better term for the outcome than "agreement".[8]

15–03 The terms settled upon in what are called Minutes of Agreement may be made at any time, whether prior to the marriage ("ante-nuptial agreements"), during it, or on or after divorce. In the past, marriage contracts were important when married women did not have the right to administer their own property[9] for they represented a device whereby parties could create their own property regime during marriage.[10] However, with changes in the law conferring rights on both husbands and wives to enjoy their own property regardless of marriage[11] the rationale for their existence disappeared and they fell into disuse.[12] However, there has been a revival, and it has been suggested that recent case law may fuel this trend[13] as a means of protecting the property of the very wealthy (mainly men) against the kind of claims their spouses might make on them on divorce. While prenuptial marriage contracts were recognised in Scotland, their status in England has been somewhat uncertain. In the English case of *F v F*[14] the court opined that such contracts were of limited significance because it was

---

[6] See Wasoff, Dobash and Marcus, *The Impact of the Family Law (Scotland) Act 1985 on Solicitors' Practice* (Scottish Central Research Unit, Edinburgh, 1990), Ch.8.

[7] F. Wasoff, "Mutual Consent: Separation Agreements and the Outcomes of Private Ordering in Divorce", 2005 J.S.W.F.L. 27, Nos 3-4. pp.237–250.

[8] *ibid.*, p.247.

[9] See Ch.10.

[10] According to E. M. Clive, *The Law of Husband and Wife in Scotland* (4th edn, W.Green, Edinburgh, 1997), "In the nineteenth century the marriage contract was widely used among the propertied classes. Its general purpose was to alter the normal property consequences of marriage": para.17.001.

[11] Family Law (Scotland) Act 1985, s.24(1) as amended by s.261(2), Sch.28, para.27 of the Civil Partnership Act 2004 to extend to civil partnerships.

[12] In the first edition of E. M. Clive, *The Law of Husband and Wife in Scotland* (Green for Scottish Law Institute, Edinburgh, 1974) it was observed that, "marriage contracts are now comparatively rare": p.345.

[13] See especially *Miller v Miller, McFarlane v McFarlane* [2006] UKHL 24.

[14] [1995] 2 F.L.R. 45, CA.

undesirable for standards that are intended to be of universal significance to be limited by private contracts. But more recently in *K v K*[15] the court took the prenuptial contract into account in so far as making an award of capital to the wife. One major consideration for entering into a prenuptial agreement, which is common in the USA,[16] is to preserve property as inheritance for the children of a previous marriage where the proposed marriage is a second or third marriage.

Agreements regulating issues on breakdown of the relationship **15–04** are also sometimes known as separation agreements, but will be referred to formally throughout this chapter as minutes of agreement. MoAs are usually registered with the consent of both parties in the Books of Council and Session for preservation and execution, or in the Sheriff Court Books. The purpose of this is not only to maintain a record of the agreement, but to enable either party to enforce the terms of the deed when the other is in default, by means of summary diligence.[17] Interestingly, MoAs are often made at least partly in order to preserve privacy and confidentiality. Yet, when MoAs are registered for execution they become public documents open for examination. MoAs are binding legal contracts[18] and as such can only be varied or withdrawn from under very special circumstances (discussed below). Around 3,000 MoAs are made in Scotland each year.[19]

Sometimes, parties will reach agreement only after the divorce is **15–05** already underway in the courts. Disputes about financial provision, in particular, often commence as defended actions in court, but end up being settled by agreement between the parties. In such cases, settlement can be reached in the form of a JMoA. It is usual to ask the court to interpone authority to a JMoA and to grant decree in terms of the arrangements in the agreement. This has the effect of transforming the parties' private agreement into a binding decree of the court. Thus, as with MoAs, neither party may unilaterally withdraw from the JMoA,[20] unless the special circumstances set out below apply. A JMoA cannot, however, deal with the ground of the divorce because that is a matter on which the court must hear evidence.[21] A JMoA is lodged with the court as part of the process rather than being publicly registered.

---

[15] [2003] 1 F.L.R. 120, Fam Div.

[16] See D. Weisberg and S. Appleton, *Modern Family Law: Cases and Materials* (2nd edn, Aspen, New York, 2002), pp.145–146.

[17] This saves time and money as a party can act immediately on the warrant contained in the document, without having to go to court to enforce the terms of the deed. When the agreement is registered for execution in the Books of Council and Session, diligence may take place anywhere in Scotland. For this reason, most MoAs are registered there rather than in Sheriff Court Books.

[18] *Anderson v Anderson*, 1991 S.L.T. (Sh. Ct.) 11.

[19] *Op. cit* above, n.5.

[20] See *Horton v Horton*, 1992 S.L.T. (Sh. Ct.) 37; *Milne v Milne*, 1987 S.L.T. 45; *Elder v Elder*, 1985 S.L.T. 471.

[21] This will usually take the form of affidavit evidence: see also para.14–04.

15–06   It can be estimated that MoAs and JMoAs are used to resolve disputes in around one-third of the total number of divorces in any year.[22] This shows that in a significant proportion of divorces it is the couple themselves who decide on the terms on which their marriage will be dissolved, rather than leaving the decision to the discretion of the courts. Now that civil partnerships are legally recognised, both MoAs and JMoAs are available to civil partners on the dissolution of their partnership

15–07   Once reached, such agreements, whether MoAs or JMoAs, are binding and cannot be varied or reduced without the consent of both parties, except in certain limited circumstances.[23] This serves to prevent reappraisal and re-negotiation of matters that have already been dealt with and provides another type of "clean break". Thus parties are free to set their own terms, which may be quite different from the kind of settlement that would be reached under the 1985 Act. Once made, agreements are binding and enforceable in law[24] (except possibly with regards to children). The image is one of party empowerment, but in these circumstances it is important to remember that women do not have the same economic and social bargaining power as men. Thus, women negotiating contracts at arm's length with male partners often find themselves in an inferior bargaining position, because of the gendered way in which they are allocated responsibility for the domestic sphere which provides them with less economic power than their male partners. What appears to be a voluntary agreement may instead be the product of unequal power relations, where compliance has been acquired under pressure (see wife's claim in *McAfee v McAfee*).[25] However, in some circumstances it would be inequitable if the agreement were treated as entirely final, and so special rules apply.

Circumstances Allowing for Variation or Reduction

Children

15–08   Under s.12 of the Children (Scotland) Act 1995, the court is directed in any matrimonial proceeding or such between civil partners where there are children under 16, to consider whether any s.11 order

---

[22] In 1992, there were approximately 3,000 MoAs and at least 1,443 JMoAs made as compared with a total divorce figure of 12,479 for that year (see Civil Courts Administration, *Civil Judicial Statistics Scotland 1992*, p.12). Civil Judicial Statistics no longer records this information.

[23] Note that where one of the parties is in material breach it may be open to the other party to rescind the agreement without the other's consent. See *Morrison v Morrison*, 2000 Fam. L.B. (42) p.6.

[24] However, where parties make a separation agreement and then reconcile, their actings may be held to be consistent with an intention to revoke the agreement and the principles of financial provision under the 1985 Act may be applied. See *Methven v Methven*, 1999 S.L.T. 117.

[25] 1990 S.C.L.R. (Notes) 805.

should be granted, such as a residence or contact order.[26] Its paramount concern in so doing must be the welfare of the child.[27] Thus, agreements reached by parents concerning their childcare arrangements are not binding on the court and, indeed, any person may apply at any time for a s.11 order notwithstanding that an agreement has already been signed about residence or contact.[28] In most cases where agreements about children have been reached, the court rubber stamps them,[29] however it has to be satisfied that the proposed arrangements are the best that can be achieved, for which weight is given to affidavit evidence such as from relatives or neighbours.

Contractual grounds for reduction

Agreements may, exceptionally, be set aside or reduced under the general law of contract where one party can establish that his or her consent was vitiated by force and fear, fraud or misrepresentation, undue influence, or facility and circumvention.[30] **15–09**

There is a heavy onus of proof on the party seeking to challenge the validity of a formal written agreement. If the challenge is successful, the agreement will be set aside. However, the longer an agreement remains in force after the divorce, the more difficult it is to challenge. A contract may also be set aside for mutual or common error, but only very rarely indeed for unilateral error, e.g. where one party thought the other had no assets and this was not due in any way to misrepresentations by that party.[31] However, if both parties agreed that a written agreement does not correctly implement what was informally or orally agreed, the court has power to rectify the agreement.[32] **15–10**

Variation of periodical allowance and aliment elements

Terms as to capital payments or transfer of property cannot, in principle, be varied once an agreement has been concluded. However, terms in MoAs allowing for a periodical allowance *can* be set aside or varied by the court but only if the parties have expressly provided that this should be allowed.[33] In contrast, if a JMoA is. converted into a decree which contains a periodical allowance element, then since it is **15–11**

---

[26] 1995 Act, s.12 as amended by s.291(2), Sch.28, para.60 of the 2004 Act where there is a child who has been accepted by both partners as a child of the family which their partnership constitutes.

[27] 1995 Act, s.11(7)(a).

[28] See *Norton v Horton*, 1992 S.L.T. (Sh. Ct.) 37.

[29] See Royal Commission on Legal Services, Cmnd.7846 (1980), Vol.1, p.157.

[30] See further, MacBryde, *The Law of Contract in Scotland* (W.Green, Edinburgh, 2001) Chs 13–17, pp.307–405.

[31] *ibid.*, p.364–365.

[32] Law Reform (Miscellaneous Provisions) (Scotland) Act 1985, ss.8 and 9.

[33] Family Law (Scotland) Act 1985, s.16(1)(a) as amended by s.261(2), Sch.28, para.22 of the 2004 Act for civil partners.

in substance a decree of the court, it may be varied or recalled like a decree, i.e. if there has been, since the date of the decree, a material change of circumstances.[34] This applies whether or not the parties contemplated variation at the time the agreement was made. Such variation on the grounds of a material change in circumstances is only permissible where the agreement forms part of a court decree. It is also important to note that a material change in circumstances must be actual and not based on a deemed or hypothetical change of circumstances brought about, for example, by the granting of decree on the basis of erroneous information.[35] The court may also vary or set aside any term relating to a periodical allowance where the payer has become bankrupt.[36]

15–12 Agreements frequently provide for the payment of aliment to children. Provision in both MoAs and JMoAs can be varied by application to the court if there had been a material change of circumstances since the date of the agreement.[37] When a maintenance calculation under the Child Support Act 1991 is made in respect of a child for whom aliment is payable under an agreement (such as happens when the parent with care becomes dependent on state benefits), this will constitute a "material change in circumstances".[38] For further discussion see Ch.5.

Statutory Challenge—s.16

15–13 Any term in an agreement relating to financial provision which was not "fair and reasonable at the time it was entered into" may be set aside or varied by the court under s.16(1)(b) of the 1985 Act. This will apply to any term of the agreement whether it relates to capital, income or transfer of property. The jurisdiction of the court to alter agreements under s.16 cannot be ousted and any term of the agreement purporting to do this will be void.[39] The power applies in respect of both MoAs and JMoAs.[40] The test of unfairness must be applied as at the time agreement was reached, and not at any other date.

---

[34] 1985 Act, s.13(4).

[35] See *Bye v Bye*, 1999 G.W.D. 33-1591.

[36] 1985 Act, s.16(3) as amended by s.261(2), Sch.28, para.22 of the 2004 Act for civil partners.

[37] See ss.7(2) and 5(1) respectively of the 1985 Act.

[38] 1985 Act, ss.7(2A) and 5(1A). However courts have refused to allow an application to the Child Support Agency when a maintenance agreement is in place, after a pronouncement by a Child Support Commissioner that an extract of a MoA registered in the Books of Council and Session constitutes a "maintenance order" for the purposes of the Act. Consequently amendments were made to ss.4(10) and 7(10) of the 1991 Act to the effect that even if there is a court order or registered MoA in place, provided that the order was made or the agreement was entered into on or after March 3, 2003 and has been in existence for more than one year, the Child Support Agency has jurisdiction to entertain an application for an assessment, even if there is a court order of registered MoA in place.

[39] 1985 Act, s.16(4).

[40] See *Jongejan v Jongejan*, 1993 S.L.T. 595.

This means that changes in the parties' circumstances *after* agreement has been reached cannot be taken into account, e.g. if one spouse acquires unforeseen financial burdens in the shape of a new family after separation.[41] An "agreement" must be a bilateral obligation and so does not include a gift.[42]

When is an agreement not "fair and reasonable"?

Independent Legal Advice

One of the major issues the court will consider is whether the **15–14** parties had independent legal advice when drawing up the agreement. If such advice was obtained, then the courts will normally assume that each party was fully appraised of his or her legal rights and understood the consequences of entering the particular agreement. However, the presence of legal advice does not necessarily mean the agreement cannot be reduced. In *McAfee v McAfee*[43] the court held that:

> "[T]he extent of a party's professional qualifications and experience and the nature of any advice received from a professional source may well be important factors to bear in mind in the judgment of what is fair and reasonable. Nevertheless, they cannot in themselves be determinative of the issue where there are other circumstances, suggesting unfair advantage or unreasonable conduct by one party to influence the other in the signing of an agreement which in its terms expressly surrenders rights which that other party would have on divorce".

This approach was upheld in *Gillon v Gillon (No.1)*.[44] In this case, **15–15** the principal issue was whether the *quality* of the legal advice had been substandard. The wife maintained that when she signed the agreement, it had not been made clear to her by her lawyers that she was entitled to a share of the value of the defender's pension rights, nor had these rights been valued. These were later found to be worth about £30,000. The court held it should consider all the circumstances surrounding the making of the agreement to see whether there was some unfair advantage taken by virtue of the relationship between the parties. If relevant information, such as the value of the pension, had been withheld, this should be taken into account even if (as here) the omission was accidental rather than fraudulent. What was to be disclosed should not be restricted to what would be

---

[41] See *Drummond v Drummond*, 1992 S.C.L.R. 473.
[42] See dicta in *Anderson v Anderson*, 1991 S.L.T. (Sh. Ct.) 11 at 13E.
[43] 1990 S.C.L.R. (Notes) 805 at 808. In this case, husband and wife were both solicitors in partnership together. The wife had also consulted a professional colleague. She argued that notwithstanding this, her husband had applied undue pressure by virtue of his superior business position.
[44] 1994 S.L.T. 978 at 983.

required in a commercial context. Accordingly, a proof of the facts was allowed.

15–16   In *Gillon v Gillon (No.3)*[45] the court attacked the merits of the case and held that notwithstanding the failure to value the pension, the agreement was fair and reasonable at the time it was entered into. Under the agreement, the wife was to purchase the husband's interest in the matrimonial home at a very substantial discount in return for renouncing any further claim on any of her husband's assets, including his pension. It was clear that the wife had been anxious to reach this agreement for fear that if she waited until the case came to court, the house would rise in value, and she would be unable to buy him out. The evidence suggested this fear was well-founded and that the wife had not done badly out of the arrangement. Taking all the facts into consideration in this case, the court refused to vary the agreement. A similar finding was made in *Inglis v Inglis*,[46] which endorsed the approach adopted in *Gillon (No.3)*, and that the agreement had been entered into by the wife in the full knowledge that she had a potential claim in her husband's pension rights but that she had renounced that claim in order to achieve what had appeared to her to be the immediate and significant advantage of the husband's departure from the matrimonial home.

The fact that both parties are advised by the same law agent does not automatically imply that the agreement drawn up was not fair or reasonable because of the conflict of interest.[47] In *Worth v Worth*[48] the parties drew up their own agreement and took it to the solicitor who had acted in their house purchase and was a mutual friend. They were advised that they should seek independent legal advice if they thought there might be a conflict of interest, but chose not to.[49] Several years after the agreement had taken effect, the wife learned that she might have had a claim on her husband's pension under the 1985 Act, an issue never raised or mentioned in the original agreement. She sought to have the agreement set aside under s.16. The court found that the solicitor had not acted improperly as he had raised the issue of conflict of interest, and had attempted to act as an "honest broker" between the parties.

---

[45] 1995 S.L.T. 678.

[46] 1999 S.L.T. (Sh Ct) 59.

[47] But note Patterson's observations on r.3 of the Solicitors (Scotland) Practice Rules dealing with professional responsibility in this matter: *Professional Responsibility: Student Manual* (2001) at p.110. See also Lord Nicholls observation in *Royal Bank of Scotland v Etridge (No.2)* [2001] 4 All E.R. 449 at 471 where he sets out the pros and cons of acquiring independent legal advice as set against the benefits of use of the same law agent, such as, less expense.

[48] 1994 S.C.L.R. (Notes) 362.

[49] Note this was also an issue in *Inglis v Inglis*, 1999 S.L.T. (Sh Ct) 59 where the court held that the wife had been given the clearest warning that it would have been in her best interests to seek separate legal representation and advice but had declined to do so without any undue pressure from her husband.

However, the agreement might still be objectively unfair even though there had been no "concealment, trickery, or pressure". The court reluctantly found that the "agreement does not fairly reflect the actual value of the parties' property or the defender's fair entitlement to it, for the defender was in law, and thus presumably in fairness, entitled to a share of the value of the pursuer's pension rights".[50] As a result a term of the agreement was reduced.

Unequal Division of Assets

The mere fact that there has been an unequal division of assets **15–17** between the parties by agreement does not of itself give rise to an inference of unfairness or unreasonableness.[51] In some cases, an unequal division may be accepted by one party against their best interests because, as in *Gillon*, they prefer the certainty of knowing precisely what they are to receive on divorce, rather than the uncertainty of waiting to see what a court settlement might produce at a future date.

An agreement can be reduced or varied under s.16 only either **15–18** before decree of divorce is granted, or within such time thereafter as the court may specify.[52] Thus, in most cases, if the s.16 plea is not made at the time of divorce the agreement will stand. This can be invidious, given that divorce is often a time of turbulence and disruption, and that the full effect of an agreement negotiated under the pressures of this period—which are unlikely to constitute legal duress sufficient to allow reduction—may not become apparent until some time later when the action is barred.[53] Furthermore, in many cases, full details as to the financial position, e.g. the value of pension rights, may only emerge after the divorce. Even where the action is raised in time, as can be seen in cases like *Gillon* and *McAfee*, the courts are most reluctant to reopen a formal written agreement reached by the parties. This is because of the ordinary principle that parties should be bound to contracts they have entered voluntarily, in the interests of certainty for both the parties themselves and third parties. It is submitted that this principle is not

---

[50] 1994 S.C.L.R. (Notes) 362 at 365.
[51] *Gillon v Gillon (No.3)*, 1995 S.L.T. 678. In *Anderson v Anderson*, 1991 S.L.T. (Sh. Ct.) 11 the husband in a fit of remorse at his conduct made a written gift of his whole share of the matrimonial property to his wife. The court held that even if this was an "agreement" under s.16(1)(b), which was dubious, it was fair and reasonable when entered into as the husband had acted voluntarily and in full knowledge of what he was doing.
[52] 1985 Act, s.16(2)(b); and see *Jongejan* above, n.21. Further, note that until amended by s.45(1), Sch.2, para.5 of the FLSA 2006, s.16(2) referred to divorce only and not dissolution, whilst referring back to s.16(1)(a) and (b) which did mention civil partnerships and dissolution.
[53] Most of the sample questioned in the *Mutual Consent* study, above (n.17) reported that they felt under stress when making their agreement, and that they made compromises which they now regretted.

as compelling in relation to domestic relationships as commercial ones, something which s.16 already reflects, but perhaps not fully enough. There is something to be said for the concept of a one-year "cooling-off" period within which a s.16 action could be brought by right *after* the divorce.[54]

15–19 In the meantime it is strongly advisable to draft any agreement as comprehensively as possible,[55] with provision built in for unforeseen material changes in either party's circumstances. Otherwise, problems may arise in connection with assets which have not been specifically dealt with in the agreement. In *Atkinson v Atkinson*,[56] for example, the agreement dealt with capital but made no mention of periodical allowance. The court found that it still had jurisdiction to make an order for a sum of periodical allowance.[57] For the avoidance of doubt, it should always be expressly provided that the agreement is to be in full settlement of all future financial claims between the parties arising out of the marriage.

PRIVATE ORDERING FOR COHABITANTS

15–20 The discussion of minutes and joint minutes has so far focused on married couples and civil partners, yet unmarried couples—including same-sex couples—may, of course, also wish to enter informal agreements about finance and property. Indeed, until the FLSA 2006 introduced a limited right to cohabitees to make a claim when their relationship terminates,[58] such cohabitants had no claim upon the other in the event of relationship failure *unless* such an agreement had been made. Despite this, however, the legal status of such agreements is not as settled as those made by married couples, nor is there the same right to have agreements reduced as not fair and reasonable as there is under s.16 of the Family Law (Scotland) Act 1985 for married persons and civil partners.[59]

---

[54] It is interesting to note that lawyers practicing collaborative law (discussed at paras 15–43 *et seq.* below) take account of the fact that their clients have "good" and "bad" days during the divorce process and make allowances for this when negotiating agreements to try and avoid clients making hasty decisions on "off" days.

[55] For styles of family law agreements, see *Butterworths Family Law Service* (Lexis Nexis, 2006), Division F, Style 11. See also G. Jamieson, *Family Law Agreement* (Tottel Publishing, 2005), especially Ch.3 on drafting, executing and registering family law agreements, p.22–33.

[56] 1988 S.C.L.R. 396.

[57] But compare *Sochart v Sochart*, 1988 S.L.T. 449 where the parties agreed by JMoA that H should make W a periodical allowance, but said nothing about any capital sums. In this case, the terms of the minute were held impliedly to dispose of all financial claims between the parties, and so H was not allowed to seek a capital sum order from the court payable by W.

[58] FLSA 2006, s.28. See also s.26 and 27 of the 2006 Act

[59] For a discussion of the property claims cohabitants may make see para.13–98.

Illegality and Immorality

Under the "illegal purposes" doctrine in contract law, all contracts **15–21**
which promote illegality are unenforceable. Nineteenth-century and
earlier case law defined illegal contracts to include any contracts
which furthered immoral purposes. These included agreements for
the provision of sexual services. Originally aimed at undermining
illicit activities such as prostitution, it is questionable whether the illegality doctrine can apply to agreements reached between cohabiting
parties who have a sexual relationship, but the matter is not free from
doubt.

To clarify the position, the Scottish Law Commission some time **15–22**
ago recommended enacting a statutory provision to the effect that:

> "A contract between cohabitants or prospective cohabitants
> relating to property or financial matters should not be void or
> unenforceable solely because it was concluded between the
> parties in, or about to enter, this type of relationship".[60]

This was not, however, included in the FLSA 2006. It is clear,
nonetheless, that unmarried couples can validly make wills in each
other's favour, give each other gifts, and take title to heritable property in common. Contractual provisions will, however, be useful when
attempting in advance of the event to distribute property not yet
acquired, or to provide for transfer of property contingent on the
breakdown of the relationship or other circumstances. While the provisions of the FLSA 2006 make some property provision for cohabitants, this is not on a par with the kind of financial provision
accorded to married couples or civil partners. Despite cohabitants'
erroneous beliefs that they are "common law" spouses and entitled to
a half share of each other's property, this is not the case in law and so
they still need to consider regulating their relationship through the
use of contract.

As things currently stand, cohabitants have no right to aliment **15–23**
from each other under the Family Law (Scotland) Act 1985 and any
attempt to claim state benefit will involve aggregation of resources
under the cohabitation rule.[61] One option that has been put forward
is for them to enter in "a cohabitants' agreement which amongst other
things, would constitute mutual obligations of aliment for a time".[62]
These obligations must be finite for there is no statutory provision (as
under the 1985 Act) to bring them to an end. It has been observed
that the court has jurisdiction to regulate and enforce private aliment

---

[60] See *Report on Family Law*, Scot. Law Com. No.135 (1992), Draft Bill, Clause 42.
  For an English attempt at drafting such legislation, see German's Cohabitation
  (Contract Enforcement) Bill, June 11, 1991, Bill 175.
[61] See paras 10–78 to 10–80.
[62] G. Jamieson, "Arbitration and Conciliation for Aliment", 2003 S.L.T. 47.

under a contract but that it has no statutory power to vary contractual aliment. For this reason "the safest course is therefore for cohabitants to arbitrate for aliment, and its subsequent variation".[63] The advantages of arbitration include speed of process and "(perhaps) cost".[64] The downside is that an arbiter has to be paid for and legal aid is not available for arbitration.

15–24   Unfortunately there is very little empirical evidence as to how many cohabitants enter into cohabitation contracts. In the study on *Mutual Consent*, only about 5 per cent of agreements were made by cohabiting couples. It would appear that lawyers have relatively rarely been called on to draft such contracts in Scotland.[65] However, some guidance on the type of issues which should be covered in a cohabitation agreement is provided by *Butterworths Lexis Family Law Service*[66] and in *Family Agreements*.[67]

Same-Sex Cohabitants

15–25   Like ordinary cohabitation contracts, contracts made by same-sex couples may possibly fall foul of the illegal purposes rule. The Scottish Law Commission's proposed enactment on cohabitation contracts said nothing about the sex of the cohabitants although it defined cohabitation as: "the relationship of a man and woman who are not legally married to each other but are living together as husband and wife, whether or not they pretend to others that they are married to each other".[68] However, given the introduction of the Human Rights Act 1998 and the ruling in *Mendoza v Ghaidan*[69] as well as the definition of cohabitant in the FLSA 2006,[70] cohabitants should now be interpreted to include same-sex as well as heterosexual couples. In any event, it is most unlikely that contracts entered into between cohabitants today would be deemed unenforceable given Recommendation No R.(88)3 of the Committee of Ministers to Member States of the Council of Europe on the validity of contracts between persons living together as an unmarried couple.[71]

---

[63] See, Jamieson, above. For style of agreement see *Butterworths Family law Service, op. cit.* above, n.53, Divison F, Style 11(v).

[64] *ibid.*

[65] See Kingdom, "Lawyers will Draft Anything: Attitudes to Cohabitation Contracts", Occasional Paper No.5 in *Issues in Sociology and Social Policy* (University of Liverpool, Department of Sociology, Social Policy and Social Work Studies, 1994). Kingdom notes that solicitors sometimes negotiate an effective cohabitation agreement when problems arise by way of a minute, or through exchange of solicitors' letters, rather than drafting a full contract in advance.

[66] See *Butterworths Family Law Service, op. cit.* above, n.53, Division F, Style 11(vi).

[67] *Op. cit.* above, n.53. *Family Law Agreements*, Ch.6, pp.46–48.

[68] *Report on Family Law*, Scot. Law Com. No.135 (1995), p.16.1, n.2.

[69] [2002] EWCA Civ 1533.

[70] s.25.

[71] Adopted March 7, 1988. See *Sutton v Mischon de Reya (a Firm)*, *The Times*, December 19, 2003.

CONTENT OF MINUTES AND JOINT MINUTES OF AGREEMENT

Where parties engage in private ordering it is useful to know what **15–26**
emerges from negotiations in the form of content for comparison
with the framework set out for division of matrimonial property in
the Family Law (Scotland) Act 1985 and its resulting case law. To
what extent do such negotiations reflect bargaining "in the shadow of
the law"?[72] Such considerations are important for they raise questions
about the extent to which parties should be able to supplant legislative standards with their own terms which may depart radically from
the established framework.[73] As Wasoff has observed, when it comes
to private ordering "little is known about bargaining outcomes or the
extent to which their substance is genuinely within 'the shadow of the
law' ".[74] While it is desirable that parties should be able to reach agreements that suit their own individual needs, when private ordering goes
beyond this to substantially extinguish rights that would arise under
the statutory framework, this can cause hardship. It is true that
agreements may be set aside on the grounds discussed above but these
are limited and can be hard to establish. Experience from the United
States has shown that prenuptial agreements may be used effectively
to extinguish a spouse's claim to almost all financial provision altogether and still be upheld.[75] Most jurisdictions in the United States
are unwilling to get into questions of the substantive aspects of such
agreements and opt instead to judge the matter on the basis of procedural safeguards such as full disclosure of assets and access to legal
advice.

Unfortunately, little is known (other than anecdotally) about the **15–27**
actual content of MoAs and JMoAs. In 1992, a study was made of
written agreements of both kinds entered into by separating and

---

[72] See R. Mnookin and L. Kornhauser, "Bargaining in the shadow of the law; the case
of divorce", 1979 Yale Law Journal, Vol.88, p.950–997 who were the first to coin this
term.

[73] See *F v F* [1995] 2 F.L.R. 45, CA where the court held that prenuptial agreements
were of limited significance because it was undesirable that standards that are
intended to be of universal significance should be limited by private contracts.
However, see *K v K (Ancillary Relief: Prenutpial Agreement)* [2003] 1 F.L.R. 120,
Fam Div where the judge took account of the prenuptial agreement when determining the amount of capital to be paid to the wife.

[74] F. Wasoff, "Mutual Consent: Separation Agreements and the Outcomes of Private
Ordering in Divorce", 2005 Journal of Social Welfare and Family Law, Vol.27(3–4),
pp.237–250 at p.238.

[75] See *Simeone v Simeone*, 581 A.2d 162 (Pa. 1990) where a 39-year-old neurosurgeon
with an income of $90,000 a year presented his 23-year-old bride who was unem-
ployed with an prenuptial agreement on the eve of the parties' wedding. This agreement limited her claims on divorce to a maximum total payment of $25,000
regardless of the period of time that elapsed between the marriage and divorce.
Without legal advice she signed the agreement and the court upheld its validity
refusing to find that the agreement had been entered into under duress and embar-
rassment of postponing the wedding. See also *In Re Marriage of Greenwald*, 454
N.W.2d 34 (Wis. Ct. App. 1990).

divorcing couples.[76] The overwhelming majority of couples in this survey made agreements while they were still married.[77] A number of important points can be distinguished.

15–28 First, those making MoAs are disproportionately home owners.[78] It is therefore unsurprising that one of the principal concerns of these agreements is the distribution or transfer of the matrimonial home. The favoured option in just under two-thirds of cases was to transfer one spouse's share in the home to the other. It is interesting to compare this to the very limited use being made of property transfer orders in the courts, especially since *Wallis v Wallis*.[79] The survey found women were more than twice as likely to continue occupying the matrimonial home after separation as men, usually because the woman was the one who continued to care for the children after divorce. About two-thirds of mothers with care of the children remained in the matrimonial home after separation.

15–29 Secondly, it was found arrangements for care of the children after divorce are an important topic in separation agreements. Almost 95 per cent of agreements made by couples with children contained discussion and agreement on which parent the children should reside with after separation. Overwhelmingly, this was the mother (in 91 per cent of agreements). There was very little support for joint custody after divorce between couples, which was agreed to in only three per cent of cases.[80] This appears to mark a notable divergence between what parties choose for themselves in childcare arrangements, and the aims of the Children (Scotland) Act 1995, which introduces a presumption of joint parental responsibility after divorce.[81] Contact arrangements were considerably more hazy than those relating to residence, with precise details of access agreed in only about one-fifth of cases involving children. As in the courts, contact was more typically left to mutual arrangement between the parties. Aliment for the children was another matter commonly agreed, especially in MoAs where

---

[76] *Op. cit.* above, n.7. This study was based on 1,042 agreements including both MoAs and JMoAs. The MoAs studied formed a representative sample, so that the findings can be taken as an accurate picture of agreements of this type.

[77] *ibid.* 83% were still married, compared with 8% divorced and 5% made by cohabiting couples.

[78] *ibid.* 77% of those who made a MoA were home owners, compared with only 48% of those making JMoAs.

[79] 1992 S.L.T. 676, affirmed by the House of Lords at 1993 S.L.T. 1348. For fuller discussion of this case and relevant reform of the valuation date of matrimonial property under s.16 of the FLSA 2006, see paras 13–22 *et seq*. Note: property transfer orders were made in only five % of ordinary divorce actions in 1992: see Morris, Gibson and Platts, *op. cit* n.1, p.28.

[80] However, see *McKechnie v McKechnie*, 1990 S.L.T. (Sc Ct) 75 in which the parents had put before a court a JMoA in which they had agreed joint custody. The court said the cases where joint custody would be in the best interests of a child must be rare and awarded custody to the mother and three consecutive residential access to the father.

[81] s.11(7)(a) of the Children (Scotland) Act 1995, as amended by s.291(2), Sch.28, para.17 of the 2004 Act to include civil partners.

aliment was discussed in 90 per cent of cases. Interestingly, evidence drawn from interviews suggested that enforcement of agreed aliment payments was less of a problem than it is when payments are ordered by the court, however this is likely to be a reflection of the quality of relationship between adults who are able to cooperate with each other and reach agreement in the first place.

Thirdly, in the survey the "clean break" philosophy underlying the **15–30** Family Law (Scotland) Act 1985 also appeared to be endorsed by couples making agreements. Periodical allowance was discussed in only 16 per cent of agreements and provided for in 10 per cent. This can be compared with the fact that court orders for periodical allowance were made in the same year in about 15 per cent of divorces.[82] The most typical duration provided for a periodical allowance was three years, which echoes the maximum time limit in s.9(1)(d) of the 1985 Act for adjustment from financial dependence. In around 90 per cent of agreements then, a "clean break" was achieved, most typically by transferring one party's share in the matrimonial home to the other, and sometimes by the additional or alternative payment of a capital lump sum. Such payments were far more commonly found in agreements, especially MoAs, than capital sum orders are in the divorce courts.[83]

Finally, one of the most conspicuous features of all the agree- **15–31** ments studied was the absence to a great extent of any mention of pension rights. Pensions were referred to in only nine per cent of agreements, and payments specifically related to pension rights were recorded in only a mere three per cent of cases.[84] This omission may be due to a verbal understanding that the wife would renounce her claims to her husband's pension in return for a transfer of his half share in the matrimonial home. A more recent survey of solicitors in Scotland and England and Wales[85] found that it was more common for pension rights to be taken into account in divorce settlements in Scotland than in England and Wales. It also found that, in practice, offsetting pension rights against other assets was the most common way of treating rights in both current occupational and personal schemes, although lump sum payments were also common for occupational schemes. In contrast, orders for payment of a capital sum in respect of rights or interests in a pension[86] in

---

[82] Morris, Gibson and Platts, *op. cit.* above, n.1, at p.32.

[83] They were found in 40% of MoAs and 17% of JMoAs. By comparison, capital sum orders were made in only 5% of ordinary divorce actions in 1992 (Morris, Gibson and Platts, *op. cit.* above, n.1, at p.28).

[84] It should be noted that the empirical study on which these data are based was carried out in 1992 before the Child Support Act 1991 and the Children (Scotland) Act 1995 came into force and before reform on pensions and divorce in the Welfare Reforms and Pensions Act 1999.

[85] J. Field, *Pensions and Divorce: The 1998 Survey*, Research Report No.117 (Corporate Document Services, Leeds, 2000).

[86] 1985 Act, s.12A as amended by s.261(2), Sch.28, para.19 of the 2004 act to extend to civil partners.

Scotland were used infrequently. Qualitative research[87] drawing on in-depth interview with thirty solicitors who took part in a 1998 survey reported that solicitors preferred offsetting pension rights against other assets rather than earmarking as this reflected the priority needs of ensuring the parties' *immediate* needs were met. Although pension sharing was seen as an improvement on earmarking there was still a preference for dealing with pensions by compensation methods.

15–32   What is clear is that it is essential that women get proper legal advice. Numbers of women who were interviewed during the 1992 Scottish survey claimed that they were ill-informed about their husband's pension rights and had been pressurised into this choice, an observation born out in *Gillon v Gillon (No.1)*.[88] Once again it is essential that before concluding an agreement that parties should be fully informed of their rights and the options that are open to them given the difficulties involved in having an agreement varied or set aside. While it may be possible to sue solicitors for negligent advice, this is a difficult and costly exercise that may prove unfruitful.[89]

REACHING AGREEMENT: MEDIATION AND COLLABORATIVE LAW

15–33   There are a number of ways in which agreements between parties may be reached. These may involve negotiated settlement by lawyers (as discussed above), mediation or the use of collaborative law. The trend in family law over the last two decades has been to encourage parties to reach their own decisions on financial provision, and on residence and contact arrangements with respect to children, so that less reliance is placed on court intervention.

Mediation

15–34   One means of achieving this goal is through mediation.[90] Mediation is,

> "a process in which an impartial third person, the mediator, assists couples considering separation or divorce to meet together to deal with the arrangements which need to be made for the future".[91]

---

[87] S. Arthur and J. Lewis, *Pensions and Divorce: Exploring Financial Settlement*, Research Report No.118 (Corporate Document Services, Leeds, 2000).

[88] 1994 S.L.T. 978.

[89] See *Dible v The Morton Fraser Partnership*, 2001 Fam. L.R. 84 and *Darrie v Duncan*, 2001 S.L.T. 941.

[90] For an up-to-date account of mediation, see *The Blackwell Handbook of Mediation: Bridging Theory, Research, and Practice* (M. Herrman (ed.), Blackwell Publishing, 2005).

[91] *Looking to the Future: Mediation and the Ground for Divorce—the Government's Proposals*, Cm.27990 (1995), para.5.4.

These include reaching agreements about childcare and financial matters. The Government's White Paper on divorce reform in England in 1995 commented that:

> "Unlike current legal processes, mediation is a flexible process which can take into account the different needs of families, and differing attitudes and positions of the parties".[92]

As such, it represents "an alternative to negotiating matters at arms length through two separate lawyers and to litigating through the courts".[93]

In England, mediation was part of the basis upon which Pt II of the **15–35** Family Law Act 1996 was constructed.[94] However, although this part of the Act was not implemented,[95] mediation continues to be promoted by the Legal Services Commission as an alternative to litigation.[96]

It has been asserted that the aim of mediation is to assist "divorc- **15–36** ing and separating couples to reach agreements amicably, especially over the arrangements for their children".[97] There has been enormous debate in Scotland in recent years about the various claims made on behalf of mediation as a preferable alternative to court-based dispute settlement, e.g. that it empowers individuals by allowing them to maintain control over their own affairs and assert their autonomy from the courts.[98] There has been a similarly hard fought debate in

---

[92] *Looking to the Future*, above, para.7.7.

[93] *ibid.*, para.5.8.

[94] For discussion, see S. M. Cretney, *Family Law* (4th edn, Sweet & Maxwell, London, 2000), pp.65–77.

[95] After disappointing results from pilot schemes that were carried out to test the - effectiveness of the new procedures the Lord Chancellor, Lord Irvine, announced on January 16, 2001 that the main provisions of the Act would not be implemented after all.

[96] Under s.29, a person seeking legal aid in matrimonial proceedings would have to attend a meeting with a mediator to determine whether mediation is suitable to deal with the issue arising. This section was repealed by the Access to Justice Act 1999 but remains part of the Legal Service's funding code.

[97] *The Scottish Family Conciliation Service (Lothian): Report of an Assessment of the First Two Years of the Service* (Scottish Central Research Unit, Edinburgh, 1986), p.2.19.

[98] See F. Raitt, "Mediation As A Form of Alternative Dispute Resolution: A Rejoinder", 1995 J.L.S.S. 40(5) at p.182; A. Dick, *"Lawyer Mediator—Interface or Interloper?"*, 1995 S.L.T. 33 at p.305; Griffiths, "The Future of Family Law: Empowerment: Rhetoric or Reality?" in *Scots Law into the 21st Century* (MacQueen (ed.), W.Green, Edinburgh, 1996), pp.193–203; M. Upton, "Mediation in Family Disputes", 1996 J.L.S.S. 41(3) at p.115; A. Oswald, "Mediation in family disputes", 1996 SCOLAG 231 at p.20; F. Raitt, "Limitation of family mediation", 1996 SCOLAG 234 at p.68; R. Ward, "CALMing the Waters—Two Years On", 1996 SCOLAG 235 at p.102; A. Oswald, "In defence of family mediation", 1996 SCOLAG 237 at p.148; F. Raitt, "Informal Justice and the Ethics of Mediating in Abusive Relationships", 1997 J.R. Vol,2 at p.76; S. Brand, "Separation and Divorce: Why Clients Should See a Solicitor Mediator", 1998 J.L.S.S. 43(2) at p.58; F. Myers and F. Wasoff, "Meeting in the Middle: Mediators' and Solicitors' Divorce Practice",

England[99] over whether the assumptions underlying mediation are justified, which may be stated with much over-simplification as the belief that the divorce process will be better, cheaper and less hostile the less lawyers have to do with it. There are also concerns about the extent to which parties are empowered to negotiate, especially women who may find themselves in a weaker bargaining position, as well as the issue of whether mediation should be used at all in cases involving domestic abuse. Over and above these considerations is the issue of children's participation in the process.[1] This latter consideration is especially pertinent given the implementation of the Human Rights Act and children's rights to be consulted about and to express a view on any major decision affecting their welfare. Unfortunately, space does not permit us to deal with these debates here.

15–37 Whatever the concerns, mediation should not be dismissed as failing to provide a just and fair result simply *because* it fails to follow the model of legal representation and judicial supervision we are familiar with in the court system. So long as established legal norms, such as the "best interests of the child" and "fair sharing of matrimonial property", play a role in shaping agreements reached through mediation, there is no reason why such agreements cannot be as respectful of legal rights as those adjudicated by courts. Furthermore, it is disingenuous to regard the courts, in comparison with mediation, as bastions of justice and rights in the divorce process. The truth is that the great majority—some 80 per cent—of ordinary divorce actions come before the courts uncontested[2] with the court required only to establish that there are grounds for divorce,[3] and that satisfactory arrangements have been made for the children.[4]

15–38 Mediation began in Scotland in 1984 under the auspices of a voluntary body, the Scottish Family Conciliation Service ("Lothian") and has since expanded to cover regions throughout Scotland, under

---

2000 S.L.T. 259; J. Scoular and C. Irvine, "A Review of 'Meeting in the Middle' ", 2001 S.L.T. 125; F. Myers and F. Wasoff, "Meeting in the Middle: A Reply to Scoular and Irvine", 2001 S.L.T. 128; A. Dick and E. Malcolm, "Let Mediation take the Strain", 2001 J.L.S.S. 46(8) at p.24; J. Sturrock and D. Semple, "Mediation a Cultural Revolution", 2001 J.L.S.S. 46(8) at p.21.

[99] See, inter alia, Roberts, "Decision-Making for Life Apart", (1995) 58 M.L.R. 714; Cretney, "The Divorce White Paper—Some Reflections", 1995 Fam. Law 302; McCarthy and Walker, "Mediation and Divorce Law Reform—The Lawyer's View", 1995 Fam. Law 361; Sclater, "The Limits of Mediation", 1995 25 Fam. Law 494; and Davis, "Divorce Reform—Peering Anxiously into the Future", 1995 25 Fam. Law 564; S. Roberts, "Family Mediation After the Act", 2001 13 C.F.L.Q. 265; R. Dingwall and D. Greatbach, "Family Mediators—What Are They Doing?" [2001] Family Law 378; G. Davies, "Reflections in the Aftermath of the Family Mediation Pilot", 2001 12 C.F.L.Q. 371.

[1] For a discussion of these issues see Edward and Griffiths, *Family Law* (W.Green, Edinburgh, 1997), pp.401–414, paras 15–14 to 15–22.

[2] Morris, Gibson and Platts, *op. cit.* above, n.1. at p.15.

[3] See also para.14–04.

[4] Children (Scotland) Act 1995, s.12.

the general supervision of a national umbrella body, Family Mediation[5] Scotland ("FMS"), which was created in 1987.[6] As the service has developed, so has its remit extended from providing mediation services only in relation to children in divorce, to providing "all-issues" mediation which deals with disputes relating to finance and property as well as children.

The mediation services in Scotland, in contrast with England, are **15–39** wholly independent of the courts. However, the courts in Scotland have the power compulsorily to refer parties involved in divorce or child-related disputes to mediation.[7] Such a referral may be made at any stage in the proceedings up until the final determination of the action.[8] However, it is important to note that only a small percentage of referrals to mediation in Scotland do come from the courts.[9] The rest come from solicitors, voluntary aid agencies, or the parties themselves.[10] Agreements reached in mediation may be embodied in MoA or JMoA in order to make them binding and enforceable. Statements made in mediation are confidential[11] unless, for example, it pertains to damage to property or personal injury during a mediation session, or the civil proceedings to which the mediation relates concerns the protection of a child with whom social services are involved.[12] The statement of outcomes or the fact that no agreement has been reached may, of course, be made public.

Mediation in Scotland is not at present an alternative to seeing a **15–40** lawyer or going to court, but rather an optional extra. A legal divorce decree as for dissolution of civil partnership must be obtained from the courts and, except in simplified divorce/dissolution, a lawyer must still institute court proceedings. Originally, FMS mediators were not usually qualified to advise on the complicated issue of finance after divorce and, for this reason, traditionally devoted their efforts to helping parties to reach agreement on disputes concerning residence

---

[5] The term "mediation" has been substituted for "conciliation" in order to avoid any confusion with reconciliation which has different aims.

[6] The current title was adopted in 1992.

[7] OCR 33.22 (as substituted by the Act of Sederunt (Family Proceedings in the Sheriff Court) 1996 (SI 1996/2167), Sch., para.12); and OCR 33A.22 for civil partners. Also, RCS 49.23 (as amended by the Act of Sederunt (Rules of the Court of Session Amendment No.3) (Miscellaneous) 1996 (SI 1996/1756), para.2(17) and by the Act of Sederunt (Rules of Court of Session Amendment No.5) (Family Actions and Miscellaneous) 1996 (SI 1996/2587), para.2(16)).

[8] See *Patterson v Patterson*, 1994 S.C.L.R. 166.

[9] See further, Garwood, *Trying To Get Us Talking, a Study of Rule of Court Referrals to Family Conciliation (Mediation) Services* (Family Conciliation Scotland, Edinburgh, 1992).

[10] In 2004–2005, 71% of cases referred to FMS were self-referrals. The remainder comprised 13% of referrals from solicitors, 5% referrals from the Sheriff Court, 0% from the Court of Session and 10% from other agencies, e.g. Citizens Advice Bureaux: 2005 FMS, *Annual Review 2005*, p.9.

[11] Civil Evidence (Family Mediation) (Scotland) Act 1995.

[12] The exclusions are at s.2 of the Civil Evidence (Family Mediation) (Scotland) Act 1995.

and contact with children of the marriage. However, as in England, it is rapidly becoming normal for experienced family lawyers to train as mediators, creating a hybrid profession of lawyer-mediators who are jointly accredited by the Law Society of Scotland and CALM ("Comprehensive Accredited Lawyer Mediators").[13] Meanwhile, traditional mediators within FMS have also begun to acquire legal expertise in order to have the background to carry out "all-issues" mediation. FMS mediators usually either work free, or are paid a nominal hourly rate, while lawyer-mediators charge commercial rates for their services. In the past, this has effectively restricted access to lawyer-mediation, as legal aid was not available for mediation services. However, since 1995 legal aid has been allowed in certain circumstances as an outlay in a solicitors account and even CALM mediation may be allowed as such an outlay.

15–41 Whatever the advantages and disadvantages associated with mediation, it is clear that it is here to stay and that it is also being used increasingly as a form of alternative dispute resolution in non-family cases.[14] Initial debates on the subject tended to become polarised around the pros and cons of mediation, as distinct from those attributed to the formal legal system.[15] However, it is important to recognise that while mediation in Scotland does not form part of the court system in the same way as it does in England, it nonetheless cannot be divorced from it. In practical terms, whatever the parties agree to in mediation, be it a memorandum of understanding[16] or a summary of mediation,[17] neither document is legally binding but must be submitted to the parties' lawyers to be made into a legally binding document in the appropriate form which allows for third party scrutiny. Similarly, when disputes come to the Sheriff Court a number of sheriffs are in favour of exploring mediation as an option and alternative to the court process.[18] For example, one such sheriff, now

---

[13] According to the CALM website, there are currently 88 trained and accredited lawyer-mediators in Scotland.

[14] See J. Sturrock and D. Semple, "Mediation a Cultural Revolution", 2001 J.L.S.S. 46(8), p.21; S. O'Neill, "Mediation and Non-Family Civil Disputes", 2002 SCOLAG 81; and E. Macolm, "Breakpoint", 2004 J.L.S.S. 49(7) 15 on the work of the Scottish Mediation Network who are exploring the growing range of disputes in Scotland that are moved forward by solicitors' strategic use of the mediation process. See also M. Hassock, "New Balls Please: Civil and Commercial Mediation", 2004 J.L.S.S. 49(7) 18. For England, see E. Harte on the Solicitors Family Law Association's first mediation conference in 2003 in "Comment: Mediation—Help or Hindrance, and What of its Future?" [2003] Fam Law 33 at p.865.

[15] For a critique of the way in which the roles of lawyers and mediators have been set off against one another see C. McEwen, N. Rogers and R. Maiman, "Bring in the Lawyers: Challenging the Dominant Approaches to Ensuring Fairness in Divorce Mediation", 1994–1995 79 Minn L. Rev. 1317.

[16] Drawn up by FMS mediators.

[17] Drawn up by CALM mediators.

[18] S. Brand, "Separation and Divorce: Why Clients Should See a Solicitor Mediator", 1998 J.L.S.S. 43(2) 58 at p.59. The Sheriff Court Rules Council set up a Mediation

retired, was sheriff Sheehan, from Falkirk Sheriff Court, who would ask at an early stage of the case—if not in chambers then at the child welfare or option hearing—if there was any possibility of mediation.[19]

What is clear is the extent to which mediation and the formal legal **15–42** process compliment one another. This is highlighted by the fact that solicitors may now take on the role of mediators. This raises questions about the extent to which the two roles may become blurred or rather lead to a change in practice on the part of their practitioners. A study on *Meeting in the Middle: a Study of Solicitors' and Mediators' Divorce Practice*[20] compared how three profession groups who assist divorcing couples in Scotland—solicitors, solicitor-mediations (CALM) and all-issues family mediations (associated with FMS)—manage disputes between the parties. While this qualitative study noted differences in approach it nonetheless found that the three groups have more common ground and are closer in practice than expected from commonly made claims about partisanship and impartiality. Rather than a strictly neutral stance, mediators depart from that norm in subtly advancing implicitly preferred options more compatible with their core values. Further, solicitors, rather than being strictly partisan, operate in a more impartial manner with clients in order to secure a reasonable negotiated agreement.[21] Such findings are in keeping with Simon Roberts' view that with the advent of mediation the courts new role is as,

> "sponsors of settlement[[22]] . . . Everything is in question: the identity of the mediator as autonomous professional, the lawyer as partisan, and the court as an instrument of third-party decision."[23]

This adaptation of roles has also been acknowledged in empirical work on the legal representation of children where researchers have noted that, although the roles of lawyer as advocate for the child and as guardian *ad litem* are distinct, the former theoretically acting on the child client's instructions and the latter promoting what is in the child's best interests, these roles tended to get blurred in practice.[24]

Committee to investigate whether the court should encourage parties to use adversarial procedures, and if so, in what circumstances; the Rules Council has yet to make recommendations based on their reports.

[19] R. MacKenzie, "Mediation: The Falkirk Experience", 2001 J.L.S.S. 46(8) at p.32.

[20] By F. Meyers and F. Wasoff for the Scottish Central Research Unit 2000.

[21] This study has been criticised by J. Scoular, and C. Irvine: "A Review of 'Meeting in the Middle'", 2001 S.L.T. 125. For a rejoinder see F. Myers, and F. Wasoff , "Meeting in the Middle: A Reply to Scoular and Irvine", 2001 S.L.T. 128.

[22] S. Roberts, "Family Mediation After the Act", 2001 C.F.L.Q. 265 at p.272.

[23] *ibid.* at p.273.

[24] For the UK see R. Gallagher, *Children and Young People's voices on Law, Legal Services and Systems in Scotland* (Scottish Child Law Centre, 1998); J. Masson, and M. Oakely, *Out of Hearing: Representing Children in Care Proceedings* (Wiley,

Collaborative law

15–43 These developments highlight the extent to which family law as a field,

> "has undergone a sea-change over the past 20 years as bitterly contested divorce hearings have given way to a much more non-confrontational approach. This draws on lawyers' negotiation and mediation skills".[25]

In keeping with this non-confrontational approach, another process for reaching agreement has been introduced into the United Kingdom[26] from the United States in the form of collaborative law. Under this process,

> "four-way meetings take place between the clients and lawyers in a search for fair, interest-based solutions, with the clients having access to legal advice throughout the process."[27]

The aim is,

> "to resolve family issues by practising law in which each of the parties to a family dispute voluntarily agree to assist in resolving conflict, using co-operative strategies rather than adversarial techniques and litigation".[28]

It adopts a holistic approach that involves,

> "considering the client and legal situation as a whole, not just considering the issue the client brings before you but all of the surrounding circumstances and the people themselves".[29]

15–44 In this process each client retains their own separate, independent lawyer for the purposes of advising, negotiating and assisting in problem-solving. It is important to note that the lawyer may be part of a team that may also involve counsellors, child therapists, inde-

---

Chichester, 1999). For the US see A. Griffiths, and R. Kandel, "Legislating for the Child's voice: Perspectives from Comparative Ethnography of Proceedings Involving Children" in *Making law for Families* (Mavis Maclean (ed.), Hart Publishing, Oxford, 2000), pp.161–183; R. Lidman and B. Hollingsworth, "The Guardian Ad Litem in Child Custody Cases: The Contours of Our Judicial System Stretched Beyond Recognition", 6 Geo. Mason L. Rev. 255 (1998); D. Prescott, "The Guardian Ad Litem in Custody and Conflict Cases: Investigator, Champion, and Referee?", 22 U. Ark. Little Rock L. Rev. 529 (2000).

[25] G. Langdon-Down, quoting K. Beatson, Chairwoman of Resolution (formerly the Solicitors Family Law Association) in "Family Fortunes", 2005 The Law Society's Gazette, Vol.102(08), p.20.

[26] For information see the website of the UK Collaborative Family Lawyers group at *www.collabfamilylaw.org.uk*.

[27] N. Laver, "Pulling together", 2004 Solicitors Journal, Vol.148(21) at p.610.

[28] K. Fretweell, "How to Get a Good Divorce", 2003 New Law Journal, Vol.153(7108), p.1877.

[29] L. Hickman, "Predicting the Law", 2004 The Law Society's Gazette, Vol.101(7), p.30.

pendent financial advisers, accountants and other professionals. According to one lawyer such an approach,

> "does not view the children in isolation from the finances. It does not tell clients that certain of their very real personal concerns are 'irrelevant', merely because these are matters upon which the court has no power to make orders".[30]

Instead, what the process offers,

> "is a humanistic view of divorce, taking into account that parties are being asked to make decisions about their futures when they are probably least equipped to do so and considering what other agencies may be used to assist with better equipping the parties, not only for their decision making but for life after divorce".[31]

The structure allows for a first individual client/solicitor consultation **15–45** covering general legal information and an explanation about the process. This includes recognition of the fact that,

> "during this period of change and uncertainty a client will experience personal ups and downs, and the need for the client to make a commitment to letting the problem solving and decision making come from the up mode."[32]

After this the two solicitors meet to discuss the setting up of a joint meeting as the process centres on four-way settlement meetings, where the clients meet with their collaborative lawyers to work on settlement issues. The pattern is,

> "for there to be individual client/solicitor meetings followed by a planning solicitor/solicitor meeting, then a joint meeting lasting no more than two hours, then a repeat of the cycle until a mutually acceptable formula is identified and set out in a written agreement".[33]

Part of this process involves making a commitment to full and honest disclosure as well as to upholding confidentiality and other provisions. Unlike mediation, it allows the lawyer to give advice to their client and help frame the solutions. This enables the lawyer to protect their client's interests and advise their client on evaluating the consequences of any particular solution.

---

[30] E. Da Costa, "Divorce With Dignity", [2005] Fam Law 35(Jun) 478 at p.479.
[31] *ibid.*
[32] A. Dick (professional briefing), "Now it's Collaborative", 2004 J.L.S.S. 49(9) at p.4.
[33] *ibid.*

15–46   Discussions between a solicitor and her/his client are confidential although the negotiation arising from this is open, for key to this process is a binding agreement entered into by the two parties and their lawyers to "to engage in frank and honest negotiations to settle the issues between them without recourse to the courts."[34] This means that should the negotiations prove unsuccessful, both lawyers must withdraw and any court proceedings will have to be undertaken with new lawyers. The advantage of this provision, which is the cornerstone of the process, is that clients and their lawyers cannot use the threat of litigation to coerce the other party to reach an agreement. By removing this threat it gives both the clients and their solicitors a vested interest in looking for constructive ways in which to resolve issues. It also frees the lawyers from having to think in terms of having a court strategy if negotiations fail which may inform the whole way in which they frame negotiation.

15–47   There is a certain amount of overlapping of skills used in the mediation and collaborative law processes but the latter allows collaborative family lawyers to retain the role of legal advisor albeit in a joint problem solving context. In addition, the collaborative law model may include referrals to external mediations if an impasse is reached and referrals to external counsellors ("coaches") to help the clients through the process. Although collaborative family law is an alternative to mediation, it can be used to compliment it, e.g. where a couple might seek the help of a mediator to agree a parenting plan whilst discussing financial matters in four-way meetings. Where the parties need to engage experts such as financial advisers, accountants, pension advisers and so on, this is agreed between them and done under joint instruction.

15–48   According to one Scots lawyer, the advantage of this form of law is that,

> "Unlike our conventional negotiation practice, it lets us concentrate on clients' interests and gives us a vested interest in adopting a constructive approach to problem solving. Unlike mediation, it provides each client with the security of his or her own representation and lets their solicitor protect their position when solutions are being discussed".[35]

Mediation and collaborative law, however, will not work with all clients and in some cases it has to be recognised that "litigation is the only option".[36] Nonetheless, very few family law cases end up involving litigation in the Scottish courts.

---

[34] F. Terry, "Working together", 2003 Solicitors Journal, Vol.147(48) 1445.
[35] S. Smith, "Comment, Collaborative Family Law—A Better Divorce?", 2004 Fam. L.B. 71–2.
[36] *ibid.*

LOOKING TO THE FUTURE

Overall, Scots family law has come a long way in developing processes **15–49** for assisting parties to reach agreement on financial and other matters on the breakdown of their relationship involving divorce or the dissolution of a civil partnership or separation at the end of cohabitation. Such processes not only involve negotiated settlement by lawyers but also the use of mediation or collaborative law. Working in tandem with the formal legal process they aim to provide a real alternative to litigation and resolution through the court process while respecting the dignity of the parties involved. As one commentator has noted:

> "Anything that may alleviate the distress of marriage and relationship breakdown is welcomed; if the process can help solve some of the problems, especially as they reflect on the children, it will be a great step forward".[37]

Whatever can be done to improve couples' experiences of the legal **15–50** process on separation is positive but it is also important to know what types of *outcome* derive from the process. It would be helpful to have more data available on the negotiated outcomes of such agreements as it would be illuminating to see to what extent their substance reflects bargaining "in the shadow of the law". Do such agreements really reflect the interests of the parties and the particular needs of each couple or are they in danger of substantially extinguishing rights that would arise under the formal statutory framework? Admittedly the chances of the latter occurring should be reduced by the fact that lawyers in Scotland draft the final written agreement (regardless of whether it represents the outcome of a negotiated settlement, or of mediation or collaborative law). However this will not solve the problem where no agreement is reached and parties, such as heterosexual and same-sex cohabiting couples, fail to have recourse to the kind of legal provisions that are in place for married couples and civil partners. For such persons, access to the third-party adjudication of the courts is only possible in limited circumstance.[38] Given the number of couples who are unmarried, cohabiting and having children, this may lead to hardship on relationship breakdown, an issue that may have to addressed by future reforms in family law.

---

[37] F. Terry, "Working Together", 2003 Solicitors Journal, Vol.147(48) 1445.
[38] See paras 10–90 to 10–99 and 13–98.

INDEX

(all references are to paragraph number)

Abortion
  fetal interests, 1–79—1–85
  introduction, 1–73—1–74
  statutory provision, 1–75—1–78
Abuse
  residence orders, and, 4–70—4–72
Access
  and see **Contact orders**
  generally, 4–17
Accommodation for children
  generally, 7–14—7–19
  parental responsibilities and rights,
    7–17
  parental rights of return, 7–20—7–23
  views of child, 7–19
Acknowledgement
  paternity, and, 3–32—3–35
Adjustment from financial dependence
  financial provision on divorce, and,
    13–70—13–76
Adoption
  adoption agencies
    approval, 6–21
    role, 6–22—6–23
  applicants
    criteria, 6–30—6–31
    'gay' couples, 6–32
    generally, 6–24
    same sex couples, 6–24
    step-parents, 6–25—6–29
    unmarried couples, 6–24
  application to court, 6–39—6–41
  consent requirement, 6–42—6–46
  court's role, 6–22—6–23
  dispensing with consent, 6–46—6–63
  effect, 6–17
  freeing for adoption
    freeing orders, 6–76—6–79
    introduction, 6–74—6–75
  'gay' couples, 6–32
  general duties and principles
    applicants, 6–24—6–32
    introduction, 6–21—6–23
    relevant children, 6–33—6–34

Adoption—*contd.*
  Houghton Committee Report, 6–15
  intercountry adoption
    generally, 6–80—6–91
    introduction, 6–20
  introduction, 6–15—6–20
  legal capacity, and, 2–28
  legislative background, 6–16
  meaning, 6–17
  open adoption
    generally, 6–65—6–73
    introduction, 6–19
  order, 6–64
  payments in consideration,
    6–36—6–37
  private placement, and, 6–35
  procedure
    application to court, 6–39—6–41
    consent requirement, 6–42—6–46
    dispensing with consent,
      6–46—6–63
    generally, 6–35—6–38
    order, 6–64
    supporting information,
      6–40—6–41
  relevant children, 6–33—6–34
  same sex couples, 6–24
  step-parents, 6–25—6–29
  supporting information,
    6–40—6–41
  trafficking, and, 6–36
  unmarried couples, 6–24
  welfare principle, and, 6–22
Adoptive parents
  see also **Adoption**
  non-parents' rights, and, 6–15
Adoptive relationships
  marriage, and, 9–21
Adultery
  divorce, and, 14–05—14–07
  residence orders, and, 4–79
Affidavits
  third party dealings with family
    home, and, 11–48—11–52

Age
children in need of care, and, 7–07
marriage, and, 9–25
s.11 orders, and
criteria for making, 4–55—4–62
residence orders, 4–85—4–86
Aliment
adults, between
amount, 10–36—10–42
backdating orders, 10–58—10–59
court actions, 10–43—10–46
death, on, 10–33
defences, 10–44—10–45
discretion, 10–31
enforcement of order, 10–62
factors determining amount,
10–36
generally, 10–34
introduction, 10–30—10–33
persons liable, 10–35
powers of court, 10–46
recall of orders, 10–47—10–57
"resources", 10–38—10–39
termination of award, 10–61
variation of orders, 10–47—10–57
voluntary agreements, 10–30
Child Support Act 1991, under
additional special cases, 5–84
appeals, 5–76
applications, 5–61—5–63
background, 5–51—5–57
capital transfers, 5–83
conclusion, 5–85—5–90
'departures' system, 5–80
enforcement, 5–77—5–79
formula approach, 5–68—5–75
jurisdiction of courts,
5–64—5–67
liable relatives, 5–52
non-resident parents, 5–60
person with care, 5–60
property/capital transfers, 5–83
quantification, 5–68—5–75
reviews, 5–76
scheme details, 5–58—5–60
special expenses, 5–82
variations, 5–80—5–84
children, for
Child Support Act 1991, under,
5–51—5–90
death of parents, on, 5–91—5–96
Family Law (Scotland) Act 1985,
under, 5–41—5–50
Family Law (Scotland) Act 1985,
under
introduction, 5–41—5–44
living apart from both parents,
5–49

Aliment—*contd.*
Family Law (Scotland) Act 1985,
under—*contd.*
living with both parents,
5–45—5–48
living with one parent, 5–50
succession, and, 5–91—5–96
Ante-natal injury
case law, 1–19—1–24
child's rights, 1–25—1–26
general principles, 1–18
statutory right to sue, 1–18
Ante-nuptial agreements
generally, 15–02
Anti-avoidance orders
financial provision on divorce, and,
13–91—13–92
Anti-social behaviour orders
generally, 8–65—8–69
Appeals
children's hearings, and,
8–63—8–64
Applications for PRRs
applicants, 4–39—4–41
criteria for making orders
age and maturity of child,
4–55—4–62
introduction, 4–49
minimum intervention,
4–51—4–54
views of the child, 4–55—4–62
welfare of the child, 4–50
generally, 4–39—4–47
jurisdiction, 4–44—4–45
nature of action, 4–44
types of order, 4–48—4–49
Artificial insemination
parenthood, and, 3–60—3–61
Assisted reproduction
artificial insemination,
3–60—3–61
death of partner, and, 3–93—3–96
genetic heritage, 3–97—3–98
in vitro fertilisation, 3–62—3–63
introduction, 3–59
maternity, 3–70
paternity, 3–71—3–77
regulation of access, 3–89—3–92
separation of partner, and,
3–93—3–96
surrogacy, 3–64—3–69

Baby-sitters
non-parents' rights, and, 6–08
Bad association
children's hearings, and, 8–21
Bank accounts
ownership, and, 12–47—12–49

Bankruptcy
ownership of family property, and,
12–21—12–25
Behaviour
divorce, and, 14–08—14–15
Beneficial interests
ownership of family home, and,
12–10—12–20
"Best interests"
and see **Welfare principle**
generally, 4–05
Blood tests
paternity, and, 3–38—3–42
Brussels II
application for PRRs, and, 4–45
divorce, and, 14–39—14–41

Capital sum orders
generally, 13–83—13–84
pensions, 13–35—13–37
Cautionary obligations
heritable creditors, and,
12–28—12–33
Child assessment orders
generally, 7–45—7–48
Child benefit
generally, 10–72—10–
Child protection orders
challenges, 7–38—7–42
conditions, 7–32—7–33
criteria for grant, 7–28—7–29
directions, 7–34—7–35
discretion, 7–28
duration, 7–38
generally, 7–28—7–32
implementation, 7–37
"looked after" children, and, 7–26
minimum intervention principle, 7–32
recall, 7–36—7–44
significant harm, 7–30
terms, 7–32—7–33
variation, 7–36—7–44
Child-minders
non-parents' rights, and, 6–08
Child welfare hearing
divorce, and, 14–53—14–54
Children
legal capacity
and see **Legal capacity**
childhood, 2–04—2–05
historical development of Scots
law, 2–17—2–20
human rights standards,
2–06—2–16
identifying the 'child', 2–75—2–79
introduction, 2–01—2–03
other aspects, 2–57—2–74
statutory provision, 2–21—2–56

Children—*contd.*
legal personality
and see **Legal personality**
commencement, 1–06—1–26
introduction, 1–01—1–05
overview, 1–86—1–88
unborn child 1–27—1–85
need of care, in
and see **Children in need of care**
accommodation, 7–14—7–23
general principles, 7–07—7–09
introduction, 7–01—7–06
local authority powers and duties,
7–10—7–13
"looked after" children,
7–24—7–28
removal of children, 7–28—7–70
non-parents, and
adoptive parents, 6–15—6–91
guardians, 6–10—6–14
introduction, 6–01—6–02
relevant persons, 6–03—6–09
parental responsibilities and rights,
and
and see **Parental responsibilities
and rights**
children's rights, and, 4–19—4–28
dispute between child and parent,
4–29—4–99
extent, 4–14—4–18
introduction, 4–01
miscellaneous, 5–01—5–34
parental power, 4–02—4–03
recipients, 3–05—3–22
welfare principle, 4–04—4–13
rights
and see **Children's rights**
generally, 4–19—4–28
Children in need of care
accommodation
generally, 7–14—7–19
parental responsibilities and rights,
7–17
parental rights of return,
7–20—7–23
views of child, 7–19
age of child, 7–07
child assessment orders, 7–45—7–48
child protection orders
challenges, 7–38—7–42
conditions, 7–32—7–33
criteria for grant, 7–28—7–29
directions, 7–34—7–35
discretion, 7–28
duration, 7–38
generally, 7–28—7–32
implementation, 7–37
"looked after" children, and, 7–26

Children in need of care—*contd.*
  child protection orders—*contd.*
    minimum intervention principle,
      7–32
    recall, 7–36—7–44
    significant harm, 7–30
    terms, 7–32—7–33
    variation, 7–36—7–44
  children's' hearings
    generally, 7–07—7–09
    introduction, 7–06
  exclusion orders
    duration, 7–57
    effect, 7–54—7–56
    generally, 7–49—7–52
    procedure, 7–53—7–57
    recall, 7–57
    sale of family home, and, 7–58
    variation, 7–57
  general principles, 7–07—7–09
  introduction, 7–01—7–06
  legislative basis, 7–05
  local authority powers and duties
    accommodation, 7–14—7–23
    assessment of, 7–66—7–70
    generally, 7–10—7–13
    introduction, 7–06
    "looked after" children,
      7–24—7–27
  "looked after" children
    emergency protection, 7–26—7–27
    generally, 7–24—7–25
  maturity of child, 7–07
  minimum intervention principle,
    7–07—7–09
  Orkney 'satanic abuse' case,
    7–01—7–04
  parental responsibilities orders
    conditions, 7–63—7–64
    discharge, 7–65
    effect, 7–63—7–64
    generally, 7–59—7–62
    variation, 7–65
  parental rights of return, 7–20—7–23
  place of safety orders, 7–27
  removal of children
    child assessment orders,
      7–45—7–48
    child protection orders,
      7–28—7–44
    exclusion orders, 7–49—7–58
    parental responsibilities orders,
      7–59—7–66
  role of courts, and
    generally, 7–07—7–09
    introduction, 7–06
  views of child
    accommodation, 7–19

Children in need of care—*contd.*
  views of child—*contd.*
    generally, 7–07
    "looked after" children, 7–25
  welfare principle
    generally, 7–07
    "looked after" children, 7–25
Children's hearings
  anti-social behaviour orders, and,
    8–65—8–69
  appeals against disposal, 8–63—8–64
  assessment of, 8–73—8–83
  attendance, 8–25—8–29
  background, 8–02—8–07
  bad association, 8–21
  child exposed to moral danger, 8–21
  child falling into bad association,
    8–21
  child is member of same household
    as victim or offender, 8–23—8–24
  child is offender, 8–19
  child is victim, 8–20
  children in need of care, and
    generally, 7–07—7–09
    introduction, 7–06
  confidentiality, 8–38—8–39
  disposal of case
    appeals, 8–63—8–64
    generally, 8–48—8–49
  establishing grounds of referral,
    8–44—8–47
  exclusion of persons, 8–38
  grounds of referral
    establishing, 8–44—8–47
    exposure to moral danger, 8–21
    falling into bad association, 8–21
    introduction, 8–15—8–18
    lack of parental care, 8–22
    member of same household as
      victim or offender, 8–23—8–24
    offender, 8–19
    victim, 8–20
  independence of tribunal, and, 8–37
  introduction, 8–01
  lack of parental care, 8–22
  legal aid, 8–32—8–34
  minimum intervention principle,
    8–40
  moral danger, 8–21
  new evidence, 8–47
  non-appearance, 8–43
  panel members, 8–09
  parenting orders, and, 8–70—8–72
  personnel, 8–09—8–15
  Principal Reporter, 8–26
  procedure
    appeals against disposal,
      8–63—8–64

Children's hearings—*contd.*
procedure—*contd.*
attendance, 8–25—8–29
confidentiality, 8–38—8–39
disposal of case, 8–48—8–49
establishing grounds of referral,
8–44—8–47
exclusion of persons, 8–38
legal aid, 8–32—8–34
new evidence, 8–47
non-appearance, 8–43
process, 8–40—8–43
representation, 8–30—8–37
s.68 proofs, 8–44—8–46
supervision, 8–48—8–62
relevant children, 8–08
Reporter, 8–09—8–13
representation, 8–30—8–37
s.68 proofs, 8–44—8–46
supervision requirements
conditions, 8–53—8–56
contact, 8–57—8–60
duration, 8–62
effect, 8–53—8–56
generally, 8–48—8–49
medical consent, 8–61
review, 8–50—8–52
views of child, 8–40
welfare principle, 8–40
Children's rights
aliment (FL(S)A 1985)
introduction, 5–41—5–44
living apart from both parents,
5–49
living with both parents,
5–45—5–48
living with one parent, 5–50
consultation, 4–24—4–28
ECHR, 4–22
generally, 4–19—4–21
introduction, 5–35
parents' marital status, and,
5–36—5–40
right not to be discriminated against
exceptions, 5–38—5–40
generally, 5–36—5–37
right to be heard, 4–24—4–25
right to financial support
Child Support Act 1991, under,
5–51—5–90
death of parents, on, 5–91—5–96
Family Law (Scotland) Act 1985,
under, 5–41—5–50
right to financial support (CSA 1991)
additional special cases, 5–84
appeals, 5–76
applications, 5–61—5–63
background, 5–51—5–57

Children's rights—*contd.*
right to financial support—*contd.*
capital transfers, 5–83
conclusion, 5–85—5–90
'departures' system, 5–80
enforcement, 5–77—5–79
formula approach, 5–68—5–75
jurisdiction of courts, 5–64—5–67
liable relatives, 5–52
non-resident parents, 5–60
person with care, 5–60
property/capital transfers, 5–83
quantification, 5–68—5–75
reviews, 5–76
scheme details, 5–58—5–60
special expenses, 5–82
variations, 5–80—5–84
right to financial support (FL(S)A
1985)
introduction, 5–41—5–44
living apart from both parents,
5–49
living with both parents,
5–45—5–48
living with one parent, 5–50
succession, 5–91—5–96
UNCRC, 4–23—4–24
Child's property
administration, 5–27—5–34
generally, 5–24—5–26
Child's wishes
children's hearings, and, 8–40
contact orders, and, 4–95
criteria for making s 11 orders, and,
4–55—4–62
residence orders, and, 4–87—4–88
Citizenship
marriage, and, 10–06—10–07
Civil ceremony
marriage, and, 9–51
Civil partnerships
*and see under individual subject
headings*
dissolution
and see **Dissolution of civil
partnerships**
grounds, 14–03
introduction, 14–03
effect on person and property of
spouses
and see **Domestic relations**
introduction, 10–01—10–02
overview, 10–98—10–99
personal status, 10–03—10–21
right to financial support,
10–30—10–62
separate property rule,
10–22—10–29

Civil partnerships—*contd.*
effect on person and property of
spouses—*contd.*
social security benefits,
10–63—10–82
succession, 10–83—10–97
eligibility, 9–61
financial provision on dissolution
and see **Financial provision on
divorce**
assessment, 13–95—13–99
court orders, 13–81—13–94
introduction, 13–01—13–04
legal framework, 13–05
s.9 principles, 13–06—13–80
gender changes, 9–63
introduction, 9–60
judicial separation, 14–31—14–35
occupation of family home
and see **Occupation of family home**
generally, 11–01—11–76
offences, 9–68—9–69
ownership of family home
and see **Ownership of family home**
beneficial interests, 12–10—12–20
generally, 12–01—12–05
trusts, 12–10—12–20
unjust enrichment, 12–06—12–09
registration
notice of proposed partnership,
9–64—9–66
partnership schedule, 9–67
restrictions, 9–62—9–63
validity, 9–70
"Clean break"
financial provision on divorce, and,
13–82
Cohabitees
financial provision on divorce, and,
13–98—13–99
occupation of family home, and
consequential and subsidiary
rights, 11–21
exclusion orders, 11–29
interdicts, 11–33
occupancy and related rights,
11–17—11–19
powers of arrest, 11–43
prohibitory interdicts, 11–33
re-entry and occupation rights,
11–17—11–19
tenancies, 11–63
ownership of family home, and, 12–05
private ordering, and
illegality, 15–21—15–24
introduction, 15–20
same-sex couples, 15–25
succession, and, 10–90—10–97

Collusion
divorce, and, 14–28
Competence as witness
marriage, and, 10–18—10–19
Conduct
financial provision on divorce, and,
13–56
Confidentiality
children's hearings, and,
8–38—8–39
Consent
adoption, and, 6–42—6–46
marriage, and, 9–26
third party dealings with family
home, and, 11–48—11–52
Consultation
children's rights, and,
4–24—4–28
Contact orders
applications
applicants, 4–39—4–41
criteria for making orders,
4–49—4–62
generally, 4–39—4–47
jurisdiction, 4–44—4–45
nature of action, 4–44
types of order, 4–48—4–49
child's wishes, 4–95
criteria for making
age and maturity of child,
4–55—4–62
introduction, 4–49
minimum intervention,
4–51—4–54
views of the child, 4–55—4–62
welfare of the child, 4–50
emigration, and, 4–84
enforcement, 4–96
generally, 4–89—4–94
overview, 4–48
Contractual relations
marriage, and, 10–13—10–17
Contributions
ownership of family home, and,
12–02
Co-owners
family home, and, 11–55—11–58
Co-tenants' position
family home, and, 11–55—11–58
Council Tax benefit
generally, 10–74—10–75
recovery from liable relatives,
10–81—10–82
Criminal liability
legal capacity, and, 2–74
Custody
and see **Residence orders**
generally, 4–17

Death of parents
  right to financial support , and,
    5–91—5–96
Death of partner
  assisted reproduction, and,
    3–93—3–96
Debts
  bankruptcy, and, 12–21—12–25
Declarator of freedom
  marriage, and, 9–59
Decree of declarator of parentage
  paternity, and, 3–36
Delegation
  parental responsibilities and rights,
    and, 4–13
Delictual liability
  legal capacity, and, 2–58—2–60
  marriage, and, 10–13—10–17
"Designer embryos"
  parenthood, and, 3–95
'Direction and guidance'
  parental responsibilities and rights,
    and, 5–05
Disposal of case
  children's hearings, and
    appeals, 8–63—8–64
    generally, 8–48—8–49
Dissolution of civil partnerships
  cross-border, 14–42—14–44
  cross-border recognition, 14–46
  financial provision
    and see **Financial provision on
      divorce**
    assessment, 13–95—13–99
    court orders, 13–81—13–94
    introduction, 13–01—13–04
    legal framework, 13–05
    s.9 principles, 13–06—13–80
  grounds, 14–03
  introduction, 14–03
  jurisdiction
    cross-border, 14–42—14–44
    generally, 14–38
  procedure
    child welfare hearing,
      14–53—14–54
    introduction, 14–51
    options hearings, 14–52
    reference to mediation, 14–55
  proof, 14–48
  registration, 14–56
  simplified procedure, 14–49—14–50
Divorce
  see also **Judicial separation**
  child welfare hearing, 14–53—14–54
  civil partnerships, and, 14–03
  collusion, and, 14–28
  cross-border, 14–42—14–44

Divorce—*contd.*
  cross-border recognition, 14–45
  financial provision
    and see **Financial provision on
      divorce**
    assessment, 13–95—13–99
    court orders, 13–81—13–94
    introduction, 13–01—13–04
    legal framework, 13–05
    s.9 principles, 13–06—13–80
  grounds
    adultery, 14–05—14–07
    behaviour, 14–08—14–15
    introduction, 14–04
    non-cohabitation for one year plus
      consent, 14–16—14–21
    non-cohabitation for two years,
      14–22—14–27
    overview, 14–02
    reforms to, 14–29—14–30
  introduction, 14–01
  jurisdiction
    Brussels II, 14–39—14–41
    cross-border, 14–42—14–44
    generally, 14–36—14–37
  options hearings, 14–52
  reference to mediation, 14–55
  overview, 14–02
  procedure
    child welfare hearing,
      14–53—14–54
    introduction, 14–51
    options hearings, 14–52
    reference to mediation, 14–55
  proof, 14–48
  recognition of overseas decree, 14–47
  reference to mediation, 14–55
  registration, 14–56
  simplified procedure, 14–49—14–50
DNA profiles
  paternity, and, 3–38—3–42
Documentary witness
  legal capacity, and, 2–73
Domestic relations
  aliment
    amount, 10–36—10–42
    backdating orders, 10–58—10–59
    court actions, 10–43—10–46
    death, on, 10–33
    defences, 10–44—10–45
    discretion, 10–31
    enforcement of order, 10–62
    factors determining amount,
      10–36
    generally, 10–34
    introduction, 10–30—10–33
    persons liable, 10–35
    powers of court, 10–46

Domestic relations—*contd.*
aliment—*contd.*
   recall of orders, 10–47—10–57
   "resources", 10–38—10–39
   termination of award, 10–61
   variation of orders, 10–47—10–57
   voluntary agreements, 10–30
household goods, 10–29
housekeeping allowance, 10–29
insurance policies, 10–29
introduction, 10–01—10–02
jus martii, and, 10–02
overview, 10–98—10–99
personal status
   citizenship, 10–06—10–07
   competence as witness,
      10–18—10–19
   contractual relations,
      10–13—10–17
   delictual relations, 10–13—10–17
   domicile, 10–03
   duty to give witness, 10–18—10–19
   fidelity, 10–04—10–05
   immigration, 10–08—10–12
   marital rape, 10–04—10–05
   name, 10–06
   naturalisation, 10–07
   residence, 10–03
   sexual relations, 10–04—10–05
   surname, 10–06
   taxation, 10–20—10–21
right to financial support
   aliment, 10–34
   amount, 10–36—10–42
   backdating orders, 10–58—10–59
   court actions, 10–43—10–46
   death, on, 10–33
   defences, 10–44—10–45
   discretion, 10–31
   enforcement of order, 10–62
   factors determining amount,
      10–36
   introduction, 10–30—10–33
   persons liable, 10–35
   powers of court, 10–46
   recall of orders, 10–47—10–57
   "resources", 10–38—10–39
   termination of award, 10–61
   variation of orders, 10–47—10–57
   voluntary agreements, 10–30
separate property rule
   aliment, and, 10–30—10–62
   exceptions, 10–29
   general rule, 10–22—10–28
social security benefits
   aggregation of resources,
      10–78—10–80
   child benefit, 10–72—10–73

Domestic relations—*contd.*
social security benefits—*contd.*
   Council Tax benefit, 10–74—10–75
   housing benefit, 10–74—10–75
   income support, 10–76—10–77
   introduction, 10–63—10–65
   jobseeker's allowance, 10–66
   recovery from liable relatives,
      10–81—10–82
   working tax credit, 10–67—10–71
succession
   cohabitants, 10–90—10–97
   intestate, 10–84—10–86
   introduction, 10–83
   testate, 10–87—10–89
   transfer of tenancy, 10–29
Domestic violence
residence orders, and, 4–70—4–72
Domicile
marriage, and, 10–03
Double dealing
third party dealings with family
   home, and, 11–53
Duress
marriage, and, 9–30—9–36
Duty to give witness
marriage, and, 10–18—10–19

Earmarking
financial provision on divorce, and,
   13–35—13–37
Economic activities and transactions
and see **Legal capacity**
child aged 16 to 18 years, 2–52
child under 16 years, 2–23—2–26
Economic advantage and contributions
financial provision on divorce, and,
   13–58—13–65
Economic burden of childcare
financial provision on divorce, and,
   13–66—13–69
Education
parental responsibilities and rights,
   and, 5–19—5–21
Emigration
s.11 orders, and, 4–84
Error
marriage, and, 9–28
**European Convention on Human Rights
(ECHR)**
children's rights, and, 4–22
legal capacity, and, 2–06—2–16
marriage, and, 9–04—9–07
Evidence
legal capacity, and
   civil proceedings, 2–65—2–71
   criminal proceedings, 2–72

Evidence—*contd.*
 legal capacity, and—*contd.*
  documentary witness, 2–73
  generally, 2–61—2–64
  "vulnerable witness" provisions,
   2–70—2–71
Exclusion of persons
 children's hearings, and, 8–38
Exclusion orders
 child's safety, and
  duration, 7–57
  effect, 7–54—7–56
  generally, 7–49—7–52
  procedure, 7–53—7–57
  recall, 7–57
  sale of family home, and, 7–58
  variation, 7–57
 family home, and
  additional orders, 11–30—11–33
  case law, 11–26—11–28
  cohabitees, 11–29
  introduction, 11–24—11–25
  prohibitory interdicts,
   11–30—11–33
  warrant for summary ejection,
   11–30

Fair sharing of economic burden of childcare
 financial provision on divorce, and,
  13–66—13–69
Fair sharing of value of property
 acquisition of property before
  marriage, 13–13—13–16
 conduct, 13–56
 excluded property, 13–13—13–20
 gifts, 13–17—13–20
 introduction, 13–07
 'matrimonial property',
  13–08—13–12
 nature of property, 13–43
 net value, 13–39
 pensions, 13–26—13–38
 realisability of property,
  13–47—13–55
 special circumstances, 13–40—13–57
 succession to property,
  13–17—13–20
 use of property, 13–44—13–46
 valuation of property, 13–21—13–34
Families
 changing approaches, 9–03—9–03
 civil partnerships
  eligibility, 9–61
  gender changes, 9–63
  introduction, 9–60
  offences, 9–68—9–69
  registration, 9–64—9–67

Families—*contd.*
 civil partnerships—*contd.*
  restrictions, 9–62—9–63
  validity, 9–70
 human rights, and, 9–04—9–07
 marriage, and
  and see **Marriage**
  introduction, 9–08
  irregular marriage, 9–56—9–59
  persons entitled to marry, 9–09
  regular marriage, 9–50—9–55
  regulatory structure, 9–10
  restrictions, 9–11—9–49
 nature, 9–01—9–02
 overview, 1–01—1–02
Family home
 occupation
  and see below
  generally, 11–01—11–76
 ownership
  beneficial interests, 12–10—12–20
  cohabitees, 12–05
  contributions in kind, 12–20
  financial contributions, 12–02
  generally, 12–01—12–05
  same-sex couples, 12–05
  trusts, 12–10—12–20
  unjust enrichment, 12–06—12–09
Family home, occupation of
 civil partners, and
  consequential and subsidiary
   rights, 11–20
  exclusion orders, 11–24—11–25
  interdicts, 11–30—11–32
  occupancy and related rights,
   11–16
  powers of arrest, 11–38—11–42
  prohibitory interdicts,
   11–30—11–32
  re-entry and occupation rights,
   11–16
  tenancies, 11–59
 consequential and subsidiary rights
  civil partners, 11–20
  cohabitees, 11–21
  spouses, 11–20
 cohabitees, and
  consequential and subsidiary
   rights, 11–21
  exclusion orders, 11–29
  interdicts, 11–33
  occupancy and related rights,
   11–17—11–19
  powers of arrest, 11–43
  prohibitory interdicts, 11–33
  re-entry and occupation rights,
   11–17—11–19
  tenancies, 11–63

Family home, occupation of—*contd.*
  co-owners' position, 11–55—11–58
  co-tenants' position, 11–55—11–58
  entitled spouses, 11–12
  exclusion orders
    additional orders, 11–30—11–33
    case law, 11–26—11–28
    cohabitees, 11–29
    introduction, 11–24—11–25
    prohibitory interdicts,
      11–30—11–33
    warrant for summary ejection,
      11–30
  general rights of occupation
    background, 11–09—11–11
    consequential and subsidiary
      rights, 11–20—11–21
    entitled spouses, 11–12
    exclusion orders, 11–24—11–37
    furniture, 11–20
    maintenance of home, 11–20
    matrimonial home,
      11–13—11–14
    mortgage payments, 11–20
    non-entitled spouses, 11–12
    occupancy and related rights,
      11–15—11–19
    powers of arrest, 11–38—11–43
    regulatory orders, 11–22—11–23
  harassment, 11–70—11–76
  interdicts
    cohabitees, 11–33
    enforcement, 11–34—11–37
    generally, 11–30—11–32
  introduction, 11–01—11–04
  Land Register of Scotland, 11–05
  legislative framework
    background, 11–05—11–11
    introduction, 11–04
    structure, 11–12—11–43
  'matrimonial home', 11–13—11–14
  mortgages, and, 11–02
  non-entitled spouses, 11–12
  occupancy and related rights
    civil partners, 11–16
    cohabitees, 11–17—11–19
    consequential and subsidiary
      rights, 11–20—11–21
    spouses, 11–15
  powers of arrest
    cohabitees, 11–43
    generally, 11–38—11–42
    protection from abuse,
      11–66—11–69
  prohibitory interdicts
    cohabitees, 11–33
    enforcement, 11–34—11–37
    generally, 11–30—11–32

Family home, occupation of—*contd.*
  protection from harassment,
    11–70—11–76
  re-entry and occupation rights
    civil partners, 11–16
    cohabitees, 11–17—11–19
    consequential and subsidiary
      rights, 11–20—11–21
    spouses, 11–15
  Register of Sasines, 11–05
  regulatory orders, 11–22—11–23
  same-sex couples, and, 11–04
  standard securities, and, 11–02
  tenancies
    cohabitees, 11–63
    introduction, 11–59
    limitations of statutory provisions,
      11–65
    termination, 11–64
    transfer, 11–60—11–62
  third party dealings
    affidavits, 11–48—11–52
    consents, 11–48—11–52
    double dealing, 11–53
    generally, 11–44—11–47
    pre-Act dealings, 11–54
    pre-marital dealings, 11–54
    renunciations, 11–48—11–52
  transfer of tenancies, 11–60—11–62
  warrant for summary ejection, 11–30
Family property ownership
  bank accounts, 12–47—12–49
  bankruptcy, 12–21—12–25
  debts, 12–21—12–25
  family home
    beneficial interests, 12–10—12–20
    cohabitees, 12–05
    contributions in kind, 12–20
    financial contributions, 12–02
    generally, 12–01—12–05
    same-sex couples, 12–05
    trusts, 12–10—12–20
    unjust enrichment, 12–06—12–09
  heritable creditors
    cautionary obligations,
      12–28—12–33
    generally, 12–26—12–27
    protection of spouses,
      12–34—12–36
    undue influence, 12–28
  household allowance, 12–50—12–52
  household goods, 12–40—12–46
  life policies
    generally, 12–53
    introduction, 12–25
  money, 12–47—12–49
  other types
    bank accounts, 12–47—12–49

Family property ownership—*contd.*
  other types—*contd.*
    household allowance,
      12–50—12–52
    household goods, 12–40—12–46
    introduction, 12–37—12–39
    life policies, 12–53
    money, 12–47—12–49
    poinding, 12–36
    savings from household allowance,
      12–50—12–52
    sequestration, 12–22—12–23
Fear
  marriage, and, 9–30—9–36
Feticide
  unborn children, and, 1–70—1–72
Fidelity
  marriage, and, 10–04—10–05
Financial contributions
  ownership of family home, and,
    12–02
Financial provision on divorce
  see also **Financial support**
  acquisition of property before
    marriage, 13–13—13–16
  adjustment from financial
    dependence, 13–70—13–76
  anti-avoidance orders, 13–91—13–92
  assessment
    cohabitants, 13–98—13–99
    generally, 13–95—13–98
  capital sum orders, 13–83—13–84
  "clean break"
    generally, 13–82
    introduction, 13–03
  conduct, 13–56
  court orders
    anti-avoidance orders,
      13–91—13–92
    capital sum, 13–83—13–84
    "clean break", 13–82
    enforcement, 13–93—13–94
    financial provision, 13–82—13–87
    incidental orders, 13–88—13–90
    interest, 13–89
    interim aliment, 13–94
    introduction, 13–81
    periodical allowance,
      13–86—13–87
    transfer of property, 13–85
  earmarking, 13–35—13–37
  economic advantage and
    contributions, 13–58—13–65
  economic burden of childcare,
    13–66—13–69
  excluded property, 13–13—13–20
  fair sharing of economic burden of
    childcare, 13–66—13–69

Financial provision on divorce—*contd.*
  fair sharing of value of property
    acquisition of property before
      marriage, 13–13—13–16
    conduct, 13–56
    excluded property, 13–13—13–20
    gifts, 13–17—13–20
    introduction, 13–07
    'matrimonial property',
      13–08—13–12
    nature of property, 13–43
    net value, 13–39
    pensions, 13–26—13–38
    realisability of property,
      13–47—13–55
    special circumstances,
      13–40—13–57
    succession to property,
      13–17—13–20
    use of property, 13–44—13–46
    valuation of property,
      13–21—13–34
  gifts, 13–17—13–20
  incidental orders, 13–88—13–90
  interest, 13–89
  interim aliment, 13–94
  introduction, 13–01—13–04
  legal framework, 13–05
  lump sum orders
    pensions, 13–35—13–37
  'matrimonial property',
    13–08—13–12
  nature of property, 14–43
  net value, 13–39
  overview, 9–30—9–36
  pension sharing orders,
    13–35—13–37
  pensions
    earmarking, 13–35—13–37
    lump sum orders, 13–35—13–37
    Pension Protection Fund, 13–38
    pension sharing orders,
      13–35—13–37
    realisability, 13–47—13–55
    valuation of property,
      13–26—13–34
  periodical allowance, 13–86—13–87
  realisability of property,
    13–47—13–55
  reasonableness, 13–05
  'resources', 13–05
  s.9 principles
    adjustment from financial
      dependence, 13–70—13–76
    economic advantage and
      contributions, 13–58—13–65
    fair sharing of economic burden of
      childcare, 13–66—13–69

Financial provision on divorce—*contd.*
  s.9 principles—*contd.*
    fair sharing of value of property,
      13–07—13–57
    introduction, 13–06
    serious financial hardship,
      13–77—13–80
  serious financial hardship,
    13–77—13–80
  special circumstances
    conduct, 13–56
    introduction, 13–40—13–42
    nature of property, 13–43
    overall, 13–57
    realisability of property,
      13–47—13–55
    use of property, 13–44—13–46
  succession to property,
    13–17—13–20
  transfer of property, 13–85
  use of property, 13–44—13–46
  valuation of property
    generally, 13–21—13–25
    pensions, 13–26—13–34
Financial support
  adults, between
    amount, 10–36—10–42
    backdating orders, 10–58—10–59
    court actions, 10–43—10–46
    death, on, 10–33
    defences, 10–44—10–45
    discretion, 10–31
    enforcement of order, 10–62
    factors determining amount,
      10–36
    generally, 10–34
    introduction, 10–30—10–33
    persons liable, 10–35
    powers of court, 10–46
    recall of orders, 10–47—10–57
    "resources", 10–38—10–39
    termination of award, 10–61
    variation of orders, 10–47—10–57
    voluntary agreements, 10–30
  Child Support Act 1991, under
    additional special cases, 5–84
    appeals, 5–76
    applications, 5–61—5–63
    background, 5–51—5–57
    capital transfers, 5–83
    conclusion, 5–85—5–90
    'departures' system, 5–80
    enforcement, 5–77—5–79
    formula approach, 5–68—5–75
    jurisdiction of courts, 5–64—5–67
    liable relatives, 5–52
    non-resident parents, 5–60
    person with care, 5–60

Financial support—*contd.*
  Child Support Act 1991—*contd.*
    property/capital transfers, 5–83
    quantification, 5–68—5–75
    reviews, 5–76
    scheme details, 5–58—5–60
    special expenses, 5–82
    variations, 5–80—5–84
  children, for
    Child Support Act 1991, under,
      5–51—5–90
    death of parents, on, 5–91—5–96
    Family Law (Scotland) Act 1985,
      under, 5–41—5–50
    divorce or dissolution, on
      and see **Financial provision on
        divorce**
      assessment, 13–95—13–99
      court orders, 13–81—13–94
      introduction, 13–01—13–04
      legal framework, 13–05
      s.9 principles, 13–06—13–80
    Family Law (Scotland) Act 1985,
      under
      introduction, 5–41—5–44
      living apart from both parents,
        5–49
      living with both parents,
        5–45—5–48
      living with one parent, 5–50
    succession, and, 5–91—5–96
Forbidden degrees of relationship
  adoptive relationships, 9–21
  affinity, 9–17—9–20
  consanguinity, 9–15—9–16
  introduction, 9–12—9–13
  policy reasoning, 9–22—9–23
  types, 9–14
Force
  marriage, and, 9–30—9–36
Foster parents
  non-parents' rights, and, 6–08
Fraud
  marriage, and, 9–28—9–29
Fraudulent misrepresentation
  legal capacity, and, 2–53—2–54
Freeing for adoption
  freeing orders, 6–76—6–79
  introduction, 6–74—6–75

'Gay' parenting
  adoption, and, 6–32
  residence orders, and, 4–73—4–78
Gender recognition
  marriage, and, 9–45—9–49
Genetic heritage
  assisted reproduction, and,
    3–97—3–98

Gifts
    financial provision on divorce, and,
        13–17—13–20
***Gillick*-competence**
    legal capacity, and, 2–30—2–36
    parental responsibilities and rights,
        and, 4–31—4–37
Grandparents
    parental responsibilities and rights,
        and
        application for PRRs, 4–39
        generally, 3–19—3–22
        introduction, 6–06—6–07
Guardians
    non-parents' rights, and, 6–10—6–14

Harassment
    family home, and, 11–70—11–76
Health and welfare
    general, 5–05—5–10
    physical punishment, 5–11—5–14
Heritable creditors
    cautionary obligations,
        12–28—12–33
    generally, 12–26—12–27
    protection of spouses, 12–34—12–36
    undue influence, 12–28
Houghton Committee Report
    adoption, and, 6–15
Household goods
    ownership of family property, and,
        12–40—12–46
    separate property rule, and, 10–29
Housekeeping allowance
    ownership of family property, and,
        12–50—12–52
    separate property rule, and, 10–29
Housing benefit
    generally, 10–74—10–75
    recovery from liable relatives,
        10–81—10–82
Human rights
    children's rights, and, 4–22
    legal capacity, and, 2–06—2–16
    marriage, and, 9–04—9–07

Immigration
    marriage, and, 10–08—10–12
In vitro fertilisation
    assisted reproduction, and,
        3–62—3–63
Incidental orders
    financial provision on divorce, and,
        13–88—13–90
Income support
    generally, 10–76—10–77
    recovery from liable relatives,
        10–81—10–82

Independence of tribunal
    children's hearings, and, 8–37
Insurance policies
    separate property rule, and, 10–29
"Intentional" parentage
    surrogacy, and, 3–88
Intercountry adoption
    generally, 6–80—6–91
    introduction, 6–20
Interdicts
    family home, and
        cohabitees, 11–33
        enforcement, 11–34—11–37
        generally, 11–30—11–32
    parental responsibilities and rights,
        and, 4–48
Interest
    financial provision on divorce, and,
        13–89
Interim aliment
    financial provision on divorce, and,
        13–94
Intestate succession
    generally, 10–84—10–86

Jobseeker's allowance
    generally, 10–66
    recovery from liable relatives,
        10–81—10–82
Joint minutes of agreement
    ante-nuptial agreements, 15–02
    circumstances allowing variation or
        reduction
        aliment, 15–11—15–12
        children, 15–08
        contractual grounds,
            15–09—15–10
        periodical allowance,
            15–11—15–12
    cohabitants, and
        illegality, 15–21—15–24
        introduction, 15–20
        same-sex couples, 15–25
    content, 15–26—15–32
    future developments,
        15–49—15–50
    independent legal advice,
        15–14—15–16
    introduction, 15–01—15–07
    procedure
        collaborative approach,
            15–43—15–48
        introduction, 15–33
        mediation, 15–34—15–42
    same-sex couples, and, 15–25
    statutory challenge, 15–13
    unequal division of assets,
        15.17—15–19

Judicial separation
see also **Divorce**
generally, 14–31—14–35
Jurisdiction
divorce, and
Brussels II, 14–39—14–41
cross-border, 14–42—14–44
generally, 14–36—14–37
Jus martii
domestic rules, and, 10–02

Lack of consent
marriage, and, 9–26
Lack of parental care
children's hearings, and, 8–22
Land Register of Scotland
family home, and, 11–05
Legal aid
children's hearings, and, 8–32—8–34
Legal capacity
adoption, 2–28
child aged 16 to 18 years
fraudulent misrepresentation,
2–53—2–54
introduction, 2–47—2–51
ratification of transactions,
2–55—2–56
transaction in course of trade,
2–52
child under 16 years
adoption, 2–28
economic activities and
transactions, 2–23—2–26
introduction, 2–22
litigation, 2–38—2–45
medical treatment, 2–29—2–37
rights ownership, 2–46
wills, 2–27
concept of "childhood"
development of Scots perception,
2–17—2–20
generally, 2–04—2–05
human rights standards,
2–06—2–16
criminal liability, 2–74
definition, 2–02
delictual liability, 2–58—2–60
documentary witness, 2–73
economic activities and transactions
child aged 16 to 18 years, 2–52
child under 16 years, 2–23—2–26
evidence
civil proceedings, 2–65—2–71
criminal proceedings, 2–72
documentary witness, 2–73
generally, 2–61—2–64
"vulnerable witness" provisions,
2–70—2–71

Legal capacity—*contd.*
fraudulent misrepresentation,
2–53—2–54
Gillick-competence, 2–30—2–36
historical development of Scots law,
2–17—2–20
human rights standards,
2–06—2–16
identifying the 'child', 2–75—2–79
introduction, 2–01—2–03
litigation, 2–38—2–45
medical treatment, 2–29—2–37
other aspects
criminal liability, 2–74
delictual liability, 2–58—2–60
documentary witness, 2–73
evidence, 2–61—2–73
introduction, 2–57
pupillarity, and, 2–17—2–19
ratification of transactions
child upon reaching 18 years, by,
2–55
court, by, 2–56
rights ownership, 2–46
statutory provision
child aged 16 to 18 years,
2–47—2–56
child under 16 years, 2–22—2–46
introduction, 2–21
summary of rights and duties, 2–03
transaction in course of trade
child aged 16 to 18 years, 2–52
child under 16 years, 2–23—2–26
"vulnerable witness" provisions,
2–70—2–71
wills, 2–27
"young persons", 2–47—2–56
Legal personality
commencement
ante-natal injury, and,
1–18—1–26
case law, 1–09—1–16
general rule, 1–06—1–08
nasciturus exception, 1–16—1–17
introduction, 1–01—1–05
overview, 1–86—1–88
unborn child
and see **Unborn child**
civil law, 1–06—1–69
criminal law, 1–70—1–85
Legal representation
children's hearings, and,
8–30—8–37
child's property, 5–24—5–34
introduction, 5–23
Liberal paternalism
parental responsibilities and powers,
and, 4–05

Life policies
  ownership of family property, and
    generally, 12–53
    introduction, 12–25
Local authority powers and duties
  children in need of care, and
    accommodation, 7–14—7–23
    assessment of, 7–66—7–70
    generally, 7–10—7–13
    introduction, 7–06
    "looked after" children, 7–24—7–27
Locus standi
  legal personality, and, 1–04
"Looked after" children
  emergency protection, 7–26—7–27
  generally, 7–24—7–25
Lump sum orders
  generally, 13–83—13–84
  pensions, 13–35—13–37

Marital rape
  marriage, and, 10–04—10–05
Marital status
  right of child not to be discriminated
    against
    exceptions, 5–38—5–40
    generally, 5–36—5–37
Marriage
  see also **Civil partnerships**
  adoptive relationships, 9–21
  age, 9–25
  changing approaches, 9–03
  civil ceremony, 9–51
  consent, 9–26
  declarator of freedom, and, 9–59
  effect on person and property of
    spouses
    and see **Domestic relations**
    introduction, 10–01—10–02
    overview, 10–98—10–99
    personal status, 10–03—10–21
    right to financial support,
      10–30—10–62
    separate property rule,
      10–22—10–29
    social security benefits,
      10–63—10–82
    succession, 10–83—10–97
  duress, 9–30—9–36
  error, 9–28
  fear, 9–30—9–36
  forbidden degrees
    adoptive relationships, 9–21
    affinity, 9–17—9–20
    consanguinity, 9–15—9–16
    introduction, 9–12—9–13
    policy reasoning, 9–22—9–23
    types, 9–14

Marriage—*contd.*
  force, 9–30—9–36
  fraud, 9–28—9–29
  gender recognition, and, 9–45—9–49
  human rights, and, 9–04—9–07
  impediments, 9–54
  introduction, 9–08
  irregular marriage, 9–56—9–59
  lack of consent, 9–26
  mental incapacity, 9–27
  persons entitled to marry, 9–09
  prior subsisting marriage, 9–24
  putting to silence, 9–59
  regular marriage
    civil ceremony, 9–51
    effect of defects, 9–55
    impediments, 9–54
    introduction, 9–50
    religious ceremony, 9–52
    unauthorised celebrant, 9–53
  regulatory structure, 9–10
  religious ceremony, 9–52
  restrictions
    adoptive relationships, 9–21
    age, 9–25
    duress, 9–30—9–36
    error, 9–28
    fear, 9–30—9–36
    forbidden degrees, 9–12—9–36
    force, 9–30—9–36
    fraud, 9–28—9–29
    introduction, 9–11
    lack of consent, 9–26
    mental incapacity, 9–27
    policy reasoning, 9–22—9–23
    prior subsisting marriage, 9–24
    same sex, 9–37—9–44
    transsexuals, 9–45—9–49
  same sex couples
    generally, 9–37—9–40
    human rights challenges,
      9–41—9–44
  transsexuals, 9–45—9–49
  unauthorised celebrant, 9–53
  validity
    defects, 9–55
    unauthorised celebrant, 9–53
Maternity
  assisted reproduction, and, 3–70
Matrimonial home
  occupation
    and see below
    generally, 11–01—11–76
  ownership
    beneficial interests, 12–10—12–20
    cohabitees, 12–05
    contributions in kind, 12–20
    financial contributions, 12–02

Matrimonial home—*contd.*
  ownership—*contd.*
    generally, 12–01—12–05
    same-sex couples, 12–05
    trusts, 12–10—12–20
    unjust enrichment, 12–06—12–09
Matrimonial home, occupation of
  civil partners, and
    consequential and subsidiary
      rights, 11–20
    exclusion orders, 11–24—11–25
    interdicts, 11–30—11–32
    occupancy and related rights,
      11–16
    powers of arrest, 11–38—11–42
    prohibitory interdicts,
      11–30—11–32
    re-entry and occupation rights,
      11–16
    tenancies, 11–59
  cohabitees, and
    consequential and subsidiary
      rights, 11–21
    exclusion orders, 11–29
    interdicts, 11–33
    occupancy and related rights,
      11–17—11–19
    powers of arrest, 11–43
    prohibitory interdicts, 11–33
    re-entry and occupation rights,
      11–17—11–19
    tenancies, 11–63
  consequential and subsidiary rights
    civil partners, 11–20
    cohabitees, 11–21
    spouses, 11–20
  co-owners' position, 11–55—11–58
  co-tenants' position, 11–55—11–58
  entitled spouses, 11–12
  exclusion orders
    additional orders, 11–30—11–33
    case law, 11–26—11–28
    cohabitees, 11–29
    introduction, 11–24—11–25
    prohibitory interdicts,
      11–30—11–33
    warrant for summary ejection,
      11–30
  general rights
    background, 11–09—11–11
    consequential and subsidiary
      rights, 11–20—11–21
    entitled spouses, 11–12
    exclusion orders, 11–24—11–37
    furniture, 11–20
    maintenance of home, 11–20
    matrimonial home, 11–13—11–14
    mortgage payments, 11–20

**Matrimonial home, occupation
of**—*contd.*
  general rights—*contd.*
    non-entitled spouses, 11–12
    occupancy and related rights,
      11–15—11–19
    powers of arrest, 11–38—11–43
    regulatory orders, 11–22—11–23
  harassment, 11–70—11–76
  interdicts
    cohabitees, 11–33
    enforcement, 11–34—11–37
    generally, 11–30—11–32
  introduction, 11–01—11–04
  Land Register of Scotland, 11–05
  legislative framework
    background, 11–05—11–11
    introduction, 11–04
    structure, 11–12—11–43
  'matrimonial home', 11–13—11–14
  mortgages, and, 11–02
  non-entitled spouses, 11–12
  occupancy and related rights
    civil partners, 11–16
    cohabitees, 11–17—11–19
    consequential and subsidiary
      rights, 11–20—11–21
    spouses, 11–15
  powers of arrest
    cohabitees, 11–43
    generally, 11–38—11–42
    protection from abuse,
      11–66—11–69
  prohibitory interdicts
    cohabitees, 11–33
    enforcement, 11–34—11–37
    generally, 11–30—11–32
  protection from harassment,
    11–70—11–76
  re-entry and occupation rights
    civil partners, 11–16
    cohabitees, 11–17—11–19
    consequential and subsidiary
      rights, 11–20—11–21
    spouses, 11–15
  Register of Sasines, 11–05
  regulatory orders, 11–22—11–23
  same-sex couples, and, 11–04
  standard securities, and, 11–02
  tenancies
    cohabitees, 11–63
    introduction, 11–59
    limitations of statutory provisions,
      11–65
    termination, 11–64
    transfer, 11–60—11–62
  third party dealings
    affidavits, 11–48—11–52

Matrimonial home, occupation of—*contd.*
third party dealings—*contd.*
consents, 11–48—11–52
double dealing, 11–53
generally, 11–44—11–47
pre-Act dealings, 11–54
pre-marital dealings, 11–54
renunciations, 11–48—11–52
transfer of tenancies, 11–60—11–62
warrant for summary ejection, 11–30
Maturity of child
children in need of care, and, 7–07
s.11 orders, and, 4–55—4–62
Mediation
divorce, and, 14–55
Medical consent
supervision requirements, and, 8–61
Mental incapacity
marriage, and, 9–27
Minimum intervention principle
children in need of care, and
child protection orders, 7–32
generally, 7–07—7–09
children's hearings, and, 8–40
s.11 orders, and, 4–51—4–54
Minutes of agreement
ante-nuptial agreements, 15–02
circumstances allowing variation or reduction
aliment, 15–11—15–12
children, 15–08
contractual grounds, 15–09—15–10
periodical allowance, 15–11—15–12
cohabitants, and
illegality, 15–21—15–24
introduction, 15–20
same-sex couples, 15–25
content, 15–26—15–32
future developments, 15–49—15–50
independent legal advice, 15–14—15–16
introduction, 15–01—15–07
procedure
collaborative approach, 15–43—15–48
introduction, 15–33
mediation, 15–34—15–42
same-sex couples, and, 15–25
statutory challenge, 15–13
unequal division of assets, 15.17—15–19
Money
ownership of family property, and, 12–47—12–49

Moral danger
children's hearings, and, 8–21
Mortgages
family home, and, 11–02

Names and surnames
marriage, and, 10–06
parental responsibilities and rights, and, 5–22
Nasciturus rule
legal personality, and, 1–16—1–17
"Natural persons"
meaning, 1–03
Naturalisation
marriage, and, 10–07
Net value
financial provision on divorce, and, 13–39
New evidence
children's hearings, and, 8–47
Non-appearance
children's hearings, and, 8–43
Non-cohabitation
divorce, and, 14–16—14–27
Non-entitled spouses
family home, and, 11–12
Non-parents
adoptive parents
see also **Adoption**
generally, 6–15—6–20
baby-sitters, and, 6–08
child-minders, and, 6–08
foster parents, and, 6–08
grandparents
application for PRRs, 4–39
generally, 3–19—3–22
introduction, 6–06—6–07
guardians, 6–10—6–14
introduction, 6–01—6–02
parental responsibilities and rights, 6–03
relevant persons, 6–03—6–09
s.11 C(S)A 1995, and, 6–03
step-parents
application for PRRs, 4–39
generally, 3–19—3–22
introduction, 6–05
unmarried fathers
application for PRRs, 4–39
generally, 3–10—3–17

Occupancy and related rights
and see **Occupation of family home**
civil partners, 11–16
cohabitees, 11–17—11–19
consequential and subsidiary rights, 11–20—11–21
spouses, 11–15

Occupation of family home
civil partners, and
  consequential and subsidiary
    rights, 11–20
  exclusion orders, 11–24—11–25
  interdicts, 11–30—11–32
  occupancy and related rights,
    11–16
  powers of arrest, 11–38—11–42
  prohibitory interdicts,
    11–30—11–32
  re-entry and occupation rights,
    11–16
  tenancies, 11–59
cohabitees, and
  consequential and subsidiary
    rights, 11–21
  exclusion orders, 11–29
  interdicts, 11–33
  occupancy and related rights,
    11–17—11–19
  powers of arrest, 11–43
  prohibitory interdicts, 11–33
  re-entry and occupation rights,
    11–17—11–19
  tenancies, 11–63
consequential and subsidiary rights
  civil partners, 11–20
  cohabitees, 11–21
  spouses, 11–20
co-owners' position, 11–55—11–58
co-tenants' position, 11–55—11–58
entitled spouses, 11–12
exclusion orders
  additional orders, 11–30—11–33
  case law, 11–26—11–28
  cohabitees, 11–29
  introduction, 11–24—11–25
  prohibitory interdicts,
    11–30—11–33
  warrant for summary ejection,
    11–30
general rights
  background, 11–09—11–11
  consequential and subsidiary
    rights, 11–20—11–21
  entitled spouses, 11–12
  exclusion orders, 11–24—11–37
  furniture, 11–20
  maintenance of home, 11–20
  matrimonial home, 11–13—11–14
  mortgage payments, 11–20
  non-entitled spouses, 11–12
  occupancy and related rights,
    11–15—11–19
  powers of arrest, 11–38—11–43
  regulatory orders, 11–22—11–23
harassment, 11–70—11–76

Occupation of family home—*contd.*
interdicts
  cohabitees, 11–33
  enforcement, 11–34—11–37
  generally, 11–30—11–32
introduction, 11–01—11–04
Land Register of Scotland, 11–05
legislative framework
  background, 11–05—11–11
  introduction, 11–04
  structure, 11–12—11–43
'matrimonial home', 11–13—11–14
mortgages, and, 11–02
non-entitled spouses, 11–12
occupancy and related rights
  civil partners, 11–16
  cohabitees, 11–17—11–19
  consequential and subsidiary
    rights, 11–20—11–21
  spouses, 11–15
powers of arrest
  cohabitees, 11–43
  generally, 11–38—11–42
  protection from abuse,
    11–66—11–69
prohibitory interdicts
  cohabitees, 11–33
  enforcement, 11–34—11–37
  generally, 11–30—11–32
protection from harassment,
  11–70—11–76
re-entry and occupation rights
  civil partners, 11–16
  cohabitees, 11–17—11–19
  consequential and subsidiary
    rights, 11–20—11–21
  spouses, 11–15
Register of Sasines, 11–05
regulatory orders, 11–22—11–23
same-sex couples, and, 11–04
standard securities, and, 11–02
tenancies
  cohabitees, 11–63
  introduction, 11–59
  limitations of statutory provisions,
    11–65
  termination, 11–64
  transfer, 11–60—11–62
third party dealings
  affidavits, 11–48—11–52
  consents, 11–48—11–52
  double dealing, 11–53
  generally, 11–44—11–47
  pre-Act dealings, 11–54
  pre-marital dealings, 11–54
  renunciations, 11–48—11–52
transfer of tenancies, 11–60—11–62
warrant for summary ejection, 11–30

Open adoption
generally, 6–65—6–73
introduction, 6–19
Options hearings
divorce, and, 14–52
Ownership of family home
beneficial interests, 12–10—12–20
cohabitees, 12–05
contributions in kind, 12–20
financial contributions, 12–02
generally, 12–01—12–05
same-sex couples, 12–05
trusts, 12–10—12–20
unjust enrichment, 12–06—12–09

Parental care, behaviour and lifestyle
residence orders, and, 4–69—4–84
Parental orders
surrogacy, and, 3–85—3–87
Parental responsibilities and rights
see also **Parenthood**
access, and
and see **Contact orders**
generally, 4–17
applications
applicants, 4–39—4–41
criteria for making orders,
4–49—4–62
generally, 4–39—4–47
jurisdiction, 4–44—4–45
nature of action, 4–44
types of order, 4–48—4–49
automatic, 3–06—3–09
"best interests"
and see **Welfare principle**
generally, 4–05
children's rights, and
consultation, 4–24—4–28
ECHR, 4–22
generally, 4–19—4–21
right to be heard, 4–24—4–25
UNCRC, 4–23—4–24
child's property
administration, 5–27—5–34
generally, 5–24—5–26
conclusions, 4–97—4–99
contact orders
child's wishes, 4–95
emigration, and, 4–84
enforcement, 4–96
generally, 4–89—4–94
overview, 4–48
court orders
applications, 4–39—4–47
contact orders, 4–89—4–96
introduction, 4–38
residence orders, 4–63—4–88
types, 4–48

**Parental responsibilities and
rights**—*contd.*
court's role, 4–19—4–20
criteria for making s 11 orders
age and maturity of child,
4–55—4–62
introduction, 4–49
minimum intervention,
4–51—4–54
views of the child, 4–55—4–62
welfare of the child, 4–50
custody, and
and see **Residence orders**
generally, 4–17
delegation, 4–13
dispute between child and parent
court orders, 4–38—4–96
generally, 4–29—4–30
Gillick-competence, 4–31—4–37
education, 5–19—5–21
extent
generally, 4–17—4–18
introduction, 4–14
responsibilities, 4–15
rights, 4–16
general responsibilities, 4–15, 5–02
general responsibilities, 4–16, 5–03
Gillick-competence, and, 4–31—4–37
grandparents
application for PRRs, 4–39
generally, 3–19—3–22
health and welfare
general, 5–05—5–10
physical punishment, 5–11—5–14
interdicts, 4–48
introduction, 4–01
legal representation
child's property, 5–24—5–34
introduction, 5–23
liberal paternalism, and, 4–05
names and surnames, 5–22
parental power, 4–02—4–03
patria potestas, and, 4–02—4–03
physical punishment, 5–11—5–14
prohibitory interdicts, 4–48
recipients
automatic, 3–06—3–09
introduction, 3–05
s.11 C(S)A 1995, under,
3–18—3–22
step-parents, 3–19—3–22
unmarried fathers, 3–10—3–17
religious upbringing, 5–15—5–18
residence orders
abuse, 4–70—4–72
adultery, 4–79
age of child, 4–85—4–86
domestic violence, 4–70—4–72

Parental responsibilities and rights—*contd.*
  residence orders—*contd.*
    emigration, and, 4–84
    'gay' parenting, and, 4–73—4–78
    overview, 4–48
    parental care, behaviour and lifestyle, 4–69—4–84
    promiscuity, 4–79
    race, 4–83
    religion, 4–80—4–82
    sex of child, 4–85—4–86
    sexuality of parents, 4–73—4–79
    status quo principle, 4–66—4–68
    support networks, 4–79
    views of the child, 4–87—4–88
    welfare principle, 4–63—4–65
  role of courts, 4–19—4–20
  s.11 C(S)A 1995, under
    applications, 4–39—4–47
    criteria for making, 4–49—4–62
    introduction, 3–18—3–22
    types, 4–48
  specific issue orders, 4–48
  step-parents, 3–19—3–22
  surnames, 5–22
  termination
    generally, 4–17
    introduction, 3–05
  unmarried fathers
    application for PRRs, 4–39
    generally, 3–10—3–17
  welfare principle
    conclusions, 4–97—4–99
    generally, 4–04—4–13
    residence orders, and, 4–63—4–65
Parental responsibilities orders
  conditions, 7–63—7–64
  discharge, 7–65
  effect, 7–63—7–64
  generally, 7–59—7–62
  variation, 7–65
Parental rights of return
  children in need of care, and, 7–20—7–23
Parenthood
  assisted reproduction
    artificial insemination, 3–60—3–61
    death of partner, and, 3–93—3–96
    genetic heritage, 3–97—3–98
    in vitro fertilisation, 3–62—3–63
    introduction, 3–59
    maternity, 3–70
    paternity, 3–71—3–77
    regulation of access, 3–89—3–92
    separation of partner, and, 3–93—3–96
    surrogacy, 3–64—3–69

Parenthood—*contd.*
  conclusions, 3–99
  "designer embryos", and, 3–95
  introduction, 3–01—3–02
  legal consequences
    generally, 3–03—3–05
    parental responsibilities and rights, 3–06—3–09
    unmarried fathers, 3–10—3–17
  "parent"
    introduction, 3–23
    maternity, 3–24—3–25
    paternity, 3–26—3–58
  parental responsibilities and rights
    and see **Parental responsibilities and rights**
    automatic, 3–06—3–09
    children's rights, and, 4–01—4–99
    introduction, 3–05
    s.11 C(S)A 1995, under, 3–18—3–22
    step-parents, 3–19—3–22
    termination, 3–05
    unmarried fathers, 3–10—3–17
  paternity
    balance of probabilities, 3–58
    blood tests, 3–38—3–42
    DNA profiles, 3–38—3–42
    evidence, 3–37
    name on birth certificate, 3–58
    non-scientific evidence, 3–57—3–58
    presumptions, 3–26—3–36
    scientific tests, 3–38—3–42
  post-death insemination, 3–93—3–96
  pre-implantation diagnosis, and, 3–95
  presumptions of paternity
    acknowledgement, 3–32—3–35
    introduction, 3–26
    marriage, 3–27—3–31
    prior decree of declarator of parentage, 3–36
    registration, 3–32—3–35
  scientific tests
    consent to sample on behalf of child, 3–43—3–50
    discretion of court on request, 3–51—3–56
    generally, 3–38—3–42
  sex selection of embryos, and, 3–95
  surrogacy
    commissioning parents' position, 3–85—3–88
    generally, 3–64—3–69
    "intentional" parentage, 3–88
    parental orders 3–85—3–87
    surrogate parents' position, 3–78—3–84

Parenting orders
children's hearings, and, 8–70—8–72
Paternity
acknowledgement, 3–32—3–35
assisted reproduction, and,
3–71—3–77
balance of probabilities, 3–58
blood tests, 3–38—3–42
decree of declarator of parentage,
3–36
DNA profiles, 3–38—3–42
evidence, 3–37
marriage, 3–27—3–31
name on birth certificate, 3–58
non-scientific evidence, 3–57—3–58
presumptions
acknowledgement, 3–32—3–35
introduction, 3–26
marriage, 3–27—3–31
prior decree of declarator of
parentage, 3–36
registration, 3–32—3–35
scientific tests
consent to sample on behalf of
child, 3–43—3–50
discretion of court on request,
3–51—3–56
generally, 3–38—3–42
Patria potestas
parental responsibilities and powers,
and, 4–02—4–03
Payments
adoption, and, 6–36—6–37
Pension sharing orders
financial provision on divorce, and,
13–35—13–37
Pensions
earmarking, 13–35—13–37
lump sum orders, 13–35—13–37
Pension Protection Fund, 13–38
pension sharing orders,
13–35—13–37
realisability, 13–47—13–55
valuation of property, 13–26—13–34
Periodical allowance
financial provision on divorce, and,
13–86—13–87
Personal status
citizenship, 10–06—10–07
competence as witness,
10–18—10–19
contractual relations, 10–13—10–17
delictual relations, 10–13—10–17
domicile, 10–03
duty to give witness, 10–18—10–19
fidelity, 10–04—10–05
immigration, 10–08—10–12
marital rape, 10–04—10–05

Personal status—*contd.*
name, 10–06
naturalisation, 10–07
residence, 10–03
sexual relations, 10–04—10–05
surname, 10–06
taxation, 10–20—10–21
Physical punishment
parental responsibilities and rights,
and, 5–11—5–14
Place of safety orders
children in need of care, and, 7–27
Poinding
ownership of family property, and,
12–36
Post-death insemination
parenthood, and, 3–93—3–96
Powers of arrest
cohabitees, 11–43
generally, 11–38—11–42
protection from abuse, 11–66—11–69
Pre-implantation diagnosis
parenthood, and, 3–95
Principal Reporter
children's hearings, and, 8–26
Private ordering
ante-nuptial agreements, 15–02
circumstances allowing variation or
reduction
aliment, 15–11—15–12
children, 15–08
contractual grounds,
15–09—15–10
periodical allowance,
15–11—15–12
cohabitants, and
illegality, 15–21—15–24
introduction, 15–20
same-sex couples, 15–25
content of minutes, 15–26—15–32
future developments, 15–49—15–50
independent legal advice,
15–14—15–16
introduction, 15–01—15–07
procedure
collaborative approach,
15–43—15–48
introduction, 15–33
mediation, 15–34—15–42
same-sex couples, and, 15–25
statutory challenge, 15–13
unequal division of assets,
15.17—15–19
Private placement
adoption, and, 6–35
Prohibitory interdicts
family home, and
cohabitees, 11–33

Prohibitory interdicts—*contd.*
 family home, and—*contd.*
  enforcement, 11–34—11–37
  generally, 11–30—11–32
Promiscuity
 residence orders, and, 4–79
Protection from harassment
 family home, and, 11–70—11–76
Punishment
 parental responsibilities and rights,
  and, 5–11—5–14
Putting to silence
 marriage, and, 9–59

Race
 residence orders, and, 4–83
Rape
 marriage, and, 10–04—10–05
Realisability of property
 financial provision on divorce, and,
  13–47—13–55
Reasonableness
 financial provision on divorce, and,
  13–05
Re-entry and occupation rights
 civil partners, 11–16
 cohabitees, 11–17—11–19
 consequential and subsidiary rights,
  11–20—11–21
 spouses, 11–15
Reference to mediation
 divorce, and, 14–55
Register of Sasines
 family home, and, 11–05
Registration
 paternity, and, 3–32—3–35
Regular marriage
 civil ceremony, 9–51
 effect of defects, 9–55
 impediments, 9–54
 introduction, 9–50
 religious ceremony, 9–52
 unauthorised celebrant, 9–53
Regulatory orders
 family home, and, 11–22—11–23
Religion
 residence orders, and, 4–80—4–82
Religious ceremony
 marriage, and, 9–52
Religious upbringing
 parental responsibilities and rights,
  and, 5–15—5–18
Removal of children
 child assessment orders, 7–45—7–48
 child protection orders
  challenges, 7–38—7–42
  conditions, 7–32—7–33
  criteria for grant, 7–28—7–29

Removal of children—*contd.*
 child protection orders—*contd.*
  directions, 7–34—7–35
  discretion, 7–28
  duration, 7–38
  generally, 7–28—7–32
  implementation, 7–37
  "looked after" children, and, 7–26
  minimum intervention principle,
   7–32
  recall, 7–36—7–44
  significant harm, 7–30
  terms, 7–32—7–33
  variation, 7–36—7–44
 exclusion orders
  duration, 7–57
  effect, 7–54—7–56
  generally, 7–49—7–52
  procedure, 7–53—7–57
  recall, 7–57
  sale of family home, and, 7–58
  variation, 7–57
 parental responsibilities orders
  conditions, 7–63—7–64
  discharge, 7–65
  effect, 7–63—7–64
  generally, 7–59—7–62
  variation, 7–65
Renunciations
 third party dealings with family
  home, and, 11–48—11–52
Reporter
 children's hearings, and, 8–09—8–13
Representation
 children's hearings, and, 8–30—8–37
 child's property, 5–24—5–34
 introduction, 5–23
Residence
 marriage, and, 10–03
Residence orders
 abuse, 4–70—4–72
 adultery, 4–79
 age of child, 4–85—4–86
 applications
  applicants, 4–39—4–41
  criteria for making orders,
   4–49—4–62
  generally, 4–39—4–47
  jurisdiction, 4–44—4–45
  nature of action, 4–44
  types of order, 4–48—4–49
 criteria for making
  age and maturity of child,
   4–55—4–62
  introduction, 4–49
  minimum intervention, 4–51—4–54
  views of the child, 4–55—4–62
  welfare of the child, 4–50

Residence orders—*contd.*
  domestic violence, 4–70—4–72
  emigration, and, 4–84
  'gay' parenting, and, 4–73—4–78
  overview, 4–48
  parental care, behaviour and lifestyle
    abuse, 4–70—4–72
    adultery, 4–79
    domestic violence, 4–70—4–72
    emigration, 4–84
    'gay' parenting, and, 4–73—4–78
    introduction, 4–69
    promiscuity, 4–79
    race, 4–83
    religion, 4–80—4–82
    sexuality of parents, 4–73—4–79
    support networks, 4–79
  promiscuity, 4–79
  race, 4–83
  religion, 4–80—4–82
  sex of child, 4–85—4–86
  sexuality of parents, 4–73—4–79
  status quo principle, 4–66—4–68
  support networks, 4–79
  views of the child, 4–87—4–88
  welfare principle, 4–63—4–65
'Resources'
  financial provision on divorce, and,
    13–05
Right to be heard
  children's rights, and, 4–24—4–25
Right to financial support
  adults, between
    amount, 10–36—10–42
    backdating orders, 10–58—10–59
    court actions, 10–43—10–46
    death, on, 10–33
    defences, 10–44—10–45
    discretion, 10–31
    enforcement of order, 10–62
    factors determining amount,
      10–36
    generally, 10–34
    introduction, 10–30—10–33
    persons liable, 10–35
    powers of court, 10–46
    recall of orders, 10–47—10–57
    "resources", 10–38—10–39
    termination of award, 10–61
    variation of orders, 10–47—10–57
    voluntary agreements, 10–30
  Child Support Act 1991, under
    additional special cases, 5–84
    appeals, 5–76
    applications, 5–61—5–63
    background, 5–51—5–57
    capital transfers, 5–83
    conclusion, 5–85—5–90

Right to financial support—*contd.*
  Child Support Act 1991—*contd.*
    'departures' system, 5–80
    enforcement, 5–77—5–79
    formula approach, 5–68—5–75
    jurisdiction of courts,
      5–64—5–67
    liable relatives, 5–52
    non-resident parents, 5–60
    person with care, 5–60
    property/capital transfers, 5–83
    quantification, 5–68—5–75
    reviews, 5–76
    scheme details, 5–58—5–60
    special expenses, 5–82
    variations, 5–80—5–84
  children, for
    Child Support Act 1991, under,
      5–51—5–90
    death of parents, on, 5–91—5–96
    Family Law (Scotland) Act 1985,
      under, 5–41—5–50
  Family Law (Scotland) Act 1985,
    under
    introduction, 5–41—5–44
    living apart from both parents,
      5–49
    living with both parents,
      5–45—5–48
    living with one parent, 5–50
    succession, and, 5–91—5–96
Rights of return
  children in need of care, and,
    7–20—7–23

s.9 principles
  adjustment from financial
    dependence, 13–70—13–76
  economic advantage and
    contributions, 13–58—13–65
  fair sharing of economic burden of
    childcare, 13–66—13–69
  fair sharing of value of property
    acquisition of property before
      marriage, 13–13—13–16
    conduct, 13–56
    excluded property, 13–13—13–20
    gifts, 13–17—13–20
    introduction, 13–07
    'matrimonial property',
      13–08—13–12
    nature of property, 13–43
    net value, 13–39
    pensions, 13–26—13–38
    realisability of property,
      13–47—13–55
    special circumstances,
      13–40—13–57

s.9 principles—*contd.*
  fair sharing of value of
    property—*contd.*
    succession to property,
      13–17—13–20
    use of property, 13–44—13–46
    valuation of property,
      13–21—13–34
  introduction, 13–06
  serious financial hardship,
    13–77—13–80
s.11 C(S)A 1995 orders
  applications
    applicants, 4–39—4–41
    criteria for making orders,
      4–49—4–62
    generally, 4–39—4–47
    jurisdiction, 4–44—4–45
    nature of action, 4–44
    types of order, 4–48—4–49
  "best interests"
    and see **Welfare principle**
    generally, 4–05
  contact orders
    child's wishes, 4–95
    emigration, and, 4–84
    enforcement, 4–96
    generally, 4–89—4–94
    overview, 4–48
  criteria for making
    age and maturity of child,
      4–55—4–62
    introduction, 4–49
    minimum intervention, 4–51—4–54
    views of the child, 4–55—4–62
    welfare of the child, 4–50
  non-parents' rights, and, 6–03
  residence orders
    abuse, 4–70—4–72
    adultery, 4–79
    age of child, 4–85—4–86
    domestic violence, 4–70—4–72
    emigration, and, 4–84
    'gay' parenting, and, 4–73—4–78
    overview, 4–48
    parental care, behaviour and
      lifestyle, 4–69—4–84
    promiscuity, 4–79
    race, 4–83
    religion, 4–80—4–82
    sex of child, 4–85—4–86
    sexuality of parents, 4–73—4–79
    status quo principle, 4–66—4–68
    support networks, 4–79
    views of the child, 4–87—4–88
    welfare principle, 4–63—4–65
  specific issue orders, 4–48
  types, 4–48

s.68 proofs
  children's hearings, and, 8–44—8–46
'Safeguard and promote'
  parental responsibilities and rights,
    and, 5–05—5–10
Same sex couples
  see also **Civil partnerships**
  adoption, and, 6–24
  marriage, and
    generally, 9–37—9–40
    human rights challenges,
      9–41—9–44
  occupation of family home, and,
    11–04
  ownership of family home, and,
    12–05
  private ordering, and, 15–25
Scientific tests
  parenthood, and
    consent to sample on behalf of
      child, 3–43—3–50
    discretion of court on request,
      3–51—3–56
    generally, 3–38—3–42
Separate property rule
  aliment, and
    amount, 10–36—10–42
    backdating orders, 10–58—10–59
    court actions, 10–43—10–46
    death, on, 10–33
    defences, 10–44—10–45
    discretion, 10–31
    enforcement of order, 10–62
    factors determining amount,
      10–36
    generally, 10–34
    introduction, 10–30—10–33
    persons liable, 10–35
    powers of court, 10–46
    recall of orders, 10–47—10–57
    "resources", 10–38—10–39
    termination of award, 10–61
    variation of orders, 10–47—10–57
    voluntary agreements, 10–30
  exceptions, 10–29
  general rule, 10–22—10–28
  household goods, 10–29
  housekeeping allowance, 10–29
  insurance policies, 10–29
  overview, 10–98—10–99
  social security benefits
    aggregation of resources,
      10–78—10–80
    child benefit, 10–72—10–73
    Council Tax benefit, 10–74—10–75
    housing benefit, 10–74—10–75
    income support, 10–76—10–77
    introduction, 10–63—10–65

Separate property rule—*contd.*
  social security benefits—*contd.*
    jobseeker's allowance, 10–66
    recovery from liable relatives,
      10–81—10–82
    working tax credit, 10–67—10–71
  succession
    cohabitants, 10–90—10–97
    intestate, 10–84—10–86
    introduction, 10–83
    testate, 10–87—10–89
  transfer of tenancy, 10–29
Separation of partner
  assisted reproduction, and,
    3–93—3–96
Sequestration
  ownership of family property, and,
    12–22—12–23
Serious financial hardship
  financial provision on divorce, and,
    13–77—13–80
Sex of child
  residence orders, and, 4–85—4–86
Sex selection of embryos
  parenthood, and, 3–95
Sexual relations
  marriage, and, 10–04—10–05
Sexuality of parents
  residence orders, and, 4–73—4–79
Social security benefits
  aggregation of resources,
    10–78—10–80
  child benefit, 10–72—10–73
  Council Tax benefit, 10–74—10–75
  housing benefit, 10–74—10–75
  income support, 10–76—10–77
  introduction, 10–63—10–65
  jobseeker's allowance, 10–66
  recovery from liable relatives,
    10–81—10–82
  working tax credit, 10–67—10–71
Special circumstances
  conduct, 13–56
  introduction, 13–40—13–42
  nature of property, 13–43
  overall, 13–57
  realisability of property,
    13–47—13–55
  use of property, 13–44—13–46
Specific issue orders
  parental responsibilities and rights,
    and, 4–48
Standard securities
  family home, and, 11–02
Status quo principle
  residence orders, and, 4–66—4–68
Step-parents
  adoption, and, 6–25—6–29

Step-parents—*contd.*
  parental responsibilities and rights,
    and
    application, 4–39
    generally, 3–19—3–22
    introduction, 6–05
Succession
  children's rights, and, 5–91—5–96
  cohabitants, 10–90—10–97
  financial provision on divorce, and,
    13–17—13–20
  intestate, 10–84—10–86
  introduction, 10–83
  testate, 10–87—10–89
Supervision requirements
  conditions, 8–53—8–56
  contact, 8–57—8–60
  duration, 8–62
  effect, 8–53—8–56
  generally, 8–48—8–49
  medical consent, 8–61
  review, 8–50—8–52
Support networks
  residence orders, and, 4–79
Surname
  marriage, and, 10–06
  parental responsibilities and rights,
    and, 5–22
Surrogacy
  commissioning parents' position,
    3–85—3–88
  generally, 3–64—3–69
  "intentional" parentage, 3–88
  parental orders 3–85—3–87
  surrogate parents' position,
    3–78—3–84

Taxation
  marriage, and, 10–20—10–21
Tenancies
  cohabitees, 11–63
  introduction, 11–59
  limitations of statutory provisions,
    11–65
  termination, 11–64
  transfer, 11–60—11–62
Testate succession
  generally, 10–87—10–89
Third party dealings
  affidavits, 11–48—11–52
  consents, 11–48–11–52
  double dealing, 11–53
  generally, 11–44—11–47
  pre-Act dealings, 11–54
  pre-marital dealings, 11–54
  renunciations, 11–48—11–52
Trafficking
  adoption, and, 6–36

Transfer of property
financial provision on divorce, and, 13–85
Transfer of tenancy
generally, 11–60—11–62
separate property rule, and, 10–29
Transsexuals
marriage, and, 9–45—9–49
Trusts
ownership of family home, , 12–10—12–20

UN Convention on the Rights of the Child (UNCRC)
children's rights, and, 4–23—4–24
legal capacity, and, 2–06—2–07
Unauthorised celebrant
marriage, and, 9–53
Unborn child
abortion
fetal interests, 1–79—1–85
introduction, 1–73—1–74
statutory provision, 1–75—1–78
ante-natal injury
case law, 1–19—1–24
child's rights, 1–25—1–26
general principles, 1–18
statutory right to sue, 1–18
civil law
ante-natal injury, 1–18—1–26
wrongful birth, 1–27—1–51
wrongful life, 1–64—1–69
wrongful pregnancy, 1–27—1–63
criminal law
abortion, 1–73—1–85
generally, 1–70—1–72
feticide, 1–70—1–72
wrongful birth
case law, 1–32—1–51
current legal position, 1–63
generally, 1–28
introduction, 1–27
legal options, 1–62
meaning, 1–28
negligence, 1–29—1–31
wrongful life
case law, 1–65—1–69
introduction, 1–64
statutory provision, 1–68
wrongful pregnancy
case law, 1–32—1–61
current legal position, 1–63
disabled child, and, 1–52—1–55
disabled parent giving birth to healthy child, and, 1–56—1–61
introduction, 1–27
legal options, 1–62
meaning, 1–27

Unborn child—*contd.*
wrongful pregnancy—*contd.*
negligence, 1–29—1–31
Undue influence
heritable creditors, and, 12–28
Unjust enrichment
ownership of family home, and, 12–06—12–09
Unmarried couples
and see **Cohabitees**
adoption, and, 6–24
Unmarried fathers
application for PRRs, 4–39
generally, 3–10—3–17
Use of property
financial provision on divorce, and, 13–44—13–46

Valuation of property
generally, 13–21—13–25
pensions, 13–26—13–34
Views of child
children in need of care, and
accommodation, 7–19
generally, 7–07
"looked after" children, 7–25
children's hearings, and, 8–40
contact orders, and, 4–95
criteria for making s 11 orders, and, 4–55—4–62
residence orders, and, 4–87—4–88

Warrant for summary ejection
family home, and, 11–30
Welfare principle
adoption, and, 6–22
children in need of care, and
generally, 7–07
"looked after" children, 7–25
children's hearings, and, 8–40
conclusions, 4–97—4–99
generally, 4–04—4–13
residence orders, and, 4–63—4–65
Working tax credit
generally, 10–67—10–71
recovery from liable relatives, 10–81—10–82
Wrongful birth
case law
introduction, 1–32
McFarlane v Tayside, 1–33—1–43
Rand v East Dorset, 1–44—1–51
current legal position, 1–63
generally, 1–28
introduction, 1–27
legal options, 1–62
meaning, 1–28
negligence, 1–29—1–31

Wrongful life
case law
  McKay v Essex AHA, 1–65—1–67
  Perruche v MACSF, 1–69
introduction, 1–64
statutory provision, 1–58
Wrongful pregnancy
case law
  introduction, 1–32
  McFarlane v Tayside, 1–33—1–38
  Parkinson v St James and Sea Croft, 1–52—1–55
  Rand v East Dorset, 1–44—1–51

Wrongful pregnancy—*contd.*
case law—*contd.*
  Rees v Darlington Memorial, 1–56—1–61
current legal position, 1–63
disabled child, and, 1–52—1–55
disabled parent giving birth to healthy child, and, 1–56—1–61
introduction, 1–27
legal options, 1–62
meaning, 1–27
negligence, 1–29—1–31